Governing Postwar Germany

Governing
Postwar Germany

By EDWARD H. LITCHFIELD

AND ASSOCIATES

ARNOLD BRECHT	A. M. HILLHOUSE
HENRY L. BRETTON	HOWARD PALFREY JONES
TAYLOR COLE	ROBERT M. W. KEMPNER
HAROLD M. DORR	HERTHA KRAUS
CARL J. FRIEDRICH	KARL LOEWENSTEIN
KURT GLASER	RODNEY L. MOTT
ALONZO G. GRACE	RICHARD M. SCAMMON
JOHN HAY	HERBERT J. SPIRO

ROGER H. WELLS

31149

Cornell University Press

ITHACA, NEW YORK

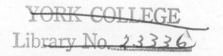

First published 1953

PRINTED IN THE UNITED STATES OF AMERICA

BY CAYUGA PRESS, INC., ITHACA, NEW YORK

TO

Lucius D. Clay

whose foresight, determination, and leadership were essentials in the growth of a democratic postwar Germany and a continuing inspiration for those who were privileged to work with him.

TO

Lucius D. Clay

whose foresight, determination, and leadership
were essentials in the growth of a democratic
postwar Germany and a continuing inspiration
for those who were privileged to work with him.

Introduction

I N THE spring of 1952, seven years after her unprecedented defeat
and unconditional surrender, Germany again emerged as a major
European power. Shorn of more than twenty million of her people and
much of her eastern territory, burdened by large-scale destruction and
a heavy influx of refugee peoples, humiliated in defeat and frustrated
by occupation, Western Germany by 1952 was nonetheless a dominating influence in that portion of Europe which was free from Soviet
control. As summer, fall, and winter pass, it becomes increasingly
clear that Western Germany's role is to grow rather than recede in the
months and years of West-East conflict which are ahead. Even now it
must be apparent that a steady economic revival, a national work
habit, a motive to guide an effort, and, perhaps, an element of the
classic German sense of destiny will combine to make the Federal
Republic at once the *bête noire* and the eastern bastion of the free
world.

Central to the structure of the enigma which is Germany is the German government and the political processes upon which it depends.
This book deals with those subjects. It is concerned with the historic
antecedents of contemporary German political life, with the impact of
the Four Power occupation, with the community forces upon which
any responsive government is dependent, and with the political processes and institutions as they are to be found in Germany today—the
period controlled by the Contractual Agreement which restores at
least Western Germany to a position of relative independence in the
community of free nations. Is it a political system which can resist
characteristic German authoritarian tendencies? Is it a government

which will take its place in the concert of other democratic nations? Is it a government upon which the other free nations can rely? Does it as a pattern of institutions and behavior mechanisms satisfy the manifest political needs of its own people? Can it control its own militarism? Has it profited by the mistakes of Weimar?

It is not possible to answer all of these questions within the covers of a single volume. Nor is it likely that answers could be undertaken upon the basis of the limited time which has elapsed since the beginnings of political revival in Western Germany. It is also improbable that adequate answers could be provided by such a small council of observers as the authors of this volume provide, however informed and careful they may be. To provide definitive answers to these and related questions is not our purpose. It is our object, however, to provide as much information and as many informed judgments as possible upon the general question of the contemporary political scene in Western Germany and, to a lesser extent, Eastern Germany.

To further this objective I have made a determined attempt to include in this volume the views of a great many of the most competent American observers of the German scene. Every contributor to this effort is a man who can claim both scholarly and practical experience with the problems of which he writes. Most have had both an academic and an official relationship to the questions which are here in issue. Every author has had some measure of responsibility for the political developments in postwar Germany. For some of us these have been "command" responsibilities the consequences of which we cannot avoid. Others need acknowledge no more than the involvements which go with "advice and counsel." In any event, to every contributor to this volume, Germany has been a personal, an academic, and an official concern.

As a consequence, the reader will recognize that we write from different and from specialized points of view. He will note that we are occasionally bitter, for some of us have worked with mixed success in German political affairs. He will observe an occasional loftiness among those of us who are perhaps overly wedded to our American way of political behavior. He will see more than a gleam of the blade as we have at one another for our respective successes and failures at a time when we were all charged with more than the commentator's responsibilities. I hope he will also not only see the foibles but perhaps find mature distillations of the intimacy of our experience with prewar and postwar German political life.

In planning and editing this volume I have tried to preserve the vitality of every man's experience without subordinating it either to editorial convenience or to the artificialities which uniformity of conclusion and a consensus of judgment would otherwise impose. Each has expressed his view without regard to the other, and those opinions have been faithfully recorded here. They spare neither Germans, the Allied governments, the editor, nor the views set forth elsewhere in the volume. This is in the best scholarly tradition, and we would hope that the reader will accept it with the tolerance which that tradition demands. We offer it also as further evidence of the value of a pluralist tradition that is so inextricably related to the larger democratic value which most of us would hope might find ultimate acceptance in a German culture too long devoted to absolutist concepts.

Reference to an absolutist tradition provides the opportunity to enter here the usual disclaimer possible in a society in which the individual is permitted an existence distinct from his life as a public servant. Those of us who have relinquished our official responsibilities obviously speak without prejudice to our former governmental agencies. Those of us who have not reserve the same privilege and therefore speak also in the name of the person and not in the name of the governmental agency with which they are affiliated.

In organizing this book we have made an effort to discuss German government from several different points of view. The casual student of the subject would expect a discussion of the several levels of governmental activity much as he would find that discussion in a textbook in the United States. This is not only an orthodox but an important way in which to consider the functioning of German or any other government. At the same time there will be those who are analytically concerned with the adequacy of the legislative, judicial, and executive processes as they occur on all levels of government. They will want to know something of the manner in which the citizen is admitted to the processes of legislative policy formulation at local, state, and federal levels and something of the way in which the civil servant performs. Others will be concerned with social security, education, labor relations, or other problems with no particular concern as to whether they have a provincial or central incidence. Consequently we have tried to discuss German government as it is today with reference to the functions, the processes, and the levels of government.

As a result of this method of organization the reader will be obliged to tolerate a certain amount of duplication of comment. When several references produce additional reflection upon the problem, the reader will find advantage in the overlapping. When the same proximity of interest produces conflict, it may be that he will profit from the juxtaposition of competitive ideas. In other cases he may recognize what the editor hopes is but a modest amount of actual repetition.

In presenting what we would hope might become a reasonably authoritative volume upon this subject we have attempted to include those documents which are essential to our purpose. We have not sought to duplicate the several documentary collections already available to the reader except as our own story has necessitated doing so. Students of this subject are referred to the excellent collection prepared by James K. Pollock, James H. Meisel, and Henry L. Bretton entitled *Germany under Occupation,* the Department of State's *Germany: The Story in Documents,* and the variety of authoritative publications which have emerged from the Historical Division of the Office of the United States High Commissioner for Germany and from the Civil Administration Division of the Office of Military Government. The documentary materials included in the appendices to this volume are therefore composed of materials which have never previously been published or collected or which are so basic to the discussion as to necessitate republication here for the constant reference of careful readers of the text. In the former category are such materials as the text of the reply of the ministers-president to the opportunity to establish a western German government and in the latter are such basic materials as the Basic Law, the Occupation Statute, and the Convention on Relations between the Three Powers and the Federal Republic of Germany. As we have kept the documentation to an absolute minimum, so we have also permitted a considerable amount of flexibility among the several authors who have documented this undertaking. In some instances they have followed their own scholarly predilections and included a substantial amount of reference material. In other instances either their own direct manner of approach or the nature of their subject matter has made extensive documentation difficult, superfluous, or even impossible. We have not written a volume for the casual reader. Neither, on the other hand, have we consciously attempted to provide a textbook for the classroom use of the professional student of German government. We have rather indulged ourselves in writing what most reviewers will refer to as a "reference" volume. At the same time we have made every effort to avoid the droning too often characteristic of works of this type. Where we have failed to sustain that objective we would hope it had been because of the essentially specific nature of our subject.

As the years of our generation wear on, it would be gratifying to believe that in this volume we had commented sentiently upon a subject of universal concern and interest. Yet, in fact, we know that the government and the political institutions with which we are concerned are no more than an articulate product of a culture which is in process of rapid change. In the turbulence of the stream of postwar German development there is much which is hopeful and much which we must view with cautious alarm. The springs of an authoritarian tradition may easily feed these waters with pressures which will drastically change the scene as we have described it. On the other hand, the contours of the contemporary European and world political topography through which the stream flows could easily direct its ultimate course into channels of democratic stability that could become models for the rest of the continent. As commentators and as occupiers we have sought constantly to recall that while political institutions are not without major importance in shaping the character of a people, in the ultimate appraisal those institutions are themselves the product of philosophic, moral, psychological, and economic threads of the fabric of a total culture. It is important that the reader accept our volume in this context.

E. H. L.

Ithaca, New York
July, 1953

Contents

Part I. Evolution of Postwar Governments

Part II. Levels of Government

[Contents]

Part III. Processes of Government

Part IV. Functions of Government

[Contents]

Illustrations

Tables

Governing Postwar Germany

Part I

EVOLUTION OF POSTWAR GOVERNMENTS

1

Political Objectives and Legal

Bases of Occupation Government

EDWARD H. LITCHFIELD

S EVEN years of Allied occupation are indelibly recorded in the
character of contemporary German political institutions. Understanding those institutions therefore requires not only an appreciation
of Germany's long and often complex history but also a more specific
knowledge of those years of foreign domination of German life.[1]
Hence, while this volume is primarily concerned with German governments and politics and not with the structures of the occupation,
it cannot proceed without first examining the permanent patterns cast

[1] By all means the most complete and authoritative of the personal accounts is
Lucius D. Clay, *Decision in Germany* (Garden City, N.Y., 1950). Responsible
analysis of military government's impact upon German life is also to be found in
W. Friedmann, *The Allied Military Government of Germany* (London, 1947);
C. J. Friedrich and associates, *American Experiences in Military Government in
World War II* (New York, 1948); Harold Zink, *American Military Government
in Germany* (New York, 1947); J. P. Nettl, *The Eastern Zone and Soviet Policy
in Germany, 1945-1950* (New York, 1951); M. Virally, *L'Administration interna-
tionale de l'Allemagne* (Paris, 1948); Sydney Connor and C. J. Friedrich, eds.,
"Military Government," in *Annals of the American Academy of Political and
Social Science*, CCLXVII (Jan., 1950). Of the official histories the most substantial are those still emerging from the office of the two chief historians (Roger H.
Wells and Harold Zink) of the Office of the United States High Commissioner for
Germany. Among these the most important for the political scientist are three by
Elmer Plischke, *History of the Allied High Commission for Germany: Its Estab-
lishment, Structure, and Procedure* (1951), *Revision of the Occupation Statute
for Germany* (1952), and *Development of Allied High Commission Relations with
the German Government* (1952).

upon the political scene by the long shadows of occupation government.

Political life in the new Germany has been influenced by two significant aspects of the occupation. Probably the most important of these was the effort at political reform undertaken at different times and to varying ends in the several parts of the truncated area. But political institutions were molded too by the manner in which the occupying powers assumed, exercised, and later returned the powers of civil government. That neither aspect of occupation effort was as effective as it might have been is today abundantly, perhaps painfully, clear. That both were considerably diluted by the diversity and conflict of objectives and the inconsistency of the pattern of occupation governance is apparent. Yet no reasonable observer could conclude that the efforts had been lost or that the impact of the occupation had been negligible. Whether for peace or war, West or East, democracy or totalitarianism, the occupation has left a mottle of bench marks, pegs, and scars which will not soon depart. It is with these influences and these direct consequences that this chapter is concerned.

POLITICAL OBJECTIVES OF THE OCCUPATION

Probably the most significant single aspect of Allied occupation of Germany is the fact that the effort was launched and completed without any agreement as to basic objectives. This was true in the political sphere as it was in the broader areas of occupation policy. When the United States entered the war against Germany, there was no agreement as to specific political objectives which we hoped to achieve by victory and subsequent occupation. With the termination of the war four years later, there was still no political program for the defeated nation beyond "peace," "democracy," and "denazification." Today, more than a decade later, it is still impossible to define a specific Allied program for political reform in Germany.

It is true that we had the Atlantic Charter, Yalta, and the Potsdam Agreement of 1945. But it is equally true that these agreements were not accepted by all four occupying governments and that they contained only the most general of objectives. The most specific was Potsdam, though even from it those who were to administer policy could extract no more than these generalities:

a. Destruction of the National Socialist party and its affiliated organizations.

b. Reconstruction of political life upon a democratic basis.

c. Reorganization of the judicial system in accordance with the principles of democracy, of justice under the law, and of equal rights for all citizens without distinction of race, nationality, or religion.

d. Decentralization of the political structure and development of local responsibility on democratic principles and by means of elective councils.

e. Encouragement of all democratic political parties.

f. Establishment of certain central administrative agencies in such fields as finance, transport, communications, foreign trade, and industry.

Had these almost meaningless generalities been buttressed by agreed specific programs prepared and negotiated during the long war years, there might have been hope for subsequent efforts to give meaning to Potsdam. However, there were no papers of this kind that had been negotiated at staff level and accepted on the levels at which policy was formulated. Indeed, such efforts at joint policy planning as had been undertaken in the "country units" of SHAEF (Supreme Headquarters, Allied Expeditionary Forces) were never able to reach the highest policy-determining levels and were ignored in other echelons of SHAEF itself. In the absence of such staff agreement, Potsdam was a disarming but dangerous sham which covered skin-deep, vast chasms of uncertainty and disagreement regarding the meaning of words, of concepts, of values, and, indeed, of life itself.

Again, even in the absence of multipartitely prepared staff papers which would have given some clue to the content of the Potsdam platitudes, it was conceivable that specific meaning might have been developed later in the Allied Control Council established in Berlin to direct the quadripartite occupation. To have assumed that this could have developed may appear naive today, but it was a reasonable assumption at that time. In any event, subsequent negotiations both in the Control Council in Berlin and in the meetings of the Council of Foreign Ministers in Moscow and London in 1947 revealed how little agreement could be reached on broad concepts of "democracy" and therefore how impossible was the development of a specific program of institutional reform. Nor was agreement reached on federalism, the nature of legislative representation, the character of the electoral process, the meaning of civil rights, the structure of the police system, the nature of the civil service, to mention but a few. This was scarcely surprising since "demilitarization" and "denazification" which everyone favored in principle were disagreed subjects to the end.

The absence of agreed political objectives was not entirely the result of West-East conflicts. Very little progress toward an agreed French, British, United States policy was achieved until the 1947 Moscow Conference of the Council of Foreign Ministers, though by that time a modest amount of progress had been made by the Military Governors of the United States and the United Kingdom. It was not until 1948, nine years after the beginning of the war and three years after its conclusion, that substantial agreement was reached among the three western Allies on certain aspects of a program for political development. That agreement, reached in London under pressure created by the Communist coup d'état in Prague, was extremely important, but it contained little which would affect problems of basic reform that already had been separately faced, solved, or ignored in the individual zones of occupation. Coming as late as it did, the agreement could do no more than specify certain of the minima upon the basis of which the proposed federal government would be built. Nineteen hundred forty-eight was at least three years too late to be developing agreed policies for the reform of the police system, for the democratization of the civil service, for the creation of new roles for the citizen, for the introduction of public hearings into the legislative process, or for the planning of a new and effective pattern of local and state government. It was too late because German minds were closed or closing, too late because in the meantime divergent patterns with consequent vested interests had been created, and too late because the influence of the occupation forces was already largely dissipated.

Beyond the questions of internal political objectives was the complete uncertainty surrounding the issue of Germany's place as a national state in the international scene. During the critical formative years after the war, agreement never moved beyond the Potsdam gesture of preparing Germany "for eventual peaceful cooperation in international life." During those years, men and governments proceeded according to very different concepts of Germany's ultimate relationship to the outside world. In 1945 and 1946, the French disinterest in the development of the central administrative agencies called for by Potsdam was clearly based upon at least the hope that some parts of former Germany might well be integrated into quite another type of political union. One of the most persistent efforts during this period was the French activity designed to draw Bavaria into an Alpine Union. It is clear now that the Soviets always intended that either the eastern portion of the country or the whole of Germany would be integrated into the Soviet satellite system. In this country, responsible officials urged a dismemberment of Germany with the understanding that the severed parts would be incorporated in a European Federation. In short, there was no basic agreement at that time as to the character of ultimate German national sovereignty or its relationship to larger international organization.

This was an issue which was to return in force in later years. The tardy decision to unite Western Germany was made about the time that the United States began to talk quietly and occasionally publicly about the need for a federation of western European nations. Tardily but positively the French came to see that the development of the latter would provide a method of controlling the dangers Paris felt to be inherent in the revival of the German nation as a sovereign force in European affairs. Subsequent enunciation of the Schumann and later the Pleven plan followed from this premise. Unnecessary difficulties followed, however, from the fact that German sovereignty and particularly German nationalism revived more rapidly than western European federation grew. A minimum of early agreement as to Germany's ultimate incorporation into such a supranational organization would have avoided this risk and might well have saved years of internal frustration.[2]

If Allied agreement was difficult and often impossible to realize, there were also conflict and confusion in the United States' own policy with reference to political change within Germany. Wartime planning for these specifics of occupation practice was carried on in a variety of places both in Washington and in the theater headquarters abroad. Only the famous directives of the Joint Chiefs of Staff actually attained sufficient status to influence field action and ultimately German practice. JCS 1067 was issued in April, 1945, and was replaced with a similar instruction to the United States Military Governor in July, 1947. The 1945 directive suffered from most of the faults of Potsdam —of which it was the prototype—in that its objectives in the political field were either negative in intent or meaningless in their use of words and concepts which had no accepted significance among the Allied governments. In certain respects it was even less constructive in its apparent motive and in its proposed methods of operation. It contained, for example, the now widely known provision, "You will strongly discourage fraternization with the German officials and population." There was manifest conflict between this and a later instruction regarding the establishment of "an affirmative program of reorientation" in the educational system and in other portions of the community. In contrast with the long and detailed policy statement contained in the economic and financial sections of the directive, political guidance beyond negative instructions regarding war criminals

[2] For subsequent developments, see Chapter 7 below.

and denazification was buried in a few lines of general instructions. Re-education and reorientation efforts which would provide the basis of genuine political reform were called for in a three-line subsection of a paragraph devoted almost entirely to closing schools, purging textbooks and personnel.

The absence of agreed Allied policy may have stemmed in part from the fact that we had no national policy for political development in Germany which was clear and consistent until General Clay, as a deputy field commander, took matters into his own hands. However much men were to differ later as to the adequacy of Clay's policy of rapid restoration of self-government without corresponding emphasis upon political and social reform, the Clay policy was clear, consistent, constructive, and determined. As such it was infinitely more than Washington had developed and far more than a government had reason to expect from a deputy theater commander. Under the circumstances, it is difficult to avoid observing the irony in later charges that he had usurped Washington's policy-determining responsibilities.

The directive issued more than two years later was better balanced, more constructive in tone and intent, and more specific in its reference to political objectives. Actually it was primarily a consolidated statement of the various policy concurrences which Washington had sent to Berlin during the intervening years in response to theater initiation. It was helpful, but it was too late to have serious effect upon the emerging political scene.

Beyond this, today's appraisal must recognize that the effectiveness of the few clear political objectives we were able to develop has been in part minimized by the about-face which has occurred in many of our other policy goals. The impact of our efforts at political change has obviously been reduced by forcing complete demilitarization at the beginning of the occupation and encouraging Germans to rearm again in 1952, by dismantling on a sweeping scale at one moment and offering economic aid to rebuild the economy on the other, by preaching nonfraternization today and large-scale educational exchange tomorrow. Whatever the reason, the fact of basic reversal in fundamental objectives in one area has necessarily undermined the acceptance of other purposes in political fields.

All through the planning and conduct of the occupation, men differed as to its objectives, and many of them are still in disagreement today. It is not with the merit of their respective positions that we are concerned here but rather with the fact that whatever the content of our political program should have been, the truth of the matter is that we arrived in Germany without one which was accepted by any of our Allies and that by the time we obtained one it was too late to accomplish many of the objectives which might otherwise have been possible. Nor are we concerned with adducing responsibility for this failure. It was surely more than an American responsibility, for none of the other governments did as much as was done by Washington representatives in formulating the content of Potsdam. Nor were our own failures to produce a more specific internal program peculiar, for Soviet policy swung from side to side, and French policy for three years was little more than a frightened negation of anything that presaged revival or stability for Germany. On the other hand, after reading the cables for the critical years 1945-1948, one could not avoid the conclusion that as far as the United States was concerned if there were failure it was not in Berlin but in Washington. Perhaps this was to be expected from an atmosphere of turnover and change which during six years of the German occupation brought seventeen different persons to the positions of Secretary and Assistant Secretary for occupation problems in the Departments of the Army and State. In Paris, too, governments came and went in rapid succession, and the French headquarters in Germany was constantly divided between professional civil servants prepared to accept the decisions of the government of the day and others with strong affinities for De Gaulle who on many occasions were more than willing to retard announced Paris policy. British policy was more consistent in that it had never embraced the strong "pastoralization" concepts of "Morgenthauism" from which to depart and, on the other hand, was less insistent than the United States upon German reconstruction. Policy-wise it had the distinct advantage also of having a government which was in a position to make seat-of-government decisions at responsible levels and to convey them to its representatives in Germany sometime prior to the fact of their need.

In any event the absence of multilateral agreement and consistent unilateral policies thought out and reconciled in advance of actual occupation meant horseback judgments by those who found themselves with problems for which no advance preparation had been made. The territorial dismemberment of Württemberg and Baden, the collapse and, indeed, disappearance of minimal political institutions from national to village level, were examples of considerable import. This confusion of political objectives also meant contradiction of practice which often neutralized the efforts in the different zones. Thus, French and American efforts to develop a strong sense of local home rule were in substantial extent vitiated by British centralism. Related questions of deconcentration of industry were equally contradictory

between zones and influenced the impact of the broader decentralization programs. American efforts to subordinate police organizations to
popular control by locating them within the organization structure of
elective units of government were minimized by British practice of
establishing *ad hoc* police districts subject to neither local nor immediate state control. For years the Americans tried to change the German
civil service while the other Allies did nothing to discourage the Germans from thinking this was but a passing fancy of one of the occupying powers. Divergence of view and practice was, of course, even
greater between the Soviet and western zones.

The absence of multipartite agreement also encouraged a tendency
to confuse one's own national practice with democratic universals.
Had there been the considered Allied attention to democratic minima
which the gravity of large-scale occupation required, much of this
provincialism might have been avoided and the general effort made
more successful as a result. The essentials of political democracy
clearly do not include the British town clerk. Nor do they demand the
existence of an independent civil service commission after an American
model styled to meet the patronage needs of a political situation without German parallel.

The absence of an articulated policy of political change was aggravated for Americans by a haunting concern for the three great
dilemmas with which any "democratic occupation" is faced. In the
minds of many there was always grave concern about the use of absolutist powers of the occupant for the purpose of combating a general acceptance of absolutism as a political value. To those persons
there was always a disturbing concern for democracy preached by
means of occupation dictatorship. Others, and I think Clay among
them, were even more troubled by a program which preached the
sanctity of the home, the dignity of the person, and the importance of
individual self-determination while slowly committing itself to a series
of activities which sought to breach a culture from the cradle to the
grave. While admitting that such a breach was clearly required if
fundamental change was to occur, these persons were nonetheless
bothered by the manifest conflict between end and means in such a
program. In later years the substance of the dilemma took on another
form. If Germany were to be genuinely democratized, she must remain subject to Allied controls. But nothing is more firmly imbedded
in democratic theory than the concept of equality. How could one
preach democracy to a mature, competent, and cultured people on
one hand and deny them national equality on the other? A sophistical
argument when applied in earlier times to backward peoples, it was

hardly satisfying when applied to twentieth-century Germans. In the wake of the dilemma came the inevitable consequence of a Germany returned to substantial sovereignty before she had made appreciable domestic change. In its several forms the problem troubled the occupation from the day fighting ceased until the preparation of the Contractual Agreement in 1952. Failing the growth of an international body into which Germany's nationality is incorporated, it will come again in the interval preceding complete and sovereign independence. The dilemma of "the democratic occupation" is a ghost which has not yet been laid.

But whether it was agreed, disagreed, or unagreed, whether it was internally consistent, whether it was made by the home government or its representative in Germany, Allied political policy was a major factor in the postwar revision of German governments from the village to the nation's several capitals. Its influence was exerted by direction, by the imposition of conditions precedent, by its own example during the months and years in which the powers of civil government were exercised by military government, and by its suggestions in later phases when power had been largely returned to German authorities. To a considerable extent these influences will be noted in all of the subsequent chapters in this book. Beyond this, however, it is necessary that we review the patterns by which the Allies themselves governed Germany and the manner in which they turned political power back to the civilian governments that they had been instrumental in creating. For it is in this process of governance and in the procedure employed in relinquishing power that many of the significant explanations of contemporary government lie.

LEGAL FOUNDATIONS OF OCCUPATION GOVERNMENT

When the Allies crossed the German frontier, they brought with them no agreed concept of the position of the occupation in international law. In the summer of 1945 there were long discussions as to the applicability of the Hague Convention on the Laws and Customs of War on Land.[3] More than a year later United States and United Kingdom political and legal directors in Berlin still debated the legal status of occupation legislation and its relationship to the body of German law then emerging from a variety of Allied-sponsored German agencies.[4] Later negotiations concerning the Occupation Statute

[3] See Charles Fahy, "Legal Problems of the German Occupation," *Michigan Law Review*, XLVII (1948), 11-22.
[4] With particular reference to the legislative powers of the *Länderrat* of the U.S. Zone compared with the then emerging bizonal administrative agencies.

and its subsequent revisions raised many of the same questions.

Much of the uncertainty resulted from the fact that existing international law did not cover the major portion of the occupation. Its assistance was limited to the traditional concepts of *occupatio bellica* and *occupatio pacifica*. Occupations in the "peaceful" category were normally undertaken as a result of a treaty or some similar agreement between the occupant government and the legally sovereign government of the state occupied. The rights and the obligations of the former were specifically set forth in the instrument of agreement, and disputes were usually adjudicated in international courts established for the purpose. Legal sovereignty was presumed to remain in the government of the occupied nation and, indeed, that government was more often than not itself retained to assist in the exercise of the occupant's assigned powers.[5] Western Europe had become familiar with peaceful occupations during the nineteenth century, for Germany had occupied France in this manner in the period 1871-1873, Austria-Hungary had occupied Bosnia and Herzegovina by treaty in 1878-1908, and the Allies had occupied the Rhineland during the years following World War I.[6]

The rules of "belligerent occupation" had also developed considerably since eighteenth-century times when "enemy territory occupied by a belligerent was in every point considered his property, so that he could do what he liked with it and its inhabitants."[7] In the intervening years the distinction between outright conquest and subjugation on the one hand and mere military occupation on the other had been noted by Vattel[8] and developed in the works of Heffter, Lieber, and other nineteenth-century writers.[9] The Lieber Code of 1863 was followed by a series of others culminating in the Hague Conventions of 1899 and 1907. When World War II opened, the laws of "belligerent occupation" were still largely in the state in which they had been embodied in Articles 42-56 of the Regulations annexed to Hague Convention IV of 1907. As thus developed they presumed that sovereign legal powers would continue in the government of the territory occupied and that the authority of the occupant would be narrowly confined to areas of largely military concern. These precepts were under-

[5] See Raymond Robin, *Des occupations militaires en dehors des occupations de guerre* (Paris, 1913, 1942).

[6] See Ernst Fraenkel, *Military Occupation and the Rule of Law* (New York, 1944).

[7] L. Oppenheim, *International Law*, 6th ed. (New York, 1940), II, 337.

[8] Vattel, *Le Droit des gens* (Neuchatel, 1773), III, 197.

[9] See Doris A. Graber, *The Development of the Law of Belligerent Occupation* (New York, 1949).

scored by the specific provisions requiring respect for the laws in force in the occupied country "unless absolutely prevented" from doing so.[10]

The Allied occupation of Germany in months prior to the cessation of hostilities was clearly undertaken in accordance with the Hague Conventions and may be considered as constituting a period of belligerent occupation. However, with the termination of actual warfare in the spring of 1945 came a series of events which drastically changed the status of the occupant powers under international law. The first of these was the "unconditional surrender" of the German High Command on May 8[11] followed immediately by the arrest of Admiral Doenitz and his colleagues with the consequent collapse of the last remnant of organized German government. Less than a month later in the Declaration of Berlin, the Allied powers assumed "supreme authority with respect to Germany, including all the powers possessed by the German Government, the High Command, and any state, municipal or local government or authority."[12] In August came the Potsdam Agreement in which the occupant powers announced their intention—and presumably claimed the authority—to abolish laws, reorganize educational, judicial, and political institutions, and reorganize the patterns of the economic life of the German people.

Several conclusions followed almost automatically from these events. In the first place, it is apparent that the belligerent occupation phase had ended for there was no longer a German belligerent. On the other hand, it was equally clear that the new period could not satisfy the conditions of *occupatio pacifica* for there was no semblance of government with which to conclude an agreement. This much is generally agreed today.[13] However, it is equally important to understand that

---

[10] See Article 43 of the Hague Land Warfare Conventions of 1907.

[11] For text, see J. K. Pollock, J. H. Meisel, and H. L. Bretton, eds., *Germany under Occupation,* rev. ed. (Ann Arbor, 1949).

[12] Declaration of Berlin, June 5, 1945, par. 5.

[13] See Fahy, *op. cit.;* John H. E. Fried, "Transfer of Civilian Manpower from Occupied Territory," *American Journal of International Law,* XL (1946), 303-331; Hans Kelsen, "The Legal Status of Germany According to the Declaration of Berlin," *Am. J. Internat. Law,* XXXIX (1945), 518-526, and "Is a Peace Treaty with Germany Legally Possible and Politically Desirable," *American Political Science Review,* XLI (1947), 1188-1193; Arnold Duncan McNair, *Legal Effects of War* (Cambridge, 1948), p. 354; Max Rheinstein, "The Legal Status of Occupied Germany," *Mich. Law R.,* XLVII (1948), 23-40; Oliver J. Shaw, "Military Government Law and British Subjects in Germany," *International Law Quarterly,* II (1948), 670-674. See also Grahame *v.* The Director of Prosecutions (c.c.cr. opp., 1947, Vol. 3, p. 168); Rex *v.* Bottrill, *ex parte* Kuechenmeister [1947] I.K.B. 41.

the same condition would probably have existed regardless of whether there had been an unconditional surrender and the arrest and trial of Doenitz *et al.* or not. The basic Allied decision to undertake sweeping internal German reform in a wide variety of fields would have transcended the power of the occupant in a state of *occupatio bellica* and would almost certainly have been refused as a treaty provision by any government which might otherwise have been willing to contemplate a "peaceful occupation." Once this primary policy had been established, occupation in the traditional meanings of international law was impossible.

But if this second phase was neither a "peaceful occupation" nor a "belligerent occupation," what was it?[14] Upon what bases could it be justified? What were its limitations? And upon what legal premises could it build? Kelsen maintained that sovereignty had passed from the German state to the Allies and that Germany had therefore "ceased to exist as a state in the sense of international law."[15] It also followed, he said, that Allied powers, having all of the attributes of sovereignty, were unlimited. His use of the term "sovereignty" in the legal sense was objected to by those who chose to use it in its political sense. Still others challenged both his claim that the German state had disappeared and his assertion of unlimited powers for the occupant governments. Rheinstein, for example, noted the substantial number of state attributes such as nationality, territoriality, and so forth which Germany retained and concluded that the state had not been destroyed. More practically, he speculated that occupation authority during this second phase was limited by two considerations. First, he said that Allied rights as military victors were affected by those Hague Regulations which limit the rights of the occupation to "the necessities of the occupation, especially those obliging the occupation to respect private property."[16] Furthermore, he claims that Allied rights as "the government of Germany" are circumscribed by the political and legal foundations of democracy particularly with respect to the inalienable rights of life, liberty, and the pursuit of happiness which he asserts are beginning to find their way into a variety of parts of international law.[17] Noting that this was neither *occupatio bellica* nor *occupatio pacifica*, Friedrich was later to suggest that the occupation be referred

[14] For a discussion of the considerable amount of German literature on the subject, see Menzel, "Zur Voelker rechtlechen Laze Deutschlands," 2 *Europe-Archiv* 1009 (1947).

[15] Kelsen, "The Legal Status of Germany According to the Declaration of Berlin," *Am. J. Internat. Law,* XXXIX (1945), 519.

[16] Rheinstein, *op. cit.,* p. 27.   [17] *Ibid.,* p. 29.

to as an *occupatio pacifica prelimnaria.*[18] Others speculated in varying vein.

To those who exercised the responsibility for the occupation much of this was of no more than academic interest. Whether Germany was a state in international law may have been doubtful, but that she was without the governmental mechanism with which to exercise traditional functions of national sovereignty was indisputable. There may have been limits imposed upon the conduct of occupation affairs, but they were the product of the culture from which the occupants came and not of international convention or articulated international law. The patent facts were that this occupation was *sui generis* and that international law had not developed as rapidly as the problems with which the victors of World War II were faced. It offered nothing more than a concept of occupation as a "subordinate incident of war."[19] It contemplated war in its nineteenth-century aspects envisaging, for example, "an invading army which is trying to 'live on the country'" when in fact modern western armies are immediately faced with the necessity of wholesale food imports in order to prevent the population from starving and with a vast array of other problems which either conflict with the premises of the Hague Conventions or are completely beyond their provisions or their apparent contemplation.[20] To the men in the field then and to the objective observer today it must be apparent that Potter was quite right in concluding that in the years since World War I there had been an unfortunate negligence in developing this aspect of the law of nations.[21]

If there was neither a clear body of law nor theory to apply to this period in the occupation, the workaday premises were nonetheless real. In reconstructing those years following termination of the period of *occupatio bellica* it is apparent that the program in Western Germany proceeded in accordance with four major though often unarticulated principles. In the first place, the Declaration of Berlin and all of subsequent practice made it clear that military victory would be used for the acquisition of what was called "supreme authority" and what was in fact legal sovereignty. Judged from almost any point of view, the representatives of the occupant governments became "the determinate sovereign whose commands and permissions establishd the law

[18] C. J. Friedrich, "Rebuilding the German Constitution," *Am. Pol. Sci. R.,* XLIII (1949), 474.

[19] See P. B. Potter, "Legal Bases and Character of Military Occupation in Germany and Japan," *Am. J. Internat. Law,* XLIII (1949), 323-325.

[20] See H. A. Smith, "Government of Occupied Territories," *British Yearbook of International Law,* XXI (1944), 151-155.   [21] Potter, *op. cit.*

and whose position was above the law."[22] In the second place, it was equally apparent that the occupants were intent upon abandoning the traditional and Atlantic Charter-repeated doctrine of the right of internal self-determination. From Yalta through Potsdam, from the London agreements down to the most recent Allied-German agreement, runs recognition of the clear intention of forcing certain basic patterns of living upon the German people. The Allies have not been willing that Germany should return to monarchical or to fascist forms of government, nor will the western Allies permit her to choose to establish a Communist government. Hence, in a primary respect the occupation during these years was erected upon a principle of a limited denial of internal self-determination.

Just as basic was a third tenet, the conviction that political or popular sovereignty had not and could not be taken from the German people, that it awaited only the opportunity to express itself again and thereby lodge political power in the institutions which might be newly created. It was upon this basis that local, state, and ultimately federal governments in Western Germany were developed. The constitutions were conceived as having been derived from the political sovereignty of the people rather than from the legal sovereignty which had fallen to the occupant governments in 1945. The latter were thought to do no more than to permit the expression and exercise of the primary powers of the people's sovereignty.

Finally, it was generally held that legal sovereignty itself was held in trust until such time as the trustees might decide that the possessors of political sovereignty were prepared to undertake its responsibilities in accordance with Allied understanding of the Potsdam minima of "life on a democratic and peaceful basis."[23] This was a concept which had been recognized early in the occupation by the Obergericht in Zurich when it said, "The state of affairs presently existing in Germany corresponds closely to a kind of fiduciary administration of the authority of the German states by the occupying powers."[24] During the first five years of occupation it was consistently maintained in the western zones that the powers of German government were held in trust until such time as they could be returned to a sovereign people.[25]

Rather than borrow from existing terminology of international law

[22] Francis Coker, "Sovereignty," *Encyclopaedia of the Social Sciences*, XIV, 265-268.

[23] Potsdam Agreement, August 2, 1945, sec. III, par. 4.

[24] 42 *Schweizerische Juristen-Zeitung* 89 (1946), reported by Rheinstein, *op. cit.*, who also develops the fiduciary concept.

[25] See, for example, letter from Gen. Lucius D. Clay to the president of the

in order to find an appropriate designation for this period of occupation which followed the belligerent occupation, it will be identified
here in terms of its principal characteristic. Hence, we shall refer to it
as a period of "Allied legal sovereignty." Extending from 1945 well
into 1953, it will probably prove to be the longest of the several intervals in this occupation. This period of Allied legal sovereignty was in
turn subdivided into phases that are distinguished from one another
by the degree to which the trusteeship was relaxed and institutions of
self-government were established by a politically sovereign German
people. In the first phase all political power was exercised directly by
military government through agencies of its own creation or designation. German personnel was utilized for consultation and for the performance of subordinate functions, but policy, general supervision,
and a considerable amount of actual performance were assumed by
Allied agencies and Allied personnel. Gradually this type of direct
occupation government was replaced in certain fields and in certain
zones by German institutions under the supervision of German officials
moving on their own initiative but in fact exercising both the legal
and political powers of the occupant governments. During this second
phase German decisions and German legislation had no sanction beyond that provided by the occupants. It was a time in which German
institutions and officials served primarily as agents of the occupation.
Quite distinct was the third phase, in which units of German government were created by and in the name of the German people. While
theirs was a limited jurisdiction and it was at all times subject to revocation by the occupants, the popular source of their power and their
sanctions in public opinion were nonetheless clear and, for this purpose, distinctive. It was a period in which the overriding legal sovereignty of the Allies had been voluntarily withdrawn to permit the
rise of popularly based institutions with the clear proviso that, glacier-
like, it might return at any time to cover and/or uproot the growth
which had occurred in the meantime.

The period of occupation legal sovereignty ended in Western Germany when the governments of the United States, France, and Great
Britain concluded an agreement with the German Federal Republic
which in fact delimited the remaining authority of the occupant governments in Western Germany. When this agreement becomes effective, the occupation will almost certainly enter a distinctly new
phase which is clearly *occupatio pacifica*. Legal as well as political

Bavarian Constitutional Assembly of October 24, 1946, which referred to "Germany as it is administered by the Allied Control Council, and as later it may be
administered by some form of German government," Appendix A.

sovereignty are recognized in the Bonn government or in the people; the jurisdiction of the occupant is specifically limited; the action is not unilateral but mutual, and provision has been made for adjudication of disputes in a court of law. Only one aspect of this third period is unusual. It contemplates the possibility that under specified circumstances the powers of governance may again be exercised by the occupying powers and withdrawn from the formerly sovereign German government. However, since this has been provided for by mutual agreement, it would seem that it satisfies the conditions of traditional concepts of "peaceful occupation." In order to be entirely consistent with the theory as we have developed it here, however, it might have been better had the agreement been approved by the people in a referendum and thus placed the stamp of approval of the political sovereign upon a document which authorizes a transfer of legal sovereignty from the constituted government back to the occupant governments. This would avoid the argument that a legal sovereign is incapable of voluntary abdication of its powers.

The occupation of Western Germany after World War II may therefore be said to have fallen into three distinct periods. From the day Allied troops crossed into German territory until May 8, 1945, we conducted a "belligerent occupation." From that time until the conclusion of the Contractual Agreement may be referred to as a period of "occupational legal sovereignty." With the conclusion of that agreement the third and final phase of "peaceful occupation" was begun. The first of these periods was largely military, had few long-run implications, was relatively brief, and would be described best in a volume dealing with the occupation per se rather than in one which is primarily concerned with German government. On the other hand, the period of *occupatio pacifica* is one in which the political institutions and processes described in this volume will be in operation. But before turning to that period and those political concerns, it is necessary that we examine the three phases which constitute the second period of Allied legal sovereignty. It is important to do so, however, with a view to the influence those phases had upon German practice rather than as an analysis in occupation administration.

2

Emergence of
German Governments

EDWARD H. LITCHFIELD

THE period of "occupation legal sovereignty" was much the longest
of the major segments of the occupation. While the characteristics
of its three phases are reasonably clear, it is not possible to specify
precise times when one began and another ended. Controls were relaxed much more rapidly in the United States Zone than they were in
the French and British zones, and all three have returned more authority to German governments than was contemplated at any time in
the Soviet satellite of Eastern Germany. Furthermore, within any one
zone, direct military government came to an end in the field of local
government before it did on state or federal levels. As a consequence
it is necessary to speak of phases with uniform characteristics rather
than phases set off as specific time intervals.

DIRECT MILITARY GOVERNMENT PHASE

During the months and years of direct military government, the
functions of civil government were exercised by individual military
governors acting unilaterally and the four acting in concert in the
Allied Control Council. In both instances, the occupiers assumed legislative, executive, and judicial powers which they exercised to the
extent of their abilities and needs. These were the governments of
Germany during those early postwar times. For some months after
the surrender and the close of the period of "belligerent occupation,"
military government continued in essentially the same hands as had
conducted it in the earlier period of actual hostilities. In the United

States Zone it was entrusted to G-5 in SHAEF and later USFET (United States Forces, European Theatre) and their field teams known as E, F, G, H, and I detachments. A modest amount of planning also fell to U.S. Group CC. This was a time of substantial confusion and internal conflict though it was also a period in which the field detachments were making decisive preliminary efforts to establish German agent governments at local and state levels.[1] In the British Zone, SHAEF military government functions passed to Control Council Group, British Element, while in the Soviet Zone responsibility remained with relatively unspecialized units of the Red Army.[2] By summer a more permanent structure was created in the form of the Soviet Military Administration. Fall brought a similar development in the United States Zone with the organization of the Office of Military Government for Germany known generally as OMGUS. These were the principal offices for the exercise of occupation powers from that time until the establishment of central German governments in 1949. The details of their internal organization and operation do not concern us here for they are questions of military rather than civil government.[3] At the same time several broad aspects of their administration had significant bearing upon the German political pattern which slowly emerged from under their weight.

Allied decision to establish the Control Council in Berlin and unilateral determinations to locate British, American, and Soviet headquarters in the same city were conclusions of major though transient political import. The definite, though by no means predominant, German desire to make a clean break with the traditions which Berlin represented and turn to Weimar, Frankfurt, or some one of the other cities of historic democratic significance was substantially discouraged by the re-emergence of the former capital as the new center of Allied governmental activity. French insistence upon maintaining their principal offices in Baden-Baden did not materially diminish the impact of

[1] See Harold Zink, *American Military Government in Germany* (New York, 1947), pp. 93-97.

[2] See J. P. Nettl, *The Eastern Zone and Soviet Policy in Germany, 1945-50* (New York, 1951), pp. 56-59; Frank Howley, *Berlin Command* (New York, 1950).

[3] See, particularly, Sydney Connor and C. J. Friedrich, eds., "Military Government," in *Annals of the American Academy of Political and Social Science*, CCLXVII (Jan., 1950); W. Friedmann, *The Allied Military Government of Germany* (London, 1947); C. J. Friedrich and associates, *American Experiences in Military Government in World War II* (New York, 1948); Hajo Holborn, *Military Government Organization and Politics* (Washington, 1947); Harold Zink, *op. cit.*

this decision. For all practical purposes the old capital was again the focal point of the news, the center of public attention, the base of principal governmental activity. Old nationalist loyalties were re-kindled and developed until the later course of West-East affairs had left Berlin a meander scar removed from the main stream of political development.

Important also was the fact that the territorial organization of German state governments was made to depend in part upon the administrative convenience of military government. At times this reached incredible proportions, as in the case of the creation of a Frankfurt Enclave made up of the old Free City of Frankfurt and pieces of *Land* Hesse, Province Hessen-Nassau, and Province Kurhessen.[4] In other circumstances, such as the dismemberment of Württemberg and Baden, there were more compelling military considerations which dictated change in the civil structure. In the substantial British Zone reorganization which resulted in the creation of an entirely new state of North Rhine–Westphalia, civil units were again adjusted in order to accommodate them to the occupant government's administrative convenience in exercising effective controls over the Ruhr. Primary changes in German government such as these have necessarily affected the federal system which subsequently grew up in Western Germany. The elimination of a spate of tiny states and the formation of a more viable unit such as North Rhine–Westphalia would appear to have contributed to a healthy federal organization even though this was not the primary reason for the change. It would also appear that however fortuitous it may have been, the actual outcome of the Württemberg-Baden-Hohenzollern reorganization will contribute to effective federalism.[5] On the other hand, one can make something of a case for the conclusion that, had military government administrative needs not dictated such change and had the former states and provinces been retained, there might have been a more determined effort to protect state interests in the Parliamentary Council which drafted the Bonn Constitution. The author's own conclusion is that any such insistence upon a more extreme states' rights point of view would have been both unlikely and unsuccessful in the face of the centralization which would have been demanded by the Social Democratic party under almost any circumstances. However little it may have been calculated for the purpose, military government's insistence upon territorial changes which would further its own objectives has probably con-

[4] See an appropriately indignant account of this abortive plan in Zink, *op. cit.*, pp. 97-98.

[5] See subsequent discussion of this whole development in Chapter 4 below.

tributed substantially to the growth of sound member units in the western federal government.

It has also been maintained that the hopes of a successful federal structure were in part retarded by the centralized structures of each of the military governments. Exponents of this point of view were most numerous in the *Land* offices of military government. They insisted that the necessity of looking constantly to Berlin for instructions encouraged the all-too-well-established German tendency of looking to the center for direction rather than exercising local initiative for the solution of local problems. Officers on *Kreis* (county and city) levels applied the same argument to centralized military government organization within the state. While it is no doubt true that greater decentralization of occupation organization would have encouraged local initiative, it is equally true that the nature of the problems of economic collapse, of public safety, of public health, and of millions of displaced and migrant persons made centralized control essential whatever its affect upon the vitality of state governments.

During this phase the examples set by occupation forces were also of considerable long-run significance in the development of postwar German political life. Wholesale disregard of the rights of the individual in the Soviet Zone,[6] in early days in Stuttgart by the French, and occasionally by American and British forces elsewhere in Germany retarded the effort to build a new concept of the value of the individual in the community more than months of patient effort by military government could develop. On the other hand, the determined efforts of the United States and British Military Governors in later years to impose a rule of law upon their troops did a considerable amount to build respect for the concept.

Perhaps most important in the impact of the unilateral administration of the powers of military government upon German political life during this early phase was the quality of the leadership of the men and women who exercised its responsibilities. Stable, experienced, and conscientious officers were able to accomplish a great deal, but their efforts were all too often nullified by the activities of others who were without either the experience or the motive essential to the accomplishment of their tasks. The quality of the leadership varied tremendously from zone to zone and office to office. There were men like Clay and Robertson whose competence, devotion, and leadership were an inspiration not only to their own staffs but to the German leaders and people as well. But there were also vain, ignorant, and self-seeking men who came to authority without a shred of claim to knowledge

[6] For example, see Nettl, *op. cit.*, p. 58, and Chapter 6 below.

or experience in the field of civil government. They too had an impact upon their countries' efforts to mold the character of postwar German politics and government. It was an uneven record which might have been tremendously improved had personnel planning been more adequate, had early military leaders been more familiar with the essential character of the occupation, and had both the United States and Great Britain not lost sight of the thousands of men whom they trained for occupation duty but who never arrived in Germany. But in spite of all the failures, the over-all impact of occupation personnel on the growth of new German governments was impressive. Throughout this volume the reader will encounter frequent reference to ideas and practices which had their origins in the efforts of individual military government officials.

During these early phases Germany was also governed by the Allied Control Council. Created by the Potsdam Agreement in the summer of 1945, the Council functioned off and on through a checkered career which came to a decisive end in the spring of 1948. The detailed story of the structure and functioning of the Council has never been fully told and cannot be undertaken here,[7] for this too belongs primarily to the story of Allied military government and not to an account of German government. For our purposes a brief description of its organization and operation and its impact upon the ultimate structure of German government is all that is required. The Control Council was composed of the four military governors who met regularly to consider problems referred to them by their subordinate bodies and subjects raised by one of the members or referred to the Control Council by the Council of Foreign Ministers in one of the latter's occasional meetings. It was supported by a so-called "co-ordinating committee," a number of directorates, and a variety of lesser committees and working parties covering the multitude of fields which were necessarily involved in the process of governing a large nation. Every unit, from working party to Council, functioned in substantially the same manner and under most of the same handicaps. Three languages were official, and German was a constant but unofficial fourth. Decisions required unanimous agreement, with the consequence that comparatively few were achieved. Each unit was assisted by secretaries, interpreters, and stenographers, and the volume of sheer paper work was staggering in many of the more active areas such as transportation, communications, finance, and a variety of economic fields. Meetings seemed interminable and after the summer of 1946 became increasingly acrimonious. After its initial

[7] See accounts in Lucius D. Clay, *Decision in Germany* (Garden City, N.Y., 1949), chaps. 6, 7, 8, and 18.

spurt the work of the Control Council and its subordinate bodies fell off to little more than an occasional piece of relatively mechanical legislation.

During its years in existence, the Council legislated on subjects as diverse as taxation, property restitution, the punishment of politically incriminated citizens, reparations removals, diet, control of shipbuilding, wages, prices, utility rates, marriage, and hundreds of other subjects with which civil governments are ordinarily faced. In these categories of substantive legislation the impact of the occupation was obviously varied. In many instances Control Council legislation in its original or slightly modified form is still the law of the land, and some of it may be expected to remain for many years to come.

Control Council legislation was executed in the different zones by the individual zone commanders. This, plus the varying practices employed in the exercise of unilateral military government powers, resulted in a diversity of governmental patterns which constitutes one of the most significant legacies of the period of occupation. Police administration, tax collection, the structure of local government, the role of citizen committees in welfare administration, the extent of state powers, the use of the budget as a planning instrument, are but illustrations of fundamentally differing practice which grew in the different zones as a result of unilateral administration of both Control Council and zonal legislation. Contributing to that diversity but also affecting the over-all patterns of government in the western zones was the forced decentralization of functions of government as a result of the refusal of the French to agree to the establishment of the central administrative agencies which had been provided for in the Potsdam Agreement. The consequence was that for some time state governments or, in some instances, zonal governments were made accustomed to the exercise of these powers. For all of the general desire to re-establish national agencies for the administration of economic, agricultural, and financial activities, this period of enforced state administration was unquestionably helpful in the rekindling of interest and at least some small measure of confidence in the competence of governmental authorities on less than national levels. Conversely, it was also the failure of the Control Council to agree on the establishment of central agencies which began the long development that culminated in the present government in Bonn.

Direct military government of Germany came to an end as a result of many factors. The heavy turnover in trained military government staff made direct governance almost an impossibility. In the United States Zone this was coupled with long-standing policy of exercising controls rather than assuming responsibility for direct performance and also with a strong aversion to the type of colonization which continued exercise of direct government powers would have necessitated. Deep in the matrix of American motivation to return power to Germans was the personal reluctance of many top officials to continue to intrude into the internal life of another people. While less concerned for the sensibilities of an occupied people, the British too were impelled toward substantial relaxation of controls by financial pressures which made it difficult to maintain large occupation installations. Combined American and British influence finally led to the capitulation of the French who were not disturbed by the responsibilities of colonization and whose policy of living partially off the land made them less interested in the financial aspects of the problem. Slowly, direct performance of the legislative and executive functions of military government gave way to performance by means of German "agent governments" functioning on behalf of the occupants.

GERMAN GOVERNMENTS AS AGENTS OF THE OCCUPATION POWERS

While there was considerable variation from level to level and zone to zone, the phase of "agent governments" in the localities and states had a common pattern. Authority for their establishment was contained in military government directives. Legislation was approved or disapproved on an individual basis and was issued in some instances by military government in its own name. Enforcement while undertaken in the first instance by the agent government was ultimately enforceable by the occupation forces. Responsibility was to the Allied sources of power and not to the German people in the area in which the agent government had jurisdiction. These organizations were accurately referred to by the British and the Soviets as "administrations" rather than as governments.

The process of creating responsible German agent governments to exercise the authority of the occupants began early in the American Zone. Within a month after the surrender and the opening of this period of "occupation sovereignty" one such agent government had been established in Bavaria and a considerable number had been created in the towns and villages.[8] By the fall of 1945 there were state and local governments of this character in the entire zone. In the Soviet Zone agent governments on these levels also appeared in mid- and late 1945, though there continued to be a considerable amount of direct SMA intrusion into internal operations of the individual units of

[8] See Zink, *op. cit.*, chap. 8.

government. In the British area responsible agents were rather slow to develop, for Control Commission officials on both state and local levels insisted upon direct exercise of their authority. However, by late 1946 relatively responsible agent governments were in existence on state level in that zone as well.[9] In many respects agent government came last in the French Zone, where in South Baden, for example, not even a semblance of legislative power was passed to the state government until late in 1946.

In the summer and fall of 1945 came the first agency governments on higher than state level. There was still no agreement in the Control Council as to the establishment of the administrative agencies contemplated by the Potsdam Agreement, and the need for uniform central administration of food, finance, transport, communication, and related problems was growing daily. To meet this increasingly critical problem, the military government in the United States Zone authorized the establishment of the *Länderrat* or Council of States.[10] The Council was made up of the ministers-president of the three and later four states in the United States Zone and was issisted by a small secretariat in the headquarters in Stuttgart. In later periods its work was materially expedited by the creation of a full-time Directorate which undertook to co-ordinate its widespread activities. As the time of government by agent drew to a close the *Länderrat* was augmented by an advisory but modestly representative Parliamentary Advisory Council[11] of twenty-four members. The limited original jurisdiction of the *Länderrat* was slowly expanded to include many of the functions of government which were ultimately to be entrusted to the federal government.[12]

The legislative process in the *Länderrat* was characteristic of agency governments. Legislation was passed by unanimous vote of the ministers-president and with the specific approval of the deputy military governor. It was ultimately issued by the individual ministers-president upon the basis of decree-making authority specifically conferred upon them by military government.[13] While it was generally referred to as

[9] See Ordinance No. 57, "Powers of *Länder* in the British Zone," November, 1946, in J. K. Pollock, J. H. Meisel, and H. L. Bretton, eds., *Germany under Occupation*, rev. ed. (Ann Arbor, 1949), pp. 182-184.

[10] Actual authorization was given in Stuttgart on October 17, 1945. For pertinent directives and *Länderrat* statutes, see Pollock, Meisel, and Bretton, *op. cit.*, pp. 101-109.

[11] Amendment to *Länderrat* Statute of February 10, 1947. For text, see Pollock, Meisel, and Bretton, *op. cit.*, p. 110.

[12] For a careful review of the work of the *Länderrat*, see Heinz Guradze, "The *Laenderrat*. Landmark of German Reconstruction," *Western Political Quarterly*, June, 1950.

[13] Proclamation No. 2, September 19, 1945, *MG Gazette*, September, 1945.

Länderrat legislation, it was in fact military government legislation prepared and issued by and in the name of designated agents of the occupation. Later this was to become still more confused when the ministers-president became duly elected public officials with constitutional mandates from the German people. Their dual legal capacity during this period was not only puzzling but also politically embarrassing.

It was during the summer and fall of 1945 that the Soviet Military Administration also began the creation of administrative agents on zone level. By October, twelve had been established in industry, transport, and communications and also in a number of noneconomic fields not called for in the Potsdam Agreement. Complete with staffs, a president, and general corporate identity, they too were no more than occupation agents or, as they were officially explained, "the prolonged executive arm" of the SMA.[14] Legislation was issued in the name of the president of the Administration but "by command of the Soviet Military Administration."[15] By early 1947 certain of the heads of the Central Administrations, some of the state officials, and a group of trade-union and farm officials had been organized into what was to become the powerful Economic Commission of the Soviet Zone. The commission was created in the first instance as a means of resolving conflicts between the state governments and the politically removed Central Administrations. The commission included a legislative body which, in Soviet fashion, did little more than ratify actions submitted to it, a secretariat which in fact was controlling, and a group of seventeen administrative departments which had been taken over from the earlier Central Administrations. Whatever the reasons for the change and whatever the institutional adjustment which the change involved, there was no change in the agency character of the German bodies which governed in the name of the Allied occupant power.

In the British area, zonal agents of the occupation were again slow in developing. The Zonal Advisory Council created in 1946 was principally an advisory body for the deputy military governor and as such belonged more to the phase of direct military government than it did to the subsequent time of responsible agents. Not until its reorganization and the establishment of the Central Economic Office in October, 1946, did it begin to assume the stature of the *Länderrat* in the United States Zone.[16] If the British were slow, the French were even farther

[14] Thus, in referring to potential conflict between these central agencies and the states, Nettl remarks, "Any protest would indeed have been futile, as it would have been a protest against the SMA itself," *op cit.*, p. 129.

[15] *Ibid.*, pp. 114-125.

[16] Ordinance No. 52; see Pollock, Meisel, and Bretton, *op cit.*, pp. 177-178.

behind for the "agency" phase in the development of central agencies never did occur in the French Zone.

By the summer of 1946 it was clear that the impasse in the Control Council's consideration of the establishment of central agencies and the related issue of treatment of Germany as an economic whole would not soon be resolved. While the *Länderrat* had been tremendously successful in the United States Zone, the general economic situation demanded a more comprehensive administrative framework within which to develop. American Military Government had come to the conclusion that "eleven months after the Potsdam Protocol, Germany was more thoroughly split into independent and isolated economic units than it was when the protocol was signed."[17] Unwilling to let the economy drift indefinitely, Secretary Byrnes in Paris in the early summer of 1946 had invited the Foreign Ministers to pool the economies of their zones with the American Zone. Only the British had accepted.[18] This invitation was repeated the same month in the Control Council,[19] and the British acceptance set off a series of conferences which were the introduction to the development of Bizonia and ultimately of the Bonn government.

In the three years from the Byrnes proposal in July of 1946 to the formal establishment of the German Federal Republic in September, 1949, three stages occurred in the development of the bizonal agent government.[20] Step one called for the organization of a series of "Executive Committees" composed of representatives of each of the eight states in the two zones. The six committees were located in a number of different cities in order to avoid the creation of a capital-city sense which might militate against an ultimate all-German development at some later date. In this first organization care was taken to specify clearly that "the German authorities in both zones must be charged with the execution of military government policy subject to policy direction and supervision by the United States and British staffs."[21] There was no debate or doubt about the agency aspect of the relationship. At this time the two military governments also created the

[17] OMGUS, *The Evolution of Bizonal Organization* (1948), p. 2; a special report prepared by the Civil Administration Division.

[18] For the background of the early development in Bizonia, see Clay, *op. cit.*, chap. 9.

[19] CONL/M (46) 19, Min. 82, "Statement by the U.S. Member on Measures to Insure the Economic Unity of Germany."

[20] Subsequent paragraphs are patterned largely upon material contained in *The Evolution of Bizonal Organization,* published by the Civil Administration Division, OMGUS, when the author was the division director.

[21] *Ibid.,* p. 2.

Bipartite Board which for the next three years was to replace the Allied Control Council in so far as the two zones were concerned. The board developed a secretariat and a series of panels in much the same way that the Control Council had been structured. By the end of the year both Allied and German organization had been crystallized in the Byrnes-Bevin Agreement[22] and a series of agreements between *Land* ministers in the United States Zone and the chief of the Central Office for Economics in the British Zone.[23]

By spring of 1947 the dismal Moscow meeting of the Council of Foreign Ministers had made it clear that an all-German organization was even more remote than it had been the preceding year. The experience with the Executive Committees had also illustrated the need for a more compact, effective, and perhaps politically acceptable German organization for Bizonia. The agencies were widely scattered and their activities were therefore in need of co-ordination.[24] Furthermore, compliance with their decisions was left entirely to the individual states, and there had been occasions in which state implementation had been substantially less than the circumstances really required. This was further aggravated by the unequal powers of the states and zonal agencies in the two zones. All things pointed to the reorganization which finally took place in May of 1947.

The Bizonal Agreement of May 29, 1947, converted the autonomous Executive Committees into departments in a consolidated structure administered by an Executive Committee and generally responsible to an Economic Council of fifty-two members selected upon a proportional basis by the state legislatures.[25] The administration of the several functions by committees was abolished, and individual directors were substituted. Perhaps most important, all agencies were moved to Frankfurt and rudimentary co-ordination of effort became possible if only as a result of proximity. Co-ordination was considerably enhanced also through the agency of an Executive Committee composed of one representative from each of the state governments.[26] Economic Council legislation became binding upon the individual citizen and upon the

[22] Byrnes-Bevin Agreement, December 2, 1946, in Pollock, Meisel, and Bretton, *op. cit.*, pp. 225-227.

[23] See, for example, "Preliminary Agreement on the Establishment of a German Economic Administration," September 5, 1946 BIB/P (46) 5 (Revise), published in *The Evolution of Bizonal Organization*, pp. 20-23.

[24] For graphic illustration, see Chart No. 1, *The Evolution of Bizonal Organization*.

[25] Agreement contained in app. A of U.S. Proclamation No. 5 (published in identical form in the British Zone); see Pollock, Meisel, and Bretton, *op. cit.*, pp. 29-52. [26] See Chart No. 2, *The Evolution of Bizonal Organization*.

states. Conflicts between bizonal legislation and state laws were resolved in favor of the former despite the fact that by this time some of the states had already moved beyond the phase of agency and were in reality exercising limited powers of sovereignty conferred upon them by popularly prepared and approved constitutions. It was specified at the time that this resulted from the fact that the Economic Council, though semirepresentative in character, was still an agent of the occupation powers and legislated with their specific approval and upon the basis of authority conferred by them. Again, with full realization of the dangers which a disproportionate centralization might bring to a future German federal government, considerable care was taken to limit rigidly the jurisdicition of the Council to the fields of finance, transport, food and agriculture, communications, and certain related economic questions. It was intended that the states should take advantage of this additional opportunity to establish their competence and their identity during this interim period in which central bodies were less effective than they would ultimately become as an integrated federal government.

While an improvement over the initial structure, this second step in the evolution of Bizonia was also to reveal serious shortcomings in practice. The Executive Committee's anomolous role as executive and also as representative of the individual states caused conflict with the politically representative Council, with the consequence that it was not long before the Council began to ignore the committee and to undertake direct supervision of the executive directors administering the several departments. This very thoroughly destroyed the delicate balance which the proclamation called for when it specified that immediate supervision of the departments should rest with the committee while ultimate responsibility of each director must be to the Council. These difficulties were compounded by the shortcomings of the Economic Council as a legislative body. Its fifty-two members found themselves too few to man the multitude of committees which the Council's work required. This plus the inexperience and partisan bickerings of many of the members resulted in a legislative product which was both meager in quantity and inadequate in content. During its eight months of existence only a handful of ordinances was passed and approved. It was during this period also that the Bipartite Board first called emphatic attention to what was to become a long-standing effort to encourage German legislative bodies to recognize the necessity of adequate legislative policy standards as a basis for subsequent administrative implementation.[27] Finally, difficulties of disturbing pro-

[27] For example, see letter from Bipartite Board to the chairmen of the Bipartite

portions developed between the increasingly independent and politically responsive states on the one hand and the bizonal organization on the other. At best, "the *Länder* complained, procrastinated and altogether too frequently attacked the authority[28] of the bizonal structure, and at worst, they actually refused to share their industrial and agricultural resources with one another and the bizonal economy. There were many who felt that the states were abusing rather than constructively using their years of relative predominance.

While reorganization was therefore dictated by internal considerations, it was also affected by the steady drift of western-Soviet relationships in Germany specifically and in the world generally. The months following the Moscow Foreign Ministers' Conference had witnessed a gradual deterioration of Control Council work. In November and December the four ministers met in London to make another effort to come to some agreement about the treatment of Germany as a whole. As far as the structure of German government was concerned it accomplished little more than a greater agreement between the United Kingdom and the United States as to the ultimate character of the federal German government.[29] Accord between the four powers proved impossible, and the Council of Foreign Ministers adjourned with clear recognition between the partners in Bizonia that the structure of that agency government must be immediately revised. Preliminary and precautionary plans, developed prior to the London Conference, were rapidly crytalized into draft proposals which were discussed with German leaders in January, 1948, and revised and published in the two zones less than a month later.[30]

Step three in bizonal organization contemplated a more elaborate structure. State interests were more specifically assured by the creation of a full-fledged second legislative chamber called a *Länderrat* with powers of initiation and veto of legislation and with limited control over the executive through participation in the appointment and removal of the chairman of the Executive Committee. Composed of the ministers-president and one other representative from each of the *Länder*, it both represented state points of view in the formulation of legislation and also provided a liaison with individual state adminis-

Control Office, *The Evolution of Bizonal Organization*, p. 6.

[28] *Ibid.*, p. 7.

[29] The text of the working paper developed in London is unfortunately still classified. It was based in considerable measure upon Moscow proposals made earlier in the year.

[30] U.S. Proclamation No. 7, February 9, 1948 (British Zone Ordinance No. 126). in Pollock, Meisel, and Bretton, *op. cit.*, pp. 238-243.

trations which, it was hoped, would encourage a greater measure of co-operation than had previously existed. The Economic Council was also altered to include an additional 52 members, making a total of 104 members selected by the state legislatures in accordance with their respective political complexions. Administrative functions of the new organization were entrusted to an Executive Committee composed of the heads of the several departments and a chairman without departmental responsibilities. Department heads were to be elected and recalled by the Council, though both actions required the specific approval of the Bipartite Board.[31]

The Economic Council and the *Länderrat* retained the powers exercised by their predecessor excepting those entrusted at about this same time to the *Bank Deutscher Länder.* They acquired authority to raise their own funds from revenues derived from customs, excise taxes, postal services, railways, and a self-established percentage of income, wage, and corporation tax revenues. They were promised and soon received general legislative powers in the fields of labor, labor relations, and wage control. The exercises of these powers continued to require the specific approval of the parent body, the Bipartite Board. While the Council's legal status was presumably clarified in German law by a provision which declared it "capable of having rights and obligations,"[32] it was equally clear from the manner of its creation, the controls over its appointments, and the necessity of approval of its legislation that it was still a creature of the occupation, still an illustration of the agency phase of the period of occupation sovereignty.

Two other important bizonal agent governing bodies were established during this same month. The first was the Bizonal High Court.[33] Earlier bizonal legislative bodies had been obliged to depend upon state courts for the trial of those who violated central legislation, with the consequence that many were never prosecuted and conflicts between states or between a state and the bizonal organization had gone unresolved. The new body was established to provide a judicial answer to the problem. The court consisted of ten members appointed by the Bipartite Board upon the basis of recommendations supplied by the Economic Council and the *Länderrat.* Again, there could be no question as to the "agent" status of the court, for if the method of its creation and the selection of its justices had not settled the matter, Article XV clearly did so. It noted that Military Government Law No. 2

[31] See Chart No. 3, *The Evolution of Bizonal Organization.*
[32] U.S. Proclamation No. 7, Article XII.
[33] U.S. Proclamation No. 8 (British Zone Ordinance No. 127), in Pollock, Meisel, and Bretton, *op. cit.,* pp. 243-248.

prohibited German courts from declaring military government law invalid and pointed out that since Economic Council legislation required Bipartite Board approval it was in fact occupation legislation and hence a determination of invalidity was beyond the competence of the court.

The second of these additional bodies was the *Bank Deutscher Länder.*[34] While *Land Central Banks* had been in existence for some time, March of 1948 marked the establishment of the first postwar interzonal banking organization. The steady growth of a bizonal economy made such an institution necessary for both public and private financial transactions. It was authorized to issue and distribute bank notes and coins, promote the solvency and liquidity of the *Land Central Banks,* regulate credit, interest, and discount rates, establish minimum reserve requirements for individual banks, settle balances among the *Länder,* buy and sell foreign exchange, and engage in a number of other functions which in the United States would normally be undertaken by the Federal Reserve Board. However, despite its performance of many essentially governmental functions, considerable care was taken to assure a position for the bank which would be relatively free from control of other governmental or quasi-governmental bodies. General review of policy and practice was vested in an agency of the Bipartite Board, the Allied Bank Commission. Here, as in the case of the Economic Council and the High Court, the governing statutes were careful to protect the primary and controlling position of the occupation powers.

During the years 1946 through mid-1949, bizonal economic and financial functions were also performed in part by the Joint Export-Import and Joint Foreign Exchange Agencies. Created as a result of the December, 1946, Byrnes-Bevin Agreement,[35] the agencies were charged with responsibility for trade promotion and foreign exchange negotiation and control. While operating in areas closely related to those for which the bizonal German agencies had been given responsibility, JEIA and JFEA were in fact parts of the bipartite military government structure since they were staffed and managed by Allied personnel, governed by Allied boards, and ultimately controlled by the Bipartite Board itself, though with the United States member exercising predominant control. For reasons resulting from Germany's uncertain position in world affairs these functions continued to be exercised by Allied agencies until the *Bank Deutscher Länder* took

[34] U.S. Military Government Law No. 6, February 15, 1948. For text, see U.S. Department of State, *Germany 1947-1949: The Story in Documents.* pp. 474-478.
[35] See note 22 above.

over a few of them as an agent in 1948 and the Federal Republic took on most of the others in late 1949. As units of military government these two joint agencies were atypical of their times and were in fact unavoidable remnants of an earlier phase of direct military government.

With occasional additional grants of authority and with growing acceptance in the community, these bizonal agencies governed the two zones on behalf of the occupying powers until the "agency" phase came to an end in the fall of 1949 with the establishment of the German Federal Republic. It had been a time which served two primary purposes beyond the immediate functions of day to day governing. In the first place it had provided an important and practical experiment in government which had enabled the United States and the United Kingdom gradually to accommodate their views regarding the broad outlines of the ultimate structure of central German political organization. Given the division of Germany into separate zones, this time of accommodation was essential to final agreement as to the direction in which the future structure would develop. But it was perhaps more important as a time in which state governments were established, gained a measure of confidence, and found voice. If the federal principle finds acceptance and a measure of success in Western Germany in the years to come, it will be in considerable measure the result of the fact that the states were permitted to grow in stature during those years of bizonal "agency" government held in close rein by the two Allied governments.

GERMAN GOVERNMENTS OF LIMITED SOVEREIGNTY

The occupation was less than a year old when the first steps were taken to re-establish governments on state level which would speak in the name of the German people, sanctions of which would rest primarily in German hands, and ultimate success of which would depend upon acceptance in German public opinion. It was characteristic of these state governments, of the Bonn government which followed, and therefore of this phase of the period of occupation sovereignty that power was derived from the people but theoretically both the people's expression of intent and the governments' exercise of assigned powers were retractable at the will of the occupant powers. In fact in the western zones, once the process had been initiated and barring unusual developments, there was no turning back. Once we had started down the long road of Germany's return to full political and legal sovereignty there was no real likelihood that the permission to express popular will through legally semisovereign institutions would ever be withdrawn.

The first step in this development came with the announcement in February, 1946, of elections to constituent assemblies in the three southern *Länder* in the United States Zone.[36] The elections themselves were held on schedule, the conventions met, framed their respective constitutions, and referred them to the people for ratification, and the governments for which they called were quickly set up.[37] Representative institutions, functioning in terms of constitutional mandates, were again a fact in German political life by the fall of 1946. Superficially these organizations may have resembled the agency governments already in existence or later to be created, but actually they were both politically and legally of a quite different character. The legislatures spoke in their own names, and their laws were intended and accepted as German and not occupation legislation. Their actions were subject to the veto of the United States Military Governor and the exercise of sovereign power was therefore limited, but legislation was nonetheless an expression of German intent conveyed through German instrumentalities. It was no longer the result of occupation desires or the work of appointed agents. These early state governments were the prototype of the Bonn government which was to come three years later.

The state constitutions in Bavaria, Hesse, and Württemberg-Baden were approved by the deputy military governor in October, 1946. In approving the documents General Clay actually did no more than to remove a restriction upon the exercise of popular sovereignty. However, the continuity of the power of ultimate restraint by the occupation authorities was clearly indicated by the several reservations which were set forth in those letters of approval.[38] This too was a suggestion of what was to occur years later when the three western military governors were to take a parallel step with reference to the Basic Law prepared in the Bonn Parliamentary Assembly. At the same time the

---

[36] OMGUS directive February 4, 1946, "Elections in the U.S. Zone," reported in Pollock, Meisel, and Bretton, *op. cit.*, pp. 119-121.

[37] See Chapter 4 below.

[38] General Clay's letter to the presidents of the Constitutional Assemblies will be found in Appendix A. All of the letters make clear the overriding powers of the occupying forces while simultaneously recognizing the constitution "to represent the will of the State of Bavaria as expressed through the elected representatives of the citizens of the State." For texts of the state constitutions in the U.S., French, and Soviet zones, see OMGUS, *Constitutions of the German Länder* (1947), a special report of the Civil Administration Division.

military government issued a directive limiting the extent of occupation powers in the fields with which the constitutions dealt and setting forth the first specific criteria of political democracy which had appeared in Allied policy pronouncements.[39] This became the forerunner of the Occupation Statute which was issued at the time the Bonn Basic Law was approved. A combination of the constitutions, the letters of approval and reservation, and the self-limiting directive set in motion the first of the postwar German governments which could claim even a limited amount of sovereign power. It was a pattern followed in detail at the time of the creation of the German Federal Republic in 1949.

The example set in the American Zone was quickly followed in both the French and Soviet zones. In the Soviet Zone popularly elected *Landtage* drafted constitutions which were approved by the Soviet Military Administration and promulgated between December, 1946, and the early spring of 1947.[40] French Zone constitutions were finally approved by military government and accepted by popular vote on May 18, 1947. On June 9 the French High Command issued Ordinance No. 95, which was intended to serve the same purposes as the September 30 directive of the preceding year.[41] In both instances the people were presumed to have spoken, and the governments established by the constitutions were held to exercise semisovereign powers subject, of course, to the overriding veto powers of the two military governments. If in both instances the governments in fact became relatively puppetlike, this was because of compelling political and military circumstances which subverted constitutional and announced occupational theory. Nevertheless these too were governments of limited sovereignty.

Whether because they were less interested in legal and constitutional theory and less willing to entrust sweeping powers to German governments than the Americans or whether they were less willing to grant powers in theory which they intended to retain in political fact than the French and the Soviets, the British were unprepared to give constitutional status to the *Länder* in their zone until many years later. During the years of growth and relative independence of the states in the United States Zone, the British Zone *Länder* limped along under the restricting provisions of Ordinance No. 57, which actually left

[39] OMGUS directive, September 30, 1946, "Relationship between Military and Civil Government (U.S. Zone) Subsequent to Adoption of *Land* Constitutions," Appendix B.

[40] See *Constitutions of the German Länder,* Part II.

[41] *Ibid.,* Part III; also for text of Ordinance No. 95, see Pollock, Meisel, and Bretton, *op. cit.,* p. 194.

them in the status of agent governments.[42] It was not until after the Basic Law was in effect in the whole of Western Germany that the British in fact granted constitutional powers and limited sovereignty to the states in that portion of Germany.

Talk of the restoration of limited sovereignty on central levels began in the Moscow meeting of the Council of Foreign Ministers in early 1947. On March 21, Secretary Marshall formally proposed the establishment of a provisional German government, the drafting of a new constitution to be reviewed in terms of specified criteria, and the ultimate organization of a permanent government of limited sovereign powers.[43] This was followed by a specific United States plan detailing those criteria in a manner which was to be followed in substance a year later when final agreement to establish a western German government was obtained.[44] During the next several weeks proposals of varying types were also submitted by the United Kingdom, the Soviet Union, and France. Whereas the American proposal had set only broad principles of constitutional government as the bases for approval of the constitution which the Germans might ultimately draw, the British proposal contained far more specific instructions as to institutional detail. The first evidence of what was later to become a major issue was contained in those provisions of the United Kingdom proposal which specified minimum powers for a central government, as distinct from the United States insistence upon other minima for the determination of state authority in a federal system. Soviet proposals closely followed Weimar, though they were accompanied by an emphatic plea for a type of functional representation in the second chamber which would have ensured disproportionate Communist representation through the bloc organizations that had already been firmly implanted in the Eastern Zone. French proposals were so hedged by qualifications as to reveal little more than an insistence upon an extreme form of decentralization in which the federal government would be entrusted with only the most essential of functions in the fields of transport, communications, food and agriculture, and several other closely related activities. Without the benefit of today's retrospect it was nonetheless clear to participants at the time that the French were intent upon delay, that Soviets were concerned with a structure which would assist their plans to dominate a united Germany, and that only in the United States and the United Kingdom proposals were there possibilities for negotiation and perhaps ultimate agreement. In any

[42] For text, see Pollock, Meisel, and Bretton, *op. cit.*, pp. 182-184.
[43] This important statement of emergent American policy has never been released for publication. [44] *Ibid.*

event the Moscow meeting proved a bitter and unproductive experience which resolved neither this nor any of the other issues which faced the conference. The delegates left Moscow with no suggestion of an agreement as to the character of the ultimate German government.

Late in 1947 the Council of Foreign Ministers convened again to consider the problem of Germany. This London conference produced no more of a meeting of minds than had been possible in Moscow, though it did provide an opportunity for the American and the British delegations to come to closer agreement regarding the German government which they hoped to see emerge from the postwar period. This took the form of an American revision of the United Kingdom's Moscow paper.[45] While it bore little specific relationship to the final agreement reached among the French, the Americans, and the British for a west German government, it did mark the turning point in the British-American thinking on a number of important points. Thus, it made it clear that the Americans were not prepared to accept the type of detailed specifications in which the British were so interested. On the other hand, however much they may have disliked it, the Americans were clearly advised of British genuine disinterest in federalism as a device for the control of German affairs.

While London produced only this small amount to further the cause of German government, it did a great deal to cement the dry wall of western intent. Here for the first time were clear indications of French, British, and American disbelief in Soviet sincerity and at least bipartite determination to proceed to build an effective structure in Western Germany. In the councils of those critical days no man in any delegation was as resolute, as informed, as clear in his conception, or as creative in his design as Lucius Clay. It was Clay who pressed for statement of the American position on governmental problems in Moscow and initiated the conferences with the British in London. It was he who urged immediate action following the failure of the London Conference. In later years it was to be Clay who pressed for German government when the British and the French would have let it go by default and when a disastrously irresponsible German move at Coblenz almost destroyed western German government in the process of conception.

London had hardly adjourned before tripartite discussions of German government were undertaken. The exchanges of this period will no doubt be of interest to the careful student of the period, but for our purposes they produced little of substantive interest. When British,

[45] *Ibid.*

French, and United States talks were reinstituted in London in early 1948, there was little that was new, and while the meetings there produced something more than had previosuly existed, they too failed to agree upon the structure of a German government which would be acceptable to the governments concerned. Subsequent conversations in Berlin also produced little until Clay negotiated a compromise with a French Foreign Office representative which paved the way for the later agreement reached in London.[46] This was the turning point in relationship between the French and the United Kingdom–United States plans for the western German government. When tripartite talks and Benelux conversations were reinstituted in London in the late spring of 1948, agreement was reached on the character of the future German government, on the Occupation Statute, and on the territorial reorganization of the states within the western areas.

Essential to that agreement to create a west German government was American acceptance of the concept of an international authority to control the Ruhr. In view of the subsequent replacement of the Ruhr Authority by the Schuman Plan for the pooling of iron and coal resources of western Europe, it is appropriate to point out that throughout the whole of the London conversations of 1948 Ambassador Robert Murphy, without instructions or effective support from the State Department, consistently and courageously raised and discussed the importance of a European pooling of coal and steel as the only sound counterpart to the demands which the creation of an authority for the Ruhr had made upon Germany.

The talks in London culminated in a series of agreements covering the character of the future federal government, the nature of controls retained by the occupation powers, the control of the Ruhr, and the reorganization of the states in the western zones.[47] Most important among these was the one which instructed the military governors to authorize the ministers-president to convene a constituent assembly representing the several states. When the content of the authorization had been conveyed to them, the heads of states met in Coblenz and adopted a series of resolutions which virtually rejected the opportunity offered by the occupation powers. Protesting that they did not wish to "increase the West-East split," the ministers-president set forth a series of counter proposals. In the covering letter it was categorically maintained that "nothing should be done to give the character of a state to the organization which is to be formed, not withstanding the grant-

[46] For a brief account, see Clay, *op. cit.*, pp. 397-400.

[47] Complete texts of these agreements are unfortunately still classified. Approximations were released in 1948 and are shown in Appendix C.

ing of the fullest possible autonomy to the population of this territory."[48] The military governors received the replies with mixed feelings,
ranging from the American view that the action represented cata-
strophic disregard of the seriousness of the total European situation
to the none too thinly disguised French relief that perhaps the London
decision might be undone after all. The determined American effort
to offset a decision taken largely as a result of the intransigence of
Socialist party leadership was almost certainly the decisive factor in
forcing a reconsideration of German views in a series of prolonged
discussions in Rüdesheim late in July.

To make the move more acceptable in German eyes the military
governors agreed that the constitution might be known as a "basic
law" and that the constituent assembly would be referred to by the less
definitive title of "Parliamentary Council." Some modifications were
also accepted for reference to governments in Paris, London, and
Washington on the subjects of constitutional ratification and the time
limits established for the change in state boundaries.[49] In early August
the ministers-president signed a protocol accepting responsibility for
the convening of a parliamentary council in Bonn on September 1.[50]
With the holding of elections to the Council during the month the
process of constitutional reconstruction was well under way. At about
the same time the ministers-president convened a group of experts in
Chiemsee who in a very short time prepared an excellent survey of
contemporary German constitutional thought which was to become
the principal working instrument of the Parliamentary Council when it
assembled the following month.

The Bonn Council was evenly divided between the Christian Democrats and Socialists; consequently any document to emerge with anything like an impressive majority required the support of both of these
major parties. Since there were fundamental differences between them,
a series of compromises was clearly required if there was to be a
constitution in Western Germany. Primary among the differences were
those concerning the powers and the composition of the upper legislative chamber and the distribution of powers between the *Länder* and
the federal government, the most important of which were in the field
of taxation. During the fall the Parliamentary Council made considerable progress on many aspects of the draft and reached a certain
amount of agreement on the character of the upper house, though the

[48] See Coblenz Resolutions July 10, 1948, in Appendix D.
[49] See Minutes of Meeting of Military Governors and Ministers-President of July
26, 1948, Appendix E.   [50] See Protocol of August 8, Appendix F.

distribution of finance powers remained substantially unsettled. In November, in order to remove at least a portion of the uncertainty in the situation, the president of the Council asked for military government views on the progress which had been made to that time. In an informal reply, the military governors conveyed the substance of the instructions they had received from their governments as a result of the original Six Power London talks. Referred to as the Aide Memoire of November 22, this document set forth the broad minima for what the occupation powers regarded as a satisfactory constitutional document. They agreed that there were "several ways in which democratic federal government can be obtained" and that they would therefore "consider the provisions of the basic law in their whole context." At the same time they indicated the specific nature of their thinking by suggesting that the ultimate constitution should to the maximum extent possible provide:

(a) for a Bicameral legislative system in which one of the houses must represent the individual states and must have sufficient power to safeguard the interests of the states;

(b) that the executive must only have those powers which are definitely prescribed by the constitution, and that emergency powers, if any, of the executive must be so limited as to require prompt legislative or judicial review;

(c) that the powers of the federal government shall be limited to those expressly enumerated in the constitution and in any case, shall not include education, cultural and religious affairs, local government and public health (except in this last case, to secure such coordination as [is] essential to safeguard the health of the people in the several states)[,] that its powers in the field of public welfare be limited to those necessary for the co-ordination of social security measures, that its powers in the police field be limited to those especially approved by the Military Governors, during the occupation period;

(d) that the powers of the federal government in the field of public finance shall be limited to the disposal of monies including the raising of revenues, for purposes for which it is responsible; that the federal government may set rates and legislate on the general principles of assessment with regard to other taxes for which uniformity is essential, the collection and utilization of such taxes being left to the individual states, and that it may appropriate funds only for the purpose for which it is responsible under the constitution;

(e) that the constitution should provide for an independent judiciary to review federal legislation, to review the exercise of federal executive power, and to adjudicate conflicts between federal and *Land* authorities as well as between *Land* authorities, and to protect the civil rights and freedom of the individual;

(f) that the powers of the federal government to establish federal agencies for the execution and administration of its responsibilities should be clearly defined and should be limited to those fields in which it is clear that state implementation is impracticable;

(g) that each citizen has access to public office, with appointment and promotion being based solely on his fitness to discharge the responsibilities of the position, and that Civil Service should be non-political in character;

(h) that a public servant, if elected to the federal legislature, shall resign his office with the agency where he is employed before he accepts election.[51]

During the next few months, the several committees of the Parliamentary Council made a determined effort to compromise their long-standing disagreements regarding the character of the second chamber and the distribution of powers between the state and federal governments. After a number of concessions on the part of both the major political parties, substantial agreement was finally reached early in February, 1949. During the weeks that followed there was great uncertainty among the military governments as to the extent to which the draft Basic Law departed from the Aide Memoire given the Council earlier in its deliberations. The disappointment was probably keenest in the American headquarters, for the apparent deviations from American concepts of federalism had to be reconciled with American desires to press ahead as rapidly as possible. The United Kingdom representatives were prepared to proceed without serious concern for the centralizing features of the document. Since the French had never acknowledged the urgency of the Bonn government to the same extent as had the British and the Americans, General Koenig's staff often appeared to be content to reject the document out of hand and thus forestall the early establishment of a western German government. After considerable discussion, the military governors finally on March 2, 1949, addressed a memorandum to a Parliamentary Council delegation invited to Frankfurt for this purpose. In taking exception to the draft Basic Law, the military governors raised eight points which they considered of major importance. Most important among these were the questions of the general distribution of powers between the federal government and the states, the distribution of specific finance authorities as among the states and the federal government, the ambiguity of the provisions relating to the independence of the judiciary, the nature of federal administrative agencies, and the place of Berlin in the federal structure.[52] As a consequence of the memorandum of March 2, a series of negotiations developed which moved ultimately from Berlin

[51] For the full text, see Appendix G.   [52] For text, see Appendix H.

and Frankfurt to the meeting of the Foreign Ministers of the three countries in Washington in early April.

Resolving the differences between the centralist Socialist party and the decentralist Christian parties within the Parliamentary Council was difficult under any circumstances. Again, resolution of the extreme French decentralist views and British unitary concepts was even more difficult. Gradually, the British and Socialist positions on constitutional questions and French and extreme Christian Socialist views came to more or less coincide. American views were somewhere in between. When agreement finally came in mid-May, it was only after all of these conflicting concepts had been resolved at the expense of a certain amount of constitutional ambiguity.[53]

The letter of approval of the Basic Law was signed by the military governors on May 12. It suspended certain of the police powers set forth in the constitution and limited the participation of greater Berlin to nonvoting membership in the legislative bodies.[54] It also clearly noted that "the powers vested in the federation by the Basic Law, as well as the powers exercised by *Länder* and local governments, are subject to the provisions of the Occupation Statute" which was simultaneously promulgated.[55] The provision made it clear that while a measure of sovereignty had been restored it was to be exercised in strict accordance with the Occupation Statute prepared unilaterally by the occupant powers. The Bonn Constitution, when approved by the people in the summer of 1949, was therefore to become the principal example of this period of German governments of limited sovereignty.

The Occupation Statute was also an outgrowth of basic decisions made in London at the time of the Six Power talks.[56] Intended as a legal definition of the condition under which German powers of government might be exercised, the statute in basic intention was a more formal repetition of the type of instrument issued in the American Zone on September 30, 1946, at the time when the constitutions in the southern *Länder* became effective. Shortly after the Parliamentary Council convened in Bonn, a Tripartite Occupation Statute Committee

[53] See, for example, the provisions of the article in which the dangers of centralism were presumably partially offset by criteria for the exercise of federal powers which it was hoped the constitutional court might judicially interpret. It was one of the few provisions which were largely Allied in origin.

[54] In response to French representation in Washington, relayed by the Department of the Army to the Theater, Clay had insisted upon Berlin representation and had concluded with characteristic force, "After all, Western Germans will need some assurance that we are men not mice."

[55] Letter of Approval of the Basic Law, May 12, 1949, Appendix J.

[56] See Appendix C.

was established by the military governors. Seven major redrafts of the committee's work and elaborate co-ordination within each of the three military governments as well as among the several departments of the home governments resolved many of the conflicting opinions regarding the appropriate provisions of the statute. However, by Christmas of 1948 final agreement among the military governors on all aspects of the proposed statute had proved impossible, and their disagreements were forwarded to governments for resolution. While some of the issues were of only temporary substantive interest, one related to a matter of fundamental concern to the future Bonn government. The French Military Governor insisted that German authorities should be permitted to legislate in fields reserved to military government only after receiving express authorization to do so. The American and British Military Governors were equally insistent that this would mean virtual frustration of the Bonn government's legislative activity in the years ahead. This was the type of fundamental disagreement among the occupation powers which characterized the reluctant co-operation of the French during the period following the London agreements.

After extensive but inconclusive discussions in London during early 1949, the question of the Occupation Statute was forwarded to the three Foreign Ministers meeting in Washington in April of that year. In those meetings the earlier texts of the statute were considerably abbreviated, and ultimately accepted and issued by the Foreign Ministers on April 8, 1949.[57] The statute contained several provisions of particular concern to the new federal government. In the first place, it granted "full legislative, executive and judicial powers" to Bonn and the several state governments. This grant of authority was limited by the following powers which were reserved to the occupation authorities:

(a) Disarmament and demilitarization, including related fields of scientific research, prohibitions and restrictions on industry, and civil aviation;

(b) Controls in regard to the Ruhr, restitution, reparations, decartelization, deconcentration, non-discrimination in trade matters, foreign interests in Germany and claims against Germany;

(c) Foreign affairs, including international agreements made by or on behalf of Germany;

(d) Displaced persons and the admission of refugees;

(e) Protection, prestige, and security of Allied Forces, dependents, employees and representatives, their immunities and satisfaction of occupation costs and of their other requirements;

(f) Respect for the Basic Law and the *Land* Constitutions;

[57] For text, see Appendix L.

(g) Control over foreign trade and exchange;

(h) Control over internal action, only to the minimum extent necessary to ensure use of funds, food and other supplies in such manner as to reduce to a minimum the need for external assistance to Germany;

(i) Control of the care and treatment in German prisons of persons charged before or sentenced by the courts or tribunals of the Occupying Powers or Occupation Authorities; over the carrying out of sentences imposed on them; and over questions of amnesty, pardon or release in relation to them.

The earlier controversy as to German legislation in these reserved fields was resolved by providing that they might legislate in these areas "after due notification to the occupation authorities" and assuming that the latter had not otherwise specifically directed and provided, of course, that such legislation would not "be inconsistent with decisions or actions taken by the occupation authorities themselves."[58] The occupation authorities continued to exercise general control over the legislative process by reserving the right to disapprove legislation which they believed inconsistent with the Basic Law, with a *Land* constitution, with the legislation of the occupation authorities themselves, or with the Occupation Statute. The statute contained a categorical reference, however, to disapproval of legislation which might also constitute "a grave threat to the basic purposes of the occupation." Beyond this, occupation authority was protected by a general reservation of the right "to resume, in whole or in part, the exercise of full authority if they consider that to do so is essential to security or to preserve democratic government in Germany."[59] It is important to an understanding of the legal position of the Bonn government to recognize that its functions were circumscribed by the Occupation Statute and that the latter was the product of agreement among the occupant governments but without either the systematic advice or certainly the consent of the peoples occupied. This was not an agreed document though in its preparation German views had been officially solicited and had in fact been informally expressed. These discussions, however, were in the nature of consultations and never were intended or accepted as negotiations. The statute was the creation of the occupation authorities, was so accepted by both the state and federal governments, and must be so recognized in analyzing the evolution of postwar German governments. In origin and in content the statute illustrated the overriding power of the occupant governments and the still-limited sovereignty of the Bonn government.

Stemming also from the London talks and paralleling the develop-

---

[58] Occupation Statute, par. 4.   [59] *Ibid.*, par. 3.

ments regarding the Basic Law and the Occupation Statute were the discussions of territorial reorganizations in the several states. The subject had been included in the London discussions largely because the American delegation had persuaded the French that reasonably viable state units were essential to an effective federal system. London had therefore provided that the constituent units should be at least roughly comparable in size, have a certain economic and political viability, and "take account of traditional patterns." It was because of the close relationship between this question and the larger federal issue that the instructions to the ministers-president provided that the reorganization should be completed in time to enable the states to establish legislative assemblies which would "determine the electoral procedure and regulations for the ratification of the constitution."

Responsibility for territorial reorganization had been vested in the ministers-president rather than the Parliamentary Council since this clearly was a problem for the individual states and for the states in relationship to one another rather than for the federal government. At the first meeting of the military governors and the ministers-president of the eleven states, the general content of the London agreements had been forwarded to the German authorities. Shortly thereafter it became apparent that the Allied hope for a substantial revision of *Länder* boundaries as the first step in the constitution-making process could not soon be realized. When the ministers-president met in Coblenz in July, they concluded that the problem needed more thorough study than could be undertaken in the period prior to the convening of a constitutional assembly. For a variety of reasons the ministers-president limited themselves to suggestions regarding the obviously unsatisfactory conditions existing in the three truncated *Länder,* Württemberg-Baden, Württemberg-Hohenzollern, and Baden.[60] The military governors explained the unsatisfactory character of this conclusion, and as a consequence the meeting held in Rüdesheim later in the month agreed to the establishment of a committee to consider proposals for change in *Länder* boundaries. The committee set up under the chairmanship of Minister-President Luedemann immediately concluded that nothing could be accomplished prior to the September meeting of the Parliamentary Council. Subsequently the military governors extended the deadline for the submission of proposals to October 15, 1948. From this time forward until the completion of the reorganization years later, serious consideration was never given to any

[60] See reply of Ministers-President of July 12, 1948, in Pollock, Meisel, and Bretton, *op. cit.,* p. 272.

aspect of the question other than that of the consolidation of the three southwest *Länder*.[61]

Notwithstanding the disappointment associated with this last effort, the student of government, looking back through seven years of occupation, would almost certainly say that substantial improvements have been made in the territorial patterns of German state government. The first of these was the consolidation of the many miscellaneous units which now make up the state of Hesse. Later, in the British Zone, came the elimination of such tiny units as Lippe and Schaumberg-Lippe and the establishment of the large and significant state of North Rhine–Westphalia. As a result of Allied prodding (or at least United States and United Kingdom prodding) the Germans themselves created a new southwest state made up of former Baden, Württemberg, and Hohenzollern. In addition, the four Allies could claim credit for having eliminated the all too dominating state of Prussia. Finally, a great deal had been added to the contiguous character of German states by the virtual elimination of the pattern of miscellaneous enclaves and exclaves which have characterized German territorial organization since the middle ages. Hence, if the efforts of the ministers-president were disappointing to those who had hoped for so much in London, the ultimate German effort combined with the decisions which the Allies themselves had made resulted in reforms which years of effort during the days of the Weimar Republic had never accomplished.[62]

While the territorial reorganization of the *Länder* had not been accomplished in either the manner or to the extent originally contemplated by the Allied enthusiasts for a viable federal state, the other portions of the Allied effort to create a western political community were generally successful. By September, 1949, both the Occupation Statute[63] and the Bonn Constitution had entered into force and Western Germany had become a political fact. For three and a half years this government of limited sovereignty has functioned in terms of the Occupation Statute and under the broad surveillance of the newly established Allied High Commission.[64] They were not years of fundamental change in the broad structure either of German government or in the

[61] Cf. Chapter 4.

[62] See Arnold Brecht, *Federalism and Regionalism in Germany* (New York, 1945).

[63] "Declaration concerning the Entry into Force of the Occupation Statute," September 21, 1949. For text, see Elmer Plischke, *History of the Allied High Commission for Germany* (1951), app. 2, p. 104.

[64] "Charter of the Allied High Commission for Germany," June 16, 1949. For text, see Plischke, *History*, app. 4, pp. 108-116.

relationship between German institutions and the occupying powers. It was rather a time in which the specified relationships were interpreted and clarified and individual occupation powers were relaxed. While these adjustments were of considerable importance, they did not change the primary character of the over-all institutional framework, nor did they alter the primary character of the existing legal relationships.

The Occupation Statute, as originally drafted, had provided that "after twelve months, and in any event within eighteen months of the effective date of this instrument, the occupying powers will undertake a review of its provisions in the light of experience with its operation and with a view to extending the jurisdiction of the German authorities in the legislative, executive and judicial fields."[65] The first of these adjustments came almost immediately after the coming into force of the Occupation Statute. In November, Allied-German relations were modified by the Petersberg Protocol which, on the one hand, contained German agreement to join the International Authority for the Ruhr and to co-operate with the Military Security Board established by the High Commission and, on the other hand, Allied agreement to relax control over shipbuilding and foreign affairs with consequent establishment of a German consular service and a curtailment of Allied dismantling programs.[66] The protocol was unusual in that it was a "negotiated" document signed by representatives of both the occupant and occupied governments. It was the only significant document of the kind to appear during the seven-year period of "occupation sovereignty." In its suggestion of *occupatio pacifica* it was distinctly out of place in the general pattern of Allied-German relationships of the period.

In May of 1950 the Foreign Ministers met again in London and reaffirmed their desire that Germany eventually "re-enter progressively the community of free peoples of Europe" and expressed a "desire to see the pace of progress toward this end as rapid as possible."[67] At the same time they made provision to accelerate this process by establishing an intergovernmental study group to begin preparatory work on a revision of the Occupation Statute and consequent relaxation of the controls exercised by the occupant powers. It was at about the same time that the federal government itself began to prepare a detailed analysis of the statute and its need for revision. As a consequence of the recommendations of the study group and of the representations

[65] Occupation Statute, par. 9.   [66] See Petersberg Protocol in Appendix M.
[67] See "Declaration of the Three Foreign Ministers in Germany," *3rd Quarterly Report on Germany,* Office of the U.S. High Commissioner for Germany (Frankfurt, 1950), pp. 76-77.

forwarded by Chancellor Adenauer, the Foreign Ministers in September announced their intention to terminate the state of war with Germany, substantially amend the Occupation Statute, and authorize the establishment of a ministry of foreign affairs and the reopening of diplomatic relations with foreign countries. Requisite to the implementation of these general conclusions were certain actions by the Federal Republic; these were not forthcoming until March, 1951, when the *Bundestag* both acknowledged responsibility for the prewar German external debt and for postwar economic assistance in the several western zones and gave assurance of willingness to co-operate in an equitable distribution of scarce materials needed for European defense purposes.

A variety of piecemeal revisions of the statute followed immediately thereafter. These included approving "the immediate establishment of a federal ministry of foreign affairs" and authorization to the federal government "to enter into direct diplomatic relations with friendly nations and to exchange diplomatic representatives with them." A series of specific reserve powers were abandoned and others in such fields as foreign trade and exchange were "considerably reduced." From the point of view of the relationships between Allied and German governments, much the most important of the decisions was that which removed the necessity for prior review of federal and *Land* legislation. At the same time ultimate power of annulment of legislation was reserved to the occupation authorities in the event they found it necessary to exercise those powers.[68] Important, too, was the promise to relinquish control designed to ensure respect for the Basic Law and state constitutions once the Federal Republic had "established a judicial authority . . . capable of effectively upholding the civil rights of the individual as defined in the basic law."[69] Additional promises of further relaxation were made at the same time.

The revisions of 1951 were deliberately designed as unilateral occupation actions rather than as negotiated agreements. Chancellor Adenauer's repeated and emphatic requests for comprehensive revision upon an assumption of contractual agreements were specifically rejected in favor of a continuation of the existing legal relationship. The example of the Petersberg Protocol was not to be repeated. Both German reaction to these revisions and clear continuing need demonstrated the accuracy of the comment of the United States High Commission's official historian that this "was merely a temporary expedi-

[68] "First Instrument of Revision of the Occupation Statute"; see Plischke, *Revision of the Occupation Statute for Germany* (1952), app. 4, pp. 78-79.
[69] See "Decision No. 10" in Plischke, *Revision,* app. 5, pp. 80-81.

ent."[70] It was equally clear that for the first time in the long process of the reconstruction of German governments the burden of initiative for major constructive change had shifted from Allied to German hands.

Several months after the revision of the Occupation Statute, the Allied High Commission announced that the governments of the western powers would take action to terminate the state of war with Germany. As a result of the earlier communiqué of the Foreign Ministers following their September, 1950, meeting, a considerable number of other nations had taken action during 1951 to terminate their own individual states of war with Germany. Reference to the earlier discussion of the legal aspects of the occupation will indicate that, while suggesting much, these actions by the individual nations did not affect the legal basis of the occupation in any way.[71] Each such action was primarily an action to alter the municipal law of the country concerned. Those actions did not and could not affect the international state of war which had in fact been concluded in 1945. The announcement on July 9 by the High Commission of the intention of the United States, the United Kingdom, and France to terminate this state of war, as far as their individual governments were concerned, may therefore have been of psychological significance within Germany but had no legal or other political significance to the occupation.

Under the very considerable pressure of western European defense problems and the articulate insistence of Chancellor Adenauer, the Allied governments announced in the fall of 1951 their intention to create "a new relationship between the Allied and the Federal Republic" which would be based upon "the substitution of contractual agreements for the occupation statute." While negotiations on the subject of a Contractual Agreement were in process prior to the announcement in September of 1951, it was not until late spring of 1952 that the agreement was finally prepared. Caught up in the problems of the Schuman plan, the development of a defense force for western Europe, and the rearmament of Germany, the Contractual Agreement (now referred to as a Convention) became a pawn in the larger West-East competition. When it finally emerged, the agreement represented a sharp departure from anything which had occurred in the first seven

[70] Plischke, *Revision,* p. 49.

[71] For a contrary view, see Chapter 5, p. 121, footnote 8. The reader will note, however, that the basic thesis is the same in both chapters. Only the place of this one series of actions regarding the termination of the state of war is differently interpreted in the two chapters.

years of the occupation. When ultimately approved it will definitely conclude the second period in the occupation which we have identified here as a time of "occupation legal sovereignty" and introduce a third period of "peaceful occupation."

THE PERIOD OF PEACEFUL OCCUPATION

The Contractual Agreement or Convention of 1952 satisfies most of the criteria of the traditional *occupatio pacifica*. It is an agreement negotiated between and accepted by both occupant and occupied governments. It sets forth their respective rights and obligations and creates an international tribunal in which disputes arising under the agreement may be adjudicated. It presumes that both legal and political sovereignty rests primarily with the occupied people and their governments. In restricting "Three Power" authority to matters of an international and military character it imposes no more restraint upon the occupant powers than were normally imposed by the Hague Conventions upon a belligerent occupant. President Truman in referring the new Convention to the Senate was therefore accurate when he said that it would "restore the Federal Republic of Germany to a status which will enable it to play a full and honorable part in the family of nations." On the other hand, one cannot accurately say that the conventions "terminate" the occupation of Western Germany,[72] for they actually do no more than to transform an occupation which was *sui generis* into a traditional form of *occupatio pacifica*. They have created a situation not dissimilar to the legal position established in Germany with the conclusion of the Peace Treaty and the Rhineland Agreement in June, 1919.[73]

The "Contractual Agreement" is in fact a "Convention on Relations between the Three Powers and the Federal Republic of Germany" and three technical agreements referred to as "related conventions." Annexed to the Convention on Relations is a charter for an "Arbitration Tribunal."[74] Closely associated with these documents are the protocol to the North Atlantic Treaty and a treaty constituting the European Defense Community, both of which are intended to cement

[72] See reference to conventions as "terminating the occupation of Western Germany" in Secretary Acheson's letter of transmittal of May 31, 1952.

[73] See Ernst Fraenkel, *Military Occupation and the Rule of Law* (New York, 1944).

[74] For text of the Convention on Relations between the Three Powers and the Federal Republic of Germany, see Appendix N. For texts of other related conventions and the protocol to the North Atlantic Treaty, see *EXECUTIVES Q and R*, 82d Congress, 2d session.

Germany's position in European affairs as described more fully in a subsequent portion of this volume.[75]

Structurally the Convention calls for the abolition of the Allied High Commission and a return to the use of customary diplomatic relations excepting on matters of general Three Power concern in which case the three ambassadors would be expected to act in concert. Legally the Convention provides for the revocation of the Occupation Statute and (in one of the related conventions) recognizes both federal and *Land* authority to repeal or amend legislation enacted by the occupation authorities during the first two periods of occupation. Exceptions to this general authorization of repeal and amendment are set out in considerable detail in supporting sections.

With the ratification of the Convention the Federal Republic will have full authority over its internal and external affairs except that the Three Powers retain their rights and powers relating to:

(a) the stationing of armed forces in Germany and the protection of their security,
(b) Berlin, and
(c) Germany as a whole, including the unification of Germany and a peace settlement.

Of far-reaching potential importance is the provision that protecting the security of the armed forces shall include the power to proclaim a state of emergency in the event of an uncontrolled attack on the Federal Republic or Berlin, a serious disturbance of public order, or a subversion of "the liberal democratic basic order." While certain minimal procedural safeguards are set forth, the extent of these "emergency powers" of the occupants is limited only by the proviso that they be measures necessary "to maintain or restore order and to ensure the security of the Forces." Thus, while the Convention contemplates a general independence of power and action in the Federal Republic, it also grants major continuing authority to the occupiers and concedes them overriding powers in the event of attack from without, serious disturbance or subversion from within, or "a grave threat of any of these events."

Disputes arising between the Three Powers and the Federal Republic under the Convention are to be adjudicated by an Arbitration Tribunal of nine members representing the Three Powers, the Federal Republic, and "neutrals." The three representatives of the occupying powers are appointed by their respective governments, the three Ger-

[75] See Chapter 7 below.

man members are appointed by the federal government, and the neutral members are selected by agreement between the Three Powers and the government of the Federal Republic. The tribunal's jurisdiction extends to all portions of the Convention except Article 2 and other parts of the document which define the reserved authority of the Three Powers. In addition to limiting the tribunal's jurisdiction, this provision is important for again it indicates the potential sweep of occupation powers generally and their "emergency" features particularly.

While the Convention substantially modifies the character of the occupation and the structure of Allied mechanisms, it does not contemplate change in the Basic Law. Indeed, every reference to the present constitutional framework must be interpreted as either a direct or an indirect confirmation of its essential adequacy under the present circumstances. In one paragraph it is asserted that "the Federal Republic . . . is determined to maintain the liberal democratic constitution which guarantees human rights and is enshrined in its Basic Law." A later paragraph provides that both the Three Powers and the Federal Republic will co-operate to achieve their common objective of a united Germany "enjoying a liberal democratic constitution like that of the Federal Republic." While by no means constituting an unqualified assurance that the present Basic Law will be retained in precisely its present form for an indefinite period, these provisions do give reasonable indication of substantial satisfaction with the present document and suggest that for the duration of the occupation no fundamental alterations need be anticipated.

It is essential to recognize the significance of the general framework of European developments within which the Convention was negotiated and without which it could not have been so quickly or so comprehensively prepared. The large measure of independence which the Convention accords the Federal Republic is conditional upon German acceptance of both the general concept of European organization and its several specific programs such as the European Coal and Steel Community and the European Defense Community. The Federal Republic thus emerges among the nations of the world in an atmosphere in which the national state is of less significance than it was after World War I or in the early years following World War II. It may be that German political revival has been more rapid than the construction of the European framework into which Germany was to be incorporated, but the fact remains that when independence came it was accompanied by a very real measure of European organization which could be expected to do much to mitigate the dangers almost inevitably inherent in the revival of a powerful if truncated German national state.

The present period of occupation and the institutions which accompany it may well last for an extended period of time. The Convention procedure was employed, since a peace treaty with only Western Germany seemed undesirable both because it would give an air of finality to the division of the country and because it might also further aggravate the Soviet Union. The same conditions may be expected to remain for as long as the present intensity of the West-East conflict holds. Similarly, the Convention necessarily reserved substantial powers to the Allies since the same West-East conflict necessitates the maintainance of large military forces in Germany, and neither now nor in the foreseeable future are France, Great Britain, or the United States apt to place large installations of their own troops at Germany's disposal. In view of the character of the West's present conflict with the Soviet Union it would therefore appear reasonable to anticipate a number of years of life for the Convention, the peaceful occupation, and the broad framework of political institutions with which this volume is concerned.

CONCLUSION

As the occupation of Germany moves into its final period, it must be clear that the impact of Allied effort has been considerable. Whether its influences are continuing or transitory, whether they have been as great as we might have hoped, whether they might have been more significant given better planning and co-ordination, are all questions which it is too early to answer definitively. For the political scientist there are other problems which require urgent examination. They include value questions such as the abandonment of the principle of self-determination and practical questions of the transferability of political institutions from one culture to another. But however uncertain the specific answers to these and similar queries may be, it is nonetheless clear that contemporary German political institutions have been materially affected by the occupation. That those institutions will in turn have influence upon our own future is equally apparent. It is to the discussion of those institutions and related political processes that the remaining chapters in this volume are devoted.

Part II

LEVELS OF GOVERNMENT

3

Local Government

ROGER H. WELLS

IN 1943 a Swiss scholar, Dr. Adolf Gasser, published a book entitled *Municipal Liberty the Salvation of Europe*.[1] Gasser argued, with words reminiscent of Jefferson and Tocqueville, that "sound" democracies have historically deep-rooted and vigorous systems of local self-government and that Nazi Germany, if it was to become truly democratic, must be reconstructed from the bottom up on strong local foundations. When the Hitler regime fell in 1945, these foundations were almost blotted out. The physical ruins of bombed-out cities were matched by the ruins of democratic institutions, not only on local levels but in such fields as civil liberties, free elections, responsible parliamentary government, local self-government (*Kommunalselbstverwaltung*), the rule of law, and voluntary labor unions, co-operatives, and other similar associations through which the democratic spirit expresses itself.

The present volume, therefore, in its discussion of the specifics of governmental organization appropriately begins with local government. The principal units of German local government are the *Gemeinde* (municipality) and the *Kreis* (county).[2] The *Gemeinde* may range in area and population from the small rural village with its surrounding territory to the largest city. The more populous

[1] *Gemeindefreiheit als Rettung Europas* (Basel, 1943).

[2] For details on these and other types of German local units, see Roger H. Wells, *German Cities* (Princeton, 1932), chap. 2, and J. F. J. Gillen, *State and Local Government in West Germany, 1945-1953*, Historical Division, Office of the U.S. High Commissioner for Germany (Bad Godesberg, 1953).

Gemeinden usually have the legal title *Stadt* (city); and if the number of inhabitants reaches a prescribed minimum, the city may become a *Stadtkreis* (city-county). The *Stadtkreis* is detached governmentally from the county in which it is located. In other words, it is relieved from the supervision of the county authorities. Other cities, as well as *Gemeinden* which are not cities, are under the supervision of the county.[3]

To distinguish the county from the city-county, the former is usually referred to as a *Landkreis* (rural county).[4] The *Landkreis* roughly corresponds to the American county but its average size is smaller. It is also occasionally called a *Gemeindeverband* because it is a union of the *Gemeinden* contained within it. Both the *Gemeinde* and the *Landkreis* are public municipal corporations having the right of local self-government.

The importance of local government as a "grass roots" approach to the problem of German reconstruction was recognized by many Allied officials who from 1942 onward concerned themselves with postwar planning. It was specifically underlined in the Potsdam Agreement (August 2, 1945) between the United States, Britain, and the Soviet Union, which stated:

> The administration of affairs in Germany should be directed towards the decentralization of the political structure and the development of local responsibility. To this end, local self-government shall be restored throughout Germany on democratic principles and in particular through elective councils as rapidly as is consistent with military security and the purposes of the occupation.[5]

The reconstruction of Germany beginning at the local level was made even more necessary than the planners had anticipated because of the conditions prevailing at the end of the war. There were no higher levels of German government left. The July 20, 1944, revolt had failed in its attempt to provide an alternative to Hitler's rule. The nihilism of the Nazis, spurred by the doctrine of unconditional surrender, led them to a truly Wagnerian *Götterdämmerung* with wanton and widespread destruction throughout the country. Coupled with this was the popular belief in Allied quarters that all Germans were con-

[3] There are 111 *Stadtkreise* in the three western zones of Germany. How large a *Stadt* must be before it can become a *Stadtkreis* has been and is a controversial question between the cities and the *Landkreise*. See Wells, *op. cit.*, pp. 23-24, 181-187. In Bavaria, the minimum population is 20,000.

[4] There are 419 *Landkreise* in the western zones of Germany.

[5] See text in J. K. Pollock, J. H. Meisel, and H. L. Bretton, ed., *Germany Under Occupation*, rev. ed. (Ann Arbor, 1949).

genitally bad. The result was a *tabula rasa,* governmentally speaking. The military governments of the Allies had no choice except to start at the bottom. Since the Potsdam Agreement directs that local self-government (*Kommunalselbstverwaltung*) shall be "restored,"[6] it is important to know how much there had been in pre-Nazi Germany. To answer this question, a brief summary of past experience is necessary.

LOCAL GOVERNMENT BEFORE 1945

Prior to 1918—In 1950 the city of Cologne proudly celebrated the anniversary of its founding by the Romans in A.D. 50. Within that span of nineteen hundred years, Cologne and other German cities had enjoyed two notable periods of self-government.[7] The first was associated with the rise of medieval cities and the Hanseatic and other leagues of cities. It reached its climax in the wide city autonomy of the twelfth and thirteenth centuries. The development and consolidation of national states under monarchical absolutism eventually proved fatal to municipal liberties. By the middle of the eighteenth century, the self-government of cities had been practically wiped out in most of Germany. Nowhere was the process of liquidation more thoroughly carried out than by the rulers of Prussia.

The second period of *Kommunalselbstverwaltung* was ushered in by Napoleon's crushing defeat of Prussia at the battle of Jena. Out of the wreckage came the Stein-Hardenburg reforms. It was Baron vom Stein who was chiefly responsible for the Prussian City Government Act (*Stadteordnung*) of 1808 which, in the course of the nineteenth century, became the cornerstone of municipal self-government all over Germany,[8] though diverse patterns of organization continued in many areas until the days of the Nazis. Under the Bismarckian Empire (1871-1918), German cities flourished in an atmosphere of relative freedom. In the United States during the same period, city government, although nominally democratic, was frequently corrupt, boss-ridden, and harassed by state legislative interference. In Germany, on the other hand, where urban population growth caused by the Industrial Revolution had been equally rapid, city government was honest,

[6] For a sharp criticism of local self-government prior to 1933 and of the "restoration" concept of the Potsdam Agreement, see William A. Robson, "Local Government in Occupied Germany," *Political Quarterly,* XVI (1945), 277-287. Robson's views foreshadowed British Military Government policies.

[7] Fritz Morstein Marx in William Anderson, ed., *Local Government in Europe* (New York, 1939), chap. 3.

[8] William H. Dawson, *Municipal Life and Government in Germany,* 2d ed. (London, 1916); Heinrich Heffter, *Die deutsche Selbstverwaltung im 19. Jahrhundert* (Stuttgart, 1949).

free from demagogic bosses, and possessed of a substantial amount of autonomy. No doubt the German system was bureaucratic; no doubt the municipal suffrage was for the most part narrow and undemocratic. Nevertheless, during this period self-government was a reality. It was most conspicuous in the case of cities but was also present to a lesser extent in other local government units where directly or indirectly elected popular representative bodies were introduced and where lay participation in both local and state administration was stressed.

Under the Weimar Constitution—The Weimar Consitution (1918-1933) thoroughly democratized the legal foundations of local government.[9] Universal, equal, direct, and secret suffrage was prescribed for all elections. Representative bodies at all levels were required to be chosen by proportional representation. The constitutions of the Reich and of the *Länder* guaranteed local self-government. According to the letter of the law, the Weimar Republic seemed to be fully equipped with the tools of democracy. During this period there were three principal forms of government in the *Gemeinden* and *Städte*. The first was a bicameral structure in which the upper chamber or *Magistrat* was entrusted with both legislative and collegial executive powers. The *Magistrat* included the *Bürgermeister* (or *Oberbürgermeister*), other leading administrative officials, and a group of lay members, all of whom were chosen by the popularly elected council or lower house. A second form in which executive powers were exercised by the *Bürgermeister* (hence referred to as *Bürgermeisterverfassung*) might be likened to the American "strong-mayor" plan. A third variation in which legislative and executive powers were combined in a single council or *Stadtrat* resembled certain aspects of the British local government system. The *Stadtrat* consisted not only of popularly elected councilmen but also the *Bürgermeister* and other leading officials chosen by the council. This system was restricted to Bavaria and Württemberg though it differed between them in that the *Bürgermeister* was elected by the council in the former and directly by the voters in the latter.

In the days of the Weimar Republic, county government also followed varying patterns and was known by several names, though the Prussian pattern and terminology (*Kreis*) was more prevalent than any other. The *Kreis* was essentially a rural government exercising both its own corporate powers and those delegated to it from *Land* level. In its typical pre-Hitler form the *Kreis* was governed by a popularly elected assembly (*Kreistag*), a county committee (*Kreisausschus*), and a county director (*Landrat*). The committee and the

[9] On city and local government under the Weimar Republic, see Wells, *op. cit.*

Landrat shared the county's administrative responsibilities though the former was elected by the assembly and the latter was normally a professional civil servant selected by the *Land* ministry of the interior.

Space does not permit discussion of the various factors, both internal and international, which contributed to the failure of the Weimar Republic. The writer does not believe that one of these factors was the failure of local self-government. The most that can be said is that *Kommunalselbstverwaltung* was impaired by forces beyond its control. In part, this was due to increasing centralization which was powerfully stimulated by World War I and was further extended in the postwar years. Nowhere was centralization more apparent than in the field of finance.[10] Local units had far less discretion as to revenues and expenditures than they had before. The associations of German local authorities, such as the *Deutscher Städtetag*, protested vigorously against these adverse developments and made many constructive but futile suggestions for improving federal-state-local relationships.

The situation became progressively worse after 1929. In the great depression, with the economy prostrate and millions unemployed, state and federal control of local government was extended in all directions. State commissioners were appointed in hundreds of municipalities with full power to take whatever financial action the state deemed necessary. Thus local self-government became too weakened to provide any effective opposition to the Nazi revolution which began when President von Hindenburg named Adolf Hitler as Chancellor. For the second time in German history, local self-government was crushed by despotism.

During National Socialism, 1933-1945—The changes which the Nazis made in local government were many and far-reaching.[11] The most important were the abolition of popularly elected local councils, the abolition of direct and indirect election of the leading executive officials, the introduction of the "leadership principle" at each local level, the subordination and strict control of local government by Reich and Nazi party agencies; and the unification of local government law throughout Germany. A discussion of this last point will also clarify the nature of the other changes. In the local field, the most famous single piece of Nazi legislation was the German Municipal Govern-

[10] See Chapter 13 below and Wells, *op. cit.*, pp. 166-174.

[11] See Marx in Anderson, *op. cit.*, chap. 3. The best and most complete account by a German is Harry Goetz, "Die deutschen Städte und Landgemeinden im Dritten Reich, 1933-1945." This is an unpublished manuscript of some 350 typed pages, written in 1946-1947 by Dr. Goetz of the Berlin Municipal Science Institute. Dr. Goetz's study also deals with *Landkreise* and with the *Deutscher Gemeindetag*.

ment Act (*Deutsche Gemeindeordnung,* hereafter cited as DGO) which the Hitler cabinet decreed in 1935.[12] Prior to 1933, under the federal form of government prevailing in the Empire and the Weimar Republic, the basic laws determining the structure and operation of local government were enacted by the state legislatures. These laws not only varied from state to state but also within a given state, Prussia being the most notable example. It was common for cities to be regulated by one statute and smaller municipalities by another. In the Nazi unitary state, this diversity was replaced by uniformity.

The DGO was comparatively brief (123 articles), but it repealed or replaced no less than 66 state laws on local government. It applied to all the approximately 50,000 *Gemeinden* in Germany except Berlin. The *Stadtkreise* were included in the DGO but not the *Landkreise.* There was much discussion of a uniform county government act (*Landkreisordnung*) for the Reich but it was never passed. The DGO, although embodying specifically Nazi features, also contained many good provisions which represented the best thinking and experience of municipal experts. From this point of view, it can be regarded as the successor of the 1925 and 1930 drafts of a Reich City Government Act which the *Deutscher Städtetag* prepared. It is important to bear in mind the non-Nazi elements of the DGO; that is why so much of the law was preserved in military government and German legislation after 1945.

Under the DGO, the three most important officials were the Reich minister of the interior, the local agent (*Beauftragter*) of the Nazi party, and the local *Bürgermeister.* The minister of the interior was the head of a hierarchy of Reich-*Land* supervisory agencies exercising control over municipalities and was vested with large discretionary powers. The local party agent was appointed by Rudolph Hess, the deputy leader, and was supposed to be the connecting link between the party and each *Gemeinde* government. In practice, the local party agent was very often the district or county leader of the party. The working out of party-municipal relationships was one of the most difficult problems in the framing of the DGO. Municipal officials, even though they were themselves party members, sometimes complained of excessive interference by party agencies. On the other hand, the party leaders would not accept the principle of local freedom from party control. Hence a compromise was embodied in the law whereby the party agent was made the sole official tie between the party and municipality, and the legal powers of the agent, although important, were strictly limited. To have given the party agent blanket authority

[12] See Marx's translation of the DGO in Anderson, *op. cit.,* pp. 277-303.

would have seriously interfered with the *Führerprinzip* represented by the *Bürgermeister* and the hierarchical control terminating in the Reich minister of the interior.

The leadership principle concentrated local legislative and administrative powers in the hands of the *Land*-level-appointed *Bürgermeister*.[13] The *Bürgermeister* enacted local ordinances after hearing the opinions of the municipal councilors. He directed the administration and appointed and dismissed all municipal officials and employees except the chief executive officers, and even these were subject to his orders. The method of appointing the chief executive officers was somewhat complicated. It is sufficient to say that the local party agent and the Reich-state supervisory authorities had the dominant role in the selection process. The local party agent was supposed to consult the municipal councilors before submitting his nominations to the supervisory authorities. No longer did the municipal councilors elect the *Bürgermeister* and the other leading officials.

The councilors themselves were not elected by the voters but were appointed by the party agent in agreement with the *Bürgermeister*. The councilors had no powers; they could only give advice which the *Bürgermeister* was free to disregard, although on certain subjects, such as the enactment of ordinances and the adoption of the budget, the *Bürgermeister*, before taking action, was required by the DGO to give the councilors an opportunity to express themselves. The vaunted *Selbstverwaltung* of the DGO did not work out in practice. The advisory councilors were almost as useless as the *Reichstag* deputies.[14] Consequently, the device of advisory councilors fell into desuetude which even a Himmler directive of 1943 could not overcome.[15] Citizens were reluctant to serve, and if they did, the *Bürgermeister* frequently did not bother to consult them. Moreover, the strict control of the press did not allow much leeway for newspaper discussion of local problems, as had been the case before 1933. The result was popular indifference, lack of understanding, and smoldering discontent.

Under the DGO, the professional character of the local civil service

[13] *Oberbürgermeister* in *Stadtkreise*. Technically, the Reich-state supervisory authorities did not appoint the *Bürgermeister*. They merely approved the appointment, but no one could be appointed without that approval. The position of the *Landrat* in the *Landkreis* was similar. He, too, was appointed, exemplified the leadership principle, and had no locally elected council (*Kreistag*) to restrain his actions.

[14] See the poem on the *Reichstag* by "Saggitarius" entitled "Solo Turn," *American Mercury*, XLVII (1939), 391.

[15] John H. Herz, "German Administration under the Nazi Regime," *American Political Science Review*, XL (1946), 682-702.

was not destroyed. In the early days of the Nazi revolution, there was a large purge of Jewish, republican, socialist, and other "unreliable" elements. This particularly affected the office of *Bürgermeister* and provided opportunities for "deserving party workers." But on the whole, the local *Beamten* continued to be a professional group as the DGO required. They "went along" with the regime, and many of them sooner or later became at least nominal party members.

Party-municipal conflicts remained a problem notwithstanding the line of demarcation drawn by the DGO. In general, the *Bürgermeister,* appointed for a long term, declared to be the sole local *Führer,* and invested with all powers of local government, was in a good position to resist party pressures beyond those authorized by the DGO. On the other hand, the very authority given the *Bürgermeister,* which was unchecked by effective citizen representation and participation, made for an increasing bureaucratization. Moreover, "municipal autonomy" was in fact *Bürgermeister* autonomy, and this proved incompatible with the vast war plans of the Nazi state. By a Hitler decree of August 28, 1939, direct state control replaced state supervision over local government.

LOCAL GOVERNMENT DURING POSTWAR YEARS

Immediate Aftermath of War, 1945-1946—The years which followed the Nazi defeat in 1945 saw the gradual emergence of local government institutions. To a large degree, these postwar institutions are similar to those of the Weimar period, but there are also significant differences reflecting the changed conditions. In 1933, when Hitler became Chancellor, the German economy was physically intact although operating at low productivity with millions unemployed. When World War II ended, the economy was physically in ruins, with widespread destruction of homes, buildings, and utilities. A second major problem had to do with "expelled" Germans, who in accordance with the Potsdam Agreement were transferred from territories now belonging to or administered by Poland, Czechoslavakia, or Hungary, and with refugees who had fled from Soviet-dominated areas, including Eastern Germany. In 1950 there were over 9,000,000 expellees and refugees in Western Germany out of a total population of almost 48,000,000. The impact of this problem upon the possibilities for local self-government and democracy was immediate and far-reaching.

The reconstruction of German local government did not begin with V-E Day. Instead, it started almost as soon as the Allied armies entered upon German soil. For example, the city of Aachen was captured by American forces on October 20, 1944. A few days later, military government appointed a German *Oberbürgermeister,* even though there were only 3,000 of the 166,000 inhabitant still residing within the ruined city. During the next six months, as the Allied troops advanced deeper into Western Germany, British and American Military Government continued to appoint the leading local officials. This was in accordance with the 1944 directive of the Combined Chiefs of Staff which called for indirect rule by military government through German personnel. Actually, owing to the chaotic conditions which prevailed in the early days of the occupation and the compelling need for effective support of Allied combat units, there was a great deal of direct rule and administration by military government and army authorities.[16]

The usual pattern was that military government named the leading local officials, such as the *Bürgermeister* and the *Landrat.* These in turn selected their subordinates subject to military government approval. The pressing needs of the moment called for a speedy restoration of orderly local administration. On the other hand, one of the major Allied objectives was denazification. It proved very difficult to reconcile the two. If trained local officials were kept from office because of their Nazi taint, there would be a great shortage of qualified personnel. But if existing administrations were retained without purging, there would be no denazification as a first step toward democracy. Such were the Scylla and Charybdis between which military government had to steer.[17]

The system of local government which resulted was in many ways like that provided by the *Deutsche Gemeindeordnung.* Military government took the place of the Nazi state and party supervisory agencies although in some areas new German state supervisory authorities were soon created. The *Bürgermeister* and the *Landrat* were still in theory the local leaders. Whereas they once were required to demonstrate unquestioned loyalty to the principles of National Socialism, they now had a similar obligation to the principles of democracy as defined in each of the four zones and to the objectives of the occupation as similarly defined. If they failed, they might be summarily dismissed and perhaps even tried and imprisoned. Under these circumstances, no great amount of German initiative in local government was developed.

[16] See Chapter 2 above.
[17] See Leonard Krieger, "The Inter-Regnum in Germany: March-August, 1945," *Political Science Quarterly,* LXIV (1949), 507-532. For a graphic account of the early days of American Military Government, see Dexter L. Freeman, *Hesse: A New German State* (Frankfurt, 1948), chap. 1.

Another feature taken over from the DGO was the use of advisory councilors. Within a short time the *Bürgermeister* or *Landrat* was asked to appoint, subject to the approval of military government, a citizens' advisory committee or council. This advisory group was supposed to represent all major interests in the community. In the Soviet Zone antifascist political parties and other democratic organizations were authorized as early as June 10, 1945, and hence could be represented in the advisory committees.[18] The western Allies were much slower in granting such authorizations. The U.S. Zone authorized political parties at *Kreis* level on August 27, 1945. Similar action was taken in the British Zone in October, 1945, and in the French Zone in December, 1945. In part, this may have been due to the unwillingness of the western powers to recognize the antifascist committees ("Antifas") which sprang up in many German cities as the war drew to a close and which usually contained strong Communist elements.[19] These groups naturally suffered from the western prohibitions on political activities. They were little used in the reconstruction of local government in the western zones, where reliance was placed on the more traditional elements. The citizens' advisory committees were meant to be temporary bodies, serving only until popular elections could take place. In some instances they rendered valuable assistance. British Military Government especially made a consistent effort to develop the committees as steppingstones to elected representative councils. From the beginning the 8,000 appointed councils of the British Zone were given something of the executive powers enjoyed by local councils in Great Britain.[20]

Period of Reconstruction, after 1946—Prior to establishment of the locally elected councils as envisaged by the Potsdam Agreement, new legal foundations had to be laid. These were provided in the *Gemeindeordnungen* and *Kreisordnungen* and election laws adopted in the various zones in 1945 and 1946 and subsequently reinforced by various articles in the *Land* and federal constitutions.[21]

[18] See Chapter 6 below for further description of the use of the "Antifas."
[19] Krieger, *op. cit.*, pp. 513-514; Moses Moskovitz, "The Political Re-education of the Germans: The Emergence of Parties and Politics in Württemberg-Baden, May 1945-June 1946," *Pol. Sci. Q.*, LXI (1946), 535-561.
[20] Harold Ingrams, "Building Democracy in Germany," *Quarterly Review*, CCLXXXV (1947), 208-222.
[21] On local government in the second stage, see Lucius D. Clay, *Decision in Germany* (Garden City, N.Y., 1950), chap. 5; Hermann Pünder, *Die deutschen Gemeinden: Gestern, Heute, und Morgen* (Cologne, 1948); Otto Gönnenwein, "Das deutsche Gemeindeverfassungsrecht," *Archiv des öffentlichen Rechts*, LXXIV (1948), 191-238; Hermann Heimerich, *Die kommunale Entwicklung seit 1945*

(1) *British Zone*—The British tried to introduce their own local government system in a zone which previously had known only the *Magistratsverfassung* and the *Bürgermeisterverfassung* types of organization referred to above.[22] After consultation with a German working party, military government promulgated Ordinance No. 21 (April 1, 1946) which, as an appendix, carried a revised text of the *Deutsche Gemeindeordnung* of 1935.[23] Military government did not enact a complete *Kreisordnung* for the zone, but the main principles of the revised *Gemeindeordnung* were uniformly applied to all *Landkreise*.[24] The British Administration and Local Government Branch of Military Government was convinced that the Potsdam Agreement was wrong in calling for the "restoration" of pre-Nazi *Kommunalselbstverwaltung*. What was needed was the British plan which elevated the role of the elected council and made the local bureaucracy subject to council control. In the Napoleonic era, the French had introduced the *Bürgermeisterverfassung* in Western Germany and it had "stuck." Could not the same thing be done again by a victorious, occupying power?[25] The British Zone local government reform program involved a number of points, the first having to do with the method of electing the councils. The second British reform aimed to split the political and administrative functions of the chief local official—the *Bürgermeister* in the *Gemeinden* and the *Landrat* in the *Landkreise*. In Britain, the mayor (or county or district chairman as the case may be) is elected yearly by the council, usually from among its own members. He receives no salary and is not a professional civil servant, although long service in the council may give him a good command of local administration.

(pamphlet, *Institut zur Förderung öffentlicher Angelegenheiten,* Frankfurt, 1950); Comstock Glaser, *Land and Local Government in the U.S. Zone of Germany* (Civil Administration Division, Office of Military Government for Germany [U.S.], Berlin, 1947); and "Local Government in Bizonia," in *Planning,* Vol. XIV, No. 277 (Jan. 23, 1948), pamphlet issued by PEP (Political and Economic Planning, London, and reprinted by the *New Republic,* New York).

[22] See S. H. Fazan, *The German Government in Process of Reconstruction* (Berlin, 1949), chaps. ii and iii.

[23] For the German text and commentary, see Hartwig F. Ziegler, ed., *Ordnung in der Gemeinde* (Hahnenklee, 1948), pp. 6-37. The English and German texts may also be found in the *Military Government Gazette, Germany, British Zone of Control,* 1946.

[24] See Military Government Instruction No. 100. Although the British Zone *Länder* now have full power to adopt their own *Kreisordnungen,* only Schleswig-Holstein (1950) has thus far done so. The other *Länder* have contented themselves with interim legislation.

[25] See J. W. F. Hill, "Local Government in Western Germany," *Pol. Q.,* XX (1949), 256-264.

Apart from presiding over the council, the mayor's legal powers are the same as those of any other council member. However, he is the "first citizen" of his city or borough and represents it on public occasions. The chief administrative officer is the nonpolitical, professional town clerk who is chosen by the council for an indefinite term. The revised *Deutsche Gemeindeordnung* copied the British system. In place of the professional but also political *Bürgemeister,* who, except in smaller *Gemeinden,* was a full-time, salaried official, there were now the political, unsalaried, lay *Bürgemeister,* annually elected by the council, and the nonpolitical, professional *Gemeindedirektor* elected by the council for terms prescribed by it.[26] The same division was made in the *Landkreise* between the political and nonprofessional *Landrat* and the professional chief administrator, the *Oberkreisdirektor.* Both were chosen by the county council, the former for one year, the latter for a longer term fixed by the council.

At the outset, the Germans protested strongly. In part, the disagreement was a matter of semantics. Had the British allowed the chief administrative officials to retain the titles of *Bürgermeister* and *Landrat* and given another designation to the council president or chairman, the reform would have been more easily understood. More serious were the difficulties about the precise division of powers between the *Bürgermeister* and *Gemeindedirektor* or between the *Landrat* and the *Oberkreisdirektor.* Finally, in the chaos and hunger of the first postwar years and with denazification in operation, it was hard to find enough qualified personnel to fill the two sets of position. The scheme eventually won some German support; but its future is questionable, and it was rejected in the Schleswig-Holstein *Gemeindeordnung* and *Kreisordnung* of 1950 though it was retained in the North Rhine–Westphalia *Gemeindeordnung* of 1952.

The third British reform was closely linked with the second. It aimed to vest all legislative and executive authority exclusively in the council. This left no room for a second legislative chamber under the old *Magistratsverfassung;* or for the veto power of the *Landrat, Magistrat,* or *Bürgermeister* over council ordinances; or for the quasi-independent position of the *Bürgermeister* or *Landrat* as head of the administration. This last point was particularly important in connection with state-delegated functions. Prior to 1933, these had been dele-

[26] In *Städte,* the director is called *Stadtdirektor;* in *Stadtkreise, Oberstadtdirektor.* In North Rhine–Westphalia, the prevailing term of office for *Oberstadtdirektor* is now twelve years, a term that was very common for leading professional officials before 1933. The *Gemeindedirektor* is not required to be a professional official in the smaller *Gemeinden.*

gated to the *Landrat, Bürgermeister,* or *Magistrat.* Under British Military Government legislation, they were delegated to the council. Finally, in the endeavor to make sure that the local professional officials were nonpolitical, they were forbidden to be active in politics in the *Gemeinde* and *Kreis* in which they were employed. In particular, they could not be elected to the *Gemeinde* council or *Kreistag.*[27]

After the adoption of the Bonn Constitution and the Occupation Statute and the termination of military government, the British Zone *Länder* were free to revise their basic local government legislation. Thus far, Schleswig-Holstein is the only British Zone *Land* to enact a completely new *Gemeindeordnung* and *Kreisordnung* (January 24, 1950).[28] The Schleswig-Holstein *Gemeindeordnung* restored the old *Magistratsverfassung* but with certain modifications. The *Magistrat* is no longer a second legislative chamber, but it does have a suspensory veto over council decisions. It is once again the collegial executive, responsible for administration under the general principles laid down by the council. As before, the council elects the lay and professional members of the *Magistrat* but with the innovation that the council may recall them before their terms have expired. Neither the *Bürgermeister* nor any other member of the *Magistrat* can be chairman of the city council. The *Burgermeister* is responsible to the state supervisory authorities for the execution of state-delegated functions. On the other hand, the North Rhine–Westphalia *Gemeindeordnung* of 1952 continues the essential features of the British reforms.

(2) *United States Zone*—Of the four occupying powers, the United States was the first to act in setting up locally elected councils. Military government directives of September 20 and November 23, 1945, requested the provisional German *Land* governments to frame local government "codes" and election laws and to submit them to military government for approval.[29] Certain general standards were laid down in the directives, but on the whole the Germans were given wide discretion—much

---

[27] This type of prohibition was a continuing source of controversy between the Germans on the one hand and British and U.S. Military Government on the other. The practice of allowing public officials to be members of legislative bodies was recognized under the Bismarckian constitution and was firmly anchored in the constitutions of the Weimar period. See Chapter 10 below for further reference to this problem.

[28] See Lauritz Lauritzen, ed., *Die Selbstverwaltung in Schleswig-Holstein: Handkommentar zur Gemeindeordnung, Amtsordnung, Kreisordnung, und Landessatzung* (Kiel, 1950). See also Lauritzen, "Die Schleswig-holsteinische Magistratsverfassung," *Der Städtetag,* New Series, III (1950), 97-100.

[29] The text of the September 20 directive may be found in Pollock, Meisel, and Bretton, *op cit.,* pp 115-119.

more so than in the other three zones. The result was a series of *Gemein-deordnungen* and *Kreisordnungen* which differed considerably from *Land* to *Land* and yet which borrowed heavily from the *Deutsche Gemeindeordnung* of 1935 and the pre-Hitler legislation.[30] Although these local government statutes of 1945 and 1946 have been subsequently amended, up to 1951 no *Land* of the U.S. Zone had adopted complete revisions of its *Gemeindeordnung* and *Kreisordnung*. Under these statutes, *Gemeinde, Landkreis,* and *Stadtkreis* officials were elected during the first five months of 1946. The method of election was left to the Germans, but military government did insist upon several positive and negative requirements for the suffrage and for eligibility to office. Of the latter, the most important was the disqualification of Nazis.

In Bavaria and Württemburg-Baden, the old *Stadtratsverfassung* of pre-Hitler days was restored with minor changes.[31] Under it, the council has from six to eighty members, depending upon the population, and is elected for four years in Bavaria and six in Württemberg-Baden, one-half retiring every three years in the latter case. The council is the legislative and executive organ of the *Gemeinde*. It appoints and dismisses all officials except the *Bürgermeister*. In Württemberg-Baden, the *Bürgermeister* is directly elected by the people, and the same is true in Bavaria for *Gemeinden* with less than 10,000 inhabitants. In the larger Bavarian *Gemeinden,* the council elects the *Bürgermeister*. The *Bürgermeister* is chairman of the council but has no veto power. He is the first citizen of the *Gemeinde* and also the chief executive officer under the council. In the larger municipalities, the *Bürgermeister* is a full-time professional official. His term of office is six years.

In Hesse, the *Gemeindeordnung* provides for the *Bürgermeisterverfassung* as the normal type but permits *Gemeinden* to adopt the old Hessian version of the *Magistratsverfassung*. When this is done, the

[30] Bavaria, *Gemeindeordnung* of December 18, 1945, and *Landkreisordnung* of February 18, 1946; Hesse, *Gemeindeordnung* of December 21, 1945, and *Kreisordnung* of January 24, 1946; Württemberg-Baden, *Gesetz über die Anwendung de Deutschen Gemeindeordnung* of December 20, 1945 (for North Württemberg), *Gesetz über die Verwaltung und Wahlen in den Gemeinden* of January 10, 1946 (for North Baden), and Württemberg-Baden *Kreisordnung* of January 24, 1946.

[31] The Bavarian *Gemeindeordnung* of 1945 has been replaced by the *Gemeindeordnung* of 1952. The latter continues the *Stadtratsverfassung* but provides for the popular election of the *Bürgermeister* in all *Gemeinden,* not just those under 10,000 inhabitants as was the rule under the *Gemeindeordnung* of 1945. Although Württemberg-Baden has now been merged in the new state of Baden-Württemberg, a new *Germeindeordnung* has not yet been enacted for the consolidated state; meanwhile the old legislation remains in effect.

Magistrat is not the second chamber of the legislative but is merely a collegial executive. In the Hessian *Bürgermeisterverfassung*, the *Bürgermeister* and not the council is the head of the administration, although the council has a general supervision. The *Bürgermeister* is the first citizen of the *Gemeinde*, presides over the council, and may veto ordinances on grounds of illegality subject to appeal by the council to the state supervisory authorities. The *Bürgermeister* and the other leading officials are elected by the council for six years if full-time professionals, otherwise for four years. The council ranges in size from seven to eight members and is elected for four years.

To turn now to county government in the U.S. Zone, the three principal organs of the *Landkreis* today, as in pre-Nazi days, are the county council (*Kreistag*), the county committee (*Kreisausschuss* or *Kreisrat* as it is called in Württemberg-Baden), and the county director. The *Kreistag* has between twenty and fifty members, depending upon the population of the county, and is directly elected by the people for a four-year term (six years in Württemberg-Baden). Unlike the *Gemeinde* council with its frequent sessions, the *Kreistag* meets only a few times each year. Much of the current work is handled by the *Kreisausschuss*. In Bavaria and Württemberg-Baden, the *Kreisausschuss* is chosen from among the members of the *Kreistag*, but in Hesse the *Kreisausschuss* members may not be simultaneously members of the *Kreistag* although they attend its sessions. The *Kreisausschuss* is a kind of collegial executive resembling the *Magistrat* under the *Magistratsverfassung*. Unlike the *Magistrat*, none of the *Kreisausschuss* members are full-time, professional officials except the *Landrat*. The *Kreisausschuss* is not only a standing committee for the Kreistag but shares with the *Landrat* in his work of supervising the *Gemeinden*.

The most important official in a U.S. Zone *Landkreis* is the *Landrat*. Before 1933, the *Landrat* was a political and professional state official appointed by the *Land* minister of the interior. He was responsible for the state functions delegated to the *Landkreis* and for supervision of the *Gemeinden* within his county which had not been legally removed from county control. At the same time, he was the chief executive officer for the self-governing functions of the *Landkreis* as vested in the *Kreistag*. In postwar years, in spite of strong German opposition, military government insisted that the *Landrat* be elected by the *Kreistag* without state confirmation, thus making for decentralization. This is still the law. The *Landrat* is chosen for four or six years. He is a full-time professional official except that Bavaria permits "honorary" *Landräte*. The *Landrat* is chairman of the council and of the committee. As chief executive, he appoints county employees and in this respect is like the *Bürgermeister* under the *Bürgermeisterverfassung.* There is some confusion as to just what the present position of the *Landrat* is. In Württemberg-Baden, he is considered a local official; but in Hesse, he is regarded as a state official and is responsible to the state-appointed official who heads the state administrative area known as the *Regierungsbezirk* and through him to the *Land* minister of the interior. His salary and pension are paid by the state. Moreover, in the three U.S. Zone *Länder,* the state has appointed a state official as the *Landrat's* assistant for state functions. In some instances, the state has removed or tried to remove the popularly elected *Landrat.*[32] On the whole, the *Landrat* in the U.S. Zone is still a key person.[33] In the writer's opinion, it would not be wise to split his office as has been done in the British Zone. *Kreistag* election of the *Landrat* should be retained, although the state could do more in prescribing qualifications for his position. He should never be an honorary official, as can happen in Bavaria, but should be a full-time professional official.

(3)*French Zone*—Partly because of the patchwork character of the French Zone[34] and partly because military government exercised more direct controls and retained them longer than in the U.S. and British zones, the restoration of local self-government lagged. However, prompt local elections in the U.S. Zone precipitated similar moves in the other zones in September and October, 1946. The dates for the French Zone local elections were the same as those for the British Zone, namely, *Gemeinde* council elections on September 15 and *Landkreis* and *Stadtkreis* council elections on October 13.

Military government ordinances established the election regulations and the local government structure.[35] In the *Gemeinden* and *Stadt-*

[32] Dr. Ludwig Bernheim was removed by the state from his post as *Landrat* of Kreis Sinsheim in Württemberg-Baden, but the administrative court invalidated the removal. Between 1945 and 1950, *Kreis* Sinsheim had no less than twelve *Landräte.* See *Neue Zeitung,* June 23, 1950. One is tempted to parody Gilbert and Sullivan and sing, "The *Landrat's* life is not a happy one!" In some cases, military government ordered the German *Land* government to remove *Landräte* and other local officials because they were legally disqualified by their Nazi background or because they obstructed military government.

[33] For a vivid description of *Landrat's* work, especially with expellees, see the article by the ex-*Landrat,* Hans Steinmetz, "The Problems of the *Landrat:* A Study of County Government in the U.S. Zone of Germany," *Journal of Politics,* XI (1949), 318-334.

[34] This chapter does not include the Saar which, for the French, was almost from the beginning a *régime exceptionnel.*

[35] The relevant military government ordinances are Nos. 44, 49, 50, 52, 53, 60, 61, 62, and 63, issued between June 15 and September 2, 1946. See *Journal officiel du commandement en chef français en Allemagne,* 1946, *passim.*

kreise, the French tried to introduce their own form of local government, much to the dislike of the Germans. The *Bürgermeister* and *"adjoints"* were required to be elected by the council from among its own members. In county government, however, the *Landrat* was continued as an appointed state official. What the Germans objected to in the *maire-et-adjoints* system for the *Gemeinden* and *Stadtkreise* was that it struck at the full-time professional top executives, the *Bürgermeister* and the other leading officials. As soon as the French Zone *Länder* had the legal opportunity, they reverted to the traditional pattern. Thus, in Rhineland-Palatinate, the *Bürgermeisterverfassung* was restored.[36] The *Landrat* is still state appointed, but the appointment requires the approval of the *Kreisversammlung* or county council.

(4) *Soviet Zone*—The Soviet Zone Municipal and County Government Acts have little significance.[37] The really important facts about the Soviet Zone are the strong Russian controls, the dominant role assigned to the Socialist Unity party among the other nominally authorized parties and mass organizations, the social revolution directed against the "bourgeois" classes, and the impact of central economic planning and centralizing tendencies generally on local institutions. The Soviet occupying power has transformed its zone into a satellite state, embodying the principles of a "people's democracy," with a secret police, concentration camps, forced labor, and all the other evils which Kremlin tyranny has devised or borrowed from the Nazis.[38]

The Soviet Zone has uniform local government legislation. When a draft *Gemeindeordnung* was prepared in Brandenburg by the *Land* government,[39] it was approved by Soviet Military Government as valid

[36] Emil Kraus, "Die Bürgermeistereiverfassung in Rheinland-Pfalz," *Der Städtetag,* New Series, II (1949), 135-137. The Rhineland-Palatinate *Gemeindeordnung* of September 29, 1948, is Part A of the *Selbstverwaltungsgesetz.* Part B is the *Amtsordnung,* and Part C the *Kreisordnung.* See *Gesetz-und Verordnungsblatt,* 1948, No. 32. Württemberg-Hohenzollern enacted a new *Gemeindeordnung* on March 14, and Baden did the same on March 25, 1947. See Wilhelm Braun and Theodor Holl, eds., *Gemeindeordnung für Württemberg-Hohenzollern* (Stuttgart, 1950).

[37] See *Government and Administration in the Soviet Zone of Germany* (Civil Administration Division, Office of Military Government for Germany [U.S.], Berlin, Nov. 1947), pp. 14-21.

[38] See Chapter 6 below for detailed discussion of the government and politics of the Soviet Zone. Both accounts reflect conditions as of 1951.

[39] According to information received by U.S. Military Government, the *Gemeindeordnung* was actually prepared at Karlshorst, Soviet Military Government headquarters. It was then taken to Potsdam and the signatures of the German *Land* government members were demanded so as to make it appear that the *Gemeindeordnung* was prepared in Potsdam.

for the whole zone although the other *Länder* did go through the form of adopting it.[40] It was the same with the *Demokratische Kreisordnung*, which was first enacted in Brandenburg on December 19, 1946, followed immediately by the other states of the Soviet Zone. The *Gemeinde* and *Stadtkreis* councils were "popularly" elected by proportional representation on September 1, 8, and 15, 1946, followed by the election of *Landkreis* councils on October 20. The elections were not "free" in the western sense of the word, but they were certainly freer than the central, state, and local elections of October 15, 1950, in which, for each legislative body chosen, there was only a single list of "bloc" candidates with no choice whatever left to the voter.

The local council is known as the *Gemeindeversammlung* in *Gemeinden,* the *Stadtverordnetenversammlung* in *Städte,* and the *Kreistag* in the *Landkreise.* The term of office is two years except for the *Kreistag,* where it is three years—but there were no elections between 1946 and 1950. The council is vested with all legislative and executive powers. Neither the *Bürgermeister* nor the *Landrat* preside over the council which elects its own chairman. There is a collegial executive (*Gemeinderat* or *Kreisrat*) consisting of the *Bürgermeister* or *Landrat* as chairman and other salaried and nonsalaried members, all of whom are elected by the council for the same term as the council. Members of the *Gemeinderat* or *Kreisrat* may simultaneously be members of the council which chooses them. This collegial type of executive suggests the *Magistrat* under the *Magistratverfassung,* but it has no independent administrative powers and its members individually and collectively require the confidence of the council. In other words, the parliamentary system is prescribed for local government. Provision is also made for the popular initiative and referendum on local ordiances and for the popular recall of the council before its term is completed. These devices of direct local democracy were found in certain German states during the Weimar period, but they have seldom been adopted in the western zones of Germany since the end of World War II.[41]

State supervision over local government is handled differently in the Soviet Zone. In the western zones of Germany, state supervision

---

[40] For example, the *Gemeindeordnung* was enacted by Saxony on February 6, 1947. For the text of the *Demokratische Gemeindeordnung für das Land Sachsen,* see *Sächsischer Landtag,* 1946/47 (Dresden, 1947), pp. 202-214. This handbook also contains the text of the *Demokratische Kreisordnung* for Saxony, pp. 189-201.

[41] Wells *op. cit.,* pp. 97-102. In Soviet Zone *Gemeinden* with less than twenty inhabitants, the voters may substitute a "town meeting" for the council. This type of direct democracy is also found in some *Gemeindeordnungen* of the western zones.

is exercised primarily by the *Land* minister of the interior acting through the *Regierungspräsident* in the case of *Stadtkreise* and *Landkreise,* and through the *Landrat* in the case of the county-supervised *Gemeinden.* However, in the Soviet Zone, state supervision is vested in the *Landtag* for the *Stadtkreise* and *Landkreise* and in the *Kreistag* for the supervised *Gemeinden.*[42]

The widespread socialization and central planning measure of the Soviet Zone have adversely affected local self-government. In 1949 all *Gemeinden, Stadtkreise,* and *Landkreise* were deprived of their municipally owned utilities, such as electricity, gas, water, transportation, markets, and slaughterhouses, and of other revenue-producing property, such as farms and forests. In the city of Leipzig alone, these holdings were valued at a half-billion marks. All such properties were expropriated and transferred to "People's Municipal Economic Undertakings," which were established under central control.[43]

A further blow at local self-government is found in the consolidations and boundary changes made by the *Land* governments without the local governments having anything to say about them.[44] Early in 1947, *Land* Saxony reduced the number of *Stadtkreise* from twenty-three to six.[45] It was argued that most cities should be under a *Landkreis* and that administrative simplification and taxsaving would result from depriving *Stadtkreise* of their independent position. In 1950 each *Land* enacted a law authorizing the state cabinet to change boundaries when and as the economic development requires.[46] In particular, the cabinet may abolish *Gemeinde* freedom from county supervision. It may be conceded that local governments in Germany, as in the United States, are too numerous and stand in need of boundary changes and consolidations. Nevertheless, the method by which this is accomplished is important. If done by central fiat and without local consultation and participation, the result can scarcely be described as being in harmony with local self-government.[47]

[42] It may also be mentioned that, in the western zones of Germany, state-delegated functions can be imposed on local governments only by law enacted by the *Landtag.* In the Soviet Zone, it can be done either by law or by cabinet decree.

[43] "Enteignung der ostdeutschen Städte," *Der Städtetag,* New Series, II (1949), 309-310.

[44] In 1950 the *Landkreis* Schmalkalden in Thuringia was peremptorily dissolved. *Ibid.,* III (1950), 330.

[45] *Tagesspiegel* (Berlin), Feb. 12, 1947.

[46] "Selbstverwaltung anderswo," *Der Städtetag,* New Series, III (1950), 235-236. For the text of the Brandenburg law, see *Gesetz- und Verordnungsblatt,* May 5, 1950.

[47] On local territorial reorganization, see Wells, *op. cit.,* chap. 8; Pünder, *op. cit.,* pp. 128-149.

CONSTITUTIONAL GUARANTEES AND LOCAL POWERS

The basic local government laws contain various statutory guarantees of local self-government. These in the main are repeated in the federal and state constitutions which were subsequently adopted. Even the Soviet Zone constitutions mention the right of local self-government but, as has just been shown, the practice is otherwise. The Bonn Constitution provides certain guarantees of local self-government.[48] Article 28 states that the *Kreise* and *Gemeinden* must have representative councils chosen by universal, direct, free, equal, and secret elections but that in *Gemeinden* the town meeting of all voters may be substituted for the elected council.[49] Article 28 continues by guaranteeing to *Gemeinden* the right to regulate all local affairs on their own responsibility and within the limits of the laws. It further provides that *Gemeindeverbände* also have the right of self-government within the limits of their legal sphere and in accordance with the laws.[50]

The west German *Land* constitutions pay greater attention to local self-government than does the Bonn Constitution.[51] More clearly than the Bonn Constitution, they recognize the two main classes of powers which the *Gemeinden* and, to a lesser extent, the *Landkreise* have.[52] This division arises from the fact that, as noted above, the *Gemeinden* and *Landkreise* are units of local self-government and, at the same time, agencies of the state for those functions for which the state has not created its own field offices. In the first class of powers are the *Selbstverwaltungsangelegenheiten;* these relate to purely local affairs and are administered by the local units on their own responsibility. In German legal theory the *Gemeinden* have all local powers without specific enumeration or grant by the state. State supervision over the exercise of these local powers is limited to ensuring compliance with the law.[53] The second class of powers is widely referred to as *Auf-*

[48] *Grundgesetz für die Bundesrepublik Deutschland,* May 23, 1949. Cf. Articles 17 and 127 of the Weimar Constitution.

[49] Hesse authorizes the town meeting for *Gemeinden* with less than 100 inhabitants.

[50] In practice, the only *Gemeindeverbände* of consequence are the *Landkreise.* The Bavarian constitution provides for self-government of the provinces, which are called *"Kreise,"* but this has not yet been organized. Elsewhere in the western zones, the examples of provincial self-government are few. See *Die Mittlestufe der Verwaltung* (*Institut zur Förderung öffentlicher Angelegenheiten,* Frankfurt, 1950), pp. 11-16, 116.

[51] Pünder, *op. cit.,* pp. 27-42.   [52] Wells, *op. cit.,* pp. 128-132.

[53] However, the Bavarian constitution of 1946 (Art. 83) also includes a long list of *Selbstverwaltungsangelegenheiten* and in this respect resembles the "home

tragsangelegenheiten; these are state functions delegated by law to the *Gemeinden* and *Landkreise* which, as state agents, are charged with their administration, subject to the orders of the higher state supervisory authorities.[54] The general principle of the twofold division of powers is clear, but the actual classification of functions into one category or the other is a matter of great difficulty and controversy.[55]

Since 1945, the sphere of local powers has been enlarged by legislation. This is most clearly shown in the case of the police which traditionally was a state function and, under the Nazis, had become highly centralized. The pressure for police decentralization came primarily from military government. Thus in the U.S. Zone each *Gemeinde* with 5,000 or more inhabitants was required to maintain and assume "total administrative responsibility for the police department," which was charged with performing "all police functions within the municipality."[56] The rural police function was assigned to the *Land,* which could delegate it to the *Regierungsbezirk* or *Landkreis* or both. Such decentralization may not endure much longer, since the militarization of East Germany is forcing larger state and federal police contingents and powers and probably armed German troops in West Germany. There is also a tendency to reduce the number of independent state field offices and to assign their work to the general units of local government.[57] For example, public health is still a state function, but the health office is now under the general administration of the *Stadtkreis* or *Landkreis* instead of being a separate field office.[58]

---

rule" provisions of certain American state constitutions. Article 11 of the Bavarian constitution contains a general grant of "home rule."

[54] On state supervision, see Wells, *op. cit.,* pp. 138-152; Pünder, *op. cit.,* pp. 181-194. Since decentralization was one of the objectives of the Potsdam Agreement, British and U.S. Military Government took positive action to weaken state supervision and control over local government. The requirement that leading local officials be elected by the local council (or by the voters) without state appointment or confirmation was an effort in this direction.

[55] See Glaser, *Land and Local Government in the U.S. Zone of Germany,* pp. 31-34.

[56] *Military Government Regulations,* Title 9, Public Safety, par. 211 as revised July 9, 1949 (Office of Military Government for Germany [U.S.], Berlin). Also see Chapter 16 below.

[57] With the repeal of war and postwar restrictions, other offices, such as the economic and food offices, have been abolished outright.

[58] Friedrich Lube, "Zur Kommunalisierung der Gesundheitsämter," *Der Städtetag,* New Series, II (1949), 279-180. On the other hand, municipal utilities, one of the oldest and most traditional of the *Selbstverwaltungsangelegenheiten,* are threatened by large-scale developments in such fields as gas and electricity. See Otto Ziebill, "Zur Selbstbehauptung der kommunalen Wirtschaft," *ibid.,* III (1950), 157-158; and Hans Storck, "Energierecht und Energieverbundwirtschaft,"

Finance is one of the most basic problems of local self-government. Do the local units have any independent powers of raising revenue through local taxation such as real estate and trade and business taxes, through fees for administrative services, and through the earnings of municipal undertakings? Can they determine at least some of the objects of expenditure, or do the state-delegated functions use up all or most of the money? How far are the local units dependent upon central grants and/or centrally collected but locally shared taxes? These are large and difficult questions which range beyond the scope of the present chapter. They involve the financial relations of the federal government and the *Länder,* a subject which is treated elsewhere in this volume.[59]

However, before the topic is left, it should be noted that the *Land* constitutions contain a number of provisions relating to local finance. Article 79 of the North Rhine–Westphalia Constitution declares that "*Gemeinden* have the right to exploit their own tax resources for the purpose of performing their functions. The *Land* is obligated to consider this claim in its legislation and to guarantee within the limits of its financial capacity an equalization of finances on a higher than *Gemeinde* level." According to the Bavarian Constitution (Art. 83), "When state functions are delegated to *Gemeinden,* the necessary financial means must at the same time be made available." There are similar expressions in the other west German *Land* constitutions. Nevertheless, in spite of these provisions, the financial demands upon the federal and *Land* governments are so great that, in the struggle for revenues, local governments are apt to fare badly.[60]

INTERGOVERNMENTAL RELATIONS AT THE LOCAL LEVEL

Area Relationships—Intergovernmental relations at the local level assume a variety of forms, some compulsory, others voluntary. In the first category are the relations between the *Landkreis* and the supervised *Gemeinden* situated within it. The *Landkreis* as a *Gemeindeverband* is a union of *Gemeinden,* and the relationships between it and its constituent units are largely imposed by state law.[61] However,

---

ibid., pp. 158-163. British cities have lost their electricity and gas works under the nationalization programs. The drastic action taken in the Soviet Zone with respect to municipal utilities has already been discussed in this chapter.

[59] See Chapter 13 below.

[60] George Berkenhoff, "Gemeinden immer noch Kostgänger des Staates," *Neue Zeitung,* June 20, 1950.

[61] This does not preclude additional voluntary arrangements between the *Landkreis* and its *Gemeinden.* The law does not require the *Landrat* to consult his

most intergovernmental relations at the local level are voluntarily assumed. These may be very informal, such as consultation and exchange of information between officials of neighboring units. They may involve contractual arrangements whereby one unit provides certain equipment or services for another or where two or more units jointly employ an official. The local governments may go further and establish a general or a special-purpose authority. For example, in the Rhineland and Westphalia, the *Amt* is a union of neighboring *Landgemeinden* for the general purposes of local government. The *Amter* are to be distinguished from the *ad hoc* authorities (*Zweckverbände*) for particular and limited functions such as the provision of electricity, gas, water, and sewage disposal. Although no recent figures are available, it was estimated that Germany in 1938 had about 14,000 *Zweckverbände*.[62]

Local Government Associations—Another type of intergovernmental relations is represented by the local government associations or unions of Western Germany, the so-called *Kommunalspitzenverbände*.[63] These associations have been created for the promotion of mutual interests and the defense of local rights against state encroachment.

The first German association of local authorities was the Hanover *Städteverein* founded in 1866 while Hanover was still an independent kingdom. In 1896 the cities of all Prussia formed the *Preussischer Städtetag*, and the Bavarian cities were also organized. In 1905 these various state associations were united into an all-German union known as the *Deutscher Städtetag*. In addition to the state associations, the larger cities were direct members of the *Städtetag*. In 1910 the small and medium-sized cities organized the *Reichstädtebund*. For the *Landkreise*, there was the *Deutscher Landkreistag* (1921), and the more rural *Gemeinden* had the *Deutscher Landgemeindetag* (1916).

These national associations with their various state-affiliated unions were dissolved in 1933 by the Nazis, who created a single compulsory organization embracing all local governments and known as the *Deutscher Gemeindetag*. The *Deutscher Gemeindetag* was not meant to be an agency of local self-government but rather was an instrument of state control exercised by the Reich minister of the interior and of

---

Bürgermeister, but a good *Landrat* will convene them in periodic conferences for the discussion of common problems and the encouragement of a co-operative spirit.

[62] Kurt Kottenberg, "Neuordnung des Zweckverbandsrechts," *Kommunalpolitik,* I (1948), 60-62. See also Wells, *op. cit.,* pp. 188-194.

[63] Roger H. Wells, "The Revival of German Unions of Local Authorities after World War II," Am. Pol. Sci. R. XLI (1947), 1181-1187.

Nazi party control exercised through the *Hauptamt für Kommunal-politik*. Because the *Deutscher Gemeindetag* was a Nazi organization, it was prohibited by Allied Control Council Law No. 2 (October 2, 1945). However, as early as the end of 1945, German local officials took the lead in re-establishing associations of local authorities like those which had existed before 1933, a step encouraged by U.S. and British Military Government. Organization began first on a *Land* basis, spread throughout the U.S. and British zones, and finally in 1949, after initial French resistance had been overcome, included the French Zone. It is reported that there are (or have been) a few similar associations in the Soviet Zone, but they have little, if any, contact with the West.

At present in West Germany, there are four principal associations corresponding to the four of the Weimar period. The first is the *Deutscher Städtetag* with headquarters in Cologne, representing, as before, the *Stadtkreise*. The *Landkreise* have the *Deutscher Land-kreistag* with headquarters at Frankfurt/Höchst. The *Deutscher Städtebund* is located in Düsseldorf and is the organization of the small and medium-sized cities. The *Landgemeinden* have established the *Deutscher Gemeindetag* (not to be confused with the Nazi organization having the same name) in Bad Godesberg. The four associations are loosely linked by a working party which has its office with the *Deutscher Städtetag*. There is no sentiment for the revival of the highly centralized Nazi *Gemeindetag*, although *Städtetag* circles feel that having the central headquarters of the associations in four different places is unfortunate. (Americans who know 1313 East 60th Street, Chicago, the common headquarters of many state and local government organizations, will sympathize with this view.) However, the other associations are inclined to be suspicious, and in fact there are real conflicts of interest between them.

The work of the revived *Spitzenverbände* is carried on through special committees of local officials and through periodic meetings and conferences to which the committees report and at which there is general discussion of common problems. The associations also publish monthly magazines filled with valuable material.[64] Because so much federal and state legislation directly or indirectly affects local govern-

---

[64] *Der Städtetag* is the official magazine of the *Deutscher Städtetag*. Since July, 1948, it has been published monthly at Cologne. The *Städtetag* has also resumed publication of the *Statistisches Jahrbuch deutscher Gemeinden*, Vol. XXXVII, 1949 (Lorch, 1950). *Die Selbstverwaltung* is the official magazine of the *Deutscher Landkreistag*. Since August, 1947, it has been published monthly at Heidelberg.

ments, the local authorities naturally wish to participate in framing the legislation or at least to have the opportunity to be heard. This applies particularly to questions of finance equalization. The Württemberg-Baden Constitution (Art. 98) specifically grants to the local authorities the right to be heard "before general questions concerning them are regulated by law." The Bavarian Constitution (Art. 35) requires that, among the sixty members of the Senate, there shall be "6 representatives of the *Gemeinden* and *Gemeindeverbände.*" But even without special constitutional provisions, the *Spitzenverbände* make their voices heard in federal and state legislative halls and executive offices.

These associations are among the most active defenders of local self-government in West Germany today. The cynic may argue that they are largely made up of professional officials who are naturally interested in defending their respective "empires" against federal and state encroachments. The writer dissents from this view. He has found most local officials genuinely interested in local self-government and anxious to develop greater interest and participation by lay citizens in their local governments. The Third General Assembly of the *Deutscher Städtetag* was held in Cologne on June 30 and July 1, 1950. The subject of the meeting was "Our Cities and Their Youth." In addition to the 150 regular delegates, there were 150 representatives of German youth organizations who took an active part in the deliberations and decisions.[65]

THE FUTURE OF GERMAN LOCAL DEMOCRACY

In spite of many adverse external factors, West Germany has made definite progress toward local self-government. The first step was the local elections of 1946. These brought into the councils many men and women who were completely without experience in their new assignments. Recognizing this, British Military Government in 1946 established self-government schools in each *Land*. There were five such schools in Lower Saxony alone, the best known being at Hahnenklee. In the first two years of the Hahnenklee school, 50 courses, each lasting five days, were held. More than 4,000 Germans participated in this school, the usual course having from 40 to 50 members. While local councilors predominated, local officials, officials from the ministry of the interior, local party leaders, and private citizens were also included. From the beginning, the school emphasized training in local self-government through lectures, round-table discussions,

[65] See the July, 1950, number of *Der Städtetag* for a series of excellent articles on German youth organizations.

model *Gemeinderat* and *Kreistag* sessions, and the like. Although the school was originally operated by British Military Government, it was managed and financed by the Germans from October, 1946, except for the expenses of one or two British lecturers participating in each course.

Following the British Zone example, self-government schools have been established in the U.S. Zone; the first was the Ettlingen school in Württemberg-Baden in November, 1949. In this connection, mention should be made of the lectures and round-table conferences arranged by the Institute of Public Affairs in Frankfurt. The institute is also publishing a series of pamphlets and studies dealing with a wide variety of current questions.[66] Perhaps of even greater importance are the British and American exchange programs under which German local officials and councilmen visit Britain and America in order to study how local government operates there.[67] Since the exchange program is a two-way process, numerous local officials from Britain and the United States and the countries of western Europe have been brought to Germany as visiting experts. Quantitatively, the exchange programs do not bulk large in terms of the size of the job to be done. Nevertheless, they have had a beneficial leavening effect and certainly represent steps in the right direction.

Traditionally, German local self-government has emphasized citizen participation, not only as voter or as elected council member, but also in administration. The pre-1933 administrative committees, such as the school committee and the youth welfare committee, often contained private citizens co-opted by the council for committee service.[68] Co-optation is also permitted under the postwar *Gemeindeordnungen.*[69] In the first postwar years, the struggle to keep body and soul together left little time for lay men and women to serve on committees or even to stand for election to the local council. However, with the improvement of economic conditions, this form of citizen participation has increased.

[66] *Institut zur Förderung öffentlicher Angelengenheiten.* The institute has fourteen German member and affiliated organizations including the four *Kommunalspitzenverbände.*

[67] Up to January, 1950, about 200 German local officials had visited the British Isles. On groups coming to the United States, see Paul van Riper, "The Cultural Exchange Program," *Annals of the American Academy of Political and Social Science, CCLXVII* (Jan., 98-105; and *Report of Panel on Governmental Affairs and Social Science* (now Governmental Affairs Institute; mimeographed, Washington, D.C., July 28, 1950).

[68] Wells, *German Cities,* pp. 50-53, 135-138.

[69] See, for example, the *Gemeindeordnung* for North Württemberg of 1945, Art. 45.

[Local Government]

The restoration of a free press and radio in West Germany has likewise contributed to the re-establishment of local self-government. So many of Germany's problems, such as housing, schools, and expellees, have a focus in each community that naturally they receive much attention in the newspapers. On the whole, the press is doing a creditable job in reporting local government. Moreover, the widespread growth of forums and public discussion groups has promoted civic interest. Increasingly, the leading local officials make speeches to citizens' groups and are subjected to questions from the floor. School children are encouraged to visit the *Rathaus* and see for themselves what goes on. Local self-government in West Germany still has a long way to go before it reaches the goal. However, it is moving in the right direction, and the progress made since 1945 gives hope for the future.

4

State Government

ROGER H. WELLS

THE preceding chapter on local government leads naturally to a consideration of the next higher governmental unit, the state or *Land*. The German *Länder* are of both historical and contemporary interest. The historical interest is reflected in the preamble of the Bavarian Consitution of 1946 which proudly recalls Bavaria's "more than one thousand years of history." Other *Länder* are of more recent vintage, but they too have no difficulty in finding an abundance of materials for their archives and museums. This is not the place to summarize the long annals of the Holy Roman Empire or to speak in detail of its "galaxy of states," to use Brecht's apt term.[1] It is sufficient to note that there were about three hundred of these "states" on the eve of the French Revolution. The work of wholesale consolidation, energetically begun by Napoleon, was carried forward by the Congress of Vienna, which in 1815 united the surviving thirty-nine states in the German Confederation. During the next half century, the number was still further reduced to twenty-seven, all of which, except Austria and Liechtenstein, became members of the German Empire in 1871.[2]

The twenty-five states of the Empire were also the constituent *Länder* of the Weimar Republic (1918), under which a new chapter in amalgamation was written. Coburg was joined with Bavaria and Waldeck with Prussia; and seven small states were combined to form

[1] Arnold Brecht, *Federalism and Regionalism in Germany: The Division of Prussia* (New York, 1945), pp. 7-8.
[2] The German Empire also included Alsace-Lorraine as a Reich territory.

the new *Land* of Thuringia. At the end of the Weimar period (1933), there were seventeen *Länder*—Prussia, Bavaria, Württemberg, Baden, Saxony, Mecklenburg-Schwerin, Mecklenburg-Strelitz, Thuringia, Hesse, Oldenburg, Brunswick, Anhalt, Lippe, Schaumburg-Lippe, and the three city-states of Hamburg, Bremen, and Lübeck. In spite of the fact that the Nazis destroyed Weimar federalism and set up a unitary and highly centralized government and in spite of the fact that they frequently talked about replacing the existing *Länder* with *Reichsgaue*, fourteen of the seventeen *Länder* survived, at least as administrative units.[3] Lübeck was incorporated in Prussia, and the two Mecklenburgs were united into a single state by that name. The most significant change, however, was in the status of Prussia. In effect, if not in theory, Prussia was abolished as a *Land*. Its ministries were merged with those of the Reich and its provinces were transformed into immediate administrative subdivisions of the Reich. Thus, when the Nazi regime fell in 1945, there were not seventeen but twenty-nine major territorial units within the boundaries of prewar Germany.

The contemporary as distinguished from the historical interest in the German *Länder* is intimately connected with the general problem of Germany. Had the Reich been dismembered in accordance with the Yalta Conference decision,[4] the *Länder*, or at any rate some of them, would have been made into independent states. Fortunately, such a dismemberment was never implemented. Instead, the Potsdam Agreement posited the unity of Germany, merely stating that "for the time being, no central German Government shall be established." How to achieve the eventual unity of the country was and is a source of great controversy. Shall Germany be a unitary state like that of National Socialism, a loose confederation of quasi-independent states (*Staatenbund*) like the German Confederation (1815-1866), or a true federal state (*Bundesstaat*), which avoids the shortcomings both of Bismarck's federal German Empire and of the federal Weimar Republic? Since the four occupying powers were not able to agree, Britain, France, and the United States, together with the three Benelux countries, reached their own decisions, which called for a federal form of government which adequately protects the rights of the re-

[3] Brecht, *op. cit.*, pp. 120-132; John H. Herz, "German Administration under the Nazi Regime," *American Political Science Review*, XL (1946), 682-702, especially pp. 695-696.

[4] Philip E. Mosely, "Dismemberment of Germany: The Allied Negotiations from Yalta to Potsdam," *Foreign Affairs*, XXVIII (1950), 484-498. Mosely points out that the division of Germany into occupation zones very soon produced a *de facto* dismemberment. Germany's territorial losses in the East and West should also be kept in mind in discussing dismemberment.

spective states, and which at the same time provides for adequate central authority and which guarantees the rights and freedoms of the individual.[5]

Federalism ideally should be based upon constituent states, each of which has sufficient area, population, and resources to maintain a vigorous self-government of its own. Moreover, the disparity between the states with respect to these factors should not be too pronounced. Unfortunately, the course of German history did not provide ideal building blocks, but instead offered an assortment of boulders and pebbles. For example, Prussia, the largest *Land,* had in 1929 an area of 113,000 square miles and a population of 38,000,000. At the other extreme was Schaumburg-Lippe with 131 square miles and 48,000 population.[6] The metaphor of "boulders and pebbles" is misleading when applied to the German *Länder* because it suggests that they were well-rounded and integrated shapes. In actual fact, the territory of a state was frequently not a consolidated area at all but was splattered over other states in the form of enclaves.[7] This explains why maps of Germany indicating *Land* boundaries have resembled patchwork quilts.

The Germans themselves have long been aware of the irrational pattern of their "quilt" and numerous proposals for territorial reorganization have been made, usually in connection with discussions of *Reichsreform,* a subject on which there is a substantial literature.[8] Prior to 1945, however, not much was actually done, not even by the Nazis. The great redrawing of the map came with the Allied occupation and the establishment of the four separate zones and of Berlin as an island under Four Power rule.[9] Upon the existing *Land* irration-

[5] See Appendix G and the discussion of London Six Power Conference Recommendations in Chapter 2, above. On postwar state government, see J. F. J. Gillen, *State and Local Government in West Germany, 1945-1953,* Historical Division, Office of the U.S. High Commissioner for Germany (Bad Godesberg, 1953).

[6] *Statistisches Jahrbuch für das Deutsche Reich, 1929* (Berlin, 1929).

[7] For example, the German *Gemeinde,* Büsingen, is completely surrounded by Swiss territory. See *Frankfurter Rundschau,* July 26, 1949. Bad Wimpfen has been a Hessian enclave since 1803. In 1945, U.S. Military Government allocated it to Württemberg-Baden, but Hesse and Württemberg-Baden are still quarreling about it. See *Neue Zeitung,* June 14, 1950. For a list of the enclaves and exclaves in West Germany, see *Die Bundesländer: Beiträge zur Neugliederung der Bundesrepublik (Institute zur Förderung öffentlicher Angelegenheiten,* Frankfurt am Main, 1950), pp. 221-233.

[8] Brecht, *op. cit.;* Robert E. Dickinson, *The Regions of Germany* (New York, 1945); Walther Vogel, *Deutsche Reichsgliederung und Reichsreform in Vergangenheit und Gegenwart* (Berlin, 1932); *Die Bundesländer.*

[9] Philip E. Mosely, "The Occupation of Germany: New Light on How the Zones Were Drawn," For. Affairs, XXVIII (1950), 508-604.

alities, new and greater zonal irrationalities were imposed by the conquerors. These zonal demarcations, which soon became "frozen," may have been unavoidable from the standpoint of military and external political considerations, but they greatly complicated the restoration of German government at state level, to say nothing of the adverse effects upon the economy as a whole. The carving out of the French Zone from areas already assigned to the Americans and British was especially harmful in breaking up existing territorial units. Moreover, zonalism was a very poor approach to the "decentralization of the political structure" envisaged by the Potsdam Agreement and to the federalism agreed to by the western Allies at the London Conference of 1948.

However, it is only fair to add that the occupying powers did some *Land* territorial reorganization of their own, both on a quadripartite and on a zonal basis. As a result, the map of Germany today is in some respects tidier than it was in 1945. Quadripartite action was limited to the legal recognition of the *de facto* abolition of the state of Prussia by the promulgation of Control Council Law No. 46 on February 25, 1947. Less than one month later Control Council action was endorsed in Moscow by the Council of Foreign Ministers in one of the few affirmative actions arising from that ill-fated conference.[10]

TERRITORIAL REORGANIZATION UNDER OCCUPATION

British Zone—At the beginning of the occupation, the British Zone consisted of the Prussian provinces of Schleswig-Holstein, Hanover, Westphalia, and the northern part of the Rhine Province, the remainder of which was assigned to the French Zone.[11] In addition, there were four small *Länder* (Oldenburg, Lippe, Schaumburg-Lippe, and Brunswick) and the city-state of Hamburg.[12] Although all of these except Schaumburg-Lippe were reconstituted, the unsatisfactory character of these units was obvious and led to various experiments.[13] On July 17, 1946, British Military Government announced the merger of North Rhine and Westphalia into the *Land* North Rhine–Westphalia.

[10] *Germany, 1947-1949: The Story in Documents* (Washington, 1950), p. 151. On March 10, 1947, the Moscow Council of Foreign Ministers approved the Control Council Law on the abolition of Prussia. Also compare with conclusions drawn on the same subject in Chapter 2 above.

[11] These provinces were raised to the status of *Länder* by British Military Government Ordinance No. 46, August 23, 1946.

[12] The city-state of Bremen is physically in the British Zone but was under American control.

[13] W. Friedmann, *The Allied Military Government of Germany* (London, 1947), pp. 84-85.

Thus for the first time the whole of the Ruhr area, together with other neighboring industrial regions, was combined under a single state government. But on the other hand a wide disparity in population among the *Länder* composing the Federal Republic of Germany was thereby produced. Four of the nine states in West Germany have less than 3,000,000 inhabitants as compared with the 13,000,000 in North Rhine–Westphalia.

Meanwhile, the ticklish question of further territorial reorganization was referred to a special committee of the German Zonal Advisory Council. This committee, under the chairmanship of Dr. Kurt Schumacher, considered numerous proposals, especially from the smaller states, which eloquently championed their "small state status." Its recommendations, presented in September, 1946, were substantially adopted by the British. By January, 1947, reorganization by Military Government Ordinance was completed. *Land* Schleswig-Holstein and *Land* Hamburg were retained with their traditional boundaries. North Rhine–Westphalia absorbed the state of Lippe.[14] The greatest change was the creation of *Land* Lower Saxony by the amalgamation of Hanover, Schaumburg-Lippe, Oldenburg, and Brunswick.[15] In area, Lower Saxony is now the second largest German state. It is too soon to conclude that particularism and local pride have been overcome and that the new *Land* will "stick together." Thus as early as 1950, Oldenburg demanded a plebiscite under Article 29-2 of the Bonn Constitution but was told by the Allied High Commission that the issue must await the conclusion of the peace treaty.

United States Zone—In the early days of the American occupation, there was uncertainty as to the number of *Länder* to be established, and several makeshift arrangements were tried.[16] By September, 1945, the doubt had been resolved in favor of three states, Bavaria, Hesse, and Württemberg-Baden.[17] For a long time the status of the city-state of Bremen, which is located in the British Zone, was uncertain, but in January, 1947, it was formally recognized as a *Land* under Ameri-

[14] Military Government Ordinance No. 77, January 21, 1947.

[15] Military Government Ordinance No. 75, November 1, 1946. Small portions of the former Prussian province of Hanover are in the Soviet Zone. The British recognized Hanover as a *Land* on November 6, 1945.

[16] These produced separate entities such as the Frankfurt enclave, *Land* Hesse, Nassau Province, Kurhessen Province, *Land* North Baden, and *Land* North Württemberg. Friedmann, *op. cit.*, p. 75, note 1.

[17] Military Governor, Proclamation No. 2, September 19, 1945; text in James K. Pollock, James H. Meisel, and Henry Bretton, eds., *Germany under Occupation*, rev. ed. (Ann Arbor, 1949).

can control.[18] Bavaria has preserved most of its original territory. To be sure, the Bavarian Palatinate was assigned to the French Zone, but this had already been lost to Bavaria when the Nazis united the Bavarian Palatinate and the Saar to form the *Gau Westmark*. When the zones of occupation were established, Bavaria also lost *Landkreis* Lindau to the French Zone, thereby providing a connecting link with the French Zone of Austria.[19] There were those in American Military Government who argued that Bavaria should be divided into two *Länder*—Bavaria proper, south of the Danube, and Northern Bavaria or Franconia—but this possibility, whatever may have been its merits, was never seriously considered. In consequence, Bavaria today is the largest German *Land* in area.

Unlike Bavaria, Hesse was a synthetic creation of military government. Three units were combined to form it, namely, the original *Land* Hesse and the Prussian provinces of Nassau and Kurhessen. The latter two were really one province historically (Hesse-Nassau), having been separated by the Nazis as recently as 1944.[20] When the zonal boundaries were fixed, the original *Land* Hesse and Nassau Province each lost four *Landkreise* to the French Zone while Kurhessen lost one *Landkreis* to the Soviet Zone.[21] In addition, the Americans and Russians made minor exchanges of territory in September, 1945, on the Kurhessen-Thuringian frontier. Although there have been difficulties in harmonizing and unifying the Prussian and Hessian legal and administrative systems throughout the new state, these have been far less than in Lower Saxony, which represents a much more diverse mixture.

The consequences of zonal partition are seen at their worst in the case of Württemberg and Baden. Here were two historic German

---

[18] Military Governor, Proclamation No. 3, January 21, 1947; in Pollock, Meisel, and Bretton, *op. cit.* Because the Americans insisted upon having a German port of their own, Bremen and the surrounding non-Bremen territory were made into an American enclave. In December, 1945, the enclave was transferred to British Military Government. In January, 1947, it was transferred back to U.S. Military Government minus the non-Bremen territory, which remained under British control. Proclamation No. 3 defined *Land* Bremen as *Stadt* Bremen, *Landgebiet* Bremen, and *Stadtkreis* Wesermünde including Bremerhaven—in other words, the traditional area.

[19] In the zonal demarcation, Bavaria lost a number of small enclaves but received the Thuringian enclave of Ostheim.

[20] Ernest Berger, *Die Kommunalwahlen in Hessen, 1948* (Wiesbaden, 1948), pp. 1-2.

[21] In 1944 the Nazis had already in effect transferred Schmalkalden to Thuringia although no change in state boundary lines was made.

states whose traditions of constitutionalism and parliamentary rule were better than in most of the other states. Yet they were arbitrarily bisected, producing four "rumps," no one of which could be considered a viable *Land* in a federal Reich. U.S. Military Government soon came to the conclusion that North Württemberg and North Baden must be united into a single *Land*. The result was the formation of Württemberg-Baden, which was a veritable "Siamese twin." At first, things did not go well.[22] The peoples of Württemberg and Baden bitterly resented the partition of their respective states. They feared that the new creation would jeopardize the eventual reunion of the original *Länder*. There are still cultural differences between Protestant Württemberg and Catholic Baden, a fact which helps to explain the opposition of the Baden Christian Democratic Union to the merger. On the other hand, the Baden parties of the Left, the Social Democrats and the Communists, tended to favor the permanent combination of the whole of the two states and hence could regard North Württemberg–Baden as a step in that direction. In such territorial amalgamations, one must also not overlook the jealousy and suspicion of the state bureaucracies concerned. This was a factor both in Lower Saxony and in Württemberg-Baden. The Karlsruhe *Beamten* had no desire to be governed from distant Stuttgart to the detriment of Baden's traditional capital, Karlsruhe, and their own jobs.

Finally, one must not neglect the role of the French, who were never happy about the zonal frontiers. It was to French interest to defend the integrity of Baden, especially if, in a revision of the zones, the whole *Land* could be brought under French control and thus become one more buffer between France and Germany. Against all these approaches, the Americans stood firmly for the zonal *status quo*, at least until the future of Germany could be clarified. U.S. Military Government "drove with a loose rein" in Württemberg–Baden, allowing a maximum of autonomy to the two parts, a fact which explains why separate *Gemeindeordnungen* and election laws were permitted in North Württemberg and North Baden. Even in a "forced marriage," the partners may develop a *modus vivendi*, as the Württemberg–Baden Constitution of 1946 well demonstrated. The Germans came to realize that Württemberg–Baden, with all its faults, was nevertheless better than the two separate "dwarf" *Länder* which the French insisted on maintaining in the south.

French Zone—Of the four zones, that carved out for the French was

[22] Moses Moskovitz, "The Political Re-education of the Germans: The Emergence of Parties and Politics in Württemberg-Baden (May, 1945-June, 1946)," *Political Science Quarterly*, LXI (1946), 535-561, especially 543-544 and 551-552.

the least satisfactory, both to the occupying power and to Germans. Whereas the British, Americans, and Russians each received one or more historic *Länder* or provinces with boundaries intact or substantially unchanged, the French were assigned only fragments. In September, 1945, the French organized[23] their zone into the following five provinces:

1. Rhineland Province; the southern part of the old Prussian Rhine Province and four *Landkreise* from the Prussian Province of Hesse–Nassau.
2. Province of Hesse–Palatinate; the Bavarian Palatinate and four *Landkreise* from *Land* Hesse.
3. Province of Baden; the southern part of *Land* Baden.
4. Province of Württemberg; the southern part of *Land* Württemberg, the Prussian enclave of Hohenzollern, and the Bavarian *Landkreis* of Lindau.
5. Saar Province; this was, however, soon separated from the French Zone of occupation and economically attached to France.

At the end of August, 1946, the Rhineland Province and the Province of Hesse–Palatinate were combined to form the *Land* Rhineland–Palatinate.[24] This "creation" was accurately described by a German as "scenically one of the finest *Länder* in Germany, rich in history and culture, in cathedrals and castles, in romance and wine, but leaving much to be desired in political, administrative, and economic relations." Although in population and area the Rhineland–Palatinate is possible as a federal unit, it represents a union of so many diversities that its long-run future is extremely questionable. The other two provinces were likewise elevated to the status of *Länder* (Baden and Württemberg–Hohenzollern), neither of which are viable as separate entities.

Soviet Zone—Prior to the 1952 reorganization resulting in abolition of the *Länder,* four of the five *Länder* of the Soviet Zone had the same names and substantially the same areas as preoccupation *Länder* and provinces. The major differences in state boundaries were those resulting from the Oder-Neisse frontier established by the Potsdam Agreement. Thus *Land* Brandenburg was the old Prussian province of Brandenburg less those parts of Brandenburg which are east of the Oder-Neisse line and hence under Polish administration. *Land* Mecklenburg was the old *Land* Mecklenburg plus the remnants of the Prus-

---

[23] Arrêtés Nos. 5, 7, 8, 9, 10, *Journal officiel du commandement en chef français en Allemagne: Gouvernement militaire de la zone française d'occupation* (Baden-Baden, 1945), *passim.*

[24]Ordonnance No. 57, August 30, 1946, *Journal officiel.*

sion Province of Pomerania. Similarly, *Land* Saxony was the old *Land* Saxony and fragments of three *Landkreise* from the Prussian Province of Lower Silesia. *Land* Thuringia was not affected by the Oder-Neisse partition, but it received accessions.[25] In addition to the old *Land* Thuringia, it included the *Regierungsbezirk* Erfurt from the Prussian province of Saxony and the *Landkreis* Schmalkalden from the Prussian province of Kurhessen.

One new state was organized in the Soviet Zone—*Land* Saxony-Anhalt.[26] The constituent elements which were united to form Saxony-Anhalt were the Prussian province of Saxony which the Nazis had divided into two provinces, Magdeburg and Halle-Merseburg; the old *Land* Anhalt, which consisted of two larger parts and five smaller enclaves; and a part of *Landkreis* Blankenburg from *Land* Brunswick, most of which is in the British Zone and is now incorporated into Lower Saxony. So far as area and population are concerned, the five *Länder* of the Soviet Zone were all suitable federal units. The largest *Land*, Bradenburg, was less than twice as big as the smallest, Thuringia. The least populous *Land*, Mecklenburg, had almost half as many inhabitants as the most populous, Saxony. Enclaves were eliminated and minor boundary rectifications were made.[27] After quadripartite agreements on the dissolution of the State of Prussia in 1947, the provinces of Brandenburg and Saxony-Anhalt received the title of *Land*.

West German Territorial Reorganization, 1948-1951—After the failure of the London Council of Foreign Ministers in December, 1947, territorial reorganization became a matter for tripartite rather than quadripartite negotiations. General Clay's memorandum of April 6, 1948, which was accepted by the British and French military governors, proposed that the west German constituent assembly be given the power to:

determine the boundaries of the several states which will form the federal government, recognizing traditional patterns and avoiding to the extent feasible the creation of states which are either too large or too small in comparison with other states composing the federal structure.[28]

This memorandum formed the basis of the London Conference agree-

[25] Thuringia was organized as a *Land* by U.S. Military Government but was transferred to Soviet control on July 14, 1945.

[26] Created March 3, 1946.

[27] Two Thuringian enclaves, Ostheim and Allstedt, went to Bavaria and Saxony-Anhalt respectively. In September, 1946, 12,000 hectares were transferred from Saxony-Anhalt to Thuringia. Berlin *Tagesspiegel*, September 26, 1946.

[28] Lucius D. Clay, *Decision in Germany* (Garden City, N.Y., 1950), p. 399. For General Clay's further discussion of the question of territorial reorganization, see pp. 402-404, 422-423, 427, 429.

ment which was communicated to the German *Land* ministers-president on July 1, 1948.[29] The ministers-president were asked to recommend *Land* boundary changes, which, if approved by the military governors, would be submitted to popular referendum in the areas concerned not later than the time when the members of the constituent assembly for West Germany were chosen. The ministers-president were unable to agree on specific recommendations within the time limit, and hence the constituent assembly was elected from the existing *Länder*.[30]

The Bonn Constitution (Art. 29) provided for territorial reorganization by federal law and plebiscite under a definite time schedule. Article 118 stated that reorganization in Baden, Württemberg–Baden, and Württemberg–Hohenzollern might be accomplished by agreement among the *Länder* concerned "in a manner deviating from the provisions of Article 29. Should an agreement not be reached, the reorganization shall be regulated by federal legislation which must provide for a referendum." In approving the Bonn Constitution, the military governors made the following reservation:

Unless the High Commissioners should unanimously agree to change this position, the powers set forth in these articles (Arts. 29 and 118) shall not be exercised and the boundaries of all the *Länder* except Württemberg–Baden and Hohenzollern shall remain as now fixed until the time of the peace treaty.[31]

The effect of this was to suspend all territorial reorganization except in Southwest Germany.

For the next year, the Germans discussed the "southwest problem." In May, 1950, the High Commission indicated that it was ready to consider an agreement between the three *Länder* concerned or, in the absence of an agreement, a federal law on a plebiscite. The three states did agree on an advisory referendum presenting two alternative questions to the voters: (a) the union of Württemberg–Baden, South Baden, and Württemberg–Hohenzollern into a southwest state or (b) the reconstruction of the old *Länder*, Württemberg including Hohenzollern, and Baden. The referendum held on September 24, with only 51 per cent of the electorate participating, was inconclusive. In both parts of Württemberg there was a combined majority of 878,296 for the southwest state. However, in North Baden the southwest majority

---

[29] See Chapter 1 above for discussion.

[30] Anton F. Pabsch and S. L. Wahrhaftig, "Constitutional Development of the Federal Republic of Germany," *Information Bulletin,* U.S. High Commission for Germany, January, 1950, pp. 7-9, 53-57, especially pp. 9 and 55.

[31] See Appendix J.

was only 85,151, while in South Baden the southwest state was rejected by a majority of 101,765.[32]

In accordance with the provisions of Article 118, the problem thereupon became one for federal legislation. Throughout the first half of 1951 parliamentary sessions in Bonn were punctuated by constant controversy, not only as to the merits of the issue of the southwest state but also as to the legality of a peripheral federal action designed to extend the life of the legislatures in the southwest states pending some solution to the reorganization question. Despite the controversy, federal legislation was finally passed calling for a plebiscite in which the issue of creating a single new state or of reverting to the former states of Württemberg and Baden would again be voted upon at the polls.

The referendum was held on December 9, 1951, and resulted in a vote similar to that of the informational plebiscite of 1950. At long last, the merger of Württemberg-Baden, Württemberg-Hohenzollern, and Baden was approved. A constitutional convention was elected on March 9, 1952, for the new *Land* which tentatively has the name Baden-Württemberg.

As a consequence of zonal and interzonal territorial reorganization, the West German *Länder* (not counting West Berlin) are now nine in number—Baden-Württemberg, Bavaria, Bremen, Hamburg, Hesse, Lower Saxony, North Rhine–Westphalia, Rhineland-Palatinate, and Schleswig-Holstein. Their populations are noted in Table 1.

GOVERNMENTAL ORGANIZATION

Land Government before 1945—In the preceding chapter, it was pointed out that the reconstruction of local government, at least in the western zones, was largely a restoration of a historically developed *Kommunalselbstverwaltung* which reached back into the nineteenth century. The problem of rebuilding *Land* government was more difficult. The adverse effects of zonal and external boundary changes upon *Land* areas have already been noted. Moreover, no traditional and well-accepted pattern of democratic *Land* government existed. Under the Empire, there was great governmental diversity among the twenty-five member states, which included four kingdoms, six grand duchies,

[32] *Information Letter of the Frankfurter Hefte,* December 1/15, 1950, pp. 20-21. On the southwest problem in general, see Karl Siegfried Bader, *Der deutsche Südwesten in seiner territorialstaatlichen Entwicklung* (Stuttgart, 1950); Theodor Eschenburg, *Das Problem der Neugliederung der deutschen Bundesrepublik: Dargesstellt am Beispiel des Südweststaates* (Institut zur Förderung öffentlicher Angelegenheiten, Frankfurt, 1950).

Table 1. Postwar *Länder* (Area and Population)

Land	Area in Square Miles	Population (1950)
Baden-Württemberg	13,820	6,461,000
Bavaria	27,112	9,112,000
Berlin	341	3,280,000
West Berlin	188	2,146,000
East Berlin	153	1,203,000
Brandenburg	10,448	2,527,000
Bremen	156	558,000
Hamburg	288	1,605,000
Hesse	7,931	4,324,000
Lower Saxony	18,226	6,794,000
Mecklenburg	8,862	2,139,000
North Rhine–Westphalia	13,153	13,147,000
Rhineland-Palatinate	7,665	2,994,000
Saxony	6,539	5,558,000
Saxony-Anhalt	9,520	4,160,000
Schleswig-Holstein	6,048	2,594,000
Thuringia	6,022	2,927,000

five duchies, seven principalities, and three free cities.[33] All except the two Mecklenburgs had written constitutions and elective legislative chambers, although the elections were frequently indirect and the suffrage restricted, as in the Prussian three-class system of voting. The common *Landtag* of the Mecklenburgs was, as Ogg put it, "a typically mediaeval assemblage of estates";[34] and there was plenty of medievalism in the appointed and *ex officio* upper houses of the larger states which followed the bicameral principle. Ministerial responsibility to a parliamentary body was unknown although Bavaria, Württemberg, and Baden, together with the city-states of Bremen, Hamburg, and Lübeck, could be described as "quasi-parliamentary." But on the whole the states of the Empire were characterized by autocracy rather than popular rule.

All this was radically changed by the Weimar Constitution, which formally abolished princely authority and standardized the basic principles of *Land* governmental organization. Article 17 of that constitution declared:

Every *Land* must have a republican constitution. The legislature (*Volksvertretung*) must be elected by universal, equal, direct, and secret suffrage

[33] For details, see Frederic A. Ogg, *The Governments of Europe* (New York, 1913), chaps. 12-14.

[34] *Ibid.*, p. 280.

of all men and women who are citizens of the Reich, according to the fundamental principles of proportional representation. The *Land* cabinet must have the confidence of the legislature.

Although bicameralism was not specifically prohibited by Article 17, all the states except Prussia established unicameral legislatures. Even in Prussia the upper house had only a limited role in lawmaking. As was done in the Reich, each *Land* had its own written constitution, adopted by a special constitutional convention or by the *Landtag* acting as a constituent body.[35] There was much similarity between these constitutions, a similarity that went far beyond the requirement of Article 17, with much copying from each other and from the language of the Weimar document.

The years 1919-1933, during which the *Land* constitutions were operative, were too short a period to allow them to become deep-rooted, especially when one remembers that the first four or five years were a time of postwar disorder and astronomical inflation and that the last four were characterized by prolonged economic depression and mass unemployment. In looking back with the benefit of hindsight, it can be argued that to require all states to have the parliamentary form of government, regardless of size and population, was unwise. If tiny Schaumburg-Lippe had to continue as a separate *Land*, why insist that it must have parliamentary government? It would have been more in the spirit of federalism to have allowed each state some choice so long as its governmental form was republican and based on a broad suffrage. The same comment may be made with respect to mandatory proportional representation. Criticism could also be directed against the federal-state distribution of powers. Too much was given to the Reich and too little to the *Länder*, particularly in the field of finance, as the subsequent financial legislation of the Reich only too well demonstrated. In consequence, there was much anemia in *Land* government. On the other hand, it must not be forgotten that the once reactionary Prussia was, under a stable Socialist-Center coalition, a bulwark of republican strength broken only by Von Papen's unlawful seizure of that state in 1932.[36]

Under the *Einheitsstaat* of National Socialism, *Land* government

[35] For the texts of the Weimar and *Land* constitutions, see Otto Ruthenberg, ed., *Verfassungsgesetze des Deutschen Reichs und der deutschen Länder* (Berlin, 1926); for further details on *Land* government, see Frederick F. Blachly and Miriam E. Oatman, *The Government and Administration of Germany* (Baltimore, 1928), chap. 9.

[36] See Arnold Brecht, *Prelude to Silence: The End of the German Republic* (New York, 1944).

was completely transformed.[37] The state legislatures were abolished. Each state was placed under a national governor appointed by Hitler. The governor enacted state laws with the approval of the national cabinet. The state cabinet members were appointed by Hitler upon nomination of the governor. Here, as elsewhere, the "leadership principle" was established. Such was the nature of *Land* government when the Nazi regime was overthrown.

Interim Land Government, 1945-1946—General Eisenhower's Proclamation No. 2 (September 19, 1945), which formally established the states of Bavaria, Hesse, and Württemberg-Baden, vested each of them with "full legislative, judicial and executive powers."[38] This grant was subject to important limitations. German authority was circumscribed on all sides by Control Council and military government laws and directives. The grant of power to the *Land* was in fact a grant to the *Land* minister-president who was selected by military government. The minister-president enacted laws with the approval of military government. He appointed the other members of the *Land* cabinet with military government confirmation. There were usually between seven and twelve ministers in the cabinet plus a number of state secretaries or deputy ministers. If a minister-president proved recalcitrant or "unco-operative," he was summarily removed, as the case of Fritz Schäffer in Bavaria well illustrates.[39]

Very soon it was discovered that "full powers" to the *Land* ministers-president were not enough, and since French objections made it impossible for the Control Council to create the central German administrative departments called for by the Potsdam Agreement, agencies for intrazonal co-ordination became imperative. This need was met in the U.S. Zone by the creation in the fall of 1945 of the *Länderrat* discussed in Chapter 1 of this volume.

In the *Land* governments as originally restored, there was no representative body. This gap was filled in January, 1946, by the creation of advisory state legislatures, popularly called *"Vorparlamente."* The members thereof were all appointed by the ministers-president and were intended to represent the various interests of the state. Thus of the 124 members of the Württemberg-Baden *Vorparlament*, twelve

[37] Roger H. Wells, "The Liquidation of the German *Länder*," *Am. Pol. Sci. R.*, XXX (1936), 350-361.

[38] The discussion which follows deals with many of the same topics discussed in Chapter 2. However, the reader will observe that the emphasis is quite different.

[39] *Land* governments had been organized in Bavaria and Württemberg-Baden prior to General Eisenhower's proclamation. The Schäffer cabinet took office in Bavaria on May 28, 1945. Schäffer was dismissed September 28 for obstructing denazification.

were from each of the four authorized political parties,[40] while twenty were representatives of professional groups such as labor unions and chambers of commerce, handicrafts and agriculture. The cities and counties were represented by their *Oberbürgermeister* and *Ländräte*. The higher institutions of learning and the churches also had their representatives. These advisory "parliaments" functioned until the state constitutional conventions were elected on June 30, 1946.[41] There was some committee organization,[42] and from time to time the entire body met in plenary session. The most active was that of Württemberg-Baden which met no less than ten times.[43]

Although the minister-president could consult his *Vorparlament* about bills which he proposed to enact, he did not ordinarily do so. Normally, legislation was drafted by the ministry concerned, reviewed in the office of the minister-president, and then presented for cabinet discussion. It was thereupon enacted by the minister-president, usually in accordance with the cabinet discussion, although he was not legally bound by such discussion. The chief value of the advisory legislature was threefold. First, it was a good step toward an elected representative body since it provided experience that was wholly lacking in *Land* government under the Nazi regime. Secondly, it offered a forum for the discussion of many urgent problems. Finally, it concentrated public attention upon issues which would never otherwise have been adequately aired.

(2) *British Zone*—The organization of interim *Land* governments in the British Zone was complicated by three factors: (a) the problem of appropriate territorial areas (already discussed in the first part of this chapter); (b) the fact that British Military Government, in spite of talk about "indirect rule," had larger staffs than those of U.S. Military Government and stayed longer in the business of direct administration than did the Americans; and (c) the British theory of local government with its sharp division between political and ceremonial head and chief administrator. According to the directive of September 10, 1945, this theory was to be applied not only to local, but also to "re-

[40] One was the Communist party. In the early *Land* cabinets prior to the "cold war," there was usually one Communist minister and one or more state secretaries.

[41] There was no elected representative body in Bremen until October 13, 1946, when the *Bürgerschaft* was elected.

[42] The Württemberg-Baden *Vorparlament* had a single standing committee. At the request of the minister-president, this committee, enlarged by the addition of certain experts, prepared a draft constitution for consideration by the constitutional convention.

[43] The advisory legislature of Hesse had four plenary sessions: that of Bavaria, three.

gional government" which was defined as "the administration of *Regierungsbezirke, Länder,* and *Provinzen.*"[44] However, the directive proved unworkable in its attempt at dualism. What emerged were *Regierungspräsidenten, Oberpräsidenten,* and *Landespräsidenten* appointed by military government with a cabinet group around each.

In the first half of 1946, representative councils appointed by military government were added at each level.[45] When the provinces were elevated to the status of *Länder,*[46] the *Land* representative bodies uniformly received the title of *Landtag* although they were still largely advisory in character. Following the *Landkreis* and *Stadtkreis* council elections on October 13, 1946, the membership of the *Landtage* was altered to correspond to the voting strength of the political parties as revealed at the polls.[47]

In November, 1946, the powers of the *Länder* were more precisely defined. Ordinance No. 57 purported to give the *Landtag* "exclusive power to make laws for the *Land.*"[48] However, three large schedules of subjects were reserved from the competence of the state legislatures. In a fourth list of subjects, military government laid down the "fundamental principles" and then it was "incumbent" on the *Landtag* to implement them. Almost the only matters left to German legislative discretion were education, health, local government, and elections, and even here military government approval of laws was required.[49] The executive authority of the *Land* government extended to all the subjects enumerated in the ordinance "save as otherwise provided by Military Government" and in addition included "all matters with respect to which the *Land* government is required to take action by Military Government."

As the *Länderrat* of the U.S. Zone eventually came to have an ad-

[44] Military Government Directive on Administrative, Local, and Regional Government, Part I, *passim.*

[45] For example, the provincial councils of Westphalia and the Rhineland each had 100 members. These two councils were combined to form the first *Landtag* of the new *Land,* North Rhine-Westphalia.

[46] British Military Government Ordinance No. 46, August 23, 1946.

[47] The first *Landtag* of the new *Land,* Lower Saxony, was appointed after these elections and consisted of eighty-six members. However, the legislatures of Bremen and Hamburg were elected on October 13 in the same way as the councils of other cities.

[48] Ordinance No. 57, Powers of *Länder* in the British Zone, published November 14, 1946; effective December 1, 1946. Pollock, Meisel, and Bretton, *op. cit.,* pp. 182-185.

[49] Stolper sarcastically remarks that Ordinance No. 57 "virtually defined the powers of the *Länder* as non-existent." Gustav Stolper, *German Realities* (New York, 1947), p. 209.

visory representative council associated with it, so the British early set up a zonal German group to advise military government. This was the Zonal Advisory Council, established in February, 1946. Military government appointed its members from four groups: (a) the political parties; (b) senior German administrative officials of the *Länder;* (c) functional representatives covering subjects formerly handled by various Reich agencies; and (d) representatives of labor unions and co-operative societies. The Council was reorganized in June, 1947, so that its members were appointed by the state legislatures on a political party basis in proportion to the votes cast for each party at the *Land* elections.

In the early days of the occupation, British Military Government directly operated most of the functions of the central Reich agencies. Between the end of 1945 and September, 1946, German zonal administrative offices were set up. While these were given the power of direction over the *Länder* in zonal matters, they were so closely supervised by military government as to be little more than adjuncts to it.

(3) *French Zone*—During most of the first two occupation years, the French Zone was characterized by large military government staffs, direct administration, and strict controls. Even if it had been desired to organize provisional *Land* governments, the fragmentary character of the territories concerned would have been an obstacle. In the fall of 1945, the French appointed *Land* secretaries which performed routine administrative work under close supervision but which had no legislative authority whatever. These were replaced in December, 1946, by French-appointed *Land* ministers-president and cabinets. A modicum of legislative power was vested in them with the clear provision that it be exercised in accordance with military government approval. There were no representative bodies until November, 1946, when *Land* consultative assemblies were indirectly elected.[50] These were to give advice on current matters and to frame *Land* constitutions. No German zonal agencies, either administrative or consultative, were created apart from two advisory boards (food, posts and communications).[51]

[50] *Journel officiel,* Ordinances Nos. 65, 66, 67, October 8, 1946, pp. 335-344. Local councils were elected in the French Zone on September 15 and October 13, 1946. In each *Land,* there were two sets of electoral colleges, one consisting of the *Kreistag* councilmen and the other of councilmen of *Gemeinden* having more than 7,000 inhabitants. These electoral colleges met on November 17, and each elected its share of the members of the *Land* consultative assembly. The consultative assemblies held their first sessions in December, 1946.

[51] It was not until April, 1948, that the French Zone ministers-president were permitted to form a zonal *Länderrat.*

(4) *Soviet Zone*—In the summer of 1945, Soviet Military Government appointed interim governments in the *Länder* and provinces of the zone. These at first were called "presidia" and later "cabinets" when the provinces were elevated to the status of *Länder*. They consisted of a president,[52] one or more vice-president, and a number of department heads. While these presidia or cabinets did have, almost from the first, the power to legislate by decree, such enactments were subject to military government approval.[53] With respect to administration, these German officials were closely controlled by their Soviet counterparts. Along with such "indirect rule," there was a great deal of direct military government both in legislation and administration.

Advisory representative bodies were not set up at *Land* level until June and July, 1946.[54] The members thereof were appointed by the *Land* president and consisted of representatives of the three authorized political parties and of "fellow traveler" organizations such as the Free German Trade Union Federation, the Free German Youth, the Peasants' Mutual Aid, and the Antifascist Women's Committees and a few persons from chambers of commerce, industry and handicrafts and the "intellectual professions." These *Vorparlamente* were soon replaced by the *Landtage* elected on October 20, 1946.[55] Although advisory, their sessions were characterized by some plain speaking on the part of Christian Democrats and Liberal Democrats. The "bloc policy" of the Socialist Unity party (SED) was not yet in good working order.[56] Soviet Zone steps paralleling American and British efforts to co-ordinate *Land* activities as a partial substitute for the creation of a federal government are discussed in greater detail in Chapter 6.

Provisional Land Constitutions—Under the Weimar Republic, each *Land* has its own written constitution duly enacted by a popularly elected state constitutional convention or legislature but without a popular referendum. In the National Socialist *Einheitsstaat*, these constitutions were superseded in fact even if not formally repealed. No

[52] *Landespräsident* or *Provinzialpräsident*. Subsequently the term "minister-president" was used. For further discussion of the structure of the Soviet Zone see Chapter 6 below.

[53] This legislative authority was confirmed by a general order of the military governor issued October 22, 1945. See *Neue Zeit* (Berlin), October 25, 1945.

[54] The first of the advisory legislatures to meet was that of Thuringia. It was convened on June 24, 1946. *Tagesspiegel* (Berlin), June 25, 1946. The others met shortly thereafter.

[55] The *Landtag* elections were preceded by *Gemeinde* and *Stadtkreis* council elections on September 1, 8, and 15, 1946. The *Landkreis* council elections were held on the same day as the *Landtag* elections. See Chapter 19 below.

[56] See "Beratende Provinzialversammlung in Sachsen," *Tagesspiegel* (Berlin), August 2, 1946.

effort was made to declare them again in force after the fall of the Hitler regime.[57] The *Länder* as originally reconstituted in 1945 has no constitutions beyond the fiat of military government, but it was recognized that sooner or later the Germans themselves would have to provide their own constitutional foundations. The Americans pressed for the early adoption of permanent *Land* constitutions, an example which the French and Russians were not slow to follow. Thus it came about that in 1946 and 1947 all the states of the U.S., French, and Soviet zones adopted permanent constitutions, and in only on instance, Hesse, were these preceded by a provisional constitution.[58]

On the other hand, the British, with their emphasis upon gradualism, favored a provisional constitution as a necessary intermediate step toward a permanent constitution. Consequently, all the British Zone *Länder* had provisional consitutions which were in effect for several years. In fact, the provisional constitution of Lower Saxony was operative until May 1, 1951.[59]

Land Constitution Making—As previously noted, U.S. Military Government took the lead in urging the early adoption of permanent *Land* Constitutions.[60] The timetable for the U.S. Zone called for the election of state constitutional conventions as soon as the election of local councils had been completed. The constitutional conventions were directly elected in Bavaria, Hesse, and Württemberg-Baden on June 30, 1946. After Bremen returned to U.S. control in January, 1947, it was originally intended to have a constitutional convention elected there. The Germans, however, requested that the regular legislative body (*Bürgerschaft*) be used for this purpose. In view of the fact that

[57] The *Land* constitutions of the Weimar period were eventually repealed by the permanent postwar constitutions, either explicitly (Baden, Art. 129; Bavaria, Art. 186), by general clause (Thuringia, Art. 80), or by implication.

[58] *Staatsgrundgesetz des Staates Gross-Hessen*, November 22, 1945, *Gesetz- und Verordnungsblatt für Gross-Hessen*, 1945, p. 3. The Bavarian provisional constitution of October 22, 1945 (*Gesetz über die vorläufige Stadtsgewalt in Bayern*), drafted by the minister-president, was disapproved by military government.

[59] The Lower Saxony provisional constitution of February 11, 1947, was known as the *Gesetz zur vorläufigen Ordnung der Niedersächischen Landesgewalt*. The provisional constitution of North Rhine–Westphalia was likewise adopted in February, 1947. The Schleswig-Holstein provisional constitution dated from September, 1946. After Bremen was transferred back to American control, its provisional constitution was replaced by the permanent constitution of October 12, 1947.

[60] For related discussion, see Chapter 2 above. For the text of the directive, "Elections in the U.S. Zone," February 4, 1946, see Pollock, Meisel, and Bretton, *op. cit.* For the German texts and English translations of the *Land* constitutions of the U.S., French, and Soviet zones, see *Constitutions of the German Länder* (Berlin, 1947), prepared by the Civil Administration Division, Office of Military Government for Germany (U.S.).

the *Bürgerschaft* had only been elected on October 13, 1946, military government agreed to allow it to function both as a legislative and as a constituent assembly. In Bavaria, Hesse, and Württemberg-Baden, the constitutional conventions were specifically prohibited from serving as lawmaking bodies, although they were permitted to act in an advisory capacity to the *Land* governments and did in fact replace the appointed *Vorparlamente*.

The constitutional conventions of Bavaria, Hesse, and Württemberg-Baden convened for the first time on July 15, 1946. Between that date and October 29, when convention action on the constitution was completed, the conventions and particularly the drafting committees of those bodies held numerous meetings. In general, the work proceeded smoothly, although there were bitter controversies over particular articles among the delegates. Throughout the process of constitution making, military government kept well in the background. Democratic procedure required that the constitutions be framed by Germans and accepted by Germans. On the other hand, military government did reserve the right to review the constitutions for the purpose of making sure that they were in accordance with the objectives of the occupation.[61] However, the veto power of military government was sparingly exercised. Various disagreements were ironed out through informal conferences between the military government liaison officers and the German drafting committees. A few additional changes were required by General Clay in his letters of approval.[62]

Military government did insist that each constitution be submitted to popular referendum. This was an innovation in German practice. The constitutions of Hesse and Württemberg-Baden were ratified by the people on November 24, 1946; that of Bavaria on December 1; and that of Bremen on October 12, 1947. The constitutions of Bavaria and Württemberg-Baden were voted upon as complete documents. In Hesse, General Clay required that the socialization article (Art. 41) be separately submitted. By vote of the Bremen constitutional convention, there was a separate submission of Article 47, the article dealing with the codetermination rights of works councils and labor unions. These separate articles and the two constitutions from which they were taken were likewise approved by the voters.

Except in Bremen, the state legislature was also elected at the time the constitution was ratified. This was a military government decision but one made with reluctance. Ideally, a constitution should be ratified before the legislature provided by that constitution is elected.

[61] See September 30, 1946, directive in Appendix B.
[62] *Constitutions of the German Länder,* pp. 12, 28, 48, 73-74.

But there had already been four sets of elections in the U.S. Zone in the first half of 1946. To add two more elections would have been an excess of democratic zeal. Hence, the fifth election was a double-barreled affair. It was stipulated that, if a constitution were defeated at the polls, the elected legislature would then serve, not as a *Landtag*, but as a new constitutional convention.

The French Zone, following the American example, likewise made use of preparatory commissions and constitutional conventions. The latter were not directly elected but were indirectly chosen by electoral colleges (November 17, 1946).[63] The constitutions were ratified by popular referendum on May 18, 1947, and the *Landtage* were elected at the same time. Article 29 of the Rhineland-Palatinate constitution dealing with schools was submitted to separate vote.

In the British and Soviet Zones, special constitutional conventions were not used. Instead, the *Landtage,* elected in the Soviet Zone on October 20, 1946, and in the British Zone on April 20, 1947, were empowered to adopt *Land* constitutions. The speediest job of constitution making was done in the Soviet Zone. On November 14, 1946, the Socialist Unity party produced a draft constitution for the future "German Democratic Republic." This was promptly published in all the Russian-controlled newspapers and formed the basis of such deliberations as took place in the various state legislatures. Although the draft was a Reich rather than a *Land* constitution, it was meant to influence the latter. The basic similarity of the Soviet *Land* constitutions springs from the common model which had to be used.[64] The first constitution adopted was that of Thuringia on December 20, 1946. Within the next two months, the other four *Länder* followed suit.[65] None of these consitutions were submitted to popular referendum.

In their zone, the British were in no hurry about permanent *Land* constitutions. No definitive action was taken until after the termination of military government and the coming into effect of the Occupation Statute on September 21, 1949. Under the Occupation Statute, the occupation authorities could still disapprove *Land* constitutions and constitutional amendments within twenty-one days after their official receipt, but they had no positive powers to force or induce German action.[66] When the Occupation Statute was amended in

[63] See note 51 above. They were not called constitutional conventions but consultative assemblies. *Journel officiel*, 1946, No. 41.

[64] Cf. Chapter 6 below.

[65] Saxony-Anhalt, January 10, 1947; Mecklenburg, January 15, 1947; Brandenburg, February 6, 1947; Saxony, February 28, 1947.

[66] Thus far, the Germans have made little use of *Land* constitutional amendments. On July 9, 1950, the voters of Hesse approved an amendment submitted

March, 1951, this was further reduced to a mere right to annul or repeal.

On December 13, 1949, the Schleswig-Holstein *Landtag* adopted a permanent constitution without popular referendum. On June 6, 1950, after three years of discussion, the *Landtag* of North Rhine–Westphalia by a narrow vote likewise enacted a permanent constitution. This was ratified by popular referendum on June 18, with 57 per cent of the votes cast in the affirmative.[67] On April 3, 1951, the legislature of Lower Saxony took similar action, but there was no popular referendum. The Hamburg provisional constitution of 1946 was replaced by a permanent constitution in 1952.

Structure of Land Government since 1947—The *Land* governments in Western Germany are now representative democracies based upon a broad suffrage and free elections. They rest upon the principle of the division of legislative, executive, and judicial powers. While accepting cabinet responsibility to the legislature, a measure of executive independence is also provided. Although most of the constitutions contain provisions for direct democracy through the initiative, referendum, and recall, thus far these have been little used. For example, in Württemberg-Baden in 1950, a group of voters attempted to force a popular vote on the dissolution of the *Landtag*. The attempt failed because the sponsors secured the signatures of only 14,202 voters instead of the 100,000 required by Article 58 of the constitution.[68]

The state legislature is the principle organ of representative democracy. It is everywhere unicameral except in Bavaria, where a "corporative" Senate, reflecting Catholic doctrine, "represents the social, economic, and cultural corporations and self-governing units of the *Land*.[69] The sixty members of the Senate are elected or appointed by

---

by the *Landtag* which permitted the *Landtag* to deviate from proportional representation in state and local election legislation (Arts. 75, 137). Only 34 per cent of the electorate participated in this referendum. The Social Democratic majority in the Schleswig-Holstein *Landtag* jammed through the permanent constitution of December, 1949, without a popular referendum. The triumph of the opposition parties in the *Landtag* election of 1950 resulted in immediate constitutional amendments by the new legislature. These downgraded the land and school reform provisions of the constitution to the status of ordinary laws so that they could be more easily changed. *Die Zeit* (Hamburg), November 23, 1950.

[67] Alois Vogel, ed., *Kommentar zur Verfassung des Landes Nordrhein-Westfalen* (Stuttgart, 1951). The *Landtag* of North Rhine–Westphalia was also elected on the same day.

[68] *Ibid.*, June 6, 1950.

[69] Constitution of Bavaria, Article 34. Articles 34-42 were implemented by the law of July 31, 1947, *Gesetz- und Verordnungsblatt*, 1947, p. 162. In several other *Länder*, unsuccessful attempts were made to introduce a second chamber. On the

the constituent groups. The senatorial term of office is six years, one-third retiring every two years. The Senate may initiate legislation and may object to bills passed by the *Landtag*. The latter "decides whether it wishes to take account of the objections" (Art. 41).

The *Landtage* (*"Bürgerschaft"* in Bremen and Hamburg) range in size from fairly small legislative chambers to 204 in Bavaria and 215 in North Rhine–Westphalia. The term of office is in most instances four years. Proportional representation is used in *Landtag* elections but with various modifications designed to discourage splinter parties.[70] The constitutions prescribe the usual qualifications and disqualifications of legislators. Unlike Britain and America, civil servants are permitted to be members without relinquishing their official positions and salaries. In the first Hessian *Landtag*, which was elected in 1946, forty-four of the ninety members, not counting cabinet ministers, were officials. While this is in accord with previous German practice, it provoked many controversies with the occupying powers. In September, 1950, the Allied High Commission provisionally disapproved the Württemberg-Baden election law because it permitted the continuance of the practice.[71] The North Rhine–Westphalia election law of 1950 forbids state officials to be members of the *Landtag*.

The internal organization and procedure of the *Landtag* follows the traditional pattern of the Weimar period with respect to such matters as officers of the legislature, standing and special committees, introduction and passage of bills, and questions to ministers. As before 1933, the members are organized into recognized party groups called *Fraktionen,* and party discipline is strong. There is much criticism of this discipline and some indication of an increasing independence on the part of the individual member. For further discussion of internal state legislative processes, the reader is referred to Chapter 8, in which their technical aspects are reviewed in detail.

With regard to executive-legislative relationships, all the west German *Länder* have a parliamentary form of government. The chief executive is the minister-president, elected by the *Landtag*. He in turn appoints and heads a cabinet responsible to the legislature.[72] Bavaria

---

Hauptwirtschaftskammer of Rhineland-Palatinate, see Articles 71-73 of the *Land* constitution.

[70] For details relating to elections, see Chapter 19 below.

[71] See further discussions of this issue in Chapter 10 below.

[72] In several former southwestern *Länder,* the minister-president has the title *Staatspräsident.* In the Bavarian constitutional convention, an unsuccessful attempt was made to have both a state president and a minister-president, the hope in some quarters being that a member of the House of Wittelsbach might grace

is an apparent exception to the rule. In that state, the *Landtag* elects the minister-president for four years. He cannot be removed by the legislature, although it may impeach him before the constitutional court. However, according to Article 44 of the constitution, the minister-president "must resign if the political situation make co-operation between him and the *Landtag* impossible." Whatever this provision was intended to mean, the parliamentary system in Bavaria operates as it does elsewhere in West Germany.

The *Land* cabinets are relatively small bodies—smaller now than they were originally when all political parties were usually represented in them. Political and administrative reasons may result in one man's holding more than one portfolio. Cabinets range in size from five members in Hesse to sixteen in Bavaria. The size of the Bavarian cabinet results from the fact that the constitution (Art. 43) declares that "the cabinet consists of the minister-president, the ministers, and the state secretaries."

Since there are numerous political parties in Western Germany, the usual situation after an election is that no one party has a majority in the *Landtag*. Hence a coalition cabinet is necessary—sometimes a "great coalition" including both major parties, the Christian Democrats and the Social Democrats; sometimes a "little coalition" built around the Christian Democrats. However, Baden and Bavaria have had experience with cabinets made up exclusively of Christian Democrats, and Hamburg, Hesse, and Schleswig-Holstein have had cabinets of Social Democrats alone.

In spite of coalitions, the cabinet is usually in a strong position with reference to the legislature. Although subjected to heated debate and questioning, it is not easily overturned. Ministerial crises and changes have occurred from time to time, but no entire cabinet has been forced out of office by *Landtag* vote. The cabinet's strength is not explained by the vesting of dissolution powers in the minister-president, for neither he nor the cabinet has been entrusted with that authority except in former Württemberg-Hohenzollern (Art. 42), where the minister-president was authorized to dissolve the legislature if two-fifths of the members of the *Landtag* supported such action.

---

the former office. As the U.S. Military Government liaison officer to the Bavarian convention, the writer remained silent during the dispute, although he was prepared to recommend a veto of the provision for a state president. Fortunately, the convention settled the question itself. On the general problem of the state president in the debates of the constitutional conventions, see Dr. Süsterhenn, "Der Staatspräsident," *Tagesspiegel* (Berlin), November 28, 1946. In Bremen, the chairman of the Senate (cabinet) is called "*Bürgermeister* and Senate president"; in Hamburg, "First *Bürgermeister*."

Cabinet strength is derived from two other types of constitutional provisions, both deliberately adopted to avoid the unhappy experiences of the Weimar period.[73] In Bavaria, Hesse, and Rhineland-Palatinate, when a minister-president resigns or is forced out, a new minister-president must be elected within a specified period of time or the *Landtag* is automatically dissolved. The second type is the "constructive vote of no confidence," found in Bremen, Hamburg, and North Rhine–Westphalia. According to the Bremen constitution (Art. 110), "The vote of confidence requires a majority of the legal number of members. It becomes valid if the *Bürgerschaft* has elected a new Senate."

The structure of government in the Soviet Zone is set out in detail in Chapter 6 and needs no further discussion here.[74]

Bills of Rights in Land Constitutions—The Weimar Constitution of August 11, 1919, with its long chapter (Arts. 109-165) on the "Fundamental Rights and Duties of Germans" was adopted prior to most of the *Land* constitutions of that period. Since these guarantees were intended to be binding upon the states, most of the *Länder* did not include separate bills of rights in their constitutions. On the other hand, in the post-Nazi era, the permanent *Land* constitutions preceded the west and east German constitutions except in the British Zone. These *Land* constitutions tended to be lengthy documents, the longest being that of Bavaria with 188 articles, the shortest that of Brandenburg with 69 articles.[75] To a large extent, the length is due to the inclusion of extension bills of rights of a political, social, and economic character. In view of the German experience under the Nazi tyranny, it is not surprising but encouraging that the constitutional fathers should stress the rights of individuals and groups.

[73] For similar efforts on federal level, see Chapter 5 below.

[74] See also an illuminating account written by a German who was formerly minister of justice in Thuringia, in H. R. Külz, "The Soviet Zone of Germany: A Study of Developments and Policies," *International Affairs*, XXVII (1951), 156-166. See also J. P. Nettl, *The Eastern Zone and Soviet Policy in Germany, 1945-50* (New York, 1951); *2nd Quarterly Report on Germany*, Office of the U.S. High Commissioner for Germany (Frankfurt, 1950), pp. 26-41; Franz L. Neumann, "Soviet Policy in Germany," *Annals of the American Academy of Political and Social Science*, CCLXIII (1949), 165-179; Henry B. Cox, "Establishment of a Soviet-sponsored East German Republic," *Department of State Bulletin*, XXI (1949), 761-764; *Confuse and Control: Soviet Techniques in Germany* (pamphlet, Department of State, 1951); *Ignotus*, "In Eastern Germany," *Contemporary Review*, CLXXIX (1951), 20-25.

[75] For detailed discussions of the bills of rights and other features of the *Land* constitutions in the U.S., French, and Soviet zones, see Harold O. Lewis, *New Constitutions in Occupied Germany* (Washington, D.C., 1948); Robert G. Neumann, "New Constitutions in Germany," *Am. Pol. Sci. R.*, XLII (1948), 448-468.

At the outset these constitutional guarantees were hardly more than aspirations. The exigencies of occupation, the emergency community conditions resulting from housing shortages, food scarcity, large-scale population movements, and the controversial issues of denazification combined to make universal recognition of constitutional rights a virtual impossibility. As a consequence a series of temporary exceptions were set forth in the documents themselves. But despite the qualifications resulting from the context within which they were prepared, the constitutional guarantees set forth in the *Land* constitutions were both impressive in themselves and an important exercise in preparation for the federal constitution making which was to come almost three years later.

BERLIN

Political life in Berlin is unusual in many respects. It is there that the West-East conflict has come to sharpest focus, and as a consequence its political orientation is anomalous vis-à-vis Western Germany. Again, it is both city and *Land,* and its institutions reflect its mixed status.

The history of Greater Berlin begins in 1912 when the central city and its surrounding satellites were loosely united into an *ad hoc* authority for city planning, recreation, and transportation purposes.[76] A real consolidation was effected by the charter of 1920 which abolished ninety-five local governments and created in their place the new corporation of Greater Berlin. Berlin was also detached from the Province of Brandenburg and given the status of a separate province; but for purposes of state supervision, it was left under the jurisdiction of the *Oberpräsident* of Brandenburg. The form of government provided was the familiar *Magistratsverfassung*[77] with *Oberbürgermeister, Magistrat,* and *Stadtverordnetenversammlung* (council).

Under the charter of 1920, Berlin was organized into twenty administrative districts or "boroughs," each with its own *Magistratsverfassung* paralleling that of the central city government. The borough government consisted of a popularly elected council; the *"Bezirksbürgermeister,* elected by the borough council; and the *Bezirksamt* (the equivalent of the *Magistrat*), the members of which were likewise elected by the borough council. The charter represented an

---

[76] On Berlin's government before 1933, see Roger H. Wells, *German Cities* (Princeton, 1932), pp. 203-217.

[77] See Chapter 3 above. Berlin's *Magistratsverfassung* was modified in 1931 by greatly increasing the powers of the *Oberbürgermeister.*

experiment in "municipal federalism" with division of powers between the central city government and the boroughs.

The Nazis allowed Berlin to retain its previous status as a province but introduced the leadership principle as they did elsewhere.[78] The elected central city and borough councils were abolished and were replaced by appointed advisory councilors. In 1936 all powers, both municipal and provincial, were vested in a single official, the *Oberbürgermeister und Stadtpräsident* named by Hitler.[79]. This official in turn appointed the *Bezirksbürgermeister* though in his dual role he was much more a state than a local official. In spite of what the law said, actually the real power was in the hands of Dr. Goebbels, the Nazi party agent for Berlin, who was called the "uncrowned king of Berlin." In 1944 the office of *Oberbürgermeister* and *Stadtpräsident* was divided into its to component parts, Goebbels himself becoming *Stadtpräsident*.[80]

When the Nazi tyranny was finally overthrown, Berlin was in ruins. Before the war, Berlin had 1,562,000 dwelling units, apartment houses or separate homes. At the end of the war, only 370,000 dwellings were undamaged, 360,000 were lightly damaged, and 832,000 were badly damaged or destroyed.[81] The destruction of public buildings, factories, places of business, and utilities was equally great. After the Soviet troops captured Berlin in May, 1945, they proceeded almost immediately to establish a provisional German administration for the city as a whole and for the twenty boroughs.[82] The *Magistrat* was restored as the central organ of the government. The Russians appointed a nonentity, Dr. Arthur Werner, as lord mayor but filled the key positions with Communists or Communist sympathizers upon whom they could rely. The same was done at the *Verwaltungsbezirk* level. Berlin was thus organized and ruled directly by Soviet Military Government and indirectly by its German appointees before the military government staffs of the western Allies arrived there in July, 1945.

[78] For a fuller description, see Harry Goetz (of the Berlin Municipal Science Institute), "Die deutschen Städte und Landgemeinden im Dritten Reich, 1933-1945 (unpublished manuscript, Berlin, 1946-1947), pp. 100-110. See also *Gesetz über die Verfassung der Hauptstadt Berlin,* June 29, 1934, *Preussische Gesetzammlung,* 1934, p. 319.

[79] *Gesetz über die Verfassung und Verwaltung der Reichshauptstadt Berlin,* December 1, 1936, *Reichsgesetzblatt,* I (1936), 957.

[80] *Ibid.,* I (1944), 175.

[81] *Tagesspiegel* (Berlin), February 7, 1947.

[82] For a vivid but highly personalized account of Berlin, 1945-1950, see Frank L. Howley, *Berlin Command* (New York, 1950), and its review in the *Saturday Review of Literature,* February 18, 1950, by the editor of this volume.

The European Advisory Commission, in its 1944 planning, had envisaged a quadripartite body (Allied *Kommandatura*) which, under the Allied Control Council, would jointly direct the administration of Greater Berlin. The Allied *Kommandatura* held its first formal meeting on July 11, 1945, and made the important decision that, pending further study, the ordinances promulgated under Soviet Military Government would remain in effect. Since all decisions of the *Kommandatura* had to be unanimous, this froze the *status quo* except where the Russians agreed to change it. Quadripartite rule involved the physical division of the twenty boroughs among the occupying powers, resulting in a situation far worse than that which had prevailed before the consolidation charter of 1920. The American Sector had six boroughs; the British, four; the French, two; and the Russians, eight. Each power had a military government detachment in each of its boroughs as well as a detachment for the sector as a whole. Although the Allied *Kommandatura* and, under it, the German *Magistrat* theoretically governed the city as a whole, there was wide scope for discretion and divergence as between the four sectors.

From the fall of 1945, the Soviet-picked *Magistrat* encountered increasing German criticism.[83] Its sessions were secret and its decisions were frequently unpopular. Representative elements were almost completely lacking in the government although in about one-fourth of the boroughs there were appointed advisory borough councils consisting of party and labor union leaders. The Germans demanded the restoration of elected councils, and this demand was supported by the western Allies, particularly the United States. However, the Russians had their own special reasons for delay. For the Russians, the first prerequisite of elections was the merger of the Social Democratic and Communist parties. After six months of agitation, this was finally "railroaded through" when the Socialist Unity party (SED) was formed on April 19-20, 1946, by methods described in detail in Chapter 19 of this volume. The western allies were not able to prevent the forced consolidation in the Soveit Zone but Berlin was another matter. They insisted upon a Social Democratic party referendum in Berlin which was carried out on March 31, 1946, but was not permitted in the Soviet Sector. Eighty-two percent of the Social Democrats who voted in the western sectors expressed themselves against the amalgamation.

Beginning in January, 1946, there was prolonged discussion of a new charter or constitution for Berlin. The first draft, prepared by the *Magistrat*, was rejected by the Local Government Committee of the

[83] See, for example, "Nominelle Magistratsdemokratie," *Tagesspiegel* (Berlin), June 20, 1946.

Kommandatura. The *Magistrat* then framed a second and a third draft after a certain amount of consultation with the political parties. These drafts were worked over and changed by the Local Government Committee, which produced a fourth draft. This finally secured Allied approval and came into effect on September 20, 1946.[84]

The Allies insisted that the constitution be designated as "temporary." The city council to be elected under it was directed to prepare the draft of a permanent constitution and to submit it "to the Allied Powers for approval before May 1, 1948" (Art. 35). The provisional constitution of 1946 carefully evaded any definition of Berlin's status as *Land* or province. It merely stated (Art. 1) that "Greater Berlin is the exclusively established public territorial corporation for the territory of the municipality (*Stadtgemeinde*) of Berlin."

In general, the temporary constitution was based on the charter of 1920. It provided for the election by proportional representation and for a two-year term of a city council of 130 members. The council in turn elected the *Magistrat* for a two-year term, the latter consisting of the *Oberbürgermeister* and nineteen additional full-time, professional members. There were no lay members of the *Magistrat* as in the typical *Magistratsverfassung*. The two-year term of office was also prescribed for the boroughs. In each, there was an elected borough council of thirty to forty-five members. The borough council elected the *Bezirksamt*—a borough "*Magistrat*" made up of the *Bezirksbürgermeister* and of not more than ten additional professional members.

Elections to the city and borough councils were held on October 20, 1946, with 90 per cent of the electorate participating. The elections were supervised by quadripartite election teams and resulted in the Social Democratic party polling 48.79 per cent of the votes cast.[85] Although the Social Democratic party was forbidden in the Soviet Zone on the ground that it had been merged with the Socialist Unity party, it was permitted to nominate candidates in the Soviet Sector of Berlin as well as in the western sectors. In return, the Socialist Unity party was allowed to put up candidates in the western sectors.

On paper, the temporary constitution was an improvement over the preceding situation, but in practice the city government was almost strangled by quadripartite controls. The Allied *Kommandatura* continued to function through its committees, which supervised the departments of the *Magistrat* and held them to the fulfillment of *Kommandatura* orders. Moreover, the *Kommandatura* committees had the

[84] For an English translation of the Berlin constitution of 1946, see Pollock, Meisel, and Bretton, *op. cit.*

[85] See Chapter 19 below.

right to issue technical instructions directly to the corresponding departments of the *Magistrat.* In each sector as before, the military government detachment was a power to be reckoned with.

The city government was further weakened by Article 36 of the constitution which stipulated that laws, ordinances, and appointments and dismissals of leading officials required the "sanction" of the *Kommandatura.* What did "sanction" mean? After much controversy which involved not only the *Kommandatura* but also the Allied Control Council, the Russian interpretation of Article 36 prevailed. This meant that almost everything had to have the prior and unanimous approval of the *Kommandatura,* with each power having a veto. Had the city government been allowed to act except in those cases where action was unanimously disapproved by the *Kommandatura,* it would have been in a much stronger position.

The system at its worst was seen with respect to the election of the *Magistrat* members by the council. On December 5, 1946, the council elected the *Magistrat* with a due distribution of posts among the four recognized political parties. The Social Democrat, Dr. Otto Ostrowski, was elected *Oberbürgermeister.* Of the three posts of *Bürgermeister,* one went to the Social Democrats (*Louise Schroeder*), one to the Christian Democrats, and one to the Socialist Unity party. The *Kommandatura* approved most of the twenty *Magistrat* members thus elected. However, it rejected one man because of his past political activities and held up the election of two others.

Once in office, the new *Magistrat* attempted to remove certain key officials who were members of the Socialist Unity party and who had been appointed prior to the adoption of the constitution. This failed because of Russian vetoes in the *Kommandatura.* Dr. Ostrowski then made a deal with the Socialist Unity party whereby, in return for certain considerations, the appointees objected to by the *Magistrat* would voluntarily resign. But Ostrowski had acted without informing his own party, the Social Democrats. When the deal became known, it provoked a violent debate in the city council. A vote of want of confidence in Ostrowski was passed, but it lacked two votes of the two-thirds majority required by the constitution for such motions. Ostrowski subsequently resigned, and the council elected as lord mayor another Social Democrat, Dr. Ernst Reuter. The Ostrowski resignation was finally approved by the Allied Control Council on June 10, 1947, but, because of Russian vetoes, it was impossible to secure Allied approval of Reuter. By default, *Bürgermeister* Louise Schroeder became acting *Oberbürgermeister.*

Although thwarted by Russian vetoes and by Socialist Unity party obstruction, the Berlin city council did carry out one of the mandates imposed upon it by the temporary constitution. It drafted and submitted to the Allied *Kommandatura* on April 30, 1948—one day before the deadline—a new constitution. This never received Four Power approval, but was lost in the deepening East-West struggle. In protest at the decisions on Germany taken by the western powers, the Russians walked out of the Allied Control Council on March 20, 1948, and out of the Allied *Kommandatura* on June 16, 1948. Quadripartite rule was at an end. A few days later, the Russians clamped a tight blockade on Berlin. The western allies responded with the airlift and with a counterblockade. The siege of Berlin—June 24, 1948–May 12, 1949—was on in earnest.

The split among the occupying powers was soon followed by a split in the city government. On June 23, 1948, Socialist Unity party mobs stormed the city council as it tried to meet in the city hall, which was located in the Soviet Sector. These tactics were repeated at three subsequent meetings, the last being on September 8. The council thereupon adjourned its sessions to the western sectors, but all the Socialist Unity party members withdrew from it. The die had been cast for developments which resulted in two completely separate city governments, one for the three sectors of West Berlin, the other for the Soviet Sector.

The East Berlin city government was hurriedly organized on November 30, 1948, just prior to the West Berlin elections of December 5. An assembly of some 2,500 persons met, deposed the existing city government, and elected a new *Magistrat* with Friedrich Ebert, son of the first president of the Weimar Republic, as *Oberbürgermeister*. The elected borough councils of the Soviet Sector were dissolved and replaced by appointed "*Volksblock*" committees. On January 21, 1949, a city council for the Soviet Sector was appointed. It was called a "bloc presidium and working committee."

After the siege began, West Berlin continued to operate under the temporary constitution of 1946. Since the first city council had been elected for only two years, a new election was held on December 5, 1948. This was boycotted by the Socialist Unity party, which refused to nominate candidates in the western sectors and prevented the election in the Soviet Sector. The election was an impressive demonstration of the fortitude of the West Berliners. In spite of threats of reprisals and of sufferings due to the blockade, 86.2 per cent of the electorate participated. The result was a great victory for the Social Democratic party, which polled almost two-thirds of the votes cast.[86]

[86] Social Democratic, Christian Democratic, and Liberal Democratic councilmen

The new city council then proceeded to elect a new three-party coalition *Magistrat* with Ernst Reuter as *Oberbürgermeister*. Borough councils which elected new *Bezirksämter* were also elected on December 5.

The process of organizing West Berlin was completed on December 21, 1948, when the Allied *Kommandatura* was formally reconstituted on a Three Power basis. Legally, it had its old authority, but its political and administrative temper was different. After all, the West Berliners and the western Allies were fighting a common battle. The new temper was soon reflected in the "Statement of Principles Governing the Relationship between the Allied *Kommandatura* and Greater Berlin," adopted May 14, 1949, and popularly known as the Berlin Occupation Statue.[87] It aimed to do for Berlin what the Occupation Statute was to do for West Germany.

The lifting of the siege of Berlin in May, 1949, by no means solved the basic problems involved. In spite of American and west German financial assistance, the city continued to be in a precarious economic position with widespread unemployment. From time to time, it has been subjected to a "creeping blockade" by the Communists and Russians who, however, always relaxed their restrictions under thread of Allied reprisals. Politically, the Berliners have been the targets of the most intense propaganda. Thus on May 26, 1950, after months of preparation, the Communist-controlled Free German Youth organizations staged mass demonstrations in East Berlin. Confronted by the Allied willingness to use force, they desisted from their original plan to demonstrate in West Berlin. The firm determination of the West was further evidenced by the symbolic dedication of the "Freedom Bell," a gift of the American people to West Berlin. The bell was hung in the West Berlin city hall and was dedicated by General Clay on October 24, 1950, as a kind of "spiritual airlift."

Meanwhile, West Berlin moved toward a permanent constitution.[88] The 1948 draft which had been vetoed by the Russians was now revised and submitted to the Allied *Kommandatura,* which approved it

---

elected from the Soviet Sector in 1946 were allowed to continue as members of the new council.

[87] On March 7, 1951, the Allied *Kommandatura* further revised and liberalized the Berlin Occupation Statute. For the text of the revision, see *6th Quarterly Report on Germany,* Office of the U.S. High Commissioner for Germany (Frankfurt, 1951), pp. 145-146.

[88] For details, see Elmer Plischke, *Berlin: Development of Its Government and Administration,* Historical Division, Office of the U.S. High Commissioner for Germany (Bad Godesberg, 1952).

on August 29, 1950. The new constitution attempted to give Berlin the status of a *Land* within the west German republic. The Allies did not object to Berlin being a *Land*, but were unwilling to incorporate it in West Germany. Hence the *Kommandatura* suspended the provision designed to accomplish that purpose, just as an analogous provision in the Bonn Constitution had been suspended by the Allied Military Governors in May, 1949. Berlin was allowed to have nonvoting representatives in the convention which framed the Bonn Constitution, and it is permitted to send nonvoting members to the *Bundestag*. Thus the final step of full incorporation is yet to be taken. However, for practical purposes, the Bonn government treats Berlin as if it were the twelfth *Land* in the *Federal Republic*.

For the city-state of Berlin, the 1950 constitution provides a parliamentary form of government not unlike that of the city-states of Bremen and Hamburg. The city council is now called the House of Representatives. It consists of 200 members (in reality 127, since 73 seats are reserved for the Soviet Sector) elected by proportional representation for a four-year term. The minister-president is called the governing *Bürgermeister* and is elected by the House of Representatives. He in turn nominates a cabinet of nineteen members, subject to the approval of the House. The House may withdraw its confidence from the cabinet as a whole or from any cabinet member, thus forcing collective resignation. Government at the borough level is much the same as before—an elected borough council of forty-five members which elects the *Bezirksamt*. One new feature is the Council of *Bezirksbürgermeister* which is designed to give the chief borough officers the opportunity to express their views on questions of legislation and administration affecting Berlin as a whole.

The House of Representatives and the borough councils in West Berlin were elected on December 3, 1950, with 90.4 per cent of the electorate participating. The Christian Democrats and the Free Democrats (formerly called Liberal Democrats) gained at the expense of the Social Democrats, whose popular vote fell from 64.5 per cent in 1948 to 44.7 per cent in 1950. For a time it seemed that the House of Representatives would not choose *Oberbürgermeister* Reuter as the governing *Bürgermeister*. However, a compromise was worked out resulting in a "great coalition" (SPD-CDU-FDP) with appropriate allocation of cabinet seats among the three parties. Reuter was elected on January 18, 1951, and his nominations for the cabinet were confirmed. In spite of controversy over domestic political questions, the coalition has thus far managed to hold together.

5

The Constitution of the

German Federal Republic

CARL J. FRIEDRICH AND HERBERT J. SPIRO

SOME time ago, in discussing the "rebuilding" of the German constitution, one of the authors suggested that the compromise which
had been arrived at is the resultant of constitutional ideas, partly German, partly English, and partly American. But German concepts of
democracy and government were undoubtedly the dominant ones.
The "prescriptive force" of tradition, in Burke's sense, is winning out
against external influences and pressures. The time which has since
elapsed has served to confirm and reinforce this verdict. The development fills many with apprehension. If the Germans, who have so continuously failed to build democracy and constitutionalism on a sound
foundation, are repeating the errors of the past, there seems slender
hope that they will achieve the goal of a stable, free, and peace-loving
community. If they do so under the further complications arising from
mounting tension between East and West, then the chances of achieving a successfully functioning constitutional democracy seem slim
indeed.[1] But perhaps there are countertrends which make the situation less unfortunate than it appears in the light of history. For one,
the immediate postwar policy of demilitarization destroyed the German military establishment and its traditions much more thoroughly
than was done after 1919. For another, the Nazi regime itself had already uprooted the bureaucratic caste which remained in background
control after World War I; its reappearance since 1948 may not lead

[1] See C. J. Friedrich, "Rebuilding the German Constitution," *American Political Science Review*, Vol. XLIII (June, 1949).

to a recapture of its former predominance. Thirdly, the annexation of the eastern German provinces by the Soviet Union and Poland and the expulsion of most of the native German populations—the refugees, expellees more strictly speaking, which crowd the German Federal Republic—have all but exterminated the junker class which, while perhaps not as powerful as sometimes assumed, nonetheless provided the backbone of the reactionary and militaristic elements that clustered around Hindenburg and encouraged him to betray the republic.[2] As a result of these three changes in the social and class structure, the constitutional and democratic forces, even though weak, do not face the same formidable opposition which wrecked the Weimar Republic. The struggle against the totalitarian oppression in Eastern Germany and the memory of the Hitler regime serve to reinforce the antidictatorial tendencies in the Federal Republic among many citizens who are lukewarm in their support of constitutional democracy. Indeed, one may sum up this curious paradox by saying that the Germans, while least certain in their support of democratic constitutionalism, are the most opposed to dictatorship in its various forms.

It is against this background that the operation of the Basic Law of the Federal German Republic during the first two years of its existence must be viewed. Many of the utterances of German politicians have an enigmatic quality for those who fail to keep these peculiarities of the German situation in mind. Thus, the rhetoric of Dr. Kurt Schumacher, the former leader of the German Social Democrats, struck many as nationalistic, and so it was. But the true meaning of these nationalistic utterances can be evaluated only if one remembers that Schumacher was combating communism and that the Communists are continually trying to exploit nationalist appeals for the Soviet party line. Furthermore, it is a truism that any people under occupation will be "nationalist." Even the pacifist Ghandi and his followers were "nationalist" as long as India was under British rule. Add to this all-pervasive fact of occupation the further fact of division of the country between the Federal German Republic and the Democratic German Republic and you have a perfect setting for patriotic oratory.

The division of the country must, in any case, be considered a dominant fact of the constitution in operation. Not only did the government at Bonn immediately create a ministry for all-German questions (see below), but the work of every ministry and of all other governmental agencies is continually concerned with problems arising from this division. Whether it be the constant flow of refugees from the

[2] For this story, see John W. Wheeler-Bennett, *The Wooden Titan* (Toronto, 1936).

Soviet satellite "democracy" of the East, or the negotiations of some barter trade between the two, or again the problem of pensions and social security payments, not to speak of such debilitating issues as the support which must be given to Western Berlin, the division of the country is truly a "brooding omnipresence in the sky." If affects every decision taken by federal and state authorities whether concerned with the past, the present, or the future. And while the eastern provinces may well be permanently lost, the division cannot last, and the Basic Law is stating a fact when it declares in its preamble that the German people in the states of the western zones "acted also on behalf of those Germans to whom participation was denied." And it hallowed the key goal of all Germans, whether leading politicians or ordinary citizens, when it declared at the same time that "the entire German people is called upon to accomplish, by free self-determination, the unity and freedom of Germany." In keeping with these general sentiments, membership in the republic is open to those states now under Soviet control, and "on their accession" the Basic Law "shall be put into force" in such other parts of Germany (Art. 23). It is generally assumed, however, that when the day of reunification arrives there will be held a new constitutional convention which will overhaul the entire constitutional structure, possibly with a view to making it more centralistic than it is at present. The prospect being remote, it seems difficult to assess these anticipations.

LEGAL FRAMEWORK FOR THE FEDERAL REPUBLIC

For all of the period under review, the Federal German Republic operated within the framework not only of the Basic Law but of the Occupation Statute as well. It is important to bear this in mind at all times and not to be guided merely by constitutional provisions as found in the Basic Law.[3] This Occupation Statute, finally agreed upon among the western Allies on April 8, 1949, was based upon previous policy announcements which are analyzed in Chapter 2 of this volume. The association of the constitution with an occupation statute was perhaps the most serious obstacle in securing agreement from the Germans to the making of a constitution or basic law. Their demand for such a statute had been based on a very different idea, namely, a treaty-like agreement between themselves and the Allies

[3] This is the shortcoming of a number of recent studies on the Basic Law and has adversely affected the generally prevailing understanding on the part of such writers on international affairs as Lippman. A substantial help is afforded by the unfortunately incomplete, but very detailed commentary of Mangoldt, *Das Bonner Grundgesetz* (1951). It covers only about the first one hundred articles.

prior to a peace treaty.[4] The underlying idea was that without such an agreement the German people were not sufficiently "sovereign" to establish a constitution. Hence, the eventual compromise of a "basic law," rather than a constitution, had to be adopted, although as a matter of fact German writings since that time have increasingly referred to the Basic Law as a constitution, and designations of specific institutions established thereunder, such as the constitutional court, have aided in this development.

The Occupation Statute as required of the Germans amounted essentially to a statement of reserved powers, linked with a grant of the remaining legislative, executive, and judicial power to the German government, subject to review by the Allies. Foreign relations, foreign trade, reparations, level of industry, decartelization, disarmament, and demilitarization, as well as the protection and security of the occupation forces, were among the major fields reserved at the time. The statute also maintained the principle that the occupation powers are primarily concerned with the maintenance of the constitutional order; indeed, it made them in effect the guardians of the constiution by requiring unanimous approval of any constitutional changes.[5] These provisions cannot be said to have worked very well, but owing to the diplomacy and skill of the men charged with their execution, open rupture was avoided. No doubt the ever-present danger from the East helped to bring about compromise. But interferences with German economic activities on the basis of older military government legislation proved difficult and largely ineffectual, as shown by the lawsuit instituted in an attempt to enforce decartelization legislation.[6] Similarly, the move to veto German tax legislation, after precipitating a crisis, had to be abandoned (see below). Generally speaking, the student of politics cannot but be critical of this setup, for any attempt to utilize the alleged "reserve powers" is likely to precipitate a conflict, as a shrewd politician can skillfully hide behind such powers

[4] In German the word *Statut* means by-laws or charter, and it was unfortunate that it should have been translated as statute. Nevertheless, the British realized the German position and tried to have it adopted, but France and the United States objected.

[5] For a sketch of the difficulties encountered in negotiating this settlement at the time, see Carl J. Friedrich's article already cited, "Rebuilding the German Constitution," pp. 473-474, as well as Chapter 2 above. There it has also been shown why the occupation cannot be readily classified in conventional terms of international law as either *pacifica* or *bellica*, and why the author of this chapter has suggested that it constituted an *occupatio pacifica prelimnaria*.

[6] See "Decartelization Law Prosecutions Filed" and "Decartelization Law Violators Fined," *Information Bulletin*, U.S. High Commissioner for Germany, July 1950 p. 38, and October, 1950, p. 82.

when he does not wish to act on a popular demand or can make himself a popular hero by advocating action which he might hesitate to undertake on his own full responsibility. In short, the blame is readily shifted to the occupying powers. The result is a division of responsibility which not only is at variance with the Allied powers' professed interest in promoting democracy, but tends to produce weak and ineffectual government. Hence it is not surprising that a revision, or indeed the abolition, of the statute became not only a primary objective of the German government but of the Allies themselves.[7] Such revision was, in fact, called for by the very terms of the statute which in its concluding article (9) provided that within twelve months, and in any event within eighteen months, of the effective date of the statute, that is, April 10, 1949, "the occupying powers will undertake a review of its provisions in the light of experience with its operation." This self-commitment the western Allies just barely lived up to when the Foreign Ministers in a meeting at New York in September, 1950, presumably agreed on such a revision. The actual date when such revision became effective, March 6, 1951, was well behind time, and gave substance to the German complaint that it was "too late." But they also complained that it was "too little." That the Allies themselves were quite aware of certain shortcomings is shown by the fact that they coupled the announcement of the actual revision with a promise of additional concessions to follow soon. In light of these, the situation must be considered highly fluid.

The most important practical forward step was to allow the Federal Republic to establish a Ministry of Foreign Affairs and to organize diplomatic missions in friendly nations, including the three occupying powers.[8] It should not be concluded from this move that the Federal Republic is granted sovereignty in conducting its foreign policy. Not only are specific restrictions placed upon it, but the Allies by reserving the right to intervene in any international negotiations relating to the fields reserved to the occupation authorities, including of course security, in effect retain ultimate authority. Foreign policy is an indivisible whole and does not consist, as some writers seem to think,

[7] See for this policy the repeated policy statements, such as Secretary of State Dean Acheson's address of April 28, 1949, reprinted in J. K. Pollock, J. H. Meisel, and H. L. Bretton, eds., *Germany under Occupation*, rev. ed. (Ann Arbor, 1949), pp. 297 ff.

[8] This step, in the view of the authors, definitely made the occupation an *occupatio pacifica*, however qualified it might be to allow for the unprecedented situation which persists. The cessation of the "state of war" between Germany and the several Allies during the summer of 1951 settled the issue still further. Cf. Chapter 2 above.

of a bundle of separate foreign policies. It is also deprived of one of its most characteristic features, namely, its confidential nature, if outsiders have " a right to be informed of any international discussion." Yet that right is reserved by the Allies, though it may be doubted whether they can enforce it.

In the field of foreign trade and exchange, the revision brought a relaxation, but not a discontinuance, of controls. These presumably will be progressively eliminated as the Federal German Republic becomes a member of such international bodies as the Monetary Fund. Relinquishment of the reserve powers over such matters as decartelization and displaced persons and refugees was made dependent upon the Germans' promulgating legislation satisfactory to the Allies in these fields. Whether such pressuring of a presumably popularly elected legislature into vital policy decisions was a sound method of procedure has been widely questioned, and not only by Germans. In the field of decartelization, for example, the considerable German support for such legislation has been hampered in becoming effective by being placed in the position of merely acquiescing in what the Allies demand. It is, of course, true that failure to insist upon such legislation may result in no legislation at all, but the insistence was itself a two-edged sword. The risk of having such "dictated" legislation eliminated as soon as the Allied supervision is further reduced seems quite as real a danger to any permanently satisfactory resolution of the problem.

Of considerable formal though perhaps not as great practical importance was the Allies' relinquishment of their powers of review of German legislation under the Occupation Statute. Under the revision, they retained the authority to repeal or annul legislation, but laws no longer were subject to a twenty-one-day period of uncertainty during which the allies may review it and raise objections. This power of specific approval was, however, being retained for federal constitutional amendments. In other words, the Allies continued in their role of guardians of the federal constitution and applied the same rules to the review of the state constitutions. As to the procedure for amending the constitution (Art. 79) which requires two-thirds of both *Bundestag* and *Bundesrat,* it seems highly unlikely that this provision was very wise. So far, no amendments have been passed, nor are they likely to pass under present political conditions, as they would call for an agreement between the two leading parties, the CDU in the government and the SPD in the opposition. If, on the other hand, an issue should present itself on which both these parties would agree it appears more than doubtful that the Allies could agree among themselves to disallow it. Hence this failure to include constitutional

amendments in the otherwise general relinquishment of Allied participation in German legislation strikes one as ill-conceived, since it does
not help the Allies to maintain their essential controls, while it tends
to weaken the German people's loyalty toward the constitution which
thereby becomes an instrumentality of foreign control, when it should
be the key to German participation in the government of the country.

Before the Allies announced this revision, they extracted from the
German government two major agreements, one thoroughly justified
and the other much more dubious. They had the German Chancellor
declare the German government's willingness to co-operate in the
equitable apportionment of the materials and services necessary for
the common defense of the West, as indeed it should. This formula
avoided a specific reference to the explosive issue of German rearmament which has since come to the fore. At the same time, the Allies
insisted that the German government assume responsibility for the
prewar external debts of the German "state" and that it acknowledge
"in principle" the debts arising from the economic assistance given to
Western Germany since the end of World War II. This acknowledg-
ment was hedged about by reference to Germany's capacity to pay,
but there seemingly was little objection to an obligation in regard to
economic aid, especially as its specific details were to be negotiated. By
contrast, an insistence that the new German democracy assume re-
sponsibilty for debts contracted by the Hitler government, largely
made in connection with preparations for war, seemed questionable indeed. It is to be surmised, however, that since these obligations are
preceded by others they are likely to receive short shrift, once the obligations of the Weimar Republic and postwar obligations have been
taken care of. For only to these latter would the argument about re-
establishing German credit seem to apply; surely the credit of the
Federal Republic and its citizens cannot be said to depend upon the
bankruptcy of the Hitler regime one way or the other.

If one examines the original Occupation Statute in light of these
revisions,[9] it can readily be seen that the changes were rather slight.
Most of the reserved fields remained reserved, constitutional amendments needed Allied approval, only procedural (as before) but no substantive civil liberties were expressly guaranteed, no concession was
made on the subject of interpretation or on that of negotiating future
changes, and while further changes were foreshadowed and negotiations regarding a "contractual agreement" eventually produced a treaty-
like agreement, no explicit commitment as to extent or effective date
was made at the time.

[9] See Appendix L.

Finally, a word should be added concerning an important relaxation which the Allies granted in the matter of constitutional restraints. Originally, in 1949, when approving the Basic Law, the Allies had refused to allow two articles to come into effect—Article 23 and Article 91, paragraph 2.[10] Article 23 proposed to include Greater Berlin among the states-members of the Federal Republic. Article 91, paragraph 2, dealt with the problem of federal authority over police of the states and reads in part as follows:

If the Land in which this danger [to the free democratic order] is imminent is not itself prepared or in a position to combat the danger, the Federal Government may place the police in that Land and the police forces of other Laender under its own instructions.

The military governors stated in their "Letter of Approval of the Basic Law" that "the police powers contained in Article 91 (2) may not be exercised until specifically approved by the Occupation Authorities." In light of increasing Allied concern over the lack of adequate security forces in Western Germany, this refusal had become obsolete by the summer of 1950, and therefore the high commissioners granted this approval somewhat belatedly in February, 1951, basing their action on the decisions made at the Foreign Ministers Conference held in New York in September, 1950. Part of the delay was due to the difficulties encountered by the Germans in reaching agreement among themselves regarding the administrative procedure under which the article could be put into effect.[11] These difficulties were, of course, closely related to the general German apprehensions concerning rearmament.

There are broader constitutional issues involved in setting up even a federal police force of any size, and owing to the difficulties of constitutional amendment, these issues are going to be hard to resolve. In the meantime, under this agreement there will be 110,000 police in the territory of the Federal Republic. Of these, 90,000 make up the police forces of the *Länder.* Ten thousand men of these *Land* police forces are to be organized as *Länderbereitschaftspolizei,* to be at the disposal of the federal government when needed under the provisions of Article 91. Another 10,000 constitute the federal frontier protection police (*Bundesgrenzschutzpolizei*). Another 10,000 are to be organized as a federal police force (*Bundesbereitschaftspolizei*) after the

---

[10] See Chapter 2 above and Lucius D. Clay, *Decision in Germany* (Garden City, N.Y., 1950), chap. 22.

[11] *Die Welt,* February 10, 1951; *Die Neue Zeitung* (Berlin ed.), same date.

Basic Law has been amended so as to make such a force constitutional.[12]

FEDERALISM

Federalism has been as controversial among Germans as among the Allies. From the radical centralism of communist doctrinaires and nationalists to the outright separatism of the Party of the Bavarians,[13] a broad middle-of-the-road group is distinguished by shades rather than by sharp contrast. Besides old and deeply rooted traditions of federalism, the present division of Germany suggests a federal system because such a system might facilitate the future reintegration. Hence Article 23 of the Basic Law provided:

For the time being, this Basic Law applies in the territory of the Laender Baden, Bavaria, Bremen, Greater Berlin, Hamburg, Hesse, Lower-Saxony, North-Rhine-Westphalia, Rineland-Palatinate, Schleswig-Holstein, Wuerttemberg-Hohenzollern. It is to be put into force in other parts of Germany on their accession. [*Dieses Grundgesetz gilt zunächst im Gebiete der Länder Baden . . . . In anderen Teilen Deutschland ist es nach deren Beitritt in Kraft zu setzen.*]

This seems a distant hope, and the prospect is complicated by the increasing centralization of the Soviet Zone.

The division has certainly had an influence upon constitutional and political development in Western Germany. In concrete terms, the effect of the division has been most noticeable in the difficulties encountered over giving the western part of Berlin proper representation in the Bonn Parliament. Both Allied opposition to including Western Berlin in the Federal Republic[14] and CDU lack of enthusiasm for having an overwhelmingly Social Democratic delegation from Berlin swell the ranks of the opposition figured in this controversy. The problem was tentatively solved by admitting nonvoting delegates from the city to both *Bundestag* and *Bundesrat*.

In the larger political arena outside the Parliament itself, the division of the country has quite naturally served to keep nationalism

[12] For further discussion of this and related police problems, see Chapter 16 below.

[13] This title is suggested as nearer the German *Bayernpartei* than the colorless "Bavarian party."

[14] See Chapters 2 and 3 above; also "Communication of the US, UK, and French Military Governor Transmitting to the Parliamentary Council the View of the Foreign Ministers on the Basic Law, 22 April 1949," in *Documents on the Creation of the German Federal Constitution,* Office of U.S. High Commissioner for Germany (Frankfurt, 1949), p. 135. This publication is cited hereafter in this chapter as *Documents*.

alive, in spite of growing European sentiment. Reunion of the country is not a debated issue; all parties favor it. Only the means and terms are debated, and even here there is substantial agreement among all parties except the Communists. The creation of a Ministry for "Questions regarding the Whole of Germany" (*Ministerium für Gesamtdeutsche Fragen*) showed that the government was much concerned with the problem. The ministry, partly located in Berlin, carries on work, both symbolic and concrete, which implies that the Soviet Zone of Germany and even the areas under Polish administration (though by treaty with the Democratic German Republic ceded to Poland in June, 1949) are under the potential jurisdiction of the Federal Republic and will soon be actually so. A steel embargo against the Soviet Zone, maintained for six months in 1949, a refusal to co-operate with the western Allies in keeping refugees from the Soviet Zone out of Western Germany, support for trade unions, churches, and other organizations working in the Soviet Zone—all these are part of a concerted effort to maintain as much contact as possible. So long as the country remains divided, the new German constitutionalism is bound to retain an aura of incompleteness and artificiality which ought to be remembered when comparing current experiences under the Bonn Basic Law with either the Weimar Republic or other constitutional democracies. Yet at the same time it gives the Federal Republic a fighting edge in face of the Soviet Zone with its totalitarian regime which it might otherwise lack.

The issue of centralism versus federalism has continued to play a role in German parliamentary politics. The CDU, as might have been expected of any government party, has been considerably more centralist in practice than it had been in theory during the constitutional debates. Only the separatist Party of the Bavarians has been advocating the kind of highly decentralized federalism, including the right to nullify and secede, which Southern states' rights partisans espoused in this country before the Civil War. But even among the remaining parties, more moderate on this point, there is a sufficient degree of difference of opinion to bring up the issue of violations of *Länder* rights whenever the federal Parliament enters a new sphere of legislation. This, for example, was the case during the debate on the federal amnesty law, when delegations of five of the states in the *Bundesrat* voted against federal jurisdiction in this matter. The issue again appeared during the debates on legislation to restore legal uniformity throughout federal territory.[15]

[15] See *Sitzungen des deutschen Bundestages*, pp. 573 ff. Erich Schmidt-Leichner, "Dia Bundesamnestie," *Neue Juristische Wochenschrift*, January 15, 1950.

Some of these difficulties trace back to the unhappy decision to make the German federal government one of specifically delegated and hence limited powers. There existed a doctrinaire tendency on the part of Americans especially to consider such a constitutional arrangement more nearly "federalistic" than one in which the *Länder* are given specific functions by the constitution. This attitude traces in part to the American constitution, where such limited delegated powers are given the federal government; it also has some fairly good grounding in older theory. But the experience under Weimar, if not that of Canada, should have served as a warning guide. Canada actually has operated a successful federal system with just such a delegation of legislative functions to the provinces. An insistence upon delegation to the federal authorities has, if the economic situation calls for considerable centralization of power, merely the effect of making the grant so broad that the question naturally arises: "What is left for the states?" Under such conditions it may be much sounder to give the states clearly defined functions which are constitutionally protected (as is done regularly with other local government authorities) than to leave their jurisdiction to the haphazard protection of judicial authorities. Actually, a more careful consideration of American constitutional history ought to have served as an object lesson in this regard; for many decades now the jurisdiction of the states of the Union has been curtailed by federal legislation which the courts have managed to blanket under one of the broad constitutional categories, such as "interstate commerce." In the case of the Basic Law, Allied insistence upon delegation to the federal authorities led to very broad and flexible provisions which leave the federal government free to take over anything, as long as it succeeds in getting the proposal through the Federal Council. It is in this Council that the real safeguard, such as it is, must now be sought. It is a negative brake, at best.

Of course, Allied and especially American attitudes and policy as concerns the whole range of problems connected with federalism have changed to some extent since the days of the adoption of the Basic Law. Not only is it more nearly felt to be an internal German concern, but in some important matters the Allies now desire more concentrated powers, notably in the field of the federal police, as analyzed above. In this respect, as in a number of others, trouble might have been avoided had the Allies realized more fully from the outset that "after all is said and done, German concepts of democracy and government [would] play a predominant role in shaping the new German constitutionalism."[16]

[16] "Rebuilding the German Constitution," as cited, p. 462. For the general

The list of concurrent legislation, as given in Article 74 of the Basic Law and implemented by Article 75, is a very long one; it does not, however, include some important matters, such as education. Essentially, all these areas of concurrent legislation may be dealt with by federal legislation, provided one of three conditions is fulfilled: if a matter cannot effectively be dealt with by *Land* law; or if such legislation by one *Land* would prejudice the interests of another *Land;* or (and this is the crucial joker) if "legal or economic unity demand it." It is hard to imagine any subject on which the federal authorities would want to legislate which could not be brought under this heading; but for good measure it was added that "the preservation of uniformity of living conditions" might also be used as a standard. The constitution might just as well have given legislative authority to the *Bund* in all these matters, but permitted *Land* legislation as long as the *Bund* had not acted. To repeat the thought stated at the outset, it is our view that more genuine *Land* authority would have resulted from spelling out in the constitution what functions it was desired to leave to the *Land*. This has been the result in Canada.

More basic than any of these formal attributions of jurisdiction is the problem of sound, healthy component units for any kind of effective federalism. Here again Allied policy has tended to disturb rather than to guide and aid sound development. The Germans were not ready to submit a reorganization plan for the federal structure, as far as *Land* boundaries were concerned, by the time the constitution was to be voted upon. Because of this, the Allies suspended (or made subject to their approval) any implementation of Article 29 of the constitution which calls for a reorganization of the *Länder* as created, mostly by military fiat, after May 8, 1945. The article specifically provides that this reorganization shall create *Länder* which by their size and potentiality are able to fulfill efficiently the functions incumbent upon them. The present structure is felt, by many Germans, not to correspond to these requirements; they frequently call for larger *Länder* as better able to stand up to the centralizing tendencies of the *Bund*. Be that as it may—and the efforts at overcoming the artificialities created in the southwest corner of Germany by the exigencies of demarcating the French and American occupation zones will be discussed presently in this chapter—the question may be counted upon to remain a subject of heated controversy for some years to come. Germans often forget that theirs is a relatively balanced structure, that in both the United States and Switzerland the range in size of the

problem of the distribution of legislative functions, see C. J. Friedrich, *Constitutional Government and Democracy* (New York, 1950), pp. 204 ff.

component units is considerably greater, and that any wholly rational scheme is apt to lack those bases in local and regional sentiment which are the life of federalism under democratic conditions.

Significantly, Article 29 contains the only provision in the Basic Law for a popular initiative in legislation. This popular initiative was to have taken place within one year after the Basic Law had come into effect, but presumably this provision will remain applicable for one year after the suspension is lifted. A draft law has been prepared.[17] It will presumably also become applicable to other parts of Germany which may join the Federal Republic in the future. One of the proposals which has been under discussion has been a union of the Rhineland-Palatinate with *Land* Hesse. The Social Democratic minister-president of Hesse advocated this union in June, 1950, mainly for reasons of economic and administrative efficiency,[18]but the political and sentimental obstacles will increase as time goes on and as the existing arrangements become settled.

To serve the special needs of the three southwestern states of the Federal Republic, Article 118 of the Basic Law provided that:

> The reorganization of the territory comprising the Laender Baden, Wuerttemberg-Baden and Wuerttemberg-Hohenzollern may be effected, by agreement between the Laender concerned, in a manner deviating from the provisions of Article 29. Failing agreement, the reorganization shall be regulated by federal legislation which must provide for a referendum.

Soon after the end of the war a movement got under way which aimed at the creation of a new southwest state out of these three *Länder*. For economic and administrative reasons, this appeared to be the best solution to many of the people concerned. It was, however, opposed by the government of Baden, which urged the restoration of Baden's prewar boundaries, mainly out of a sense of tradition, reinforced by local vested interests and French preferences. Minorities elsewhere shared this view. It was supported by the French, originally because they hoped to detach Baden (like the Saar), but in any case because they favor a high degree of decentralization for their eastern neighbor. The Catholic archbishop of Freiburg also was favorably inclined.[19]

By June, 1950, the three state parliaments had passed laws authorizing a consultative plebiscite which, after a spirited campaign, took place in September.[20] Only slightly more than 50 per cent of the

---

[17] *Deutschland im Wiederaufbau*, p. 18.
[18] *Die Welt*, June 7, 1950.
[19] *Die Welt*, September 13, 1950. See also *Die Zeit*, August 3, 1950.
[20] See *Die Welt*, June 21, 1950, and September 26, 1950.

eligible voters in the three states went to the polls, as compared with 78.5 per cent who voted in the *Bundestag* elections. While the vote throughout the territory favored formation of the southwest state by about 70 per cent, the proposal was defeated by a small majority in (south) Baden. As a result, the governments of the three now-existing states did not complete their negotiations, in which the outcome of the plebiscite was supposed to serve them as a guide. Since they failed to reach agreement, the federal Parliament had to provide the solution to this problem by legislation, passed on May 4, 1951, which set September 16 as the date for the final plebiscite. The *Land* government of Baden, however, supported by that of the Rhineland-Palatinate, tried by a bill introduced in the *Bundesrat* to have this plebiscite postponed, on grounds that no decision could be rendered on the constitutionality of the plebiscite legislation since the federal constitutional court had not yet been established.[21] In October the court held the reorganization law to be constitutional, and December, 1951, was set for the plebiscite.[22] The more general reorganization would, it seems, get under way as soon as the suspension of Article 29 is removed, presumably in connection with the elimination of the Occupation Statute. In the meantime, general discussions are held and plans are shaped up in various conferences, such as that held by the *Institut zur Förderung öffentlicher Angelegenheiten.*[23]

ELECTION LAW

The election law under which the present *Bundestag* was elected constituted a compromise between the two major parties.[24] The CDU wanted election by simple majority in single constituencies as practiced in Great Britain and the United States, while the SPD favored a proportional representation system along the lines of that used during the days of the Weimar Republic. Under the compromise,[25] 60 per cent of the seats in each *Land* were allocated on a simple majority basis. The remaining 40 per cent were allocated proportionally among the parties on the basis of all the votes cast in each *Land*. But from the number of seats which would go to each party on this proportional basis were subtracted the number of seats which it had already won

[21] *Frankfurter Allgemeine Zeitung,* September 1, 1951.

[22] The subject of territorial reorganization is dealt with in detail in Chapter 4 above.

[23] See *Die Bundesländer: Beiträge zur Neugliederung der Bundesrepublik* (1950).

[24] "Das Bonner Wahlgesetz," *Archiv des öffentlichen Rechts* (1949), p. 360. See also Chapter 19 below for detailed discussion of electoral practice.

[25] See *Documents,* pp. 140-154.

on the majority principle. In two cases, this system resulted in a party's gain of a surplus of one seat, which explains the fact that the present *Bundestag* has 402 members instead of the 400 for which the law provided. There were no federal lists of candidates as under Weimar. Moreover, in order to have its *Land* list considered in the proportional assignment of seats in any one of the *Länder,* a party was required to have received at least 5 per cent of the total *Land* vote.

The results of the *Bundestag* election of August 14, 1949, might be said to show that both CDU and SPD had been right in advocating their respective election schemes. The CDU won 115 seats from individual constituencies and 24 from *Land* lists. The SPD, on the other hand, won only ninety-six seats in single constituencies but thirty-five on the proportional representation basis. But the CDU position opposed to proportional representation is reinforced by the results achieved by the third largest party, the FDP, which gained only twelve seats from single constituencies but forty from *Land* lists.[26] To be sure, Adenauer's government has rested upon these, and it remains an open question as to what a straight majority system might have brought. However, it seems unlikely that these votes would have gone to the SPD.

As for the federal elections in the future, it appears that the government, considering that the law under which the present *Bundestag* was elected was restricted to that election, has prepared a new draft, since a new law is "required." Regarding this matter, an official document declares that "first of all, the basic decision must be prepared as to which electoral system (whether PR or MR) is preferred."[27]

PARLIAMENT AND THE GOVERNMENT

Bundestag—Parliamentary assemblies throughout the western world resemble one another to a considerable degree, and in many respects the new *Bundestag* goes about its business in a manner not at all unlike that of its older French and British counterparts. There is the same heckling which keeps speakers in the House of Commons ever on the *qui vive,* as well as the same occasional fistfight around the rostrum which disgraces the French Assembly. Nevertheless, the *Bundestag* does have distinctive aspects which give it its own individuality. Most striking among these characteristics is the tenor of the major debates which have taken place in this chamber. We doubt whether there exists another parliamentary assembly whose members

[26] "Die Bundestagswahl vom 14. 8. 49," *Archiv des öffentlichen Rechts* (1949), pp. 221-224.
[27] *Deutschland im Wiederaufbau,* p. 19.

have as deep and serious a consciousness and understanding of their historical role as do the *Bundestag* deputies. Speaker after speaker will trace his own or his party's intellectual, social, and political pedigree, often in the most learned terms. This theoretical self-consciousness has, of course, been an attribute of previous German parliamentary gatherings since 1848.

Perhaps this phenomenon may be explained in terms of the high proportion of professional men among the body's 402 members. Its roster lists 114 who hold a doctor's degree, including three who are listed as "Dr. Dr." This is a somewhat higher proportion than the Weimar *Reichstag* had during most of its existence, a fact which need not surprise us since Germany's so-called doctoral proletariat was produced during the interwar period and may therefore be expected to have flowered to full bloom by now. This doctoral quarter of the *Bundestag* cannot be explained away by pointing to the fact that most German lawyers have a doctor's degree. There are only thitry-four lawyers in the House. But there are seventeen professors, sixteen teachers, and forty literary men of one sort or another, and all of these undoubtedly contribute their share of professional learnedness. Most prominently represented among the other vocational groups are agricultural proprietors, of whom there are thirty-eight, wage earners of various occupations being next in numerical strength with thirty-seven. There are thirty-five businessmen, twenty manufacturers, and fifteen mayors of towns and cities. Among thirty women members, there are fourteen housewives. Fifteen members list jobs with their party as their occupation, while nineteen are trade-union functionaries. About sixty members are expellees or refugees. Deputies receive a monthly salary of DM600 in addition to a *per diem* allowances of DM30 while in attendance at Bonn and free railroad travel.

The *Bundestag* adopted the rules of procedure of the Weimar *Reichstag,* but since then some significant changes have been made to adapt these rules to the new constitution and the changed political circumstances with which it must cope.[28] The only important changes which were made at the outset are the reduction of parliamentary "groups" (*Fraktion*) from fifteen to ten members; establishment of thirty-nine committees instead of the *Reichstag's* fifteen standing committees; empowering the *Bundestag* President to ban members from the chamber for up to thirty days, instead of twenty, for gross viola-

[28] *Sitzungen des deutschen Bundestages, Drucksache No. 18;* see also Chapter 8 below for general discussion of legislative processes.

tions of order; and extending to members of the cabinet and the *Bundestag* or their deputies the right of addressing the *Bundestag* on their own initiative. The novel constitutional provision for a "constructive" vote of no-confidence caused omission of that paragraph of the old procedural rules which regulated no-confidence votes. Since the new rules thus obviously failed to spell out most of the major changes in governmental structure and procedure which the Bonn Basic Law has brought about, insistent demand for a complete overhauling has led to special work and proposals for a set of rules.

Of the new assembly's first tasks was the organization of its committees.[29] Thirty-nine of these bodies were established, varying in size from twenty-seven to twenty-one, fifteen, or seven members. A bitter battle was fought over the method by which seats on these committees were to be allocated to the various parties represented in the *Bundestag*. The system which was finally adopted favors the three large parties and is designed, in several particulars, to discriminate especially against the Communist party. Drafts of new legislation, after they have had their first reading in the House, are usually referred to the proper committee or committees for further detailed work before their second and third readings. *Bundestag* committees may, and often do, collaborate with parallel committees of the *Bundesrat* in this work. In May, 1950, a mediation committee between *Bundestag* and *Bundesrat* was established. It consists of twenty-four members, half of them from each house, and has as its special task the resolution of differences arising between the two houses of the federal Parliament.[30] So far the committees do not appear to have approached either the power of French committees or the usefuless of American Congressional committees. A trend in this direction may be indicated, however, in at least one case by Adenauer's complaint that the SPD's Carlo Schmid, as chairman of the Foreign Affairs Committee, had attempted to usurp executive functions.[31]

The *Bundestag* has been much concerned with a number of problems arising out of the constitutional provisions for rights and privileges of its members. In several instances it refused to waive immunity from criminal prosecution of members involved in legal suits of a primarily political character. But it did not hesitate to make possible the prosecution of deputies from both extremes of the political spectrum under the provisions of Article 18, which denies the basic rights to

[29] *Sitzungen,* pp. 180 ff.   [30] *Die Welt,* May 12, 1950.
[31] *Ibid.,* p. 144. See also *New York Times,* December 16, 1950, and Chapter 8 below for further discussion of committee activities.

those who abuse them for anticonstitutional purposes. Nor has it permitted its members by virtue of their parliamentary immunity to evade criminal prosecution for alleged financial irregularities.[32]

The first President of the *Bundestag*, a member of the CDU, made frequent use of his procedural right to exclude unruly members from the House for up to thirty days. Even Dr. Schumacher was once briefly excluded from the sittings, motivating the Social Democrats to move the then President's ouster from the presidency.[33] In the main, the exclusion rule has been applied for the most part to Communist (KPD) members. During September, 1950, six KPD deputies were banned from the floor for varying periods of time, a situation which conveniently enabled the Council of Elders, which arranges the order of the day, to rule that the nine Communists remaining in the House did not constitute a *Fraktion* and could therefore not move any resolutions or bills.[34]

Members of the *Bundesrat* have occasionally availed themselves of the constitutional provision entitling them to the floor of the *Bundestag* upon their request, despite constitutionally invalid Communist protests against this practice.[35] An interesting constitutional problem might some day arise out of the presence in the *Bundestag*, as regular deputies, of five ministers of *Land* governments who are entitled to represent their states in the *Bundesrat*.[36] Neither the Weimar Constitution nor the present Basic Law provides for incompatibility of membership in the lower house with membership in the upper house, but the Free Democratic party has already come out strongly for making simultaneous membership in both houses unconstitutional.

The *Bundestag* has jealously, but not always successfully, defended its position vis-à-vis the Chancellor, who has been strengthened very much by Article 67 of the Basic Law which provides the crucial restrictions on no-confidence votes that have given rise to the term "constructive" no-confidence vote. The article reads as follows:

The Bundestag may express its lack of confidence in the Federal Chancellor only by electing a successor with the majority of its members and submitting a request to the Federal President for the dismissal of the Federal Chancellor. The Federal President must comply with the request and appoint the person elected.[37]

[32] See *Die Welt*, March 30 and May 31, 1950; *Neue Zeitung*, July 28, 1950.

[33] *Die Welt*, March 2, 1950. [34] *Ibid.*, September 12, 1950.

[35] *Sitzungen*, p. 295.

[36] Partsch and Genzer, "Inkompatibilität der Mitgliedschaft in Bundestag und Bundesrat," *Archiv des öffentlichen Rechts* (1950), pp. 186 ff.

[37] See Chapter VI below for discussion of somewhat similar provision in Eastern Germany.

This provision made it possible for Dr. Adenauer, when the *Bundestag* demanded the right to ratify all commercial treaties concluded between the federal government and other states, to deny this privilege except in the case of the agreement with the Economic Cooperation Administration.[38] Articles 112 and 113 of the Basic Law, which, somewhat like Special Order 63 of the House of Commons, make increases in budgetary expenditures dependent upon government approval, have also restricted the effectiveness of the *Bundestag*. This rule has not yet, as a matter of fact, been very scrupulously observed. Nevertheless, when a majority of the House voted to continue a broad subsidy in opposition to cabinet policy, it was unable either to pass a law to this effect or to defeat the government on the issue.[39] Nor was a vote of no-confidence in Dr. Erhard, the federal minister of Economics, any more effective.[40]

The clumsy procedure of the *Bundestag* regarding allotment of time for speeches has gone far towards re-earning the new body the epithet *"Quasselbude"* (Blabber Shack), often and not altogether inappropriately applied to the *Reichstag*. In every major debate, spokesmen of each party, regardless of its strength in the Parliament, are granted a maximum speaking time of one hour, a limit which, moreover, is enforced none too strictly. As a result, more than nine hours of the valuable time of the House are taken up by the initial policy declarations of the nine parties on every major issue that arises.

Statistically, the first year's record of the *Bundestag* looks as follows: 81 plenary sessions and 1,073 committee meetings were held. There were 1,300 drafts of laws, resolutions and interpellations presented. Of 150 drafted bills, the government submitted 97, the parties 61, and 76 were passed. The House also passed 278 resolutions and 113 inquiries and witnessed 39 interpellations.[41] Its major legislative achievements of the year consisted of ratification of the ECA agreement and the Federal Republic's joining the Council of Europe and passage of a veterans' and a civil service law, the so-called minor tax reform, and the important laws for the restoration of legal uniformity and for the protection of the constitution.

Bundesrat—When the *Bundesrat* convened for the first of the thirty-four meetings which it held during the first year of its existence, some observers doubted whether it would succeed in its constitutional function of enabling the *Länder* to participate in federal legislation

[38] *Neue Zeitung,* June 26, 1950.
[39] *Ibid.,* July 20, 1950.
[40] *Die Welt,* September 6, 1950; *Die Zeit,* same date.
[41] *Die Welt,* September 6, 1950.

and administration.[42] They felt that the party composition of the upper house would make it nothing more than a miniature replica of the *Bundestag*[43] after due allowance had been made for the absence of the lesser parties. Indeed, the even balance of twenty Social Democrats and twenty Christian Democratic and Christian Socialist (CDU-CSU) members, with two Free Democrats and one Center deputy thrown in to tip the scales slightly to the right, might well have led one to expect that party discipline would outweigh *Land* interests, had it not been for the constitutional requirement, under Article 51, which obliges each state to cast its votes as a unit.

In fact, the *Bundesrat* has turned out to be a truly "federal" body. One legislative example in particular illustrates this quality of the upper house. When the Adenauer government presented an amnesty bill to the legislature, the issue was raised, as has already been mentioned, whether the federal government had the constitutional power to pass such legislation. The vote on this issue found the delegations of five *Länder* in opposition, and they were a composite assortment of SPD and CDU: Bavaria's delegation of five CDU-CSU ministers; Baden's of three CLU ministers; the Rhineland-Palatinate's of two CDU and two SPD men; Württemberg-Hohenzollern's delegation, consisting of two CDU and one SPD ministers; and Hamburg's group of three SPD senators. These eighteen votes were defeated by twenty-three in favor of the bill and of federal jurisdiction in this field; and this majority, made up of the votes of the remaining six *Länder,* was just as composite a coalition as the minority.[44]

Adenauer had apparently hoped to be able to dispose of the position of president of the *Bundesrat* as part of his original coalition deal. He wanted the job to go to Bavaria's minister-president, Hans Ehard. The *Bundesrat* preferred, however, to elect Rhineland-Westphalia's minister-president, Karl Arnold, who, as leader of the left wing of the CDU, was less acceptable to the Chancellor.[45] The defeat of the Basic Law in the Bavarian *Landtag* served as a convenient "out." However, at the end of his one-year term in this office and after his political position in his home state had become less secure, Arnold was succeeded by Ehard.[46]

The *Bundesrat,* just as the more numerous *Bundestag,* worries a

[42] Article 50, Basic Law. "*Durch den Bundesrat wirken die Länder bei der Gesetzgebung und Verwaltung des Bundes mit.*"
[43] "Die Konstituierung der westdeutschen Bundesorgane," *Archiv des öffentlichen Rechts* (1949), pp. 332-346.
[44] *Sitzungen,* p. 578.   [45] *Archiv des öffentlichen Rechts, loc. cit.*
[46] *Die Welt,* September 9, 1950.

good deal over asserting its prerogatives vis-à-vis the cabinet, and with just as good cause. Under article 53 of the Basic Law, for example, cabinet members are obliged to meet with committees of the upper house. In June, 1950, however, Adenauer actually instructed the federal minister for food not to attend any meetings of the food committee of the *Bundesrat* so long as the food minister of Lower Saxony, Gereke, was chairman of that committee. Gereke at that time was about to be excluded from the CDU for an attempt to conclude a trade agreement with the east German government.[47] Despite the resentment of the *Bundesrat* of this rather peremptory disregard of its constitutional privileges by the Chancellor, the latter had his way in this case just as in his dealings with the lower house. The general atmosphere of the *Bundesrat* contrasts with that prevailing in the *Bundestag* by being somewhat less partisan and more objective, a fact probably due mainly to its smaller size and its lesser exposure to the glare of publicity. So far it seems to have well fulfilled its functions within the federal scheme.

The Government—The constitutional fathers of Bonn, intent upon correcting those provisions of the Weimar Constitution which, by making the President strong, were generally believed to have facilitated Hitler's coming into power, drastically reduced the powers of the President. If effective government was to be had, this could only be done by making the Chancellor stronger. As a consequence the powers of the Chancellor under the Basic Law in fact resemble those of the American President, since he leads cabinet, Parliament, and parties.

The federal President was elected, as provided in Article 54, by the Federal Convention, consisting of the membership of the *Bundestag* and an equal number of electors sent by the eleven *Länder* on the basis of the proportional strength achieved by the several parties in either the *Bundestag* election or recent *Land* elections. Professor Theodor Heuss, the leader of the Free Democratic party, was elected on the second ballot by a majority of 416 out of 800 votes. Three days later, the leader of the Christian Democratic Union, Dr. Konrad Adenauer, was elected to the chancellorship by a coalition of CDU-CSU, FDP and the German party. Two hundred and two deputies voted for Adenauer, while 144 opposed him, the remaining members either abstaining or remaining silent. While he thus obtained a substantial majority of those voting, he was in fact elected by a one-vote majority, since Article 63 of the Basic Law states that "the person obtaining

[47] *Ibid.,* June 17, 1950.

the majority of votes of the *Bundestag* members is elected."[48] Two hundred and one votes would have constituted just half of the members. Adenauer's survival as Chancellor, in spite of this insecure majority, of tension within the coalition, and of dissension which has since developed in his own party, may well be due mainly to the provisions of Article 67 set forth above.

The new Chancellor asserted the independence of his position from the very beginning by selecting members of his cabinet with the consent but, in several instances, against the advice of President Heuss. Adenauer quite literally interpreted the provisions of Article 64, according to which "the Federal Ministers are appointed and dismissed by the Federal President upon the proposal of the Federal Chancellor." Heuss felt that he should do more than merely provide an automatic approval for Adenauer's nominees but did not succeed in making this conception of presidential prerogatives prevail.[49] Nor did the Chancellor permit his own party to dictate the composition of his cabinet. He selected eight members of the CDU-CSU, three members of the FDP, and two of the German party to constitute his government. There was opposition from the SPD to the creation of three new ministries in excess of the "classical" ten—the Ministries for the Marshall Plan, for Liaison with the *Bundesrat* and for "Questions regarding the Whole of Germany." The Chancellor did not, however, submit himself to a vote of confidence after announcing the size and composition of his government, nor was he required to do so under the Basic Law.

In his relations with the cabinet, Adenauer has certainly assumed a role similar to that of the American President. And since Article 65 makes him alone responsible for general policy, this was to be expected. Nor should occasional dissatisfaction with, or grumbling at, the Chancellor's dominant position in the cabinet on the part of its other members come entirely as a surprise. Complaints about premature policy statements on vital issues by the Chancellor have come not only from the *Bundestag* but also from his ministers. Thus, Adenauer issued his memorandum on German rearmament without prior consultation with the cabinet.[50] Although the resignation of Dr. Heinemann, the minister of the interior, in October, 1950, was ostensibly the result of the latter's disagreement with Adenauer's rearmament policy, it has been suggested that Heinemann was also protesting against the existing relationship between cabinet and Chancellor, which in turn is

---

[48] *"Gewählt ist, wer die Stimmen der Mehrheit der Mitglieder des Bundestages auf sich vereint."* See also Article 121.
[49] *Archiv des öffentlichen Rechts, loc. cit.* [50] *Die Zeit,* September 14, 1950.

related to disagreement between right and left in the CDU, as highlighted by the cabinet change in North Rhine–Westphalia. That the ministers do not take Adenauer's firm hand with complete docility is again indicated by his own recent complaint about Sunday speeches of several cabinet members who dared to make deviationist policy statements without obtaining his prior approval.[51]

On the other hand, the Chancellor has firmly backed up his ministers in the face of strong *Bundestag* attacks upon one or the other among them. Thus, he retained Economics Minister Ludwig Erhard despite a vote of censure against him after his "defeat" on the bread subsidy issue already mentioned.[52] Similarly, Adenauer supported Dr. Fritz Schäffer, his finance minister, against whom the Party of the Bavarians moved a vote of censure. He exercised his strong influence upon the President of the *Bundestag* to have debate on this motion postponed several times on rather flimsy technical grounds.[53]

The two houses of the legislature have also repeatedly had reason to express their unhappiness over the Chancellor's position. His role is so strong that he has been able to slight with impunity some of their prerogatives. Thus, for example, members of the cabinet have on occasion failed to follow with alacrity, to say the least, the provisions of Articles 43 and 53 of the Basic Law which require them to attend the proceedings of the two houses upon requests to that effect.[54] In this connection, though it is not a constitutional issue, we might mention complaints in the *Bundestag* about the generally unpopular and allegedly overstaffed press office of the government, which has sometimes made important announcements to press and general public without prior notification to the *Bundestag* through members of the cabinet, as when the German currency was devalued following the devaluation of the British pound.

The present Chancellor is fully aware of the fact that he is the kingpin of the constitutional setup and makes no bones about wielding the power which his position gives him. This becomes most apparent in his relations with the parliamentary delegation of his own party. In May, 1950, the CDU group in the *Bundestag* dared to present for consideration the draft of a bill dealing with labor's participation in management, a very hot issue of great concern to the more progressive elements in the CDU.[55] This move went counter to Adenauer's conception of the role of the government party in the legislature, according to which legislative initiative rested either with the cabinet itself

[51] *Die Welt,* September 22, 1950. [52] *Ibid.,* September 6, 1950.
[53] *Ibid.,* September 13 and 22, 1950. [54] *Sitzungen,* p. 359.
[55] See further discussion in Chapter 14 below.

or with the opposition in the House[56]—a conception much in line with current British parliamentary practice, though the British cabinet is more of a collegiate body and more exposed to party opinion than its counterpart in Bonn.

In parliamentary practice, the new constitutional provisions and the party constellation have thus served to make the Chancellor stronger than he has ever been. He is, in contrast to the Chancellors of Weimar days, virtually completely independent of the President as long as no majority for another Chancellor exists in the *Bundestag*. In the present situation this is partly due to the President's being leader of the minor party (FDP) supporting the coalition which it cannot leave without giving up participation in the government. The Chancellor dominates his cabinet. Although elected by the slim margin of one vote, Adenauer may well serve his four-year term, for it is unlikely that the *Bundestag*, as presently composed, will ever be able to get a majority to agree upon a replacement for him. This situation in turn contributed towards promoting his ascendancy over his own party. It is well to keep this in mind as we next focus our attention on the party system in Parliament which has taken shape under the new German constitutionalism.

PARTIES AND PARLIAMENT

The outcome of the first *Bundestag* elections, in which the two major parties, CDU and SPD, won 139 and 131 seats respectively, might have led one to expect that a coalition government would be formed by these two, while the opposition would consist of the minor parties which controlled the remaining 132 seats. And this is precisely what happened in three of the *Länder*—North Rhine–Westphalia, Lower Saxony, and Hesse—where the so-called "great coalition," consisting of CDU and SPD, controlled the cabinets. In the first of these states, this coalition could not survive the election of June, 1950, whose principal result was a gain for the Free Democratic party at the expense of the two leading parties. But the CDU's Minister-President Arnold continued in office, first with an all-CDU cabinet and later with a so-called "smallest coalition," made up of CDU and the Center party. The FDP moved a non-confidence vote against him in September but failed to carry it because both SPD and KPD abstained. Since, moreover, North Rhineland–Westphalia's constitution contains a clause which closely resembles Article 67 of the Basic Law, it is unlikely that Arnold could be forced out of office except by a firm

[56] *Die Welt,* May 24, 1950.

or "constructive" coalition of SPD and FDP which would be prepared to take over the government of the state.[57]

Be that as it may, we can be sure that Chancellor Adenauer favored the breakup of the "great coalition" in Düsseldorf, for he is opposed to the idea as a matter of principle, both at the *Land* and federal levels. At one time he applied considerable pressure, unsuccessfully, on the Lower Saxony branch of his own party to make them withdraw from the coalition government in that state.[58] And in this one respect at least, Adenauer and his Social Democratic adversary, Schumacher, were in agreement. The latter was as much opposed to SPD/CDU coalitions as the former. This relationship between the major parties is also reflected in the field of legislation. Only rarely, as in February, 1950, have SPD and CDU voted together in the *Bundestag*, in this instance in order to defeat a coalition of FPD and German Party on a bill regulating property relations in the coal-mining industry.[59] Otherwise, on the federal level at least, the SDP has maintained the role of an opposition party, the proper definition of which was debated at the very first meeting of the *Bundestag*. Adenauer welcomed the presence of an opposition party in the House and expressed the opinion that it was better for this opposition to show its true colors in the *Bundestag* than that "it should run wild outside of Parliament in an uncontrollable manner because, gagged by a broad coalition, it cannot express itself to any extent in the Parliament." Dr. Schumacher, on the other hand, placed more emphasis on what he considered the essential function of the opposition—namely, to oppose the government. He stated that the SPD would refuse to permit the government parties to shift to its shoulders responsibility for some particular, perhaps unpopular, policy which they wanted to enact but did not want to defend before the country without the opposition's support.[60]

The Social Democrats have followed the course which their leader indicated for them and have collaborated in a parliamentary fashion with the government parties only on very rare occasions, such as the one mentioned above. The personal antagonism which at first existed between Adenauer and Schumacher was for a while eased, and these two met regularly for exchanging information, a practice which, it is said, was suggested to them by the former British High Commissioner, Sir Brian Robertson, who impressed them with the kind of relation

[57] See *Die Welt*, September 8 and 23, 1950; *Die Zeit*, September 21, 1950.
[58] *Neue Zeitung*, February 16, 1950.   [59] *Ibid.*
[60] See *Germany's Parliament in Action*, U.S. High Commissioner for Germany, (Frankfurt, 1950), pp. 20 and 29.

which exists between government and opposition in his own country.[61] On the whole, this trend of relationships between the government and a distinctive and articulate opposition is a wholesome one and should contribute to strengthening constitutional democracy in Germany. It provides more clear-cut responsibility and enables the voter to exercise a genuine choice.

Among the minor parties in the *Bundestag*, the Communists have been the most troublesome. Like other western constitutional democracies, the new German state has had to be concerned with the problem of limiting the freedom of those who would use constitutional rights as a means for the subversion of the constitutional order itself. Two articles of the Basic Law deal with this question. Article 18 provides that persons who abuse the basic constitutional rights "in order to attack the free, democratic basic order" shall forfeit these rights. According to Article 21:

> Parties which, according to their aims and the conduct of their members, seek to impair or abolish the free and democratic basic order or to jeopardize the existence of the Federal Republic of Germany are unconstitutional. The Federal Constitutional Court shall decide on the question of unconstitutionality.[62]

Since at the outset the Federal Constitutional Court had not yet been established, the government had to seek other means of dealing with the anticonstitutional menace of the German Communist party. We have already seen how the rules of procedure of the *Bundestag* have been used against the KPD's parliamentary delegation. In September, 1950, the government took drastic measures to cope with this danger outside of Parliament as well. It ordered the dismissal from the civil service of all "democratically unreliable officials" (*demokratisch nicht zuverlässige Beamte*"), that is, members of any one of thirteen organizations. Eleven of these were Communist or Communist-dominated, the other two being the neofascist Socialist Reich party and Otto Strasser's Black Front. The decree stipulated that formal official proceedings, simultaneously with tentative dismissal from the service and retention of salaries, were to be instituted against civil servants with permanent tenure, while other classes were simply to be dismissed. Several *Land* governments immediately followed suit at the federal

[61] *Die Welt*, September 6, 1950; also April 8, 1950.
[62] *Parteien, die nach ihren Zielen oder nach dem Verhalten ihrer Anhänger darauf ausgehen, die freiheitliche demokratische Grundordnung zu beeinträchtigen oder zu beseitigen oder den Bestand der Bundesrepublik Deutschland zu gefährden, sind verfassungswidrig. Über die Frage der Verfassungswidrigkeit entscheidet das Bundesverfassungsgericht.*

government's request, and even the General Federation of Trade Unions announced their agreement with the move, although they would have preferred to have been consulted about it beforehand.[63] By itself, this measure would not appear to endanger general respect for constitutionalism in Germany. The problem in Germany in many respects parallels that in the United States, whose antisubversive legislation has had effects similar to those intended by the German decree.

THE CONSTITUTIONAL COURT

The law establishing the Federal Constitutional Court provided for by Article 93 of the Basic Law was passed by the *Bundestag* on February 1, 1951, and by bipartisan majorities.[64] Owing to the revision of the Occupation Statute it has since become law. The long delay in establishing this court does not mean, however, that it has failed to play a role in the Federal Republic's first year of politics. Recourse to this court has been threatened so often that one German commentator thought only the court's nonexistence tempted politicians to mention it so often. Now that the court has actually begun effective operation, these same men may prefer to settle their controversies by legislative rather than judicial decision.[65]

The court consists of two chambers of twelve judges each, all of whom must be lawyers and experienced in constitutional and public law. They will be elected half and half by the *Bundesrat* and *Bundestag* respectively, two-thirds for eight years, and the other third from among the judges of the higher federal courts for the period of their tenure of office. The judisdiction of the court is very extensive and includes the right to determine the constitutionality of federal as well as state legislation. In accordance with the government draft, individuals can bring suit before the court if they consider that their constitutional rights have been infringed. Local government bodies likewise can call upon the court to protect their local autonomy as guaranteed by the constitution. The various governmental authorities, both federal and state, can sue before the court in support of their claims for constitutional jurisdiction. In short, to a very large extent the American tradition of the constitutional judiciary, that is to say of the

[63] *Die Welt,* September 20, 1950; *Neue Zeitung,* September 21, 1950.

[64] See *Die Neue Zeitung* (Berlin ed.), March 3, 1951, p. 3, where Friedrich Glum discusses this legislation under the heading "Die Aufgaben des Bundesverfassungsgerichts."

[65] Hermann Jahrreiss, "Das Bundesverfassungsgericht soll 'Hüter der Verfassung' sein," *Justiz und Verwaltung,* June, 1950.

judiciary as the guardian of the constitution, has taken hold and may serve to establish a real framework of a working constitutional order in Germany. The court is also charged with impeachments and with the giving of advisory opinions. This is, of course, the continental tradition; one must hope that these political tasks will not impinge too much upon the court's legal task or serve to undermine its authority as the ultimate fountain of basic law. As one scholarly commentator rightly observed:

Decisions of the greatest political consequences are to be expected from the Constitutional Court. It is to be hoped, therefore, that judges will be found who will, in their decisions . . . display the wisdom, both legally and politically, which characterized the famous decisions of the United States Court.[66]

Under the Occupation Statute, as we have seen, the occupation authorities retained the right to disapprove legislation "inconsistent with the Basic Law, a *Land* constitution, legislation or other directives of the Occupation Authorities themselves or the provisions of this instrument." In other words, the three high commissioners constituted a kind of supreme constitutional guardian. Hence it became all the more important, after the Occupation Statute had been revised to limit this authority, that the law establishing the Federal Constitutional Court should be passed. Great difficulties were encountered in settling the problems of membership and especially that of the presidency (chief justice). With Dr. Höpker-Aschoff in that post, the court was finally inaugurated on September 28, 1951.[67]

Allegedly in order to fill to some extent the gap in the implementation of the Basic Law which the nonexistence of the court had left, a law was passed in July, 1950, establishing a Federal Office for the Protection of the Constitution (*Bundesverfassungsschutzamt*), under the jurisdiction of the Federal Ministry of the Interior. The law provided for collaboration between this federal bureau and corresponding *Land* offices, but it restricted the activity of both these agencies to the collection and evaluation of information about unconstitutional and anticonstitutional developments. The bureau has no police or control functions under the law.[68] Nor, for that matter, does it have any judicial aspects, and those who even thought of this organization in connection with the Constitutional Court obviously labored under a

[66] Glum, *loc. cit.* The court has since moved into a very crucial position. It has declared the neo-Nazi Socialist Reich party incompatible with the Constitution (December, 1952) and has been deeply involved in the issue of the constitutionality of the Community Defense Treaty and the Contractual Agreement.

[67] See *Frankfurter Allgemeine Zeitung,* September 1 and 9, 1951; also *New York Times,* September 29, 1951.

[68] *Neue Zeitung,* July 20, 1950. *Bundesgesetzblatt,* No. 42, September 28, 1950.

misconception of the role of the judiciary. But even in its assigned sphere, the Federal Office for the Protection of the Constitution has apparently not been conspicuously successful. It began its operations by having the high commissioners reject ten out of nineteen men recommended for the job by Dr. Heinemann, then federal minister of the Interior. The *Länder* were also reluctant to co-operate, and when Heinemann resigned in September, 1950, one newspaper suggested that one of the reasons had been the failure of the *Verfassungsschutzamt*.[69]

As long as there was no Federal Constitutional Court, the beginnings of judicial constitutional interpretation had to be made by state constitutional courts, among which that of Bavaria has been particularly active. The decisions of this court may perhaps provide a preview of future decisions of the federal tribunal, especially since some German jurists seem to have been of the opinion that state courts ought consciously to perform some of the functions of the Federal Constitutional Court until this body came into existence.[70] With one exception, the Bavarian court's decisions have been fairly conventional. One dealt with the constitutionality of a new election law; another decided whether a law passed by the Bavarian *Landtag* had changed the state constitution.[71] In one case the court decided that a Reich law of the Hitler period which prohibited midwives to engage in their profession after reaching a certain age was in conflict with the equality provisions of the Bavarian constitution. The court handed down one particularly interesting decision, however, in a case in which the constitutionality of an article of the Bavarian constitution itself was challenged. Article 184 of this document provides that "the validity of laws which are aimed at National Socialism or militarism or which are intended to set aside their effect are not affected or limited by this Constitution."[72] This was attacked as incompatible with the basic rights guaranteed by the constitution. While the court rejected this particular claim, its decision did contain the following significant dictum:

There are constitutional principles which are so fundamental, and which

[69] *Echo der Woche*, September 8, 1950.

[70] Erich Schmidt-Leichner, "Die Bundesamnestie," *Neue Juristische Wochenschrift*, January 15, 1950.

[71] *Bayerisches Gesetz- und Verordnungsblatt*, Nr. 1/1950, January 10, 1950. Walter Roemer, "Zur Rechtssprechung des Bayer: Verfassungsgerichtshofes," *Süddeutsche Juristen Zeitung*, August, 1950.

[72] *Die Gültigkeit von Gesetzen, die gegen Nationalsozialismus oder Militarismus gerichtet sind oder ihre Folgen beseitigen wollen, wird durch diese Verfassung nicht berührt oder beschränkt.*

give expression to a law which precedes even the constitution, that they bind the constitutional legislator himself, with the result that other constitutional provisions which do not deserve this rank may be null and void because they violate these fundamental principles.[73]

This decision is in line with a great, albeit now obsolete, English tradition, the so-called Higher Law Doctrine of Sir Edward Coke and others.[74] While related to natural-law thinking, it is distinct from it. Its recent revival hangs together with what has rightly been called the "revival of natural law."[75]

In general, we may conclude that the new German constitutionalism has not yet matured sufficiently to have developed an appreciable or consistent body of judicial practice or decisions. But the developments which have taken place so far indicate that, if given a chance, the constitutional courts may well play an important role under the Basic Law.

CIVIL SERVICE IN THE BASIC LAW

The character of the new civil service of the German republic has been a major bone of contention between the occupation authorities, British as well as American, and the Bonn government.[76] British and American ideas on the civil service have been employed as yardsticks of a "democratic" public service with scant regard for the differences in institutional setting and tradition. The Allied viewpoint found its expression in an Aide Memoire of the military governors, left with the president of the Parliamentary Council on November 22, 1948, which insisted *inter alias:*

(1) that each citizen has access to public office, with appointment and promotion being based solely on his fitness to discharge the responsibilities of the position, and that the Civil Service should be non-political in character;

[73] *Bayerisches Gesetz- und Verordnungsblatt,* Nr. 16/1950, July 24, 1950: *Es gibt Verfassungsgrundsätze, die so elementar und so sehr Ausdruck eines auch der Verfassung vorausliegenden Rechtes sind, dass sie den Verfassungsgesetzgeber selbst binden und dass andere Verfassungsbestimmungen, denen dieser Rang nicht zukommt, wegen ihres Verstosses gegen sie nichtig sein können."* See also Roemer, *op. cit.*

[74] See John Dickinson, *Administrative Justice and the Supremacy of Law in the United States* (Cambridge, Mass., 1927), chap. IV.

[75] See Charles G. Haines, *The Revival of Natural Law Concepts* (Cambridge, Mass., 1930).

[76] This subject is discussed in greater detail and from another point of view in Chapter 10 below.

(2) that a public servant, if elected to the federal legislature, shall resign his office with the agency where he is employed before he accepts election.[77]

The first of these paragraphs is reflected in the Basic Law. Article 33, paragraph 2, states that:

Every German shall have equal access to any public office in accordance with his suitability, ability and professional achievements.

The Parliamentary Council also made a concession with regard to the second demand, by inserting a draft article which provided that certain classes of higher officials would have to transfer to inactive status before accepting office.[78] The final version of the Basic Law, however, omitted this paragraph.

This circumvention did not solve the problem; it returned with the drafting of the electoral law, Article 5, paragraph 2, of which contained a similar provision. This still failed to satisfy the military governors, who in a message to the ministers-president stated, on May 28, 1949, that they had

agreed to issue Laws and Ordinances in their respective Zones which will require all Civil Servants and Judges to resign their Civil Service Offices immediately prior to accepting membership in the *Bundestag*.[79]

The ministers-president, in turn, thought this provision to be in conflict with Article 48, paragraph 2, of the Basic Law, which reads:

No one may be prevented from assuming and exercising the office of a deputy. Notice of dismissal or dismissal (from employment) for this reason shall be inadmissible.

In their reply, the military governors repeated their previous reasoning.[80] Thus, while the original provision of Article 5, paragraph 2, of the electoral law was left in the final version of that document, the military governors nevertheless proceeded to issue the ordinances

[77] *Documents,* p. 106.

[78] "Proposals of the Committee of Seven, 17 March 1949," in *Documents,* p. 112; Article 65 (former Art. 62); "Any official exercising public authority (*Hoheitsbefugnisse*) must, before accepting his election to the *Volkstag* [the term used at that stage to designate the *Bundestag*], request his transfer to the inactive status. The transfer shall be valid for the duration of his membership in the *Volkstag,* without a claim to inactive status pay; the claim to reemployment, however, shall be maintained. These provisions shall apply appropriately to employees in public service. The provisions of sentence 1 shall not apply to officials elected for a limited period of time. Details shall be regulated by a federal law."

[79] *Documents,* p. 148.

[80] "Answer of the Military Governors to the Ministers President, 1 June 1949," in *Documents,* p. 150.

which required civil servants to resign upon accepting an elective federal office.

This failure to resolve the disagreement recurred a third time, when the civil service law, passed by the *Bundestag* in April, 1950, was provisionally rejected by the High Commission on essentially the same grounds: the law failed to provide for resignation in case of election to the federal Parliament.[81] This provisional veto later was lifted by the high commissioners because, according to Mr. McCloy, the federal government had promised a "good law." At the same time, however, he warned the Germans that civil service posts should be available to all, "irrespective of fraternities and social connections."[82] In this case the United States High Commissioner used words which later were to be echoed by Dr. Schumacher in an attack upon the government's civil service policies.[83]

The American insistence that civil servants who are elected to a legislature permanently resign from the service might well cause the quality of the legislatures to suffer. In some instances the best qualified and most interested candidates are to be found among the bureaucracy. But these men would hesitate to run for elective office if they cannot expect to return later on to their former civil service status. The difficulty of the American, and to a lesser extent the British, position is to be found in the apparent incompatibility of its two main aims, that is, to have a civil service which is both nonpolitical and democratic. By a nonpolitical service is meant one whose members are not closely affiliated with political parties. A democratic civil service is one recruited not alone from the upper classes of society. In order to make the German civil service democratic, it would have to admit to its higher levels members of lower income groups who possess the necessary training and experience. It so happens that many of these people are active Social Democrats. Consequently, if the emphasis is placed on the nonpolitical aspects of the civil service, its more important functionaries would have to be drawn mainly from the upper and more conservative classes, and this would militate against the democratic characteristics of the service. As a result, the civil service might well return to its former tradition of exclusiveness, especially in the higher ranks, with its attendant evil of a lack of "human" connection with the people at large.

Added to this dilemma in the theory which has been motivating American interferences with west German civil service legislation are

[81] See *New York Times*, April 18, 1950; also Chapter 10 below.
[82] See *New York Times*, May 23, 1950.
[83] *Neue Zeitung*, July 13, 1950.

the results of the actual American conduct of affairs. The needs of military government when dealing first with the Council of States[84] and later with the several bizonal bodies which existed before the creation of the Federal Republic have of themselves tended to strengthen and solidify the new officialdom. The military apparatus itself constituted a bureaucracy, and it was only natural that its officials should have found it most convenient to deal with their German opposites, that is, the German bureaucracy. In the end, the chances are that the Germans will have their way, since neither of the major parties agrees with the American view of the matter, which clashes with German and general European tradition and with their specific interests at this time.

CONCLUSION

In conclusion, it may be well to consider the prospects and prevailing trends. The Federal Republic is not a strong government, although more stable than that of either France or Italy. The presence of large and increasing contingents of foreign troops upon German territory, while at the present time giving the German government the backbone of concrete force without which no government can live, provides sources of friction which feed a nationalist revival. At the same time, the insistence of the western Allies upon a German "defense contribution" as a *quid pro quo* for German autonomy—the word constantly used is "independence," but there will not be German "independence" for many a year—is a tragic reversal of the previous Allied policy of demilitarization. For not only is this a matter of soldiers, of an army and all its paraphernalia, but also involved is a program of increasing "defense" production, meaning the re-establishment of plants and industries providing either military weapons or at least basic constituents of such weapons.

The new "Contractual Agreement" which takes the place of the Occupation Statute has not yet become effective. However, it is clear that, outside the military field of security, the restrictions on German autonomy will be very limited indeed. At this writing, it is not possible to say just how the German contribution to western defense will be worked out. Owing to Allied pressure, the constitution contains no provisions even for a federal police. The organization of any kind of military establishment may conceivably require a constitutional amendment, which cannot be passed without the concurrence of the two major parties because of the two-thirds majority requirement. This

[84] See Heinz Guradze, "The Laenderrat: Landmark of German Reconstruction," *Western Political Quarterly*, June, 1950, p. 190.

will depend upon a decision of the constitutional courts. The leader of the Social Democratic opposition has made it amply clear that his party will not consent to any rearmament of Germany without full equality of status; it is difficult to unravel the complex skein of motivation which is at the bottom of this attitude. Clearly it is not simply a matter of "nationalism" as so many outside observers are inclined to surmise.

There is widespread dissatisfaction in the German Federal Republic with the workings of the Basic Law, as well as the performance of the present government. Apart from the substantial but specific criticism of the Social Democratic opposition, there is much general "popular" dislike of, and even disgust with, "Bonn." The continued Allied occupation bears its share of responsibility for this outlook and point of view. Radical elements of left and right are in the habit of talking about the government as *"Lizenzdemokraten"* or licensed democrats, that is to say, men who, like Quisling for the Nazis, operate a democratic government by license from the occupying powers. It is this atmosphere which motivated Dr. Schumacher in making some of his more bitter speeches. But so far these aversions and hostilities have not crystallized into any significant political movement. To be sure, the success of the Socialist Reich party (SRP) at the polls in the election in *Land* Lower Saxony in May, 1951, where they secured over 11 per cent of the votes, produced something of a shock both in Germany and abroad.[85] The simultaneous collapse of the Communists, who received less than 2 per cent in the election, was generally overlooked. Yet these two changes must be taken together; for they mean that the percentage willing to try dictatorship once again remains around 10 per cent in Germany, or rather even in this corner of Germany where the influx of eastern refugees has been a particularly formidable and upsetting factor. It is also significant, and quite at variance with what happened in the twenties, that the government immediately took rather strong action by bringing suit against the leader of this Neo-Nazi group, General Remer, who was subsequently condemned to a term in jail. It also challenged the constitutionality of the party before the court which eventually "outlawed" the neo-Nazi group. At the same time, the government pushed its amendments to the criminal law to tighten up control on subversive groups, and several of the *Land* governments took specific action to curb the irresponsible action of the SRP group. It seems clear from these events that one must expect further troubles from unreformed Nazis and recalcitrant militarists, but it seems equally clear that the government is much more

[85] For further discussion see Chapter 19 below.

alert to the problems such political activities create for the maintenance of democratic government in Germany.

All in all, it appears reasonably clear that the German government
and a large majority of the German people as well are committed not
only to a western course, but also to the fullest possible integration of
Germany into a United Europe. Indeed, the difficulties and hesitations
which developed in 1950-1951 in the progress toward this goal were
at least in part responsible for the nationalist revivals that appeared
recently. They serve to underline the soundness of the French insistence, which is also the official German position, that the future of
German democracy is closely linked to the establishment of an effective European governmental system for the control of a European
army and of a European coal and steel program as envisaged under
the Schuman Plan, as well as other such policies which are, it is hoped,
to follow fairly soon.[86] Fortunately, there are no constitutional obstacles to such European developments, as the Basic Law clearly
enunciates, in its Article 24, that sovereign powers may be transferred
to international institutions, that, in order to preserve peace, Germany
may join in a system of mutual collective security, and that she will,
in this connection, consent to such limitations of her sovereignty as
may help to bring about a more peaceful order in Europe. If, therefore, the European organization could be made secure, even a German
participation in a European army might not require a constitutional
amendment. The situation is certainly a perplexing and difficult one.
But anyone surveying the first two years of the German Federal Republic will, if he weighs all the factors involved, come to the conclusion that the weak and faltering structure which came into existence
in 1949 may yet prove again the old French dictum that *rien ne
persiste que le provisoire.*

[86] This subject is set forth in detail in Chapter 7 below.

6

Governments of

Soviet Germany

KURT GLASER

THE Deutsche Demokratische Republik (hereinafter referred to as the DDR) is territorially identical with the Soviet Zone of Occupation in Germany. This area, which does not include any part of the city of Berlin, contains 107,805 square kilometers, or 30.2 per cent of Germany west of the Oder-Neisse line. In October, 1946, the population of the Soviet Zone was 17,313,581, or 26.3 per cent of that of the four zones together. Since then the increase due to arrival of refugees and to excess of births has been approximately balanced by large-scale migration to Western Germany.[1]

The DDR has five states, Brandenburg, Mecklenburg, Saxony, Saxony-Anhalt, and Thuringia. These are very largely agricultural in their nature, but there are concentrations of heavy industry in Saxony and of fine industry and textiles in Saxony and Thuringia. The uranium deposits along the Czech border have been heavily exploited and publicized but are actually rather unproductive. The principal cities of the DDR are Leipzig, Dresden, and Chemnitz in Saxony, Halle and Magdeburg in Saxony-Anhalt, and Weimar and Jena in Thuringia.

Although the parliament of the DDR meets in the Soviet Sector of Berlin and its ministries are located there, no attempt has yet been made to incorporate Berlin officially into the DDR. If and when West

[1] This chapter is based largely on investigations undertaken by the author while an official in the Civil Administration Division of the Office of Military Government for Germany (U.S.). As a consequence it will not always be possible to cite documentary authority to support the conclusions drawn,

Berlin is officially declared to be a part of the Federal Republic of Germany, a parallel move of the DDR with respect to the Soviet Sector can be expected. Actually the special status of Berlin makes little difference. The industry of the Soviet Sector is integrated with that of the Soviet Zone, the Berlin organization of the Socialist Unity party functions as a *Land* group within the zonal party, and the political police operate in the sector exactly as they do in the zone.

To understand the political development and the governmental institutions of the Soviet Zone it is necessary to keep in mind one basic fact—that the Soviets and their Communist allies in Germany have never regarded the establishment of a Soviet state in Eastern Germany as more than an immediate objective. In long-run Communist strategy the Soviet Zone is a jumping-off-place from which it is hoped to accomplish the sovietization of all of Germany. If this cannot be achieved by political infiltration there is always the possibility of using military force. Not only the Soviets but also the free nations know that the sovietization of Germany would be the first step toward the sovietization of Europe. This knowledge has led to the changes in British, American, and French foreign policy which we have witnessed during the past several years.

INITIAL SOVIET POLITICAL POLICY

The Soviet plan for a Communist Germany appears to have originated shortly after Hitler invaded Russia on June 22, 1941. On July 3 of that year Stalin made a speech in which he appealed to the German people to co-operate with the Soviet Union in destroying the fascist tyranny. Shortly after this the "Free Germany Committee" (*Nationalkomitee freies Deutschland*) was organized in Moscow. It consisted at first of German Communist exiles such as Wilhelm Pieck and Walter Ulbricht, but was later expanded to include numerous military figures such as Field Marshal von Paulus, captured at Stalingrad, and Generals von Seydlitz and Einsiedel.

Although the Soviets had evidently considered using the Free Germany Committee as the basis of a Soviet-oriented government upon their arrival in Germany, they were induced to shelve this plan by a variety of factors. In the first place, the Potsdam Agreement of August, 1945, postponed indefinitely the creation of a central German government. Secondly, the military character of the Free Germany Committee was inconsistent with the agreement for the complete demilitarization of Germany to which the Soviet Union was a party. An open alliance of the Communists with military elements would also have obstructed the unification of the Communist and Social Democratic parties—this unification was a basic element in Communist strategy not only in Germany but also in Poland, Czechoslovakia, and Italy. Lastly, the Soviets appear to have supposed, as the German Communists firmly believed, that the German people were ripe for communism and that the German comrades could bring about their conversion. This erroneous optimism, which was doubtless influenced by the isolation to which the German Communists in Russia had been subjected, set the tone for initial Soviet political policy in Germany.

On June 15, 1945, without consulting the other occupying powers, the Soviet Military Administration (SMA) issued an order permitting the organization of political parties and trade unions in the Soviet Zone. Within a short time, four parties were licensed: the Communist party (KPD), the Social Democratic party (SPD), the Christian Democratic Union (CDU), and the Liberal Democratic party (LDP). There was no ideological difference at that time between the CDU and the LDP which would have justified two parties. Soviet political officers, however, insisted that the two working-class parties be balanced by two bourgeois parties since a single antisocialist party might have become too powerful.

Whatever chance the Communist party may have had to accomplish the voluntary conversion of the Germans was ruined by the behavior of Soviet troops and by the booty and reparations practices of the Soviet Union. The invading Soviet soldiers engaged in an orgy of plunder and rape without regard to the laws and usages of war. Furthermore, the Soviet army appropriated for its needs whatever it thought necessary, without considering the needs of the civilian economy. While the western Allies brought their rations with them, the Soviet army's policy of "living off the land" resulted in a food shortage which created serious discontent. Without waiting for the end of hostilities or the allocation of capital equipment by the Allied Control Authority, the Soviets began the frantic dismantling of all kinds of industrial equipment, much of which could not be moved without being ruined in the process. The result of all this was that the Communist party, which was identified by the public as an instrument of Soviet policy, was unable to make any significant headway in free competition with other parties.

By the end of 1945 the Soviets began to realize that communism could be propagated in Germany only by force. They changed their tactics accordingly and began a campaign of pressure and bribery designed to force the merger of the Communist party with its most important competitor, the Social Democratic party. Although a referendum held in March, 1946, in the western sectors of Berlin indicated that over 80 per cent of the members of the Social Democratic party opposed the merger, the SPD members in the Soviet Zone never had a chance to vote on the question.[2] The Soviet Military Administration saw to it that those party functionaries in the zone who opposed the merger were removed from office, arrested, or intimidated into silence. On April 19 and 20 a so-called "national convention" (which was boycotted by leaders from West Berlin and the western zones) voted to merge the Social Democratic party with the Communist party. At the same time the latter held a similar convention and on April 21, 1946, the two groups joined to form the Socialist Unity party (SED).

The new party was initially organized on the principle of equal representation of former members of the KPD and of the SPD in all offices and committees, beginning with the fourteen-member secretariat which was to rule the party. Actually this scheme favored the Communists, since the SPD had been numerically much larger than KPD. There were two chairmen. The Communist chairman was Wilhelm Pieck, who together with Ernst Thälmann had ruled the KPD before 1933 and who since 1945 had been its leading public figure. It was generally agreed, however, that the actual power was wielded by Walter Ulbricht, an individual of considerably greater energy and acumen who was also apparently on closer terms with the Soviet political advisers. On the Social Democratic side, the chairman (with authority supposedly equal to Pieck's) was Otto Grotewohl, leader of the party in the Soviet Zone; other important figures were Max Fechner and Erich Gniffke. All three of these had been formally read out of the SPD by its new Berlin Central Committee, elected on April 7, 1946, by a convention of antimerger delegates.

The SED is the chosen instrument for Soviet domination of the DDR and for the co-ordination of infiltration, sabotage, and public disturbances in Western Germany. It operates according to the Leninist-Stalinist principle of "democratic centralism." The individual party member is bound to iron discipline (backed up by an internal party "thought police" and a system of concentration camps) without regard to his own opinion or conscience.

Like all other Communist parties, the Socialist Unity party has organized and controls a number of "mass organizations." These organizations were originally devices for assisting the SED to gain political power. Now that this power has been achieved, they tend to function as instruments of government. The most important of these organizations are as follows:

[2] For additional discussion of elections and parties in the Soviet Zone, see Chapters 19 and 20 below.

a. *The Free German Trade Union Federation*—The FDGB is a trade-union monopoly with about 5,000,000 members and resembling the Nazi-controlled German Labor Front. The member unions are controlled closely by the Central Board of the FDGB, which regulates their finances under a consolidated budget. The FDGB has propagandized extensively for an all-German trade-union body, but unions in Western Germany and West Berlin refuse to join an organization dominated by Communists. Of late, the FDGB has concentrated on propaganda for the economic plans of the DDR and for the piece-work system. It is an instrument for controlling the workers, not for representing them.

b. *The Free German Youth (FDJ)*—This organization has a monopoly of all youth activities, including sports and recreation, and is subsidized by the government and the SED. Young people in the DDR are put under considerable pressure to join. Recently the FDJ has been used for political purposes, such as attempting to break the Berlin (S-Bahn) rapid-transit strike in 1949 and "marching on Berlin" at Whitsuntide in 1950. It has secured a foothold in Western Germany.

c. *The Democratic Womens' Association (DFD)*—The DFD has about 200,000 members. It has succeeded in drawing large numbers of women into public life and specializes in "peace" activities.

d. *The Peasants' Mutual Aid (VdGB)*—This is an organization which farmers must join in order to receive seed and fertilizer and to be assigned delivery quotas which they can fulfill. It also plays a role in the gradual collectivization of agriculture. Because of its farmer membership the VdGB has at times been more unruly than the other "mass organizations."

e. *The Cultural League for the Democratic Renewal of Germany*—The "Kulturbund" undertakes to co-ordinate art, literature, and music in accordance with Stalinist principles and endeavors to see to it that the artist is politically conscious, that he reflects "triumphant socialism" in his work, and that he does not commit the sin of "formalism."[3]

f. *Association of Victims of the Nazi Regime (VVN)*—This associa-

---

[3] Although Soviet savants have written elaborate treatises on the subject of "formalism" (for instance, J. Fried, "Formalism as the Enemy of Art" in the July, 1948, issue of *Soviet Literature*), the term refers essentially to art which is considered to be decadent while not class conscious and particularly to art which cannot be easily understood by the masses. Surrealist and abstract painting, psychoanalytical and existentialist fiction and drama, and atonal music fall under this latter taboo. The hue and cry against "formalism" was apparently started by Stalin. After hearing Shostakovich's unconventional opera Lady Macbeth of Mzinsk, he is reported to have rebuked the composer by telling him: "I want you to compose a tune which I can whistle."

tion of persons imprisoned or otherwise injured by the Nazis exists all through Germany. In the western zones it has been rent by internal dissensions, and its non-Communist leaders have resigned. In the Soviet Zone it is firmly controlled by the SED.

One of the principal devices introduced during the early occupation period for the purpose of achieving Communist domination of the Soviet Zone was the Unity Committee of Antifascist Democratic Parties, known as the "Antifa." The Central Committee of the "Antifa" was founded in 1945 with equal representation for each of the four licensed parties. Similar committees were then established for each *Land,* each county, and each community. The purpose of the "Antifa" was to agree in advance on important decisions to be taken by parliaments, county or city councils, and executive organs. In practice this meant agreeing to the decisions wanted by the Communists since they were known to have the support of the SMA, the political police (MGB) of which was becoming increasingly active.

Following the merger of the KPD and SPD to form the SED, the "Antifas" were enlarged by the inclusion of the SED-controlled "mass organizations" with voting powers equal to those of the political parties. This maneuver gave the SED a firm control over the "Antifas" and also served to undermine the parliamentary system. While officially being the repositories of public power, the *Landtage,* county assemblies, and municipal councils actually degenerated to the status of rubber stamps approving the decisions made in private by small committees under Communist domination.

In 1946 the Soviets were not yet ready to make an open break with the principle of free political activity. They allowed the *Land* and local elections in October of that year to be held in at least reasonable conformity with democratic standards, counting on the candidates of the "mass organizations" (the true nature of which was not yet fully recognized) to bolster the SED so as to give that party a working majority in all representative bodies. They did, however, begin a policy of repression against the Christian Democratic Union and the Liberal Democratic party designed to bring the SED gradually into a position of absolute political dominance. By requiring local groups of the bourgeois parties to register with the SMA and then refusing to accept the registration, it was possible to restrict the extent of their activity. In many cases bourgeois candidates for municipal and county office were disapproved without any reason being given. It was possible, by attending internal party meetings and ordering the dismissal of functionaries who displayed effective opposition to the SED, to reduce the CDU and the LDP gradually to the status of puppet parties.

The system of "bloc politics" under the aegis of the "Antifas" and later of the "People's Committees" served to reduce further their effectiveness by depriving them of the opportunity to challenge SED policies in public. The SMA also took care that SED members were given preference in public employment, only small quotas of positions being "allocated" to the other parties.

THE GERMAN CENTRAL AGENCIES OF THE SOVIET ZONE

On July 27, 1945, Marshal Zhukov, then Commander in Chief of the Soviet Military Administration, issued an ordinance establishing twelve German central agencies for the Soviet Zone, with headquarters in Berlin. These agencies were completely independent from one another. At this time the course of the negotiations taking place at Potsdam indicated that a series of German central agencies for all four zones would be established under quadripartite Allied control. This project was blocked in 1945 and early 1946 not so much by the Soviets as by the French, who were not a party to the Potsdam Agreement. It was evident that the Soviets intended to steal a march on the Allies by presenting them with a series of complete and functioning government departments, staffed with officials whom the Soviets had selected.[4]

Each agency had a president and one or more vice-presidents. The number of employees of the larger agencies varied between 200 and 600. From time to time new agencies were added; the complete list as of June, 1947, was as follows:

a. Transportation
b. Post and Telegraph
c. Fuel and Power
d. Trade and Supply
e. Industry
f. Finance
g. Agriculture and Forests
h. Labor and Social Welfare
i. Culture
j. Justice
k. Health
l. Interior
m. Statistics
n. Resettlement
o. Interzonal and Foreign Trade

The contention that the agencies were established for political rather than administrative reasons is supported by the fact (reported repeat-

[4] To make the agencies acceptable to the other occupying powers, the Soviets appointed several prominent non-Communists to important positions, such as Dr. Friedensburg (CDU, later *Bürgermeister* of Berlin) to the presidency of the Central Administration for Fuel and Power and Dr. Buschmann (SPD) to that of the Central Administration for Trade and Supply. In September, 1946, the Soviets dismissed Friedensburg; shortly afterward Buschmann (who had joined the SED but was in disagreement with the party leadership) resigned.

edly by West Berlin papers) that the employees had relatively little to do. In default of actual duties they spent considerable time studying Russian, dialectical materialism, and other educational subjects. During a period of extreme shortages they were granted special rations of liquor and of potatoes and other foods, priorities for railroad tickets, and special rates at vacation resorts.

During the period up to June, 1947, the German central agencies were purely advisory. They had no power to issue or enforce orders to the *Land* governments. Such orders as were given from Berlin to the *Länder* were issued by the SMA itself. The number of formal ordinances issued by Marshal Zhukov and his successor Marshal Sokolovsky totaled at least 125 during 1945, and during the next two years it was considerably larger. Even if the Soviets had given the agencies a free hand, it would have been difficult for them to establish effective control over their counterpart ministries in the *Länder*. During the early period of the occupation, the railroad system in the Soviet Zone was in such a chaotic condition that traveling was slow and uncertain. Practically all the telephones and telegraph equipment had been dismantled or requisitioned for military use, and motor vehicles and gasoline were almost unobtainable. These difficulties of communication would have in any case prevented effective administrative control.

The result was that the central agencies functioned mainly as planning groups. They proposed policies and orders to the respective branches of the SMA at Berlin-Karlshorst, which made the decisions and transmitted them through the *Land* SMA's to the German *Land* governments. The Communist party and later the SED participated in the negotiations between the central agency officials and their Soviet opposites; Walter Ulbricht was said to be one of the principal middlemen between the central agencies and the Soviets. Unfortunately much of this planning was thrown out of joint by the fact that Soviet policy and action in different functional fields are often badly coordinated. Each of the operating divisions of the SMA was controlled to a considerable extent by a functional ministry in Moscow which could give it orders over the head of the Soviet Commander in Chief in Germany. In particular, the agency responsible for economic planning was not co-ordinated with the agency which collected reparations. The result was that economic plans were repeatedly thrown into confusion by the unexpected dismantling and removal of industrial equipment needed for their execution.

The authority of the central agencies was further restricted by the principle, apparently sanctioned by the Soviets, that they were not really governmental bodies. In the April, 1947, issue of *Die Versorgung*, organ of the Central Administration for Trade and Supply, it was declared that the central agencies were not *Behörden* (governmental administrative offices) since they did not represent any legal territorial organization. The *Länder* had no control over them, and the zone itself was not an entity in German law so long as it had no constitution. The conclusion was drawn that the agencies were independent public corporations deriving their powers exclusively by delegation from the SMA.[5]

During 1946 several central agencies began to establish a degree of administrative control over their counterpart ministries on *Land* level. The first of these was the Central Administration for Trade and Supply, which set up a corps of inspectors to check food distribution in the cities and rural counties as well as administrative operations in *Land* food offices. In November, 1946, the SMA authorized the Central Administration for Labor and Social Welfare to issue ordinances and instructions to the *Länder* concerning labor affairs, wages, welfare, and social insurance. In October, 1946, a new Central Administration for the Interior was established for the express purpose of taking over direct control of all police forces in the Soviet Zone. While the agency originally was kept carefully under wraps it now functions under the euphemistic title "People's Police" (*Volkspolizei*).

THE GERMAN ECONOMIC COMMISSION (DWK)

By the end of 1946 it was apparent that the original quadripartite plan to establish German central agencies under the aegis of the Allied Control Council would not be realized within the foreseeable future. The French had been brought into line, but now the Soviets were refusing to co-operate. In December, 1946, Secretary of State Byrnes and Foreign Minister Bevin concluded their agreement for economic fusion of the United States and British zones of Germany. While maintaining a steady barrage of newspaper and radio propaganda and of protests in the Control Council and through diplomatic channels against the bizonal merger, the Soviets refused to take advantage of the clause in the Byrnes-Bevin agreement permitting other zones to join in economic fusion. Instead, they began the first steps toward creation of their own zonal economic adminsitration. In February, 1947, the SMA dictated an "agreement" between the German central agencies and the *Land* governments by which the former were assigned definite responsibilities in the fields of planning, control of raw

[5] See discussion of German governments as "agents" of occupation in Chapter 2 above.

materials, and production goals as well as over-all control over the coal industry. This "agreement" was entered into somewhat grudgingly by the *Land* governments.

In June, 1947, presumably as a countermove to the establishment of the Bizonal Economic Council at Frankfurt, Marshal Sokolovsky announced the formation of a permanent Economic Commission for the Soviet Zone, the operations of which were to be based on the February agreement. This commission consisted of the presidents of the Central Administrations for Industry, Transportation, Fuel and Power, Agriculture and Forests, and Trade and Supply plus the chairmen of two "mass organizations," the Free German Trade Union Federation and the Peasants' Mutual Aid. At its first meeting, held June 24, 1947, the commission elected Bruno Leuschner, general secretary of the SED, as its administrative offcer.

In spite of a lively start, the Economic Commission failed to establish its authority over the *Land* governments, and the *Land* SMA's continued to give out orders which conflicted with those of the commission. The one accomplishment of the commission during the summer of 1947, a directive on food distribution, was invalidated on September 1 by the SMA. The statement of reasons for this action was so flimsy as to suggest that the SMA did not care to state the real reason. Evidently there had been a change in Soviet policy immediately after the establishment of the commission. Moscow was still trying to obtain a unified Germany (under Communist control) and considered it too early to create a powerful governmental body in the Soviet Zone. With the breakdown of the London Conference of Foregin Ministers in December, 1947, and the subsequent steps of U.S. and British Military Government to strengthen the Bizonal Economic Council, Soviet policy changed again. This time the signals were set for all-out centralization.

On February 12, 1948, Marshal Sokolovsky issued Order No. 32, reorganizing and expanding the functions of the Economic Commission and renaming it "German Economic Commission" (*Deutsche Wirtschafts-Kommission* or DWK.) The commission was enlarged by the addition of the Central Administrations for Post and Telegraph, Labor and Social Welfare, Finance, Interzonal and Foreign Trade, Statistics, and Resettlement and of one representative each from the five *Länder* of the Soviet Zone. Its functions were (a) to co-ordinate the activities of the Central Economic Administration, (b) to supervise the punctual delivery of reparations and to fulfill the needs of the occupation forces, and (c) to issue instructions (pursuant to SMA orders) legally binding on all levels of German government. Although order No. 32 suggested that the central agencies would continue to exist as before, the DWK issued after its first meeting a series of regulations converting them into subordinate main divisions (*Hauptabteilungen*) of the DWK. The entire administration was placed under the supervision of the new full-time president of the DWK, one Heinrich Rau, a gentleman whose name has been repeatedly mentioned by the Berlin press in connection with unsavory financial transactions. Rau began immediately to purge all high officials whose subservience to the SMA was doubtful, such as President Skrzypczynski and Vice-President Mischler of the Central Administration for Industry and Vice-Presidents Ziegelmeier, Benecke, and Gleitze of the Central Administrations of Trade and Supply, Agriculture and Forests and Finance, respectively.

As of May, 1948, the DWK had the following main divisions:

a. Coal and Gasoline
b. Electricity and Gas
c. Metallurgy
d. Machine Tools and Electrical Industry
e. Chemical Industry
f. Light Industry
g. Stone and Earth Industries
h. Agriculture and Forestry
i. Transportation
j. Interzonal and Foreign Trade
k. Post and Telegraph
l. Trade and Supply
m. Finance and Banking
n. Labor and Social Welfare
o. Public Health
p. Statistics
q. Material Supply
r. Economic Planning

Each main division was headed by a director with one or more deputies.

Although an administrative agency, the DWK was given substantial legislative powers. On the basis of these powers it proceeded to enact a series of laws designed to destroy private enterprise and to pave the way for complete socialization in the Soviet Zone. The two most important of these laws were:

a. *The Economic Punishment Law* (*Wirtschaftsstrafgesetz*)—This law established a series of commissions, supervised by the DWK, with the power to determine administratively that a businessman was guilty of "economic sabotage" and to order confiscation of his property. The crime of "economic sabotage" was not defined in the law, and no appeal could brought against decisions of the commissions.

b. *The Requisitioning Law* (*Anforderungsgesetz*)—This law, which expanded the provisions of the Nazi requisitioning law (*Reichsleistungsgesetz*), empowered the DWK or any *Land* minister of economics to issue administrative orders requiring any business concern to

rent or sell movable or immovable objects at administratively determined prices, to surrender legal rights, to conclude or refrain from
concluding contracts, or to cease business altogether.

Shortly after granting the DWK its increased powers, the SMA
issued Directive No. 234 calling for the increase of production, supposedly through the introduction of more efficient methods. The real
purpose of this order was revealed by Chairman Pieck of the SED,
who declared to the students of the Karl Marx School that although
the Communists in the west would continue to fight the piecework
system as "capitalistic exploitation of the workers" they would themselves introduce it in Eastern Germany. The piecework system was,
said Pieck, "the only system for getting efficient production." In September, 1947, the DWK issued a series of "Principles for Production"
implementing the Soviet directive.

The essence of the legislation enacted by the DWK was to grant
itself greater and greater power. The final step in the development of
an absolute economic dictatorship was the consolidation of most of the
larger factories, which had already been socialized by SED-dominated
Land governments, into the "Unions of Public Enterprises" (*Verein-
igungen der volkseigenen Betriebe*). These giant trusts, which were
later taken over by the Ministry of Industry of the DDR, control in
their own right 40 per cent of the industrial production of the Soviet
Zone. Their operations are kept secret by the fact that all audits and investigations are made by the "Auditing and Trustee Office (*Revisions-
und Treuhandanstalt*) of Leipzig which was itself owned by the DWK
and has since been taken over by the government of the DDR as a
subordinate executive agency. The DWK achieved further control
over Soviet Zone industry by establishing the German Investment
Bank and granting that institution power to approve or disapprove all
capital expenditures over 10,000 marks.

The only three German central agencies of the Soviet Zone which
remained outside the DWK were the Central Administrations for the
Interior, for Justice, and for Popular Education. These were not granted any powers to legislate, but they were given such extensive administrative powers as to make legislative authority superfluous. In
addition to exercising powers specifically granted to them by Soviet
ordinance, all three of these agencies adopted the practice of holding
monthly meetings of the *Land* ministers in their respective fields. At
these meetings "decisions" were adopted which were then considered
to be binding on the individual *Land* ministers. This procedure, which
sidetracked both the *Landtage* and the *Land* cabinets, was dependent
on the Communist principle of "democratic centralism" and on the

fact that the SED provided an effective vehicle for enforcing the decisions. Since the "decisions" officially made by the ministers were regularly prepared in advance by the Central Administration in collaboration with the Central Secretariat of the SED, the effect was to nullify both the federalist principle and the *Land* constitutions. As SED leader Ulbricht stated in a speech during the summer of 1948, the *Land* authorities were from now on to undertake new activities only after consultation with the appropriate central agency.

THE VOLKSKONGRESS MOVEMENT

Although it is evident from the foregoing that the Soviet Zone had in fact a zonal government by the middle of 1948, this government was still operating on the basis of authority granted directly by the SMA. The necessary steps toward the legitimation of this "unofficial" government as an official German government were undertaken by the SED. Inasmuch as the Communist theory of "people's democracy" demanded the appearance of a popular movement, the party leadership was faced with the task of producing and manipulating a "spontaneous" upsurge of the people. The first steps in this direction took place late in 1947. At this time the fifth session of the Council of Foreign Ministers was still in progress at London, and none of the western Allies had made any official statements about a constitution for Western Germany.

On November 26, 1947, the Central Committee of the SED held an extraordinary meeting which passed unanimously a resolution introduced by Cochairman Pieck, calling for the formation of a "German People's Congress for the Unity of Germany and a Just Peace." The first meeting of this People's Congress (*Volkskongress*) was opened on December 6 in the Soviet Sector of Berlin. The 2,215 delegates, some of whom represented the KPD and other leftist organizations in Western Germany, had been selected so as to permit the SED, with the help of its controlled "mass organizations," to wield an easy majority. The Congress elected a Permanent Committee and passed a resolution, conforming exactly to the demands of Foreign Minister Molotov, which was to be presented to the London Conference as the wish of the German people. Upon refusal of the three western Foreign Ministers to receive the delegation from the *Volkskongress*, the London Conference of the Council of Foreign Ministers broke up in disagreement.

Early in January, 1948, the Permanent Committee of the *Volkskongress* planned a second session of the Congress to be held early in March and began the organization of a series of "People's Committees" on *Land,* county, and municipal level. These committees were in their membership largely identical with the already existing "Antifa Committees" and, like their predecessors, had the function of carrying on the "bloc politics" within their respective governmental units. The extension of *Volkskongress* activity into the western zones and the western sectors of Berlin was prohibited by the occupying powers. The SMA did, however, manage to circulate on January 19 in parts of West Berlin a petition calling for a new People's Congress. On January 21 a "People's Congress of Greater Berlin" resolved to demand a referendum to be held throughout Germany on the "Unity of Germany" and on the formation of a so-called German People's Council (*Deutscher Volksrat*).

On March 17, 1948, the second *Volkskongress* met in Berlin and passed two resolutions prepared by the Permanent Committee. The first of these called for election of a German People's Council of 400 members with advisory and some executive powers. The second called for the circulation between May 23 and June 13 of initiative petitions on the question of "German unity." The *Volksrat,* which was elected by the *Volkskongress* the following day, established a Presidium with Wilhelm Pieck (SED), Wilhelm Kuelz (LDP), and Otto Nuschke (CDU) as cochairmen. It also set up committees for the drafting of a constitution, the peace treaty, economics, justice, cultural affairs, and socialization. In spite of the declaration of General Clay that canvassing for signatures to the initiative petition would not be permitted in areas under U.S. control, the Presidium began to make plans for circulating it in all parts of Germany. On April 27 the Constitutional Committee began the drafting of a constitution for the Soviet Zone and, by implication, for the whole of Germany.

The initiative petition was circulated according to plan throughout the Soviet Zone between May 23 and June 13, 1948, the canvassing methods being such that those who refused to sign were subjected to threats of political or economic persecution. A small number of petitions were circulated illegally in the western sectors and zones. On June 14 the Soviet-licensed news agency ADN reported that 13,000,000 signatures had been collected, a figure which cannot be verified, since the names were counted in secret.

During the rest of 1948 the *Volksrat* and its Presidium engaged in continuous and energetic propaganda activity. The *Volksrat* passed from time to time resolutions demanding abandonment of plans for a west German state and establishment of an all-German government, a uniform currency, and full accounting for reparations. In each case the wording of the resolution was such as to suggest that the western powers had prevented the realization of these objectives. The *Volksrat* also concerned itself with "settlement" of the dispute on the Berlin blockade, with revising the distribution system in the Soviet Zone so as to provide a new "free market" with higher-than-normal prices, and with the issuance of new identity cards. Emphasis was also placed on the demand for conclusion of a peace treaty and withdrawal of occupation troops, and much was made of the fact that the Soviet Union was already in the process of withdrawing its troops from North Korea.

A degree of co-ordination between the *Volksrat* and the German Economic Commission (DWK) was achieved through an order of Marshal Sokolovsky of November 26, 1948, by which the full body of the DWK was expanded to 101 members, including 48 from the political parties and 10 from the SED-controlled mass organizations. The result was an overlapping of the DWK with the *Volksrat*, particularly with its Economic Committee. Simultaneously President Rau of the DWK began the practice of submitting reports to the *Volksrat* as though it were an official zonal parliament.

Professor Steiniger of Berlin University (SED), Dr. Polak (SED), and Dr. Brandt (CDU) had been charged with preparing the first draft of a constitution for the Soviet Zone government. This draft was discussed at a meeting of the Constitution Committee on July 6, 1948, and a "statement of principles" adopted. The committee continued its work throughout the summer and autumn, and future developments were indicated by a resolution passed by an expanded meeting of another committee of the *Volksrat* calling for the election of delegates to a third *Volkskongress* to be held in Berlin. On October 29 the completed constitution was given its first publication in the overt Soviet organ *Tägliche Rundschau* under the title "A Constitution for the German Democratic Republic." The implication that the constitution was intended for the whole of Germany was underlined by the action taken by the Peace Committee of the *Volksrat* on the following day. On the occasion of Stalin's statement that agreement on the Berlin situation had twice been rejected by the western powers, the committee appealed to "democratic" public opinion in America, Britain, and France to induce the governments of these countries to reconvene the Council of Foreign Ministers for the immediate preparation of a German peace treaty.

On March 19, 1949, Wilhelm Pieck announced at a meeting of the *Volksrat* that a third *Volkskongress* would be elected shortly to take action on establishing a government for the Soviet Zone. The same meeting adopted the draft constitution without argument. The me-

chanics of the election were explained on the following day in the
Tägliche Rundschau by Wilhelm Koenen of the *Volksrat's* Secretariat.
Seats in the new Congress were to be apportioned in advance between
the parties and the mass organizations, and there would be only one
list of candidates on which the citizens could vote "yes" or "no." The
SED allotted itself only 450 out of an estimated 2,000 delegates. The
addition of the mass organizations and of two new satellite parties,
the National Democratic party (NDP) and the Democratic Peasants'
party (DBP), both controlled behind the scenes by the SED, assured
that the forthcoming Congress would be as tightly controlled as in the
past.

The action of the *Volksrat* provided the occasion for much vehement
criticism in the West Berlin press and radio. Emphasis was placed on
the fact that the constitution closely resembled that of the U.S.S.R.
and that *Volkskongress* and *Volksrat* were both puppet organizations
which only echoed the policies already formulated in Moscow. It was
also evident that considerable opposition to the constitution existed in
both the Liberal Democratic party and the Christian Democratic
Union in the Soviet Zone, in spite of the fact that the SMA had removed independent party leaders, such as Kaiser and Lemmer of the
CDU, who had objected to the tactics of the *Volkskongress*. To combat this unfavorable publicity, the *Volksrat* and the SED launched a
high-pressure propaganda campaign in the Soviet Zone press and
radio, distributed millions of pamphlets, and subjected the citizens to
almost daily political rallies at which attendance was compulsory.
The *Volksrat* also attempted to have the election held in all four
sectors of Berlin, but this was flatly refused by the western comman-
dants.

The election of delegates to the third *Volkskongress* was held on
May 15 and 16, 1949, in the Soviet Zone and the Soviet Sector of
Berlin. In spite of a number of irregularities in vote counting and a
ballot which made it difficult for voters to know whether they were
voting "yes" or "no," there was at least some opportunity for the voters
to express their opinions. The new *Volkskongress* was legitimated by
at most 58.7 per cent of the voters (not taking into account the numerous claims that the returns had been falsified), and the Presidium
of the *Volksrat* proceeded to call it into session on May 20 and 30,
1949, to act upon the agenda as planned. Since the membership included a number of Communist-selected delegates from Western
Germany, the *Volkskongress* proceeded to announce that it was "the
only national, all-German governmental representation."

On May 30, 1949, the third *Volkskongress* elected a new *Volksrat* consisting of 400 members, 70 of whom were from Western Germany. The election was by unanimous ballot on the basis of a single list following closely the percentages of delegates making up the Congress itself. The Presidium of the *Volksrat* was simultaneously enlarged from twenty-nine to thirty-eight, all from the Soviet Zone. On the same day the *Volkskongress* approved the constitution of the German Democratic Republic though it took no steps to put this constitution into effect.

PROVISIONAL GOVERNMENT OF THE DEUTSCHE DEMOKRATISCHE REPUBLIK

The *Volksrat* met twice during the summer of 1949. In one meeting it protested against the August 14 elections in the German Federal Republic. In the other it "recognized" the Oder-Neisse boundary with Poland. The *Volksrat* did nothing about putting the constitution of the German Democratic Republic into effect: the problem of doing so without an election was a difficult one. Eventually a solution for the problem was found and put into effect. October 2, 1949, was proclaimed as "World Peace Day," and on this day the workers in shops, offices, and factories as well as the local branches of political parties and "mass organizations" began to pass resolutions demanding the formation of a "provisional democratic government for the whole of Germany." The Presidium of the *Volksrat* then called a plenary session of that body for October 7, 1949. At the same time it resolved to request the *Volksrat* to assume the functions of a "provisional People's Chamber" (*Volkskammer*) on the basis of the constitution and to form a "constitutional government of the German Democratic Republic." This resolution was passed only after a bitter struggle in which the LDP and the CDU had demanded the holding of elections, only to meet with an absolute veto from the Soviets.

The *Volksrat* met on October 7 as scheduled. Before taking up its other business it adopted a "Manifesto of the National Front," the significance of which is explained further on, and a resolution addressed to the foreign ministers of the four occupying powers. The *Volksrat* then adopted a "Law on the Formation of the Provisional People's Chamber of the German Democratic Republic." Through this "law" it transformed itself into a provisional People's Chamber (*Volkskammer*) and authorized itself to exercise the functions of that body until the next elections, which in the meantime had been set for October 15, 1950. After electing a new Presidium, the *Volksrat*—now the *Volkskammer*—passed a "Law on the Provisional Government of the German Democratic" which determined the composition of the cabinet. It then passed a "Law on the Formation of the Provisional *Länder* Chamber" and a "Law on the Constitution of the German Democratic Republic." The latter had the effect of putting the constitution into effect simultaneously with the passage of the law, this is, after the *Volksrat* had assumed the functions of the *Volkskammer*. The provisional *Volkskammer* concluded its session by electing Otto Grotewohl Minister-President.

The next step in the organization of the DDR was the calling of a special session of the *Landtag* in each of the five *Länder*, for the purpose of electing delegates representing the *Land* in the provisional *Länder* chamber (*Länderkammer*). These sessions, which were held October 10, 1949, also passed identical laws (which were in open conflict with the *Land* constitutions) postponing the *Landtag* and local government elections to correspond with the *Volkskammer* election on October 15, 1950. On the same day the Commander in Chief of the SMA, General Tschuikov, informed the Presidium of the *Volkskammer* that the Soviet Union had decided to transfer to the provisional government of the DDR those functions which up to then had been exercised by the SMA. The Soviet Military Administration itself would be replaced by a Soviet Control Commission, which would supervise the fulfillment of the Potsdam Agreement and other quadripartite decisions concerning Germany. The *Volkskammer* and the *Länderkammer* held a joint meeting on October 11 in which, by prearrangement, Wilhelm Pieck was elected unanimously as President of the German Democratic Republic.

The final step in the organization of the provisional government of the DDR was a session of the *Volkskammer* on October 12, 1949, at which Minister-President Grotewohl introduced his cabinet. Having introduced his cabinet and declared the policy of his government, Minister-President Grotewohl then obtained a unanimous vote of confidence from the *Volkskammer*. A "Law on the Transfer of the Administration" was then passed. This law clothed the cabinet with the functions of former DWK and transferred the operating divisions of the DWK as well as the Central Administrations for the Interior, Justice, and Popular Education to the appropriate ministries of the DDR. The cabinet was authorized to develop the necessary organization plans to implement the law; these plans were to be "laid before" the *Volkskammer*. A further provision of the law continued the budget of the DWK as the budget of the DDR and authorized the cabinet to determine administratively any necessary changes. On the evening of October 12 the cabinet was formally sworn into office by President Pieck.

The constitution of the German Democratic Republic is based in its essential points on the "Stalin Consitution" adopted in 1936 in the Soviet Union. The most significant structural feature which the constitution of the DDR borrows from the Soviet Constitution is the emphatic rejection of the separation-of-powers principle and the granting of complete and unlimited governmental power to the parliamentary bodies on the national, state, and local levels. This principle had already made its appearance in the constitutions and local government laws adopted by the *Länder* of the Soviet Zone in 1946 and 1947.

Both the Soviet Russian and Soviet German constitutions provide a theoretically all-powerful parliament. The cabinet is in theory very weak; it can be removed at any time by a vote of nonconfidence in the parliament and has no power to dissolve that body. In practice, this type of constitutional structure is unworkable without the parallel, extraconstitutional, principle of "democratic centralism." That is to say, the parliament must itself be controlled behind the scenes by a single party or a tightly knit political bloc which is, for practical purposes, identical with the cabinet. To put it another way, the structure incorporated in the constiution of the DDR seems at first to be extremely democratic though actually it is made to order for a democratic "front" coupled with a behind-the-scenes dictatorship.

The constitution of the DDR is strictly centralistic. It prescribes the constitutional structure of the *Länder* (which the Basic Law of the German Federal Republic does not) and also gives the national parliament wide powers to change *Land* boundaries without the consent of the *Länder* concerned. In addition to a long list of subjects on which the DDR has the exclusive right to legislate, it also has a right of legislation, concurrent with that of the *Länder*, for all other subjects.[6] The DDR has, furthermore, the right to take over the direct administration of whatever governmental functions it chooses and to establish its own regional and field offices for this purpose. So far as the *Länder* are charged with administration of the laws of the DDR, the central government has an unlimited right of instruction and supervision. It may also send its own commissars into the *Land* agencies with authority to give orders to *Land* officials. These provisions stand in sharpest contrast to those of the west German Basic Law.

The principal house of the parliament of the DDR is the *Volkskammer,* which consists of 400 members elected directly by the voters

[6] Note the contrast with the distribution of powers set out in the Bonn Constitution articles.

for four years, theoretically by secret ballot and proportional representation. Its powers are:

   a. To determine the principles of governmental policy and the methods for its execution.

   b. To confirm, supervise, and recall the cabinet.

   c. To determine the principles of administration and to supervise the entire activity of the State.

   d. To enact legislation, except as laws may be enacted by referendum.

   e. To decide on the budget, the economic plan, loans, and credits of the DDR and to ratify international treaties.

   f. To declare amnesties.

   g. In joint session with the *Länderkammer* to elect the President of the DDR.

   h. To elect and recall the members of the Supreme Court and the Attorney General of the DDR.

The upper house of the parliament is the *Länderkammer* (Chamber of States), the members of which are elected by the *Landtage* (*Land* parliaments), normally from among their own members. Inasmuch as this election must be proportional to the party strength in the *Landtage,* the political composition of the *Länderkammer* is likely to be similar to that of the *Volkskammer*. The *Länderkammer* may veto legislation passed by the *Volkskammer,* but the *Volkskammer* may override the veto by a simple majority vote in normal cases. A two-thirds majority of those present in the *Volkskammer* is required when the *Länderkammer* has adopted its veto by such a majority.

Constitutional amendments are adopted by a two-thirds majority of members present in the *Volkskammer* (with a quorum of two-thirds of the legal number of members) or by simple majority vote followed by a referendum of the voters. The constitution makes a concession to German tradition by providing a President of the DDR. The President has, however, no substantial powers and can be removed at any time by vote of two-thirds of the legal number of members of both houses of parliament.

The Soviet Military Administration has generally insisted that the Minister-President be designated by the party having the largest individual parliamentary fraction (the SED). This principle is incorporated specifically in the constitution of the DDR. All fractions with forty or more members in the *Volkskammer* are entitled to seats on the cabinet if they choose to participate in the government, including any fractions of "mass organizations" which reach that figure. Theoretically the cabinet may be dismissed by a vote of nonconfidence.

The nonconfidence motion must, however, be coupled with the nomination of a new Minister-President. Should the candidate so elected fail to assume office within twenty-one days after passage of the motion, the vote of nonconfidence is automatically canceled. This provision, coupled with the provision that the largest fraction must designate the Minister-President, provides a method whereby the majority, if it should conceivably revolt against Communist domination, could not remove the Communist cabinet. If the *Volkskammer* should wish to remove the SED Minister-President, it would have to ask the SED to propose a new candidate for that office and the SED could produce a deadlock by refusing to do so.

The constitution contains a reasonably adequate bill of rights, including many of the "rights of labor" which appear in the Soviet Russian Constitution. These rights are not, however, backed up by any effective judicial review: judges are specifically denied the right to question the constitutionality of a law. There is a Constitutional Committee charged with examining the validity of laws, but this committee is elected by the *Volkskammer* and is only advisory, the final decision remaining with the *Volkskammer* itself. The independence of the judiciary is negated by a provision that all judges are subject to recall at any time by the political bodies which elect them, whenever the political body considers that a judge has "neglected his duties."

The provisions of the constitution concerning political parties are designed to perpetuate the system of "bloc politics" which was introduced by the Soviets at the beginning of the occupation. Under this system not only political parties but also "democratic mass organizations" may nominate candidates for the various parliaments. It is then expected that the fractions will settle all important questions in secret "informal" meetings before they are discussed in open sessions of the representative bodies. The decision as to what organizations are "democratic" and therefore eligible to nominate candidates is left to the *Volkskammer* (presumably to the *Landtag* if the issue arises on *Land* level).

The constitution of the DDR contains other communistic touches. One of these is a provision declaring war propaganda and propaganda "inciting to the boycott of democratic organizations" or "inciting to the murder of democratic politicians" to be criminal acts. This language makes it a crime for anyone to organize an independent trade union in competition with the official "free" German Trade Union Federation. The establishment of the non-Communist "Independent Trade-Union Organization" (UGO) in West Berlin was clearly considered by the Soviet German politicians to be a criminal act. The constitution permits the abridgement of the most basic civil rights by legislation. It also states clearly that there will be socialization and economic planning and that the right of private property is limited to whatever the State chooses to allow.

THE ESTABLISHMENT OF ABSOLUTE
PARTY DICTATORSHIP

The adoption of the constitution and the creation of the provisional government of the German Democratic Republic did not complete the process of making Soviet Germany what it is today. These actions provided only the legal framework within which it was possible for the SED to complete the "revolutionary" process of establishing a "dictatorship of the proletariat," that is to say, a dictatorship of the Politburo. This process required reform within the SED itself. Since the beginning of the occupation, the SMA and the SED had followed the policy of giving SED members preference in public employment and of dismissing non-SED public servants when the slightest excuse (or often no excuse) could be found for doing so. This policy had been applied particularly sharply in 1948, at which time at least half of the non-SED employees of the Central Administrations for Justice and for Popular Culture and all of the 200 non-members in the Central Administration of the Interior had been dismissed, with the exception of those who promptly took out party cards. The same policy was applied in the *Land* and local governments, in the school system, in socialized enterprises, and in granting licenses, contracts, and supplies to private merchants and tradesmen.

The result of the foregoing policy was that the SED expanded to a total membership of approximately 1,800,000, the majority of which consisted of nominal members. There were few really active members outside the corps of about 250,000 functionaries, of whom, according to SPD circles, about 10 per cent receive direct or indirect remuneration. In view of the much smaller size of the Communist party in the Soviet Union and in most other countries, it seemed desirable to reduce the membership of the SED and simultaneously to develop the smaller party into a disciplined force. This change in tactics was first indicated at a party conference in the summer of 1948 by Walter Ulbricht, who stated the need for a "new technical intelligentsia" of the SED which could assume the direction of the Soviet Zone economy. Early in 1949 the shift was made official under the slogan of building a "party of the new type." There was established a Bureau for Political Education at headquarters, with organized "cadres" extending down to the cell of ten people. At the same time the substantial powers of the Central Secretariat were transferred to a seven-man "Politburo" containing only two former Social Democrats. At this time the policy of equal representation of the SPD and KPD elements in the SED was abandoned.

Shortly afterward the SED carried out its first "purge," which involved at least 100,000 members. Some of these had violated laws or regulations, but most of them were charged with "deviation" or with "not belonging economically to the working class." At the same time it was decided that candidates for party membership would have to serve a probationary period—one year for workers, two years for others. At the same time the SED undertook steps to strengthen its control over the "mass organizations." One of these, the Peasant's Mutual Aid (VdGB), had become increasingly independent and many of its local branches had developed into forums for anti-Communist sentiments. To correct this situation, the SED ordered the control of co-operative farm-machinery stations taken away from the local branches of the VdGB and centralized in district offices in charge of loyal SED officials. These were then able to restore discipline by withholding farm machinery from whose who strayed from the party line.

The reorganization of the SED on a hierarchical and disciplined basis was accompanied by a closer integration of the party with the Communist parties of the Soviet Union and of the Soviet satellites. Members of the SED Politburo attended several Cominform meetings as "observers," and numerous visitors from the Soviet Union and the Cominform countries appeared at the SED party convention in July, 1950. It was, however, apparent that the SED could never expect to base its power on genuine intellectual leadership, but would have to rely essentially on brute force. While this phenomenon is undoubtedly a constitutional disease of Communist parties generally, there were certain factors in the history of German communism which prevented the emergence in the SED of genuine intellectuals such as exist in the French Communist party. In order to understand more clearly the development of the SED it is desirable to go briefly into this historical background.

There is no doubt that many of the German Communists of the Weimar period were moved by genuine democratic ideals. There was a "left wing" within the party which carried on the tradition of the "Spartacus movement" and which operated under the motto "Independence from Stresemann and Stalin." By the end of the Weimar period this opposition had been fairly effectively liquidated, and the party was under the firm control of Ernst Thälmann and Wilhelm Pieck, both close adherents of Stalin. After the Nazis had assumed power in 1933, a number of German Communists who at one time or another had opposed Pieck and Thälmann sought refuge, nevertheless, in the Soviet Union. In 1939, after the Hitler-Stalin Pact had been concluded, the Soviet government, with Pieck's concurrence, turned 170 leading German Communists over to the Gestapo. Other German Communists, including many members of the *Reichstag*, were executed in Soviet concentration camps. The Moscow purges of the late thirties affected the exiles in the Soviet Union as much as the Russians. Only the more mediocre German Communists survived, and they found it necessary to become more or less "russified" as a means of becoming less conspicuous. Most of them assumed Soviet citizenship, many of them married Russian women, and a large number became officers in the Soviet army. When these functionaries returned to Germany, speaking German with a Russian accent, they were simply not accepted. Nor were they able to adapt their propaganda methods to German psychology. They were so infatuated with the Soviet Union and with Stalin that they attempted the impossible: to transplant the Stakhanov movement to Germany and to secure German approval of the cession of territories east of the Oder and the Neisse.

Since the SED was condemned by its own internal structure to be an instrument of Soviet colonial policy—German communism having long since been liquidated—there was nothing for it to do but purge those within its ranks who showed any independence. Since the SPD had been swallowed, it was necessary to get rid of those former SPD leaders who had believed that the SED would really be a *united* party. In the spring of 1950 there was a purge of public officials: from April to June forty-one mayors and twelve county commissioners (*Landräte*) were removed from the party and from office. The principal activity of the 1950 party conference was heretic hunting, and following the conference a number of other important party members were expelled.

Parallel with the "reform" of the SED the Deutsche Demokratische Republik has witnessed the growth of the complete apparatus of a police state of Soviet Russian type. On February 17, 1950, a new Ministry for State Security was established under the direction of the Training Section of the *Volks Polizei*. This individual, one Wilhelm Zaisser, had previously earned a reputation as "General Gomez," leader of the international brigades in the Spanish civil war. The Ministry for State Security, which corresponds to the ministry of the same name in the Soviet Union, has charge of the secret police and is in close touch with (and probably under the direction of) its Russian counterpart. A closely related agency is the State Control Commission, which exercises supervision over economic planning, the remnants of private enterprise, the combating of "industrial sabotage" and the like. A central Personnel Administration has been established in the Interior Ministry to screen the political records of all candidates for public employment. These controls extend into the *Land* and local governments, which have by now been reduced to the status of field offices of the central government of the DDR.

One of the most recent developments has been the creation of a corps of political commissars who are attached to the various administrative offices of the *Land* and local governments and who perform the functions formerly exercised by Soviet officers attached to the SMA. These commissars, known as *Instrukteure,* are organized on a centralized basis in each *Land.* The cabinet of Brandenburg, for instance, adopted on April 22, 1950, an ordinance requiring that the *Instrukteure* be qualified propagandists for the planned objectives of the State as well as for the "National Front." These officers constitute a "state within the State," a disciplined, tightly organized corps responsible for manipulating all affairs of government, economics, culture and social life in the DDR. Insofar as the *Instrukteure* are assigned to local governments, they are officially classified as assistants to the *Landräte* and *Oberbürgermeister.* Actually they have the power to give orders to these officials. The *Instrukteure* are controlled by the Division for Organizational Instruction in the *Land* ministry of the interior and are called together by that division for conferences once every two months.

It would be impossible within the scope of this single chapter to describe all the various ways in which the SED has expanded governmental power in the DDR so as to reach into every phase of society and to regulate the life of every citizen. Nor is there space to describe in detail the techniques used to regiment public opinion. An illustration in a single field, which may be taken as typical, is the activity of the SED-controlled government in the field of education and youth activities. As early as 1948 the organizational structure and functions of the Nazi Ministry for Science, Education, and Popular Culture had been revived, not only in general terms but also in detail, by the Central Administration for Popular Culture which has since become the ministry of the same name. This agency not only operates a practical monopoly of the printing and publishing business and controls the allocation of paper to the few private publishers who are permitted to operate, but also exercises ideological control over the school system. The educational policy was expressed in March, 1949, in the *Sächische Zeitung* as follows: "In the final analysis it is necessary to understand that the educational reform of the years before 1933 which concentrated on the needs of the child is entirely obsolete." The article goes on to demand that teachers be re-educated to form an "activist movement" as "flag bearers of the future."

THE NATIONAL FRONT—COMMUNIST INFILTRATION IN WESTERN GERMANY

It was mentioned at the beginning of this chapter that the Soviets view the Deutsche Demokratische Republik not only as a colony in its present status but also as a springboard for the conquest of Western Germany and eventually of Europe. The vehicle for this expansionism is the "National Front," which has already been mentioned several times before. The theory behind the National Front is the "spontaneous" upsurge of the German people to restore the unity of their nation and to combat capitalist aggression in collaboration with the Soviet Union and other peaceful nations.

During the summer of 1949 the idea of a National Front was mentioned by various politicians of the SED without much explanation of what was meant by the term. By October the idea had taken definite shape: Otto Grotewohl launched the National Front officially at the *Volksrat* meeting of October 7, 1949, at which he explained that "this front must now preserve a political force of sufficient strength to bridge existing differences between the two governments or governmental camps, in order to continue the struggle for national unity on a higher level." As its last act before it transformed itself into the *Volkskammer,* the *Volksrat* adopted a Manifesto of the National Front. This document indicated that an organization under that name would be established and contained twenty demands, some of the most important of which were:

a. Restoration of German unity, abolition of West German State, repeal of Ruhr Statute, abolition of Saar autonomy, creation of all-German government.

b. Speedy conclusion of peace treaty and withdrawal of occupation troops.

c. Restoration of full German sovereignty.

d. Implacable fight against warmongers, agents of American imperialism, and splitters of Germany.

e. Restoration of unity and normalization of life in Berlin.

f. Uniform currency, free movement of persons and goods throughout Germany.

g. Stopping of dismantling, abolition of limitations placed on German economy.

h. Promotion of trade with the Soviet Union and eastern Europe.

i. Freedom of press, radio, and film, abolition of Anglo-American censorship.

The political ammunition of the National Front includes not only the purely Communist SED party line but also a parallel and equally irrational nationalist line harking back to dreams of former Prussian glory and to Bismarck's idea of an alliance between Germany and Russia. To mobilize this nationalistic element, the SED organized some time ago a satellite party, the National Democratic party (NDP), under the leadership of Dr. Lothar Bolz and former *Reichswehr General* Vincenz Mueller. Since this party did little more than to sing the song in another key, its appeal was limited. It was necessary to emphasize nationalism, to point out the advantages which Germany could supposedly secure from an agreement with Russia, and to cultivate the opportunists and the dreamers, the discontented officers and the romantic professors. For this purpose Professor Ernst Niekisch of the Soviet Sector Berlin University, a former intellectual leader of the Nazi movement,[7] was charged with preparing the ideological basis for the National Front. In December, 1949, and January, 1950, Niekisch made an extensive trip in the western zones, during which he visited a large number of former generals and other high officers. He also made contact with the "Nauheim Circle" headed by Professor Ulrich Noack of Würzburg and with other intellectuals of leftish or pro-Russian leanings. In the meantime preparations were being made in the DDR; the principal measure was the reorganization of the People's Committees for German Unity and a Just Peace as Committees of the National Front.

On February 3, 1950, the National Council of the National Front was founded at a conference opened by Professor Niekisch in the

[7] Professor Niekisch was well qualified to expound the advantages of a Russo-German alliance. In his book *Decision* (*Entscheidung;* Berlin, 1930) he had written: "Only the Prussian form of self-discipline, applied to the mighty Germanic-Slavic bloc, will endow the latter with the iron power which it needs to measure up to the encirclement of the Roman training of the will with its great powers of resistance. The Prussian 'Ordnung' harmonizes with the Russian 'Herrschaft.' The spirit of Prussian order must be extended from the Urals to the Elbe, in order to chase the spirit of democracy back over the Rhine and the Alps. . . . Germany's independence can only be regained against Europe. Germany can only recover its freedom if it favors the Russian-Asiatic advance against Europe."

Haus der Nationalen Front in the Soviet Sector of Berlin. Ironically enough, this building was Goebbels' old Propaganda Ministry which been refurnished for the occasion. This *Nationalrat* consists of sixty-five members, all from the Soviet Zone, and has a Presidium of ten, five of whom are cabinet ministers of the DDR. On February 15 the *Nationalrat* held a second meeting with a number of west German guests, at which it adopted a lengthy program. This program amplified the points covered in the manifesto of October 7, 1949, and set forth the claim of the National Front to represent all Germans, including those who had the misfortune to live in the Federal Republic.

Since its organization the National Front has been active in two fields. One of them has been the cultivation of "national consciousness," that is, the unquestioned acceptance of the policy and objectives of the Soviet Union.[8] For this purpose, it continues the door-to-door work of the "Antifias" and People's Committees. It operates Enlightenment Centers in most communities and sends its "agitators" to address neighborhood meetings and to distribute literature. Because the National Front has the backing of the SED and the secret police, it does not meet with any open opposition.

The other function of the National Front is the co-ordination of Communist propaganda, sabotage, and "scare rumors" in Western Germany. As is well known, the SED controls the west German KPD and its affiliated Free German Youth. It has given the KPD specific instructions for infiltration in the trade-union movement[9] and has from time to time conjured up demonstrations and riots which have given local executives and police officials unpleasant moments. The National Front is concerned with another level of activity, that is, with individuals and groups which are not overtly Communits or which even adopt the cloak of anticommunism. This "indirect" activity takes different forms, but is always recognizable by its violently anti-American line; it centers in the Nauheim Circle of Professor Noack, about which a fairly extensive network of small groups has assembled. While some members of these groups undoubtedly are misguided idealists, the key personalities in the network are either professional

[8] The political commentator Salter, writing in the January 12, 1950, issue of *Die Neue Zeitung,* suggested that the National Democrats were from a Soviet Russian point of view more reliable than the run-of-the-mill SED functionaries. Because of their socialist background, SED officials have a weakness for "deviationism," that is, their ideals interfere with their party loyalty and they tend, at least secretly, to reject the militarization of the DDR.

[9] The Central Office of the German Trade Union Federation in Düsseldorf issued on October 23, 1950, a "White Book" containing documents illustrating Communist plans for infiltration of the trade unions in Western Germany.

Communist functionaries or, as in the case of Professor Noack and the Reverend Dr. Rossaint (ideological leader of the Free German Youth in Western Germany), are alleged to have direct contacts with and receive money from the SED as well as Soviet agencies. A leading role is played by disgruntled Social Democrats, most of whom were expelled from the SPD because of their Communist sympathies. The network also includes a number of ultrarightist groups such as certain sectors of the Socialist Reich party.

THE "ELECTION" OF OCTOBER 15, 1950

The SED was at least realistic enough to know that it could not possibly win a free election in the DDR.[10] After four years of undisputed control in the Soviet Zone, it had to assume the responsibility for a long list of unpopular measures. Its economic policies had wrecked private business and turned the independent tradesman or shopkeeper into an employee, without producing the constantly improving standard of living enjoyed by the "capitalistic" west. It had corrupted the judicial system and had conducted propaganda trials at Waldheim[11] and other places where guilty verdicts by the hundreds were turned out under a "production quota" system. It had reopened scores of Nazi concentration camps and imprisoned tens of thousands of its political opponents without trial. It had revived the political terror of the Third Reich in which everyone was expected to spy on his neighbor and anyone could overnight become the victim of a "denunciation." Finally, it had shown conclusively that it was not a German, but a Soviet Russian party. These factors, combined with the ray of hope afforded by the overcoming of the Berlin blockade, made it clear that a free and secret election as provided in the constitution of the DDR would result in an overwhelming victory for the "bourgeois" parties. The only way in which the SED could win on October 15, 1950, was to use a "unity list" such as that used in the last Czechoslovakian election, that is, to determine the election result in advance.

The job of providing a propaganda basis for the "unity list" was turned over to the National Front. By handing down orders to its *Land*

[10] See also Chapter 19 below.

[11] The Waldheim trials, which caused a sensation in Berlin in July, 1950, came to light through the flight of the court stenographer to West Berlin. In 220 trials some 3,500 political prisoners, of whom 3,000 were according to available documents not guilty of any offenses, were without exception sentenced to imprisonment or (in seven cases) death. There were no witnesses; the only evidence admitted was the protocol of the Soviet investigators. The average trial lasted twenty minutes.

and local National Front Committees and by forcing the citizens to attend meetings and to pass resolutions, the National Front was able to call forth a "spontaneous" demand for a "unity list." After it was made clear that those who opposed this list would be considered "saboteurs" or "imperialist agents" (that is, subjected to arrest and imprisonment without trial), it was possible for the SED, on July 7, 1950, to secure the agreement of the CDU and LDP to a combined list for the *Volkskammer* based on the following quotas:

	SED	(Socialist Unity party)	25%
	CDU	(Christian Democratic Union)	15%
	LDP	(Liberal Democratic party)	15%
SED satellite	NDP	(National Democratic party)	7.5%
parties	DBP	(Democratic Peasants' party)	7.5%
	FDGB	(Free German Trade Union Fed.)	10%
	FDJ	(Free German Youth)	5%
SED-controlled	KB	(Kulturbund)	5%
"mass"	DFD	(Democratic Women's Association)	3.7%
organizations	VVN	(Victims of Nazi Regime)	3.7%
	VdGB	(Peasants' Mutual Aid)	1.3%
	LwG	(Rural Co-operatives)	1.3%

The result of this division is a 70 per cent majority for the SED, with 30 per cent for the two parties which (in spite of repeated purging by the SMA) might conceivably vote occasionally against SED-sponsored measures. Similar quotas were adopted for the *Landtage* and local assemblies, which were to be elected on October 15, 1950, simultaneously with the *Volkskammer*.

It was originally reported that the DDR would use a ballot similar to that used by the Nazis at their elections and plebiscites, with a large circle for "ja" and a small circle for "nein." In August, 1950, the SED party offices began, however, to make statements to the effect that since it was the "obvious duty of every German patriot to pledge his allegiance to the national program, the election does not necessarily need to take place in secret." This propaganda was intensified to the point where it was quite clear that those who used the election booths would be branded as "enemies of democracy"; those who supported the National Front would not be afraid to give their votes in public.

That an election held under these conditions would result in a practically unanimous vote for the National Front was a foregone conclusion. On October 12 the cabinet of the German Federal Republic and the *Bundestag*'s Committee for All-German Questions issued a joint statement declaring the east German election to be null and void. The committee also addressed an appeal to the voters of the DDR, suggesting that they should vote "no" or invalidate their ballots where this could be done without personal danger. On the day before election the Berlin Group for the Struggle against Inhumanity announced that it had learned of instructions that the names of all persons using the voting booths should be reported to the Ministry of State Security. It therefore urged the voters not to use the booths.

On October 15 the SED and its associated "mass organizations" mobilized their entire apparatus to get out a 100 per cent vote. At the polling places the voters were handed a ballot containing no places for marking "yes" or "no" but simply the statement: "By depositing this ballot without change I hereby vote for the proposed list." In most polling places there were no voting booths. Where booths were available they were not used, except by a number of pastors whose names were, as predicted, reported. The vote of 99.6 per cent in favor of the National Front candidates, reported by the government of the DDR, has no significance whatever as an indication of what the people of the DDR think about their government or the SED.

What the people under Soviet rule really think was indicated by the plebiscite held in the Soviet Sector of Berlin the week before the election. The *Magistrat* of West Berlin addressed an appeal to the population of the Soviet Sector, urging all those who were opposed to the October 15 election in the zone and who wished free elections in all of Berlin to mail the stubs of their September ration cards to the West Berlin government. The Soviets tried to block this referendum by announcing a special ration of clothing in exchange for the stub. In spite of this and in spite of the difficulty involved for East Berliners to mail their ration stubs in the western sectors (since such letters mailed in the Soviet Sector were liable to interception), more than 400,000 of the 600,000-odd voters in East Berlin sent in their ration stubs or letters explaining that the stubs had already been destroyed. This two-thirds participation in a voluntary referendum is the clearest possible answer to the forced "election" result in the zone.

CONCLUSION

The story of the Deutsche Demokratische Republik is not an edifying one. Since this has been a discussion of governmental institutions and political processes and not a treatise on human rights, judicial institutions, or the morality of civil servants, the reader has been spared many unpleasant details he would otherwise would had to read. The German citizen in the DDR is not spared these details. He has been made the unwilling victim of a Soviet Russian plan to establish a subservient puppet state in eastern Germany and to use this state as a starting point for further expansion. The only encouraging thing which can be said is that neither the Soviets nor the SED have succeeded in making communism popular. As Charles E. Merriam wrote many years ago: "Power is not strongest when it uses violence, but weakest. It is strongest when it employs the instruments of substitution and counter attraction, of allurement, of participation rather than exclusion, of education rather than annihilation. Rape is not an evidence of irresistible power in politics or in sex."[12] If Merriam's thesis is correct, then we may confidently predict that the effort of Soviet Russia to create a Soviet Germany will, in the long run, prove to be a failure.

[12] *Political Power* (New York, 1934), p. 180.

7

Germany in International

Organization

JOHN HAY

WITH the German surrender in 1945 and assumption of supreme authority by the United States, the United Kingdom, the Soviet Union, and France, Germany as a sovereign nation ceased to exist. Authority over its international affairs, among other sovereign powers, was assumed by the Four Powers acting through the respective commanders of their occupation forces in Germany.[1] Under terms of an agreement of September 20, 1945, the Four Powers proclaimed that their representatives would henceforth regulate all matters affecting Germany's relations with other countries. No foreign obligations or commitments were to be undertaken on behalf of German authorities without Allied sanction. The Allied representatives also acquired authority over all treaty matters affecting Germany, terminated diplomatic, consular, and commercial relations of the German state, recalled all German missions abroad, and otherwise assumed complete control over official contact of Germany with the outside world.[2]

Until the breakdown of quadripartite rule in March, 1948, authority over the administration of Germany's external affairs was vested in the Allied Control Council. The repeated failures of the three western powers and the Soviet Union to reach agreement on any vital issue concerning the future development of a democratic Germany served

[1] See Chapter 1 above; for text of "Declaration regarding Defeat of Germany and Assumption of Supreme Authority by Allied Powers," see J. K. Pollock, J. H. Meisel, and H. L. Bretton, eds., *Germany under Occupation*, rev. ed. (Ann Arbor, 1949).

[2] *Ibid.*, p. 25.

only to reinforce the conviction, now commonly accepted, that the Soviet Union would only accept conditions which would ensure that any future central German government would be under Communist domination. The three western powers, determined to thwart any further encroachment of Soviet power in Europe and fearing that further delays would lead to political and economic disintegration, decided at London in 1948 to permit the three western zones to be united under a central west German government. This decision and subsequent steps taken to bring a German state back into the European community were designed to fulfill two major objectives. The first was to rebuild Europe to a position of sufficient economic and political strength so that it might be able to withstand the threats of Communist expansion from without and to cope with Communist erosion from within. The second objective was to ensure that a revitalized self-governing Germany would not also be restored to a position of independent power which might permit her at some future date again to become a threat to her neighbors. These objectives led logically to the conclusion that, if western Europe were to survive, a greater unity would have to be established among its member states, including Western Germany.

As a consequence, a long series of steps have been taken to bring Western Germany within the pattern of a developing European community. Common institutions such as the Organization for European Economic Cooperation, the European Payments Union, and the European Coal and Steel Community have been created in the economic field, and plans have been proposed to create additional European organizations in such fields as agricultural production and marketing, transport, civil aviation, manpower, postal services, and scientific research. A Council of Europe has been established in which European statesmen may propose and debate various plans for European unification; and a treaty has been signed to create a European Defense Community in which Western Germany will participate. The various steps taken and institutions being created to bring Western Germany within the framework of a European community are described below. Some will require a surrender of sovereignty to a central European authority. Others are purely intergovernmental agencies which require the unanimous consent of member governments before common action can be taken. All are expected to contribute to the strengthening of ties between Western Germany and other free nations of Europe and to the integration of Europe itself by providing for a more efficient integration of resources, by removing restraints on commerce, and by otherwise furthering common political and social aims.

The first definite step to bring Western Germany into the international community was taken in 1948 when agreement was reached by the Foreign Ministers at London to permit the creation of a federal west German government. The Foreign Ministers authorized the Germans to convene a constituent assembly (later to be called a Parliamentary Council) which, in May, 1949, produced a constitution or Basic Law setting forth, *inter alia*, the powers of the federal west German government and *Länder* in foreign affairs. Under the Basic Law the federal government has exclusive jurisdiction over foreign affairs, although in treaty matters it is obliged to consult with the *Länder* governments if their interests are affected. With the approval of the federal government the *Länder* may also conclude treaties in matters falling within their competence.[3] In matters concerning international law the President technically represents the federation. He is given power to conclude treaties with foreign states and to accredit and receive envoys.[4] It is the Chancellor, as head and chief policy maker of the government, however, who plays the dominant role in the conduct of the Federal Republic's foreign relations.[5] A unique provision of the Basic Law (Art. 24) permits the transfer of German sovereignty to international organizations by ordinary legislation. This article also provides that the Federal Republic may, for the maintenance of peace, join a system of mutual collective security and "consent to those limitations of its sovereign powers which will bring about and secure a peaceful and lasting order in Europe and among the nations of the world." The Federal Republic is further empowered to accede to conventions concerning a general comprehensive system of international arbitration. These provisions, governing the transfer of German sovereignty to supranational organizations by ordinary legislation, facilitated the ratification of the treaty creating the Coal and Steel Community and may prove to be equally useful in implementing future plans involving the integration of Germany with western Europe.

While the Basic Law grants the Federal Republic the normal powers over foreign relations usually enjoyed by sovereign nations, these powers were in effect suspended by the provisions of the Occupation Statute of September 21, 1949, which reserved to the Allied powers supreme authority over Western Germany's foreign relations, includ-

---

[3] Basic Law, Article 32.   [4] *Ibid.*, Article 59.

[5] This does not follow from constitutional necessity but is due to the preference and character of the encumbent Chancellor, who also retains the post of foreign minister. For a discussion of the Chancellor's powers and functions, see Chapter 5 above.

ing the power to conclude international agreements and to control foreign trade and exchange.[6] The three Allied powers continued to retain complete control over Western Germany's foreign affairs until the revision of the Occupation Statute in March, 1951. Under the revision the exercise of reserved powers in this field was limited so as to permit the Federal Republic to conduct relations with foreign countries "to the full extent compatible with the requirements of security, other reserved powers, and the obligations of the occupying powers relating to Germany." The Allied powers also modified their controls over foreign trade and exchange, retaining only those necessary (a) to meet the needs of security, (b) to ensure observance of the principles of certain international organizations in the field of trade and finance, and (c) to provide for the orderly settlement of claims against Germany.[7]

The instrument of revision of the Occupation Statute was supplemented by Decision 11 of the Allied High Commission defining the area of competence of the Federal Republic in the field of foreign affairs. The Decision, which became effective on March 7, 1951, authorized the Federal Republic to establish a Ministry of Foreign Affairs. While the power of prior approval was retained with regard to the establishment of the federal government's diplomatic, consular, and trade missions, the Decision permitted the west German government to reopen diplomatic missions in those countries (other than the United States, United Kingdom, and France) in which it had been previously authorized to establish consular offices. It likewise permitted the establishment, without approval, of consular offices and trade missions in the countries with which the Federal Republic already had diplomatic or consular relations. In the capitals of the United States, the United Kingdom, and France, the federal government was authorized to appoint "official agents."[8] The status of foreign missions in the territory of the Federal Republic also was changed to

[6] For text of Occupation Statute, see Appendix L.

[7] Under the Revision, controls over foreign trade were retained until the Federal Republic adhered to the General Agreement on Tariffs and Trade (GATT) in October, 1951. Control over the exchange rate was relinquished as soon as the Federal Republic became a member of the International Monetary Fund (IMF) in August, 1952. For the text of the Instrument of Revision of the Occupation statute, see "Documents on the Revision of the Occupation Statute," *6th Quarterly Report on Germany,* Office of the U.S. High Commissioner for Germany (Frankfurt, 1951), pp. 128-140.

[8] Later they were accorded diplomatic status with the title of chargé d' affaires. As of February, 1953, the Federal Republic had restored diplomatic and consular relations with forty nations.

permit direct accreditation to the federal government with certain exceptions.[9] Finally, the occupation authorities retained the right to be kept informed of any international negotiations in which the federal or *Land* governments might participate, as well as the right to intervene in negotiations relating to the fields reserved to them under the Occupation Statute, as amended. Negotiations are currently under way to grant Western Germany a fuller measure of equality with the western powers. If they should be successfully concluded, the Occupation Statute will be repealed and the occupation regime terminated, giving the Federal Republic almost complete control over her foreign relations. In all probability the only restrictions that will be retained will concern basic security matters or subjects such as boundaries which can be dealt with only in the final peace settlement.

The policy of integrating Germany into the European community was first stated explicitly in the Petersberg Protocol, an agreement signed by the Allied High Commissioners and Chancellor Adenauer on November 22, 1949.[10] Under the agreement the representatives of the Four Powers stated that their primary objective was the incorporation of the Federal Republic as a peaceful member of the European community and "to this end German association with the countries of western Europe in all fields should be diligently pursued by means of her entry into appropriate international bodies and the exchange of commercial and consular representatives with other countries." The Petersberg Protocol was the first agreement entered into between the Germans and the Allied powers since the war and may be said to be the starting point of western Germany's return to the international community. Since then the Federal Republic has joined many regional and international organizations, the most important of which are discussed below.

INTERNATIONAL ORGANIZATIONS—
ECONOMIC AND FINANCIAL

Organization for European Economic Cooperation (OEEC)—In response to Secretary Marshall's Harvard speech of June 5, 1947, the representatives of sixteen European nations assembled at Paris as the Committee on European Economic Cooperation (CEEC) to prepare a report on their recovery needs and resources. The CEEC produced a Convention in April, 1948, which bound the participating nations to work in close economic co-operation with each other and estab-

[9] As of March, 1953, thirty-seven foreign governments and the Holy See had diplomatic missions accredited to the Federal Republic.
[10] See Appendix M.

lished the OEEC as the intergovernmental organization through which the aid program would be administered and other co-operative economic efforts carried out. Western Germany was represented in the OEEC by Allied delegates from the French and U.S.-U.K. combined zones until the creation of the Federal Republic. In accepting an invitation to join the OEEC on October 1, 1948, Western Germany entered its first postwar international organization.

The principal organs of the OEEC are the Council, the Executive Committee, the technical committees, and the Secretariat. The Council represents the participating governments. It is the decision-making body of the organization and acts by unanimity, although members may refrain from voting or may approve a decision with stated reservations. When a decision is taken, however, it becomes binding upon the members who have participated. The Executive Committee directs the day to day activities of the OEEC. It is composed of seven members chosen by the Council, reviews all matters referred to the Council, prepares its agenda, and has been delegated an increasingly wide area of direct responsibility in administering the Organization's affairs. The technical committees are generally of two types: "horizontal committees," which deal with general problems, and "vertical committees," which handle industry or special-commodity problems.[11] The committees also work on the principle of unanimity and have the power of recommendation only. Both the committees and the Council are served by an internationally staffed Secretariat. In addition to having representation on the Council and the Executive Committee in the person of Vice-Chancellor Blücher, the Federal Republic is represented on all the technical committees with the exception of the Committee on Overseas Territories. The Federal Republic has also established at Bonn a Federal Ministry for the Marshall Plan and in a number of ministries has set up working groups and special committees roughly comparable to the horizontal and technical committees of the OEEC in Paris.

The OEEC has served as the first in a number of organizations to assist the economic recovery and integration of western Europe. That the recovery program has been singularly successful needs no comment here and is beyond the scope of this text.[12] Progress toward

[11] The so-called "horizontal" committees are Manpower, Intra-European Payments, Trade, and Economic. The "vertical" committees are Inland Transport, Maritime Transport, Tourism, Food and Agriculture, Coal, Electricity, Oil, Iron and Steel, Nonferrous Metals, Timber, Pulp and Paper, Textiles, Chemical Products, Machinery, and Miscellaneous Products.

[12] See, however, Howard S. Ellis, *The Economics of Freedom* (New York, 1950).

economic unity, however, has been modest, although the creation of the European Payments Union and measures taken to liberalize intra-European trade among OEEC members by the progressive reduction of quantitative restrictions on imports represent commendable accomplishments. Through its special studies the OEEC has given each participating nation a greater knowledge and understanding of the others' economic problems. It has also served as a meeting ground where, albeit with some difficulty, compromises have been brought about in the interest of the European community. However, as a structure for permanent economic integration the OEEC leaves much to be desired, for it suffers from the common weakness of all coalitions—the necessity of obtaining the unanimous approval of governments in the decision-making process. Its ultimate success thus is dependent upon the continued voluntary co-operation of member governments and their ability and willingness to subordinate conflicting national interests to the common good.

European Payments Union (EPU)—Western Germany took another step toward European economic integration by joining the EPU as an original member on September 19, 1950.[13] The EPU was established by the OEEC to overcome the difficulties inherent in a cumbersome system based on bilateral clearing in foreign trade. The principle on which EPU operates is simple although the mechanics, as set forth in the agreement, are somewhat complex. Western Germany, as well as other OEEC countries belonging to the Union, are no longer required to settle their trade debts with each other but settle them multilaterally through the Union. Each month the central banks of each of the member nations report to the Bank for International Settlements at Basle the balances resulting from transactions between it and other members. The bank cancels the trade debits and credits multilaterally so that each member is left with a single net position with the Union. After compensating for resources which the members hold in each other's currencies, any deficit position still outstanding is settled by the receipt of credit from and payment of gold to the Union. The administration of the EPU rests with a managing board of seven members, responsible to the Council of the OEEC. It reaches its decisions

---

Useful comparative data are also contained in the three annual reports of the OEEC: *Interim Report on the European Recovery Programme* (Paris, 1948); *European Recovery Programme: Second Report of the O.E.E.C.* (Paris, 1950); *Economic Progress and Problems of Western Europe* (Paris, 1951). Also see the quarterly reports to Congress of the Economic Cooperation Administration and *Report of the German Federal Government on the Progress of the Marshall Plan* (Bonn, 1951).

[13] The agreement was, however, made retroactive to July 1, 1951.

by majority vote. While the EPU has been in existence less than three years, it has already proven its value as an international payments mechanism in the absence of freely convertible currencies. During its first year ending June 30, 1951, $2.1 billion of a total of $3.2 billion in monthly bilateral surpluses and deficits were settled by adjustment within the EPU, leaving $1.1 billion to be settled by credit or gold payments. Discrimination against Western Germany and other countries on currency grounds has been eliminated, trading policies of member states have been liberalized, and the volume of intra-European trade has substantially increased.[14]

International Authority for the Ruhr (IAR)—The problem of controlling the industrial Ruhr has been a major consideration of the Great Powers since the earliest days of the occupation. Concentrated in a small area of North Rhine–Westphalia are most of Germany's coal and steel resources, possessing an enormous potential for peace or war. The U.S.S.R. first advanced a proposal for quadripartite control of the Ruhr at Potsdam in 1945. Molotov repeated the proposal at the Moscow Conference of the Foreign Ministers in 1947, where its acceptance was made conditional upon the attainment of economic unity—a condition which has never been realized. At the same conference the French proposed a plan for internationalizing the Ruhr, but that scheme was also rejected. Meanwhile the British had seized the Ruhr resources at the beginning of the occupation and continued to control them unilaterally until 1947 when, following the creation of the Bizone, control over the coal industries passed to the U.S.-U.K. Coal Group. A year later control over the steel industries was assumed by the U.S.-U.K. Steel Group. In 1949, with the admission of the French, the Coal and Steel Groups became tripartite in character and were made responsible to the Allied High Commission.[15] The basic idea of the Ruhr Authority was proposed at the tripartite Foreign Ministers' Conference in 1948. The Benelux nations were later brought into the discussions, and after several months of negotiations, an agreement was signed by the six powers on April 28, 1949, creating the

[14] The text of the agreement establishing the EPU, the OEEC directive covering the operation of the EPU agreement, and related documents may be found in the *Ninth Report to Congress of the Economic Cooperation Administration: Supplement* (Washington, 1951). The activities of the EPU during its first year of operation are described in *European Payments Union: First Annual Report of the Managing Board* (Paris, 1951).

[15] A useful brief description of the German coal and steel industries, early forms of regulation, and Allied-German relationships in these fields may be found in the *Monthly Report of the Control Commission for Germany (British Element)*, Office of U.K. High Commissioner, Vol. V, nos. 2 and 5.

International Authority for the Ruhr.[16] Membership in the Authority was limited to the six signatory governments and Western Germany. Since its creation preceded the setting up of the Federal Republic by several months, provision was made for the voting rights of Germany to be exercised by a representative of the occupation authorities jointly agreed upon, pending Germany's accession to the agreement. The German Chancellor first signified the Federal Republic's intention of adhering to the Ruhr Agreement by signing the Petersberg Protocol. On December 16, 1949, the Chancellor transmitted a letter to the Allied High Commission indicating that the Federal Republic had assumed the rights and obligations arising out of the agreement and had named Vice-Chancellor Blücher as the German representative on the Authority.[17]

The purpose of the Authority as stated in the Ruhr Agreement was to ensure that the resources of the Ruhr industrial area would be used solely for peace and the closer co-ordination of the economic life of western Europe. The Authority's principal function was to make a division, by periodic allocation, of the coal, coke, and steel from the Ruhr as between German consumption and export, in order to provide adequate access of these supplies to those countries "cooperating in the common good." Other functions related to preventing discriminatory practices and to the protection of foreign interests. In actual practice the Authority was concerned chiefly with allocating solid fuels and to some extent with the problem of dual pricing of coal.

The Council was composed of the representatives of the six signatory governments and the Federal Republic. The chairmanship was assumed in rotation by the representatives of the signatory governments. Working as a permanent body, the Council met approximately every three weeks. Directly responsible to the Council were three permanent committees, the Permanent Consultative Financial Committee, the Working Party on Minutes of the Council, and the Press Relations Committee. Other problems were handled by *ad hoc* working parties whose terms of reference were fixed by the Council. The Secretariat consisted of the executive secretary and his office and four functional divisions —Steel, Solid Fuels, Trade Practices and Protection of Foreign Interests, Statistics and Investigation. While the Ruhr Authority did serve a useful if limited function in the distribution of the Ruhr's coal output, it seems likely to be viewed historically as a relatively

[16] For text of the Ruhr Agreement, see *Germany, 1947-1949: The Story in Documents* (Washington, D.C., 1950), pp. 334-343.

[17] The Ruhr Authority was terminated in February, 1953, with the creation of the common market for coal of the European Coal and Steel Community. ·

unimportant experiment in international control. Its usefulness was severely limited in that its scope of operations was restricted to Germany alone and to certain areas of jurisdiction with respect to the Ruhr industries.[18] The Authority's usefulness was hardly put to a final test because during most of its existence steel shortages and, until recently, coal shortages were nonexistent.

European Coal and Steel Community (Schuman Plan)—This highly significant experiment in relating Western Germany to the European community was proposed on May 9, 1950, by French Foreign Minister Schuman, who spoke of the plan as laying "the first concrete foundation for a European Federation . . . so indispensable for the preservation of peace." Less than a year later, on April 18, 1951, a treaty had been drawn up and signed by the foreign ministers of the six participating nations—the Federal Republic, France, Italy, Luxembourg, Belgium, and the Netherlands.[19] The treaty, which will extend for fifty years, was effective July, 1952, after approval by the parliaments of the participating nations.[20] Under its terms the signatory nations have agreed to create a western European community for coal, iron, and steel based upon a common market, common objectives, and common institutions. In doing so the member countries relinquished to the Community regulatory powers over their iron, coal, and steel resources in Europe, without disturbing ownership or management of the industries. The mission of the Community is to contribute to economic expansion, increased employment, and improved living stand-

[18] It should be noted that the Allied High Commission also exercised independent and concurrent powers over the Ruhr coal and steel industries. It retained as a reserved power "controls over the Ruhr" (see Occupation Statute, par. 2[b]), was responsible for the reorganization of the coal, iron, and steel industries (Law No. 27) through the Economics Committee and Combined Coal and Combined Steel Groups, and exercised control over German steel capacity and production through the Military Security Board. The High Authority also had concurrent jurisdiction with the Ruhr Authority in matters relating to foreign interests and trade discrimination.

[19] For text of the treaty and supporting documents, see *EXECUTIVES Q and R*, 82d Congress, 2d session, pp. 255-328.

[20] The Federal Republic was the first nation to complete the ratification of the treaty. *Bundestag* approval followed a lively debate extending over three days. The final vote was 232 in favor, 143 in opposition, with three abstentions. Strictly following party lines, the government coalition (CDU-CSU, FDP, and DP) and the Union of Federalists (Center and Bavarian party) endorsed the treaty, as did three members of the BHE and three independent deputies. The opposing votes were cast by the SPD, KPD, and five right-wing delegates. Final ratification became complete on February 1, 1952, when the *Bundesrat* failed to exercise its constitutional privilege of demanding further consideration of the measure by a joint committee of both houses. (See Basic Law, Arts. 77[2] and 78.)

ards in the six countries through the institution of a single market for these products. To achieve a single market the treaty abolishes within the Community import and export duties, quantitative restrictions on the movement of iron, coal, and steel, all discriminatory practices among producers, buyers, and consumers, all subsidies or charges imposed by the state, and other restrictive practices which tend to divide the market or exploit the consumer. In a positive sense the principal function of the organization is to ensure the observance of normal conditions of a competitive market and to take direct action in controlling production and distribution only when compelled by unusual circumstances to do so. The treaty did not become operative immediately. After it was ratified a "preparatory period" of several months, as expected, elapsed before the common market was formed. During this period the various institutions were set up, negotiations with nonmember countries were conducted, and special studies by the High Authority were made. At the end of the "preparatory period" a so-called "transition period" of five years was begun permitting certain high-cost producers receiving subsidies and other aids to adapt themselves generally to the demands of the single market. The common market and five-year transition period for coal, iron ore, and scrap, began on February 10, 1953; for steel, on May 1, 1953.

The treaty provided for the creation of several institutions: a High Authority, to be assisted by a Consultative Committee; a Common Assembly; a Council of Ministers; and a Court of Justice. The High Authority consists of nine members, eight of whom are designated by governments of the member states and the ninth selected by majority vote of the eight members. The Consultative Committee consists of thirty to fifty-one producers, workers, consumers, and dealers in equal numbers. The treaty obliges the members of the High Authority to exercise their function in complete independence. They are bound not to accept or solicit instructions from any government or organization; and the member states are similarly bound not to influence the members of the Authority in the execution of their duties. As the executive organ of the Community, the High Authority executes the terms of the treaty. It acts by majority vote. Its powers include the right to issue directives binding on the individual enterprises and the member states and to fine enterprises violating its orders. It it to have unhindered access to records of the industries under its jurisdiction. It may borrow, lend, receive grants, and place levies on the production of coal and steel. Member states have agreed to use their police powers to enforce the directives of the Authority. In the fields of gathering information, preventing the growth of private cartels, and preventing mergers which violate the nondiscriminatory aims of the treaty the High Authority is given almost unlimited power. It is also provided with fairly substantial powers over the allocation of the Community's products during periods of shortage or surplus.

The members of the Common Assembly are selected each year by one of two methods. The parliament of a member state may designate them from among its own membership; or a state may provide for their election by universal suffrage. Germany, France, and Italy have been allotted eighteen members, Belgium and the Netherlands ten apiece, and Luxembourg four. The Assembly meets annually to discuss the report of the High Authority, but it may be convoked in extraordinary session at the request of the Council, by a majority of its members, or by the High Authority. The Assembly may demand replies to all questions it chooses to ask the Authority and may adopt a motion of censure on the High Authority's report. If the motion should be supported by two-thirds of the members present and voting, representing a majority of the total membership, the High Authority must resign in a body.

The Council of Ministers is composed of representatives of the member states, each designating one of the members of its government. The body is empowered to consult and exchange information with the High Authority with a view to harmonizing the acts of the Authority with those of the member states, particularly in the field of general economic policy. Under many provisions of the treaty the High Authority's decisions require the concurrence of the Council. The Council's powers are greatest in the fields of market control and industry development. Except when unanimity is specified, the Council votes by a "qualified majority," defined so as to include either France or Germany in any absolute majority vote, or both France and Germany in any equal division of votes.

The Court of Justice is composed of seven judges appointed for six years by agreement among the governments of the member states. Its function is to ensure that the rule of law applies in the interpretation and application of the treaty and its implementing regulations. It has jurisdiction over appeals by a member state or by the Council and may amend decisions of the High Authority on grounds of lack of legal competence, substantial procedural violation, treaty violation, or abuse of power. In cases of alleged abuse of power affecting them, enterprises and associations also enjoy the right of appeal to the court.

It is still too early to predict, however, the extent to which the Authority will exercise truly supranational powers. It would seem to be provided with all the necessary powers to permit it to carry out the aims of the treaty. It came into being without incident or resistance. This is encouraging, but another test will come at the end of the transition period. Some critics of the treaty attack it on the grounds that it has created a giant cartel, endowed with enormous powers which may be used more for restriction than for expansion. Others take the view that the organization will not be too powerful, but on the contrary too weak. They cite as supporting arguments the many instances in which the High Authority must obtain the concurrence of the Council (that is, governments) and the existence of temporary exceptional measures which they fear may become permanent. It is too early to answer these questions. The success of this unique experiment in supranational control will depend upon a number of factors, including the continued co-operation of the participating nations and the ability of the members of the Authority to withstand local pressures and to execute the treaty provisions with faithful regard for the interests of the whole Community. Apart from the purely economic advantages which are expected to accrue from the single market, this venture will prove to be a remarkable achievement if only it fulfills the promise of Robert Schuman that any war between Germany and France will become "not only unthinkable but in actual fact impossible." Aside from the possibility of repudiation of the treaty by either of the principal members, there would seem to be cause for reasonable optimism that this promise may be fulfilled.

INTERNATIONAL ORGANIZATIONS—POLITICAL AND MILITARY

Council of Europe—Unlike its active part in the creation of the Coal and Steel Community, the Federal Republic did not participate in the formation of the Council of Europe. However, west Germans were among the European delegates who assembled at The Hague in May, 1948, to participate in the unofficial Congress of Europe.[21] Among the many resolutions adopted by the Congress was a measure put forward by its Political Committee proposing the creation of a European Assembly, to be selected by parliaments of the participating nations. Two months later Bidault officially proposed in the Consultative Council of the Brussels Treaty Powers the creation of a European parliament. No action was taken on this proposal, but at its next meeting in October, 1948, the Consultative Council agreed to set up a Committee

[21] For details of the meeting at The Hague and resolutions adopted, see *European Movement and the Council of Europe* (London, 1951) and *Europe Unites* (London, 1950).

for the Study of European Unity. The French and Belgian delegates of the study group put forward a plan for a European Assembly. This was matched by a British counterproposal for a ministerial council to be named by the governments rather than parliaments. The committee was unable to agree, but the ministers finally reached a compromise in January, 1949, which consisted of combining both proposals. The task of drafting the convention was then assigned to the Permanent Commission of the Brussels Treaty Organization.

The Statute of the Council of Europe signed at London on May 5, 1949, consists of a preamble and forty-two articles.[22] The aim of the organization as set forth in the Statute is to achieve a greater unity among its members in order to preserve their common heritage and to further their economic and social progress. The principal organs of the Council of Europe consist of a Committee of Ministers and a Consultative Assembly. They are served by a common Secretariat. The Committee of Ministers is composed of the foreign ministers of the respective member states. It is the decision-making body of the Council of Europe. Except in certain procedural matters the committee acts on the principle of unanimity, although individual members may abstain from voting on any particular issue. The committee acts on recommendations submitted to it by the Consultative Assembly and on the basis of those proposals or on its own initiative may direct its recommendations to member governments for consideration. The Consultative Assembly is the deliberative organ of the Council. It is composed of representatives elected by the parliaments of the respective member states. On all important matters it reaches decisions by a two-thirds majority of its membership. The president of the Assembly represents it before the Committee of Ministers. He, with the six vice-presidents, constitute the Bureau which controls the day to day activities of the Assembly. In addition, the Bureau proposes to the Assembly the composition of the six general committees: General Affairs, Rules of Procedure and Privileges, Economic Questions, Social Questions, Cultural and Scientific Questions, and Legal and Administrative Questions. The chairmen of these committees, the vice-president, president, and fifteen other representatives comprise the Standing Committee which meets between sessions to facilitate the work of the Assembly. Finally, a Joint Committee, consisting of five members of the Commit-

[22] The text of the Council of Europe statute may be found in a number of secondary sources. See *American Journal of International Law*, XLIII (Oct., 1949), 162-172; *Bulletin*, Dept of State, Dec. 5, 1949; *Congressional Record* (Oct. 13, 1949), pp. 14755-14759; *European Movement and the Council of Europe*, pp. 169-183.

tee of Ministers and seven members of the Assembly has been established to co-ordinate the activities of the two bodies and to maintain
good relations between them.

The association of western Germany with the Council of Europe
began in 1950. Both the Federal Republic and the Saar government
were extended membership in the Consultative Assembly (but not the
Committee of Ministers) on April 1, 1950. Both accepted, the Federal
Republic with some hesitation in view of the limited association permitted and the fact that the Saar was also offered associate membership.[23] While Federal Republic membership in the Committee of
Ministers was deferred, provision was made for its representation on
special occasions. The limitation was removed in November, 1950,
when the ministers agreed that German representatives would be
permitted at all meetings of the committee. Finally, on May 2, 1951,
the Federal Republic was granted the status of full membership, and
Chancellor Adenauer took his seat on the Council. Since their entry
into the Council of Europe the Germans have participated actively
in its work. They are represented on all of the important committees
including the Standing and Joint Committees, and Heinrich von Bren-
tano, leader of the CDU faction in the *Bundestag*, is one of the six
vice-presidents of the Assembly.

Whether or not the Council of Europe is constituted to fulfill the
aims of the Statute has been a subject of debate almost since the institution was founded. Those who are impatient for an early political
federation of Europe express dismay at the apparent lack of accomplishment made thus far in that direction. Others, who are inclined
toward a gradual approach to federation or who conceive of unity
in terms of intergovernmental agreements, find satisfaction in the
Council's accomplishments. This disparity in sentiment is most apparent in the Assembly, where so-called "Federalist" and "Functionalist" factions have opposed each other to gain control. Up to the present time the "Federalists" have not succeeded either in extending significantly the Assembly's powers or in convincing the member governments to part with their sovereignty in the interest of a United
Europe. With the exception of the Social Democrats, the German

[23] Despite the offer of qualified membership the *Bundesrat* approved a bill to
join the Assembly on May 25, 1950, by a vote of twenty-seven to sixteen. The
final *Bundestag* vote, taken on June 15, 1950, was 218 to 51 in favor of entry,
with the Social Democrats, Center party, Communists, and extreme right-wing
deputies voting in opposition. On July 18, 1950, the *Bundestag* selected a delegation of eighteen from its own membership, consisting of seven CDU-CSU, seven
SPD, three FDP, and one DP, who joined the August session of the Consultative
Assembly.

delegates are among the Assembly representatives who have pleaded the cause of European federation.[24] The Assembly now seems to be committed to the "Functionalist" approach to integration, a policy which finds favor with the British, Benelux, and Scandinavian countries. However, despite the limited progress being made in the Council toward political federation, the organization serves a useful purpose in many other respects. It provides a meeting place where Germans, Frenchmen, and other Europeans may debate and exchange ideas. As long as it exists it will provide a medium through which the idea of European unification may be kept alive. Its deliberations are bound to influence European public opinion as well as the parliaments of the member states. It has produced at least two conventions which are noteworthy achievements—a Charter on Human Rights and a Convention on Full Employment. Moreover, it has endorsed measures furthering integration such as the Schuman Plan and the Pleven Plan in addition to advancing scores of proposals of its own designed to further European unity.[25]

European Defense Community (EDC)—The plan of the western powers to bring the Federal Republic into the defense arrangement for Europe gave rise to the Pleven proposal in November, 1950, for a European Defense Community. Western Germany, Italy, Belgium, and Luxembourg responded to the French invitation to discuss a draft treaty proposal put forward by the French. The discussions began on February 15, 1951, and the treaty was signed on May 27, 1953. During the early stages of the conference the Netherlands government was represented only by observers, but in October, 1951, became a participant on the same basis as the other five members. In simple terms, the plan of the EDC seeks to bring about a fusion of the national military establishments of the five participating nations (Germany having none) under the supranational control of a European

[24] On two occasions before the German delegation left for Strasbourg the *Bundestag* voted resolutions authorizing the delegation to participate in the drafting of a convention for European federation.

[25] A complete account of the Council of Europe's activities may be found in the numerous publications of the Consultative Assembly. For an excellent brief article, see Frederick L. Schuman, "The Council of Europe," *American Political Science Review*, Vol. XLV, No. 3 (Sept., 1951). See also Susan Strange, "Strasbourg in Retrospect," *World Affairs*, Vol. IV, No. 1 (Jan., 1950). For views of a British Labor delegate, see Maurice Edelman, "The Council of Europe 1950," *International Affairs*, Vol. XXVII, No. 1 (Jan., 1951). Also see George L. Powell, "The Council of Europe," *International Law Quarterly*, Vol. III, No. 2 (London, 1950). Reference should also be made to the excellent summaries of the activities of the Council of Europe contained in each quarterly issue since 1949 of *International Organization* (Boston).

Defense Community.[26] Within the structure thus created German divisions (*groupements*), tactical air units, defensive naval forces, and similar forces of other member nations will be brought together under international command responsible to the Supreme Allied Commander (SACEUR), who in turn is responsible to the North Atlantic Treaty Organization (NATO). The objectives of the EDC are to secure the advantages of a German defense contribution without the necessity of recreating a German national army, to gain the strength which flows from unity, and to obtain the economies which follow from the elimination of the duplicating features of national military establishments. If the plan materializes, the armies of the six nations will serve as European soldiers. They will wear a common uniform. Recruitment and training will take place under common standards, and European training schools will be created. The EDC will be financed through a European defense budget, and a common system of supply will be worked out which will include European control of armament production and distribution.

The institutions to be created under the EDC are analogous to those of the European Coal and Steel Community. There is to be a Council consisting of six ministers, a Commissariat (or Commission), a Common Assembly, and a Court of Justice. The Council of Ministers will represent the participating nations. The task of the Council will be to harmonize the actions of the Commissariat with the policies of the governments of the member states. Except as specifically provided for under the treaty, the Council will act by majority vote. Many vital matters will require the unanimous consent of the Council. The Commissariat will consist of nine members of whom no more than two may be nationals of a single state. It will serve as the executive body of the EDC and will implement the provisions of the treaty. The Assembly will be composed of all of the members of the Coal and Steel Community, plus three additional delegates each from the Federal Republic, France, and Italy. The EDC Assembly will meet in annual session. By a two-thirds majority it may, on a vote of censure, require the Commissariat to resign. The Assembly will also have certain limited powers over the budget of the Community. The Court of the Coal and Steel Community will also serve the EDC and perform similar functions. Whether or not the EDC treaty will be ratified by the six nations is extremely uncertain. Unusual obstacles and technical difficulties have been overcome, but political difficulties remain. The

[26] Certain armed forces may be retained under national control for the defense of overseas territories.

German parliament alone had approved the treaty within the first year of signing. But even in the Federal Republic ratification has been withheld pending a court suit on the constitutionality of the Treaty. France has been unable, thus far, to cross the political Rubicon; and the remaining nations seem reluctant to proceed until the prospects of ratification in Western Germany and France appear more certain.

European Political Community (EPC)—The framers of the EDC Treaty recognized the essential anomaly in granting sovereign powers to a defense community with only limited and indirect political responsibility to the peoples of the six nations from which it derives those powers. The treaty therefore provided (Art. 38) for a study to determine the powers and structure of an assembly which would have a more popular basis, provide for suitable representation by the states, and not prejudice the subsequent creation of a federal or confederal structure having a bicameral legislature and employing the separation of powers principle.

By a later agreement the six powers authorized the setting up of an *ad hoc* assembly consisting of the present members of the Coal and Steel Community assembly, plus three additional delegates from France, Italy, and Western Germany. The *ad hoc* assembly convened in September, 1952, and after several months of study produced a draft statute for a European Political Community. Under this statute, which must yet be approved by the governments and parliaments of the six nations, the EPC would succeed to the powers and duties of the Coal and Steel Community and the European Defense Community and propose to governments additional plans for the progressive achievement of a common market.

United Nations and Other Organizations—The Federal Republic is not a member of the United Nations, but has become associated with many of its specialized agencies. In several, the Federal Republic has obtained full membership; in others her representatives participate as observers. At a special session of the Food and Agriculture Organization (FAO) in November, 1950, the Federal Republic was admitted to full membership. In May, 1951, she was admitted to the World Health Organization (WHO), and in the following month to the International Labor Organization (ILO) and the United Nations Educational, Scientific, and Cultural Organization (UNESCO). In October, 1951, the Federal Republic acceded to the General Agreement on Tariffs and Trade (GATT). Consideration is now pending with respect to German membership in the International Monetary Fund (IMF), the International Bank for Reconstruction (IBR), and the

International Telecommunications Union (ITU), all of which western Germany is expected to join in the near future. The Federal Republic has also joined many other international and regional organizations of lesser importance such as the International Wheat Council (IWC), the Central Rhine Commission (CRC), and the European Customs Union Study Group.

EASTERN GERMANY

Unlike western Germany, the course of eastern Germany's relationship with other countries and international organizations has been narrowly restricted. From June, 1945, until November, 1949, Eastern Germany's foreign relations were under the absolute control of the Soviet Military Administration. With the setting up of the puppet German Democratic Republic, the Soviet Control Commission (which then replaced the Soviet Military Administration) authorized the German Democratic Republic to enter into trade and other relations with foreign countries, subject to what it chose to call "necessary supervision." The Republic has been equipped with a Foreign Ministry, nominally headed by Georg Dertlinger, a CDU deputy. Real control in the ministry is exercised by his deputy, Anton Ackermann, who is a member of the Central Committee of the Communist party and Politburo. Thus, for all practical purposes the Foreign Ministry is simply a façade behind which eastern Germany's foreign policy is dictated by the Soviet Union through the new Supreme Commissar.[27] While the German Democratic Republic has established diplomatic representations in other countries, they have been accorded only the status of "diplomatic missions," and even these are limited to the U.S.S.R., Poland, Czechoslovakia, Hungary, Bulgaria, Rumania, and China. The Republic has not been granted recognition by the western democratic countries and does not have representation in any international organization. Among Soviet-sponsored regional organizations the Republic participates (as a member) only in the Council for Mutual Economic Assistance (CEMA), to which she was admitted in September, 1950.[28]

[27] A former official of the Czechoslovak Ministry of Foreign Affairs, Dr. Bedrich Bruegel, presents a revealing account of the techniques and administrative machinery employed by the Soviet Union in transmitting policy decisions from its Politburo to the deputy foreign minister of each satellite country by intermediary of the Party Secretariat and Ministry of State Security. See his "Methods of Soviet Domination in Satellite States," *Internat. Affairs,* Vol. XXVII, No 1 (Jan., 1951).

[28] For a report on the activities and objectives of this organization, see C. Alexandrowicz, "Comecon," *World Affairs,* IV, No. 1 (Jan., 1950), 35 ff.

CONCLUSION

In reflecting upon the postwar international relations of Germany, the most obvious impression one gets is the striking contrast between developments in Eastern and Western Germany. In the former, relations with other governments have been narrowly confined substantively and have been restricted to a few Communist-dominated states. There has also been no discernible increase in the activity of the German Democratic Republic in the international field since the government was set up by the Soviet authorities in 1949. In Western Germany, on the other hand, there has been a progressive release of control by the western powers and a corresponding increase in the Federal Republic's competence and influence in international affairs. Unlike the German Democratic Republic, the Federal Republic has been accorded full diplomatic status in a large number of countries and has representation in most of the technical organizations of the United Nations. But indeed the most remarkable development in the international field is the progress that has been made toward integrating Germany with western Europe. Even in the current early stages of development of such European organizations as the Schuman Plan and EDC, efforts of the past three years have yielded greater practical results leading to European unification than have the labors of the previous six centuries. Whether these western achievements will be supplemented by equally imaginative plans for unification in other areas leading ultimately to full political federation of western Europe is, of course, an open question. At least first steps have been taken, and it is not inconceivable that the urge of western European nations to find united strength in the face of the common danger and their desire to prevent the resurgence of nationalist Germany may well be the catalytic agents that will hasten the process of uniting Europe.

Part III

PROCESSES OF GOVERNMENT

8

*Legislation**

HAROLD M. DORR AND HENRY L. BRETTON

IT HAS been said that German political thought, in its practical aspects, has always lacked a basic concept of democracy. German commentators, viewing the North American political scene, have long observed that the major political parties, whatever their political objectives, are agreed on the fundamentals of democracy. Not so in Germany: here the residue of monarchism and, as of late, fascism, plus religious differences, have prevented a consolidation of political thought on the grounds of democracy. If there is no agreement on the principles of government which are to prevail in a given area and if the differences are as deep seated as they are in Germany, political, economic, and social problems are not likely to be solved to meet practical requirements of statecraft but will rather be used to bring ideological differences to the fore. Such a development will in turn result in a lack of political elasticity—for only basic agreement among all forces concerned will permit elasticity—and will inevitably lead to a petrification of all major institutions of government. Under such conditions, minor legislative issues will tend to be magnified to the point where discussion will shake the foundations of the state. By the same token, major legislative projects will fall short of full realization because of

* The chapters in Part III are concerned with governmental processes which are common to governments on local, state, and federal levels in both West and East Germany. While they necessarily refer to some of the same subjects treated in Part II, their primary interests are with the universals of the processes rather than with the integration of the several processes into any given governmental structure.—EDITOR.

the failure on the part of the political parties to compromise on fundamental concepts.[1] The legislative practice followed under the Weimar Republic as well as that evident during the first years of the Bonn Republic shows that the deficiency mentioned constitutes one of the major obstacles to an expeditious functioning of parliamentary government in the German state.

There is reason to believe that the institutions of parliamentary government have not yet become organic parts of the German body politic. The basic attitudes of German legislators, aside from fundamental ideological differences—and, by the same token, the attitudes of the German public toward their legislatures—show a certain lack of appreciation of the rudimentary aspects of parliamentarism. Between the Scylla of widespread apathy with regard to the sinews of democratic life and the Charybdis of ideological divergences, the ship of the new Bonn Republic faces grave dangers before it can embark upon the voyage envisaged by the western Allies. In its structural outline, the new federal legislature closely resembles its predecessor of Weimar. The adoption of certain federalist terminologies, such as the prefix *Bund* for both parts of the new parliament, is expressive of the emphasis which has been placed upon federalism.[2]

FEDERAL LEGISLATIVE ORGANIZATION

The Bundesrat—The *Bundesrat* or Federal Council is the principal organ of federalism sharing certain legislative powers and functions with the *Bundestag*. Since the Bonn Republic rests upon the premises of democracy, the more representative part of the legislature has been endowed with the major share of legislative prerogatives.[3] The legislative powers assigned to the *Bundesrat* are restricted to certain enumerated instances.[4] Consequently, participation by the states in the legislative processes through their representatives in the *Bundesrat* does not necessarily establish a bicameral legislature at Bonn.[5] One

[1] The debates, in the Bonn Republic, on the "Work Councils" and on the subject of industrial codetermination by unions and management are cases in point. See *3rd Quarterly Report on Germany*, Office of the U.S. High Commissioner for Germany (Frankfurt, 1950), pp. 35-38.

[2] The *Bundesrat* of the Bismarck constitution of 1871 (Art. 6 *et seq.*) represented the federative principle with this important difference: since sovereignty in the Empire did not rest upon democratic premises, the upper chamber was also representative of an alliance among "sovereign" states.

[3] See Friedrich Giese, *Grundgesetz fur die Bundesrepublik Deutschland* (Frankfurt am Main, 1949), p. 50.

[4] Carl J. Friedrich, "Rebuilding the German Constitution," *American Political Science Review*, XLIII (1949), 713.

[5] Giese, *op. cit.*, p. 51.

authority even goes so far as to call the Council a "governmental college" rather than a representative assembly.[6]

The members of the Council are appointed by the respective state governments, are instructed by them, derive their power from them, and may be recalled by them. The principles of representation along democratic lines are preserved inasmuch as the state governments are responsible to elected state legislatures (*Landtage*). The outstanding single improvement of the *Bundesrat* over its predecessor the Weimar *Reichsrat* has been the reapportionment of seats in the interest of a more equitable representation of the states.[7] Because the votes of each *Land* delegation are cast as a block, party lines are not adhered to since a given delegation may be made up of representatives of several parties.[8]

The state representatives who have so far been appointed to the *Bundesrat* represent the pick of available trained officials. This permitted the Council, during the early phases of the Bonn Republic, to carry on with the functions of government before either the executive branch or the Federal Diet had settled down to their unfamiliar roles.[9] Should the *Bundestag* be unable to fulfill the functions assigned to it under the Basic Law, the possibility exists that the "upper house," by virtue of its more professional character and make-up, will once again, like its predecessor, exert considerable influence at the national level.[10] Since, in our view, the emphasis in the Council is more upon efficiency than upon close adherence to democratic procedures, that branch of parliament cannot be expected to yield much in the way of progressive democratization.[11] The fourteen committees, in each of which the nine states are represented by a member, are open

---

[6] *Ibid.* Cf. conclusions drawn in Chapter 5 above.

[7] Article 51 (2), Basic Law. Prussia was abolished as a state by Control Council Law No. 46. The text of that law and other materials related to the pre-1950 phases of the Bonn Republic can be found in James K. Pollock, James H. Meisel, and Henry L. Bretton, eds., *Germany under Occupation*, rev. ed. (Ann Arbor, 1949).

The representation in the present Federal Council is apportioned as follows: Bavaria, 5; Lower Saxony, 5; North Rhine–Westphalia, 5; Hesse, 4; Schleswig-Holstein, 4; Rhineland-Palatinate, 4; Bremen, 3; Hamburg, 3; Baden-Württemberg, 5; Berlin (observers without voting privileges), 4.

[8] Article 51 (3), Basic Law. Cf. *5th Quarterly Report on Germany*, Office of the U.S. High Commissioner for Germany (Frankfurt, 1950), p. 36.

[9] *4th Quarterly Report on Germany* (Frankfurt, 1950), p. 24.

[10] See Gerhard Anschütz, *Die Verfassung des Deutschen Reichs vom 11 August 1919*, 4th ed. (Berlin, 1932), pp. 335-357; also Willibald Apelt, *Geschichte der Weimarer Verfassung* (München, 1946), pp. 216-224.

[11] For a concise critique of the Weimar *Reichsrat*, see Apelt, *op. cit.*, p. 382.

to representatives of the executive branch of the federal government.[12] It can be expected that, under the circumstances, committee meetings on the Council level will reflect at least equally the executive point of view.

The Bundestag—The *Bundestag* or Federal Diet is, in constitutional theory, the central governing agency of the German Federal Republic and the principal legislative organ. Yet in the early days of its existence, the Federal Diet was overshadowed by the executive branch of the federal government.[13] Once it had grown to adequate stature and with gentle prodding by occupation authorities, more attention was paid to the proposition that democracy calls for a vigorous defense of parliamentary prerogatives against encroachments by the executive. The lack of vigilance in this respect may be considered one of the greatest evils of the Weimar system as it worked out in practice.[14]

(1) *Election*—Contrary to the practice followed under the Weimar Republic, the more representative "lower house" is no longer elected on the basis of proportional representation alone. The legal minimum of the *Bundestag's* membership is 400.[15] The seats are allotted to each state in accordance with its respective popular strength. Three-fifths of the seats are filled through elections in single-member constituencies, and two-fifths by proportional distribution of the total vote cast in each state. An attempt has also been made to reduce the number of splinter parties in the legislature by making it mandatory for a party to poll at least 5 per cent of the total vote cast before it is qualified to compete for the distribution of available seats.[16]

It cannot yet be stated with certainty whether the democratic tradition in Germany has been enhanced by the changes in the election procedure. The Weimar Republic suffered from a continuous splintering process which disrupted its party life and tended to remove parliament from the clear focus of the voting public. The present system of proportional representation and of state-wide party tickets does not necessarily close the gap which has always existed between the parties and the people. Nominees are still hand-picked by the party organiza-

[12] Article 53, Basic Law. The Council has presently thirteen standing committees and one Joint Conference Committee for meetings with the *Bundestag.*
[13] *4th Quarterly Report on Germany*, p. 24, and Chapter 5 above.
[14] For an appraisal of the weaknesses of the Weimar Republic, see Apelt, *op. cit.*, pp. 369-385.
[15] For the text of the Electoral Law, see *Germany, 1947-1949: The Story in Documents* (Washington, D.C., 1950), p. 310.
[16] Article 10 (4,5), Electoral Law. For a critique of the election procedure under Weimar, see Apelt, *op. cit.*, pp. 178-185.

tion. The voter still does not in any real sense vote for an individual candidate and still cannot split his ticket. The deputy elected at large, and responsible to the voters only in a nebulous sense, still has to develop a personal relationship to the electorate.[17]

There is as yet no evidence that the German voter is less inclined to form special-interest groups which will then seek special representation—not necessarily on the grounds of the prevailing form of government—with concomitant effects upon the public's esteem of parliamentary institutions. The picture as it could be seen after the first election of August 14, 1949, is certainly not too encouraging. The diffusion of the popular mandate among some fourteen parties, some old and some new, does not tend to strengthen the democratic tradition. It remains to be seen whether the parliamentary coalitions which can be formed have the innate political strength to give Western Germany the essential benefits of a two- or three-party system.[18]

Since the details concerning the elections are to be determined by federal legislation, much will depend upon the success of the democratic tradition in other spheres of political life. This is as true here as it is in the case of all other constitutional provisions. Democratic principles as laid down in the Basic Law do not and cannot extend beyond the stipulation that elections are to be "universal, direct, free, equal, and secret."[19] The question of a more precise correlation of the popular will with parliamentary representation can only be answered by the people in their collective attitude toward the principles of democracy and parliamentary government.[20] There is no doubt that the major share of the responsibility for the task of making parliamentary government palatable to the German masses rests with the leadership of the major parties.

(2) *Organization*—The organization of the *Bundestag* is partly regulated by the Basic Law[21] and partly by its own Rules of Procedure.[22] According to Article 38 of the Basic Law, the representatives are "not

[17] For a thorough discussion of proposals for electoral reform prior to the 1953 election, see chapter 20 and *Bundestag, Sitzungsberichte,* 253d session (March 5, 1953), pp. 12180-12191, and 254th session (March 18, 1953), pp. 12203-12235.

[18] Cf. Chapter 5 above and Chapters 19 and 20 below.

[19] Article 38 (1), Basic Law. Cf. Article 21 of Weimar Constitution.

[20] Dr. Franz Richter of the *Deutsche Reichspartei* has already complained bitterly against what he called the *"Demokratur"* under the Bonn system. "Comments on the Statement of Policy of the Federal Government Delivered in the *Bundestag* of September 22, 1949," *Germany's Parliament in Action,* U.S. High Commissioner for Germany (Frankfurt, 1950), pp. 85-86.

[21] Articles 40-49.

[22] *Geschäftsordnung des Deutschen Bundestages* (Bonn, 1952).

bound by orders and instructions, and [are] subject only to their conscience." The Weimar Constitution restricted parties and interest groups in a similar manner. Yet, in practice, the real legislative work as far as the *Reichstag* was concerned was carried on in the party caucus, by the *Fraktion*, and was more often than not subject to *"Fraktionszwang."* Voting in committee or in the *Fraktion* room was too often subject to orders and instructions handed down by the party leadership.[23] It is held by some that the Basic Law does not permit resort to the debatable practice of the *Fraktionszwang.*[24] The Rules of Procedure, while mentioning *Fraktions* and discussing their role in the legislative processes, do not attempt to regulate voting in committee.[25] There is no reason to believe, however, that the overpowering role of the parliamentary *Fraktion,* as it became all too evident under Weimar, will be curtailed by the present Diet.[26] The party leadership will again seek party solidarity whenever parliamentary strategy calls for it. Given certain crucial issues or situations, the party leaders will throw the combined strength of their respective parliamentary parties into the scale, and the only way this can be done, under a system which makes coalitions mandatory for survival, is by invocation of party discipline or *Fraktionszwang.*[27]

Any attempt to break the power of the *Fraktions* in favor of individual, unfettered representation will have to originate outside of parliament. Too many of the present parliamentarians are steeped in the old traditions and are not prepared to accept incisive changes. Further, the Rules of Procedure lower the minimum membership of a *Fraktion* from fifteen to ten and stipulate that seats on committees, on the Presidium, and on other functional and procedural bodies are to be allocated in accordance with the strength of the *Fraktion.* Under Weimar the minimum strength of a *Fraktion* was fifteen. The reduced minimum, it is believed, will tend to weaken legislative efficiency, with little benefit accruing to the observance of democratic traditions.[28] Whatever the future may hold, *Fraktion* meetings are called with regularity and are a recognized feature of the total legislative process.

The three most powerful and influential organs of the *Bundestag* are the presidency, the Presidium, and the Council of Elders.[29] The President, elected by secret ballot, is the official head of the house

[23] Apelt, *op. cit.,* p. 192. [24] Giese, *op. cit.,* p. 41, notes.

[25] *Geschäftsordnung,* pars. 60-74. [26] Anschütz, *op. cit.,* pp. 180 ff.

[27] Ludwig Bergsträsser, *Die Problematik des deutschen Parlamentarismus* (Schriftenreihe der Hochschule für Politische Wissenschaften, No. 7; München, 1950), p. 9.

[28] Sänger, *Die Volksvertretung* (Stuttgart, 1949), p. 71.

[29] *Geschäftsordnung,* pars. 5-15.

in matters respecting its rights, prerogatives, and internal order. German parliamentary tradition makes this last function a most crucial one.[30] One innovation of the Weimar Constitution which has been carried over into the Basic Law is the assignment of police powers to the President,[31] a power which has been interpreted as vesting in him the authority to exclude deputies from the session of parliament for as long as thirty days.[32] The President's powers were more adequately defined in the Weimar Constitution. However, as one author points out, the exercise of the *Hausrecht* coupled with that of police powers and interpreted in the light of the legal development under Weimar is sufficient for the President to keep order on the premises of the Diet.[33]

The President is assisted in his functions by the Secretariat and the Council of Elders. The latter is responsible for the distribution of committee chairmanships, a fair share of which are assigned to the opposition. Furthermore, the Council of Elders is given the task of facilitating *inter-Fraktional* agreements concerning the distribution of work in the Diet. In other words, it fulfills in some respects the functions of a steering committee. The *Fraktions* select their delegates to the Council on the basis of age seniority rather than length of service or parliamentary tenure. The Presidium, consisting of the President, his alternates, and the members of the Secretariat, is primarily concerned with budgetary questions and with technical matters concerning order in the lower house.

(3) *Immunities*—Seeking to avoid the notorious abuses of parliamentary privilege by the radical deputies in the *Reichstag* and to remind the deputies of their role as the people's representatives, the Bonn Basic Law introduces a notable exception to the enjoyment of parliamentary immunity. Article 46 states that the usual privileges "shall not apply in the case of defamatory insults." The danger inherent in such a constitutional restriction is self-evident. In the light of paragraph 2 of the same article, it would appear, however, that the *Bundestag* itself is to be the sole judge of what should be considered "defamatory." The Weimar Constitution stated rather carelessly that a deputy could not be prosecuted "for any expression which

[30] Cf. *Germany's Parliament in Action*, pp. 70-71. The word *Präsident* is frequently, but not correctly, translated as "speaker."
[31] Cf. Articles 26 and 28 of the Weimar Constitution and Article 40 of the Bonn Basic Law. Also see Anschütz, *op. cit.*, pp. 202-207; Apelt, *op. cit.*, p. 191; Giese, *op. cit.*, pp. 42-43.
[32] See case of Dr. Kurt Schumacher, *Bundestag, Sitzungsberichte*, 18th session (Nov. 24, 1949), pp. 525-526.
[33] Giese, *op. cit.*, p. 42, note 3.

he has employed in carrying out his functions." Such vagueness lent itself to much abuse. Any political or personal utterance could be hidden behind that provision, regardless of whether it was made in or out of parliament. To fill this gap, the Basic Law stipulates clearly that the material immunity extends only to a "vote given or an utterance made . . . in the Bundestag or one of its committees." The consent of the *Bundestag* is also required in all other cases where a deputy's freedom of movement may be restricted by outside authorities or where he is threatened with the loss of his basic rights guaranteed in the Basic Law.[34]

Parliamentary practice has shown that the degree to which a parliament shows responsibility and discretion in the application of provisions granting immunities to its members depends largely upon the kind of pressure brought to bear upon the legislative body by the executive branch of the government. A parliament aroused to defend its integrity against encroachments, especially by the executive, will tend to protect its members under all circumstances, provided, of course, that it is free to do so. Thus, while the new provision cannot be considered an ironclad rule against abuse of parliamentary privileges, it may nevertheless serve as a reminder of parliamentary responsibility. There is no guarantee that under the immunity provisions a majority may not at one time in the future ignore the rights of a minority. The only reliable guarantee against such a development can be found in a proper stimulation of the forces which, in turn, generate the moods and attitudes found at the level of parliament—an alert electorate.

Again, the Weimar Constitution did not make it sufficiently clear that deputies can never be held legally responsible for actions or utterances which are based upon their official status and which occurred while parliament was in session.[35] This omission is corrected by the specific statement that "a representative may at no time be proceeded against . . . outside the *Bundestag*," if official acts are at the base of threatened legal action.[36] Finally, to protect the interests of

[34] See Anschütz, *op. cit.*, p. 227; Giese, *op. cit.*, p. 47, note 3. The case of federal deputy Wolfgang Hedler may be cited in this connection. The deputy was charged with preaching racism and nationalism, with malicious slander, libel, disparagement of the dead, and incitement to class struggle. The offensive remarks had been made at a political rally in Einfeld, Schleswig-Holstein, on November 25, 1949. Hedler's parliamentary immunity was lifted shortly thereafter to permit criminal prosecution. See "The Hedler Case," *Information Bulletin*, U.S. High Commissioner for Germany, April, 1950, pp. 43-45. The deputy was also expelled from his party.

[35] Article 37. Cf. Anschütz, *op. cit.*, p. 230.   [36] Article 46, Basic Law.

the *Bundestag* between legislative terms, these immunities and certain prerogatives of members are extended to members of the Presidium, members of the parliamentary "watchdog" committee, and their chief deputies during those intervening periods.

Legislation—Bills may be introduced in the *Bundestag* by the government, by individual members, or by the *Bundesrat*.[37] Bills originating with the government must first be submitted to the *Bundesrat* before they can be forwarded to the *Bundestag*. Bills originating with the *Bundesrat* are submitted to the lower house by the government, which must add a statement of its own views. Legislative projects, budgetary proposals, and international treaties are considered in three readings.[38] The first reading of bills and treaties is devoted to a discussion of basic principles only, subject to some separation into compartments. Changes in the proposed law may not be brought up before the end of the first reading and not at all in the case of international treaties. The committee stage follows a favorable vote at the end of the first reading.[39] The second reading does not involve a detailed discussion of the bill unless ordered by the *Bundestag*. Each separate discussion of principles, headings, introduction, and title is concluded by a vote on the matter under discussion. Changes in the order of the discussion, regroupings, or summary discussions may be decided upon by the house itself. Amendments may be introduced as long as the discussion of the original passage has not been terminated. Only international treaties must be discussed as a whole; they may not be compartmented.

The third reading is opened with a discussion of the principles which is followed by a separate debate on the component parts of the bill under consideration. Amendments may be considered at this

[37] Even though practices vary somewhat, there is a common pattern of legislative organization and procedure throughout Western Germany. To avoid repetition, these features of the legislative process are generally stated here and are elaborated in the section dealing with *Land* legislatures.

For a critical analysis of the "mechanization" of parliamentary procedure under the Bonn Republic, see Bergsträsser, *op. cit.*, pp. 11-13. In this connection, a passage from the *4th Quarterly Report on Germany* may be cited: "In the second six months, the rate of legislative accomplishments (of the Federal Diet) was increased by reason of more frequent meetings, stricter procedural rules, more limited debate, and better cooperation in committee between the Government parties and those of the opposition."

[38] See Sänger, *op. cit.*, pp. 78-81.

[39] By the end of 1952, there were thirty-nine functional committees in the *Bundestag*. Membership varied from seven to twenty-seven. Under paragraph 38 of the Rules of Procedure, a measure may be submitted to several committees at the same time.

stage provided that at least ten members pledge their support. The final vote comes at the end of the third reading. Unanimous agreement of all members present is required to rush all three readings through in the course of one day. No speaker may extend his remarks beyond one hour unless permission is granted by resolution supported by a majority of the members. The duration of the debate on certain items may be curtailed upon suggestion by the Council of Elders. Fifty members may move a roll call except on certain procedural matters such as a vote on adjournment or on termination of debate. Finally, the rules may be suspended or adapted to suit a given situation but only by unanimous consent. Following the final vote, the bill is submitted to the *Bundesrat* by the President of the *Bundestag*.

Upon request of the *Bundesrat*, if made within two weeks of the receipt of a bill, a conference must be convoked to iron out any conflicting views separating the two branches of parliament.[40] If legislation does not require the consent of the second chamber, that body may exercise a suspensive veto. If the veto is sustained by a two-thirds majority in the *Bundesrat*, a like majority in the *Bundestag* is required to override the veto. In all other cases, with the exception of amendments to the Basic Law, a simple majority of the members of the *Bundestag* is sufficient to override the veto. Laws enacted by the *Bundestag* are engrossed by the President upon receipt of the appropriate ministerial countersignature and are promulgated in the *Federal Gazette*. The Basic Law does not grant a delaying veto to the federal President.

The principle of parliamentary government and, closely allied with it, the principle of ministerial responsibility depend for effective functioning upon a certain independence of parliament from the executive. Legislative initiative is reserved to members of parliament as well as to members of the executive and the *Bundesrat*.[41] In the light of certain developments under the Weimar Republic and in view of the long absence of parliamentary government from the German political scene, it was doubly important to endow the popular house with independent powers in the field of legislation. Yet the constitutionally conferred authority has not been adequately implemented. The *Bundestag* cannot successfully wrest the initiative from the cabinet if its

[40] The veto procedure is contained in Article 77 (3-4), Basic Law. For a list of draft laws brought before the joint conference committee, see Elmer Plischke, *The West German Government* (Bonn, 1952), pp. 73-76.

[41] Since legislative proposals originating in an executive department must first be submitted to the Federal Council, it has become a frequent practice to introduce executive bills through individual members of the lower house.

members are not equipped to check legislative proposals coming from the government or to draft their own proposals in an intelligent and expert manner. Some German scholars and legislators, especially those who had occasion to study the American legislative reference services and the legislative councils, are aware of the need for such services in German parliamentary practice.[42] Dependence upon the several ministries for technical assistance and legal information tends to weaken the hand of the people's representatives and to undermine its confidence in its own proper functioning. The Rules of Procedure make but scant reference to legislative research by legislators. All that is provided for is a library committee of nine members. There are, however, a well-organized and growing archives section and a small library which is in the process of reorganization and expansion.

Legislative Review of Executive Action—In Western Germany, as elsewhere in the world, the effort of the legislature to maintain control of at least a portion of the executive structure has created specific devices for review and control. Traditional among these is the power to create special legislative committees for investigation purposes. The Weimar Constitution stipulated that the *Reichstag* could authorize the creation of such committees by a vote of one-fifth of its membership.[43] The Basic Law, however, has increased the minimum requirements to the point where one-fourth of the membership must support the creation of such a committee.[44] This change in minimum requirements, while indicating a desire to eliminate "nuisance" investigations by irresponsible groups, may nevertheless have an adverse effect upon effective legislative development. On the other hand, the stipulation that the decisions of the investigating committees are not subject to judicial review represents an improvement over corresponding provisions of the Weimar Constitution and is indicative of a strengthened faith in the ability of the legislature to exercise its functions in a responsible manner.

The rights and prerogatives of the legislature are protected further by the constitutionally conferred power to create a standing (watchdog) committee. This committee, appointed by the *Bundestag*, is to "safeguard the rights of the Bundestag in relation to the Federal Government in the interval between legislative terms." It is also endowed with the powers of an investigating committee.[45] Whether the failure of the Basic Law to provide for a standing committee on foreign af-

[42] Willibald Apelt, *Die Gesetzgebungstechnik* (Schriftenreihe der Hochschule für Politische Wissenschaften, No. 5; München, 1950), pp. 12-14.
[43] Article 34, Weimar Constitution. [44] Article 44 (1-4), Basic Law.
[45] Article 45, Basic Law.

fairs constitutes a further weakening of the legislature as against the government cannot yet be ascertained.[46] It would perhaps have been expedient to continue the Weimar practice of letting a foreign affairs committee check on that vital phase of the government's activities in the event of a dissolution of the legislature as well as at all other times. On the other hand, the Weimar committee, especially during the years when Gustav Stresemann was in charge of foreign affairs, rarely amounted to more than a sounding board for the minister.

Another control over the executive, albeit an insufficient one, is provided in the interpellation and question procedures. Thirty members of the *Bundestag* may address an interpellation through the President of that body to the government. If fifty members support the motion, a debate may proceed following the reply by the government representative. A motion based upon the interpellation or the government reply may be voted upon provided that thirty members are willing to support it. In the event that the government shows no inclination to reply to the interpellation, the Diet may decide to place it on the calendar for debate. Questions of lesser weight than interpellations may be brought up by as few as ten members of the Diet, but in these cases debate is not permitted on the government reply.

Aside from these political aspects of the relationships between legislature and executive, the Basic Law stipulates, as was done under Weimar, certain technical procedures designed to facilitate close cooperation between the two branches of government. The *Bundestag* has the right to demand the presence of members of the government at its plenary sessions as well as at meetings of its committees.[47] The government, on the other hand, as well as the members of the *Bundesrat*, are guaranteed access to all meetings of the *Bundestag* and its committees and cannot be denied a hearing if they seek one.

The Weight of Public Opinion—German legislatures have always shown a notable lack of appreciation of the role of public opinion in the legislative process. They have developed few techniques to facilitate effective utilization of public opinion in the formulation of legal norms. For example, with the exception of the committees of investigation (which may be closed to the public), committee meetings are not public, reports are not readily accessible, and public hearings are not regarded as essential to the legislative process.[48] By the same token, no means are available to marshal public opinion in support

[46] Article 35 (1) of the Weimar Constitution.

[47] However, as noted in Chapter 5 above, the first Chancellor ignored this provision on occasion.

[48] German scholars, returned from a study tour in the United States, are already

of the legislature against executive predominance.[49] It is assumed that public opinion is properly represented by the parties. The more controversial an issue, the less inclination can be found to inquire as to the state of public opinion. The fallacy becomes evident upon close examination of common procedures. Party discipline at the top is so overpowering as to leave little or no influence to the rank and file, not to speak of the voter. National headquarters of the parties do in fact determine the course to be followed in the legislature, and since no party represents a true cross section of the population—they are generally restricted to certain class, religious, or otherwise delimited interest groups—public opinion as such is not a potent factor in the legislative process. Because of certain distinct dividing lines, even the major parties, such as the CDU and SPD, cannot be considered as truly representative of the public as a whole. If an intergovernmental balance sufficient to preserve an independent legislature is to be secured, it is probable that the *Bundestag* will be required to seek a closer alliance with a cultivated public opinion.

STATE LEGISLATURES

A discussion of the legislative processes on the state level must take into account the fact that the majority of state constitutions were promulgated prior to the birth of the Bonn Republic. The differential occupation policies, applied by the several occupying powers in their respective zones, left their mark upon the constitutions, governmental structures, and political scenes of the several states.[50] Not to be overlooked either are the basic, traditional differences between the several areas. The tremendous amount of legislation thrown on state legislatures after 1946, necessitated by the collapse of federal authority, forced the states to enact much legislation which normally would have been a federal function and overburdened the legislative institutions in the states. The situation was conditioned further by the pressures for action contributed to by the confusion of postwar Germany and the race against time, especially in the American Zone, by the occupying powers. Yet out of these diverse factors and trying circumstances a rather uniform pattern of legislative organization, practices, and

---

calling for a more extensive application of public hearings to the legislative process. See Apelt, *Die Gesetzgebungstechnik*, pp. 14-15.

[49] Cf. Apelt, *Geschichte der Weimarer Verfassung*, p. 190.

[50] A comparison of the relatively progressive policies followed in the U.S. Zone of Occupation with the policies applied in the British and French Zones would serve to establish this point clearly. Cf. Harold O. Lewis, *New Constitutions in Occupied Germany* (Washington, D.C., 1948), Chaps. 2 and 3 above.

procedures is developing among the German states. Final judgment on the democratic or undemocratic characteristics of these developments must be delayed pending a further consolidation of present tendencies.

General Characteristics of State Legislatures—Constitutionally speaking, the power to govern is derived from the people and vested in unicameral legislatures which select the governments and assume responsibility for policies and administration. In only one state, Bavaria, is there a second chamber, and here the Senate, as it is called, in no true sense assumes any governing responsibilities. The Bavarian Senate was created to provide a secondary constituency ensuring representation for certain economic, social, and cultural interests. Conceived largely as a policy forum for these interests, its powers were limited to initiating, reviewing, and advising. It is not vested with co-ordinate legislative powers. The *Landtag* is under no legal obligation to consider legislation initiated by the Senate or to accept or even to listen to Senate advice. Consequently, the Senate has had little influence and the legislature in Bavaria, as in other German states, is essentially unicameral. The word "senate" is associated also with the legislature in the city-states of Bremen and Hamburg, but in these cities the word denotes no legislative functions but refers rather to "the government" or the organization of the administrative branch.

In terms of size, occupational spread, and educational attainments, German legislatures approximate the pattern of state legislatures in the United States. The average membership is 125 representatives, with a spread of from 215 to 204 in North Rhine–Westphalia and Bavaria, respectively, to 60 each in Baden and Württemberg-Hohenzollern. As in the United States, the legal profession is well represented in all legislatures. The occupational spread is otherwise conditioned, but not necessarily governed, by the dominant economic forces in the state. Again, as in the United States, the professionally trained constitute the bulk of the university-educated members. Although severely and widely criticized as undemocratic and unrepresentative, the German state legislatures provide a fairly representative cross section of postwar German society.

The legislatures selected in the first postwar elections were criticized (especially in the American Zone and with the encouragement of the occupying forces) because of the advanced age of the members, party domination, and the number of seats occupied by members holding other public positions, many in the executive branch of the government. This disregard of separation and division of powers was opposed in the American Zone as inconsistent with democratic principles and was for this and other reasons at least frowned upon in other sections of West Germany. At one time 38 per cent of the members of the Hessian legislature held at the same time another public office. The average number of officeholders sitting in the legislatures in the American Zone approximated 28 per cent of the total membership. The sharpest criticisms were directed against civil servants, with elective local officers being subject to censure to a somewhat lesser degree.[51]

Advanced age and party domination were largely attributable to the confused political picture, traditional party cleavages and discipline, and the early electoral system. In the search for confirmed, democratically inclined candidates it was felt necessary to reach back over the better part of a generation of Nazi domination to Weimar times. As a result "age" became in many cases a necessary qualification. Consequently, both the average and mean ages were unusually high, a fact resented and openly criticized especially among the younger elements of the population. In 1949, in the Hessian *Landtag*, two-thirds of the members were fifty years of age or older. Only six of the ninety members were under forty years of age. A similar situation was to be found in Bavaria, where 60 per cent of the members were fifty years of age or over and 28 per cent had exceeded threescore years. Only 14 of the 180 members were under forty years of age.

The reintroduction of proportional representation and the tacit encouragement given to the rise of parties in the image of their prototypes of an earlier era assured the return to Germany of bitter political differences, strict party discipline, and hierarchic and even autocratic party control.[52] The reflections of this general political situation in the legislative assemblies invited charges of undemocratic and nonpopular government. The situation has, however, been at least partially corrected. The recent elections have brought younger men into the assemblies, and electoral reforms have allegedly introduced a degree of political independence. The *Beamten* influences have been somewhat mitigated by the adoption of regulations in the majority of states which require civil servants to be placed on the inactive list before accepting legislative seats.

The Election of Legislators—The system of proportional representation was reintroduced in Germany in the postwar state constitutions. Although the constitutional provisions have a sense of permanency, the legislatures are permitted to provide for an "improved system of proportional representation." Under the guise of improving the earlier system, a majority of the states have adopted split systems which retain proportional representation in part but introduce also the single-mem-

[51] Cf. Chapters 4 and 5 above and 10 below.   [52] Cf. Chapter 20 below.

ber district, plurality election system.[53] Although the number of legislators selected by the one method or the other differs somewhat from state to state, the numbers gravitate about a norm of 50 per cent. The deviations in either direction represent concessions to dominant groups without introducing basic electoral differences. Party splintering, generally regarded as inimical to democratic development and governmental stability, is an acknowledged characteristic of German political life. With an eye to the past and alarmed by the rise of numerous party groups, the state legislatures have moved to protect their own stability. The device used, similar to the one used in federal elections, is a provision which requires the polling of a stated minimum of the total votes cast to obtain representation in the state legislature. The constitutions of some states stipulate the necessary minimum; in others the constitutions direct that the distribution of seats may be made dependent upon the polling of an unspecified per cent of the total vote, with the details left to legislative discretion.[54] In general, postwar electoral developments on the state level bear evidence of a strong desire to avoid the atomization of party life which had so considerably contributed to the demise of the Weimar Republic. Realization of these desires is still to be attained. Recent election returns gave seats in the state legislatures to a host of parties. In Lower Saxony ten of the eleven competing parties won places in the *Landtag.*

Leadership in the Landtag—As in the case of the federal legislature, the presiding officer and the key person in the state legislature is the president. Generally the position of the president is comparatively strong. What can be made of the office is, however, in most states a matter of personality and party fortunes. He is chosen by secret ballot from the house membership upon nomination by his party, and with one exception he serves for four years with little possibility of serious challenge to his position.[55] As the representative of the strongest party, his influence in the legislature depends in large measure upon the fortunes of that party, his position in it, and the attitude of the party toward the office. The president usually enjoys a strong position in the councils of his party, occupying a place just below the *Fraktion* leader.

[53] See Chapter 19 below for an extended discussion of the whole subject of electoral systems in postwar Germany.

[54] See R. Nebinger, *Kommentar zur Verfassung fuer Württemberg-Baden* (Stuttgart, 1949), pp. 188-190 (Art. 52).

[55] The president of the Hamburg legislature is elected for one year only. In the Rhineland-Palatinate he is selected first for four weeks and then for the remainder of the election period.

The president does not, on assuming the office, forfeit his membership prerogatives. He may vacate the chair to participate in debates and may attend all legislative committee meetings with the privilege of speaking but without vote. Generally regarded as something of an expert on parliamentary affairs, he speaks with considerable authority in committee and *Fraktion* meetings and on the floor. The president has in the several states, but in varying degrees, power to arrange the legislative agenda and to establish the order of speakers in debate. He employs all legislative personnel and in a general way directs and supervises their activities. He is responsible for maintaining order and possesses some policing powers over the chamber and the properties and papers of the legislature even in periods when the legislature is not in session. In spite of these rather liberal grants of power and the dignity of the office, he is neither a party boss nor a legislative dictator.[56] Both in stature and in authority, he ranks well below the minister-president. He suffers from German political tradition and faces at every turn the demands of the ministry and the interests of party *Fraktions*. The president is assisted by one or more deputies and several assistants (*Schriftführer*). The latter are as a rule younger members chosen on a proportional basis from the parties' representatives in the legislature. Neither the deputies nor the assistants share the special prerogatives of the president, nor do they draw an equal salary.

The functions and powers of legislative management are not lodged exclusively in the president and his assistants. In every west German state there is a special committee charged with policy questions relating to legislative work. This committee is composed of the president, his deputies, and a varying number of assistants. The groups are vested with authority, again in varying degree, over the administration of affairs in the legislature such as budget, printing, personnel, archives, and room assignments, but do not as a group have a voice in the determination of legislative business. This group, sometimes called "the Presidium," conducts the routine business of the *Landtag* between sessions and in theory protects its prerogatives against executive encroachments.

There is, in addition, the Council of Elders or, as it is called in some states, the Legislative Policy Committee. This body varies in size, with an approximate range of from seven to sixteen members. It con-

---

[56] A recent survey of state legislatures in West Germany indicated that most presidents make extensive use of their legal powers. As in the case of the federal legislature, however, the presidents will not oppose the government in such a way as to invite a clash between the two branches of the government.

sists of the president and leading members of the political parties represented in the legislature. Because of its influence on policy decisions and political differences, membership is distributed among the several parties strictly in proportion to their respective votes in the chamber. A meeting of the Council may be regarded as a caucus of *Fraktion* leaders augmented by enough other influential members to ensure relative interparty balance. It provides the arena for political (party) decisions and may be realistically viewed as the seat of ultimate legislative authority. Here interparty feuds are compromised, highly controversial issues resolved, and the dignity of the chamber preserved when threatened by disorder or individual misconduct. The Council has supreme authority over the order of legislative business including the agenda, speakers, and the time allotted to debate. It sits in review on contested rulings from the chair. It resolves all controversial issues of legislative strategy and policy and may designate the chairmen of the standing committees. The Council sometimes serves in the capacity of a standing committee, especially when a highly controversial measure must be recommitted. Its power emanates from the dominant role of German political parties rather than from constitutional sources. The Council, the apex of legislative authority and potentially antithetical to democratic government, can, but rarely does, rule arbitrarily. Its meetings may be infrequent, as infrequent as one meeting in two months. If the president enjoys their confidence, most of the Council functions are then performed under his direction. But when it chooses to act, its decisions are rarely questioned. As a rule, opposition to any measure dissolves almost magically before an announcement by the president of the Council's decision. While some might say that the device is potentially undemocratic, it differs little from the casual interparty caucuses used in all democratic legislatures. It is to be distinguished primarily in formal organization, the strong partisan loyalties of its members, and the felt necessity for opportunities to compromise party differences free from the temptation to make political thunder.

The System of Legislative Committees—Aside from the consequences of the more intense struggle for partisan advantage, the system of German state legislative committees bears a strong resemblance to its American counterpart in origin, purpose, and procedure. Each legislature has a number of standing committees created to prepare legislation for the plenary sessions. Each committee is charged with this task within a specified subject-matter area. In general, there is a committee for each major division or ministry in the executive branch of the state government. The strength or legislative influence as well as the number of these committees varies greatly, but there are almost always standing committees on budget and legal affairs and on social, cultural, and agricultural matters. A recent count revealed a range of standing committees of from four in Hamburg to twenty in Bremen. In addition to the standing committees, special or *ad hoc* committees are sometimes created by the legislature to explore certain areas which do not fall clearly within the jurisdiction of one of the standing committees. The division of labor is more widely distributed by the practice of forming subcommittees to ensure a thorough examination of all important bills. A German tradition is continued under the prevailing practice of creating a so-called "permanent committee" or "Presidium" to assist the president in safeguarding the interests of the legislature and in protecting its prerogatives against executive interference between legislative sessions.

Partisan influences and the consequences of the struggle for partisan advantage here as elsewhere in the world are distinguishing characteristics of the committee system and are initially reflected in the filling of committees and in the selection of chairmen. Parties with any show of strength are proportionately represented on all standing committees. Chairmanships are likewise distributed according to party strength. Each of at least the stronger parties is entitled to the chairmanship of one or more committees. This is normally true even in legislatures where one party has an absolute majority. The chairman is formally elected by the committee even though the choice may be limited to the single member designated by the Council of Elders. Consequently, the committee chairman does not provide any substantial legislative leadership. In fact, his position may be relatively weak. He does not control the committee agenda, and as a rule he does not report bills to the chamber nor does he assume the role of legislative manager. These functions and responsibilities, usually associated with committee chairmanships in the United States, are frequently delegated to a spokesman of the dominant party.

Executive or ministerial influence is liberally injected throughout the legislative process. Yet it is nowhere more apparent than at the committee level. In all states, members of the executive, that is, ministers or their representatives, may attend all committee meetings and speak at any time even outside the normal order of business. In most cases, the committees are authorized to call members of the executive branch in order to explain and elaborate their policies or to defend bills originating in the ministries. In several states, committee sessions are seldom held in the absence of the executive representative. Executive representatives have a tendency to exercise excessive influence at

committee meetings. This is particularly true in all cases where complicated matters of administration, including budgetary matters, are
involved.[57] By virtue of their superior knowledge and command of
relevant facts and figures, representatives of the executive are in a
favored position vis-à-vis the relatively uninformed legislator.[58]

Further opportunities for intrusions into committee proceedings
are found in the practice of permitting the presiding officer (the president) to appear at will to speak before any committee and to admit
other legislators as observers. Committee solidarity is weakened also
by absenteeism. Alternates are nominated and may be called in to
form a quorum. These practices sap the strength of the committee and
invite domination by party "regulars," specialists, and representatives
from the ministries. Cabinet members as well as high-ranking representatives of the bureaucracy who represent their ministries before
the legislature usually focus attention upon the committees rather
than the legislature as a whole. In the first place, most of the standing
committees are composed of members with special interests and
knowledge in the particular field assigned to the committee. In the
second place, a primary responsibility of the ministry representative
is to guide carefully prepared government legislation through the tor-
tuous legislative process. By reason of the closer scrutiny encouraged
by the relative secrecy of the committee room, these executive-initi-
ated bills run greater risks of mutilation, rearrangement, and amendment at this stage. It is here, then, that the ministry must be most
alert.

In prevailing circumstances, these close working relationships are
not devoid of advantages and benefits to the committee. A kind of
esprit de corps develops among representatives of the executive branch
and the committee "regulars." Furthermore, this close liaison with the
executive assures to the committee members access to technical data
otherwise unobtainable because of the lack of legislative reference
services and sufficient technical and clerical staffs and thus, paradoxi-
cally, ensures more penetrating investigations of government bills than

[57] It should be noted that budgetary practices have so far prevented real control by the legislature inasmuch as budgets, because of postwar circumstances,
have very often been submitted only after the expenditures had been made. See
Chapter 12 below.

[58] An extreme example is found in Schleswig-Holstein, where the minutes of
committees at one time were prepared not by employees of the legislature but by
representatives of the ministries. As a result the executive was placed in a position of undue influence over legislative procedures through the medium of the
committee report. This malpractice, however, has been discontinued, and the
committees are now taking care of their own business.

would otherwise be possible. Finally, the position of a given minister in his party and the strength of that party in the committee will establish to a considerable extent the degree of influence a representative of the executive may have over the work of the committee. The situation can well result in healthy legislative co-operation rather than outright executive domination.

In all states except Bavaria, committee meetings are secret.[59] Full minutes including debate and votes are not usually taken, but a rather full report on important legislation is prepared. This report is regarded as the exclusive property of the legislature. Copies are not given to the press, nor can they be examined by nonlegislative persons or taken from the premises except by special permission, which is not readily granted. Committee procedures are, however, not entirely unknown.

The burden of legislative work is carried by the committees. All bills are faithfully investigated and if necessary revised and rearranged. Because of the perfunctory and strictly partisan character of debate in the house, discussions leading to a meeting of minds on the merits of legislation come almost always at committee stage. Political differences are also compromised even though highly explosive situations are usually resolved by the Council of Elders, whose decisions are apparently not seriously questioned in committee. Bills together with committee amendments are reported to the chamber by a member of the committee specially assigned. If there is a strong dissent, a co-reporter will be appointed to present the case for the minority. In the case of important bills, presentations are made through formal reports which outline the principal features of the bill, set forth the issues, and carry the supporting arguments.

Committee procedures and practices differ from state to state and from situation to situation. Some reports reveal little more than a parade of party members mouthing the party line formulated in *Fraktion* meetings. In such sessions all decisions are strictly party decisions. Amendments are proposed and supported or opposed by party groupings, and occasionally, when tempers get out of control, a delegation withdraws. Such tactics do not, however, best characterize committee sessions. If basic party differences can be compromised, the members take off, or at least unbutton, their party coats and engage in a collective study of pending legislation, striving earnestly to arrive at conclusions which will promote the public interest. Although votes in

[59] In Bavaria, the public may be excluded by vote of the committee. The investigating committees authorized in all German constitutions are expected to conduct open sessions, and such sessions can be closed by the committee only by the vote of an extraordinary majority.

committee tend to reflect party divisions, the crossing of party lines in committee is far more frequent than in plenary sessions. Likewise, in the face of constant executive pressures in support of the government's legislative program, the committees demonstrate real independence of mind. Even though they are far too dependent upon the ministries for technical assistance, the committees undertake independent investigations. Individual members have some understanding of the proposals and some private sources of information. Their questioning of executive representatives can be penetrating and revealing. Formal or informal questioning of nongovernment "experts" is not uncommon though by no means as well developed as in Congressional practice in the United States.

The results of committee activities are difficult to appraise. Significant changes in government-initiated bills afford one type of test. Such an inventory will provide uneven results and perhaps indecisive answers. In some states and in certain circumstances ministry bills escape almost unscathed. This result may be anticipated when a single party dominates both branches of the state government, but with political strength divided, significant changes may be made in as much as 60 per cent or more of the government's legislative program. The results revealed by an accurate tabulation of amendments would be inconclusive. Some government-sponsored bills are *Fraktion* inspired. Others are introduced only after a careful canvassing of political opinion permits intelligent revision. Government bills, if vigorously attacked, may be withdrawn. Committee influence cannot be easily measured. It is, nevertheless, always significant, and many times it is the decisive factor in the shaping of specific legislation. Almost all legislation originates in the ministries, and in spite of committee vigilance, the legislative pattern is determined there. However effective or ineffective their activities may be, the committees constitute the only reliable check on government-sponsored legislation. Only occasionally does the government's program encounter difficulties in the chamber.

The Origin of Legislation—The cabinet in the German states assumes the power to govern, including the initiation of legislative policies. In no state is the responsibility limited to general policy declarations. Programs are delivered to the legislature in a series of carefully prepared bills. This right to initiate a legislative program is specifically granted in the state constitutions, but in no state is it made the exclusive function of the executive. Initiation by party groups and individual legislators is likewise recognized. Rules of procedure usually permit a party *Fraktion* the privilege of introducing bills without reference to the voting strength of the party but require five or more endorsements or cosponsors for bills offered by individual members. Political practices and pressures, without denying the right, practically require the individual to seek party endorsement rather than independent cosponsors.[60]

Legislative tradition, the existence of a well-established bureaucracy, and an absence of technical services for the legislatures encourage leaving the initiation of legislation almost exclusively to the executive branch of the government. Since the initial postwar reorganization of state governments, almost 90 per cent of all laws enacted were originated in the ministries. Of the total number of bills introduced, including those which did not become law, 50 to 80 per cent are originated by the government. Further, the small number of nongovernment bills which are passed is not a true index of the relative significance of the originating sources. In the first place, some of the laws originating in the chamber are rather inconsequential in the formulation of general public policy. A very few represent a kind of ganging-up of the major parties as a rebuke to the government, and some are introduced by the *Fraktions* with the knowledge, if not the blessing, of the executive branch and in many cases may be regarded as part and parcel of over-all political strategy. The general situation can be illustrated by reference to the history of legislation in almost any state. In the period beginning in December, 1946, to the end of May, 1949, 168 bills were introduced in the Hessian *Landtag*. One hundred nineteen of these were government-sponsored bills; forty were introduced by *Fraktions*, seven by members, and two by a special committee. Of the total number of bills introduced, 107 were passed; 92 of these were government sponsored. Eight of the *Fraktion* bills and five of the member bills became law. The two bills introduced by the special committee were enacted with government support. In North Rhine–Westphalia in the period from April, 1947, to June, 1950, ninety-six laws were enacted. Eighty-seven of these originated in the government; seven originated in the *Fraktions;* and one each was introduced by the president and a standing committee. Executive domination in Schleswig-Holstein was somewhat more evident. One hundred thirty-two of the first 135 laws enacted in that state were government sponsored.

The superiority of the resources of the ministries is nowhere more evident than in the preparation and drafting of the legislative program. The executive branch is as adequately equipped to formulate

[60] In Bavaria, bills may be introduced at the request of the Senate. The *Landtag* is, however, under no constitutional obligation to consider such bills. Consequently, Senate bills are not really significant.

policy as to supervise its execution. One process is as carefully and thoroughly administered as the other. The formulation of significant legislation is preceded by thorough studies of the problem, an appraisal of public and party opinion, and the taking of testimony from "experts." As a rule, a qualified person in a ministry is responsible for these preliminary studies and for drafting the proposal in correct legal form. This draft is discussed within the ministry, with the several department heads, and finally with the minister. The latter, in general, confines his comments to observations of a political nature. When he is satisfied, he submits the proposal to his colleagues for consideration at a cabinet meeting. It must not be assumed that cabinet consideration is a mere formality. Important bills are carefully considered, frequently revised, and sometimes returned to the ministry for further study or reformulation. Some proposals are rejected. If approved, the measure will be introduced into the legislature (presented to the president) as a government-sponsored bill. Almost all constitutions require that these bills be introduced only on recommendation of the cabinet. The legal formality is by far outweighed by the practical advantage of a united front and the prestige of tacit approval by the minister-president.

As a rule it can be said that there are no provisions for priority of legislation with regard to subject matter or source. For all practical purposes, however, government bills which have *ipso facto* support of the majority will be handled with more speed and urgency than other matters.[61] In addition, some constitutions endow the executive with delaying veto powers. This, coupled with the usual prestige attached to the executive, tends toward preferential treatment of government bills in practice. In any case, much of the legislation which occupies the time of the legislature both in committee and in plenary session is offered in support of the executive's program and is moved along under pressure from that branch of the government. Nongovernment bills are frequently opposed by ministry representatives either by a frontal assault or by the presentation of a bewildering mass of damning facts and figures.[62]

[61] In Bremen, executive bills marked "urgent" have priority over all other matters before the legislature. In Hesse, the Council of Elders may declare a bill as urgent with the effect of placing the measure at the head of the agenda. In Württemberg-Baden, there were no provisions for priority. However, the rules gave preference to executive bills inasmuch as motions to set such bills back on the agenda were not permissible. The latter arrangement is rather widespread.

[62] A story current in German parliamentary circles has the member of the executive say: "Mr. Delegate, your proposal sounds quite interesting but unfortunately you are not in possession of all the facts." Whereupon he launches an

Procedures in Plenary Sessions—Although the president may at his discretion refer certain lesser, noncontroversial measures directly to a committee, all important bills begin their legislative careers by presentation to the plenum, usually by distribution of printed copies and a reading of the title. Consideration at this time is not the usual course, but general discussion may ensue on petition (request or motion) supported by some stipulated number of members. The discussion must be confined to the general merits of the legislation. Amendment is not in order. The rules require always two or three readings, these to be separated by a period of at least several days. But as German legislators so frequently declare, "exceptions may be made." Introduction may or may not be one of the required readings, depending on the rules of the several states. After consideration in committee, bills are returned to the chamber together with the committee's report. The bill is in charge of a designated spokesman who may be required to supplement the written report by oral argument. Committee drafts of bills or recommended amendments must be printed before reintroduction on the floor. Amendments from the floor are in order, usually, until the time of the final vote. Procedures differ from state to state, but in general, bills are considered section by section on second reading. A vote closes the discussion on each section. Procedure on last reading directs attention to the over-all merits of the bill and is concluded by a vote to pass or to reject the bill as a whole. If passed, the bill is sent to the cabinet for promulgation. The responsibility for promulgation and publication is generally imposed upon the minister-president and the appropriate minister.

The pattern of debate, determined by the legislative procedures, is characterized by executive participation and rigid party discipline. Procedures at first and second readings provide some opportunity for informal discussion, but common practices limit these discussions largely to explanations and elaborations. Procedure in Committee of the Whole is not used. Speakers are usually selected in party caucuses and divide their limited time between expounding the position of the party and pleading for popular support for that position. These speeches are, with few exceptions, prepared in advance and delivered rather too formally from the rostrum in the front of the chamber. The debates are not designed, and on controversial issues are not calculated, to provide opportunities for "give and take" or to influence votes. There are two exceptions to this general pattern. When local

---

avalanche of facts and figures, smothering all arguments against the executive's proposal, and forces the legislator, who cannot answer and prefers not to look like a fool, to withdraw his motion.

issues upon which the parties have not taken stands or when tangential issues arise unexpectedly, debates become significant, and members occasionally cross party lines. The debate, likewise, assumes a more significant character when the budget is presented. The occasion provides an opportunity for a full and thorough discussion of government policies. These debates are regarded as of great political significance, equaled only by the debates on its policy statement when a new government comes to power.

The government concentrates its attention on the committee stage but does not neglect the plenary sessions. Representatives of the executive (sometimes limited by the rules to those who hold seats in the chamber) take the lead in opening and directing the debate in defense of its own measures and in opposing bills which do not have government support. They may take the floor on any occasion and are not required under the rules to adhere strictly to the order of business. Debates may be reopened, amendments may be offered at any time and a measure may be recommitted by request.[63] The cabinet seats in the front of the chamber may not always be filled, but "resource persons" are at hand and certain parliamentary advantages, which permit the government to direct the debate and to delay decisions, allow the ministers time to mobilize their resources in case of a threatened legislative crisis.

The executive veto, common in American states, is not required in Germany to provide balance in the field of legislative affairs. Yet the constitutions of several states provide either a modified type of executive veto or other opportunities for legislative maneuvering which, if evoked, would increase the measure of advantage already enjoyed by the cabinet. The constitution of Hesse declares unequivocally: "The Cabinet has the right to veto a law enacted by the *Landtag*."[64] The veto may be overridden by a simple majority, but it may be withdrawn up to the time of the opening of debate on the issue. One type or another of public referendum is supplied in the constitutions of several states. In Württemberg-Baden, for example, legislation was referred for popular decision if requested by one-third of the members of the *Landtag*.[65] It may be noted in passing that bills may be initiated by popular petition in several states. Reference to popular participation

---

[63] Only in Schleswig-Holstein, and perhaps in one other state under a strict interpretation of the rules, is the privilege of the floor denied to executive representatives who are not members of the cabinet. In Bremen, executive spokesmen must address themselves to the business before the chamber and may not reopen debate.

[64] Article 119.   [65] Article 83.

and the executive veto is made here, not with an intent to discuss these matters on their merits, but to emphasize the harassments to which an independently minded legislature might be subjected in the face of executive or politically inspired opposition.

Constituency Responsibility and Public Pressures—Neither party life nor political tradition has encouraged the development of a sense of continuing popular interest in the legislative processes or, conversely, established a strong sense of constituency responsibility. Nor have conditions in postwar Germany been conducive to the awakening of new political attitudes and relationships. Consequently, one of the most disappointing aspects of recent legislative development in the German states has been the continuing popular lethargy and the failure of the legislator to acknowledge a primary loyalty to a broad popular constituency. Both candidates and parties encourage the widely held idea that the responsibilities of the voter are discharged at the polling booth, at which point the victorious candidates and parties assume that a mandate to govern has been conferred.

Although the legislative processes are formally closed against popular participation, the process is more sensitive to popular reactions than the procedures indicate; the impact of popular pressures, however, is almost always transmitted through the political party or the executive. The German legislator's incoming mail is not heavy. An examination of petitions filed with two state legislatures over a two-year period revealed little popular interest in the legislative process. The record is not entirely negative, however. A government-sponsored bill in Württemberg-Baden, for example, was defeated in a close vote following a debate filled with references to the consequences of unfavorable popular reaction. On the other hand (and still the rule throughout Germany), those who profess to speak for a popular constituency are too frequently ridiculed for listening to "noises from the street."

Despite the materials set forth above, the situation is not entirely hopeless. Electoral reforms have encouraged a degree of political independence. The political activities and the rather weak party affiliations of certain refugee groups have compelled candidates in some cases to focus more sharply upon the unpredictable voter groups. The cultural exchange program, the "town hall" type of meeting, and the local government schools (especially in the British Zone) have also left their marks. There are reports, although too frequently unconfirmed, of informal legislator-constituency meetings in which the delegate seeks to inform, answer questions, and test the opinion of his constituency without reference to party lines or other forms of political affiliation. There is as yet, however, no substantial record which reveals a new identity of interests or demonstrates a markedly changed attitude toward legislative responsibility. When responsibility to the political party is challenged, the challenge arises most frequently from loyalties to trade and professional groups rather than popular constituencies.

Only in Bavaria are committee meetings open to the public. Nowhere are public hearings on pending legislation recognized in the legislative process, although one or more such hearings have been permitted. In spite of much public discussion and some reference to the matter on the floor, especially in the American Zone, the typical German legislator is sincerely skeptical of the procedure. He doubts the validity of the hearing and fears that the public airing of legislative questions will lead to confusion, loss of prestige, and political reprisals. The committee does not, on the other hand, completely insulate itself against outside opinion. In all but two states, the rules permit the calling of experts from outside the government. Testimony is taken, sometimes to balance or to test the opinions of government witnesses, but always behind closed doors. Committees are reported to have made on-the-spot investigations. The seeking of information and advice by individual members is a common practice. Because these practices are identified with the privileged affairs of the committee they receive no real publicity and are, consequently, difficult to evaluate either in terms of extent or significance.

Lobbying in the American sense is almost unknown in Germany. Pressure groups, real and potential, are both numerous and active but for a number of reasons avoid a concentration of effort on the legislature. In the first place, German legislatures regard themselves as representatives of, or as acting for, the population as a whole during the period of their mandate. In the second place, pressure groups, more obviously than in the United States, identify their special interest with party objectives. But, more important, these groups in Germany as in the United States direct their efforts to the vulnerable spots in the legislative process. Because of the primacy of its legislative position, the cabinet becomes the target for pressure activities.

Public relations, with special reference to press and radio, are distinctly inadequate. Public reporting of parliamentary affairs is adequate, but the activities of state legislatures receive little public notice except in highly controversial areas where the press is alleged by the legislators to be unduly critical, uncomplimentary, and unsympathetic. The press pleads scarcity of paper and too much routine. Although the press section in the public galleries is usually occupied and all public sessions are covered, the procedures do not provide news. Radio broadcast of debates in state legislatures has been abandoned. On the other hand, official reporting is excellent, the archives are well organized, public-address systems have been installed, and the public galleries are at times crowded. Yet on the whole and outside Bonn, the public, like the press and radio, demonstrate little interest in legislative affairs.

CONCLUSION

Constitutionally speaking, and in terms of structure and organization, German legislatures are democratic. Operationally, they leave much to be desired. Executive domination and party dictatorship contrive to move the lawmaking process out of its democratic setting into the hands of the manipulators. Political tradition argues against legislative independence and popular control. Postwar instability has not provided an atmosphere conducive to democratic development. Yet progress has been made, and the situation is not entirely discouraging. The German response to outside pressures for a greater degree of separation of powers has not been enthusiastic. The dangers inherent in continued executive domination and undue party influences have, however, been recognized. Among certain legislative elements these influences are resented and have been resisted. The resistance movement seeks only greater legislative independence within the existing governmental framework rather than constitutional separation of powers. Proponents of the movement, generally speaking, advocate election reforms, public hearings, adequate reference services, and sufficient legislative staff to permit a more thorough review of government policies and some check on the administration. This approach is sound. The unfinished job in Germany relates largely to fanning the spark of enthusiasm for popular control and kindling the spirit in the democratic structure.

9

Justice

KARL LOEWENSTEIN

OCCUPATION objectives in the reconstruction of the administration of justice in Germany were set forth by the Potsdam Declaration: "The judicial system will be reorganized in accordance with the principles of democracy, of justice under law, and of equal rights for all citizens without distinction of race, nationality or religion."[1] Prior to Potsdam, the famous JCS 1067 of 1945, dealing specifically with the part of Germany occupied by the United States forces, had directed the closing of all ordinary criminal, civil, and administrative courts except those previously re-established by American Military Government and the immediate abolition of all extraordinary courts and Nazi party courts.[2] Reopening of the ordinary courts was to be permitted only after the elimination of Nazi features and personnel and the establishment of appropriate controls, including the power to review and veto decisions. Both the Potsdam Declaration and JCS 1067 called for the abrogation of all peculiarly Nazi legislation.

The Directive of July 16, 1947,[3] addressed to the military governor,

---

[1] Report on the Tripartite Conference of Berlin, August 2, 1945, Article III(A) (8), in *Official Gazette of the Control Council* (Supp. No. 1, April, 1946), p. 15. For a full discussion of the reconstruction of the judiciary after 1945 (covering events until the middle of 1948), see Karl Loewenstein, "Reconstruction of the Administration of Justice in American-occupied Germany," *Harvard Law Review*, LXI (1948), 419-467.

[2] On the extraordinary courts, see Karl Loewenstein, "Law in the Third Reich," *Yale Law Journal*, XLV (1936), 808.

[3] See J. K. Pollock, J. H. Meisel, and H. L. Bretton, *Germany under Occupation*, rev. ed. (Ann Arbor, 1949).

General Clay, and superseding JCS 1067, articulated and summarized the occupation policies as they had developed under the impact of reality since unconditional surrender. It was based on the recognition of German self-government and the assumption of direct responsibility by German agencies constituted in accordance with democratic processes. To foster the independence of the German judiciary, control measures maintained by American Military Government in the legal field were to be reduced to "the minimum consistent with the accomplishment of the aims of the occupation." The basic objective of the occupation was to be the re-establishment of the rule of law. With the entering into force of the Occupation Statute on September 21, 1949,[4] German regained, under the Basic Law, full sovereignty in the field of the administration of justice with the exception of judicial powers retained by the occupation powers in the fields reserved to them in the Occupation Statute.[5]

REORGANIZATION OF THE GERMAN COURTS

The Ordinary Courts—Unconditional surrender resulted in a complete standstill of justice, a situation without parallel in modern times in any organized state. This situation was brought about in the United States Zone by Military Government Law No. 2,[6] which ordered the temporary closing of the courts of appeal (*Oberlandesgerichte*) together with all courts over which they exercised appellate or supervisory jurisdiction, the administrative courts, and all courts not dissolved as party courts or extraordinary courts.[7] American Military Government was authorized, however, to reopen the ordinary courts.

In October, 1945, the detailed Plan for the Administration of Justice in the United States Zone[8] was issued, which, in conformity with Military Government Proclamation No. 2 of September 19, 1945,[9]

[4] See *ibid.* for both this directive and JCS 1067 of 1945.
[5] See Law No. 13 on "Judicial Powers in the Reserved Fields" of November 25, 1949, *Official Gazette of the Allied High Commission for Germany,* pp. 54 ff.
[6] The following abbreviations are used throughout this chapter: MGR for Military Government Regulations; OGCC for *Official Gazette of the Control Council;* MGG for *Military Government Gazette* (United States); RGBl. for *Reichsgesetzblatt* (official law bulletin of German Reich); GVBl. for *Gesetz- und Verordnungsblatt* (official law bulletin of the *Länder*); SJZ for *Süddeutsche Juristenzeitung;* DJZ for *Deutsche Juristenzeitung.*
[7] Military Government Law No. 2, Articles I and II, in MGG (Issue A, June, 1946), p. 10.
[8] Plan for the Administration of Justice, U.S. Zone, transmitted with AG 014.1 GEC-AGO (Oct. 4, 1945; Letter to Commanding Generals of Eastern and Western Military Districts).
[9] Article III in MGG (Issue A, June, 1946), p. 3.

transferred full responsibility for the operation of the judicial system to the German authorities, in particular to the *Land* ministers of justice.[10] Thus, at long last some degree of uniformity and administrative concentration was achieved. By June, 1946, the majority of courts that had existed prior to the collapse were open for business.

The corresponding measure on the quadripartite level, Control Council Proclamation No. 3 of October 20, 1945, on Fundamental Principles of Judicial Reform[11]—credo of the Four Powers in judicial matters—required that the judicial system be based on the achievement of democracy, civilization, and justice. Embodying the principles of due process of law, it prohibited determination of guilt by "analogy" or by the "sound instinct of the people," as was permissible under Nazi law; the accused is to enjoy all rights recognized by democratic procedure. Sentences on persons convicted under the Hitler regime on racial or political grounds must be quashed. Judges are to be independent of executive control and owe obedience only to the law. The judicial office is accessible to all who "accept democratic principles," and the promotion of judges must be based solely on merit and legal qualifications.

While Control Council Proclamation No. 3 sets forth the general principles, the subsequent Control Council Law No. 4 of October 30, 1945, on Reorganization of the Judicial System,[12] presented a general frame of reference for the actual conduct of the administration of justice, valid for Germany as a whole. The carrying out of this reorganization was left to the discretion of the zone commanders. In general, the German judicial system was restored to the situation that existed prior to Hitler, in line with the Judicature Act of 1877,[13] ordinary courts being the district court (*Amtsgericht*), regional court (*Landgericht*), and court of appeals (*Oberlandesgericht*).[14]

In the final analysis, the reorganization of courts as accomplished after 1945 provided adequate judicial services and reasonable remedies. But the opportunity of cutting out numerous superfluous courts by an energetic consolidation of judicial districts was neglected. The ministers of justice were authorized to effect such a move[15] but failed to do so. The most tangible defect, however, was the absence of a

[10] MGR 5-400.3, 5-421. [11] OGCC No. 1 (Oct., 1945), p. 22.

[12] OGCC No. 2 (Nov., 1945), p. 26.

[13] In its modernized version, Law of March 24, 1924, in RGB1. (1924), I, p. 299.

[14] For a survey of the structure of German courts before Hitler, see R. C. K. Ensor, *Courts and Judges in France, Germany, and England* (London, 1933), pp. 52 ff.

[15] MGR 5-405.

supreme court, such as the *Reichsgericht* for all Germany, which was discontinued by the Allies with unconditional surrender.[16] Failure to establish it contributed much to the unprecedented legal diversity within the United States Zone, not to mention in Germany as a whole.

On the other hand, in the British Zone the functions of the former Reichsgericht of serving as a court of appeal in matters of law only was taken over, in 1947, by a High Court (*Oberster Gerichtshof*) located in Cologne[17]; this court, in terms of jurisprudential excellence, became, under the presidency of Ernst Wolff (a prominent former Berlin attorney-at-law), the most respected of all German courts. Likewise, on the bizonal level, a German High Court for the Combined Economic Area was established[18] with jurisdiction over all civil and criminal matters coming under the administration of the bizonal Economic Council; but in actual practice this court was a stillborn child and had very little work.

Administrative Courts—For several generations, administrative courts, patterned on the French precedent, had become an integrated feature of the German court system. First introduced in the *Länder*— with Baden, in 1863, taking the lead—they had gradually been extended to some special fields of Reich administration, for example, patent matters, social insurance, and finance, culminating in the Reich Finance Tribunal (*Reichsfinanzgerichtshof*). Even under the Nazis, administrative courts continued to operate with relatively few changes. However, a general Reich Administrative Court, prescribed by the Weimar Constitution (Art. 107), remained a legislative promise until 1941, when the Nazis created it; the war prevented its limited jurisdiction from coming into full operation. Administrative courts adjudicating controversies concerning rights alleged to be affected by an act of a public authority and also controversies between public authorities or bodies had proved themselves protectors against administrative arbitrariness (by no means confined to what in Anglo-Saxon countries is understood by the term "civil liberties"), and helped to safeguard the rule of law in the conduct of public administration. The public regarded them as ordinary courts, and they were as respected and independent of governmental control as were the ordinary courts.

To round out a comprehensive system of independent courts, re-

---

[16] This court, formerly located in Leipzig (now in the Russian Zone), was not reopened because under the Potsdam Agreement central agencies were not permitted to be re-established. See Chapter 2 above.

[17] See Ordinance of the *Zentral-Justizamt* of November 11, 1947.

[18] See Proclamation No. 8 of February 9, 1948, in Pollock, Meisel, and Bretton, *op. cit.*

establishment of administrative courts was envisaged by the Four Powers at an early date. But what finally emerged from their conflicting approaches was a colorless and vague compromise. Control Council Law No. 36[19] confined itself to the general statement that administrative courts should be established in all four zones and in Berlin, but left structure, jurisdiction, and procedure to the determination of the respective zone commanders and, for Berlin, to the Allied *Kommandatura.* Moreover, the action of the Control Council was pointless since, in the meantime, administrative courts had been opened in all four zones. In the U.S. Zone, the *Länderrat,* under American Military Government instructions and assistance, managed to harmonize the traditional differences in technique and jurisdiction between the three south German states, thus creating, for the first time, a uniform regulation of the matter in the entire area, one of the few instances where American Military Government actively and successfully promoted legal unity.[20] Substantially, the reorganization followed the well-tried pattern that had existed before 1933, as was also the case of the administrative courts subsequently re-established in the British and French zones.[21] Of the Supreme Administrative Courts provided for by the Bonn Constitution (Art. 96, par. 1) for general administration, social insurance, and finances, the last named has been established (1950) as *Bundesfinanzgerichtshof* in Munich, while the *Bundesverwaltungsgericht,* with its seat in Western Berlin, began operation in 1952.

In the Soviet Zone, administrative courts were not altogether discontinued but were confined to specific cases, to be decided by a single court (without inferior instances).[22] But the ineffectiveness of constitutional guarantees in a one-party controlled state is vividly demonstrated by the experience in Thuringia, in which the Supreme Administrative Court within less than two years was wholly subjugated by the Communist party.[23] The constitution of the German Democratic Republic (Art. 138) envisages "protection of the citizens

[19] Of October 10, 1946, OGCC No. 11 (Oct., 1946), p. 183.

[20] For Bavaria, see Law No. 59 of September 25, 1946 (GVBl., pp. 281 ff.); the versions in Württemberg-Baden, Hessen, and Breman differ only in minor points.

[21] For the British Zone, see Ordinances Nos. 141 (OG BMG 1948, p. 111) and 165 (VOBl. B.Z. 1948, p. 263). For the French Zone, see Ordinance No. 76 of July 2, 1947 (*Journal officiel,* p. 256).

[22] See Order of the SMA of July 8, 1947, No. 173/47.

[23] The story is compellingly told by the (then and subsequently resigned) president of the *Oberverwaltungsgericht,* Helmuth Loening, "Kampf um den Rechtsstaat in Thüringen," *Archiv des öffentlichen Rechts,* LXXV (1949), 56 ff.

against unlawful administrative measures by virtue of the control exercised by the legislature and through recourse to administrative courts" whose structure and jurisdiction is to be regulated by special law (not yet enacted at the time of this writing). But the ominous juxtaposition of protection by the political organs which control identically the administration and the administrative court has proved to be largely destructive of the rule of law in the Soviet sphere.

The regulation of administrative justice in the western German *Länder* varies considerably. The basic differences lie in the adoption of the so-called "general clause" system or of the principle of enumerated and specified complaints. Under the former, whoever feels adversely affected by an administrative decision or act alleged to be in violation of the law or to exceed legitimate administrative discretion, may invoke the administrative jurisdiction (such as in Württemberg-Baden, Art. 90); under the latter system, redress by administrative courts is confined to specified (and enumerated) cases of administrative actions or decisions (this device, for example, is applied in Hamburg). Attention should also be called to the differentiation of procedural technique. Under the system of the so-called "elective complaint" (*Wahlklage*) the complainant may either invoke the administrative court or seek redress of grievance through the superordinated agency in the administrative hierarchy. Under the system of the "terminal complaint" (*Schlussklage*) the administrative jurisdiction comes into play only after the normal administrative remedies have been exhausted through *Verwaltungsbeschwerde* (this, for example, in Württemberg-Hohenzollern). Another variant, for the complainant probably the best, is setting in motion concurrently both chains of redress—before the administrative court and the administrative authorities (for example, in Baden). Two important categories of cases are traditionally withdrawn from administrative adjudication, namely, disciplinary action against public officials, for which special disciplinary courts exist everywhere, and claims of damages against the state in case an official, acting in such capacity, violates with regard to third persons his official duties. In this case the state is liable and suable before the ordinary courts; there is no such thing as the "immune sovereign" on the European continent, a heritage of the French Revolution. The state, however, if held liable by the ordinary court, may seek compensation from the official, again through the ordinary courts (Weimar Constitution, Art. 131; Bonn Constitution, Art. 34). On the whole, the administrative justice has reverted, without much difficulties, to what had been customary before 1933.

Labor Courts—Under Weimar, Germany possessed a model system of courts for the settlement of labor disputes, established by the notable Labor Courts Law of 1926.[24] In substitution for this system, the Nazis subjected labor to the totalitarian control of the huge Labor Front, established by the "labor charter," the Law for the Organization of National Labor of 1934.[25] After unconditional surrender, restoration of independent labor courts was not urgent, since organized labor had been disintegrated. In the United States Zone, provisionally, the district courts (*Amtsgerichte*) discharged the functions of the former labor courts.[26] However, the revival and reorganization of the trade-union movement was favored by all the powers; as a result, Control Council Law No. 21 of March 30, 1946, on German labor courts,[27] decreed uniform principles on a quadripartite basis. Under the jurisdiction of the local and appellate labor courts which the law provided were the following kinds of disputes: those arising out of a collective agreement or relative to the existence or nonexistence of such; those between employers and employees arising out of the employment relationship; those concerning working conditions, including health and safety measures; and those concerning the interpretation of agreements concluded between works councils[28] and employers. The judges are to be selected by an elaborate system of panels in which representatives of management and of the unions participate. For an interim period, the German Labor Court Law of 1926 continued, in so far as it was not inconsistent with the Control Council law.[29]

Military Government Courts—In view of the fact that the reconstruction of a denazified German court organization would require

[24] 1 RGBl. 507 (1926). See Nathan Reich, *Labour Relations in Republican Germany* (New York, 1938); Frieda Wunderlich, *German Labor Courts* (Chapel Hill, 1946).

[25] RGBl. 45 (1934), I, p. 45.   [26] MGR 5-409.5.

[27] OGCC No. 5 (March, 1946), p. 124.

[28] On works councils, see Control Council Law No. 22 (April 10, 1946), p. 133. In connection with the legislative introduction of "codetermination" of the employees in the management of business and industrial enterprises (*Betriebsverfassungsgesetz* of October 11, 1952), the labor courts were assigned additional jurisdictional tasks: see Otto Koellreutter, *Deutsches Staatsrecht* (Stuttgart–Cologne, 1952), pp. 266 ff. A bill for the establishment of a Federal Supreme Court for Labor Affairs was not passed by the end of 1952; on the draft, see *Juristenzeitung* 1952, p. 155.

[29] Within the frame of Control Council Law No. 21 there existed a great diversity of regulations zone-wise and even intrazonally. See, for example, Bavarian Law of December 12, 1946; Württemberg-Hohenzollern Law of October 24, 1946. However, all *Länder* provide for at least one superior Labor Court. In the Soviet Zone, which introduced labor courts as early as by the SMA Order of January 25, 1946, a unification law is under preparation.

time and that, meanwhile, law and order had to be preserved, military courts operated from the beginning of the occupation,[30] divided, according to the kind of sentences they could mete out, into general, intermediate, and summary courts. They were given jurisdiction over all offenses committed by persons in the occupied area with the exception of the members of the Allied armed forces. It extended not only to all violations of military government legislation but as well to all offenses against German law. The procedures adopted were a mixture of courts—martial and the German and Anglo-Saxon techniques. To eliminate continuing abuses of judicial powers these courts were enjoined, by Directive of July 16, 1947, to conduct themselves in full conformity with the principles of due process at home. Finally, all persons indicted before military government courts in the U.S. Zone were formally accorded, by Military Government Ordinance No. 23 on "Relief from Unlawful Restraint on Personal Liberty" of January 7, 1948,[31] the fullest extent of the protection of habeas corpus. Although during the first years of the occupation a relatively high percentage of the total cases occurring in the U.S. Zone were tried by military government courts (27.5 per cent in 1946 and 15.9 per cent in 1947), more and more entire categories of criminal acts were transferred to the reconstituted German courts. The progressive restoration of judicial sovereignty to the German authorities required in due course the setting up by OMGUS (Office of Military Government, United States) of a completely new system of military government courts, leading (August 18, 1948) to a civilianized and independent organization.[32] The United States Area of Control was divided into eleven judicial districts with district courts, under a Court of Appeals whose Chief Justice is the highest judicial authority of the entire area. District courts, consisting of three members, have criminal as well as civil jurisdiction (the latter substantially unimportant). The criminal jurisdiction extends to all persons in the U.S. Area of Control except military and naval personnel, including, therefore, dependents of U.S. personnel as well as all Germans and displaced persons. Materially the courts can deal with all violation of Allied and German legislation. A complete system of judicial review by the Court of Appeals (consisting of the Chief Justice and six Associate Justices) was likewise installed.

[30] Ordinance No. 2, MGG (Issue A, June, 1946), p. 60. For a full discussion of military government courts, see Eli N. Nobleman, "American Military Government Courts in Germany," *Annals of the American Academy of Political and Social Sciences,* CCLXVII (Jan., 1950), 87 ff.

[31] OGG Issue H (Jan. 16, 1948), pp. 7 ff.

[32] Military Government Ordinances Nos. 31, 32, 33, MGG Issue K (Sept. 1, 1948), pp. 35, 44, 55.

On the whole, the military government courts, after the elimination of the initial inequities, have worked well and gained the respect of the Germans, who were impressed by certain features of American legal technique (cross examination) and by the impartiality of the judge toward both the prosecuting authority and the defendant. In view of the progressive self-restraint which the Allies exercised towards Germany under the Occupation Statute, these American courts in Germany confined their jurisdiction primarily to offenses against the interests of the occupation in the widest sense of security.[33] Still excluded, however, and this in conformity with what may be called the natural law of occupation, were members of the Allied forces or persons officially connected with the Allied High Commission and their dependents, in criminal matters and in civil affairs.[34] Moreover, Law No. 13 decreed further restrictions on German judicial autonomy, all emanating from the fact of the occupation, namely: the validity of Allied legislation in the widest sense is beyond challenge of the German courts. Allied personnel is not obligated to testify before German courts except by explicit authorization of the Office of the High Commissioner for Germany (HICOG); the occupation authorities may request production of any German court record and may attend any German court hearing. Concerning the persons protected by Article No. 2 of the Occupation Statute (such as displaced persons or refugees), the occupation authorities may suspend a trial or a court decision and may withdraw a case from a German court or transfer it to an occupation court. Under this article any German court decision may be nullified or amended or a trial or retrial by a German court ordered. Simultaneously, Control Council Law No. 4 and the preceding Allied military government court legislation were rescinded.[35]

Appraised in their entirety, the still-existing restrictions on German judicial sovereignty[36] are of minor importance and affect only a limited number of persons and acts. Since 1949 no case of exercising the right of intervention in German court proceedings by either HICOG

[33] HICOG Law No. 14 on "Offenses against the Interests of the Occupation" of November 25, 1949, *HICOG Official Gazette,* p. 59.

[34] HICOG Law No. 13 on "Judicial Powers on the Reserved Fields" of November 25, 1949, *HICOG Official Gazette,* p. 54. There are various technical reservations which cannot be discussed here.

[35] For a full discussion of previous American supervisory powers, see Karl Loewenstein's article, already cited, in *Harvard Law R.,* pp. 438 ff.

[36] An American court (the situation is similar in the other western zones) is also the Court of Appeals in restitution matters under Military Government Law No. 65 on "Restitution of Identifiable Property" of November 10, 1947, OGG Issue G, pp. 1 ff.

or any of the individual occupation powers has been reported. In the case of a decision of the *Oberlandesgericht* Stuttgart *re Kaess* in which the court had failed to prosecute a person incriminated of bribery in a widely discussed denazification scandal, the U.S. High Commissioner John J. McCloy "seriously considered intervening." He abstained, however, from removing the case to an Allied court "because an intervention by the Occupying Power is no adequate substitute for native protection of the principle of the equality before the law."[37]

PROBLEMS OF JUDICIAL PERSONNEL

Denazification of the Judiciary—Denazification, in the legal field, involved both purging German law of Nazi concepts and practices[38] and elimination of Nazi-tainted personnel from the legal services. A brief analysis of this fundamental issue of the occupation is indispensable for the present-day appraisal of the German judiciary. When the Nazis set out to revolutionize the *Rechtsstaat*, the new regime was accepted by the legal profession with no less approval or complacency than by other influential classes. Active nonconformists were expelled at once by the Law of April 7, 1933, misnamed the Law for the Restoration of the Professional Civil Service.[39] Aside from those outsed for racial or political reasons, only a handful of mostly older judges resigned voluntarily. On May 1, 1937, the Public Officials Act entered into force. While not explicitly requiring party membership for public officials, it suspended permanently over their heads the sword of dismissal for "political unreliability."[40] Consequently, the vast majority of the bench took out membership badges or otherwise demonstrated their allegiance to the party.[41]

Entry into the party, in many cases, was not motivated by the acceptance of its tenets. Rather, it was a sort of insurance policy against

---

[37] The letter addressed to the minister of justice in Württemberg-Baden, Joseph Beyerle, is published in *Information Bulletin*, U.S. High Commissioner for Germany, December, 1950, p. 84. The case belonged to the complex of deviations from the democratic processes of justice connected with glaringly lax law enforcement by the denazification tribunals.

[38] For a full discussion of the denazification of law, see Karl Loewenstein, "Law and the Legislative Process in Occupied Germany," *Yale Law J.*, LVII (1948), 734 ff., 994 ff.

[39] *Gesetz zur Wiederherstellung des Berufsbeamtentums* in 1 RGB1. 175 (1933); see Karl Loewenstein, "Law in the Third Reich," *Yale Law J.*, XLV (1936), 779, 794.

[40] See *Berufsbeamtengesetz*, sec. 171 (Jan. 26, 1937) in 1 RGB1. 39 (1937).

[41] Automatically and irrespective of membership in the party, all judges were enrolled in the Civil Servants Association (*Reichsbeamtenbund*), an organization supervised by the party. No special organization for judges existed.

dismissal, a guarantee of continued promotion within the service, together with the gratification of belonging to the ruling class. In the case of older men with families and tenure at stake, such opportunism may seem understandable and even condonable, for though a judge may have disagreed inwardly with the regime and recoiled from enforcing its arbitrary rules, he may have lacked the strength to resist pressure exerted by the president of his court, who invariably was a hand-picked Nazi zealot.[42] Some, of course, did not require crude persuasion. They were, however, a decided minority. For the younger men entering the profession, there was almost no chance of appointment without membership, at least after 1938. All in all, it was found that the overwhelming majority of the legal officials were members of the party.

There were, of course, factors tending to offset the human explanations for the prostration of the judiciary before the Nazi Leviathan. Not a single case occurred in which a judge who resigned was sent to a concentration camp or even lost his pension. If he wished, he could leave the service and "sit the regime out" on his pension. Moreover, there were some judges, particularly among the older generation, who, neither resigning nor yielding, resisted pressure to the end.[43] Nor were nonparty members among the judiciary invariably denied promotion.

(1) *The American Phase of Denazification*—Little is gained by repeating known facts concerning the chaos of denazification management in the early period after unconditional surrender. Article IV of Control Council Law No. 4 of October 30, 1945, on "the Reorganization of the Judicial System,"[44] stipulated that "to effect the reorganization of the judicial system, all former members of the Nazi party who have been more than nominal participants in its activities and all other persons who directly followed the punitive practices of the Hitler regime must be dismissed from appointments as judges and prosecutors and will not be admitted to these appointments." Military Government Law No. 2[45] dealt with the issue of indirection only, stating that no person shall act as judge, prosecutor, notary, or lawyer without military government consent and that military government

---

[42] For example, in the district of the *Oberlandesgericht* Bamberg, which had been saddled with a particularly fanatical Nazi president, only 7 among the 302 judges and public prosecutors had not joined. See Monthly Report No. 14 (Sept. 1946), Legal and Judicial Affairs (AMG), p. 9.

[43] For example, in the office of the public prosecutor of the important *Landgericht* I in Munich, three out of five ranking officials were not party members at the time of the collapse.

[44] OGCC No. 2 (Nov., 1945), p. 27. [45] See MGG (Issue A, June, 1946), p. 7.

had the power to dismiss or suspend any German judge, prosecutor, or court official and to disbar from practice any lawyer or notary.

Yet American Military Government authorities were not left without guidance as to the removal and ineligibility of former Nazis. Incumbents of certain enumerated offices (*Beamtenstellungen*) at any time on or after January 30, 1933, were automatically excluded from continuing in, or admission into, public service. Included were practically all of the leading positions in the administration (*höhere Verwaltung*) for which legal training is traditionally a prerequisite and the ranking positions in the various courts. In setting this date for the presumption of Nazi activity, disregard of German history caused a grave injustice because the leading positions were still held by men appointed under the Weimar Republic. It took months to have this grievous error remedied. Control Council Directive No. 24 of January 12, 1946, finally limited exclusion of officials from public service to "any person who has been appointed to any of the following positions *since* January 30, 1933 *and any person who was an incumbent on that date and survived the successive Nazi purges which followed.*"[46]

Schematic tests for what constituted an "active" Nazi brought hardships, however, in numerous individual cases and left the cardinal issue, that of determining who among the rank and file of the lower judiciary was only a nominal Nazi, very much where it had been before—within the discretion of the military government officer in charge of denazification in the particular instance. Intensive experimentation failed to develop foolproof tests. The most convenient criterion, known as the "vintage" principle, proceeded from the belief that the earlier the date of entry, the greater the entrant's sympathy with the party. On the other hand, for many in American Military Government there was some truth in the contention of many early Nazis that their initial enthusiasm soon had paled and they had become anti-Nazis, though they had not risked leaving the party after their "conversion." The only defensible date made use of under application of the vintage doctrine was May, 1937,[47] after which date officials could be forced to join the party—or at least it was so believed—under the Public Officials Act. Persons who joined after this date were excepted in due course from the compulsory removal and exclusion categories.

[46] Paragraphs 10(53)–10(86) (Jan. 12, 1946) in OGCC No. 5 (March, 1946), p. 106; (italics supplied). Paragraphs 10(87)–10(89) deal specifically with legal personnel.

[47] This date was officially recognized by Control Council Directive No. 24, paragraph 10(2)(b) (Jan. 12, 1946) in OGCC No. 5 (March, 1946), p. 102.

When the appointive power in the judicial field was transferred from American Military Government to the ministers of justice at the end of 1945, it carried with it, implicitly, the responsibility of denazification. While it is true that for the time being no appointment could be made without American Military Government approval,[48] in actual practice the presidents of the *Oberlandesgerichte* and the *Landgerichte* selected the personnel for their courts in conjunction with the ministers of justice and the skeleton ministerial bureaucracy, with American Military Government, however, retaining the function of screening the applicants. The candidate for office had to submit a yard-long questionnaire or *Fragebogen,* that ubiquitous symbol of the "revolution by bureaucracy." A special *Fragebogen* existed for the legal profession, though it never revealed, in the case of a judge with an impeccable paper record, how he had behaved in office, in what decisions he had participated, or whether his opinions reflected subservience to the regime.

In fact, therefore, denazification of legal personnel shifted to the judicial class. The judges knew best who among them had "kowtowed" more than was necessary, who had gained unmerited recognition and promotion, who had been a "profiteer." But here entered a socio-psychological element which military government was unable to neutralize —the class solidarity of the judiciary, which, subconsciously or consciously, began to balance and outweigh what desire for political cleanliness may have existed. In fact, under the impact of the occupation, a national solidarity emerged, not merely in the civil service but among all classes, which tried to save as many colleagues as possible from the clutches of denazification.[49] Only a relatively small minority of fanatics was considered permanently disqualified—men who did not dare to apply for re-employment anyway. Moreover, if a man was a good judge, his redemption and readmission to the depleted ranks were made easy. The judicial caste has not failed its members.

(2) *The German Phase of Denazification*—The strong undercurrent of tolerance towards the past sinners among the judiciary broke into the open with the deliberate transfer of responsibility for denazification to the Germans by the Law of the Liberation from National Socialism and Militarism of March 5, 1946.[50] This law contained in an appendix an elaborate list of positions and offices whose former hold-

[48] MGR 5-415.1.

[49] See Karl Loewenstein, "Denazification Report," *New York Times,* December 2, 1946, p. 10E, col. 5.

[50] For text, see MGR 24-500; Bavaria, GVBl. 197 (1946); Württemberg-Baden, RGBl. 75 (1946); Greater Hesse, GVBl. 57 (1946).

ers were considered, on rebuttable presumption, to be either major offenders (Class I) or offenders (Class II). Class I included the top-ranking judicial and administrative officials, all judges and prosecutors of the *Volksgerichte,* and presidents and general prosecutors of the *Oberlandesgerichte,* appointed after December 31, 1938. In Class II were all members of the National Socialist party (NSDAP) who joined prior to May, 1937, judges and prosecutors of the *Sondergerichte,* presidents and chief prosecutors of the *Landgerichte.* All these positions, it can be definitely stated, could be held, at least after 1937, only by tested Nazis.

From these examples, it may be seen that the categories of prima-facie disqualified legal officials were narrowly defined. The total number of persons in such offices, though it may run close to 2,000, is insignificant when compared with the number of legal officials who joined the party. The vast majority of all holders of judicial office were shoved by the denazification tribunals into minor categories. As a rule, the individual was classified as a follower or fully exonerated. For civil servants classified as followers, the penalties, at first transfer to retirement or to an office with an inferior rank or rescission of a promotion received under the Nazis, were later reduced to the payment of a nominal fine.

(3) *The End of Denazification*—Although official statistical breakdowns concerning individual professions are unobtainable, there is no reason to believe that the judicial profession fared worse than others whom their "peers" in the denazification tribunals treated leniently to begin with, assiduously graded down according to the various relaxations of the statute, and provided with the benefit of doubt where it was possible and frequently also where it seemed impossible. The over-all result is that while at first the ministries of justice showed reticence in readmitting former Nazis to the higher positions in the courts, at the present time they have reinfiltrated into the entire fabric of the administration of justice, with the exception, in some of the *Länder,* of the ministries of justice proper, a praise, however, that does not extend to the Federal Ministry of Justice in Bonn. Private statistics of the *Land* commissioners reveal that up to 85 per cent of the acting judges and a somewhat lesser percentage of the prosecutors are former Nazis. It is a corresponding reflection on the state of affairs in Western Germany that the *Länder* had to be induced by Allied prodding to enact legislation to provide employment for persons who were openly boycotted because of their participation in the denazification procedure.[51] By placing this situation in the proper relief it is not intended

[51] See, for example, Bavaria, Ordinance of April 30, 1950 (GVBl., p. 79);

to emphasize past mistakes; the writer's object is rather to elucidate the subsequent attitudes of certain sections of the German judiciary in the fulfillment of their judicial duties.

Judicial Independence—Independence of the judiciary, since the British Act of Settlement (1701), is recognized among civilized nations as the cornerstone of justice and the supreme guarantee of the rule of law. Under the Nazis the judges had been increasingly exposed to interference by the Ministry of Justice or by their presiding judge, acting through judicial conferences (*Richterbesprechungen*) and judicial instructions (*Richteranweisungen*) which determined, in criminal cases, guilt of the indicted and the measure of punishment in advance. Restoration of judicial independence, therefore, was one of the primary occupation objectives in the field of legal reconstruction.

Control Council Proclamation No. 3 of October 20, 1945, explicitly ordained that "judges will be independent from executive control when exercising their functions and are obedient only to the law."[52] Correspondingly, in the American Zone the ministers of justice were enjoined not to instruct judges with respect to the exercise of their functions.[53] In due course, all *Land* constitutions, including those in the Soviet Zone, were equipped with the stereotyped formula that "the judges are independent and subject only to the law."[54]

Under the conditions of the occupation the formal independence of the judiciary was subject, at least during the stage in which German sovereignty was not fully restored, to some potential restrictions by the right of the occupying powers to supervise and eventually to intervene in the administration of justice.[55] This is understandable since there existed no prima-facie evidence that the judicial personnel reinstated by either military government or German procedures would

Hesse, May 10, 1950 (GVBl., p. 91).

[52] Article IV, OGCC No. 11, p. 22 (Oct., 1945).

[53] MGR 5.324. On the position of the ministers of justice who, in accordance with German administrative traditions, are much more integrated in the operation of the judicial function than, for example, the Atttorney General in this country, see Karl Loewenstein's article, already cited, in *Harvard Law R.*, p. 419. In the British Zone also, at least until 1949, an attempt had been made to loosen the administrative hold of the ministries of justice on the courts and to increase judicial autonomy of the presidents of the individual *Oberlandesgerichte*. After the establishment of the Bonn Constitution, however, the traditional connection between courts and the ministries of justice seemingly was restored also in the British Zone.

[54] See, for example, Hesse, Article 126, paragraph 2; Brandenburg, Article 40. Identical provisions are found in both the Bonn (Art. 97, par. 1) and the Eastern German Constitution (Art. 127).

[55] For details, see Karl Loewenstein, article in *Harvard Law R.*, pp. 438 ff.

guarantee the adequate performance of a democratically oriented administration of justice. In the American Zone, supervision could lead to direct intervention (by reversing or revising a court decision) only in the extreme case of a flagrant violation of military government policies by a German court.[56] After March, 1947, even supervisory activities of military government were cut back sharply. The British from the start were less confident that the reinstated judiciary would perform according to democratic expectations. Here the General Instructions to Judges (*Allgemeine Anweisungen an die Richter No. 1*)[57] kept, for several years, close tab on judicial activities in criminal matters. But the order lost its validity on September 21, 1949. Under the Occupation Statute the right of the occupying powers to withdraw a case from German jurisdiction (*evocatio*), according to HICOG Law No. 13,[58] is confined to cases concerning persons referred to in the reserved fields. Thus to all practical intents and purposes the independence of the German judge from outside interference is now fully guaranteed.

Even while Allied control of German court activities existed in full the German judge did not feel hampered by it in the exercise of his independent functions. The Allied authorities were so reserved in the exercise of this right that the general public was scarcely aware of its existence. In the American Zone intervention hardly ever occurred.[59] A politically important case, however, was the unceremonial removal by the French Military Government of the judge who had quashed the murder indictment against the assassin of the republican political leader Erzberger.

Aside from these temporary and no longer effective limitations under the occupation, judicial independence requires a fuller discussion here because, beyond being indispensable for a democratic administration of justice in a state under the rule of law, it raises, in the German environment, perplexing problems and grave difficulties

---

[56] See the elaborate provisions in MGR 5.433.

[57] See, for example, Hellmuth von Weber, in SJZ 1946, p. 238, and his "Das Ende der AAR No. 1," DJZ 1950, p. 217.

[58] See DJZ 1950, p. 36.

[59] The most notorious case was that of a former police official named Bose. The criminal division of the *Landgericht* Mannheim had sentenced him to only two years in prison for the execution of a number of civilians who, on the approach of Allied troops, had hoisted white flags. Military government (March, 1946) rescinded the decision and required retrial in which only judges were to participate who had not been party members or acted as judges of the *Sondergerichte*. See *Deutschland Jahrbuch 1949*, ed. by Klaus Mehnert and Heinrich Schulte (Essen, 1949), p. 93.

which cannot be dismissed lightly by reference to the paper provisions of the judicial codes and constitutions. It may well seem an understatement that independence was granted a judiciary not thoroughly grounded in democratic judicial attitudes.

Proper evaluation of this problem requires a projection against the sociological background of the German judiciary. Contrary to superficial conclusions drawn from Nazi "justice," the German judge is far from being inclined toward arbitrariness. On the contrary, his traditional virtue—which is also his traditional vice—is his unmitigated positivism. Class antecedents and training have accustomed him to administering justice in scrupulous accordance with the law, and the law is what the state commands. Not even the Nazi regime was given to arbitrariness in the sense that the judge could decide as he pleased.[60] The truly exasperating feature of the Nazi legal system lay in the fact that the most arbitrary and unjust of its acts were couched in the form of a statute, decree, or similar enactment, which, because of its formal character as a legal norm, was applied by the judge as "law" regardless of its inherently arbitrary character. The German judge slavishly follows its letter. Unaffected by intellectual doubts as to the intrinsic justice of the legal rule he has to apply, provided it is enacted by the authority of the state, he does not question whether the authority is legitimate or not.[61] In this attitude he is confirmed by his professional class situation much more than in Anglo-Saxon countries, where the judge at one time or another has been a member of the bar and, as such, has usually participated in trials combating the state.

It is true that under the Weimar Republic the class monopoly of the judiciary had been somewhat mitigated. Access to a legal career had become more democratic in the sense that the members of the court hierarchy no longer stemmed exclusively from the upper and the upper middle classes. But widening of the social portals did not bring a change of the class mentality or automatic acceptance of democratic

[60] As to the important distinction between the "prerogative" and the "normative" state in Nazi Germany, see Ernst Fraenkel, *The Dual State* (New York, 1941). By the former is meant the governmental system characterized by arbitrariness and violence unchecked by any legal guarantees; by the latter, an administrative system in which elaborate powers for safeguarding the legal order are expressed in statutes, decisions of the courts, and activities of the administrative agencies.

[61] Significantly, after the collapse the reaction against excessive positivism gave rise to the rethinking on the natural law basis of justice which, however, was largely confined to theoretical and academic discussions as yet unreflected by the practice of the courts. See M. Guggumos, "Ober Sinn und Wert des Studiums der Rechtsphilosophie und des Naturrechts," *Juristenzeitung* 1951, p. 108 (with literature).

values. With rare exceptions, the newcomers from other classes took on the coloration of the caste which had admitted them. Positivism created by education and tradition was reinforced by membership in a class which served and supported the state.

It would, perhaps, be unfair to characterize the majority of the judicial caste serving under Weimar as "reactionary," although the number of jurists joining the Republican Association of Judges (*Republikanischer Richterbund*), membership in which was a ground for subsequent dismissal by the Nazis, was small. But the combination of these factors made the German judges nationalistic. Excellent legal technicians they were bound to become under their long and exacting training, but they felt and acted as servants of the state and not as the trustees of an abstract humanitarian ideal or of justice per se. They could not reasonably be expected to be democrats; the educational system of the "republic without republicans" was unwilling to impart democratic values.

Unfortunately, there is little evidence that the situation today is much different from what it was under Weimar. Of this basic defect some of the soul-searching members of the German judiciary did not remain unaware, then and now. Recently one of this group, Chief Prosecutor (*Generalstaatsanwalt*) Richard Schmid, of Stuttgart, in commenting on legislation for the protection of the state proposed by the federal government, had this to say:

The motives of the government bill consider a better protection of the state against criminal acts necessary *"lest the Federal Republic suffer the fate of the Weimar Republic."* In my opinion in this sentence lies a grave historical error. . . . It was not the laws that failed, but the courts. The reasons for that failure consisted in that the German judges and prosecutors, to a regrettably large extent, were possessed, instead of a positive approach, by a markedly negative attitude towards the republican, democratic and parliamentary state and the ideologies of its constitution. . . . The aversion to, and the conscious or unconscious rejection of, the political ideas that were represented by the Weimar Republic were evidenced by the highest as well as by the inferior courts. . . . The German judicial body—and unfortunately this not only in individual instances, but in its large part—was in opposition to the anti-monarchical, anti-military, international and parliamentary ingredients of the new concept of the state, and this opposition made them excessively partial towards the so-called national and folkish opposition. . . . These observations were necessary to prove that the problem of the protection of the democratic state today *is less one of legislation than one of judicial and political behavior. It is essential to implant the basic ideas in the personnel charged with judicial decision and criminal prosecution.*[62]

[62] Richard Schmid, "Das politische Strafrecht," DJZ 1950, pp. 337 ff. (transla-

For those who remember, like the author of the foregoing quota-tion, the experience of the deliberate sabotage of the Weimar democ-racy by a judiciary which used its positivism to make nationalism triumphant, it is plain that what its members require now is indoc-trination with democratic values and the awareness that they serve not the state as an abstraction, but that they should serve the state representing social justice and the democratic ideal. What is essential, therefore, is not only the independence of office or of the judicial function, but, more important, the independence of the individual judicial character, the release from the fetters of the positive law regard-less of the results of its application, and the opening of the judicial mind to the postulates of humanitarian morality.[63]

To attain these superior judicial aims the German judiciary has to go a long way. It is unlikely, and perhaps humanly impossible, that the present generation of judges and prosecutors who applied Nazi law with unflinching loyalty because it was state-commanded law could be expected to undergo the deep intellectual conversion which the retreat from their positivist position would require. It is at this point that the failure of the denazification policy, which perhaps like-wise was beyond the humanly possible, will make itself felt for a long time to come.

Unfortunate evidence of this today is to be found in the chain of recent court decisions which represent gross miscarriage of justice. Thus, the reopened courts bitterly disappointed those who had ex-pected that they would mete out just retribution to their own war criminals. Authorized to undertake the punishment of war criminals by Control Council Law No. 10 in 1945,[64] the indictments all too often permitted the accused to evade substantial punishment under posi-tivist interpretations of German law in effect at the time when the crime was committed. In the Tillessen case, French Military Govern-ment was obliged to cancel a decision, depose a judge, and order the retrial of the assassin of a Weimar official who had been released by the court upon the basis of an amnesty granted by Hitler in 1933, even though it had already been repealed by Control Council Law No. 1 repealing Nazi laws.[65]

While this sad list could be continued, it should not lead to the erroneous conclusion that the German public, in particular the dem-

---

tion by this writer; italics are *not* supplied).

[63] See Gustav Radbruch, *Die Erneuerung des Rechts, Die Wandlung* (1947), p. 8, and also his *Gesetzliches Unrecht und übergesetzliches Recht* (Heidelberg, 1946).

[64] OGCC No. 3, p. 50 (Jan., 1946). [65] OGCC No. 1, p. 7 (Oct., 1945).

ocratic press and the law journals resuscitated to their pre-Hitler excellence, were unaware of the inherent dangers of the excessive legalism of the judiciary. It is encouraging to note that a vigilant and alerted public opinion is most critical of such abuses of judicial discretion, so much so that increasingly the German administration of justice is moving into what is properly called a *Krise der Justiz,* a crisis of judicial reputation which, once the liquidation of the unsavory past has been completed, may induce the German judiciary to temper legal positivism with the consciousness of democratic and humanitarian values.

If the hope of the architects of a new Germany lies in the training of a democratic new generation of judicial personnel by democratically oriented law schools of the universities, it may well suffer bitter disappointment. The discussion of the attempted reform of legal training is beyond the compass of this study.[66] But it can be stated that the pattern visible in the reconstruction of the administration of justice is repeated, according to experience to date, in the law schools where "denazified" law professors, returned, with few exceptions, to their old chairs, impart about the same kind of technically perfected positivism as before 1933. It is still unsupported by any tangible conviction of the preference of democratic over authoritarian modes of government.

THE JUDICIAL BRANCH UNDER THE BONN CONSTITUTION

In spite of its programmatic independence, the judiciary, in German constitutional tradition, had been rather co-ordinated with the executive than constituted as a separate power, reflecting, thus, more Locke's arrangement of powers than the strict separation of Montesquieu. In the Bonn Constitution, the judiciary is raised, for the first time, to the rank of a third power coequal to the other two. The principle of the separation of organs representing the totality of sovereignty (*Staatsgewalt*) is explicitly expressed in Article 20, paragraph 2, and the rule of law is given practical value by the provision (Art. 19, par. 4) to the effect that whoever feels affected in his rights by an act of the public authority has the right of redress through the courts. This is spoken of in German constitutional jurisprudence as the truly "royal" article of the constitution. Consequently, the provisions concerning the administration of justice (*Rechtspflege*) are now brought together in a separate section of the Basic Law (Arts. 92-104). It con-

[66] See Karl Loewenstein, article in *Harvard Law R.,* pp. 458 ff. A case in point is the effort of military government to introduce political science into the curriculum of the law schools.

tains, different from other constitutions, organizational and substantive provisions and also others which actually are to be classified as civil liberties.

Organization of Courts—The organization of the judicial branch is governed by the federal principle in that judicial sovereignty (*Justizhoheit*) belongs primarily to the *Länder*. The federal courts, being the exception, are enumerated exhaustively (Art. 92). The creation of a new federal court requires the consent of the *Bundesrat*. The Basic Law provides for a Federal Constitutional Tribunal (*Bundesverfassungsgericht;* Arts. 93, 94), a Federal Supreme Court (*Oberstes Bundesgericht;* Art. 95), and superior courts in the fields of administration, finance, labor, and social insurance and, for the federal officials, a federal disciplinary court (Art. 96). Since the primary function of all federal courts consists in the preservation of legal uniformity on the individual fields, all lower and intermediary courts are subject to *Land* autonomy.

(1) *The Federal Constitutional Tribunal*—Wholly separated both as to personnel and jurisdiction from the Federal Supreme Court, the Constitutional Tribunal is charged with several kinds of functions (Art. 93). (a) It is responsible for the interpretation of the Basic Law on occasion of disputes concerning the rights and duties of the supreme federal organs. Such controversies necessarily will not always be easily subject to a justiciable decision but may rather pertain to what in this country are called "political questions" or in France "*actes de gouvernement.*" (b) The tribunal has further jurisdiction (Art. 93, No. 3) in controversies concerning the rights and duties of the federal state and the *Länder,* in particular concerning the execution of federal functions by the *Länder* and the supervision of *Land* action by the federal authorities in so far as permissible under the constitution; this genuinely "federal" aspect of the jurisdiction of the Constitutional Tribunal cannot be dispensed with in any federal organization. Likewise (Art. 93, No. 4) it has jurisdiction in all other controversies of public law character between the federal state and the *Länder,* or between different *Länder,* or even within an individual *Land,* provided there are no other legal methods for straightening them out; however, in Western Germany almost all *Länder* have assigned "domestic" constitutional controversies to their own *Land* constitutional courts.[67] (c) In numerous cases the Basic Law itself assigns judicial functions to the Federal Constitutional Tribunal, in specific cases of which the constitution mentions no fewer than eleven, for example the

[67] An exception is Schleswig-Holstein where, therefore, the Federal Constitutional Tribunal is charged with the functions of a *Land* constitutional court.

decision that a political party is illegal (Art. 21, par. 2). Furthermore, future federal legislation may create new cases of such jurisdiction. (d) To all intents and purposes, however, the most important assignment of the Constitutional Court consists in deciding on the compatibility (formally and substantially) of federal and *Land* law with the constitution (Art. 93, No. 2) and of *Land* law with federal law. To invoke this procedure, either a formal motion is required of the federal government, a *Land* government, or one-third of the members of the *Bundestag*, or, evidently the much more frequent occurrence, a motion of any court before which it is alleged that a legal rule is in conflict with the federal constitution. In this case the court must suspend the trial until the Constitutional Court has decided on the issue of constitutionality (Art. 100, par. 1). The Bonn Constitution thus formally introduces judicial review of the constitutionality of federal and *Land* law which, under the Weimar Constitution, was theoretically admitted though practically never exercised. The German system which, in the interest of an accelerated decision and uniformity in interpretation, concentrates judicial review in a single court may seem preferable to the practice of dispersed and unlimited judicial review of every court as in the United States. It should be noted, however, that for the compatibility of *Land* legislation with the *Land* constitution the *Land* constitutional courts exercise the same jurisdiction for the respective *Land*.

The Federal Constitutional Tribunal consists (Art. 94, par. 1) of federal judges and "other members," presumably law professors, politicians, or dignitaries. One-half is elected by the federal parliament, one-half by the Federal Council. These and other organizational details will be regulated by a special federal statute.[68] Judicial review of *Land* legislation is also being exercised widely and, as far as can be judged, effectively by the *Land* constitutional courts. As a matter of fact, the Germans have taken to this novel experience like fish to water; this is hardly surprising in view of the tremendous legal insecurity created by the hectic activity of a variety of competitive legislative bodies since the collapse. The jurisprudence of the constitutional courts, however, deals only to a limited extent with what is called civil liberties in this country, not because no violations are al-

[68] Election procedures, internal organization, and distribution of the jurisdictional assignments among the two "senates," each composed of twelve judges, were regulated in the law on the Federal Constitutional Court of March 12, 1951. See *Bundesgesetzblatt* (BGBl.) 1951, p. 243, and also Otto Koellreutter, *op. cit.*, pp. 211 ff. The Federal Constitutional Court established in 1951 in Karlsruhe energetically assumed its role of "Custodian of the Constitution" and has dealt with such questions as the formation of the new southwest state.

leged, but because they are often wrapped up in controversies concerning the jurisdictional competence of an organ to issue a rule.[69]

(2) *The Federal Supreme Court*—This court is laid out to be the successor of the defunct *Reichsgericht*, primarily intended for the preservation of legal uniformity (*Rechtseinheit*; Art. 95). While the Constitutional Tribunal is the capstone of the entire political structure, the Federal Supreme Court, with its strictly legal and limited assignments, will hardly grow to the stature of the former *Reichsgericht*. A novelty is the method of appointment of the federal judges of this court: a judicial election committee is to be formed consisting of an equal number of members appointed by the *Land* ministries of justice and elected by the *Bundestag*. This committee, together with the federal minister of justice, undertakes the final selection. The Election Committee has already been constituted.[70] The court, as the first of the several federal courts under the Basic Law, was established in Karlsruhe and entered into operation on October 8, 1950.[71] Among its about thirty judges (the number is not fixed by law) is one woman.

Position of the Judiciary—Concerning the position of the judiciary, the Bonn instrument differs little from Weimar. All judges (including also those of the *Länder*) are guaranteed independence, and they are subject only to the law (Art. 97). No judge, before the end of his life tenure—the fixation of a retirement age is permissible—can be dismissed, against his will be transferred to another office, or be temporarily or permanently suspended or pensioned unless by virtue of a judicial (disciplinary) decision and on statutory grounds (Art. 97, par. 2.). But a momentous innovation looms in the fact that the position of the federal judge in future will no longer be identical with that of a public official. Their legal status is to be regulated by a special federal law (*Richtergesetz*) for the federal courts and by special *Land* laws for the *Land* judiciaries.[72] How far this reform will help towards the emancipation of judges from the spirit of officialdom or, contrariwise, deepen his caste mentality remains to be seen. In retrospective

---

[69] For a survey of the Constitutional Court in Bavaria, see Wilhelm Römer, SJZ 1949, pp. 24, 184; 1950, pp. 569 ff. For Rhineland-Palatinate, see Hans Schäfer, *Juristenzeitung* 1951, pp. 58, 88 ff.

[70] *Richterwahlgesetz* of August 28, 1950, BGBl. 1950, p. 368; see also *Archiv des öffentlichen Rechts*, LXXVI (1950), 232 ff.

[71] See SJZ 1950, pp. 848 ff.

[72] For an important discussion of the needed reform in the position of the judiciary, see Eugen Schiffer, *Die deutsche Justiz*, 2d ed. (Munich-Berlin, 1949); the author was one of the most respected progressive judges of the Weimar period and served as the head of the Legal Central Office in the Soviet Zone. See also the critical comments by Hans Schulz, SJZ 1950, pp. 414 ff.

answer to the undermining of the Weimar Constitution by a democracy-resistant judiciary, the Bonn Constitution brings the further innovation of the impeachment of the judges (*Richteranklage;* Art. 98, par. 2, for the federal judges only), in case a judge violates in or outside his office the constitutional principles of the Basic Law or the constitutional order of a *Land.* The impeachment, set in motion by a two-thirds majority of the *Bundestag,* is to be tried by the Federal Constitutional Tribunal. One would think that the guilty judge would be dismissed and punished. Not so under the Bonn democracy. The penalty consists merely in transfer to another office or retirement. Only in case of a deliberate violation can he be dismissed, and not even then is he subject to other penalties. It is needless to state that even this modest precaution against a repetition of the Weimar experience is violently assailed by the spokesmen of the profession as a threat to judicial independence.

Legal Protection of the Individual—The section on the judiciary of the Basic Law includes a number of personal guarantees of due process and equal protection by the law which must be considered an implementation of the section on basic rights. They do not go much beyond the Weimar situation and add little new. Extraordinary courts (Art. 101, par. 1), retroactive laws (Art. 103, par. 2), and double jeopardy (Art. 103, par. 3) are not permissible. The habeas-corpus provisions which heretofore had been spelled out in the code of criminal procedure rather than in the constitution and which, in their totality, are as effective as in any othel legal civilization are now written into the constitution proper (Art. 104). The death penalty is abolished (Art. 102), perhaps as is now contended, prematurely. A consultation of the people might have been preferable.

Legal Unification—In and after 1945 no fewer than thirty-eight lawmaking authorities had been operating in all Germany; of these, twenty-nine had jurisdiction in or over the western zones.[73] Much of this political and legislative fragmentation was due to the unprecedented collapse of the civilian authority in Germany after uncondi-

---

[73] SHEAF (for Western Germany only); Control Council (for all four zones); the respective zone commander for each of the four zones; the Allied *Kommandatura* (for all sectors of Berlin); the Economic Council and its apparatus (for the combined British and American Zone); the Central Office of Justice (for the British Zone); the Central Administrations (for the Soviet Zone); the governments and parliaments of the four *Länder* in the British, four in the American, five in the Soviet, and (with the Saar) four in the French zones; the city government of Berlin (split in two after 1948); the eight presidents of the *Oberlandesgerichte* in the British Zone (until Oct. 10, 1946); finally, the German Federal Republic and the German Democratic Republic.

tional surrender, but as much to the occupation powers which, each trying to re-create its zone in its image, wrought unconscionable havoc with German legal unity and uniformity, a precious possession to all Germans regardless of political persuasion. In particular, in the field of civil law, legal unity had existed at least since 1900 (the entering into force of the Civil Code); in commercial and criminal law and in civil and criminal procedure the Bismarck empire had in the seventies established a legal system common to all Germans.

Consequently, the first major task to which the German Federal Republic had to devote itself was the restoration of legal unity in the major fields of law. The result is the so-called "Unification Law" (*Vereinheitlichungsgesetz*) of September 12, 1950,[74] an accomplishment which shows the ministerial bureaucracy in Bonn at its best. Technically, the German legislator was confronted with the difficult choice as to whether to return to the situation that had existed before the advent to power in 1933, while salvaging and incorporating what useful and democratically justified innovations had occurred during the Nazi regime, or to use the opportunity of new legislation for a large-scale substantive reform of the entire subject matter. The federal bureaucracy decided in favor of the first alternative for about the same reasons that had governed the legislative strategy of the foreign lawyers of the various military governments and the Control Council in their—piecemeal—rewriting of German law at the time when German authorities were not yet available.[75] In addition, the new legislation had not only to eliminate Nazi-tainted or war-conditioned provisions of before 1945 but also to harmonize and unify the excessively fragmented legislation of the numerous postsurrender legislative bodies.[76]

Of the four fields of reform to which the Unification Law pertains—organization of courts, civil procedure, criminal procedure, costs of judicial activities—only the first mentioned is of interest here. The pre-Hitler system of four levels of courts is restored, consisting of district courts (*Amtsgericht*), regional courts (*Landgericht*), Court of Appeals (*Oberlandesgericht*), and the single Federal Supreme Court.

[74] The full title reads: *Gesetz zur Wiederherstellung der Rechtseinheit auf dem Gebiete der Gerichtsverfassung, der bürgerlichen Rechtspflege, des Strafverfahrens und des Kostenrechts*, BGBl. 1950, pp. 455-512. For a competent discussion, see Willi Geiger, "Das Vereinheitlichungsgesetz," SJZ 1950, p. 708 ff; Adolf Schönke, *Die Wiederherstellung der Rechtseinheit im Gerichtsverfassungsrecht und im Strafprozessrecht der Bundesrepublik Deutschland* (1950), pp. 433 ff.

[75] See, on this dilemma, Karl Loewenstein, *Yale Law J.*, LVII (1948), pp. 735 ff.

[76] No fewer than eighty-seven different enactments were repealed. See Article 8. Neither military government nor Control Council was directly affected.

There are, as a rule, three instances: appeal to a superior court is granted invariably. In the trial on appeal, new evidence and facts not considered below are admissible. In case a question of law (and not of fact) is appealed—which the Germans call "revision" (the French *cessation*)—the Federal Supreme Court acts as the court of revision. In civil matters with a value in controversy above DM 6,000, revision is generally granted and, in other cases, if the Court of Appeals has certified its advisability (because of the legal importance of the issue). Revision is mandatory if the Court of Appeals deviates from a decision of the Federal Supreme Court (there is no system of absolutely binding precendents in Germany). The same holds true for criminal cases in which the Court of Appeals deviates from the decision either of another such court or of the Federal Supreme Court.

Governed by tradition are also the regulations concerning the organization of the criminal courts, and much experimentation undertaken by several *Länder* since 1945 is thereby eliminated. Criminal courts of the first instance (*Amtsgericht* and *Landgericht*), with jurisdiction according to the character of the crime, have both professional judges and lay assessors; the lower court (*Schöffengericht*) is composed of one professional judge and two lay assessors (*Schöffen*), the upper court (*Schwurgericht*) of two professional judges and seven laymen (*Geschworene*). But in both cases the system differs basically from the Anglo-Saxon courts with juries in that laymen and professionals sit as a single bench, deciding together on the facts as well as on the law. The Anglo Saxon court, on the whole, is confined to crimes against life in the widest sense. The return to the classical jury system, in which the jurors decide on guilt or innocence and the professionals apply to it the law, has not been favored; the tendency away from the jury system is almost universal on the European continent, including lately also France. For the composition of both lists of lay assessors (*Schöffen* and *Geschworene*) an innovation is introduced; the communal representative bodies set up lists of persons suitable for this service, instead of the formerly existing selection from among a list containing all veniremen of the district. Whether this reform, which in practice plays the composition of the lists into the hands of the political parties, is preferable remains to be seen.

To the foreign observer both the system of courts and the opportunities for appeal seem too luxurious and elaborate, requiring judicial manpower in large amount and encouraging the litigiousness of the people. But evidently the conservative trend, visible in practically all aspects of German reconstruction since 1945, demanded here also the return to the pre-Hitler pattern. And it should be noted in conclusion that the—at times—rather close symbiosis of the Germans with foreign systems and techniques of law through their contacts with the occupation authorities has left little trace on the legislation.

The Limits of Judicialization—Even the most casual student of the Bonn Constitution is struck by the prominence given throughout to the judicial element. Not only do courts and judges control, as they should, the domain of adjudication in their proper fields, but they are assigned, in the case of the Federal Constitutional Tribunal, vast functions in the regularization of political dynamics far beyond the practice of most other constitutions. The German Federal Republic claims more than emphatically to be a state under the rule of law. In many instances in which, in other political civilizations ,the compromise of conflicting interests is left to the natural dynamism of political forces (parties, state organs, public opinion) the judges are called upon to decide. The intrinsic reasons for this development may lie partly in the memory of the lawlessness of the Nazi period. Partly, however, they lie also in the distrust of the Germans in the ability of their politicians, who are less trusted than the judges. One may well speak of a judicialization of political dynamics or, as some Germans do, confront, not without misgivings, the state under the rule of law (*Rechtsstaat*) with the state under the rule of the judiciary (*Justizstaat*).[77]

The experience with Weimar where, in the conflict between the Reich government of Von Papen and the Prussian government, the Supreme Court failed signally in controlling naked power is none too encouraging. Wherever a political deadlock may loom, the effort is made to "neutralize" it by opening what is believed to be the safety valve of a judicial decision. The Germans exhibit an amazing confidence in the political wisdom, expert knowledge, and neutrality of their judiciary. Neither the Romans nor the British, both the most law-minded peoples on record, have gone so far. To raise the judge high above the policy makers and the people is the mark of either a very mature or a very primitive political civilization. Whether the confidence in the judiciary will be justified only history can tell.

[77] See Wilhelm Grewe, "Gehen wir einem Justizstaat entgegen?" *Deutsche Zeitung*, December 10, 1950, p. 4.

10

Personnel Management

ARNOLD BRECHT

THE German civil service was able during the greater part of its existence to hold the high esteem, if not the outright admiration, of the entire world. Its members enjoyed the reputation of being incorrupt and incorruptible, of working hard for moderate salaries in an anonymous and self-effacing manner and with an unfailing devotion both to their country and to the work on hand, and of quickly adapting themselves to the ever-changing requirements of the industrial age.[1]

So high had this universal esteem remained even after World War I that the Weimar Constitution bowed to it by guaranteeing the civil servants their "vested rights," including their life tenure. That guaran-

[1] An invitation extended by the Department of State and a leave of absence granted by the Graduate Faculty, New School for Social Research, have made research on the spot possible. German ministries, parliamentarians, and civil service organizations have readily lent their support, as have various HICOG offices. I am particularly indebted to Ellsworth Wolfsperger, then Civil Service Officer, Internal Political and Governmental Affairs Division, HICOG, who contributed generously from his long experience to the data here assembled, especially regarding actions taken by the occupation authorities. Most helpful in checking on a number of factual statements were also the German Institute of Public Affairs in Frankfurt and Ministerial Director Dr. Kurt Oppler, head of the Bizonal Personnel Office. Professor Rodney L. Mott of Colgate University made valuable suggestions. The following translations of German terms are used throughout: *Beamtentum*, civil service; *Beamte*, officials, civil servants, or members of the civil service (these three are used as synonyms in the strict sense of the German term *Beamte*); *öffentlicher Dienst*, public service; *Angestellte*, contractual employees or, simply, employees.

tee (Art. 129) was a unique feature within modern democratic constitutions. It was also one of the major mistakes made in Weimar, for it placed a heavy handicap on the young democracy from the beginning. No radical change either in the structure of the civil service as a whole or in the staffing of individual offices could be effected under it. Old officials were to be continued in office if they would simply take an oath of allegiance to the new constitution. A cloud of suspicion hung over the German civil service ever after, since there was obvious reason to doubt whether all its members were indeed as reliable servants of the democratic republic as they had been of the semi-authoritarian monarchy.

The reputation of the German civil servants was not, however, completely destroyed abroad until Hitler exploited their professional skill for his own immoral purposes. The strongly worded oath which he in turn had them swear—the third one in the official lives of most of them—demanded personal obedience to him. Ideals of political neutrality that had shielded them during the Weimar period were no longer tolerated. Loyalty to their country, which they were expected to demonstrate at all times, in and out of office, became equated with "national reliability,"[2] and the latter with "National Socialist reliability."[3]

Most officials that stayed in office in these circumstances did so "with a heavy heart." But they worked as hard and anonymously as ever. They still fancied that they did so for their country. Yet all their work was, in effect, for the greater glory of the Nazi party, for the ruin of their country, and for the destruction of their own reputation.

By the end of the Hitler era the German civil service had become a world-wide epithet for irresponsible servility, for turncoat opportunism, for bureaucratic self-preservation, and for an utterly undemocratic type of authoritarianism. Its renowned incorruptibility had been shown to have an unexpected limit. While its members could not be bribed individually, as a group they had surrendered to the corruption of their work by the governing party. Gone with the storm was the admiration of the world.

Several points can be made in partial defense of the German officials. Most of them fell into a status of totalitarian servitude by political passivity rather than by any active ill will of their own. Nor was their passivity altogether voluntary. They were paralyzed by the legalistic disguise under which the Hitler regime made its appearance,

[2] Act to Restore the Professional Civil Service, of April 7, 1933, sec. 2-4.

[3] Civil Service Act of January 26, 1937, sec. 26, No. 3. "No one can become a civil servant unless . . . there is full guarantee in his person that he will, without reservations, support the National Socialist state at any time."

with the cabinet duly appointed by the legitimate Reich President, with an enabling act passed by parliamentary majorities capable of amending the constitution, and—last but not least, and this should not be overlooked—with the Hitler government recognized by the foreign powers, even to the extent of great concessions made to it in treaties like that with Great Britain on the expansion of Germany's naval forces.[4]

The fact that up to one-fourth and more of the administrative officials in the higher ranks of many agencies either quit or were removed or demoted[5] must be noted on the credit side of the ledger. Actually, all leading positions, including those of personnel officers, of chiefs and deputy chiefs in provincial offices, and of county executives (*Landräte*), were filled with Nazis or their closest affiliates. The bulk of republican policemen was simply transferred to the growing army, and Nazi storm troopers were selected to take over the regular police jobs.

While many of those officials who stayed were not free from the reproach that they flattered and fawned before the representatives of a party whose unethical principles they knew and disapproved, others showed considerable courage under trying conditions. No doubt, the majority suffered intensely under the immorality of the regime and from the feeling of their own weakness. It must be acknowledged in retrospect that they were exposed to very strong pressure. Open insurrection was threatened with such cruel reprisals that only saints could be expected to go the limits of active resistance;[6] nevertheless, there was a considerable number of civil servants among the rebels of July 20, 1944, who were subsequently tortured and hanged. Secret sabotage during the war, as practiced by the resistance movements in many foreign countries, was stifled in Germany by the patriotic dilemma that there it helped the external enemy as much as it hit the internal foe. The experience of people as virile as those of Czechoslovakia and Hungary—first under the Nazi rule and later under Communist pressure—has shown that Germans were not alone in their inability to overthrow a modern dictatorship from the inside.

All such apologetic reflections could not, however, dispel the deep shadow that had darkened the once so brilliant picture. Germany's

---

[4] See Arnold Brecht, *Prelude to Silence: The End of the German Republic* (New York, 1944), p. 105 (German translation under the title *Vorspiel zum Schweigen*, Wien, 1948).

[5] *Ibid.*, p. 110.

[6] Cf. Chapter 9 above and report on civil servants in the German resistance in *Das Parlament, Sonderausgabe* (Bonn, July 20, 1952).

collapse in World War II, therefore, seemed to ring the death knell of the old civil service. If Hitler had broken its backbone, the occupation authorities cut off its head. All leading officials, including all ministerial counselors, were either arrested or, at least, banned from office. This action tended to eliminate also the particular skill which had made the clock of German administration tick. For top administrators had been concentrated within the national and state ministries; little administrative genius was to be found in the provincial officials, who were wont to look to headquarters for detailed direction.

No wonder, then, that foreign administrators in their contacts with the remnants of the German administrative machinery obtained the impression that the high professional reputation of German administrators had been a mere illusion. Soon it became fashionable to speak of it as an exploded myth. This clearly was an erroneous generalization drawn from inconclusive appearances. Would not, in the United States too, the federal administration appear confused, poorly organized, and professionally little qualified for over-all work if departmental headquarters in Washington were eliminated and all the leading officials removed?

Yet there is no denying the historical fact that as a result of the Hitler regime the German civil service had lost face as well as structure. Obviously, the great task that arose after the war had a dual aspect, one merely personal, eliminating the politically undesirable persons, the other structural, rebuilding the official apparatus in such a way as to avoid the old defects as far as possible.

ELIMINATION OF THE POLITICALLY UNFIT

Fate of the Former Nazi Officials—The methods that were applied by the military governments in order to eliminate politically undesirable persons from public offices had naturally to be summary and rough in the beginning. When they gradually came to be formalized and their administration transferred to the German *Land* governments, it was probably a mistake of considerable consequence that elimination in this second stage was closely tied to the results of quasi-penal procedures, which had been established chiefly for the different purpose of meting out penalties for criminal or quasi-criminal acts. In other words, unfitness for public office was treated as a kind of penalty to be pronounced by tribunals in the same formal procedures as other sanctions.

The denazification law of March 5, 1946—uniformly proclaimed by the *Länder* of the American Zone and subsequently followed generally also in the other zones—provided in some detail as has been noted earlier in the volume that "major offenders" and "offenders," if so classified by the tribunals under the law, shall be permanently ineligible to hold public office and shall lose any legal claims to pensions or other allowances paid from public funds. "Lesser offenders," however, also called "probationers," were to be transferred to retirement or otherwise to be curtailed in their rights only at the discretion of the tribunal and only for a two to three year period of probation, after which they had to be allotted finally to some other category. Likewise a mere "follower" could be retired or curtailed in rights at the discretion of the tribunal.[7]

This is not the place to criticize the penal aspects of the act.[8] What matters in the present context, however, is the fact that relatively few persons under it finally lost their eligibility for democratic office, because (1) sweeping amnesties exempted all persons born after January 1, 1919, and soon also many others—together some 1,900,000 people in the United States Zone alone—from punishment as mere "followers"; (2) amendments of October, 1947, and March, 1948, approved by OMGUS, permitted the treatment of offenders as mere "followers"; (3) the tribunals tended to avoid punishment in minor cases, the more so after many a person generally considered a major offender had gone free; (4) they made little use of their power to exclude mere "followers" from public office; and (5) the maximum period for which minor offenders or "followers" either could be or actually were barred from office was so short that it had generally expired even before the federal government was re-established in Germany.

Originally about 53,000 civil servants had been removed from their positions in Western Germany because of their Nazi affiliations. But only 67 were subsequently classified as major offenders, and no more than 1,004 were classified as offenders by the tribunals and therewith excluded from eligibility for the public service.[9] All others, except for a few temporary disqualifications, have remained eligible.[10]

[7] Articles 15, 16, 17, and 18.

[8] I have done so at some length in the article "Civil Service Reform in Germany: Problems and Suggestions," *Personnel Administration*, IX (Jan., 1947), 3, 4.

[9] Report of the German *Statistische Amt* of June 10, 1950—VII 7/2.

[10] The number of *all* persons, including those in business and industry, that had been originally removed was of course much higher. It amounted to almost 375,-000 in the American Zone alone. More than one-fourth (28 per cent) of the adult population in Bavaria was "affected" (*betroffen*) by the Denazification Act. The total of persons sentenced within the entire zone as major offenders (1,600) or offenders (21,600) was 23,200. There were 22,700 still ineligible to hold public office by the end of 1949. Yet only a minor fraction of them had been in the

The tie established between political fitness for public office and the results of quasi-criminal procedures tended to paralyze the democratic reform of personnel management. It should be obvious that a person not subject to punishment may still be politically unfit to hold a responsible job with a democratic administration, at least in a transitional stage after a change-over from totalitarian rule. Actually, the law of March 5, 1946, stated explicitly that no person declared to be a lesser offender or "follower" could claim either reinstitution in public office or damages because of his removal (Art. 64). The final decision on his reappointment was left to the personnel management of the new democratic governments.

Consequently the individual *Länder* governments developed principles of their own about reappointment. Typical was the Bavarian ordinance of January 29, 1947,[11] which said (Art. 3) that an official removed from office may not be reinstated unless he not only fulfills professional requirements but also has the personal qualities for the job. These must include "the guarantee that he will cooperate positively in building up, and assuring permanent foundations to, a democratic form of government" and, in case he is to serve in the higher brackets, that he "owns the political, liberal and moral qualities which justify the expectation that he will contribute to the promotion of democracy in Germany." It was added (Art. 4) that, if removed by the military government, he could be reinstated only with its written consent.

These principles were perfect in theory. But in practice there prevailed a notable tendency not to go beyond the results of the judicial procedures in rejecting candidates for political reasons. On the local level the *Land* governments had not even the legal power to do so, since the military governments, in their laudable zeal of promoting local government, had freed local elections of mayors and county executives from the old need of confirmation by the *Land* government.

As a result, by the end of 1950, four types of German governmental units could be distinguished with regard to the status of denazification. There were, first, those units where the government had tried to maintain ideals of political neutrality in personnel management, but precisely by so doing had allowed persons of little democratic

civil service. On the general figures, see William E. Griffith, "Denazification in the United States Zone of Germany," *Annals of the American Academy of Political and Social Science,* CCLXVII (Jan., 1950), 69, 70, 73.

[11] This ordinance was declared invalid by the Bavarian Constitutional Court on April 24, 1950, because it had been passed by the cabinet only, but it was subsequently confirmed retroactively by the legislature on July 27, 1950.

fiber to slip back in responsible positions. This situation prevailed in many federal and *Länder* ministries. Secondly, there were those where democratic parties in power had engaged in a more or less systematic patronage. There one would find few former Nazis restored to office but considerable weaknesses of another kind described in greater detail below. A great number of municipal governments, and also some departments on higher levels, fell into this category. Thirdly, there were those municipalities that had elected former Nazis or reactionaries to the mayoralty. And finally, there were also administrations that had done a good job in every respect.

The Reinstatement Act of 1951—Even these meager and spotty achievements in the process of elimination have been endangered through the passage of the Reinstatement Act of May 11, 1951,[12] which was designed to relieve the plight of former German civil servants who had lost their jobs through evacuation, expulsion, or flight from the eastern sections of Germany (or former Germany) or from Czechoslovakia or through discontinuance of public offices. This remarkable piece of legislation forced every governmental unit in Western Germany, including local units of more than 3,000 inhabitants, to fill vacancies up to 20 per cent of all positions in their public services with those now-unemployed old civil servants by reinstating them according to their old status in rank and salary grouping.

In establishing these priority rights the *Bundestag* went beyond the proposals of the Adenauer cabinet by failing to admit proper distinctions according to political background. The act denies priority rights only to those officials (1) who have been disqualified by the denazification tribunals (see above), or (2) who had been appointed into the civil service merely "because of their close connection with National Socialism" (sec. 7), or (3) whose only appointment had been to the *Gestapo* (secret Nazi police). This placed all German governmental units under the obligation of reactivating all former officials that had turned Nazi within the span of a normal civil service career, or have otherwise an undemocratic record, provided only that they declared their willingness now to support the democratic form of government.

True, other applicants were not completely barred. Victims of National Socialism may be appointed to any vacant position for which they qualify, and other qualified applicants to every second or third vacancy.[13] In addition, the cabinets may disregard priority rights of

[12] *Gesetz zur Regelung der Rechtsverhältnisse der unter Artikel 131 des Grundgesetzes fallenden Personen* (*Bundesgesetzblatt* 1951, p. 307).

[13] Two out of every three vacancies are to be filled with the privileged candi-

old officials in appointing federal judges, members of the police forces, state secretaries, ministerial directors, and leading officers in the foreign service outside Germany. But in filling any other offices, including such politically important ones as those of ministerial counselors, of nonleading officials in the foreign service abroad, and also of judges in the *Länder*, the priorities of the old civil servants must be heeded. Special scientific or artistic needs may warrant an individual deviation, but the political need of democratization may not.

Strong teeth, too, have been put in the law to ensure enforcement. Governmental units that fill vacancies in contravention of it must pay equalization fees in the full amount of the respective salaries until they have caught up with their obligations. In order to accelerate absorption it has been stipulated, in addition, that *Länder* or municipalities which, at a certain date after the law went into force, did not spend at least 20 per cent of their entire payrolls for the privileged categories must pay 25 per cent of the difference to the federal treasury.

All this has been done, not just in favor of former Nazis, of course, but primarily in the interest of decent public servants put out of jobs through accidental circumstances and to relieve the financial burden arising from their claims for pensions or salaries. But many old officials with politically objectionable records will profit from the reinstatement act, which has indeed destroyed any hope that such persons will be kept away from democratic offices beyond the scanty exclusions pronounced by the tribunals in atonement procedures.

Not only have the old Nazi officials been assured of their reappointment if still able to work; they now also receive full pensions in current *Deutsche* marks if over sixty-five or incapacitated, and regular allowances will be paid to their families after their death.[14] Those able to work receive transitional payments until they find reappointment.[15] After all, with the exception of *Gestapo* members and of those few

dates as long as a total of less than 10 per cent of all positions within the respective unit have gone to them; therafter, one out of every two. There are reservations for the priority rights of war veterans and for promotions in hardship cases.

[14] Some minor deviations from the general pension laws, such as requirement of at least ten years of service, exclusion of pensions over 75 per cent of the last salary, and reduction of payments for widows in case of great differences in age, were merely meant to anticipate changes to be made also in the general civil service act.

[15] The transitional pay equals the pension as earned on May 8, 1945, to the extent that only DM150 a month and half of the balance are to be paid. Payments are lower if the person is less than fifty years old. Outside earnings are deducted under the act under principles more severe than those applying to officials in general. Most of these discriminations are about to be abolished.

that have been declared ineligible by the tribunals, the treatment of the former Nazi officials could not have been more generous, or less vigilant from the democratic viewpoint.

Denazification's Balance Sheet—It would be a great mistake, however, if one drew from this unsatisfactory picture the conclusion that a major part, or even the majority, of the present-day civil servants in Germany are Nazis.[16] Any statement on the number of Nazis now in office depends to a very considerable extent upon definitions. If all those who formally had been members of the party or of any of its affiliated organizations are counted as Nazis, one reaches fantastic figures, which in certain categories approach 90 per cent of the officials.[17] If, on the other hand, estimates are limited to those who still today fully approve of all Nazi policies, including the horror of the concentration camps, the number would be so small as to be negligible.

It is, therefore, better to abandon the counting of "Nazis" and instead to say exactly what one wishes to estimate. If it is the percentage of those that entertain authoritarian patterns of thought, the estimate would have to be higher for German officials than for the German people at large (where it could not be quite low either), and so would, consequently, the estimate of those whose basic inclinations prefer a form of government slightly to the right of democracy, with the executive arm less controlled by parliamentary majorities. If it is desired, however, to know the percentage of those officials whose authoritarian tendencies go so far as to make them wish to see abolished the rule of law (*Rechtsstaat*) and the bill of rights, the estimate would have to be very low; for the German civil service has a *Rechtsstaat* tradition reaching far back into the monarchic period.

The inherent danger in the German civil service is not nazification; it is bureaucratization. There is danger of sympathy, not with totalitarian principles, but with tendencies toward bureaucratic authority and bureaucratic privilege. There is a certain innate lack of understanding, not so much for ideals of liberty as for the practices of equality and of the democratic process. It is this which must give us continuing concern.

Allegiance to the Principles of Democracy—Some unexpected help

[16] See, on this question, the author's *Prelude to Silence*.

[17] Griffith, *op. cit.*, p. 74, says: "From 40 to 80 percent of the officials in many branches of public administration are now reinstated former Nazis." See also John H. Herz, "The Fiasco of Denazification in Germany," *Political Science Quarterly*, LXIII (Dec., 1948), 569. On the other hand, cf. Eugen Kogon, "Das Recht auf den politischen Irrtum," *Frankfurter Hefte*, II (July, 1947), 641.

in the process of adjustment may arise from a noteworthy change in the legal situation. Under the Weimar Constitution, which guaranteed all members of the civil service their vested rights and full freedom of opinion, German officials had claimed the right to remain or to become opponents of the democratic form of government. In contrast, all post-Hitler civil service acts have come to include clauses which demand of civil servants a positive commitment toward democracy. For example, the Military Government Law No. 15, as discussed below, said with regard to bizonal officials that "allegiance to the principles of democratic government, evident in the over-all conduct of the public servant, shall be a prerequisite for employment in the Administration. Apart from this, political convictions shall not be taken into consideration." The corresponding clause in the Federal Civil Service Act of 1953—paralleled by similar passages in the new civil service acts of the *Länder*—reads: "The official, through his entire behavior, must show his adherence (*sich bekennen*) to the liberal democratic basic order as established in the Basic Law and support (*eintreten für*) its preservation."

Therewith an entirely different basis for the behavior pattern of German civil servants has been established. It is no longer legal for them to engage in antidemocratic activities of any kind or to support antidemocratic movements. In view of the strong influence of legalism on the German bureaucracy it may be expected that the new legal obligation will affect its group morals and its ethical code. As a matter of fact, civil service associations as well as individual officials have been anxious to assert their loyalty to the democratic cause or at least to meet any doubts in this respect with strong protests. Although this may mean mere lip service for some and may tend to lead to a broad interpretation of the concept of democracy by many, the effect of the change should not be underrated. German civil servants are legalistic—even in their behavior patterns.

CIVIL SERVICE REFORM EFFORTS

Common Features of European Civil Service Systems—Public employment in Germany differs from that in the United States in a number of distinctive traits, several of which it shares with public employment in all European democracies, while others are peculiar to the German scene. It is advisable to distinguish between these two categories. The following four features are common to European democracies. First of all, generally speaking, no vacancies may be created within the internal civilian ranks of the national service through dismissals without cause, for mere reasons of party patronage. This is not to say that party patronage has been completely eliminated in Europe. Vacancies are often filled under its influence in both Germany and France, and in local services also in Great Britain. But no vacancies may be artificially created in European democracies by *dismissals* for reasons of patronage. More exactly speaking, less than one hundred positions in the internal national service are subject to political dismissals in Germany today, and no greater number was removable in imperial and Weimar Germany.[18]

Second, recruitment to the civil service in the European countries is closely tied to their educational system, so that normally university studies are required for the highest administrative positions and secondary education for the next higher groups. Third, normal recruitment, meant to initiate a "career," is limited to youthful candidates. Fourth, entrance examinations are to test, not ability for specific jobs but aptitude for the entire career. Consequently, the term "professional civil service" (*Berufsbeamtentum*) in European democracies signifies a career service normally begun at an early stage of life on the basis of a required form of education and of an entrance examination not directly related to any specific job.[19]

German Peculiarities—The traditional peculiarities which distinguished the German civil service not only from the American but also from that of some or all European democracies may be enumerated as follows: (1) monopoly of legal education for the higher brackets; (2) systematic in-service training of several years' duration prior to the final examination for permanent appointment; (3) unusually strong protection of tenure and rank; (4) steepness of the hierarchic pyramid; (5) unusual nature of pension rights; (6) wide gaps in objective methods of selection and absence of over-all control; (7) sharp distinction between civil servants and contractual employees; (8) equally sharp differentiation between career men and outsiders; and (9) lack of political neutrality.

These institutional characteristics added their influence in the past to the authoritarian German traditions to make the German civil service probably the least democratic and the most bureaucratic within the western democratic systems—least democratic in that the difference between other citizens and civil servants has been greater than elsewhere, most bureaucratic in that the structure of the German

[18] See Arnold Brecht, "The Relevance of Foreign Experience," in F. M. Marx, ed., *Public Management in the New Democracy* (New York, 1940), pp. 107 ff., for American, British, French, and German figures. See also note 48 below.

[19] For an appraisal of the relative merits and demerits of the two systems see the author's article cited in the preceding note.

civil service is highly conducive to authoritarian and esoteric tendencies. This is not to say that all the specific features are individually bad; systematic in-service training, for instance, is fundamentally good. However, before analyzing the problems of reform in detail, it is advisable to review past legislation and the efforts which the Allies made to reform the German civil service.

Efforts toward Reform—Stability of traditions is mirrored in the stability of legal rules. The imperial Civil Service Act of 1873, amended and republished in 1907,[20] stayed in force during the entire period of the Weimar Republic with only a few modifications, some which followed from the Weimar Constitution itself and some which were amendments concerning special points.[21] True, a new civil service bill and a new disciplinary code were being prepared in hundreds of conferences; but—in view of the constitutional guarantee of vested rights— they were to effect a number of minor reforms rather than a change in the traditional structure of the civil service, and they never passed the parliamentary stage.

Even the Hitler government, while quick to eliminate "nationally unreliable" elements by special amendments, otherwise for some time continued to govern on the basis of the older acts. Not until 1937 was a new comprehensive civil service act issued, a mixture of clauses taken from the pre-Hitler acts, from the reform drafts worked out during the republican period, and from National Socialist principles.[22] This law was not simply invalidated after the war. Only those provisions that discriminated against the Jews or others or required obedience to National Socialist principles were nullified as a consequence of general occupation laws, without being specifically ruled out. The pre-Hitler acts had applied to federal employees only; the *Länder* had their own laws.[23] The 1937 act, for the first time, extended to all

[20] See Carl J. Friedrich, "The German and the Prussian Civil Service," in Leonard D. White, *The Civil Service in the Modern State* (Chicago, 1930); Fritz M. Marx, "Civil Service in Germany," in L. D. White and others, *Civil Service Abroad* (New York, 1935); and, on the history of the German civil service, Herman Finer, *Theory and Practice of Modern Government* (London, 1932), II, 1183 ff., 1252 ff.

[21] In particular the Act on Duties of Civil Service to Protect the Republic of July 21, 1921; the *Personalabbau-Verordnung* (Retrenchment Ordinance) of October 27, 1923; and the *Besoldungsordnung* (Salary Act) of December 16, 1927.

[22] *Deutsches Beamtengesetz* of January 26, 1937 (translation by J. K. Pollock and A. V. Boerner under the title *The German Civil Service Act*, Chicago, 1938). On the same day a new Disciplinary Code (*Reichsdienststrafordnung*) was issued, dealing separately with matters that had been included in the former acts.

[23] For example, Prussian *Allgemeines Landrecht* of 1794, Part II, title 10; Prus-

federal, state, and local officials. With German defeat and the advent of occupation came a pressure for new and comprehensive reform. The three major *Länder* of the American Zone soon passed new acts for their respective state and municipal services.[24] Wurttemberg-Hohenzollern and Rheinland-Pfalz in the French Zone followed suit in 1949.

At the instigation of military government, the bizonal government too started soon to draft a new civil service act. A preliminary bill of June, 1948, was approved by the occupation authorities in the expectation of a better final act. When work on the latter dragged along, the United States and United Kingdom governments decided to accelerate legislation and to secure its modern character by proclaiming Military Government Law No. 15 on February 18, 1949.

Therewith six post-Hitler civil service acts came into existence, which included many novel ideas, to be discussed below. But the 1937 act was not yet a dead letter. It continued to be in force, if subject to special amendments, in six of the western *Länder*,[25] and by the time the new federal constitution was adopted it was still the only law that dealt with the old Reich officials.

Law No. 15 met with much resentment within the old civil service, especially because it eliminated the traditional German distinction between civil servants and mere employees, created a personnel office with powers independent of the individual department heads, and excluded active civil servants from candidacies for parliamentary seats. The fact that such novelties had been "imposed" served to kindle resistance. Consequently, the Bonn Basic Law came to include in its Article 33 mandatory provisions to the effect that the relation between the civil servant and his employer must be one of public law and not of private law only and that legislation on public service must regard the "traditional principles" of the German civil service, in particular its professional character.

Unparalleled in the entire range of non-German democratic constitutions, these constitutional limitations, vague as they are, make it possible for civil servants to denounce any reform of the old system as being in conflict with traditional principles and, therefore, with

---

sian Disciplinary Codes of 1851 and 1852; Prussian Pension Laws of 1872 and 1882; Prussian *Kommunalbeamtengesetz* of July 30, 1899.

[24] Bavaria, law of October 28, 1946; Hesse, laws of November 12, 1946, and June 25, 1948; Württemberg-Baden, law of November 19, 1946.

[25] North Rhine–Westphalia, Lower Saxony, Schleswig-Holstein, Baden, Hamburg, and Bremen.

the Basic Law. They thus furnish the officials a foothold from which to establish themselves as a fourth branch of government, if not as the first.[26] Although objections were raised by the United States Military Government during the formative stages of the law, the final "Letter of Approval," in which the three military governors consented to the Basic Law, did not mention these clauses among the points to which reservations were made.[27] Therefore, they now form an essential item in the legal situation. Only wise moderation in their interpretation by all three, legislators, civil servants, and constitutional court, can make a progressive reform of the German civil service at all possible in these circumstances.[28]

Pending preparation of a new federal law, the occupation authorities wished to see Law No. 15 applied to all federal officials; as that Law dealt with bizonal employees only, an order issued by all three military governors (September 12, 1949) extended it to the employees of the federal government until an adequate federal civil service act would be passed. The Adenauer cabinet, however, placed before the parliament a transition bill, which was to give it authority until the new law was passed, to apply not Law No. 15, but the 1937 act, with a number of particularly urgent amendments included, and to republish that act and the discipinary code of the same year as expurgated and amended. In order to placate the occupation authorities, the validity of the transition bill originally was limited to 1950, and the cabinet undertook by formal correspondence with the high commissioners to inaugurate a series of reforms. Only then was permission

---

[26] See Arnold Brecht, "The New German Constitution," *Social Research,* XVI (Dec., 1949), 415, and section on "Debureaucratization," p. 468.

[27] "Letter of Approval" of May 12, 1949. See Arnold Brecht, "Re-establishing German Government." *Annals of the American Academy of Political and Social Science,* CCLXVII (Jan., 1950), 35, and also Appendix J of this volume.

[28] Professor Gerhard Wacke, "Entstehungsgeschichte und Inhalt des Artikels 33 Abs. 5," in *Neues Beamtentum, ed. by Institut zur Förderung öffentlicher Angelegenheiten* (Frankfurt, 1951), p. 152, argues that all the statements in the Weimar Constitution on civil service rights must be considered "traditional principles," unless there is a cogent reason against it in the individual case. Hermann von Mangoldt in his *Kommentar zum Bonner Grundgesetz* (Berlin and Frankfurt, 1950, p. 211) goes so far as explicitly to declare the Weimar guarantee of vested rights a "traditional principle," therewith reinterpreting that old limitation of legislative power into the new constitution. The Weinheim Conference of the Institute of Public Affairs enumerated the following traditional principles: public law relationship; profession for life; career service; life tenure as a rule; pensions and allowances for widows normally to be calculated from the last salary; and formal disciplinary procedure in case of removal. See below, note 35.

given to publish the Transition Act,[29] and a special Allied High Commission Law of May 31, 1950, was issued which suspended the provisions of Law No. 15 until December 31, 1950, for federal officials. Subsequently, the two 1937 acts (German Civil Service Act and Disciplinary Code) were republished as expurgated and amended.[30] In this form they constituted the basis of the federal service in Germany until the passage of new acts.

The Adenauer cabinet, in its memorandum of May 12, 1950, promised to include the following points in its program, either in the legislative stage or in implementing regulations: (1) equal access to public service and appointment according to merit;[31] (2) public advertising of all openings, as a rule; (3) legal training to be required only where necessary; (4) due moderation and restraint in political activities;[32] (5) retirement when entering campaigns for parliamentary seats; and (6) establishment of an independent personnel authority.[33]

The first four of these promises were tentatively fulfilled by incorporation of the respective points in implementing regulations.[34] In the

---

[29] *Bundespersonalgesetz* of May 17, 1950 (*Bundesgesetzblatt*, p. 207). Its full title is *Gesetz zur vorläufigen Regelung der Rechtsverhältnisse der im Dienst des Bundes stehenden Personen.* The act's validity was later extended beyond 1950.

[30] *Bundesgesetzblatt*, p. 281. A new disciplinary code (*Bundesdisziplinarordnung*) was promulgated on November 28, 1952 (*Bundesgesetzblatt* p. 761).

[31] "Any citizen who adheres [*sich bekennt*] to the democratic idea of government [*demokratische Staatsauffassung*] shall have access to the public service." He "shall have equal access to any public office in accordance with his aptitude, ability, and professional achievements [*Eignung, Befähigung und fachliche Leistung*]." The candidate who is found in the selective process (*durch Auslese ermittelt*) to be best qualified for the position shall obtain it.

[32] Officials shall especially "not present themselves publicly as active supporters of a particular political party or program."

[33] The cabinet "will propose establishment of an independent personnel authority [*unabhängiges Personalamt*], which shall supervise, and assure impartial and correct application of the law in all ministries, and also function as an impartial board of appeal [*Beschewerdeinstanz*]." Pending legislation, certain of these functions shall be performed by a federal personnel committee (*Bundespersonalausschuss*) to consist of the president of the Federal Court of Accounts, the chiefs of the appropriate divisions in the Ministries of Interior and Finance, and two representatives of the organizations of federal public employees. The final committee under the 1953 act is to have two more members, one of them also to be nominated by the civil service organizations. All members now must be federal officials.

[34] *Verordnung zur Durchführung des Deutschen Beamtengesetzes* of June 29, 1937, as amended and republished October 28, 1950 (*Bundesgesetzblatt*, p. 733). See in particular the implementing regulations to sections 3 and 26 of the Civil Service Act. Points 1, 3, 4, and 5 were modified by the 1953 act.

same manner the preliminary Federal Personnel Committee was being set in operation. Exclusion of parliamentary candidates from office after nomination and final establishment of the independent Personnel Authority, however, were postponed on the ground that the decision on these points had to be left to the regular legislative process.

The Institute of Public Affairs in Frankfurt, founded in 1948 at the instigation and with the active support of the Civil Administration Division of OMGUS, held a two-day conference in Weinheim, Baden, on December 2 and 3, 1950, where some ninety leading German officials discussed the problems of the civil service reform and ended up with a number of progressive resolutions.[35] This meeting was preceded by a similar conference held under the sponsorship of the German Personnel Society in the same town on December 1, to hear reports on reform movements in the British, French, and United States civil services.[36]

The prevailing temper within the majority parties of the *Bundestag*, however, seems to be still positively hostile to any major reform, even one of the moderate character as proposed in Weinheim. This, in turn, can be easily traced to the strong influence exercised by the civil servants themselves, be it individually or through their representatives in the ministries and in the *Bundestag* or through the forceful campaigns conducted by their professional organizations. Consequently, the new Federal Civil Service Act (*Bundesbeamtengesetz*) of July 14, 1953, has become a basically conservative document. In several points it has remained behind the Adenauer pledges. Almost all major problems of reform are still unresolved.

BASIC PROBLEMS OF REFORM

The Four Careers—The common European practice of recruiting candidates for entire careers rather than individual jobs logically implies the linking together of several positions in typical chains, or careers. This is in contrast with the American system where the thousands of individual positions are not so interconnected, because each job, or at least each kind of job, may be filled separately through open competitive examination. The four careers distinguished in the Ger-

[35] The procedures of the Weinheim conference, including the introductory reports by Arnold Brecht and H. Mestern, the discussions, resolutions, and a number of valuable memoranda, have been published under the title *Neues Beamtentum*, ed. by *Institut zur Förderung öffentlicher Angelegenheiten* (Frankfurt, 1951).

[36] The three reports, presented by Walter Fliess (London), Maurice Lagrange (Paris), and Arnold Brecht have been published under the title *Probleme des öffentlichen Dienstes in England, Frankreich, und den Vereinigten Staaten von Amerika*, ed. by *Deutsche Gesellschaft für Personalwesen* (Frankfurt, 1951).

man civil service are: (1) the "higher service" (*höhere Dienst*), normally based on university studies; (2) the "elevated service" (*gehobener Dienst*), including responsible services of an assistant or auxiliary character; (3) the "middle service" (*mittlerer Dienst*), covering auxiliary or assistant services of a lower degree of responsibility;[37] and (4) the "simple service" (*einfacher Dienst*), that is, custodians, postmen, messengers, and the like.

Each of these four has its normal avenue of access, regulated for the upper three in great detail with regard to educational requirements, age limits, in-service training, and examinations. The general regulations[38] are supplemented by particular ones issued by the individual ministries. Extraordinary access by promotion from lower careers or through appointment of "outsiders" is possible, but has always been constituted an exception and is frowned upon by the regular career men.

Each career runs through several stages, called salary groups, with distinct titles and salary scales. As a rule, the official receives regular increments in salary every two years up to a maximum for the individual stage. Yet he can climb from that stage to the next higher one in his career by promotion only; and he may or may not reach the top group of the respective career in this way. Salary groups and titles are established in the Salary Ordinance of December 16, 1927, as amended. All salaries were converted into *Deutsche* marks after the 1948 currency reform at a one-for-one ratio. Except for the repeal of several reductions made during Brüning's chancellorship, salaries remained more or less unchanged until April, 1951. Typical monthly salaries until the recent revision ranged from DM400 to DM1050 in the higher service, DM 233 to DM650 in the elevated service, DM175 to DM350 in the middle service, and DM133 to DM212 in the simple service. These are the so-called basic salaries, to which are added rental allowances,[39] children allowances,[40] and a special allowance granted officials who work within a ministry. Since April 1, 1951, the basic salaries have been increased by 40 per cent.

[37] The middle and elevated services had long formed only one career until they were finally divided in 1939. Several municipal units abandoned the division after the war.

[38] *Verordnung über die Vorbildung und die Laufbahnen der deutschen Beamten* of February 28, 1939 (*Reichsgesetzblatt*, p. 274). Its continued validity was expressly stated in the first implementing ordinance of June 17, 1950 (*Bundesgesetzblatt*, p. 274), under the 1950 Transition Act.

[39] Varying from DM13 to DM210 a month for married officials according to their salary group and the town of residence.

[40] DM20 a month for each child.

The Monopoly of Legal Education—It would go too far to say that lawyers enjoyed a monopoly in Germany's higher service. Yet legal education did. Whenever nonlawyers were appointed to higher positions, chiefly of an administrative character, they entered the administrative career clearly as "outsiders," because the study of law was the only study which authorized a candidate to apply for the general entrance examination toward the higher administrative service (*Referendarprüfung*), prerequisite for the ensuing in-service training and the final examination thereafter (*Assessorprüfung* or *grosse Staatsprüfung*). This had been so during the imperial era, and it remained that way during the entire Weimar period and under the Nazis down to World War II. The "regulations regarding education toward the higher service in the general and interior administration" of June 26, 1937, issued in pursuance of the 1937 act, merely confirmed the old tradition; once more they designated the study of law as the only preparation for the entrance (*Referendar*) examination toward both the legal profession and the higher administrative service. Not until 1942, shortly before the end of the Hitler regime, were certain economic diplomas (*Diplomprüfung für Volkswirte*) put on a par with the study of law for the appointment as *Regierungsreferendar* (an apprentice for administrative services; see next section). Yet this change came too late to influence realities.[41]

Legal education no doubt provides a valuable type of higher administrator. When privileged to the degree of monopoly, however, it affects the breadth of the horizon within which a country's bureaucracy operates. It also tends to confer on administrators the group character of a fraternity. The German civil service has always lacked within its own professional ranks especially that broad knowledge and vision which a systematic study of world history, of history of political institutions and of political ideas, of comparative government and related fields, infuses in the ranks of the British and in part also the American and French services.[42] Germany will hardly go as far as Great Britain, which admits to the entrance examination for its administrative class candidates from all university faculties. Candidates for the higher service in Germany should, however, at least have a choice among three fields—law; political science (including

[41] Even within the postal service, 34 per cent of all the higher officials still were lawyers in 1950, and so were 20 per cent within the railroad service (memorandum of the Adenauer cabinet of May 12, 1950). They hold the most important administrative positions. The percentage in other ministries is much higher—in some divisions around 80 to 90 per cent.

[42] See also Chapter 9 above for further discussion of stultifying influences of German legal training.

history of political institutions, history of political ideas, comparative government and administration, and international affairs); and economics, including public finance.

Examinations in these optional fields should be of equal rigidity, and the selected best candidates should be treated on a par in the ensuing training. All of them, lawyers no less than others, will learn their administrative technique in that period and on the job. Administration is not law; it is discretion skillfully applied within the limits set by the law. Legal study does not teach the administrator how to apply his administrative discretion within those limits. At best it teaches him what the limits are. Inclusion of political science among the optional fields would stimulate and even force the universities to establish adequate faculties and curricula of political science, which have been almost completely absent in the past.[43]

Internship Training—Neither in the United States nor in Great Britain or France has in-service training been applied to such an extent and with such methodical care as it was and still is in Germany. There it has assumed a particularly thorough character in the three years of internship training that are required of all regular candidates for the higher levels of public administration. The training period initiates the young employee in many aspects of judicial and administrative work. Watching and assisting the work of his seniors on various jobs in numerous stations and subject to weekly group instruction, he acquires the know-how of practical work and also the difficult art—so exceedingly valuable in public administration—of reporting, orally or in writing, on complex situations and problems in a well-organized and strictly objective manner, logically and succintly, conscientiously separating disputed from undisputed facts, both of these from the evidence, and all three from opinion.[44]

Trainees are given the choice in most of the *Länder* between a predominantly legal cycle of offices (*Gerichtsreferendare*) and a predominantly administrative cycle which, while also including several months at a law court, otherwise centers in administrative agencies (*Regierungsreferendare,* more recently called *Verwaltungsreferen-*

[43] The Weinheim conference already referred to adopted the above suggestions. They were also incorporated in the new federal draft (sec. 19, par. 2) and adopted by the Federal Council. But the *Bundestag* ruled out political science as a separate alternative. Instead the "social sciences" were added to "economics" and "public finance" to form the only alternative to the study of law—a heavily overloaded omnibus.

[44] For details, see Arnold Brecht, "Civil Service," *Soc. Research*, III (1936), 202, and "Relevance of Foreign Experience," as cited above. The trainees, originally unpaid, now receive small monthly allowances.

dare). Prussia discontinued the division in 1930, but reintroduced it in 1933, and the Nazi legislation of 1937 prescribed it for the whole of Germany. After the war Bavaria switched to the single track of legal training, while most of the other *Länder* preserved the division.

Recently, several *Länder* have developed the notable practice of having *Verwaltungsreferendare* enroll for periods from one term to two years in some "academy of administration," especially that in Speyer, where their legal education is supplemented by instruction in principles of administration, political science, and economics.[45] This practice serves as a valuable substitute for the missing education in political science.[46] But if limited to only one term it is obviously insufficient, and if extended to two years it cuts too deeply into the three-year period of systematic training on the job.

Excessive Protection of Tenure—Nothing less than a formal procedure before a disciplinary court enables the German government, in normal times, to get rid of a regular official against his will before he reaches the age limit or is disabled. In other words, the German official need not fear that he may some day receive a letter of dismissal for some cause preferred against him by his superiors and then find himself out of office with no remedy left but that of a costly appeal to the courts. Once appointed for life and sworn in, he cannot be dismissed, not even for cause, unless the facts are first established before a disciplinary court and the court finds him to have violated his duties so gravely as to justify a sentence of dismissal. This protection is strong not only because a formal procedure with all the usual guarantees of the judicial process (even publicity, which had been denied in the past, will be granted under the new federal act) must precede dismissal, but also on the additional ground that the court's composition ensures the official of a high degree of objectivity, tempered only by regard for the class interests of the civil service.[47] It is true that by

[45] Two of the *Länder* in the French Zone (Rhineland-Pfalz and Baden) do so for two years, Lower Saxony and Schleswig-Holstein for one or two semesters. In Rheinland-Pfalz alone is this training required for all *Verwaltungsreferendare;* the other *Länder* send only some of theirs. Bavaria, Hesse, Lower Saxony, and Schleswig-Holstein send also *Assessoren*. In addition, the academies of administration train for the higher service candidates from the elevated service.

[46] So does the academic work done by the *Hochschulen für Politik* in Berlin and Munich.

[47] Two of the three members (including the one presiding) must be regular judges with life tenure in either ordinary or administrative courts, and the third must be another official with life tenure. At least one of the three must belong to the same career as the accused person—a requirement which in the case of a procedure against a member of the higher service is automatically fulfilled by the presence of the two judicial members—and shall, if feasible, belong also to the

administrative action the official may be tentatively removed and up to one-half of his salary be withheld "if his dismissal by the court is to be expected"; but such action is narrowly limited by the requirement that the formal procedure must be set going at the same time.

Only a very small number of highest officials may be transferred to inactive status at any time. Within the federal administration these exemptions are limited in the new act to state secretaries, ministerial directors, ministerial counselors in the foreign office and their equals in the foreign service, chiefs of the Office for the Protection of the Constitution and of the Federal Press Relations Office and their alternates, and federal attorneys. All others, including even ministerial counselors, enjoy the strong guarantees of tenure as here described.[48] Consequently, dismissals of permanently appointed officials have been extremely rare in normal times. The powers of dismissal assumed by the Nazi regime and, after its collapse, by the new authorities in the denazification procedures were entirely extraordinary in the light of German traditions. Not only is the official's tenure rigidly protected, so is his classification within a definite salary group; he may not be transferred to a position of lower rank (final salary) without his consent. This made it next to impossible for the democratic ministers in the Weimar period to remove democratically unreliable ministerial counselors from their high positions, and the same difficulty is clearly developing in the Bonn Republic.

Requiring a formal disciplinary procedure before an official can be dismissed on charges of violation of duties is a sound feature of the German law, which deserves imitation. But violation of duties should not be the only valid cause for interference. Officials who do not live up to reasonable standards should be replaceable irrespective of whether their failure is the result of negligence or of ineptitude.[49] Security reasons, too, should make removal possible under due procedural guarantees. This need is obviously greater in a country that

same branch of the public service. The sentence can be appealed to a higher court (*Disziplinarhof*), where three members of the judiciary and two other officials pass on the case.

[48] Freely removable officials receive in inactive status their earned pension with a minimum guaranteed for five years of 50 per cent of a ministerial counselor's terminal salary. Ministerial directors, who were formerly also freely removable, will remain so under the 1953 act, as resolved only at its third reading.

[49] The new federal draft (sec. 75), following the model of Law No. 15, directed the department heads to delay automatic salary increases, or to set the official back in the salary scales of his group, or even to demote him to a lower category, if his achievements lag behind standards reasonably required. However, the final version of the act eliminated this provision.

has just emerged from fascism and is immediately threatened by communism than it is in the United States, where removal for security reasons is comparatively easy, perhaps too easy.

Steepness of the Hierarchic Pyramid—While guarantees of tenure and rank add to the security and prestige of the German career official, he is kept in his due place within the hierarchic pyramid by a number of rules, called "Reich Principles of Recruitment, Appointment, and Promotion," which block too early appointments and too rapid promotions.[50] These rules are not rigid, it is true. Deviations are possible; they are merely centralized by the requirement that they need the approval, formerly of the ministers of the interior and finance, now of the Personnel Commission. As a matter of analysis it must be admitted that in the absence of objective methods of selection and over-all control nothing less could be done to prevent the individual departments from running wild with arbitarary appointments and promotions. Yet precisely because of their general normative character the principles serve to illustrate the steepness and rigidity of the pyramid formed by the German civil service.

The first principle is that no one can skip the lowest rung of the ladder of a career into which he seeks appointment. No outsider, therefore, can immediately be appointed *Ministerialrat*. He can, at the most, be made a *Regierungsrat*. He must at least have been three years in office even before this can happen to him. Neither can a career man obtain such appointment immediately after he has passed the *Assessor* examination. He must wait at least four years and spend half of that time in the field. In addition, it is stipulated that no one may be appointed to any ministerial position unless he has served in the ministry at least one year. Access to the position of a *Ministerialrat* is made more difficult by further handicaps. No one can be appointed to that office unless he has served at least six years in positions of a *Regierungsrat* or *Oberregierungsrat* (half of the time in the field), and he must be at least thirty-five years old.

Promotion to the higher service from a lower career is quite unreasonably restricted by the last principle (No. 15), which says that no official of the middle or elevated service may be promoted even to the entrance position of the higher service at an age of less than forty and before he has served at least twenty years. No promotions of any

---

[50] *Reichsgrundsätze über Einstellung, Anstellung und Beförderung der Reichs- und Landesbeamten* of October 14, 1936, still in force for federal officials according to the first implementing order of June 17, 1950, under the 1950 Transition Act, and republished in 1951 with nazistic clauses expurgated. The *Länder,* too, continue to apply these principles. See note 63 below.

kind are to be made within the last three years prior to the age limit. One cannot fail to realize the towering height of the position of *Ministerialrat* within this pyramid. Truly, only members of that group could have drafted these principles. They obviously did so in defense against the appetite of Nazi outsiders for high offices. But the Nazis took their revenge. For they inserted into the principles several clauses to give members of the Nazi party at least part-time credit for service in Nazi organizations and—worse—added another provision to the effect that no career man could be promoted unless he had shown that "at all times he supports, and effectively represents, the National Socialist state." These Nazi clauses are no longer in force, of course. If read as mere directives for guiding normal careers in the interest of efficiency, some of the "principles" are acceptable. But if read, as they must be, as formal conditions of selection, they are a very poor, and in part even ridiculous, substitute for objective methods. To that extent they should be abandoned in favor of objective procedures.

Height and steepness of the bureaucratic pyramid are kept continuously on the minds of both officials and the general public by the constant uses of titles. Far from soberly describing actual functions,[51] the titles are actually full-sounding keywords indicating each official's present place within a definite career. No one can talk to German officials, nor can they talk to one another, without being reminded of their relative positions. Democratization would be aided materially if the use of titles in addressing civil servants were discontinued. All reasonable Germans should by now be aware of the backwardness and ludicrous nature of that usage and, as a token of maturity, renounce it gladly. However, there is little chance that this will happen.

Unusual Pension Scheme—The schedule of payments to German civil servants has to this day been influenced by a specific ideology. In accepting appointment, so it is argued, the citizen enters into a particular relationship with the state. On the one hand, he pledges a higher degree of loyalty to permeate his entire life, public and private, than that expected of ordinary citizens; on the other, the state takes away from him the ordinary human fear regarding the vicissitudes of life by assuring him of continuous service up to incapacity or retirement age and of adequate provision for him and his family thereafter, including considerable allowances for his wife and minor children after his death. This ideology has led to a unique pension system. German officials receive a much higher percentage of their salaries as pensions without paying contributions themselves than do officials in most

[51] The republican Prussian Prime Minister, Otto Braun, Social Democrat, used to joke that an *Inspektor* inspects nobody but is himself inspected.

other countries. Under the 1937 act (in force until mid-1953) the pension annuity was at least 35 per cent of the last salary plus average rental allowance, provided only that the official is twenty-seven years of age or older when he is disabled or retired. The annuity increased—after a waiting period of three years in the higher and of two in the elevated service—by 2 per cent a year for fifteen or (higher service) sixteen years of service and by 1 per cent for every year thereafter. The maximum was 80 per cent, but sank to 75 per cent when the official is sixty-five years old.

The 1953 federal act restores the pre-Hitler condition of at least ten years of service for any pension claims and reduces the maximum pension to 75 per cent, the annual increase over the minimum pension of 35 per cent to be uniformly 2 per cent for fifteen years (after the ten-year waiting period) and 1 per cent for every year thereafter. With these slight modifications, the old system is to be continued. As in the past, practically all officials retiring at the age of sixty-five will receive 75 per cent of their last salary annually as a life pension.[52] The widow receives 60 per cent of her husband's pension up to a maximum which, under the new federal law, will be 60 per cent of a *Ministerialrat's* terminal salary; and children get one-third or one-fifth of the widow's allowance until their eighteenth year.[53] In consequence of this generous scheme the budgetary amount of pensions paid on all governmental levels to former civil servants and their dependents gradually rose by the end of the interwar period to more than 30 per cent of the salaries paid to active officials, in spite of the sharply growing number of the latter.[54] Now, pension payrolls may have reached 50 per cent of the salary payrolls.

While total payments to individual officials are, generally speaking,

[52] Before a member of the U.S. civil service can draw a pension of 35 per cent of his salary, he must have served about twenty-four years and himself contributed 6 per cent each year. After the same twenty-four years of service, his German colleague would receive as much as 63 per cent of his last salary as a noncontributory pension. The maximum of 75 per cent is as a rule reached at an age of about fifty-six to fifty-eight.

[53] As before, all pensions are calculated from the salary of the last position, provided only that it had been held for at least one year; even this short waiting period does not apply in the case of death. Only one promotion is counted in every six years. Pensions may be canceled when the receiver becomes active against the liberal democratic constitutional order. The plenary meeting of the *Bundestag* ruled that promotions of postwar appointees prior to the new act will be counted even where there was more than one such promotion within six years.

[54] The percentage had been only about 17 per cent until World War I and increased thereafter to about 24 per cent. Figures provided by courtesy of the former ministerial director, Karl Wever, of the Reich Finance Ministry.

certainly not too high, the salary-pension ratio makes them appear far lower than they actually are. Ordinary citizens would have to suffer heavy reductions in case they tried to provide for similar pensions through commercial underwriters. Consequently, pension rights have assumed in Germany the character of a unique *privilege,* which separates civil servants from ordinary mortals and especially from contractual employees.[55] The privilege, however, often turned into a scourge. Pension rights were forfeited when an official voluntarily withdrew from the service prior to normal retirement age. This kept older officials in a peculiar kind of pension servitude. They could not afford to withdraw. Many officials who stayed in the service under Hitler did so only as a consequence of this pension servitude.

Reform would be surprisingly simple. All salaries could be nominally raised and all pensions reduced correspondingly through a stroke of the legislative pen, so that the sum total of salary and pension payments remained the same according to actuarial standards. The individual official might even be obligated to leave the additional amount of his salary in a pension pool and be assured that he would receive his old pension—but thenceforth to an ever-growing extent as a consequence of his own contribution rather than as a privilege. If he resigned, he could claim reimbursement to the amount of his own contributions plus interest.

The threefold advantage of such a reform would be that (1) payments to public servants, both individually and *in toto,* would be made more accurately visible; (2) salaries and pensions of civil servants and other employees could be more easily compared and adjusted; and (3) older civil servants would be relieved to a reasonable degree from their present depressive pension servitude.[56]

Gaps in Objective Methods of Selection and Absence of Over-all Control—The Germanic states had been among the first to develop the idea of a civil service based on merit principles, and along with it severe and objective examinations. Consequently, independent examination commissions have played a considerable role in Germany for more than two hundred years. Their passing marks constituted the condition for appointments to the normal career service. Over-all personnel management, however, was practically nonexistent. Selection

[55] Only Hamburg grants contractual employees the same pensions as civil servants.

[56] The Weinheim conference recommended consideration of this proposal. The new federal draft, however, preserved the traditional pension system with only minor changes, and the accompanying message passed over the objections rather cavalierly, though "without prejudice for the future" (*Begründung,* p. 35).

of candidates from the reservoirs of *Assessoren* for the higher service was left to the individual departments; so were promotions and the entire personnel management of the lower grades. This system left three gaps in objective methods of selection. No independent agency (1) made or prepared the final selection from career candidates who had passed the examination, or (2) certified the adequacy of noncareer candidates, or (3) made selections in competition between career and noncareer men. Nor were openings publicly advertised as a rule, except for some positions in the municipal service.

At the request of the occupation authorities, independent personnel offices were established in the *Länder* of the American Zone and in the bizonal administration. They were of the commission type in Bavaria and Württemberg-Baden.[57] Hesse used a mixed system. In the bizonal administration, the personnel director (Ministerial Director Dr. Kurt Oppler) was merely "advised" by a committee.

The powers vary. Bavaria's commission, strongest among the *Länder,* may independently regulate and supervise examinations and establish lists of successful candidates. Originally it had the right to certify the three top candidates, from whom the appointing department had to make its selection. But this power met with so much resistance on the side of the departments that it was eliminated by amendment in December, 1950.

The director of bizonal personnel had more extensive powers. He could regulate entrance qualifications, prepare training programs after due consultation, assign positions to definite classes, determine the proportion in which positions should be assigned to outsiders, and rule on exceptions from the public advertising of openings. His regulations needed the approval of the bizonal cabinet, however, where the majority of the department heads could overrule him. His powers, therefore, were far from dictatorial.

The other western *Länder,* with the exception of Hamburg,[58] con-

[57] The Bavarian Personnel Commission consists of seven members, who are appointed by the minister-president in overlapping terms of six years and must normally include a judge, an official each for the interior and finance administrations, a university professor, a representative of civil servants' associations to be nominated by them, and two nonofficials. All members are independent; one is appointed chairman.

[58] Hamburg has a central personnel office with which two independent commissions are connected—an examination commission of seven, which has done notable work, especially through the ample use of aptitude tests; and an appointment commission, alone authorized to submit proposals to the Senate, which may reject but not act without them. In Berlin, a central office for personnel questions can carry objections to departmental appointments either before the entire Senate or a committee, from which further appeal lies to the Senate.

tinue to operate technically along traditional lines. The federal government, too, has made no more than timid approaches to over-all control. True, the personnel commission has been assigned the function, previously performed by the Ministries of the Interior and of Finance, of granting or denying exceptions from principles or rules. But it has neither helped nor substantially controlled the individual departments in their selections. The three gaps in objective methods of selection still exist. The Weinheim conference recommended the closing of all three, but only the qualifying examination for outsiders has been included in the new federal law. Any interference with free selection among qualified candidates, career or outsider, is still exposed to the heavy resistance of the departments.

Distinction between Officials and Contractual Employees—German government departments have developed the practice of supplementing their contingents of officials with contractual employees and workers whose legal position differs sharply from that of the official. Their tenure is definitely less secure, and payments in the event of removal, incapacity, or old age are far below the amounts granted officials. On the other hand, salaries and wages during their active service are sometimes higher than those paid officials for equal work.[59] It is, therefore, difficult to compare the financial situation. Even so, the question remains as to why arrangements should be so different. Rational principles have been sought in order to decide which positions should be filled with civil servants and which with employees. Section 4 of the 1053 federal law, substantially repeating section 148 of the 1937 law, states that "an appointment into the civil service may not be made unless it be for the execution (1) of sovereign functions [*hoheitsrechtlicher Aufgaben*] or (2) of such functions as for reasons of the security of the state or of the public life may not be committed exclusively to the charge of persons who work under private-law contracts." This limitation has never been strictly observed, however. All groups of public servants are fanatic in emphasizing their sovereign functions. The final effect has been to increase class consciousness and self-complacency.

Bent on reform, Military Government Law No. 15 recognized only two categories, officials and wage earners. Yet all the *Länder* continue to use the three traditional categories, and the new federal law follows this general trend.[60] It has, therefore, become the more impor-

[59] For a fuller discussion, reference is made to the author's mimeographed report (HICOG, 1950) and a German version (HICOG, 1951), distributed by the *Deutsche Gesellschaft für Personalwesen*, Frankfurt.

[60] Hamburg was the only *Land* to vote in the Federal Council for abolishing the

tant to make certain that all artificial differences in the rights and duties of civil servants, employees, and workers are leveled down. Nothing will be more helpful in this respect than a relatively normal salary-pension ratio in the payment of officials and, on the other hand, the renunciation by all public employees, rather than by civil servants alone, of the right to strike against the democratic government.

Outsiders—One of the most undesirable implications of the career concept is that, in stamping every noncareer man an outsider, it caters to class instincts. The Basic Law (Art. 33, par. 2) promises every German "equal access to any public office in accordance with his aptitude, ability and professional achievements." So did the Weimar Constitution (Art. 128). Yet all such principles leave wide loopholes which have been amply used. Requirements are, as a rule, determined so narrowly as to exclude noncareer men. Admission of outsiders for political reasons or patronage without qualifying examinations has only aggravated the resistance because of undeniable mistakes made.

If career men have to fear that their long preparatory work will be of little value because outsiders will get most of the better jobs, fewer brilliant young men and women will be attracted to education for the public service. Here lies a crucial problem. The solution might be found in an appropriate ratio between positions reserved for career men and those open to others. A reasonable percentage of openings should be advertised in such a way as neither to require nor to exclude the normal education and training of a career candidate. The Weinheim conference adopted these views in principle, leaving the determination of the ratio to the personnel office. The new federal law has disregarded them. However, a clause permitting the appointment of non-career men only "when no suitable career men are available" or the appointment is "of particular advantage in the interests of the service," was ruled out at the third reading, fortunately.

Civil Servants as Members of Parliaments—Under both the Imperial and Weimar constitutions German civil servants did not need to resign when elected to parliamentary bodies. Consequently, they exercised great influence in political parties and served on many parliamentary committees, particularly those dealing with the public service. This dualism undermined the separation of powers and the

---

distinction between officials and employees in line with Law No. 15. The *Bundestag* in a plenary meeting in May, 1953, inserted a paragraph in the new act which permitted contractual employees less than forty years of age but with not less than ten years and not more than fifteen years of service to transfer to civil service status, yet this was eliminated at the third reading, June 2.

political neutrality of civil servants. Once some were permitted to campaign as party candidates in public elections, none could be asked to maintain external standards of impartiality and neutrality in party affairs.

American and British advisers tried hard to persuade the German political parties to abandon these practices, but met with little success. Civil servants have continued to pour into parliamentary bodies.[61] Military Government Law No. 15 prescribed that any bizonal official who wanted to be a candidate for public elections had to withdraw from the service on acceptance of the nomination. The federal constitution did not, however, incorporate the same principle but relegated the problem to simple legislation (Election Law of June 15, 1949). Subsequently, the Allies published a law of their own, excluding members of the *Bundestag* from civil service positions at all levels—federal, state, and local—but again limiting incompatibility to the time after election. As a matter of fact, fifty-eight (14.5 per cent) of the members elected to the present *Bundestag* either were civil servants until their acceptance of the election or had been so in the past.

Only North Rhine–Westphalia (law of April 6, 1950) and Berlin require resignation, at least of their own public servants, before they enter an election campaign for the respective *Land* parliament. Hesse has not gone farther than to say, in a 1950 law, that after election civil servants shall lose their active status for the duration of their membership in parliament, but will still receive half of their salaries. In Württemberg-Baden, according to another 1950 law, they are to lose their salaries entirely. But these concessions in no way remove the chief evil—active partisanship of executive officials, free to campaign before resigning their official status. Consequently, the neutrality of the entire German civil service has remained problematic.

The Adenauer cabinet, in its correspondence with the high commissioners, had promised to introduce a bill requiring resignation of any civil servant before he accepts nomination as a candidate for elective office. As mentioned before, the cabinet did indeed insert

---

[61] There were, for example, 25 active officials, 2 in inactive status, and 6 retired, together 33 per cent, among the 100 members of the first Württemberg-Baden *Landtag*. The *Landtag* of Rheinland-Pfalz had 20 per cent active and 13 per cent inactive or former officials (also 33 per cent). Not much better, the first *Landtag* of Hesse counted 20 per cent active and 2 per cent inactive or former officials among its members, and that of Bavaria 13 per cent active officials. See also H. Schuster, "Beamte und Funktionäre in den europäischen Parlamenten," *Neues Beaumtentum*, p. 243. No objections can, of course, be raised against the presence of *former* officials.

such a section in its draft (sec. 53). The Federal Council, however, restored the traditional right of federal officials to become a candidate for, and sit in, state or local legislatures without losing their federal jobs and postponed their duty to resign in federal elections to the stage after their acceptance of the election, therewith killing the principle of political neutrality of active civil servants in party affairs. They consequently eliminated also a clause in the governmental draft saying that an official must not be conspicuous in the public eye as an active adherent of a political party. Unfortunately, the Adenauer cabinet, ignoring its pledge, accepted these changes in the letter of transmittal by which it passed the bill on to the *Bundestag*. The *Bundestag* has left it at that.

CONCLUSION

The main defect of the German civil service today lies in the lingering conflict between its authoritarian tradition and its bureaucratic structure on the one side and the basic principles of a democratic society on the other. Exactly those characteristics that under the monarchy and the totalitarian regime had constituted its strength—class instincts, exclusiveness, and a steep hierarchic structure—limit its value in a democratic society. This defect is bound to be noticeable for some time to come, despite sincere efforts of many officials to serve democratic ideals faithfully and to forego personally all feelings of class superiority and all claims to privilege. The group nature of the inherent defect is too strong for the individual to overcome. Once this situation is clearly understood and thus removed from an atmosphere of inarticulate irritation and resentment, it can be met through combined efforts from both sides—a democratic society and the civil service. But it cannot be remedied within a few months or years by means of external measures. At best it will be a long and slow process.

Success cannot be hoped for unless political governments based on democratic principles will be in power in Germany for a sufficiently long period in unbroken succession. It took France at least thirty years after 1870 to republicanize its civil service. France, too, could not have succeeded in the face of monarchistic tradition, Boulangerism, the Dreyfus crisis, and other symptoms of surviving authoritarianism, had not democratic cabinets held the reins—after President MacMahon's resignation in 1879—through those thirty years and longer. We must realize that Germany may also need such a thirty-year period of adjustment between bureaucracy and democracy. The thirteen years of the Weimar Republic, with a prodemocratic majority in the *Reichstag* only during the first year,[62] were too short for the completion of this task. But with a much longer chain of democratic governments at the helm, the situation would by no means be hopeless. There exists much good will on the side of the bureaucracy—though more good will than actual awareness of defects. It is in such a perspective that all proposals for structural changes must be examined. Structural reforms alone cannot democratize the civil service. Nevertheless, they are of great importance. The petrification of the traditional structure in the 1953 act will make democratization very difficult, though not, let us hope, impossible.[63]

The act is to go into force on September 1, 1953.

[62] The elections of 1920 reduced the 1919 majority of the three prodemocratic parties (Social Democrats, Democrats, and the Catholic Center party) to a minority in the *Reichstag*, and such they remained to the end of the Weimar Republic. See *Prelude to Silence: The End of The German Republic* and Arnold Brecht, "Walther Rathenau and the German People," *Journal of Politics*, X (1948), 20.

[63] The principle that no rung of the hierarchical ladder must be skipped in appointments and promotions, formerly a mere executive regulation, has even been incorporated in the new 1953 statute so as to form a part of the civil service act itself. The legislature has further raised this forbidding barrier to outsiders in advanced years by adding that no outsider can be finally appointed even to the lowest position within a career before the expiration of at least three years of service. Both limitations are subject to exceptions which may be granted by the Federal Personnel Commission.

11

Organization and

Methods Control

KURT GLASER

NEITHER the Federal Republic of Germany nor any of its *Länder* has an agency similar to the Division of Administrative Management of the United States Bureau of the Budget or to a well-developed state management planning agency. Nor do the federal or *Land* ministries have divisions comparable to organization and procedure divisions in the United States. This does not necessarily mean that German administration is more backward than American administration.[1] What it does mean is that the Germans approach administrative problems in a manner somewhat different from that of the Americans. An appreciation of these differences is the first step toward mutual understanding.

The functions of specialized administrative management agencies (or divisions) in the United States generally include at least the following specific activities:

a. The study of organization problems and the planning of organizational structure.

b. The development of regulations and procedural instructions to achieve economical, efficient, and rapid administration.

c. The application of work-measurement techniques to adjust staff to work load and to avoid "bottlenecks."

d. The co-ordination of printed forms.

[1] German ministerial officials claim, with some justification, that they have had insufficient time since the war to recover a normal standard of operating efficiency. With regard to German administrative practices which may have value for the

e. The development of efficient office procedures, including the most efficient use of space, office machines, files and communication facilities, equipment and supplies.

An important feature of American administrative management is its status as a staff function. Granted that the operating official must have some administrative ability in order to get his job done, it is still felt that he needs, from time to time, the services of an administrative mechanic, someone who "puts the machinery in order." While the staff officials have no authority to give direct orders to the line administrator, it is generally expected that he will take their advice.

German administrative science is based predominantly on legal rather than operative norms. It does not share the American emphasis on "getting the job done."[2] One very good reason for this is that German ministries do not have the same job to do as American federal government departments. Unlike their American counterparts, which administer most of their functions directly through their own regional and field offices, German federal ministries are as a rule limited to seeing that the administration of federal law by the *Länder* conforms to the statutes and the Basic Law of the German Federal Republic. The Basic Law itself is quite clear on this point. Article 83 states: "The *Länder* execute the federal laws as matters of their own concern insofar as this Basic Law does not otherwise provide or permit." A general right of federal instruction and supervision over *Land* administration of federal law, such as was granted by Article 15 of the Weimar Constitution, is omitted in the present Basic Law. Even under the Weimar Constitution, the activity of the Reich ministries was largely limited to the preparation of regulations and the solution of legal and technical questions arising under them. Direct federal administration was (prior to 1933) and is limited essentially to the postal service, the railways, the customs, and the federal financial administration. Even these are not operated directly by the ministries, but by semi-autonomous, detached subordinate agencies. Even on *Land* level, the volume of detailed administrative activity is limited, since the bulk of administration is delegated downward to counties and municipalities.[3]

United States, see Arnold Brecht and Kurt Glaser, *The Art and Technique of Administration in German Ministries* (Cambridge, Mass., 1940).

[2] This statement is not intended to disparage the element of legality in American administration, which is perhaps little emphasized because it is taken for granted. See Fritz Morstein Marx, "Administrative Ethics and the Rule of Law," *American Political Science Review*, December, 1949, pp. 1119-1144.

[3] For a detailed comparison between German and American administrative structure, see Kurt Glaser and W. Kurtz, *Land and Local Government in the Federal Republic of Germany*. Office of U.S. High Commissioner for Germany

The result of the German system of delegation to the *Länder,* or to subordinate *Obere Bundesbehörden* where direct federal administration is involved, is that German ministries are small and do not have as many administrative problems as American departments.[4] The Federal Ministry of the Interior, for instance, has at present six divisions, one of which is divided into three subdivisions (Constitution, Administration, and Public Safety). The functional activities of these divisions are divided among forty-two *Referate,* each of which is managed by a *Referent* or subject-matter specialist. The *Referent* does not have a large staff; in fact, he usually operates alone with the help of a clerk and a stenographer who, if the work load is not large, also serve other *Referenten.* Since several *Referenten* have two or more *Referate* (sometimes in different divisions), the total number of executive-type personel in the entire ministry is not more than fifty, although it may expand to sixty when the ministry is fully staffed.

Since the *Referenten* are concerned not with the detailed administration of individual cases but rather with interpreting the law, advising their counterparts in the *Länder,* and preparing such regulations as the ministry may legally issue, the volume of work does not present a management problem in itself. The assignment of functions is therefore not so much a question of administrative feasibility or of analysis from a "production engineering" point of view as a matter of determining where a given subject matter falls within the logical classification of functions (*Zuständigkeit*). German administrators have traditionally given much thought to the problem of *Zuständigkeit:* each ministry has a carefully worked out "plan for the distribution of functions" (*Geschäftsverteilungsplan*). The development and periodic revision of this plan is usually the responsibility of the permanent undersecretary (*Staatssekretär*), who always obtains the recommendations of the division chiefs before making any changes.

Each division chief in a German ministry is held responsible for the efficiency of his internal organization and his operating procedures. This is considered such an integral part of the over-all job of administering that the injection of a procedure division with authority to survey, to inspect, and to review administrative instructions would be considered cumbersome and unnecessary. If we are willing to look at ourselves a moment as others see us, we may well consider the opinion of an *Oberregierungsrat* who remarked to the author: "I have studied American administration and have come to the conclusion that

(Frankfurt; publication pending).

[4] See Arnold Brecht, "Smaller Departments," *Public Administration Review,* Summer, 1941, pp. 363-373.

the need for procedure divisions is a symptom of administrative weakness. You people allow your administration to become so complicated that you need an administrative technician to straighten out the mess. We avoid the need for him by keeping our administration simple and decentralized in the first place." Of course the *Oberregierungsrat* exaggerated the contrast somewhat—there is more centralization in German government, particularly on the *Land* level, than he would care to admit. He also failed to consider that a procedure which may be very simple from the point of view of the agency may be complicated for the citizen who has to obtain not one, but a series of permissions for doing a single thing (such as building a house or moving from one town to another). The statement does, nevertheless, have considerable justification.

The responsibility for administrative management in German government is diffused and merged with the responsibility for over-all administration. The Germans have not in the past recognized any specialized phases of management as staff functions; in fact, they make no conscious distinction between "line" and "staff" functions such as is common in American and British practice. They do recognize a specialized service function of office management, and they also recognize the need for continuous and systematic study of administrative methods. They feel, however, that administrative technique should be understood and applied by the operating official rather than by an administrative technician representing a staff division.

THE *MINISTERIALBÜRODIREKTOR* AND THE *ORGANISATIONSREFERENT*

The business management functions of each federal ministry are consolidated under a *Ministerialbürodirektor,* whose rank and functions approximate those of an American chief clerk. The *Ministerialbürodirektor* usually belongs to a "General Administrative Division" which also includes the Personnel and Budget Offices and a *Pressestelle* which issues news releases and the official gazette of the ministry. The organization of his office is shown in Figure 1.

The *Ministerialbürodirektor* is responsible for providing the services indicated. With regard to their utilization, another official steps into the picture, the *Organisationsreferent* or "specialist for organizational questions." This official, who may or may not be in the General Administrative Division, observes whether clerical and stenographic personnel are assigned according to actual work load. He recommends to the *Ministerialbürodirektor* from time to time such reassignments as appear to be necessary. He also advises and in some ministries has a

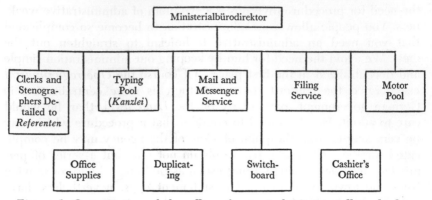

Figure 1. Organization of the office of a typical *Ministerialbürodirektor.*

right of clearance on instructions concerning internal operation of the ministry (for example, office hours, filing, use of motor vehicles) which are issued by the *Ministerialbürodirektor.* In addition, the *Organisationreferent* is frequently given assignments which do not belong to the *Zuständigkeit* of any other *Referent.* The *Organisationsreferent* of the Ministry of the Interior was, for instance, recently engaged on working out with the *Land* interior ministries a consolidated schedule for charity drives throughout the federal territory.

The functions of the *Organisationsreferent* are more limited than his title would suggest. He does not, for instance, review regulations and circulars prepared by the operating divisions for issue to the *Länder.* These are checked for legality by the legal adviser of the ministry and signed by the minister or the *Staatssekretär.* The chief of the operating division is held responsible for their administrative feasibility insofar as this is not questioned by higher officials. Nor does the *Organsationsreferent* have any authority over printed forms, except those relating to the business management of the ministry. Although the old Reich ministries were empowered to prescribe forms used in the administration of federal law, the present Basic Law vests this authority in the *Länder*—the federal ministries can only recommend the forms to be used. The important exceptions to this rule are in the sphere of direct federal administration (post, railways, and the like) and in the fields of foreign trade and currency exchange. In the latter cases detailed regulations and forms are prescribed by the Federal Ministry of Economics and the *Bank Deutscher Länder* respectively. In other fields, the technical specialists of the *Länder* meet from time to time to agree voluntarily on standard procedures and forms. These meetings are presided over by the competent subject-matter specialists in the federal ministries. The *Organisationsreferenten* usually do not participate. The *Organisationsreferent* has nothing to do with the preparation of the ministerial budget or with the control of expenditures. These are the exclusive province of the budget *Referent*. The budget has in the past been usd for purely fiscal planning and control; the possibilities of using it as a device for over-all management are just beginning to be explored.

THE CODE OF ADMINISTRATIVE PROCEDURE— ADMINISTRATIVE PRACTICES

The most significant current activity of the *Organsationsreferenten* is the revision of the Common Code of Administrative Procedure (GGO) of the federal ministries. By general agreement, the old GGO of September 2, 1926,[5] has been applied, *mutatis mutandis,* to the ministries of the new German Federal Republic. A committee of all the *Organisationsreferenten* under the chairmanship of the representative of the Ministry of the Interior, *Regierungsdirektor* Dullien, is now revising the GGO for the approval of the cabinet. The present revision is limited to the "General Part" (GGO I) concerning internal operations of the ministries. The "Special Part" (GGO I) covering relations between the ministries and the parliament will be revised later, after the *Bundestag* and the *Bundesrat* have finally settled their own rules of procedure. The new GGO will be somewhat more detailed than the 1926 document in order to provide necessary information to the many new officials in the federal service. The basic principles of the old GGO will, however, be retained since they have proven their value over a number of years.

To return to our *Oberregierungsrat* who claimed that German administration was simpler than American, it is interesting to compare a few basic administrative practices set forth in the GGO with the equivalent practices of our own federal government. For one thing, Germans do not have the American habit of making numerous carbon copies of every letter. In the typical American office, a carbon is held by the originator, one by the section chief, and one by the division chief, in addition to the official "file copy" which is deposited in the central files. This proliferation of carbon copies is due to the fact that most American government executives and files supervisors have never been able to achieve a satisfactory working relationship with each other. The files supervisor sets up a mnemonic classification which may be useful for the file clerks, but which has no necessary relation to the

[5] An English translation of the "General Part" (GGO I) is contained in Brecht and Glaser, *op. cit.,* pp. 47-113.

administrative classification of functions. The executives are not given copies of this classification, nor are they expected to know it. If they give instructions as to how a letter should be filed, they would be encroaching on the *Zuständigkeit* of the files supervisor. The result is that nine out of ten executives have no confidence that they can secure from the central files specific material when they need it. Therefore they have their secretaries maintain special files, a practice which is abetted by the free and easy distribution of filing cabinets.

The German GGO solves this problem by coordinating the files index with the "plan for the distribution of business" in such a way that the symbols designating the divisions and *Referate* are themselves the basic file symbols. Within each *Referat* additional symbols for subclassifications are added as necessary. The files are under central supervision but are physically decentralized—to the divisions in the Ministry of the Interior and to the *Referate* in most other ministries. In either case the *Referenten* have immediate access to the files they need. The files index, the maintenance of which is a joint responsibility of the *Ministerialbürodirektor* and the *Organsationsreferent*, is distributed to all executives, so that all are informed where the file on a particular subject may be found. By sticking to the principle "one letter—one subject" it is possible to prepare outgoing communications with one carbon copy.

The Germans have developed a number of multiple-use forms. For example, instead of using a "request for travel order" and a separate "travel order" form, each of which is usually filled out in several copies, the latter by a central travel section, the German ministries use a combined request and travel order which is made up in original only. Since the ministries consider their executives to be adults, authority to approve travel is generally delegated to division chiefs. The traveler fills out the form indicating where, when, and why he needs to travel, and the division chief endorses the application with "approved." The approved application then serves as a travel order, as authorization for a travel advance, and as support for the expense voucher upon completion of the trip. A similar multi-purpose form is the payroll voucher, which has two carbon copies. The second of these is perforated, and the strips are torn apart and given to each employee in lieu of the special "payroll change slip" used in the United States.

A further desirable German practice is the decentralization of authority to sign correspondence. Instead of preparing letters to the public or to other agencies for the signature of a few high officials, the German *Referent*, as the person responsible for a given subject matter, conducts in his own name the bulk of routine correspondence with the *Länder*, with other agencies, and with the public. He is expected to know the limits of his own competence and to bring all important or controversial subjects to the attention of his division chief and, if necessary, the *Staatssekretär* or minister. This decentralization replaces the system of institutionalized control with a practice of self-control, thereby improving considerably the morale and the sense of responsibility of subordinate executives. The individual who receives the communication knows exactly with whom he is dealing—the anonymity of "the government" is replaced by a personal contact.

ADMINISTRATIVE SURVEYS BY THE RECHNUNGSHOF

Large-scale administrative surveys have traditionally been a function of the Court of Accounts (*Rechnungshof*), an agency which resembles the General Accounting Office in the United States. Like its American counterpart, the *Rechsnungshof* is an instrument of parliamentary control over the executive. Its president, vice-president, directors, and *Ministerialräte* are appointed by the President of the Federal Republic, enjoy judicial independence, and can be removed only for cause. Its important decisions are made collectively, in so-called "Senates" established for various functional fields and a "Greater Senate" for matters of major importance.

In addition to having advisory powers on matters relating to the execution of the budget law within the ministries and general power to audit all expenditures for conformity with the budget and with the law, the *Rechnungshof* has authority to make administrative surveys. This authority is based on Article 96 of the Reich Budget Act (*Reichshaushaltsordnung*) of December 31, 1922,[6] which authorizes the *Rechnungshof* to determine not only whether the budget and the accounting regulations have been observed, but also whether receipts and expenditures have been in accord with accepted principles of administration and governmental economy and particularly "whether agencies or offices are maintained, or other expenditures incurred, which could be reduced or abolished without endangering the essential purposes of administration." Article 101 states that the *Rechsnungshof* may be charged by the Reich ministers or the *Reichstag* with rendering advisory opinions on questions which are "significant in relationship to the management of Reich funds." In 1933 the *Rechnungshof* took over the functions of the former Reich commissioner for economy (*Reichssparkommissar*).

[6] *Reichsgesetzblatt* II (1923), 17. Official reference edition (Berlin, 1938) contains amendments through April 30, 1938.

After the collapse of the Reich in 1945, a number of key *Rechnungshof* personnel were reassembled in the *Rechnungshof* for the British Zone at Hamburg. Following establishment of the Bizonal Economic Area, this agency moved to Frankfurt and became the *Rechnungshof* for the agencies attached to the Economic Council. The bizonal law establishing the *Rechnungshof*[7] re-enacted by reference the entire *Reichshaushaltsordnung* as did the law later passed by the *Bundestag* which established the *Rechnungshof* for the German Federal Republic.[8]

Since its re-establishment, the *Rechnungshof* has made a number of administrative surveys of entire agencies. The most important of these was a review of the Bizonal Economic Administration (*Verwaltung für Wirtschaft*—VfW). A team of five spent two months (from April 20 to June 16, 1948) investigating and prepared a report recommending a general reorganization of the VfW under three rather than the previous five main divisions, the abolition or transfer to the *Länder* of numerous activities, and a personnel reduction from 1,943 to 795 employees. The recommendations went into great detail, indicating not only which offices should be eliminated or consolidated but also which positions should be abolished and how the remaining positions should be classified. It also considered such points as the custody of rationing documents, the reorganization of files, and the utilization of transportation. The investigators took great pains to relate their recommendations to the needs which the VfW was expected to serve—this required a prognosis of the development of the German economy after the currency reform.

The absorption of the bizonal agencies into the federal government presented the *Rechnungshof* with a new task, which was undertaken late in 1948. At the request of the Conference of Ministers-President, the *Rechnungshof* developed detailed plans for the organization of the future federal ministries, indicating which bizonal offices should be taken over and which should be dropped. The report, which recommended a total of eight ministries rather than the thirteen actually established, has never been made public.

Although an accurate prediction is impossible, federal officials estimate that the *Rechnungshof*, once it has been granted the status of a federal agency, will make at least one major survey of a federal

[7] *Gesetz über die Errichtung eines Rechnungshofes für das Vereinigte Wirtschaftsgebiet in Gesetzblatt der Verwaltung des Vereinigten Wirtschaftsgebietes,* 1948, No. 24 (Nov. 10), pp. 115-116.

[8] *Gesetz über die Errichtung und Aufgaben des Bundesrechnungshofes,* November 27, 1950 (BGBL. 765). Pending enactment of this law, the bizonal *Rechnungshof* was already functioning in fact as the *Rechnungshof* of the German Federal Republic.

ministry each year. In addition to its federal work, the *Rechnungshof* also undertakes surveys of *Land* and local governments when requested by their executive or representative organs. Although the *Länder* have *Rechnungshöfe* of their own, it is sometimes preferred to have a survey made by an outside agency. In 1950 and 1951 the *Rechnungshof* surveyed the government of Schleswig-Holstein, and this survey was to be followed by one in Niedersachsen. A number of local surveys have been made, two of the most interesting being specialized investigations of the municipal cultural enterprises (theater, opera, and concerts) in Hamburg and in Freiburg. In the field of municipal surveys, the *Rechnungshof* meets with competition, since the German Cities' Association (*Deutscher Städtetag*) also maintains an advisory and survey staff called the Joint Municipal Office for Administrative Simplification (*Kommunale Gemeinschaftsstelle für Verwaltungsvereinfachung*).

One of the difficulties faced by the *Rechnungshof* is the recruitment of personnel for its survey activities. A cardinal point in a survey is to determine not only how a given governmental activity may be more efficiently conducted but whether it should be conducted at all. The public demand for governmental services and the technical problems involved in these services must be accurately appraised. This means that the members of survey teams must not only be experts in administrative law and management practices but must have a knowledge of the subject-matter fields investigated. Traditionally the *Rechnungshof* has had members qualified in administration plus music.[9] The increasing specialization and vocationalization of German education makes it difficult to replace such personnel.

THE COMMITTEE FOR EFFICIENT ADMINISTRATION

Because the responsibility for management is diffused in German government, the role played by voluntary associations in improving administrative practices is rather greater than in the United States. A number of activities which in America are performed by the Bureau of the Budget, the Civil Service Commission, and the management and personnel branches of federal agencies and state governments fall within the purview of the Committee for Efficient Administration

[9] The City of Berlin once asked the *Rechnungshof* to determine how many musicians the Philharmonic Orchestra should have, how much these musicians should be paid, and how much should be budgeted for soloists. Fortunately the *Rechnungshof* had an administrative analyst who had studied musicology. This individual managed to convince Mr. Furtwängler that he should get along with fifteen musicians fewer than he had originally asked for.

(*Ausschuss für Wirtschaftliche Verwaltung*), known by the abbreviation AWV. The AWV, which is the successor of the former Reich Committee for Economical Administration (also AWV), has absorbed the activities of the former German Institute for Economy in Administration (DIWIV).

The AWV is itself a member society in the Committee for Economic Rationalization (*Rationalisationskuratorium der deutschen Wirtschaft*), known as the RKW. The RKW also includes the REFA, which specializes in scientific management and time study applied to industrial production. Another member is the German Committee on Norms, which develops standard specifications for nuts and bolts, electrical and plumbing fixtures, radio tubes, and all other products which are most serviceable when interchangeable. The RKW concerns itself with co-ordinating the rationalization efforts of its members and with directing attention to the most urgent problems of the day. It does not itself engage in investigations or surveys, but leaves this to its member organizations. The RKW and its member societies receive small subsidies from the federal government. These subsidies, which totaled only DM300,000 for the fiscal year 1950, barely cover the cost of maintaining a small secretariat for each society. While the REFA and the Committee on Norms receive some income from the manufacturers they service, the AWV is largely dependent on the unpaid work of its members.

The AWV, which has its main office in Frankfurt under the direction of Harry Lilje, has members representing the federal ministries and the *Rechnungshof*, several *Land* governments, and a large number of institutes, technical schools, trade associations, and private firms. Its objectives were briefly stated in an article in the April, 1950, issue of the magazine *Rationalisierung* as follows:

The AWV is interested in the development of the best procedures for performing clerical tasks and also in the simplification of adminstrative processes. The object is to develop the most efficient office methods for public agencies, banks, industrial producers, merchants, and even lawyers, doctors, etc. In this connection particular attention is to be paid the conditions under which work is performed. It is intended that the employee will not feel oppressed but will enjoy his work because he knows that he is being considered as an individual.

This problem is not restricted to any branch of activity, such as industry, commerce, banks, or insurance or public agencies. It is a matter of techniques of work and of administration which are common to all fields of activity.

In order to carry out its rather extensive program, the AWV has a series of technical committees, which have the function of developing and recommending standard practices in various fields. As of this writing, the committees (and those subcommittees which are of interest to public administrators) are as follows:

a. Principles of Administrative and Industrial Organization—including personnel organization, assignment of functions and responsibilities, organization and arrangement of office space, subject-matter classification, graphic presentation (organization charts), basic organizational problems.

b. Vocational Guidance and Training—vocational guidance, in-service training (preparation of teaching materials on basis of work of other committees), customer service of private business and public contacts of governmental agencies.

c. Procurement and Warehousing.

d. Bookkeeping.

e. Office Machines and Equipment.

f. Communications and Files.

g. Business and Governmental Forms.

h. Numerical Systems.

i. Consultation, demonstration, and training subcommittees on office organization, specialized training in efficiency work, office methods exhibition, short courses for practitioners.

In order to secure results, the committees and subcommittees must assign to their individual members investigations, study projects, and the writing of reports. Such work depends to some extent on the willingness of employers to have office time used for that purpose. So far as the German federal government is concerned, it appears to be official policy to regard as official business work done in the AWV on problems which are of interest to the government. Government representatives in AWV committees are granted travel orders to attend meetings and are allowed (within reason, of course) to use office time and facilities for their individual projects.

CONCLUSION

To sum up, it may be said that although the Germans have not developed the American type of staff offices concerned with administrative management, they are aware of the problems existing in this field and have developed some valuable devices for dealing with them. They have not developed the concept of the management responsibilities of top governmental executives (on which concept modern staff organization is based); there are, however, two reasons why this concept may not be entirely applicable to German conditions.

One is the smaller size of federal departments occasioned by the delegation of administration to the *Länder*. The other is the fact that the minister, unlike his American counterpart, is a parliamentarian and is not considered traditionally (nor is he equipped to be) the "manager" of his ministry. While some strengthening of the ministerial *Organisationsreferenten* appears desirable, there appears little need for elaborate staff services in the offices of the ministers. In the field of administrative surveys, the *Rechnungshof* has accomplished results which compare favorably with the best American practice. It is, however, apparent that this agency will have to enlarge its survey staff if it is to meet the demands placed upon it. The AWV appears to have made a good start toward regaining its former effectiveness as a forum in which management problems are solved through co-operative effort.

Officials in the federal ministries, in the *Rechnungshof,* and in the AWV have expressed considerable interest in learning more about American administrative methods and in gaining access to our literature on the subject. The fields in which our experience would probably be most valuable to them are the use of the budget as an instrument of executive control and the development of administrative cost standards. In so far as such standards are applied to administration in the *Länder* under federal grants, it is important that the standards be developed and applied by co-operative committees of *Länder* representatives, since to apply them "from the top down" would conflict with the principle of federalism as it exists in Germany. It is also evident that the Americans can learn from the Germans, particularly in regard to eliminating unnecessary paper work.

12

Budget Management[1]

A. M. HILLHOUSE

BUDGETING is a well-developed process in Western Germany and is fairly uniform for the nine *Länder* governments and the federal government because practices are based on the old Reich Budget Ordinance (*Reichshaushaltsordnung*)[2] and its implementing regulations[3] and on basic and similar provisions in the federal and state constitutions. There is also a high degree of uniformity in local government budgeting owing to the fact that, although the *Deutsche Gemeindeordnung*[4] was repealed, the *Länder* legislation enacted to take its place retained essentially the former finance sections. An American who has watched German budgeting in operation for any length of time is impressed not only by the basic uniformities found, but perhaps equally by features which permit the finance ministers, whether federal or *Länder*, wide latitude. Executive responsibility for the budget in Germany is closer to the British than to the American pattern; large powers are placed in the hands of the finance minister, as in the case of the British chancellor of the Exchequer, and the minister's position in the German cabinet, second only to that of the

[1] For constructive suggestions and criticisms of this chapter in the draft stage, the author is indebted to Dr. Wilhelmina Dreissig, of the *Bank Deutscher Länder;* to Dr. Karl Lang, tax consultant, Frankfurt am Main; and to Miss Lottie Bristow, of the British Treasury.

[2] Cited as RHO. The RHO was not repealed by Allied Control Council legislation since it antedated the Nazis.

[3] *Wirtschaftsbestimmungen für die Reichsbehörden,* cited as RWB.

[4] Cited as DGO.

Chancellor, or minister-president in a *Land*,[5] is rooted (as in the United Kingdom) in long tradition and experience. These aspects of German budgeting in particular, but also other major characteristics, warrant attention.

OPERATION WITHOUT A FORMAL BUDGET

The Basic Law and the *Länder* constitutions require in principle that budgets be passed prior to the beginning of the fiscal year (April 1), but permit delays in the establishment of a formal budget.[6] In case enactment of a budget is delayed, a provisional budget law (*Vorläufige Haushaltsführung*) is passed early in the fiscal year which adopts the prior year's budget as a basis for operation. If the delay is extended, the provisional budget law is also extended.[7] The final budget law constitutes the legal basis for the final appropriation account and for post auditing. In practice, however, if the budget is established prior to the close of the fiscal year to which it applies,[8] the legal requirement is satisfied, and a basis is established for enacting a provisional budget law for the next year's operations. Thus the sound principle of prompt enactment of a budget can be, and often is, set aside.

During the postwar years the *Länder* have had varying records for promptness or lateness in budget preparation. It has been rare for the budget to be prepared prior to the beginning of the fiscal year. Even governments with prompt records—Bremen, Hamburg, Hesse, North Rhine-Westphalia, and the Berlin *Magistrat*—have usually required an extra quarter. The majority of *Länder* have been even more dilatory with their budget preparation. Rhineland-Palatinate, for example, has repeatedly delayed its budget until the end of the year. Bavaria has done well some years, but in 1949/50 its budget was enacted only nine days before the end of the fiscal year. It would be an oversimplification, however, to charge lateness in budgeting to south German or Rhineland "*Schlamperei*" or to credit promptness to Prussian efficiency. In postwar times it was more nearly a question of the "rich" *Länder* who could produce a satisfactory budget without difficulty and the "poor" who delayed in the hope that a better solution could be found. The Bizonal Economic Administration was late with its first

[5] In some instances, however, this second position is contested by the minister of economics.

[6] See Basic Law, Articles 110 and 111.

[7] In 1948 for example, the provisional budget law for the Bizonal Economic Administration was extended three times.

[8] In the difficult years immediately after the war it sometimes happened that the final budget was not enacted until after the close of the fiscal year.

budget but fairly prompt with its second. The federal budgets for both 1950/51 and 1951/52 met with serious legislative delays.

The years from 1945 to 1952 have not been favorable years for good budget practices. Aside from lack of experienced personnel, particularly in the earlier period, there have been in every year some special disturbing influences making prompt budgeting rather difficult. In 1945/46 came capitulation and the disruption of most governmental machinery; in 1946/47 the Control Council imposed new and drastic tax legislation and new state governments were created; 1947/48 saw the establishment of the Bizone and new proposals for equalization between the states and the two zones; in the following year came currency and tax reform, followed in 1949/50 by the establishment of the federal government, state equalization, and a series of income tax concessions. In 1950/51 there were further income tax reductions accompanied by extensive shifts of tax sources and expenditures from the states to the new federal government. Uncertainty in 1951/52 resulted from proposals by the federal government to take from the *Länder* between 25 and 31 per cent of income tax receipts, abolition of the *Interessenquota*,[9] and uncertainty over occupation and/or defense costs. On the other hand, the delays in *Länder* budget preparation during the earlier years of the occupation were due in some instances to a desire to avoid Allied budget review. A budget submitted at the end of the budget year offered to the Allies less opportunity for disapproval.

POWERS GRANTED IN THE BUDGET LAWS

The net result of delayed budget legislation is to give the finance minister during the provisional period broad powers over expenditure authorizations, thereby substituting executive for legislative control. For example, the provisional budget law of the Bizonal Economic Administration in 1948/49 gave the director of the Department for Finance extensive control over the recurring material expenditures. Nonrecurring expenditures in excess of DM50,000 under one *Titel* (line item in the budget) required approval of the Budget Committee.

Moreover, provisions will generally be found in the final budget law (*Haushaltsgesetz*) which give the finance minister broad powers. The following are illustrative:

a. The last 10 per cent authorized for material and general administrative expenditures can be disbursed only with the special approval of the finance minister.

[9] These were percentages of war-induced and certain social burdens in the 1950/51 budget which the *Länder* agreed to bear.

b. The last 25 per cent provided for in the table of organization for officials may be used only with the finance minister's consent.

c. Expenditures of amounts marked "blocked" under the individual budget titles likewise require his approval.

d. The finance minister may, at his discretion, transfer within major divisions of the budget (*Einzelpläne*—single plans) unspent appropriations for personnel from one item to another.[10]

In addition to powers obtained through the budget law, the RHO grants certain discretionary powers to the finance minister. He may authorize expenditures outside the budget (*Haushaltsüberschreitungen*),[11] either those for which there are no appropriation items (*Ausserplanmässige Ausgaben*) or those which are an overstepping of the amounts appropriated in the budget (*Überplanmässige Ausgaben*). The final appropriation account, however, must contain justifications for these actions.[12] Article 112 of the Basic Law also covers this grant of power: "Expenditures exceeding the budget and any extraordinary expenditures require the approval of the Federal Minister of Finance. It may only be given in case of unforeseen and compelling necessity." Determination of whether such a situation has arisen lies within the discretion of the finance minister.

BACKBOOKINGS

The German system of keeping the accounts open for backbookings was designed to permit the charging of revenues and expenditures to the fiscal (budget) year in which they originate. Backbookings do not include personnel and one-time, nonrecurring expenditures, but apply to the large class of recurring, material expenditures. An important practical by-product has been to give some flexibility to the use of such material expenditure appropriations. If all these appropriations had to be spent by March 31, there might be a rush toward the end of the year to spend all balances, and this would result in uneconomical practices. Within the discretion of the finance minister the books may be kept open, and during this extended period expenditures which are chargeable to the preceding year's appropriations can continue. A three-month period is normal, but sometimes backbookings continue into September.[13] Both revenues and expenditures can be

[10] The budget law may also give this power to the operating ministry or agency. Shifts between single plans, however, are not authorized.

[11] Section 33 of the RHO requires quarterly reports to the Budget Committee on expenditure authorizations in the amount of DM10,000 or more.

[12] Section 80 of the RHO; RWB par. 71 (1) and (2).

[13] For example, the *Länder* backbooked to fiscal 1949/50 approximately DM1.1 billion (receipts and expenditures) from April to September, 1950.

backbooked, though retroactive bookings of expenditures are more important. The finance minister may in planning his budget determine in advance upon a closing date and estimate the volume of backbookings; again, the decision may grow out of circumstances during the year. The closing date also affects planning for the next succeeding year. However, in normal times the closing date remains the same from year to year. The system of backbooking is a substitute in the German system for the practice in budgeting in many jurisdictions in the United States of carrying over appropriations for one or two years and of permitting all expenditures which are in liquidation of obligations or commitments entered into prior to the close of the fiscal year to be charged against the prior-year appropriations. In the American system the rush is only to commit or obligate the funds prior to the fiscal year's end.

The basic purpose of the backbooking system and some of its practical results are sound. The power to determine when the books shall be closed, however, could result in confused reporting and lack of comparability from year to year. To achieve a short-run objective the finance minister could, within limits set by the true budget surplus or deficit, make the budget of a year "come out" anyway he wanted. Thus:

a. If the budget tended to run a deficit, he could close the books early and thereby throw more expenditures into next year's budget; or he could go further toward minimizing the deficit if he closed the books for expenditures but kept them open for revenues.

b. If the budget tended to run a surplus, he could keep the books open for expenditures, backbooking three or four months' expenditures to the preceding year, and thus reduce the surplus.

c. The budget could be balanced right down to the last *Deutsche* mark.

As inferred, this power of fixing the closing date could be used for political purposes. If, for example, the minister had made commitments that the budget for a given year would be balanced,[14] there would be an incentive to close the books early. Similarly, if under the occupation the federal finance minister wanted to throw as much of the Allied occupation costs as possible on a given fiscal year, he could do so. A listing of these possibilities is not to imply that this type of manipulation has been customary. Quite the contrary. The backbooking system should not be confused with the American system of liquidation of obligations, with clearing the *Vorschussbuch* (see be-

---

[14] Such a commitment was given by the federal finance minister to the Allied High Commission in April, 1950.

low), or with accounting adjustments and rectification after close of the fiscal year of accounting errors.

RESERVES AND THE BALANCED BUDGET

The Basic Law and the *Länder* constitutions require balanced budgets. Payments into and out of reserves may be used to balance the budget. This practice is unusual, but was resorted to by *Länder* in the American Zone prior to currency reform. Payments into reserves at the end of the fiscal year constituted a method of reducing surpluses and avoidance of carry-overs into the next year's budget. Similarly, at least in one *Land*, the carry-over of an operating deficit was made unnecessary by withdrawals from a general prior year's reserve. In normal practice, however, reserves are not used by the federal government or the *Länder*. The former Reich also made no use of reserves.[15] On the other hand, reserves are not uncommon in local governments. *Gemeinden* and *Kreise* are permitted out of current receipts to build up reserves for extraordinary expenditures.

USE OF THE SUSPENSE BOOK

The *Reichskassenordnung* (RKO; still in force) provides for a suspense book. In this *Vorschussbuch* and its counterpart—the *Hinterlegungsbuch*—are temporarily recorded authorized expenditures and receipts which are true governmental expenditures or receipts but which cannot yet be booked directly to a budgetary account classification, either because such classification does not exist or because the exact nature of the transaction is not known.[16] An example of the former would include new expenditures authorized by the finance minister but not yet approved by the parliamentary budget committee. The suspense book is cleared periodically. At the end of the fiscal year there is the normal volume of uncleared items, which in totals (receipts and expenditures) may or may not be merged with any reported figures on backbookings. To this extent they may confuse the cash reporting analysis though, as already noted, the suspense book is not a part of the backbooking system.

FINAL APPROPRIATION ACCOUNT AND THE CAMERALISTIC SYSTEM

The finance minister must prepare and submit to the parliament

[15] The Bizonal Economic Administration, however, in its 1949/50 budget appropriated DM37 million for reserves, partly for a general working fund and partly for a general equalization fund.

[16] Cash offices are permitted to book receipts and expenditures in the regular books only when it is known to which item of the budget they can be booked.

within a year following the end of the budget year a final account of assets and liabilities and of all revenues and expenditures.[17] The purpose of the final account is accountability to parliament and establishment of a basis for the discharge of the finance minister. Since the Audit Court or Court of Accounts (*Rechnungshof*) in its audit is required to determine whether the budget plan was strictly followed,[18] the final account is set up to facilitate this determination. For each line item in the budget, each chapter, and each *Einzelplan* (single plan or major division) and for the entire ordinary and extraordinary budget, there is a comparison of the actual result with the budgeted amount and a reckoning in each case of whether the actual result was more or less than the budget estimate. These "mores" and "lesses" are then summated. The comparison in fact also takes into account the remainder carried forward, so that the full comparison is as follows:

Budgeted	*Actual*
Estimated revenues	Actual revenues
plus	*plus*
Revenues carried forward from previous year	Revenues carried forward to next year
Expenditure authorizations	Actual expenditures
plus	*plus*
Expenditures carried forward from previous year	Expenditures carried forward to next year

The purpose of the reckoning, which is an application of the Cameralistic system of bookkeeping to governmental budgetary accounting, is to arrive at a proof that the difference in actual operations and the planned program equals the over-all "accounting" surplus or deficit derived from comparing actual receipts with actual expenditures.

The final account is always a bulky document. The *Land* Hesse final account for the fiscal year 1949/50, for example, totals 914 printed pages. Included in each final account are the same single plans, chapters, and titles as in the original budget plan; also included are justifications, for approval by the finance minister, of expenditures not appropriated by parliament and expenditures in excess of the ap-

[17] Article 114 of the Basic Law and similar provisions in the *Länder* constitutions.
[18] Sections 87 *et seq.* of the RHO govern the work of the *Rechnungshof* relative to the final account, as well as sections 69-72 of the RWB.

propriations.[19] Two facts should be emphasized. First, the budget surplus or deficit arrived at by the Cameralistic reckoning is the one carried over usually not into the next year's budget but into the next but one. It is carried over after the *Vorschussbuch* has been cleared and after all accounting errors and adjustments and all backbookings have been made. Second, this surplus or deficit is not the same as a cash reporting surplus or deficit for a given calendar period. The latter, not the former, answers the question: How much in cash was received and spent by the government during, say, the quarter April 1 to June 30, regardless of the budget to which the transactions were booked? The former is an administrative-accounting concept tied to a given budget; the latter is an economist's statistical cash-flow concept geared to a time period. The two serve two different purposes and "never the twain shall meet." No little confusion arose in the Allied High Commission from the fact that the German governments report on one concept and the ECA Special Mission used the second concept.

ROLE OF THE AUDIT COURT IN THE BUDGETARY PROCESS

The Federal Audit Court (*Bundesrechnungshof*) and the *Länder Rechnungshöfe*[20] perform post audits currently and after the closing of the books following the fiscal year's end and termination of all backbookings. The main role of the Audit Court in budgeting is to audit the final accounts under the budget and to report to the finance minister on its findings.[21] The post audits of the court are not only financial audits, but also administrative audits.[22] The federal finance minister annually must submit a final account to parliament and to the *Rechnungshof*.[23] After the court has completed its audit, its findings in two parts ("comments" and an attached "memorandum") are submitted to the finance minister, who must place them before parliament. The audited final account forms the basis for the final discharge or release of the finance minister and his responsible officials.[24] The *Rechnungshof* reports to the finance minister usually a year or eigh-

[19] Section 80 of the RHO; par. 71 of the RWB.

[20] The Schleswig-Holstein Audit Court is known as the *Rechnungskammer*.

[21] Sections 87 *et seq.* of the RHO govern the auditing of the final account.

[22] These include the determination of whether funds were used economically.

[23] This goes to both houses. The Budget Committee of the *Bundestag* will discuss and decide upon the *Haushaltsüberschreitungen* without waiting for the audit report.

[24] Article 114 of the Basic Law. Similar provisions are in the *Länder* constitutions. See also section 108 of the RHO.

teen months after the close of the fiscal year, and the formal discharge comes two or three years after the fiscal year's end.

During the course of current hearings, the parliamentary budget committee may also ask the *Rechnungshof* for its opinion[25] as to whether certain proposed expenditure estimates are economical or not or whether changes in organization or methods are advisable.[26] While budget hearings are in process, the Audit Court may also be asked to undertake a special investigation of alleged waste, inefficiency, or fraud. The *Rechnungshof* is an independent body; it is responsible only to the parliament, and its main officials have life tenure. It is a useful and respected institution in German financial management.

BUDGET REPORTING

As in most governments, German external public finance reports are designed and published primarily for the specialist. Very little publicity directed to the average citizen is given to budget estimates and budget results. The Federal Finance Ministry publishes monthly a report on the "accounting" receipts and expenditures of the federal government; it also issues a special report on *Länder* accounting receipts and expenditures. Federal and *Länder* tax receipts are included in the *Bundessteuerblatt* and *Bundesanzeiger*, and federal debt figures quarterly in the latter publication. The monthly *Wirtschaft und Statistik*[27] and the monthly report of the central bank (*Bank Deutscher Länder*) contain some of the data, and the *Bundesgesetzblatt* carries the text of the budget and tax laws. Prior to 1933, very good consolidated reports on federal, *Länder,* and local government finances also were available, but these reports have not been completely resumed in the postwar period.

The cash basis of accounting (receipts and disbursements), the modified cash basis, and the accrual basis (income and expenditures) are all known in German public finance. Known, too, are the merits of

---

[25] Opinions may be required by either house of parliament, the cabinet, or the finance minister. Section 8 of the law on the establishment and the functions of the Federal Audit Court, November 27, 1950.

[26] Section 26 (1) of the RHO requires economical administration. A special department of the federal *Rechnungshof,* the *Gutachtenabteilung,* has been established to perform the functions of the *Reichssparkommissar* (Savings commissioner) of the Weimar period. Cf. chapter 11 above.

[27] Official statistical publication of the federal government issued by the *Statistisches Bundesamt.* A quarterly functional classification of Länder expenditures in this publication and a monthly breakdown of federal expenditures by *Einzelpläne* and by functions are useful.

reports and statements prepared on the accrual basis and their use by policy makers. The newer reporting device—the cash-consolidated budget—based on a cash-flow-time-period concept, is familiar at least to German economists, but those interested in fiscal policy must derive their cash figures, as far as possible, from the conventional published reports. In practice the difficulty lies with state reporting. The back-bookings of some states are not completed until about August, although a three months' period is more normal. In three to five months of the new fiscal year, therefore, the current reports of some *Länder* show only cash receipts and expenditures applying to the current budget, but not total cash finances. The figures backbooked (and therefore omitted from current reporting) can only be derived later from the final accounts for the last three months of the preceding fiscal year. This delays and complicates the establishment of a sound basis for forecasting *Länder* cash receipts and expenditures.

One cannot even be sure that all figures reported as backbookings (when reported) are solely backbookings. The states in prewar times published separately the volume of *Vorschussbuch* clearances and the backbookings, but this practice has not yet been resumed. Today, without published figures on changes in state cash balances and in indebtedness, external checks against any derived state cash figures are lacking. Since April, 1951, the Federal Finance Ministry has made available for the federal government separate figures on backbookings and suspense-book clearances so that the true federal cash figures for a period can be derived. This is a big forward step in budget reporting. The federal figures after adjustments are made can also be checked with the published *Bank Deutscher Länder* figures. Since the central banking system is the sole fiscal agent for the federal government, the German railways, and the Immediate Aid Program, the central bank is in a good position to follow closely the federal government's cash finances.

TYPES OF BUDGETS

The original budget (*Hauptbudget or Haupthaushaltsplan*) and the supplementary budget (*Nachtrag*) may each be subdivided into two main parts, an ordinary budget and an extraordinary budget. This division is found, for example, in the federal government's 1951/52 estimates. Thus, to find the total of Allied occupation costs one must look in three parts of two budgets—Main Budget-Ordinary, Supplemental Budget-Ordinary, and Supplemental Budget-Extraordinary. So complicated a budget form could easily be misinterpreted. Capital expenditures may be financed from loans or from surpluses in the ordinary budget transferred to the extraordinary budget. Proceeds from the sale of capital assets also appear on the receipts side. Capital construction and capital investment constitute the main items on the expenditure side of the extraordinary budget.[28]

During the period prior to currency reform, the British introduced two other terms into German budgeting, a "zonal budget" and an "emergency budget." The former was a centralized budget for the British Zone which included occupation costs, mandatory expenditures, coal subsidies, and so forth and certain revenues and administrative expenditures not redistributed to the *Länder*. This budget, abolished on March 31, 1948, after creation of the Bizonal Economic Administration, equalized revenue sources and expenditure burdens between the four *Länder* of that zone. The "emergency budget" was simply one of the three divisions of the zonal budget—ordinary, extraordinary, and emergency. The last part included occupation costs and mandatory expenditures, those expenditures which were not considered true *Länder* expenditures but as a burden chargeable to a "higher level" and therefore subject to equalization between the several zones. Also prior to currency reform, so-called "extraordinary budgets" in the U.S. Zone were not restricted to loans and capital construction. They were an attempt to segregate the war-induced burdens, such as occupation costs, mandatory expenditures, and refugee expenditures, from the normal governmental expenditures.

PREPARATION OF BUDGETS

The actual budget estimates are prepared in the operating ministries or agencies by the technical budget officers and are submitted after proper approval to the Finance Ministry. The finance minister prescribes the date when estimates must be submitted.[29] The Finance Ministry is responsible for preparing the total budgetary proposals, drafting the budget law, presenting the draft budget to the cabinet, and defending the estimates before the parliamentary committees. Discussions with each of the operating ministries and agencies are held in the Finance Ministry, and any unresolved disagreements between the Finance Ministry and the operating ministry are referred to the cabinet. This can be done in advance of submitting the entire draft budget. The views of the finance minister will prevail in the

---

[28] Capital construction expenditures financed from current revenues are provided for in individual *Einzelpläne* (single plans or major divisions of the budget) or under General Finance Administration (a special *Einzelplan* under the Finance Ministry).

[29] Section 19 of the RHO; see also par. 7 of the RWB.

cabinet unless upon a second vote he is opposed by all other members including the Chancellor. He cannot be overruled on the estimates so long as he retains the support of the Chancellor (or minister-president in a *Land*). This power in the cabinet on financial matters is strongly rooted in German tradition.

The budget preparation process usually requires a little more than twelve months. The budget calendar of most units of German government will approximate[30] the following:

June 1	— Advance notifications by ministries and agencies of lump-sum requirements for the next budget year.
August 15	— Submission of preliminary estimates with supporting data to the Finance Ministry.[31]
August 15	— Discussions with the operating ministries and agencies begin in the Finance Ministry.
October 1	— Ministries and agencies must have completed submission of all data.[32]
December 20	— Estimates of proposed budget submitted to the cabinet.
January 5	— Proposed budget submitted to parliament.
January 15	— First reading and referral to the Budget Committee.
March 15-31	— Enactment on the second and third readings should be completed.[33]
July 1 – August 15	— More customary dates for enactment of the budget.

FORM OF THE BUDGET

The main divisions of the budget are usually preceded by a summary plan which recapitulates the total estimates. Then follow the *Einzelpläne* (single plans), with a single plan for each individual ministry or agency, and also single plans for certain major categories of revenues and expenditures, for example, "Debt," "Occupation Costs." The federal budget for 1950/51 contained twenty-six *Einzelpläne,* but there are only eighteen ministries and agencies. The *Einzelpläne* are divided into chapters which correspond to the departments or subdivisions of the ministry or agency, together with chapters for special

[30] Section 22 of the RHO.
[31] Par. 7 of the RWB prescribes the June 1 and August 15 dates.
[32] Par. 8 of the RWB.
[33] A former Reich official states that the Reich budget only once in his memory was enacted prior to the beginning of the fiscal year (April 1).

functions. The "single plans" and the chapters thus reflect the general organization structure of the government but at the same time are more than an organizational classification. The chapters are further subdivided into line items with uniform code numbers, which constitute a mixed activity and object classification. Any further breakdowns of line items are included in the budget justifications.

On the revenue side, the administrative receipts follow the same chapters as on the expenditure side. The *Titels* or line items for administrative receipts, however, differ. All other receipts, classified by type, go into a special *Einzelplan* for General Finance Administration. The expenditures are subdivided into recurring expenditures and nonrecurring expenditures. Each chapter of the recurring expenditures is further subdivided into:

    a. Administrative expenditures

        1. Personal

        2. Material or nonpersonal

    b. General budget expenditures

The major functional and object classifications (or a combination of the two) as used in American governmental accounting and budgeting are not followed. It is very difficult, for example, to take the nine *Länder* budgets, because of different ministerial structures and budget categories, and compile total expenditures for General Administration, Protection and Safety, Welfare, and the like or by major objects, such as "Equipment," "Capital Construction," and "Debt Payments." On the other hand, Germany has gone much farther than the United States in establishing uniform classifications and terminology for regional and local authorities.

Written explanatory notes or budget justifications are included in the printed budget comments following the section to which they apply. They must contain an explanation of increases over the previous year and other matters,[34] but they may, and generally do, go much further. Generally the following will be found in the *Erläuterungen:*

    a. A table of organization giving the number in each personnel grade.

    b. The various allowances to officials.

    c. A more detailed breakdown of the material expenditures, for example, travel, communications, printing.

    d. An explanation and further breakdown of each major category of general budget expenditures, for example, road maintenance, bridge construction, subsidies to agriculture.

[34] Section 8 of the RHO.

e. Details which show how the net results of the public enterprises were arrived at.[35]

These *Erläuterungen* bind the government in so far as they were important for parliamentary approval of the appropriations. For example, the table of organization and the breakdown of the principal, general budget expenditure categories are binding.

Various annexes also may be included in the budget. Some are required in connection with the single plan to which they apply; others may be added at the end of the budget. In some cases these contain explanatory statistics which supplement the *Erläuterungen*. The final printed document is usually not assembled and bound until the budget is enacted. The budget law itself is usually a very short document containing the estimates in total and incorporating by reference the complete budget document.[36]

INCLUSIONS AND EXCLUSIONS FROM THE BUDGET

The Basic Law and the *Länder* constitutions require in principle that all revenues and expenditures have to be included in the budget. In the case of special properties and institutions of the government, the budget plans have to be annexed to the single plans of the ministry or department concerned.[37] In the case of public utilities or economic enterprises, only the net result must be carried in the budget proper— profits or surpluses as receipts and government contributions for losses or deficits as expenditures[38]—but the budget justifications must contain the details showing how the net was derived.

The *Bundesbahn* (federal railways) and the *Bundespost* (federal post and telegraph) are special cases. These two enterprises are required to make a contribution to the federal government, and these contributions show in the federal revenue estimates. If these enterprises operate at a deficit, they must borrow on their own credit.[39] The federal government exercises only a limited review over their "economic plan"[40] to the cabinet and, for information only, to the par-

---

[35] Required by section 15 of the RHO.

[36] The complete Berlin budget document in 1950 was 1393 printed pages; the federal budget was over 1300 pages.

[37] Sections 9(a) and (b) of the RHO.

[38] Section 15 of the RHO. If the public utility of a municipality has a separate legal status, only the surplus or deficit will be shown; when there is no separate legal status, the practice varies (for example, the budget of the enterprise may appear in full in an annex).

[39] A new *Bundesbahn* law now pending provides, however, for loans to the *Bundesbahn* from the federal budget.

[40] The economic plan (*Wirtschaftsplan*) and economic reckoning (*Wirtschafts-*

liament. The federal alcohol monopoly is also a special case. The net profits are shown in the federal revenue estimates.

On the whole the German budgets are fairly inclusive, although some programs are left outside the budgets. Guarantees by the state or federal government are not shown in total, but the RHO requires that a precentage for possible liabilities under the guarantees during the budget year be included under expenditures.[41] The federal government omits from its budget the Immediate Aid Program. This is partially the result of the wording in the currency reform laws which required the equalization-of-burden legislation. The Marshall Plan counterpart funds are included in a special budget which requires a final account and an audit by the *Rechnungshof.*

CARRY-OVERS

Budget authorizations in general refer only to the year for which they are granted. Provision is made, however, for possible "carry-overs." Revenue estimated but not received, and certain to be collected the next budget year, must with the consent of the finance minister be carried forward. Similarly, unexpended balances of extendible expenditure authorizations, less budgetary anticipations (deductions in advance from the expenditure authorizations provided in the next budget for the same purpose), may be carried forward. Other unexpended expenditure balances will be allowed to lapse unless special consent for their further use is obtained from the finance minister.

These budgetary balances carried over require no reappropriation, are not included in the new estimates, and customarily are not mentioned in the justifications for new appropriations. A plan for the utilization of expenditure balances carried forward must, however, be submitted to the finance minister. Attached to the preliminary estimates must be a statement showing the extendible expenditure authorizations, the expenditure balance carried forward, and the budgetary anticipations.

Recurring expenditures constitute the bulk of most budgets and generally are not extendible. Such an expenditure authorization can be designated as "extendible" in the controlling notations only if it can be proved that the possibility of extending the expenditures will facilitate a more economical administration thereof. However, nonrecurring expenditures are extendible. The major type of nonrecurring

---

rechnung) are similar to a proposed income and expense statement and a final profit and loss statement. The economic reckoning is audited by the *Rechnungshof.*

[41] The percentage is left to the discretion of the finance minister. Section 8 (b) of the RHO.

expenditure is for capital construction. When a capital project, for example a bridge, is contracted for, say in the amount of DM900,000, and it is estimated that it will take three years to construct the bridge, the normal practice is to include DM300,000 in three annual budgets.[42] However, if in a given year not all of the DM300,000 is spent, the balance is carried over into the next fiscal year and is without reappropriation available for expenditure. If progress is faster, a budgetary anticipation may be permitted. The concept of nonrecurring expenditure may extend to the purchase of permanent equipment, such as the outfitting of a new office building. Normally, furniture and like requirements are budgeted as a recurring expenditure. Balances of extendible expenditure authorizations can be used up to the end of the third year following the final authorization, but only with the consent of the finance minister. If not spent in the year following their establishment, they appear on the revenue, as well as on the expenditure, side of the final account of the next year as offsetting items.

The principle of the balanced budget (which implies more than balanced estimates) requires that a budget deficit or surplus be carried over and that a budgetary equilibrium be arrived at over a period of time. Therefore the RHO has provided that a deficit must be covered as an ordinary expenditure in the next budget year or in the next but one.[43] Any surplus in a given year must be used either for reduction of borrowing requirements or for debt amortization purposes. In the latter case it must show as an extraordinary receipt in the budget for the next year but one at the latest.

INTERNAL CONTROLS

The budgetary controls are centered in the chief of the budget department in the Finance Ministry and in technical budget officers within the operating ministries and agencies. The appropriations are direct to the individual ministries and agencies, subject, however, to the controls granted the finance minister either in the annual or provisional budget laws or in the RHO and RWB. Suballocations of budgetary authorizations and establishments are made within the ministries and agencies, records are kept of such allotments, and the *Rechnungshof* is informed thereof. Execution of expenditure authorizations according to the internal control plan is by means of "budget control lists" in which actual expenditures, advances, and earmarkings of authorizations are entered. An establishment control list, a register

---

[42] The entire DM900,000 may be appropriated in the first year and the unspent balance carried over.

[43] Section 75 of the RHO.

showing how the establishments are filled, and a list of administrative receipts "ordered" are the other records kept.

The ministry and agency budget officers send to the Finance Ministry monthly their requirement advices. Forecasts of anticipated requirements may be required for a longer period. Monthly allotments are made to each ministry and agency by letters of authorization. In turn, these allotments may be suballocated to subordinate authorities. The Finance Ministry requires each ministry and agency to submit two summary reports of their results, namely at the end of the second and third quarters, comparing by budget headings the actual results with the authorizations. Corresponding internal reports are required within the ministries and agencies.

The cash plan is used as an internal administrative control tool by many German governments, but is not a reporting document. Administrative receipts must be accounted for by each operating department or agency and cannot be set off against expenditures; expenditures are budgeted and accounted for on a gross basis. Only in exceptional cases are receipts dedicated to particular expenditure purposes. Even departmental receipts are reckoned as general revenues and not as receipts available solely to the collecting department. Notations which are included under individual headings of the budget (for example, remarks regarding extendible expenditure authorizations, reciprocally transferable authorizations, future cancelability, self-administration) govern the administration of these particular expenditure authorizations.

PARLIAMENTARY CONSIDERATION OF BUDGETS

The budget as a whole (printed by single plans but unbound) goes to the parliament from the cabinet and is subjected to three readings.[44] On motion at the first reading it is referred, usually without much debate, to the budget committee.[45] Hearings before the committee are by *Einzelpläne*. These hearings are not open hearings, and very little publicity is given the proceedings although the chairman or ranking minority member may make statements to the press from time to time.

The finance minister or his staff and representatives of the ministry or department whose budget is under discussion will be present at all

[44] In contrast, the cabinet, not the *Reichstag*, finalized the Reich budget during Nazi times.

[45] The federal government has a budget committee in the lower house and a finance committee in the upper house. The relationship between the two houses has created special problems in much federal legislation. Article 76 of the Basic Law requires all legislation, including the budget, to go first to the *Bundesrat;* then within three weeks the *Bundesrat* must give its opinion to the *Bundestag.*

the hearings and will be called upon to defend the proposals. The Budget Committee may amend the proposals or initiate new proposals, provided the budget estimates are balanced. Essentially, however, the budget is an executive and not a legislative budget. The committees, or parliament, may in general not add expenditure burdens without providing additional revenues. Article 113 of the Basic Law and *Bundestag* rules of procedure require that if expenditures are increased, the parliament must at the same time provide new revenues to meet the increased expenditures. This is a check to prevent parliament from voting expenditures and leaving the finance minister with the problem of finding revenue sources. In the *Länder* constitutions there is no similar provision, but the same result is achieved through parliamentary rules of order.

The committee process may take two or three months or longer and may result in investigations by the *Rechnungshof*. From observation one concludes that the main purpose served by the committee hearings is to focus attention on irregularities and bring to the forefront uneconomical operations, thus acting as an effective and often courageous watchdog of the government.

The appropriation act, or budget law, as presented by the cabinet, is also often amended. This law is usually only two or three printed pages with eight to twelve paragraphs. Only the total budget figures are included, but the printed budget estimates are annexed. Included in the budget law are usually an authorization for operational credits and loans for the extraordinary budget, special powers granted the finance minister, and the specific contributions to be made to, or received from, other governments.

The budget estimates and the appropriation act may be bound into one document for presentation to parliament for the second and third readings, but are more apt to go in printed form by single plans. The chairman of the Budget Committee presents the final decisions of the committee to the parliament in his speech,[46] and the debates follow on motions at the second reading. This process may go on for days. The budget may be amended at this stage, but this will happen only on very important or controversial issues. The finance minister and his parliamentary (state) secretary will take part in the debates. The third reading follows closely on the second, and by this time all the motions have generally been debated.

CONCLUSION

In concluding this brief survey of German budgetary practices, the

[46] The speech is written and has the agreement of the committee.

conviction can be recorded that both the Americans and the Germans might profitably learn from each other's practices. On the German side, something would be gained from redesigning budgetary reporting in order to include the cash-consolidated budget concept and to serve the economic policy maker as well as the administrator. The German federal and state budgets would be more useful documents if expenditures were recapitulated in the documents according to a uniform functional classification, uniform object classification, and a uniform national accounts classification. Much needs to be done in both countries to give the budget publicity and to use it as a method of interesting the citizen in the finances of his government. Unfortunately, the Allied occupation authorities contributed little if anything toward the adoption of new ideas. Now, with negotiation for the defense contract, the removal of compulsion, and the beginning of a period of friendly co-operation, the atmosphere for progress should be healthier.

Since in most countries during recent years budgetary progress has been disappointingly slow, it would not be difficult for Western Germany to overcome quickly any handicap in this field which might be due to long isolation under the Third Reich from the scientific budget literature of other countries. Under the aegis of a new federal government, rapid strides could make Western Germany the leader in budgetary reform. A higher degree of uniformity than in most countries and an experienced central audit agency are useful instruments at hand. Recapitulations of budget estimates and results in order to make budget information useful not only for the operating administrator but also for purposes of economic planning and for fiscal policy; a proper separation of current and capital expenditures in the estimates and the accounts to meet the requirements of economic planning—these and other approaches require scientific refinement and implementation everywhere.[47]

On the United States side, the American federal and state governments could with profit adopt from German practice the concept of final appropriation accounts. This would greatly strengthen accountability to Congress and the state legislatures. The role of the *Rechnungshof* in the budgetary process is also superior to anything in American practice. The entire work of this German institution warrants more careful study and adaptation to American governmental needs. A *modus operandi* must also be sought by American public administrators to attain greater uniformity in budgetary practices. The desirable uniformities which have been achieved in Germany through the RHO and the RWB constitute a distinct challenge.

[47] See John Richard Hicks, *The Problem of Budgetary Reform* (Oxford, 1948).

13

Public Finance

RODNEY L. MOTT

THE minister of finance is the principal financial official in the German government. Under him is organized a major governmental department which was called during the Empire, Weimar, and Nazi periods the Imperial Ministry of Finance and during the postwar period the Federal Ministry of Finance. In addition to the national ministry, each of the constituent states now has its own ministry of finance.[1]

The types of functions of the ministries of finance fall into two main classes, the formulation of general governmental policies and the administration of various financial services. The administrative tasks of the ministry in some areas, such as the budget, are so closely related to its functions of policy formulation that it is hardly profitable to separate them. In other areas, such as banking, the ministry participates in the formulation of policies which are administered by other agencies such as the *Bank Deutscher Länder*. There have been cases in which the ministry of finance carried out policies largely determined by other departments. The administrative activities of the Finance Ministry also vary widely. In connection with the collection of customs duties and taxes, it has extensive administrative responsibilities including the operation of the customs offices, the recruitment, training, and supervision of customs offices and border guards, and the prosecution of offenders.

The range of functions which the ministry performs in Germany is

[1] In Hamburg and Bremen the head of the finance department has the title *Senator für Finanzen*.

somewhat broader and more diverse than functions performed by similar agencies in other countries. In addition to the traditional financial functions of collecting customs duties and taxes and the preparation and supervision of the budget, the ministry performs some functions which are only indirectly related to public finance, such as the determination of pay scales and pension rates for public employees and civil servants and the formulation of accounting regulations for agencies handling public funds. Some of its tasks are even more remote from its primary duties. In this class fall the supervision of the mint, the alcohol monopoly, and of the gambling casinos; the management of public property; and the supervision of public construction. The principal functions of the Federal Ministry of Finance at the end of 1950 are listed in Table 2. This chart also indicates the type of

Table 2. Functions of the Federal Ministry of Finance

Field	Formulates Policies	Participates in Policy Formulation	Supervises Administration	Conducts Adm. Operations
Customs Duties	x			x
Taxes and Excises	x			x
Budget	x			x
Official Pay and Pensions	x			
Public Debt	x			
Treasury	x		x	
International Finance	x			
Alcohol Monopoly	x		x	
Casinos	x		x	
Public Property	x			x
Construction of Public Buildings	x		x	
Accounting of Public Agencies		x*		
Banking		x†		
Insurance	x		x	
Credit and Economic Policy		x‡		
Equalization of Burdens	x			
Occupation Costs		x§		
War Burdens		x		

* With Auditing Court (*Rechnungshof*).
† With *Bank Deutscher Länder*.
‡ With *Bank Deutscher Länder* and Ministry of Economics.
§ With High Commission.

activity which the ministry performs with respect to each of the principal fields.

The Nazi Ministry of Finance had ceased to exist at the end of World War II. Its personnel was scattered throughout the country; its buildings were destroyed; and its records were either burned, lost, or impounded by the conquering army. In spite of this cataclysm, the financial functions of the national government were so important that five years later a newly organized Federal Ministry of Finance was able to gather to itself a large part of the tasks which its predecessor had performed. However, it no longer administers the wide range of personal and business taxes, which have been given to the states under the Basic Law. Its functions with respect to debt supervision, the control of foreign exchange, and international financial policies also have been eliminated or sharply reduced by postwar events.

The Federal Ministry of Finance has increased its activity in some areas. During the Nazi period, the Ministry of Finance steadily lost ground with respect to the formulation of banking, insurance, economic, and credit policies. While the new ministry has not obtained exclusive control over these fields, its influence in them has become very much larger than it was during the war. In other areas, the ministry has traded one function for another. It no longer determines the formulas under which the centrally collected tax revenues are returned to the local communities in subsidies—this task now falls to the states. It has acquired, however, the fully as difficult problem of preparing a plan for any equalizing of financial burdens among the western states of varying size, industrial potential, and wealth. The problems of war financing and the financial policies in occupied territories no longer plague the ministry, but they have been replaced by the even thornier problems of meeting the financial consequences of the war such as the support of refugees, the payment of occupation costs, and the equalization of the burden of war destruction. All in all, except in the field of taxation, the Federal Ministry of Finance has as important a range of functions as did the corresponding agency before the war.

These changes in the activities of the Ministry of Finance are reflected in the size and character of the personnel attached to the central office of the ministry. The Imperial Ministry of Finance in 1943 employed 862 officers and clerical workers in its Berlin office, apart from nearly 137,000 who were employed in its field offices. The Berlin employees may be compared with the 415 persons employed by the Federal Ministry of Finance in Bonn in 1950. Thus, the 1950 staff is nearly half as large as the wartime staff; it serves an area 42 per cent as large and a population 59 per cent as great as were served just be-

fore the war. It is clear that either the postwar ministry has not suffered a significant decline of functions or else it is overstaffed.[2] If there
is overstaffing, it cannot be said that it is due to the retention of former officials and employees on the pay roll. Only one in six (17 per
cent) of the postwar employees of the Ministry of Finance in Bonn
held positions in the former Imperial Ministry in Berlin. Although the
proportion of branch chiefs and division directors is slightly higher—
nearly one in four (23 per cent) having seen prewar service—it is not
high enough to indicate any padding of the pay roll.

In spite of its broad range of authority, the Federal Ministry of
Finance does not include all the financial operations of the federal
government. The Federal Debt Administration is a separate agency,
as is the *Bank Deutscher Länder*. Outside its control also is the Auditing Court, a quasi-judicial body which has been reconstituted as an
independent agency to audit the accounts of the governmental officials, including those in the Ministry of Finance and its field offices.
In addition, various other governmental agencies have important financial operations which are incidental to their main functions but
which lie outside the general control of the Finance Ministry. The
postal system conducts a savings bank and also machinery for the easy
transfer of funds from one patron to another (the Giro System). The
railroads and waterways have extensive financial operations. There
are agencies of social insurance which have broader authority than
some of the single states.

The postwar agencies with incidental financial operations are few
compared with the plethora of Nazi instruments which had financial
powers. The special Nazi banks, the Four Year Plan, the Ministry for
Ecclesiastical Affairs, the Patent Office, the Labor Trustees, the Food
Estate, and the Trustees of Property in occupied countries all had important financial aspects. The Nazi party, as a state within a state,
was itself a financial giant. At one time the party, with its subordinate
organizations, owned about one-fifth of all the property in Germany.[3]

[2] The Public Finance Branch of OMGUS in April, 1946, suggested a central
finance agency of 157 employees. *Central German Agencies: Special Report to the
Military Governor*, May 1, 1946, p. xviii. The Organization Committee of the Bureau of Ministers-President recommended a Ministry of Finance of 280 employees.
Monthly Report of the Military Governor, No. 49, July, 1949, p. 135. The financial functions in 1950 were obviously more extensive than had been anticipated
four years or even one year earlier. The figures given do not, of course, include
the staffs of the nine state ministries of finance, which would substantially increase the postwar figures.

[3] The *Deutsche Arbeitsfront* alone owned or controlled through ownership about
15 per cent of the German economy. *Property Control: Special Report to the
Military Governor*, 1948, p. 14.

This policy of dispersing financial authority among a large number of new organizations was developed because the Nazis felt they could not trust the Ministry of Finance when they first took over the government. By the time the Nazis really obtained control of the Finance Ministry, the other financial agencies were so deeply entrenched that it required a military defeat and collapse of the regime to unseat them. It was natural, therefore, that postwar Germany should reverse the Nazi policy and concentrate financial functions in the Ministry of Finance, where responsibility for them could be more clearly fixed.

While changes in the organization of the financial functions have been extensive in postwar Germany, the methods of work of the ministry itself have changed but little. In connection with its tasks of formulating financial policies, the staff engages in the kind of research, legal and statistical, which characterized the former organization. It prepares reports, draws up regulations, and drafts laws to implement its findings. Both at Bonn and in the state capitals, nearly all of the financial legislation is prepared in the offices of the ministry and is introduced in the legislature with the approval of the cabinet. Indeed, financial measures are generally so technical that many of the members of the legislative bodies do not understand them. For this reason it is not uncommon to find the financial proposals of the cabinet passed with very little change and without any really effective criticism.

Such control of fiscal matters as does exist in the national legislature is largely the result of the work of the Committee on Budget and Finance in the lower house and the Finance Committee in the upper house. Since the latter consists of the state finance ministers or their deputies, it has considerable technical knowledge and frequently is able to effect changes in the laws prepared by the Finance Ministry. On the whole, however, the tendency of German lawmakers to accept domination by the administrative departments is nowhere more marked than in the field of financial legislation.

There are numerous areas where the Ministry of Finance has direct responsibility for formulating policy and need not wait for formal legislative approval to put its decisions into effect. An example of this is to be found in the clause in the Basic Law (Art. 112) which permits extraordinary expenditure for unforeseen emergencies which are not provided for in the budget. Such expenditures can be made only if the minister of finance approves, and it follows that the policies under which such approval is granted will be determined by him. In addition to these inherent powers, the ministry has been given extensive authority to implement legislation by drawing up and promulgating regulations and ordinances, a power which is itself recognized in the

Basic Law (Art. 82). While these regulations must conform to the general policies of the statutes, lest they be held void by the Supreme Finance Court, there is a wide latitude for supplementary policy determination by the ministry. Because of the technical nature of financial problems, this latitude is even greater for the Ministry of Finance than for many other ministries.

The new ministry even prescribes policies for the state governments in the field of tax collection. Although the trade and personal taxes are collected by the states, the federation has an interest in them since some of the proceeds are allocated to it. The constitution specifically gives the Ministry of Finance (Art. 108 [4]) the power to supervise the collection of the portion of those taxes which accrue to it and to give instructions to the tax collecting offices in the field with respect to such taxes.

Within the federal government itself, there are numerous examples of situations in which the Finance Ministry makes policies which are administered by other agencies. Thus, it determines the policies with respect to the construction of public buildings, although much of the actual construction lies outside its administrative sphere. Policies with respect to the alcohol monopoly and the gambling casinos originate in the ministry but are carried out by other agencies, although under the ministry's general supervision. Much more surprising, however, is the fact that the administration of functions which are much more strictly financial is left to agencies outside the ministry, but under policies determined by it. This is the situation with respect to the collection and processing of certain financial statistics, although the ministry must of necessity be one of the chief users of the statistical data. It is also the case with respect to the administration of the public debt and the operation of the mint.

These tendencies to reduce the field of administration of the Federal Ministry of Finance and at the same time to enlarge its field of policy formulation may pose some interesting problems. When policies are made by one branch of the administration and executed by another, friction is very likely to result. The policy makers will blame those who carry out the policies for any failures and the administrators may feel that those who made the policies have imposed impossible conditions on their execution. Under such an arrangement it becomes extremely difficult for the legislature, not to mention the public, to fix responsibility for failure to attain the major goals it has set. This is particularly serious in a country, such as Germany, where the administrative departments have traditionally had a large share in the formulation of policies.

The immediate disadvantages of this separation of operations from policy formulation, within the administrative branch, is less evident in Germany than it would be in a country such as the United States. The highly disciplined character of the German people and their respect for and ready acceptance of authority tend to ensure a punctilious execution of the policy mandates. This is re-enforced in the case of the bureaucracy by engrained habits of obedience to customary and legal rules, habits which are in part the result of the educational preparation of the civil servants.

ORGANIZATION OF THE MINISTRY

German administrative practice, in common with that of other modern states, does not follow any single principle of organization exclusively (see Figure 2). Practical considerations dictate the use of a variety of principles in order to obtain the most effective administration. Thus the budget subdivision is organized on the basis of the governmental departments whose budgets are analyzed and supervised, while the tax divisions are organized on the basis of the kinds of taxes levied. In some cases, diverse matters with very little functional relationship are combined in one administrative unit. Thus the control of federal property and the formulation of policies regarding the public debt and the mint make up a single subdivision of the Public Financial Policy Division in the postwar federal ministry.

Less effort is made to reduce the span of control for top executives in German public administration than in either the United States or Great Britain. There are, for example, sixteen branches in the Customs and Consumption Tax Division and twelve branches in the General Administrative Division. Before the war, some beginnings were made toward subdividing the larger divisions, but these prewar subdivisions were usually embryo divisions or groups of branches designed to meet special situations rather than deliberate efforts to make the supervisory work of the division director more manageable. Subdivisions of the prewar kind still exist in the Federal Ministry of Finance—for example, the Insurance Group in the Money, Banks, Insurance, and Credit Division. An application of modern administrative principles is to be found, on the other hand, in the Public Financial Policy Division. Here twenty-three branches are organized into two groups and three subdivisions, thus reducing the supervisory and co-ordination tasks of the division director.

Traditional German administrative practice does not recognize the distinction between line and staff, or overhead functions, which is so basic to modern administrative theory. Staff functions have, of course,

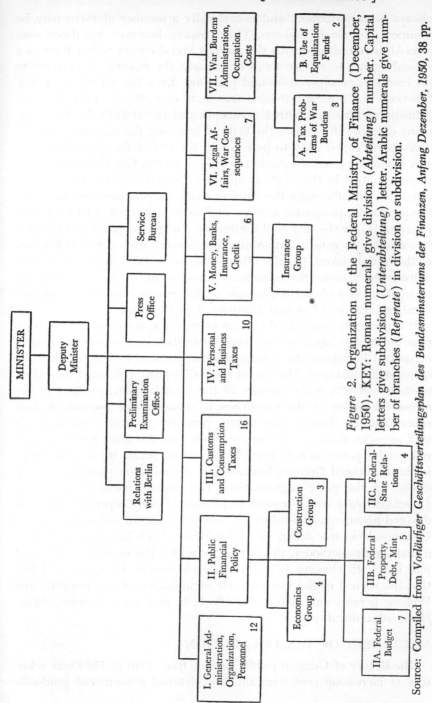

Figure 2. Organization of the Federal Ministry of Finance (December, 1950). KEY: Roman numerals give division (*Abteilung*) number. Capital letters give subdivision (*Unterabteilung*) letter. Arabic numerals give number of branches (*Referate*) in division or subdivision.

Source: Compiled from *Vorläufiger Geschäftsverteilungsplan des Bundesministeriums der Finanzen, Anfang Dezember, 1950*, 38 pp.

always been performed, and occasionally a number of them may be grouped in a single division. This division, however, has been considered as co-ordinate with the various line divisions rather than as a special agency to service them or to assist the director in performing his functions of supervision and planning. Even the grouping of staff functions in a separate division was quite exceptional in the Imperial Ministry of Finance. With the exception of the statistical office, Germany did not differentiate the tasks of servicing the ministry from the tasks it was called upon to perform for the rest of the government.

A beginning has been made toward the recognition of line and staff responsibilities in the postwar ministry. A service bureau has been organized directly under the chief executive to provide office facilities, transportation, paymaster service, and some aspects of personnel service records—for the rest of the ministry. Budget preparation and matters relating to general organization, however, are located in the first of the line divisions. On the other hand, the establishment of a press office directly under the minister, a direct result of the impact of the occupation, is a clear-cut example of the penetration of new administrative ideas into German administrative thinking.

It is generally recognized that an executive can control a large unit, plan for its development, and co-ordinate its activities only if his span of control is reduced to manageable proportions and if he has adequate staff assistance. The use of large divisions, with many branches, tends to strengthen the powers of the branch specialists and to decrease the ability of the executives to influence the policies of their subordinates. Likewise, the failure properly to utilize overhead or staff agencies throws an excessive burden on the chief executive and reduces his power of direction. The Nazis overcame these deficiencies in the traditional German bureaucratic organization through the discipline of the party organization. The deputy minister of finance (*Staatssekretär*) was a trusted and fanatical party representative and devoted his energies to enforcing Nazi policy in the ministry. Postwar Germany lacks the strong party discipline of the Nazi period. Unless a democratic method is developed by which the ministry is brought into line with changes in political developments, Germany will find that the revival of the bureaucratic organization of the Imperial and Weimar periods may defeat the efforts to produce a genuine democratic administration.

MACHINERY OF TAX COLLECTION

The history of German public finance from 1910 to 1945 was a history of increasing centralization. The national government gradually monopolized both the sources of public revenue and the machinery for their collection. This process of centralization began during World War I, was accelerated under the Weimar Republic, and was consummated by the Nazi regime. In three decades a century-old policy of local financial autonomy had been completely reversed.[4]

Before World War I, the revenues of the national government were limited to customs duties and a few excise taxes. All other taxes were levied by the states or the local communities and if the national authorities needed additional funds, requisitions were made on the states for them. By 1945 the tables had been completely turned. The states had lost all of their taxes, and the local communities continued to levy only two important ones—the real estate tax and the trade tax. Even with respect to these, local autonomy was far from complete. The real estate tax was assessed according to principles prescribed by national law, and the trade tax was collected by national tax collection offices. Before the end of World War II, the states and the communities were more dependent on the national government for funds than was the old Imperial government dependent on the states. In the accompanying table, from figures prepared by Mabel Newcomer,[5] is shown this revolution in public finance.

Table 3. German Tax Revenue Collection

Year	National Government	State and Local Governments
1913/14	40.3%	59.7%
1928/29	67.6%	32.4%
1937/38	78.5%	21.5%
1943/44	95.0%	5.0%

The absorption of tax revenues by the national government was accompanied by a centralization of tax collection machinery. Before 1919 all taxes, except customs duties and a few excise taxes, were collected by state or local tax offices, and the sums collected were paid to the community or state treasuries. The field agencies of the national Ministry of Finance were limited to its customs houses, to which the excise taxes levied by the national government were also paid. The centralization of revenues made possible by the Weimar Consti-

[4] See Mabel Newcomer, *Central and Local Finance in Germany and England* (New York, 1937), chaps. 2-3.
[5] "War and Postwar Developments in the German Tax System," *National Tax Journal*, I, No. 1 (March, 1948), 4. Somewhat different figures are given in *Report of the Military Governor: Finance Cumulative Review*, No. 24 (July, 1946–June, 1947) p. 5, but both sets of data show the same general trend.

tution was effected by a series of measures passed in 1919 and 1920 which have been known as the *Erzberger* reforms. One of the most important of these was a new tax collection statute which transferred the assessment and collection of taxes from the state agencies to a newly established group of federal offices. These tax collection offices were combined with the existing customs administration agencies into major supervisory districts under a chief financial officer (*Oberfinanzpräsident*).

The purpose of these reforms was to place the new government on a strong financial foundation. If it was to combat communism, solve its postwar financial problems, and meet reparation payments, it needed all the financial help it could have. But as is so often the case, machinery which was declared necessary to cope with an emergency became a regular feature of administrative life. The powers of the chief financial officer steadily increased as efforts were made to tighten the administration of taxes, to prevent evasion, and to add new taxes to the list of sources of revenues taken from the states.

The Nazis were not slow to recognize the importance of this machinery, and they made sure that the post of chief financial officer was occupied by a strong party man. He was given the task of collecting the special levies on the Jews, of administering the tax on capital taken out of the country, and of granting foreign exchange permits. In addition to these financial duties, he acquired responsibilities with respect to the administration of national property and the construction of public buildings. There were limits, however, to the extent to which even the Nazis were willing to go in strengthening the powers of this kingpin in the German financial machinery. The construction of the railroads, railroad buildings, and the *Autobahn* and the administration of forest properties were never given to him. Nor did the Nazi party trust the administration of the extensive party properties to the chief financial officers.

During World War II, Germany and Austria were divided into 28 major supervisory districts, 14 of which were located in what is now the Federal Republic. Under these 28 districts were grouped some 500 tax collection offices and some 200 chief customs offices (*Hauptzollämter*). These latter in turn supervised the activities of the 1,300 customs houses which blanketed the nation. The organization of the chief financial office followed rather closely that of the national Ministry of Finance. The historical division between customs and excise taxes on the one hand and the remaining national taxes on the other hand was continued. To these two major divisions a property and construction division was added, together with a cashier's office through which funds were sent from the customs and tax collecting agencies to the Ministry of Finance. An administration and personnel division serviced the major supervisory district and its subordinate offices. There were also separate bureaus to supervise various aspects of the work of the local foreign exchange offices. An important supervisory office, such as that at Cologne, might have as many as 35 officers, in addition to clerical personnel, to supervise the 4,000 officers and employees in its subordinate offices.

The collapse of the Nazi government in 1945 seriously disrupted the administration of public finance. During the war, various divisions of the national ministry were moved to small towns less subject to attack and bombing than was Berlin. Although the central treasury remained in Berlin, it no longer received taxes from southern or western Germany or made payments to these areas. Some of the superior financial offices were destroyed by bombing, others were moved to new locations, and many were unable to communicate with the local tax collection offices. These local offices, however, continued to operate without any substantial break. Orders to destroy their records before they could be captured by Allied forces were generally ignored when the Nazi leaders fled, and the military government officers were able to utilize these offices for the continued collection of taxes in accordance with their directives. As a result sizable tax collections were made each month, even during the last weeks of the fighting and the first weeks of the occupation.

The flow of money, however, was stopped at the lowest level. The local tax collection offices were unable to forward their receipts to Berlin, and they were without authority to turn them over to any unit of local government. Thus the states, counties, and even the state governments which were set up by the occupation armies were unable to meet their ordinary budget payments, let alone the extraordinary burdens resulting from war destruction and occupation. Local military government officers met this problem in various ways. The British occupation authorities continued the centralized administration of tax collection. A new head office was set up in Hamburg into which revenues were paid and from which allocations of funds were made. This office became in effect a ministry of finance for the British Zone. The American and French authorities followed a decentralized policy. In June, 1945, the superior financial officers were reconstituted in the American Zone, with orders to remit their receipts to the state treasuries for allocation by the state ministers of finance. Under this policy the superior financial offices and their subordinate field offices became agencies of the state ministries.

The state constitutions which have been adopted since 1946 made very little provision for financial administration. They generally required the cabinet to submit a budget, provided for an audit under a court of audit (*Rechnungshof*), limited borrowing without the consent of the legislature, contained provisions regarding deficiency appropriations, and laid down various tax principles. Similarly, the members of the state legislatures were naturally reluctant to crystallize the structure or powers of the state financial administrations until the federal government was established. Nevertheless, ministries of finance were created in each of the states, and they assumed supervision of the tax collection agencies. For four years Western Germany had a system of public finance which was decentralized on either a zonal or a state basis.[6]

DIVISION OF TAX POWERS

The Basic Law with its compromises resulted in complicated financial arrangements. Instead of assigning the complete power over each specific tax to a single level of government—federal, state, or local—the taxing power is divided into its component elements, namely power to legislate concerning the tax, administration of the machinery for collecting the tax, and receipt of the revenues from the tax. The levels of government thus are given various aspects of the taxing power rather than complete power over individual taxes. The distribution of the component parts of each tax, as given in Table 4, shows the intricate public finance arrangements which result from it. A striking feature of this allocation of taxing powers is the extent to which ultimate control over the taxes is given to the federal government through the grant to it of concurrent legislative power. It is evident that the framers of the Basic Law attempted to ensure a large measure of tax uniformity and at the same time to provide the states and local units with substantial revenues. In doing this they have accomplished, at least for the time being, a degree of fiscal decentralization.

The federal government was given the exclusive power to legislate concerning customs duties and the financial monopolies, but it was also given concurrent legislative power over most of the other important tax sources (Art. 105). The only exceptions are certain taxes of localized application, such as the real estate sales tax, and these localized taxes do not include the chief local tax sources (*Realsteuern*) which

[6] A review of the institutional developments at the state and local levels during the occupation is given in *Report of the Military Governor: Finance Cumulative Review*, No. 24 (July, 1946–June, 1947), pp. 10-11, 27-32.

Table 4. Principal German Taxes

Tax	Law Enacted by — Federal	Law Enacted by — Federal and State Concurrently	Law Enacted by — State	Tax Collected by — Federal	Tax Collected by — Federal and State Jointly	Tax Collected by — Local	Proceeds Paid to — Federal	Proceeds Paid to — State	Proceeds Paid to — Local
Customs Duties	x			x			x		
Alcohol Monopoly	x			x			x		
Direct Taxes on									
Income	x			†	x		†	x	
Corporation	x			†	x		†	x	
Property	x				x			x	
Inheritance	x				x			x	
Real Estate	*					x			x
Trade	*					x			x
Transactions Taxes on									
Turnover	x			x			x		
Real Estate Transfer			x		x			x	x
Capital Transactions	x			x				x	
Negotiable Instruments	x			x			x		
Motor Vehicle	x				x		x		
Transport	x			x			x		
Insurance	x			x				x	
Fire Protection			x	x				x	
Betting	x				x			x	
Increment Value			x		x			x	x
Amusements Tax			x			x			x
Excise Taxes on									
Tobacco	x			x			x		
Coffee and Tea	x			x			x		
Sugar	x			x			x		
Salt	x			x			x		
Beer	x			x				x	
Matches	x			x			x		
Mineral Oil	x			x			x		
Playing Cards	x			x			x		

* Federal government may not fix rates.
† Federal government may administer tax to extent it claims part of proceeds.
Sources: Basic Law of 1949, Articles 105,106,108. H. W. M. Copeman, *Handbook to German Taxation* (Frankfurt am Main, Nov., 1949), p. 8.

are subject to federal law, although the rates may be fixed locally. The sole protection which the states have against federal interference with most of their taxes is the requirement that many of the laws must have the approval of the upper house of the federal legislature (representing the governments of the states). Experience has shown that upper chambers are slight obstacles to centralization if the dominant groups will gain thereby.[7]

The federal government is also given access to the more important tax revenue sources. It receives all the collections from customs duties, from excise taxes (except the beer tax), and from the turnover and transportation taxes. The states and local governments are given the income and corporation taxes, the inheritance tax, the property tax, the beer tax, and the local taxes. These are substantial revenue producers, and if the states were given the exclusive right to them, they might indeed be "self-supporting" and mutually "independent" with regard to their budget economy (Art. 109). But since the federal government may claim part of the income and corporation taxes and since, if necessary to equalize burdens between the states, it may even encroach on the other tax sources (Art. 106), it is doubtful if this ideal of fiscal federalism will be realized.

The extent to which the fiscal resources of the federal government tend to overshadow those of the states and the localities is shown in Table 5. During its first year, the central government received substantially more revenue than either the states or the communities; indeed, its receipts were nearly as much as those of all the subordinate units together. With its heavy armament expenses and large appropriations for overseas aid, the government of the United States in 1952 required only 68 per cent of the American tax revenues, while the German central government received 47 per cent of the tax receipts at the outset. There was no year prior to World War II in which the American federal government took as large a slice of the tax pie as did the German federal government in 1949/50.

Table 5. Distribution of Federal, State, and Local
Tax Receipts, Year Ending March 31, 1950

	Amount (in Million DM)	Per Cent
Federal Receipts	8,192	47.3
State Receipts	6,892	39.8
Local Receipts	2,231	12.9
Total Tax Collections	17,315	100.0

Sources: H. W. M. Copeman, *Handbook to German Taxation* (Frankfurt am Main, Nov., 1949; revised to Nov., 1950), pp. 9-10. *Statistische Berichte: Die Einnahmen und Ausgaben der Gemeinden und Gemeindeverbände,* published by *Statistisches Bundesamt* (1950).

[7] See K. C. Wheare, *Federal Government* (New York, 1947), pp. 25, 94. Cf. Chapter V above for discussion of effectiveness of the upper house.

It is evident that these complexities in the tax structure will produce serious administrative problems.[8] The federal government is given the exclusive power to administer the taxes which it monopolizes, and for this purpose it has taken over the customs and excise tax offices from the states. In addition, it is given concurrent administrative powers over the collection of income and corporation taxes if it claims part of the revenues from them. These administrative powers extend to the giving of instructions to the individual tax collection offices as well as to the chief financial officers. The remaining taxes are to be administered by the state authorities, but even here the federal government has extensive administrative control. It may regulate the structure of the state tax collection machinery; it may prescribe the procedure which the state officers must follow; and it may force them to take a uniform course of training in federal schools (Art. 108). Here again the only protection afforded the state lies in the necessity of approval by the upper house of the federal legisltature of laws prescribing this federal supervision.

With this intricate pattern of taxation arrangements, the chief financial officer must play a difficult role. Under the Financial Administration Law which implements the financial clauses of the Basic Law, he becomes the servant of two masters, the state minister of finance and the federal minister of finance (Figure 3). It is difficult to see how this could be avoided under the provisions of the Basic Law if any semblance of federalism in fiscal matters is to be retained. The federal government could hardly be expected to rely on the states for the collection of its revenues or to give up the right to supervise the collection of taxes in which it may claim a share. Furthermore, there are obvious administrative advantages in combining customs and excise tax collection with the collection of personal and business taxes.

The law provides for a considerable amount of co-operation between the federal and state financial authorities. Both ministers of finance must agree with regard to the boundaries of the financial supervisory districts. They jointly select the chief financial officers and their deputies. The salary of these officers is determined by joint agreement, and they can be discharged only if both ministers agree. Half of the salaries of the chief financial officers, the deputies, and the chief cashiers are to be paid by the federal government and half by the states. The costs of collecting federal taxes are to be borne by the federal government as well as the costs of administering federal property. The states are required to bear the costs of administering their own

[8] See Gerhard Wacke, *Dan Finanzwesen der Bundesrepublik* (Tübingen, 1950), p. 47.

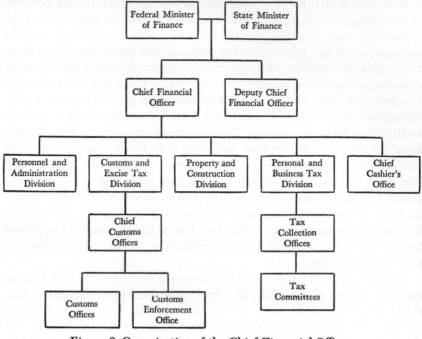

Figure 3. Organization of the Chief Financial Offices
(law of September 6, 1950).

Source: *Gesetz über die Finanzverwaltung* (FVG), September 6, 1950, in *Bundesgesetzblatt*, 1950, 448.

taxes and various overhead costs as well. In view of the fact that some
of the federal taxes are collected by the same agency which collects
most of the state taxes, there may be difficulty in separating the costs,
especially since the technique of cost accounting is by no means as
fully developed in Germany as perhaps it should be. If the financial
needs of the federal government continue to grow—and this seems very
likely—it will probably claim larger shares of additional taxes. As a
result, its influence over the financial administration will certainly increase, and the chief financial officer may come more and more under
federal control. With federal supervision of a major part of his work,
with the law which he must follow a federal statute, and with large
federal interests involved in the operation of his office, the control of
the states over the chief financial officer is apt to decline. In the end,
the Germans may have succeeded in thwarting the basic occupation
policy of promoting fiscal federalism.

NATIONAL AND STATE TAXES

The most striking feature of the German tax structure is the heavy reliance on indirect or excise taxes for governmental revenues. As shown in Table 6, more than half the tax receipts of the federal and state governments are from indirect sources.[9] This is in sharp contrast with the situation in the United States, where direct taxes comprise 70 per cent of the total tax collections. The corporate income tax produces twice as large a proportion of governmental revenue in the United States as in Germany, and the individual income and wages taxes produce 50 per cent more. The amount received from inheritance taxes in Germany is negligible, being even less than the tea or salt taxes.

The turnover tax is the largest revenue producer among the German indirect taxes. This tax is levied on sales, whether of goods or personal services and whether the sale is made by the manufacturer, wholesaler, or retailer. Less than 20 per cent of the sales are exempt (chiefly wholesale transactions in basic commodities, public utility services, and items imported or exported), and the normal rate on taxable sales or services is 4 per cent. Since the tax is assessed each time goods change hands, the cumulative effect of the tax on the price to the consumer is considerable. The turnover tax probably increases the price of food or clothing by about 10 per cent.

The general character of the German tax structure has not been substantially changed since the Weimar period. The Nazi impact on taxation resulted in a greater centralization of finances, in the granting of favors to privileged groups, and in the imposition of discriminatory taxes on persecuted groups, rather than in a revision of the general system. At the outbreak of World War II the level of taxation in Germany was fairly high in comparison with the level in England or the United States. There was some increase of taxes during the war—the income tax was raised 50 per cent, and there were increases in the beer and tobacco taxes. In general, however, the Nazis preferred to finance the war largely by revenues from occupied territories and on borrowings through the banking system instead of making direct levies on the population. Tax collections in Germany covered but 26 per cent of the expenditures during the war years, whereas in the United States they covered 40 per cent, and in Great Britain 61 per cent of the governmental payments.[10]

[9] These figures are for the west German republic. An even higher reliance on indirect taxes was found in the Soviet Zone—66 per cent in 1947/48. *Finance Quarterly Review: Report of the Military Governor*, No. 32 (Oct.-Dec., 1947), p. 3.

[10] Mabel Newcomer, "War and Postwar Developments in the German Tax System," *National Tax Journal*, I, No. 1 (March, 1948), 1-11.

Table 6. Federal and State Tax Receipts, Year Ending March 31, 1950

	Amount (in Million DM)	Per cent
Direct Taxes on	6,120	40.6
Income	4,530	30.1
Corporation	1,448	9.7
Property	115	.7
Inheritance	19	.1
Other Direct Taxes	8	
Transaction Taxes on	4,757	31.6
Turnover	3,991	26.6
Real Estate Transfer	26	.2
Capital Transactions	13	.1
Negotiable Instruments	34	.2
Motor Vehicle	282	1.9
Transport	262	1.7
Insurance	56	.3
Fire Protection	18	.1
Betting	75	.5
Excise Taxes on	3,860	25.5
Alcohol Monopoly	502	3.3
Tobacco	2,191	14.5
Coffee	281	1.9
Tea	22	.1
Sugar	378	2.5
Salt	36	.2
Beer	302	2.0
Matches	54	.4
Mineral Oil	49	.3
Other Excise Taxes	45	.3
Customs Duties	347	2.3
Total Taxes and Customs	15,084	100.0

Source: H. W. M. Copeman; *Handbook to German Taxation* (Frankfurt am Main, 1950), pp. 9-10.

As a result of this system of "noiseless financing," the occupying powers found the country with a relatively low level of taxation and a high level of inflation. It was evident that sharp increases would have to be made if budgets were to be balanced and if further inflation were to be avoided. Under the Potsdam Agreement the Allies agreed to establish common policies with regard to taxation and customs, and one of the first committees established by the Control Council in the fall of 1945 was a quadripartite taxation committee to study means of raising additional revenues. The work of this committee resulted in increases in all the major taxes within the next six months.

The general character of the changes in the tax laws since 1945[11] is shown in Table 7. Many of the German taxes are extremely complicated, and in order to present the general trend of tax development it has been necessary to oversimplify them for tabular purposes. Most of the tax rates are *ad valorem*—that is, they are levied as a percentage of income, value of property, or price of sales. Some taxes, however, are specific and are levied on the basis of the quantity of the taxable item. Thus the taxes on alcohol and beer are assessed in marks per

Table 7. Comparative Tax Rates under Nazi, Control Council, and Federal Tax Laws*

Tax	Nazi Law 1945	Control Council Law 1946	Federal Law 1950
Individual Income Tax			
Yearly Income of 1,000M	12%	17%	10%
Yearly Income of 9,000M	42%	55%	40%
Yearly Income of 70,000M	67%	95%	70%
Corporate Income Tax	30-55%	35-65%	50%
Property Tax	.5%	1-2.5%	¾ of 1%
Inheritance Tax	2-60%	14-60%	4-80%
Turnover Tax	2%	3%	3%
Tobacco Tax	35-75%	80-90%	30-60%
Alcohol Tax	475RM	11,470RM	1,000DM
Beer Tax	1-13RM	35-118RM	2-15DM
Sugar Tax	21RM	40RM	30.5DM
Coffee Tax	None	None	10-13DM
Transport Tax	2-14%	2-14%	2-14%
Motor Vehicles	8-30RM	12-45RM	12-45DM

* The proportion of national income (as reported in official German statistics) absorbed by taxes rose steadily from 1929 to 1946 and has declined since that date. The percentages are: 1929—19%; 1930—20%; 1932—23%; 1936—24%; 1938—27%; 1939—30%; 1944—35%; 1946—44%; 1948—35% (estimated). M. Gottlieb, "German Economic Potential," *Journal of Social Research*, XVII (March, 1950), 72.

hectoliter, and the tax on motor vehicles on piston displacement or weight. It will be observed that many of the taxes were increased by 50 per cent or more under the first Control Council laws, but that there was little general change in the character of German taxation.

[11] For details of changes in the tax laws between 1945 and 1950 reference is made to the following: *Report of the Military Governor: Finance and Property Control*, No. 8, (March, 1946) pp. 2-4; Eugene L. Gomberg, *Germany: Postwar Tax Program*, Public Finance Branch, OMGUS, June 10, 1946, mimeographed, 60 pp.; H. W. M. Copeman, *Handbook to German Taxation* (Frankfurt am Main, Nov., 1949), mimeographed, 102 pp.

The taxes levied by the Control Council were considered excessive, and even punitive, by many Germans. The receipts from them, however, provided sufficient revenue to enable the states to balance their budgets and to meet the necessary relief payments, subsidize coal and steel industries, and cover the internal costs of the occupation.[12] While there were some difficulties in administering the new rates, there is no evidence that they caused any serious increase in tax evasion or that they retarded German recovery nearly as much as numerous other factors, such as general disruption of economic life. Indeed, the large yield from them belies any claim that they caused a breakdown in administration.

On June 20, 1948, the western powers put into effect a drastic program of monetary reform which involved more than a 90 per cent contraction of the money supply. By means of a currency conversion some 135 billion reichmarks were canceled, and in their place 12.6 billion *Deutsche* marks were created. It was anticipated that the high levels of the Control Council taxes would become unbearable under this sharp reduction in purchasing power.[13] With so much of the public revenue coming from indirect and excise taxes, the high level might even result in smaller receipts should business activity not respond as was hoped. Accordingly, substantial reductions were made in the income, inheritance, property, and tobacco taxes to help cushion the impact of the monetary reform. The Germans continued to press for further tax reductions and especially urged that income tax concessions be made to encourage savings and to facilitate long-term investment. An ordinance incorporating these proposals was approved in April, 1949, and resulted in a substantial reduction in the effective income tax rate. Still further reductions in the income tax were made by the Federal Income Tax Reform of April, 2 1950, in spite of strong objections on the part of the occupation authorities. These three successive reductions in the income tax in as many years seriously undermined it as a dependable revenue source.[14] It soon became evident that the fiscal soundness of the government would be threatened unless the income tax were strengthened, and on July 1, 1951, a series of modifications was made which eliminated several exemptions and deductions and raised the corporate rate from 50 to 60 per cent. These

[12] *Economic Developments since Currency Reform: Special Report of the Military Governor (Germany)*, November, 1948, p. 15.

[13] *Ibid.*, p. 16.

[14] Mabel Newcomer, *Tax Revenues and the Refugee Program in the Integration of Refugees into German Life*, ECA Technical Assistance Commission Report, March 21, 1951, p. 85.

slight concessions were more than offset by an increase in the turnover tax from 3 to 4 per cent. As a result of these changes an even higher proportion of governmental revenues will probably come from indirect tax sources.

A second feature of the German tax structure is the extensive use of fiscal provisions to achieve various economic and social goals. The Nazis made full use of the power to tax in order to favor various groups and to penalize others. Tax concessions for large families, tax benefits for farmers, and favorable tax arrangements for holding companies and those developing the country's war potential were illustrations of this tax philosophy. While many of the Nazi objectives are no longer approved, their philosophy continues to permeate the tax laws in both the Soviet and the western zones. Thus, there are numerous provisions of the federal income tax law designed to stimulate saving, such as permitting the deduction from taxable income of insurance premiums, of building and loan association contributions, and of investments in co-operative societies. Accelerated depreciation is permitted for the replacement of business assets destroyed during the war and for investments in housing, ships, and farm buildings. It is often possible to avoid high tax rates by ploughing back earnings into the business, particularly if the enterprise is one which requires a large capital investment. Another category of concessions is designed to aid some groups who are in special need. Accordingly, in addition to exemptions based on family status and age, additional personal exemptions are given to wage earners, refugees, and expellees. Still another type of concession is made to encourage extra work by professional men and overtime work by employees. A special low scale of rates is applied to subsidiary earnings, and some of the overtime pay is completely tax-free.

These concessions are invariably subsidies in disguise and may open the door to substantial tax evasion.[15] There has been considerable complaint about the decline of tax morale in Germany and about the general spirit of tax evasion which prevailed. A study by the Public Finance Branch of OMGUS in December, 1948, indicated that evasion in the period immediately following the currency reforms may have amounted to 35 per cent of the assessed income and turnover tax liability, though there was no evidence of a general tax breakdown.[16] There are undoubtedly numerous causes for the lower tax morality in postwar

[15] Walter W. Heller, "Tax and Monetary Reform in Occupied Germany," *National Tax Journal*, II, No. 3 (Sept., 1949), 215-231.
[16] *Tax Revenues since Currency Reform*, Public Finance Branch, Bipartite Control Office, December 6, 1948, mimeographed, p. 10.

Germany. In part it may be due to general decline in political morality, evidenced most sharply by the black-marketeering which sprouted under the Nazi regime and blossomed after the war. In part it may be due to the excessively complicated character of German tax legislation. With a shortage of trained personnel, the German tax offices are often unable to audit returns as fully as might be desirable. The numerous provisions of the law which seem unfair to the citizen and the arrogance of some tax collectors who sometimes treat the taxpayers as a lower order of human beings have led to the development of an extensive independent profession of tax advisers. Some of these advisers are very skillful in helping the larger taxpayers, who can afford to pay their fees, to take full advantage of the loopholes in the law. Thus the generous deductions which are permitted as business expenses and the favorable treatment given holding companies opened the door to extensive tax avoidance.

A final characteristic of German taxation is the heavy weight it lays on the lower income groups. In October, 1945, the Control Council Taxation Committee unanimously agreed to reverse the Nazi taxation policy and "to lay the greatest burden of taxation on the large incomes and the large accumulations of capital which have supported Nazism and militarism in Germany in the past."[17] Thus, the tobacco tax, the property tax, and the corporate income tax were each classified in such a manner as to levy a higher percentage tax on the larger taxpayers. The fantastic rates levied on alcohol were justified on the ground that it was solely a luxury in postwar Germany. The very low inheritance tax rates were sharply increased, especially for large estates. In many respects, however, it was not possible to graduate taxes according to progressive principles. Quite apart from German opposition and Soviet indifference to steeply graduated rates, the need for large sums of new revenue and the desire to curb inflation made it necessary to increase those taxes which would produce the largest receipts. Accordingly, the beer tax, the sugar tax, and the turnover tax were increased by 5 per cent or more, although all of those levies bore heaviest on the low income groups. Furthermore, the percentage increase in the income tax rates was as great for the workers as for most of the larger taxpayers. As a result the Control Council legislation increased the tax bill of the German worker to half as much again as it had been during the war.[18]

The tax reductions which were effective between June, 1948, and

[17] Eugene L. Gomberg, *Germany—Postwar Tax Program* (1946), p. 3.
[18] *Report of the Military Governor: Finance Cumulative Review*, No. 24 (June, 1946-July, 1947).

June, 1951, did benefit the workers as much as the wealthier taxpayers. Nearly all brackets, except the very highest, had lower income tax rates than during the war, but the reduction for the workers was less than for persons in the upper middle brackets.[19] The progressive features in the corporate income tax, tobacco tax, and property tax have been repealed. Practically all the Control Council increases have been wiped out or sharply reduced except for the most regressive tax of all —the turnover tax, which was increased to 4 per cent in 1951. Two new excise taxes, on coffee and on tea, have been levied. Finally, owners of business and industry can avoid income tax rates in excess of 50 per cent by utilizing the capital formation exemptions in the present law.

The German tax structure has become a barrier, rather than an aid, to the development of democratic government. Partial emasculation of the income and inheritance taxes as progressive revenue instruments, the heavy use of indirect taxes, and the large number of tax loopholes which the law provides—all foster the growth of large fortunes. Any increase in the gap between the rich and the poor is a serious menace to a democracy. Unless the workers receive generous benefits from an existing regime they are likely to cast their lot in another direction. German democracy can ill afford to undermine support from the base of its social pyramid.

The policy of relying on indirect rather than direct taxes is also undesirable. Excise and transactions taxes are paid by manufacturers or merchants and are passed on to the consumers disguised in higher prices. The public is thus unaware of the cost of the governmental services it receives and is less able to balance the need for them against their cost. Efforts are being made in Germany to focus public attention on the fiscal problems of the national and state governments, but it is uphill work because the public does not feel the direct impact of the bulk of the taxes. Democracy rests on as large a public participation in government as possible, and a fiscal system which discourages public interest raises a barrier to effective democratic procedures.

In the third place, the extensive use of exceptions and special privileges to favored groups is a most dangerous practice. Autocratic government can be conducted in secret, and special benefits can be given to small groups without arousing serious antagonism from the public at large. But by its very nature, democratic government must be conducted in broad daylight. If some citizens receive tax favors, others

[19] Rudolf Binder, *Die Belastung durch die persönliche Einkommensteuer* (Kiel, 1950), pp. 18-20; W. W. Heller, "Role of Fiscal-Monetary Policy in German Economic Recovery." *American Economic Review*, XL (May, 1950), 543.

will be quick to demand them, and the process of government will become a mad bickering of special interests. It is the essence of democratic statesmanship to resolve the major conflicts of interests in society, but when energy must be given to granting minor favors, there may be little left for the solution of more important issues. Furthermore, the public rapidly comes to distrust a government in which statesmanship degenerates into bartering.

SOURCES OF LOCAL REVENUES

Most communities obtain their chief revenues from taxes and grants from the state.[20] These sources are often supplemented by fees and earnings from local enterprises and occasionally by the sale of public property or by borrowing. The amounts received from each of these sources vary from city to city and from state to state, but on the average taxes produce about one-third of the revenues, state grants provide about one-third, and fees bring in about one fourth.

The principal local taxes are called *Realsteuern* and consist of the tax on real estate (*Grundsteuer*) and the trade tax (*Gewerbesteuer*) which is levied on business. These two taxes produce about 90 per cent of the tax revenue (or about 30 per cent of the total revenue) of the communities. The first step in levying the real property tax is to determine the real value index (*Einheitswert*) of the land and buildings on each piece of property. This is done by the state tax collection office with the advice of a local committee, according to rules laid down in the valuation law.

Under German legislation, tax advantages are given to different pieces of real estate according to the use which is made of them. Agricultural land is generally taxed at a lower rate than is urban property: old buildings and multi-family buildings are assessed higher than buildings constructed since 1924 or than single family houses, and property in large cities is assessed less than property in small towns. This is accomplished by multiplying the value index by a differential factor or weight, a process which is also done in the state tax collection office. Thus, if a piece of property in a large city has a multi-family building erected before 1924, the value is multiplied by 10/1000, whereas if it has a single family building erected since 1924 the value is multiplied by only 5/1000. The resulting figure is the tax base (*Steuermessbetrag*) and is never more than 1 per cent of the value of the property.

The rate of tax which is finally levied on the tax base is, however, determined by the local council within limits fixed by state law. This

[20] Cf. Chapters 3 and 4 above.

rate generally lies between 150 and 250 per cent of the tax base (1.5 per cent to 2.5 per cent of the value of the property as weighted for tax purposes), the higher rates being generally levied in the larger cities. The rate is normally not changed much from year to year, but remains relatively fixed except under unusual conditions. In some states the community officials must secure the approval of the supervisory authority (usually the *Landrat* or *Regierungspräsident*) if they wish to make a sharp increase in the tax rate.

The trade tax is levied on the conduct of business of all kinds, whether by a corporation or by an individual. Part of this tax is based on the amount of profits which the business made in the preceding period, and part is based on the amount of capital used in the business. The two parts of the trade tax are combined by means of a formula which adds together a percentage of the profits (usually between 2 and 5 per cent) and a ratio of the capital (usually between two and five per thousand). The resulting figure is the trade tax base.

The assessment of the trade tax is made by the state tax collection office advised by a local committee, which also hears and decides protests against assessment inequities. However, the committee is so limited by legislation and administrative regulations that it has little real power. It appears to be an agency to which the tax office may shift blame for assessments rather than a real authority in local tax matters. The rate of tax is determined by the local council and is commonly between 200 and 300 per cent. State limitations on the amount of this rate are similar to those on the real property tax, and the state commonly supervises sharp increases or decreases in the rate. In addition, some states permit their communities to levy a tax on the total wage bill of businesses and thus decrease the rate of the profits and capital of the trade tax.

The communities of Western Germany receive about 45 per cent of their tax income from real property taxes and about an equal per cent from all forms of the trade tax. There is, however, considerable variation between communities in this respect. Thus the trade tax is naturally much less lucrative in communities with less than 10,000 inhabitants than it is in the larger cities. In addition to these major taxes, communities may be permitted to levy a number of taxes of lesser importance, including those on theater tickets, beverages, and profit on land sales.

Grants from the state are equal in importance to taxes as sources of community revenues. They fall into three general categories. The first consists of general or "key" grants paid to the communities to compensate them in part for the administraive tasks they perform for the state as well as to equalize to some extent the tax burden between poor and rich communities (*Finanzausgleich*). These grants are paid under a state law prescribing a complicated formula by which the state ministry of finance calculates the amount each unit is to receive. The formula varies from state to state, but all formulas seek to combine various indexes of necessary expenditures with an index of the ability of the community to pay taxes.

Grants are also made for particular purposes. These grants may be administered by the Ministry of Finance, the Ministry of the Interior, or the particular bureau concerned. Such grants are chiefly for highways, police, school salaries, welfare, repair of war damage, and support of health offices. There is no uniformity among the various states with respect either to the purposes of these special grants, the agencies which administer them, or the formula followed in their distribution. In general, the grants for particular purposes give the communities about twice the revenue they receive from the general or key grants.

A third type of state grant is used to meet the emergency needs of communities or to relieve special inequities resulting from the particular key-grant formula. This emergency fund may be administered by the minister of finance, by joint action of the ministers of finance and interior, or by a committee on which the communities themselves are represented. Although the fund is not usually large in relation to the total grants to communities (about 5 per cent of the total grants), it may be exceedingly important to some local governments. Fear of losing part of their former grants under this fund may be an important factor in persuading the local officials to follow the official administrative line.

Administrative fees and miscellaneous revenues form an important item in local budgets even though the individual items are small. The fees consist of charges for various administrative services (of which there are a large number and considerable variety from state to state). The amounts of these fees are generally fixed by state law or ordinance. Other revenues received by the communities consist of rents for the use of community property and interest paid to the community. Earnings of municipal enterprises have tended to decline as important sources of local revenues. The difficulty which communities have had in increasing public utility rates in spite of increasing costs has reduced the earnings of those enterprises even where they are as efficiently managed as formerly. Some communities, particularly in rural areas, receive substantial revenues from their forests.

The counties in Germany are not financed through independent tax sources of their own. In some counties small amounts are raised from the hunting tax, but the few minor taxes which the counties may levy account for less than .5 per cent of their revenues. A major source of county revenues are the grants made to them by the state. These also are of three principal kinds: general or key grants distributed to the counties on a formula similar in general respects to the formula for the general or key grants to the communities; special grants made to the counties to help cover the cost of governmental services which the state thinks are of special importance, such as welfare, health, police, and roads; reimbursement for some of the services the counties perform for the state (for example, the relief of refugees). The general or key grants form a smaller per cent of county income than of community revenues, while a larger share of county revenues come from grants for particular objects. All the grants together cover more than half the average county budget.

Somewhat over one-fourth of the county's revenues come from a levy which it makes on the communities comprising it. The amount of this levy is determined by the *Kreistag* at the request of the *Landrat*. The only influence which the communities have over this levy comes from the election of the *Kreistag* members. The amount of the levy depends on the revenues from other sources, the costs of providing the services required of the county, and the skill with which county finances are managed. Once the total amount of the levy has been determined, it is apportioned among the constituent communities by means of a formula which makes use of the factors in the equalization formula for the key grants.

PROBLEMS OF LOCAL FINANCE

One of the chief problems in local finance grows out of the tendency of both local and state officials to treat taxation, equalization of revenues, and particularly budgeting as a secret science. The German citizen finds it very difficult to obtain any detailed intelligible information concerning the financing of his community, and positive attempts to enlighten him are usually lacking. The budgets are generally prepared by a local official who has little understanding of the citizen's role in a democracy and who conceives of his function merely as one to ensure that the necessary funds are available to pay the bills. As it has not been the custom to give publicity to the proposed budget in advance of its final approval, the budget official sees no reason to inaugurate a procedure which might cause him trouble. Cases have been reported, indeed, in which the council itself has been asked to vote the budget without being given a full copy for study. In one community the council, to the chagrin of the budget officer, refused to approve the budget on the basis of a single-page summary and demanded that a copy of the complete document be given each of the political parties represented on the council. This tradition of financial secrecy naturally awakens a suspicion that there are features of the local financial picture which will not bear the light of day. To avoid this suspicion, the officials try to make as few changes as possible from the preceding year. Thus tax increases on the one hand or changes in expenditures on the other are resisted to the utmost, and local administration tends to become stagnant.

There are encouraging signs that budget procedures may be improved in the future.[21] A few municipal administrations, of which Hamburg and Frankfurt are notable examples, make definite efforts to give publicity to financial information. A privately financed organization in Bonn has a competent staff engaged in the analysis of both state and city budgets. Occasionally the release of budget information has led to general public consideration of proposed expenditures in mass meetings which have definitely affected official action.

The numerous payments which are made between different levels of government complicate local finance in other ways. The grants from the states may take three or four forms. They are never brought together in any one place, and current accounting procedures make it difficult to ascertain the total amount of the grants without an excessive amount of work. Each of the grants is made under a diffierent law, and the regulations governing them may be administered by different state departments. Furthermore, the grants are made without relation to the other interlevel payments which may be required from the local units of governments. Thus in Lower Saxony, for example, the state makes grants to the communities and then takes all or part of the money away from many communities for its equalization fund. In Bavaria a substantial number of communities never see the money granted by the state, for it is held in transit by the counties; the communities must, however, include the grants in their budgets. The accounts of the counties handling these grants cannot be audited by the communities.

Whatever purpose these interdepartmental and intergovernmental payments served when they were originally instituted, their general effect at the present time is seriously to increase the complexity of local finance and to make it almost impossible for the citizen to explore what is to him a dark continent. Perhaps the crowning complexity in this maze of local finance is the system of general financial equalization by which the states assist the poorer communities to meet

[21] Cf. Chapter 12 above.

their governmental obligations. A considerable part of the equalization complexities grow out of the attempt to incorporate in a single formula several variable factors, each with a different weight. On the one hand, several factors of need (number of children, extent of bomb damage to public buildings, number of refugees, number of aged persons) are included at varying weights. On the other hand, these are balanced against two other factors (real property valuation and the amount of collections from the trade tax) which are thought to indicate the ability of the community to support the necessary public services. The inclusion of each of these elements in the formula is defended on the ground that it is more accurate thereby. The items in the formula are carefully set forth in the equalization law which is passed by the state legislature on the recommendation of the ministry.

Each of these equalization elements presents an important question of financial policy. If the legislators were asked to decide them individually, one at a time, an intelligent and responsible determination could be made. But instead of being asked to vote on the merits of a single type of community aid—for example, aid to communities with large numbers of refugees—the legislator is asked to approve a multiple measure which links such disparate items as the community's many children, extensive war damage, and small revenues from the trade tax. Since different weights must be assigned to each of the items in the formula, the legislator soon finds it impossible to make an intelligent decision and comes to accept the proposal of the ministry as something "sacred." A ministry which is skillful enough to placate the important groups in the legislature generally has little difficulty in securing the enactment of this pork-barrel legislation. The more complex the formula becomes, the more technical it seems to be and the less understood by the legislators. Under these circumstances there is little effort on the part of the ministry officials to resist the inclusion of complicating factors in the formula. Indeed, the increasing complexity of equalization since 1933, and even since 1945, is due not merely to the additional problems which have been thrust on German communities, but also to the usefulness of confusion in thwarting democratic responsibility.

The application of the equalization key, after its adoption by the legislature, is largely automatic. The computations of the amount to be paid each community are made with meticulous care and are entirely objective. But since such complicated formulas may work hardship on certain communities, the equalization law sets up a fund from which the ministry may make supplemental grants where it finds them needed. To receive aid under these discretionary grants the community must convince the ministry that the local finances are well administered and that there is a necessity for the aid requested. In some states, as many as half of the communities apply for these supplemental grants, and the amounts available for distribution may run as high as 10 per cent of the total amount of state aid. Since this aid is essential to the revenues of so many communities, the ministry has in it a powerful weapon by which it can control local financial affairs.

There is also extensive state control over the expenditure side of local budgets. In Bavaria the functions which local governments perform are divided into three categories: state functions which are performed by the localities; local functions which the state requires the community to perform; and services which the community is free to undertake or not as it wishes. A community has complete control over only the third type of these functions. Not only must it provide the first two classes of services, but any serious attempt to reduce the level of expenditures for them is likely to be met with opposition by the state supervisory authority. During the war, the number of tasks required of local governments steadily increased, and the trend has continued. These obligations have frequently placed such a heavy burden on the community that it must reduce its other expenditures to meet them. There are no statistics giving the proportion of local budgets which must be devoted to state-mandated services. In the counties it may run as high as 80 per cent of the total budget, and in towns and cities it may reach one-third to one-half of the total expenditures. The state grants of various types, which may run to a third of the community budget, often do not cover expenditures which the state requires the local government to make.

The mandated expenditure most resented by the communities is the amount which the county assesses them to meet its budget. This levy is apportioned among the communities on the basis of the assessed valuation of their real estate and the amount of the trade tax which they collect. Since the county is largely a state agency and performs state functions, the communities feel that its budget should be borne by the state rather than the local taxpayers. Bavarian communities are required to pay about one-fourth of the county expenses and to do so must set aside nearly 15 per cent of their own revenues. In Lower Saxony there has been, in addition to the county levy, a general state levy on the communities and also a special state levy to provide aid to bombed areas. These levies seriously restrict local self-government and often place the local financial officer in a strait jacket at budget-making time.

The taxing powers of the communities are also severely limited either by law, by action of the state supervisory authority, or by custom. They have very little power to select new types of taxes to supplement the traditional sources of revenue. In general the power to levy a new tax must be expressly granted by the legislature, and in practice it may even require the approval of the state supervisory authority. Since the state itself has pre-empted the more lucrative types of taxation, the communities find it difficult to tap new sources of revenues. Real estate and trade taxes have minimum and maximum rates fixed by state law; revenues from fees are not large enough to be of much help; and profits from the operation of local enterprises such as utilities and forests may be restricted by state price-control regulations. It is impossible to produce a balanced budget unless there are elements of flexibility at the disposal of the budget-maker. If the income is fixed, he can balance the budget only by reducing the items of expenditure. If the expenditures are mandated, a balance is impossible unless revenues can be increased or decreased. When both expenditures and revenues are rigid, as in Germany, the local budget officer is faced with but a single alternative—he must seek outside help. This help must come from the state, for it is the only agency with residual funds. Under these circumstances, local self-government ceases to have reality.

German local finance is exceedingly impervious to democratic influences. In part this is due to the lack of local control, and in part to the inflexibility of both the sources of revenue and the required expenditures. When citizens demand additional or better governmental services, the answer of the budget officer is that they will cost money and that taxes cannot be raised to provide the necessary funds. When they demand economies in government and lower taxes, the answer is that the tasks imposed by the state are so great that lower taxes are impossible. If the citizens persist in their demands in the face of these obstacles, they are told that they must take their requests to the state ministries of finance and interior. Here they are met with a barrage of technical jargon and an evasion of responsibility, and even the most aggressive citizens are likely to succumb to the force of inertia. It would be difficult to contrive a financial system which would more effectively shield a bureaucracy from public influence and criticism than that used in German local finance.

Dark as this picture may seem, it is by no means entirely black. There are indications that some Germans are becoming increasingly aware of the squirrel cage in which they are caught and are trying to free themselves from it. The system of levies by one level of government on another is particularly disliked, and organizations of local officials are waging a campaign against them. Both the ministries and the state supervisory authorities are dissatisfied with the slowness of communities in preparing their budgets. Taxpayer groups have become increasingly effective in demanding greater publicity for municipal finance and access to full budgetary information before the appropriations are made and taxes voted. As a result of local criticism, several cities have called upon outside agencies to make administrative surveys of their activities and to recommend more economical procedures.

The demand for independent sources of local revenues is very general and is buttressed by the obvious intention of the Basic Law of 1949 to provide them. In general, the local officials want a share of the state income tax, rather than greater flexibility in the use of taxes which have traditionally been levied. In Bavaria, however, the legislature has removed local tax limits, and communities in that state may raise or lower local taxes as they wish. While ministry officials generally favor an increasingly complicated equalization formula, local officials have some reservations about the matter. In some states they have resisted attempts to add elements to it and have successfully thwarted further confusion of the financial scene.

CONCLUSION

A fair appraisal of local finance in Germany must lead to the conclusion that the efforts of the occupation authorities to promote more democratic methods have been only moderately successful. In view of the strongly entrenched local and state bureaucracy, it is not to be expected that a revolution in local finance could be effected quickly. Nevertheless, some advances have been made, and the German people are becoming increasingly aware of the conflict between their financial procedures and a genuine democracy. It is entirely possible that the dissatisfaction generated by the occupation authorities may result in German-led reforms which will once more enable that country to take the lead in efficient democratic local self-government.

Part IV

FUNCTIONS OF GOVERNMENT

14

*Labor Relations**

TAYLOR COLE

THE significance of the transition from the Weimar Republic to the Third Reich is nowhere more strikingly illustrated than in the field of labor relations. The transition from the Third Reich, after an interlude, to the Federal Republic has witnessed a return toward the system of labor relations which had evolved during the Weimar Republic, although the consequences of military defeat in World War II and Allied occupation policies have combined to add certain new features. It will be the purpose of this chapter to point out the chief postwar developments in labor relations in Western Germany, with special emphasis upon the role of organized labor.

The right of association, anchored in the Weimar Constitution, furnished the basis for the whole system of labor legislation after 1919. It is true that the new social and economic order, which some had read into Article 165 of the Weimar Constitution, never materialized and that labor failed to receive an effective right to equal participation with employers in the control of industry and in the regulation of wages and conditions of work. Nevertheless, there emerged during the period from 1919 to 1933 a body of labor law which placed a heavy emphasis upon collective bargaining, arbitration and conciliation, and employee representation in workshop and labor court. A strong trade-union organization, albeit one marked by bureaucratic weaknesses and divided within itself furnished a bulwark for the sys-

* This chapter was originally written in 1951. In view of the absence of the author from the United States at the time of publication, only a few minor changes and additions to the footnotes could be made.

tem of labor relations and a counterpart to the effectively organized German employers.

The developments which followed the designation of Adolph Hitler as Reich Chancellor on January 30, 1933, and which found early expression in the National Labor Law of January 30, 1934, are well known. Democratic processes vanished before the leader principle, while authoritarian prohibitions and guidance eliminated self-help and collaboration on the part of the employee. Furthermore, the demands of the new economy reduced the independent role of the employer to a most restricted one. The Nazi system of labor relations, which replaced the previous arrangements under the Weimar Republic, in turn went through the various contortions culminating in the wartime changes after 1939.

In Nazi Germany, membership in the German Labor Front was virtually compulsory; wages and conditions of work were determined by agencies over which the workers had no direct control. Almost the last vestige of a free market was removed by the successive steps taken to deal with the unemployment situation, to cope with labor shortages under the Four Year Plan of 1936, and to meet wartime labor requirements. The war economy (*Wehrwirtschaft*) of prewar days had largely accomplished the task of freezing wages and of allocating and confining the laborer to such employment as state officials designated. The general task of channeling, training, and supervising labor and of determining its material and nonmaterial returns involved a large number of agencies, most of which were swept away on the heels of the military collapse of 1945.

POLICIES AND LEGISLATION OF THE OCCUPYING AUTHORITIES

The over-all policies of the Allied Military Governments in regard to trade unionism date back to the draft directive to the Allied Commanders in Chief by the European Advisory Commission on October 23, 1944: "You will permit workers to establish organizations for the purpose of collective bargaining and mutual social and economic assistance." Article 10 of the Potsdam Agreement contained phraseology of a similar character when it stated: "Subject likewise to the maintenance of military security, the formation of free trade unions shall be permitted." These general injunctions and others of like nature were implemented through various media, such as the Allied Control Council laws, directives, and instructions. Illustrations of significant Control Council laws were No. 21, regarding labor courts; No. 22, dealing with works councils; No. 35, providing for conciliation and arbitration procedures; and No. 40, repealing the National Socialist National Labor Law. Important directives were No. 14 on wage policy, No. 26 on the regulation of working hours, and No. 31 on the establishment of federations of trade unions. In addition to the laws and directives, there were numerous policy statements from the separate military governments in the three western zones, as well as directives affecting the evolution of trade unionism which emanated from the respective Manpower Divisions of the military governments. In essence, these policy statements and directives at the different governmental levels guaranteed freedom of association and the right to strike, subject to certain limitations, and stressed collective bargaining as a desirable means for settling labor disputes. Some of the provisions were incorporated in the constitutions and legislation of the *Länder* after 1946, when constitutions were adopted in the U.S. and French zones.

It was obvious that the descending hierarchy of norms, ranging down from the Control Council laws and directives, covered only certain matters of importance in the labor relations field and allowed considerable latitude for independent action by the respective military governments. Even the general policies upon which there had presumably been common agreement were at times interpreted in different ways in order to accord with the national policies of the several powers. Thus, the British authorities originally favored a single all-inclusive trade-union organization in their zone. The U.S. authorities placed a heavier emphasis upon a federalistic solution, encouraging the development of separate trade-union federations in the several *Länder*. The French position resulted in an even heavier emphasis upon autonomous federations in the three *Länder* in that zone. The British Military Government was considered by trade-union authorities to be more sympathetic toward a program of socialization than were either the U.S. or French authorities. At the same time the U.S. officials took the initiative in returning control in the field of labor relations to the Germans. The trend toward granting greater autonomy to the German agencies in the labor field was reflected in the steps taken in August, 1948, when the British and U.S. Military Governments granted approval to an ordinance of the German Bizonal Economic Council providing for the creation of a German Manpower Department. A more final step was taken when approval was given to the Basic Law of the Federal Republic, which recognized the field of "labor law, including the legal organization of enterprise, protection of workers and provision of employment"[1] as one of the concurrent

[1] Article 74, par. 12. It is to be noted that "in the field of concurrent legislation,"

powers of the Federal Republic and *Länder*. In the absence of any provisions in the Occupation Statute which bore directly upon the competence of the German authorities to legislate in the labor field, general control of labor relations was thus left largely in the hands of the German federal and *Länder* authorities.

In view of the nature and rapidity of changes and jurisdictional un-certainties since 1945, there are still broad areas in which legislation is either lacking or incomplete. However, the federal and *Länder* governments are moving rapidly to fill the many gaps in labor legisla-tion.[2] At the same time, the High Commission frequently suspended the operation of various of the Control Council laws in individual *Länder* to remove any restrictions which they might impose upon free legislative action in labor matters.[3] In short, while the Bonn Constitu-tion provided the framework and while the revised Occupation Statute and the decisions of the High Commission provided the primary re-strictions, both federal and *Länder* governments by 1951 were filling the remaining legislative vacuums in the labor relations field.[4]

POSTWAR TRADE-UNION REVIVAL

The movement to re-establish the trade unions in Germany was started by the Allied governments shortly after victory had been won. Old trade unionists and well-known antifascists were called from cover to serve as the heads of the first unions, some of which were formed originally on an area basis. Common experience in opposing the Nazis and fear of dissipation of strength through internal division were fac-tors making for unity and for discouragement of an initial organiza-tion of the unions along pre-1933 lines. In contrast to the early policy in the Soviet Zone, where trade-union organization was created by fiat

the *Länder* have the power to legislate so long and so far as the Federation makes no use of its legislative right. Article 72, par. 1. For general comment on Article 72, see Chapter 5 above.

[2] See "Gesetzgebung auf dem Gebiete des Arbeitsrechts," *Recht der Arbeit*, July, 1950, pp. 270 ff.; Oscar Weigert, "Die westdeutsche Arbeitsgesetzgebung unter der Besatzung," *ibid.*, September, 1951, pp. 340-343.

[3] See *ibid.*, June, 1950, p. 233, for action of the Allied High Commission in suspending the operation of Control Council Law No. 22 in Württemberg-Hohen-zollern and Schleswig-Holstein.

[4] Each issue of *Recht der Arbeit*, edited by Professor H. C. Nipperdey, contains a summary of some of the current legislative developments. Significant federal laws passed between 1951 and 1953 include the law for the protection against dis-missals, the law providing for the fixing of minimum employment conditions under certain circumstances, and others.

from above, considerable weight was placed upon initiative from be-low in the establishment of the first unions at the local level in the western zones. Soon after the collapse in 1945 and before the unions were recognized, so-called "shop stewards" appeared in many plants without any official recognition to serve as "spokesmen" for the work-ers.[5] Decrees were soon issued by the military governments which regulated the nomination and election of union officers by popular vote and secret ballot, the formation of federations, and so forth. The unions which finally developed in all three of the western zones were usually of the industrial type. As indicated, the trade unions in the British Zone had at their peak a unified zonal federation. In contrast, in the less industrialized U.S. and French zones separate federations for each *Land* were developed. A loose intrazonal organization was provided in the U.S. Zone, and less formal relationships were grudg-ingly permitted to evolve between the federations in the French Zone.

The trade unions of the three zones were subjected to the ever-increasing internal German pressures to amalgamate. In September, 1949, the seven trade-union federations, three each in the U.S. and French zones and the one federation in the British Zone, voted to dissolve themselves at the end of the year. Various problems in estab-lishing an over-all unified trade-union organization for Western Ger-many were examined by a Preparatory Commission and were finally settled at a convention in Munich on October 12-14, 1949, when the German Trade Union Federation (DGB) was officially founded. Its membership, composed of around 5,000,000 individuals at the end of 1949, was divided into sixteen unions of an industrial or multi-indus-trial character. About 40 per cent of the wage earners in the western zones were thus included in this organization, which began functioning under the chairmanship of the late Hans Boeckler, the former chairman of the Trade Union Federation in the British Zone, and an Executive Committee of twenty-seven members composed of eleven full-time officers and the sixteen chairmen of the affiliated unions. All except a handful of the original members of the Executive Committee had Social Democratic leanings. A few others acknowledged Christian Democratic affiliation. While the DGB has no formal connections with any political party, its members have substantial ties with the Social Democratic party (SPD) and with the left wing of the Christian Democratic Union (CDU); indeed, some 74 per cent of the SPD and

[5] See *Industrial Relations in Germany, 1945-1949*, Cmd. 7923 (Germany No. 1, 1950), pp. 5 ff.; Matthew A. Kelly, "The Reconstitution of the German Trade Union Movement," *Political Science Quarterly*, LXIV (March, 1949), 24-49.

26 per cent of the CDU-CSU representatives in the German *Bundestag* were listed in August, 1951, as trade-union members.[6]

There are several trade-union organizations outside the ranks of the DGB. These include the Salaried Employees Organization (DAG), established in Western Germany in April, 1949, on the basis of a previously existing organization which was created in the British Zone. Some of the membership of the Independent Trade-Union Organization (UGO) in Berlin are also affiliated with the DAG.[7] In addition, there are other groups not affiliated with the DGB, such as the German Civil Servants Federation. As yet there has not been any division of the bulk of German workers and employees into groupings comparable to those prior to 1933. It is true that there has been some demand for the creation of Catholic unions.[8] While the pressure diminished during 1950-1951 in the face of growing Soviet dangers from abroad and declining Communist influence from within, the establishment of independent Christian unions is a possibility which cannot be entirely ignored.[9] The German Trade Union Federation has been accepted in the fold of the international organizations. The DGB and also the UGO were active participants when the non-Communist International Confederation of Free Trade Unions was founded in November, 1949.

The top leaders of the DGB are largely old-line trade unionists who made their mark in the pre-1933 trade-union movement. Originally hand-picked by the military governments in 1945, they owe their present positions to election by the unions. Some of them have shown an unwillingness to encourage youthful leadership in the unions[10] and an incapacity for devolving responsibility on subordinates. Their aver-

---

[6] For comment on the most important differences in policies of the DGB and the Social Democratic party, see Sidney Lens, "Social Democracy and Labor in Germany," *Foreign Policy Reports*, (Nov. 15, 1950), 150.

[7] U.S. Department of Labor, *Notes on Labor Abroad*, No. 13 (Dec., 1949), pp. 31-32; *ibid.*, No. 14 (March, 1950), p. 36.

[8] Cf. the comments in the author's *Labor Relations in Western Germany*, OMGUS Manpower Division Visiting Expert Series No. 2 (1948), p. 11, with comments of Cardinal Frings in *Frankfurter Rundschau*, April 13, 1950. Note also *Industrial Relations in Germany, 1945-1949*, p. 8.

[9] The selection of Walter Freitag as chairman of the DGB at its convention in October, 1952, has been followed by considerable discussion of this possibility. Note especially the "Text of Statement of German Catholic Bishops on Unified Labor Movement," HICOG, *Labor Headline News*, December 19, 1952, pp. 1-2, and the subsequent controversy which this statement provoked.

[10] Cf. Algot Joensson, *Organized Labor and Democracy in Germany*, OMGUS Manpower Division Visiting Expert Series No. 15 (1949), pp. 12 ff., and Alice Hanson Cook, *Bavarian Trade Union Youth*, OMGUS Manpower Division Visiting Expert Series No. 17 (1950).

age age is high. The early evidences of outside assistance have disappeared as the unions have tended to develop a more vigorous internal life of their own. Some of the bureaucratic features of union organization, which were in such marked evidence prior to 1933, are again recognizable, and friendly critics are already foreseeing the same bureaucratic malaise which produced such passivity in 1933 when the unions were dissolved by the Nazis. On the basis of various contacts in Germany with union leaders and members, however, the writer is of the opinion that, despite considerable handicaps, the unions have developed a reasonably healthy and vigorous organizational life.

The early efforts of the Communists to dominate the labor movement in Germany, especially through their control of the shop stewards and the work councils, did not prove successful. The results of elections, both in the unions and in the works councils, show a steady decline of Communist voting strength since 1947. For this development, there are various explanations. The strong opposition measures taken by the western powers, the Marshall Plan, the fate of the trade unions in neighboring countries which fell under the domination of the Soviet Union, and the economic improvement in Germany after the currency reform in 1948 all helped to contribute their share to this decline.[11]

Generally speaking, the program of the trade unions is a mildly Marxist, non-Communist, evolutionary socialist one.[12] The language of the trade-union leaders is today closer to that of Bernstein than to that of the younger Kautsky, and their program is not far removed from one which could be acceptable to British trade unions. The DGB has stressed the need for centralized planning, co-determination, the socialization of extractive industries, the integration into the national economic life of the millions of refugees, freedom of association, the right of collective bargaining, and a uniform labor code.

The early policy of the Allied Military Governments did not permit the formation of employer associations. The history and record of the activities of various members of the old German employers' groups were too fresh in the minds of the authorities in 1945 to allow for any different course of action. The first steps in the re-creation of the employers' associations were those taken in the British Zone in the fall of 1945 when "economic organizations" were permitted in order to

[11] Matthew A. Kelly, "Communists in German Labor Organizations," *Journal of Political Economy*, LVII (June, 1949), 215 ff.

[12] "Konstruktives Gewerkschaftsprogramm," *Die Quelle*, October, 1950, pp. 497-500; cf. Franz L. Neumann, "German Democracy 1950," *International Conciliation*, No. 411 (May, 1950), pp. 266 ff.

furnish advice to the military administration and to pass on to their members governmental instructions.[13] Some organizations consisting of membership from several industries began to form in a clandestine fashion. With the end of the wage stop, a process begun in 1946 and completed in 1948, the need for employers' organizations became more evident, as wage questions made collective bargaining more meaningful. The first employers' organizations openly appeared in the British Zone, where official objections were less evident than in the other two zones. Certain of these early groups, with somewhat variegated purposes, included the Employers' Association Committee of North Rhine–Westphalia, the central office of the Trade Association of Lower Saxony, and the Social Political Committee of Employers' Associations of Greater Hamburg. These were combined into a zonal *Arbeitsgemeinschaft* of employers, with headquarters in Düsseldorf, and served as a zonal counterpart of the zonal Trade Union Federation. At a later date, the same types of organizations began to appear in the U.S. and French zones. Eventually these *Länder* and zonal organizations in the U.S. and British zones were merged in January, 1949, at the bizonal level to form a Working Committee of the Combined Economic Areas. This committee was an important step toward the formation for Western Germany of the Federation of German Employers' Associations.[14] By the middle of 1951, the federation was composed of over 800 member associations.

Thus, under somewhat different names and with some functional divergencies, there had been re-established by the end of 1950 in Western Germany types of organizations representing employers and management which resembled those of pre-Hitler days. These organizations have taken a negative attitude toward most proposals which would increase the control of the government or of labor over industry, especially those which would result either in increasing socialization or in greater employee economic codetermination. As the chair-

[13] D. F. MacDonald, *Employers' Associations in Western Germany,* OMGUS Manpower Division Visiting Expert Series No. 9 (1949), pp. 7 ff.

[14] The relationship between the employers' associations which have sociopolitical functions and the economic associations is a complex one, especially at the lower levels. At the top level in 1951, there were three main "pillars" in the organization of the German economy from the management side. The first of these "pillars" was the aforementioned Federation of German Employers' Associations with its several central functional organizations of employers. The second "pillar" was the German Industry and Commerce Diet, established in October, 1949. The third "pillar" was the Economic and Trade Associations. "Die Organisation der Wirtschaft (Westzonen)," *Der Betriebs-Berater,* April 10, 1950, p. 235. For a comparison with the organization of business in the Weimar Republic, see Franz L. Neumann, *Behemoth* (New York, 1942), pp. 235-240.

man of the Federation of German Employers' Associations said, "the employers' drive is motivated by their fear of losing their managerial prerogatives and rights, particularly the right of managerial free initiative."[15]

COLLECTIVE BARGAINING

It was not until the currency reform of June 20, 1948, and the end of the wage stop on November 3, 1948, that collective bargaining began to acquire a serious content. After these changes in 1948, however, the Bizonal Economic Council, late in 1948, enacted Ordinance No. 68 regarding collective agreements. In essence, this ordinance recognized the binding force of such agreements and permitted the director of the Bizonal Manpower Department to exercise the controversial power of extending under given circumstances the provisions of a collective agreement to an entire industry.[16] After amendments in 1949 which resulted from demands of the military governments and which affected primarily the matter of extension of agreements, the Law on Collective Agreements of April 9, 1949 (No. 11), was finally enacted. In accordance with the provisions of Article 125 of the Basic Law, this Law on Collective Agreements became a federal law applicable within the *Länder* of the British and U.S. zones; and under Article 127 of the Basic Law, its provisions could be extended to the *Länder* of the French Zone with the approval of the *Länder* governments. In the eyes of one member of the DGB, this law contains "nothing fundamental that is new. . . . It is in reality a codification of the results of forty years of experience and legal development."[17] Subsequent records indicate that collective bargaining has again assumed a role of

[15] In *Der Arbeitgeber,* July 15, 1951, pp. 28 ff.; for an expression of the point of view of the Federation of German Employers' Associations on certain matters discussed at the Maria-Laach Conference with the trade-union representatives in 1950, see *Recht der Arbeit,* July, 1950, pp. 267-268.

[16] George Philipp Dietrich, *The Trade Union Role in the Reconstruction of Germany,* OMGUS Manpower Division Visiting Expert Series No. 6 (1949), pp. 13 ff.; *Industrial Relations in Germany, 1945-1949,* p. 14.

[17] "Die gesetzliche Regelung des Tarifvertrages," *Die Quelle,* August-September, 1949, pp. 368-372; Heinz Goldschmidt, "Tarifvertragsgesetz und Allgemeinverbindlichkeit von Tarifverträgen," *Bundesarbeitsblatt,* January, 1950, pp. 14-17. In early 1952 an amendment to the Law on Collective Agreements, which permits the "extension" of collective agreements in cases of "social emergency," was enacted. The amendment, similar to one which was deleted in 1949 in the draft of the original law on the insistence of the British and American Military Governments, was designed to deal primarily with the problems of agricultural workers. Its passage reflects the strength of the "Weimar pattern." U.S. Department of Labor, *Notes on Labor Abroad,* No. 26 (April, 1952), pp. 2 ff.

real significance. In early 1950 two of the most significant collective agreements operative across zonal lines were those which granted wage increases to some 22,000 brown-coal miners and to some 400,000 hard-coal miners.[18]

Implicit in these legal developments has been the transition from *Tarifordnung* to *Tarifvertrag*. Control Council Law No. 40 of November 30, 1946, had nullified the National Labor Law of 1934 under which the Trustees of Labor had been authorized to issue the wage decrees. Most of these authoritarian wage decrees were necessarily continued in effect long after 1945; indeed, some are still in effect today. In the British Zone, the powers of the Nazi Trustees of Labor over wage schedules were entrusted to the presidents of the Regional Labor Offices, and such changes as were made in the wage schedules were approved by them. These officials were assisted in the performance of their duties by advisory councils, on which representatives of the employers and trade unions were included. With the passage of the Law on Collective Contracts in 1949 in the Bizone, this power vested in the *Land* labor officials was withdrawn by action of the British Military Government.[19] Consequently, with the re-creation of the unions and employer organizations and with the acceptance of collective bargaining, the *Tarifvertrag* is again the recognized legal instrument for determining wages and work conditions.[20] In this development lies one of the most marked evidences of the return from the Third Reich to the Weimar Republic.

The collective wage agreements in Germany today usually provide for termination dates from four to six months after the dates on which they go into effect. After the Korean conflict, however, a small but increasing number of collective agreements began incorporating provisions which permit either party to terminate them before the designated date if consumer prices rise or drop beyond a certain point. These provisions differ from "escalator clauses" in collective agreements in the United States in that the adjustments are not automatic but have to depend upon contract renegotiation.

CONCILIATION AND ARBITRATION

Another glance back to the Weimar Republic was made in Control

---

[18] *2nd Quarterly Report on Germany*, Office of the U.S. High Commissioner for Germany (Frankfurt, 1950), p. 14.

[19] *Recht der Arbeit*, February, 1950, p. 71.

[20] The relationships between new *Tarifverträge* and the existing *Tarifordnungen* (which were to be replaced by the former) were covered in Article 9 of the Law on Collective Agreements of April 9, 1949.

Council Law No. 35 providing for the establishment of conciliation and arbitration machinery in the *Länder*. In the absence of federal legislation, Law No. 35, except where suspended by action of the Allied High Commission, continues in effect with such implementation as it has received in *Länder* legislation.[21] While numerous conciliation and arbitration agencies had been set up and while there has been some growing use made of them during the most recent period, only limited resort to these devices was in evidence up to 1948. Several reasons may be ascribed for this neglect. One was their relatively recent creation. Up to currency reform in 1948, there was little occasion to resort to conciliation and arbitration. A more basic factor was the lack in some quarters of acceptance of, or understanding for, conciliation and arbitration arrangements based on voluntary agreement in the absence of detailed statutory provisions—that is to say, a lack of sympathy for British and U.S. efforts to direct German thinking away from the compulsory features of the network of arbitration and conciliation agencies set up in accordance with the decree of October 30, 1923.[22] Thus, in 1950, one of the *Land* arbitration laws, that of South Baden, illustrated a tendency in the *Länder* of the French Zone "to re-create arbitration procedures on the basis of the accepted pre-1933 thought and practice," especially in permitting the compulsory participation of parties and the compulsory imposition of awards.[23] On the other hand, at the Hattenheimer Conference in January, 1950, representatives of both the trade unions and employers' organizations agreed that a "Reich law on arbitration was not absolutely necessary in the immediate future" and that state compulsion in this field was inconsistent with "responsible social self-administration."[24]

RE-ESTABLISHMENT OF LABOR COURTS

German labor courts have been successfully reconstituted in all three of the western zones along essentially pre-1933 lines.[25] The jurisdiction of this special system of courts, which includes disputes involving collective agreements between employers and employees, is somewhat broader than that of the courts under the Labor Court Act of 1926. By 1951 legislation had been passed in certain of the

[21] For illustrations, see *Labor Relations in Western Germany*, pp. 5, 16-17, 23-24. See also Chapter 9 above.

[22] *Industrial Relations in Germany, 1945-1949*, p. 15.

[23] Hessel, "Das neue Badische Schlichtungsgesetz," *Recht der Arbeit*, April, 1950, p. 134.

[24] *Ibid.*, February, 1950, p. 68. See note 17 above.

[25] Cf. the author's "National Socialism and the German Labor Courts," *Journal of Politics*, III (May, 1941), 169 ff.

Länder, especially in the U.S. and French zones, to implement and supplement Control Council Law No. 21, a law which embodied with some important variations the main features of the Act of 1926. Otherwise, as in the *Länder* of the British Zone, the labor courts were set up on the basis of the authorization of Control Council Law No. 21 without any specific legislative action by the *Länder.*

The chief criticisms of the labor courts as they were thus established were directed at the three-year term for labor court judges (by the judges themselves), the lack of the required legal training of the judges (by the legally trained judges), the sharp separation of the labor courts from the ordinary courts, and the control over the courts by the ministers of labor rather than by the ministers of justice (by employers and by certain of the legally trained labor court judges). All parties have been critical for one reason or another of the lack of a supreme labor court. Exclusion of lawyers from the labor courts of first instance is the solution to a question which has been controversial from the beginning and which has provoked expected reactions from many lawyers and legally trained judges.[26] Although several preliminary moves were made to establish a supreme labor court,[27] there is as yet no provision for one. Among the *Länder* labor courts considerable reliance must be placed upon meetings of the judges and professional writings in the field of labor law to produce some uniformity.[28] The legal situation has consequently been chaotic, and courts have continued to decide cases involving questions of occupational risk of the enterprise, protection against dismissal, and so forth in quite contradictory ways. Conflicting decisions in applying *Länder* legislation to the personnel of such agencies as the federal railways[29] have created uncertainties. On the whole, however, the activities of labor courts have met with the approval of all interested parties in Germany.

[26] *Der Betriebs-Berater,* February 20, 1950, p. 119; cf. the discussion of this point in "Zur Reform der Arbeitsgerichtsbarkeit," *ibid.,* May 20, 1950, pp. 342-344.

[27] Article 96, par. 1, of the Basic Law provides that "high federal courts shall be established in the spheres of ordinary, administrative, finance, labor and social jurisdiction." A labor court bill which included provision for the establishment of a federal labor court as an independent appeals tribunal was introduced in Parliament in 1952, and in April, 1953, federal Labor Minister Storch anticipated its passage during the "current *Bundestag* session." HICOG, *Labor Headline News,* August 28, 1952, p. 3; October 22, 1952, pp. 3-4; April 10, 1953, p. 1.

[28] Note the program of the Conference of Presidents and Chairmen of *Land* Labor Courts on April 20-22, 1950. *Recht der Arbeit,* April, 1950, p. 149.

[29] Cf. the decision of the *Land* Labor Court of Frankfurt am Main, LAG, IV 130/50 (June 27, 1950), with that of the *Land* Labor Court of Stuttgart, LAG, II Sa 243/49 (Nov. 11, 1949).

WORKS COUNCILS AND CODETERMINATION

The works councils, which have been established in all of the *Länder* in Western Germany, have roots in the developments which preceded the Works Council Law of 1920. Though the works councils under this law did not achieve many of the objectives for which their more radical sponsors had hoped, especially the socialization of the economy, they nevertheless did establish institutional precedents which endured. After World War II, works councils were recognized officially during the spring of 1946 through Control Council Law No. 22. As compared to the law of 1920, Law No. 22 contained several provisions which increased the degree of union control over the works councils. The Control Council Law left most functions of the works councils to be determined by negotiation with the workshop managements and, largely as a result of pressure from the trade unions, it was supplemented by legislation in a number of the west German *Länder* from 1947 to 1951.[30] Schleswig-Holstein, with the passage of a law in May, 1950, and Bavaria with one in October, 1950, were late additions to other *Länder* in the U.S. Zone and to the three *Länder* in the French Zone which have enacted special works council legislation. The most advanced provisions were those included in such early legislation as that of Hesse of May 31, 1948, which provided for employee codetermination in social, personnel, and economic matters. The most controversial aspects of this legislation involved the economic codetermination provisions for employee participation in the board of directors which decides upon the economic policies of the enterprise and the like.

Because of the significance of the codetermination controversy in Germany, some special observations may be justified regarding it. In the first place, the demand for "codetermination" is not basically different from that for "economic democracy" during the early days of the Weimar period. Both slogans, then and today, implied an important degree of employee participation in the control of various activities of the enterprise. Second, the U.S. Military Government in September, 1948, suspended the operation of the economic codetermination provisions of the Hesse and Württemberg-Baden laws on the stated grounds that future unity would be jeopardized if each *Land* were permitted to pass its own works council legislation, incorporating economic codetermination prior to the establishment of a central

[30] For a comparison of the provisions of this legislation, see HICOG R-1534-1 August 1950 1 C (Chart). Note the discussion of one aspect of this *Länder* legislation by Rolf Dietz, "Betriebsratsmitglieder im Aufsichtsrat, nach den heute geltenden Landesgesetzen," *Der Betriebs-Berater,* June 30, 1950, pp. 454-456.

government in the west. After the federal government had begun its operations in September, 1949, the *Bundestag* requested a draft law from the government dealing with the right of codetermination. The federal minister of labor made several unsuccessful efforts to get the union and employer groups to agree on a common proposal. In consequence of these repeated delays, the U.S. High Commissioner on April 7, 1950, revoked the suspension of the provisions of the legislation in Hesse and Württemberg-Baden, much to the delight of the trade unionists and to the dissatisfaction of employer groups.[31]

Third, in 1950 and 1951, there were several major proposals on codetermination which emanated from various quarters in Western Germany. Special mention might be made of those which came from the German Trade Union Federation, the Social Democratic party, the CDU-CSU coalition in the *Bundestag*, the federal Ministry of Labor, and the Federation of German Employers' Associations.[32] The plans presented by the German Trade Union Federation and the Federation of German Employers' Associations would have applied beyond the plant level, that is, they involved the adoption of possible district, *Land* and federal economic councils. The gradations of influence and control to be vested in the works councils ranged in these proposals from the right of information, through consultation and co-operation, to codetermination. Generally speaking, the unions have favored very wide codetermination in social, personnel, and economic matters, as well as equal representation with the employers in the supervisory agencies of the larger plants. The employers' associations would limit the role of the works councils to the provision of information, consultation, and co-operation and would exclude the works councils from codetermination in economic matters.

Fourth, the early hopes of the Communists to use the works councils as levers in the attainment of their objectives in Western Germany have been dashed by the results of works councils elections since 1947. The statistics of the Hamburg area, with its traditional Communist strength among the dockworkers, showed a decline between 1947 and 1948 from 392 to 192 Communist works councils members. Evidence from 1948 to the present time indicates continued (though,

[31] *3rd Quarterly Report on Germany*, Office of the U.S. High Commissioner for Germany (Frankfurt, 1950), p. 38. In effect, this action represented a State Department reversal of the policies approved by General Clay. See HICOG, Historical Division, *Labor Problems in West Germany* (1952), pp. 37 ff., especially note 112.

[32] HICOG R-1534-1 August 1950 1 C (Chart). Cf. *Betriebs-Berater,* September 10, 1950, pp. 646-649; *Sopade,* August, 1950, pp. 4-15; *Arbeit und Freiheit,* August, 1950, pp. 7-8.

during the elections in 1951, decreasing) losses by the Communists in works councils elections, resulting from improved trade-union election tactics and from the general factors which have been responsible for the decline in Communist strength.[33] As a result, some of the early postwar beliefs that the control and objectives of the works councils might jeopardize the attainment of the aims of the trade unions are no longer as seriously held as they once were.[34] The chief reservations in trade-union quarters as to the desirability of codetermination at the plant level have accordingly disappeared, and the union leaders now agree that the works councils should play an important role, albeit subsidiary to the unions, in the future control of German industry.

Finally, agreements on certain other issues, which may prove of considerable importance in the future, have developed from the efforts of the unions and employers' organizations to work out a compromise on codetermination above the plant level. For example, agreement was reached on the creation of *Land* and federal economic councils or chambers which will be composed of equal numbers of employers and employees.[35] Suggestions from Chancellor Adenauer for the creation of a federal economic council have been received in DGB circles as "the first step towards fulfillment of the trade union demands for codetermination on supra-plant levels."[36] Obviously, such a system of advisory councils is a far cry from that envisaged under Article 165 of the Weimar Constitution, but they could, nevertheless, prove to be important instruments in the future handling of labor relations problems.

But by far the most significant development in the federal field up to 1951 was the enactment of legislation to provide for codetermination in the coal-mining and iron and steel industries. By the fall of 1950, the plans to terminate the Allied control of the iron and steel companies, in the supervisory agencies of which the trade unions had occupied an important place, left the unions faced with the possibility of a loss of this position—in other words, with a loss of their existing rights of codetermination.[37] With no immediate national legis-

[33] *Arbeit und Freiheit*, August, 1950, pp. 9 ff.; *New York Times*, June 17, 1951, p. 19. For more recent reports, see HICOG, *Labor Headline News*, May 4, 1953, p. 3; May 26, 1953, p. 1.

[34] Note the able discussion on this point in Paul Fischer, *Works Councils in Germany*, HICOG Office of Labor Affairs Visiting Expert Series No. 18 (1951), pp. 18-32.

[35] *3rd Quarterly Report on Germany*, Office of the U.S. High Commissioner for Germany (Frankfurt, 1950), p. 38.

[36] HICOG, *Labor Headline News*, August 24, 1951, p. 2.

[37] For a brief discussion of the role of the unions in the boards of directors of

lation in sight, a strike vote was taken by the metalworkers in November, 1950, and by the mineworkers in January, 1951, to compel a guarantee of certain demanded powers of codetermination. Faced by these strikes, Chancellor Adenauer, after various conferences, made certain commitments regarding the provisions of a bill which was drafted by the federal cabinet. With several important changes in parliament, the bill was finally enacted after considerable political maneuvering by the *Bundestag* on April 10, 1951.[38]

The legislation, as enacted, applies to coal mining and to iron and steel enterprises which employ over 1,000 persons. The board of directors (*Aufsichtsrat*) of each enterprise is to consist of eleven members, five selected by the owners and five by labor. Two of the labor members are to be chosen by the works councils, and the three others by the national unions. A very complicated procedure was devised for the selection of the crucial eleventh member, an arrangement which labor leaders have bitterly criticized as favoring the ownership directors. In addition, special provisions were included to assure that the personnel manager, one of the members of the management committee, should meet the approval of the labor directors. After each company is released from the control of the occupation authorities, the provisions of this "codetermination law" are to apply.

Hardly had the ink dried on this controversial statute before other unions began to present demands. Employees in the chemical and railway enterprises, backed by the DGB, moved into the vanguard of the movement to secure an extension to their industries of codetermination arrangements comparable to those provided in coal-mining and iron and steel industries. The meaning of this new legislation and of these current demands cannot be finally evaluated today, but their significance should not be underestimated.[39] On one point the conclu-

---

the "severance companies" set up in 1947, consult *6th Quarterly Report on Germany*, Office of the U.S. High Commissioner for Germany (Frankfurt, 1951), pp. 61-66.

[38] A good English translation of this "Law concerning Codetermination in the Boards of Directors and Executive Management of Enterprises in the Mining and in the Iron and Steel-producing Industries" may be found in HICOG, *Labor Headline News*, April 11, 1951, pp. 2-7; for an excellent analysis of this law, see William H. McPherson, "Codetermination: Germany's Move toward a New Economy," *Industrial and Labor Relations Review*, V (Oct., 1951), 20ff. Cf. Gerhard Bold, "Das Mitbestimmungsrecht im Eisen und Kohle," *Recht der Arbeit*, May, 1951, pp. 159-174.

[39] After a bitter struggle, marked by strike action and the strong opposition of the Social Democratic party in both houses of the German Parliament, a general "Law Concerning the Reorganization of the Relations between Employees and Employers" was passed by the *Bundestag* on July 19, 1952, and by the *Bundesrat* on July 30,

sion of a competent critic merits quotation: "Codetermination ... may be more likely to reduce than to increase the probability of any future adoption of socialism. It is scarcely socialistic in character, for it involves no change in the identity of ownership and no increase in the authority or functions of government. ... Codetermination might be regarded as a step toward syndicalism but certainly not toward state socialism."[40]

CONCLUSION

By way of summary, the most significant characteristic of the present system of labor relations is its basic similarity to that which emerged during the first decade after the defeat of Germany in World War I. Collective bargaining, based on relative freedom of association, labor courts, conciliation and arbitration agencies, and works councils provide a collectivity of official agencies and procedures which are reminiscent of the earlier ones existing in 1928.

But the setting is different in that Germany is now divided territorially between an East and a West, and there are still other dissimilarities between the institutions of today and those which functioned over three decades ago. Among these might be mentioned the fact that the parties today, a least on the trade-union side, are not as divided either organizationally or ideologically as they were in 1928. For this and other reasons, the union's position is potentially stronger than under the Weimar Republic. Furthermore, national legislation in the field of labor relations has not as yet extended to some of the areas which were covered by legislation in 1928. For this situation there is one very simple explanation, namely, the shortness of time during which the Basic Law has been in effect. At the same time there may also be slightly less faith in the efficiency of legislative enactments and less determination to smother the field of labor rela-

---

1952. The law provided for the setting up of works councils in all "establishments employing as a rule not less than 5 permanent employees." The works councils, ranging in size from 1 to 35, were to be representative of the wage earners and the salaried employees, as well as of the sexes, in so far as possible according to their numerical strength. In addition to general tasks, the works councils were given specified responsibilities in social affairs, personnel affairs, and economic affairs. One-third of the members of the board of directors of each company must consist of employee representatives, provisions of the law to which the DGB took violent exception as providing inadequate labor representation. An acceptable unofficial English translation of the law is included in HICOG, *Labor Headline News,* Special Issue, August 11, 1952. See *ibid.,* March 23, 1953, p. 2, for reference to the executive ordinance for carrying out the works council elections.

[40] McPherson, *op. cit.,* p. 31.

tions with statutory provisions. The sustained efforts of the British, U.S., and French manpower officials to encourage the Germans to allow a broader sphere than formerly for voluntary co-operation on a nonlegislative basis may have borne some fruit. There are also important differences in the structure of the agencies operative then and now. For example, there is less state compulsion possible under the arbitration provisions effective in most of Western Germany than in 1928; labor court judges, who may or may not be legally trained today, are operating administratively under the aegis of labor rather than of justice ministers, and there is no national court of appeal in labor matters; the works councils today are not separated for workers and salaried employees, as they were under the law of 1920.

In terms of their objectives, the occupation powers have probably been more successful in Germany in the labor relations field than in any other. A part of the explanation lies in the fact that here Germany had a reasonably satisfactory precedent to which she might turn and one which the Allied military authorities were willing to see resurrected. The encouragement and support offered the trade unions during their formative years have left an organization which, comparatively considered, furnishes today one of the strongest numerically, best organized, most vigorously anti-Nazi and anti-Communist (despite its Communist membership), and most consistently pro-western (despite its nationalistic meanderings) forces in Western Germany. In short, these achievements in the field of labor relations can be attributed in large part to the fact that Germans were permitted to build upon German foundations.

Though there were frequent threats and vigorous flurries from time to time, the years from 1945 to 1950 were relatively peaceful in the labor relations sphere. Up to the currency reform and the suspension of the wage stop in 1948, there was little solid ground for employer-employee disagreements. Furthermore, during this early period the employers' organizations, as a result of their late revival, were weaker than the trade unions as bargaining agencies. The presence and the role of the occupation powers, whose objectives demanded industrial peace, certainly helped discourage industrial unrest. A rapid improvement in economic conditions since 1948, with the industrial production index in February, 1951, at 132 (1936 = 100), coupled with the rapid return to German hands of control over various phases of its economy, probably helped to hold down industrial unrest. Considerable weight must also be given to the moderating role of the leaders of the trade unions, which originally favored an "energetic price policy" and other governmental reforms rather than a wage struggle, and also to that of the employers' organizations, which have not wished to jeopardize other objectives by economic war.

However, it was clearly evident by the middle of 1951 that there were difficulties ahead, as both the trade unions and employer organizations began to feel their strength and to throw off overt evidences of friendship which could formerly be artifically produced at joint meetings sponsored by the occupation authorities. On August 28, 1950, Germany's hardest and most important post-war strike began. Spearheaded by the walkout of 20,000 Frankfurt building construction workers, who demanded an increase in hourly wages, the strike spread rapidly to other parts of Germany after negotiations at the federal level to solve the dispute had failed. The strike was finally settled on September 9, after an arbitration board had awarded a 10 per cent increase in hourly wages to the workers.[41] The metalworkers and coal miners in the Ruhr later indicated their willingness to strike on the codetermination issue. Subsequent strike moves and threats, including one in August and September, 1951, involving 50,000 metalworkers in Hesse, assumed serious proportions. In the quarter ending September 30, 1950, the second round of wage increases was begun, with approximately 2,700,000 clerical and manual workers receiving increases of around 10 per cent.

To judge by statements emanating from the DGB and the Federation of German Employer's Associations, the tension between the major parties was definitely growing in 1950.[42] Various steps were taken by the Adenauer government to avoid serious developments. On April 9, 1951, for example, Chancellor Adenauer met in Bonn for the first time with union and employer representatives to discuss various social and economic measures of the government. On August 21, 1951, Christian Fette, the successor to Hans Boeckler as chairman of the German Trade Union Federation, held his first meeting with Walter Raymond, the chairman of the Federation of German Employer's Associations, to discuss "a higher standard of living and the economic bases of the present wage situation."[43] But these and other efforts can hardly conceal the frictions which can well be deepened in the period

[41] *Handelsblatt*, September 11, 1950; *4th Quarterly Report on Germany*, Office of the U.S. High Commissioner for Germany (Frankfurt, 1950), p. 29.

[42] Cf. *Die Neue Zeitung*, September 22, 1950, for the DGB and the *Süddeutsche Zeitung*, October 14, 1950, for the Federation of German Employers' Associations.

[43] *Frankfurter Neue Presse*, August 22, 1951; see also "Offener Brief an Herrn Christian Fette von Dr. Walter Raymond," *Der Arbeitgeber*, September 15, 1951, pp. 8-9.

immediately ahead—especially in the light of organized labor's increasingly aggressive demands for wage adjustments.[44]

The control of labor relations in the German Federal Republic is now almost entirely in the hands of the Germans themselves. Additional changes in the already revised Occupation Statute and the abolition of such agencies as the International Ruhr Authority will further reduce the jurisdiction of the occupation powers.[45] Under these circumstances, the Germans will have an opportunity not only to evaluate for themselves the present strength and weaknesses but also to determine the future evolution of their system of labor relations.

[44] The year 1952 and the first half of 1953 were marked by a number of actual and threatened strikes. The general position of the DGB at the end of 1952 was that the gross national product had been increasing and that in view of the very low (though rising) real wages of labor major adjustments were necessary. The position of the average laborer has been directly affected by the tax policy of the government, which has been directed more immediately toward an increase of exports and investments rather than consumption.

[45] In April, 1952, the U.S. Office of Labor Affairs of HICOG was replaced by the Office of Labor Attaché. See *Labor Problems of West Germany*, p. 90. The nature of the more recent developments is indicated by the designation of the U.S. High Commissioner as "Ambassador" in June, 1953.

15

Health and Welfare

HERTHA KRAUS

HEALTH and welfare services have been an important activity of German government for many years, predominantly on the local and regional levels. Community services, frequently nation-wide, tax supported, and based on social legislation of long standing, form a weighty sector of a government whose structure has changed rather little since the days of the Weimar Republic. Under the impact of tremendous population movements, of a lost war, of destruction and widespread loss of property, an increasing part of the population is vitally affected by the quality of its functioning.

Of a population of roughly 48,000,000 people, at least 16 per cent[1] have moved in from outside the present territory—expellees and refugees in need of new homes, employment, and reliable means of support and also in need of personal adjustment to a difficult and complex situation, affecting every aspect of their lives. In addition to the common and repetitive needs of ill health, chronic disability, unemployment, homelessness, and destitution, new and poignant needs have developed among all population groups personally or indirectly affected by war events and have called for the organization and operation of new community services. Other needs have become more widely spread, largely owing to war-related events. They represent greater pressures, affect many more people, and are thus an increased challenge to the traditional services. Between 11,000,000 to 12,000,000

[1] *Statistiche Berichte,* published by *Statistische Amt des Vereinigten Wirtschafts- gebietes,* June 29, 1950.

people[2] now derive their major income from social assistance and social insurance benefits; at least 5,000,000 family units[3] are housed in temporary quarters only or under conditions of overcrowding or family separation that call for prompt remedy. While they continue to wait for the achievements of the government housing program, which is handicapped by lack of investment capital, their needs call for temporary measures, inadequate at the best but still urgently needed, providing support and emergency solutions.

The various victims of political persecution, of war and war-related events, have developed highly organized self-help groups; and although they may represent special and frequently conflicting interests, their demands have become increasingly articulate.[4] In response to such pressures some variations of traditional social policy have been introduced, certain new services have been developed. Other variations of the traditional services reflect essential adjustments to postwar changes in the total governmental structure; still others, though not very numerous and of rather minor significance, result from specific requests of the occupying powers and reflect their policy decisions.[5]

All told, the structure and patterns of postwar services in health and welfare, under public auspices, do not vary greatly from the earlier pattern: nor have their conceptual backgrounds changed sufficiently to warrant their independent study. In order to understand present and future trends and to see them with reasonable accuracy and in true perspective, it seems essential to review briefly their historic developments.

THE PERIOD OF THE EMPIRE

Ever since Bismarck's days the German government has operated two parallel service programs[6] which deal with certain recognized

[2] *Nachrichtendienst des Deutschen Vereins für Öffentliche und Private Fürsorge*, July, 1950; report of the German National Committee to the International Conference of Social Work. The quoted figures include the beneficiaries of the Emergency Aid Program (*Soforthilfe*).

[3] *Ibid.*

[4] See, among others, the *Conference Report of the First National Conference of Self Help and Mutual Aid Associations* (Frankfurt am Main, Sept., 1950).

[5] For example, the abolition of categorical public assistance and the transfer to the State Employment Service of assistance to the unemployed.

[6] According to another classification of a third type of program may be added, offering pensions in recognition of damages suffered in connection with meritorious service (*Versorgung*). Claims for public aid in the form of such pensions, not to be based on individual need or on contributions in money, have been presented increasingly in recent years, especially by the victims of persecution, war, and war-related events.

needs on the basis of national legislation—a nation-wide scheme of social assistance, rather uniform in character, and another, also nation-wide, of social insurance, extremely complex in structure and developing gradually by numerous additions and amendments.

Social Assistance—The federal law on Legal Settlement for Public Assistance (*Unterstützungs-Wohnsitz-Gesetz* v. 6.6.1870–UWG) had required all states to establish within their boundaries a complete network of public aid centers on two levels of government, local and regional. The local center (*Bezirksfürsorgeverband*)[7] had to function through local self-government, operating through a municipal department to which the state function of public assistance was delegated. A self-government unit on the regional level (*Landesfürsorgeverband*) became responsible for the reimbursement of expenditures incurred for clients without local settlement and for the operation of a number of institutional services for long-time care. Thus all cities and towns and also the rural units (*Kreise*) maintained a Public Welfare Department as a center of all public aid activities. This would, in addition to administering public assistance to individuals and families in their own homes, also be responsible for the management of various institutions, including hospitals, shelters, and other community services, developed independently of national or state legislation, on local initiative.

Social Insurance—First introduced by the Imperial Message of 1881, an equally complete but much more intricate network of specialized social insurance facilities has been developed through independent local and regional channels, operating agencies of its own. Health insurance, established since 1883, has the most numerous and most decentralized set of local units; the *Ortskrankenkasse* is the most important, servicing the largest population group and rendering certain auxiliary services to several other branches of social insurance. Workmen's compensation (*Unfallversicherung*), established since 1884; the social insurance funds of the miners (*Knappschaftsversicherung*) and of other occupational groups; employees' insurance for the salaried white-collar group (*Angestelltenversicherung*), developed since 1911 —each created its own channels.

The multiplicity of schemes and of operating agencies, highly confusing to the outsider, reflects the German tradition of utilizing within the public and compulsory social insurance schemes, as far as possible, existent mutual aid, such as trade and industrial associations, thus al-

---

[7] Instead of the original, slightly different terminology using consistently the term *Arm* (pauper), the current designations are used in the text. They were first introduced by legislation in 1924 and are still in use.

lowing for flexibility and self-governing operations. In contrast to these plans, old age, disability, and survivors insurance (*Altersund Invalidenversicherung*), initiated in 1889 and expanded significantly in 1911, represents a highly centralized plan, operating largely through regional, multiple-purpose units (*Landesversicherungsanstalt*—LVA), which have through the years been given an increasingly wide and important range of functions.

While this is not the place for reviewing the validity of the original German social insurance pattern—its gradual expansion and its various setbacks, its growing need for simplification or standardization if not for unification—one of its major contributions to the total of public health and welfare services should be underlined. Social insurance benefits and services for the majority of the disabled and handicapped, for the support of most of the aged, widows, and orphans, and for those temporarily out of work because of disabling illness provided an important freedom from heavy financial responsibilities to German local welfare departments, a freedom enjoyed in a far slighter degree, if at all, by other countries during the early part of this century. Any comparative study of service programs should not fail to appreciate the meaning of such freedom from chronic financial pressures with a top-ranking priority. It accounts largely for Germany's formerly high social welfare potential and for her early interest in more differentiated services.

Many large and medium-sized German cities had indeed developed, before the period of the Weimar Republic, quite progressive welfare and health services and considerable social experimentation far beyond the meager minimum as required by the 1870 law. Their status as self-governing units, implemented by substantial tax powers and other local revenues, as well as greater freedom gained by social insurance, made it possible for the interested cities to establish pioneer health and welfare services. With strong and articulate citizen participation[8] and under outstanding socially minded leadership, they initiated or supported, among others, modern public day-care centers for children, public health centers for mothers and infants, convalescent care for children and adults, vocational counseling and guidance, public employment service and vocational rehabilitation for tubercular

[8] The municipal system of self-government, revived and strengthened in 1808, has assigned to the "voluntary" citizen a rather important place in all of German local government. In the social welfare area (up to 1933) highly respected unpaid officials were used in large numbers with the intention of humanizing and localizing public aid. For a brief interpretation, particularly of the famous Elberfeld system, see Hertha Kraus, "Lay Participation in Social Work from the Point of View of Public Agencies," *Public Health Nursing*, October, 1934.

and mental patients and for other persons with serious handicaps. They also established nonprofit, public small-loan services, collective professional guardianship for children born out of wedlock (*Berufsvormundshaft*), rehabilitative work camps for transients (*Wanderarbeitsstätten*), and many other modern units far too numerous to list.

Health Services—The ever-growing expenditures of a comprehensive social insurance system and its nation-wide records of the actual cost of disabling illness and premature death demonstrated the potential significance of prevention, of early diagnosis, and of comprehensive treatment, aiming at the very causes of these conditions. At the same time recent discoveries of medical science indicated new ways and means by which some injuries might be brought under control or even completely prevented. All these factors created a favorable climate for social experimentation and for an expanding and increasingly balanced health and welfare program under public auspices. Nation-wide coverage of social insurance and social assistance, nation-wide expenditures, nation-wide statistics, indicating the very large numbers of people in need of attention and the large numbers of health incidents, were in general taken as adequate proof for accepting public responsibility for further expansion of resources in line with social change and modern technology.

Municipal health departments, gradually emerging as separate units from the public welfare departments, in charge of sanitation, health inspection, public hospitals and laboratories, immediately put newly won scientific knowledge to the test for the improvement of the common lot. They acquired high status, always interested in obtaining first-rate personnel and first-rate equipment, in eager competition with each other and with the more limited number of voluntary nonprofit hospitals. Municipal hospitals in Germany had escaped the long shadow of the almshouse, of the city hospital for the paupers. Thanks to public assistance and to health and disability insurance, all of which in Germany covered the cost of hospital care, they were also widely free from the responsibility for unpaid service to the needy sick. They could count on a regular income for most of their services as offered to the entire population.

Changing Social Concepts—While progress was by no means uniform and very often did not touch rural areas or small towns, the influence of progressive cities with a dynamic social welfare program began to be felt all over the country. There was a lively exchange of thought and experience carried on especially under the auspices of the German Association for Public and Private Welfare[9] founded in 1880

[9] For many years the association has carried on a very comprehensive publica-

(*Deutscher Verein für Öffentliche und Private Fürsorge*). The association, under farsighted leadership, offered a common meeting ground in which directors of public health and welfare agencies, city and county commissioners, and federal, state, and local government officials would meet freely with the leaders of voluntary services of every type and background. In its annual conferences, in the meetings of its permanent executive committee and of many subcommittees working on current studies and legislative drafts, slowly but consistently the underlying concepts of social welfare were changed and new objectives established. Leadership contributed by social administrators from progressive cities, taking an active part in these deliberations over many years, brought convincing illustrations from their own tested, but in many ways still experimental, service units. Such services might be expanded and become much more widely available only if changing legislation would interpret changing concepts and provide authority and funds to apply them on a nation-wide scale. The practices of the leading cities, but only theirs, expressed a continuously broadening concept of public responsibility for modern social welfare: a new interest in raising the standard of living of the working population who helped to produce so much of the nation's wealth; new opportunities for everyone for better health, better vocational and professional education, for better homes and part-time supplements of family homes as needed—all of these to be less and less dependent on individual ability to pay for service.

This was in marked contrast to public assistance traditions based on the 1870 law and also to the attitudes of Bismarck and his contemporaries who had conceived of social insurance as a happy means of narrowing the gap between the "haves" and "have nots." Primarily they had hoped to eliminate much of the economic insecurity inherent in industrial employment and urban living which gave the working population a constant reason for fighting an aggressive capitalist society. Social insurance, as seen by Bismarck, was planned as an instrument to undermine the very base on which the theory of permanent class conflict was built. He hoped to weaken essentially, if not actually to destroy, the labor movement. Early social policy was thus definitely planned to serve the ends of the dominant groups and of

---

tion program. This includes numerous social studies of functional areas and of legislative materials, detailed reports on their annual meetings, and basic commentaries on social legislation. Its monthly magazine provides important current information and authoritative studies on legislative plans and is considered the best informed source of information: *Nachrichtendienst des Deutschen Vereins für Offentliche und Private Fürsorge.*

the state which in a paternalistic manner tried to reconcile a substantial part of its population to its plans and actions. Much of the early labor legislation in Germany, of laws on public health and sanitation, followed the same line.

Social pioneering in urban communities and a new awareness of the inevitable interdependence of all groups had gradually revealed the necessity for equalizing opportunities far beyond prevalent traditions. Experience of modern services based on local experimentation in selected cities during the last years of German monarchy and legislative drafts for expanding such activities on a nation-wide scale were already available at the outbreak of World War I. A national conference of the German Association for Public and Private Welfare, meeting in 1913 in Stuttgart, approved the basic outline of a completely modernized National Public Welfare Bill in substitution for the outdated Welfare Law of 1870. Much of this material entered into the new social legislation of the Weimar Republic.

DEVELOPMENTS DURING WEIMAR

World War I brought the breakdown of the monarchy and of the paternal role of feudal benefactors especially in social welfare activities in rural areas and small towns. It built up the influence of the working man, of the urban dweller, of women. A combination of these factors made it possible for the young Weimar Republic, in a period of rapid change, to establish promptly the legislative basis for an integrated and rather complete set of health and welfare services—modern in concept—under public auspices.

The Weimar Republic thus brought to fruition a growth of many years. Changes in concept and in social design became more widely acceptable in a period of transition which aimed at recognizing more fully the right and dignity of the common man and also his pressing needs. The needy were now also a much more numerous group than in prewar times, expanded by various categories of victims of war and inflation; they were predominantly people in excellent standing in their own communities, much better known and more highly respected than the traditional "poor" at the bottom of the social ladder. Needs affecting one's neighbors, friends, and colleagues or one's own family became truly important and demanded attention. The political climate was favorable to action. The vanishing capital of the insurance funds, of the charitable foundations and city trusts, of the voluntary institutions and agencies, and, last but not least, the multitudes of victims of war and of inflation[10] made action imperative.

[10] Because uncontrolled inflation created emergency conditions in 1923, the

Two basic federal laws of 1922 and 1924 (the Federal Law for Child and Youth Welfare [*Reichgesetz für Jugendwohlfahrt* v. 9.7.1922 –RJWG] and the Federal Law on the Responsibility for Public Aid [*Reichsverodnung über die Fürsogepflicht* v. 13.2.1924–RVF] and the introduction of unemployment insurance in 1927 provided the legal framework for the modernized health and welfare services of the Weimar Republic. With minor changes and after removing modifications introduced during the Hitler period, this Weimar legislation and the two national social insurance laws of 1911 are still in effect.

In accordance with German tradition, the federal laws established jurisdictional units and defined the population groups and needs to which they apply. They also spell out in some detail basic principles which should underlie their operations, without calling for specific procedure. The states, in turn, were expected to supplement the framework of federal legislation, filling in some details applicable to their own areas. Both federal and state legislation, however, would leave the self-governing units on the local and regional levels rather free to interpret the legislative objectives and principles in different ways and to provide their own services beyond the mandatory minimum, in interpretation of optional requirements and of over-all service objectives.

Relationship between Public and Private Agencies—For the first time in German legislation, public agencies were reminded of the importance of close co-operation between the public and the voluntary agencies. Public agencies on the local level were given the responsibility for co-operative planning and for serving as a continuing center for such planning (RJWG, par. 11, and RVF, par. 5). Under these laws public agencies were free to delegate individual services or entire service programs to responsible private agencies—just as federal and state government in Germany have always delegated functions to the local or regional self-governmental units. Such delegation, however, implied compensation for expenses involved. This policy has related voluntary German agencies to the public agencies in a peculiar way: many, if not the majority, of the services which they produce are performed for specified payments, usually on a per capita or per diem basis. Such fees frequently become a matter of negotiation, especially in times of rising costs. And while the voluntary and public

---

Reich was given special authorization for legislation introducing additional taxes and a new distribution of taxes among the three levels of government. The passing of new social legislation became possible only in connection with this reorganization of revenues for local government and actually took place in close connection with fiscal legislation. (*Ermächtigungsgesetz vom* 8.12.1923 *zum Vollzuge der* 3. *Steuer-Notverordnung.*)

agencies are undoubtedly partners in a common enterprise, the weight of the German public partner with his power of holding the purse strings is recognized quite realistically. The public partner may withdraw a delegated function if he is dissatisfied with the quality of performance or with its cost. He may, and usually he must, establish standards and enforce them by supervision and inspection. His standards may be superior to those of the private agency, and he may have a controlling influence on the private agency's budget, policy, and planning.

The financial relationship between the public and private agencies has become even more complicated since the devastating inflation and resulting currency reform of 1923. In wiping out much of the operating and other cash capital of the voluntary agencies, governmental currency manipulation resulted in a new claim of voluntary agencies against the German government, which was duly recognized.[11] Its settlement provided the major agencies with a fifteen-year annual income from federal funds (since 1927) in partial recognition of the severe capital losses suffered. In order to enforce their joint claim, the scattered voluntary agencies rallied around the leadership of six associations,[12] which quickly developed into very powerful national federations representing a form of assembly of national agencies, with a rather united front against the federal government. The leadership exerted by the national associations and strengthened by their successful negotiations for the "welfare annuity" permeated all voluntary agencies down to the last local unit and affected their attitudes and policies, especially in all matters relating to co-operation with the corresponding local government units. The national policy also established a pattern for requesting and obtaining on other government

[11] The major sectarian agencies and the German Red Cross received in the period 1924–1927 a total of 37 million marks from the federal government before the annuity program went into effect. See *Erinnerungsschrift des Reichsarbeitsministeriums: Deutsche Sozialpolitik, 1918-1928,* p. 260.

[12] The six associations forming the *Deutsche Liga der freien Wohlfahrtspflege* were: (1) *Innere Mission* (Protestant); (2) *Deutscher Caritas Verband* (Catholic); (3) *Zentralwohlfahrtsstelle der deutschen Juden* (Jewish); (4) *Deutsches Rotes Kreuz;* (5) *Fünfter Wohlfahrtsverband* (a combination of nonsectarian and non labor agencies; (6) *Zentralwohlfahrtsausschuss der christlichen Arbeiterschaft* (welfare agency of the nonsocialist labor organizations). Not an original member of the League but of importance as a new voluntary service was also the *Hauptausschuss für Arbeiterwohlfahrt,* the welfare organization of the Free Trade Unions and other socialist labor groups. Since the post-Hitler period this organization has joined the League while the Jewish group has not yet joined. Also outside the League is the influential voluntary organization of the Soviet Zone, *Volkssolidarität.*

levels very substantial government grants-in-aid for capital expansion, especially for modernization and for the development of new institutions.

The expansion of voluntary facilities thus became throughout the entire period of the Weimar Republic and up to the present time a matter of highly competitive activities. Competition was and is strong between the sectarian and the nonsectarian agencies. There continues to be competition between the Catholic and Protestant services, both wanting to expand in areas of mixed populations. There is conflict and competition between the public agency's desire to expand its own direct services and the pressures of the voluntary agencies for allocating capital funds, plus operating fees, in order to make expansion possible. Each decision in allocating funds for the expansion of community services primarily reflected the influence of the major political parties with which the voluntary agencies were aligned and their balance of power on every level of government. These factors were often more important than the quality of professional leadership available on either side or than realistic interagency planning for the better coverage of defined needs.

Personnel Problems in Social Administration during the Weimar Republic—Modernized public health and welfare legislation stressed integration of all services focusing on the family as the basic unit and increased attention to the individual aspects of each problem. The leading social administrators and other professional workers engaged in these services widely agreed with this emphasis and the broad new objectives in public social service. They did not succeed, however, within the few years at their disposal, in changing traditional attitudes concerning social welfare and social insurance, which were ingrained in the minds of the civil service bureaucracy on the operational level of the public agencies. Civil servants could quickly master the letter of the new laws on public aid, child welfare, the public employment service, but only rarely the spirit of such legislation. Where the legislative framework called for individualizing and liberal interpretation of the underlying basic and very positive concepts, they would often take pride in narrowing them down, inserting rigid rulings in conflict with any attempts at individualizing aid.[13] The progressive tendencies of the basic social legislation of the Weimar Republic thus became completely overshadowed by the reality of a social practice which

[13] Trained professional social workers began to be employed in sizable numbers in the early days of the Weimar Republic, but they were assigned limited functions, for the most part those of social investigation and visiting. In general, they ranged below the civil service career men on the intermediate level.

could never yield satisfaction to either clients or staff because of the stringent needs of economy.[14]

IMPACT OF NATIONAL SOCIALIST REGIME

Public and voluntary agencies were relieved from overwhelming pressures borne during the long depression years when, starting in 1934, the full employment and mobilization program of the Hitler regime eliminated all employables from the rolls. In line with a ruthless population policy, Hitler's planned neglect and, in many instances, physical destruction of the unemployables and of defective client groups eased another part of the welfare load. Thus the Third Reich actually freed the public social services from many of the earlier pressures which so severely had crippled their development. In fact, some services, in line with the official racial and population policy, were permitted to expand, for instance infant and maternity programs and the care of families with numerous children. Social policy was aligned with the objectives of the Third Reich, and social agencies were made to serve as their instruments.[15] Those which were neither willing nor able to adapt were eliminated, such as the Socialist Labor Welfare and all voluntary Jewish agencies. In the case of the Protestant and Catholic voluntary agencies, their services were drastically curtailed by law.

THE POSTWAR PERIOD

Amidst the chaos of total defeat, widespread destruction, and displacement and under the control of the occupying powers, public and private welfare agencies continued to operate without any break. Again they had to assume heavy responsibilities with completely inadequate means—a minimum of experienced personnel and a minimum of material resources—but with some encouragement by international aid. The comprehensive service program of the highly organized National Socialist nongovernmental organization vanished overnight. The voluntary agencies of the labor movement which had been driven underground, deprived of all property and prohibited during the Hitler period, made a dramatic comeback and mobilized—as did other volunteer organizations—vast numbers of untiring helpers. Social workers on the staffs of public and private agencies worked without specific

[14] For a comprehensive and technical analysis of the social policy and programs of the Weimar Republic (with major emphasis on labor legislation), see Ludwig Preller, *Sozialpolitik in der Weimarer Republik* (Stuttgart, 1949), 560 pp.

[15] A clear and factual presentation of the basic tenets may be found in an article by Dr. Ralf Zeitler, vice-president of the German Federation of Cities: "Grundzüge der öffentlichen Fürsorge im Dritten Reich," *Deutsche Zeitschrift für Wohlfahrtspflege,* March, 1939, 14:12.

direction or plan, using their own initiative, tremendous resourcefulness, and perseverance. Their ability to improvise and to find at least temporary solutions was strained to the limit, but produced amazing results. This was particularly impressive at a moment when the staffs of public welfare departments often lost more than half their personnel because of previous Nazi affiliation. The places of those now ineligible for public service were quickly filled by less experienced employees or by civil servants from other departments who immediately had to assume major responsibilities—without any orientation to over-all objectives or to the long-range functions of their agencies.

Thus, since the end of the Nazi regime, a new personnel problem in public welfare and public health has been added to the personnel problem so significant under the Weimar Republic: a basic lack of orientation to broader social welfare goals and often a substantial lack of professional knowledge and skills. In addition to this accumulated problem, special attention should be paid to the insidious and continuing influence of National Socialist concepts which have been widely and often unconsciously absorbed.

As already stated, the postwar structure of government service in the health and welfare area is not substantially different from the earlier pattern. A summary of organization and major activities on the different levels of government may provide some orientation to the prevalent pattern, with some brief inserts specifically related to functional programs.

Local Level—Health and welfare services are heavily concentrated on the local level and as part of local self-government. Within local units an all-inclusive social welfare department is widely considered as the most desirable structure[16] and is frequently firmly established. Such a department aims at the greatest possible integration in administering (1) social assistance (including the management of certain institutions), (2) child and youth welfare services, and (3) public health services. The first-named functions may be in charge of a subdivision called *Fürsorgeamt;* the second group in charge of the *Jugendamt;* the third in charge of the *Gesundheitsamt.*

In the better-organized communities all divisions are supplemented by the *Familienfürsorge,* a special unit for family social service staffed by professional social workers who will provide counseling, social investigation, and various auxiliary services for all three subdivisions of the social welfare department and also for institutions, hospitals,

---

[16] See Chapter 3 above. See also the pertinent presentation in a recent textbook for students of public administration seeking factual material, Ernst Otto and Willy Kister, *Fürsorge und Jugenwohlfahrt: Sozialversicherung* (Göttingen, 1950).

schools, and courts of their area. This generic service, replacing earlier specialized social services, represents an important social design at variance with the principles and practices of individualizing social service of other countries, though it is by no means inferior. It is possible only when the educational preparation of professional social workers is in line with the generic function, including preprofessional nursing education. The performance of the *Familienfürsorge* is also conditioned by a limitation of the districts to be serviced by each individual worker. This, according to the best German estimates, should not exceed a population of 8,000 to 10,000 per worker. Obviously, such factors as the density and distribution of the population, transportation facilities, and numbers of schools, hospitals, children's homes, and health centers to be serviced within the area will also need to be considered. In order to work effectively, the unit of generic family social workers requires direction by a qualified chief social worker of similar experience and professional education who should be independent of, and equal in status to, the directors of the three major subdivisions of the social welfare department as listed.

Unfortunately, many local communities have not yet realized this basic pattern. While it corresponds to the basic principles and objectives of established social legislation and had been widely tested in the pre-Hitler period, it was disrupted by the separation of the health services during the Nazi period. At the time (1934) of the transfer of the municipal public health functions to state public health departments, many of the family social workers were transferred simultaneously. Although in many instances theoretically they continued to be available to the other divisions continuing under local self-government, they actually returned to the highly specialized service pattern of a much earlier period and became health visitors[17] only. This left the other branches of the social welfare departments practically unserviced until the transferred staff was replaced by new sets of social workers. These in turn became more or less specialized, carrying on rather limited functions as visitors and social investigators, while the major responsibility and the power of decisions as to type and scope of aid continued to be vested in the hands of civil service officials without professional preparation. The leading professional association of social workers as well as the German Federation of Cities and

---

[17] Public health nursing as a separate profession does not exist in Germany. Most of its functions except for bedside nursing are carried on by the family social worker (*Familienfürsorgerin*) or the health visitor (*Gesundheitsfürsorgerin*). Free or low cost bedside nursing is provided by community nurses in the employment of local churches, women's organizations, or social welfare departments.

Counties and the German Association for Public and Private Welfare are in agreement that the traditional plans of an integrated professional family service on the local level should be fully re-established[18] and strengthened by qualified supervision and constructive districting.

While the comprehensive social welfare department with four parts as sketched represents the most desirable solution, in many communities, depending on local tradition and political pressures, each of the listed units may have remained an independent department, without adequate correlation and frequently lacking a joint social policy. Whether integrated or separated, the substantive content of the four activities remains substantially as follows.

(1) *Social Assistance*—State legislation related to the 1924 Public Welfare Law has divided these responsibilities (both general assistance and various categorical programs) between local units of self-government and certain regional offices. While the local ones are in the main identical with the local public welfare departments, it is possible that the state may delegate certain functions to social insurance agencies or even to voluntary agencies. Such transfer of function is also within the competence of the local unit, although final responsibility will continue to be lodged with the public agency. Local public welfare agencies are specifically designated as centers of all public welfare services within the local community and as connecting links between the voluntary and the public social services.

In addition to providing personal and material aid, as needed, for all indigent, the public welfare units are specifically required to provide social assistance to veterans and their families, to the beneficiaries of employee, old age, and survivors insurance, and to other groups of aged affected by currency devaluation. They must also offer rehabilitative care and employment service to the severely handicapped, aid for dependent children, and, finally, maternity care for those not eligible for the maternity programs of the insurance systems. It is characteristic of the progressive spirit of this law that it required client participation in the appeals procedure and in the development of standard budgets.

An especially difficult task added in 1948 (but in all likelihood of very temporary character) has been the emergency program[19] for the

---

[18] See *Nachrichtendienst,* August and September, 1948; also Dr. Hans Muthesius, *Reichsjugendwohlfahrtsgesetz* Stuttgart, 1950), p. 1, and same author in *Stadtetag,* No. 3, 1950.

[19] See "Der Lastenausgleich als soziales Problem," *Nachrichtendienst,* April and May, 1950. The entire issue of August, 1949, of the same journal deals with all technical aspects of the program.

victims of war, persecution, displacement, and currency devaluation. This is a scheme of administering temporary allowances, similar to public assistance but by no means identical and following a specific set of eligibility requirements. In addition, this program includes the administration of grants and loans for purposes of education, vocational rehabilitation, re-equipment, rehousing, and resettlement. Theoretically, these programs of "immediate aid" (*Soforthilfe*) are to be administered by separate immediate aid departments on the local level, but in each case the public welfare department has added this function to its traditional tasks. Expenditures under this program are largely reimbursed from certain federal funds. In 1952 the emergency program has been replaced by a permanent one operating, however, through the same local channels. (Equalization Law, August 18, 1952.)

The problems of long-time care with special emphasis on institutions for the severely handicapped and the problems of re-employment and sheltered employment for the same group continue to be handled in co-operation with the regional offices. In many instances, they will reimburse the expenditures of the local units which carry the major responsibility for actual service operations.

(2) *Child and Youth Welfare Services*—The federal law[20] on child and youth welfare (1922) established a unique set of public service units focusing attention on all children and youth of a given community, healthy as well as handicapped. It provides the legal and operational base for a rather comprehensive approach to all children's needs. This law, preceding the general public welfare law of 1924, expressed the same progressive attitude and many identical principles. Thus there was a certain amount of duplication and overlapping; it may well be questioned whether a specialized agency, for children and youth only, would have been stipulated if the modernized social welfare department could have been expected. The friends of the child and youth welfare law have rarely been satisfied, however, unless a community developed a clearly defined and separate unit for child welfare. This unit, which will now be found either as a subdivision of the social welfare department or functioning independently, serves the objective of safeguarding the constitutional rights of each German child to receive an "education for physical, spiritual, and social effectiveness." As permanent functions of the public child welfare agencies, the law includes care of foster children, co-operative services in

[20] Muthesius, *Reichsjugendwohlfahrtsgesetz,* is the most authoritative contemporary commentary. For a very adequate earlier American interpretation, see Earl D. Myers and Walter Friedlander, *Child Welfare in Germany before and after Nazism* (Chicago, 1940).

guardianship, co-operative services in probation and correctional education, co-operative services for the juvenile courts, co-operative services in the supervision and inspection of child labor and the employment of young workers, co-operative services in the care of war orphans and children of veterans, and co-operative services with the local police.

Among German experts there is wide agreement that it is important to preserve the major concept of the law,[21] which combines a general approach to youth with special attention to the physically, mentally, or socially handicapped groups. This emphasis upon the entire child and youth population is particularly important because in the German tradition the public school has only a restricted function and covers only a quite limited age range. A flexible generic agency with a clear social focus and a child-centered policy seems—at least under German conditions—a most valuable supplement.

(3) *Public Health Services*—Since 1934 Germany has had a complete network of public health departments on the local level, though numerous public health departments had existed before that time as subdivisions of local self-government. The 1934 legislation standardized structure and function and completed the program. At the same time all public health departments were brought under the administration of the states. All of the health divisions or departments were under the jurisdiction of public health bureaus, which form part of the ministries of the interior of the several states. Local public health departments combine the functions related to environmental hygiene and the enforcement of health regulations with health education and individualizing services for various age and population groups. Among others, they service the school system, the social welfare including child welfare departments, the state employment service, and certain social insurance programs. In accord with recent state legislation all public health departments in certain states have again been returned to local governments; other states now have corresponding permissive legislation.

(4) *Social Insurance*—The local agency servicing most of the social

---

[21] A Joint Memorandum on Recommendations for the Amendment of the Child Welfare Law was published as a special supplement to the *Nachrichtendienst* in June, 1950. The *Nachrichtendienst* of February, 1950, brought a leading article on the basic concepts underlying the planned changes, "Die Grundgedanken der RJWG-Reform." The annual meeting of the German Federation of Cities (June 30-July 1, 1950) was devoted in its entirety to such discussions with the leitmotiv: a new spirit in our child welfare departments. A printed preconference report containing many excellent papers is available from the main office of the *Deutscher Städtetag*, Cologne.

insurance programs is now the social insurance department (*Versicherungsamt*). Its functions, however, are quite limited. It serves as information center, accepts applications for old age, disability, and survivors insurance, and handles appeals. It also has certain supervisory functions regarding local health insurance funds. Finally, it serves as an administrative court settling predominantly health insurance claims. This agency, whose structure is defined in the basic social insurance law, is under the direction of an administrative board composed of employers and workers in equal numbers with a municipal commissioner as an impartial chairman.

Regional Self-Government—Regional self-government, the so-called "medium level," represents a rather important unit of administration in social welfare. Providing a broader financial basis than local self-government, these units have facilitated the development and stable operation of a number of specialized service programs frequently of institutional character and of high professional caliber. As regional units corresponding to the local public welfare departments, they may operate regional work centers, camps for migrants, institutions for the chronically ill, and mental hospitals. In the area of veterans' aid, they are primarily responsible for vocational rehabilitation and employment service to the handicapped. As regional child welfare and youth departments, they administer correctional education in public institutions and develop regional policies and a program of grants-in-aid for the promotion of many child welfare services, serving at the same time as a standard-setting instrumentality. As regional departments of old age and disability insurance, they are in charge of programs of convalescent care and rehabilitation and of many forms of intensive, prolonged treatment, necessitating special funds. They also operate specialized hospitals, convalescent homes, and other facilities of the insurance institutions, both for adults and for children.

State Level—In contrast to these regional units of self-government, but often identical as far as territory is concerned, each of the states has established a bureau for public welfare services and a bureau for public health, in most instances within the state ministry of the interior. Other states have developed similar units within a special state department for social affairs which, in this case, is likely to include labor affairs.[22] The structure and program of these state bureaus are not yet clearly defined since, with the exception of Bavaria, they are on the whole of very recent origin. Within the former Prussian territory the newly developed states have taken over many of the functions originally handled by the old Prussian Department for Social

[22] See Chapter 14 above.

Welfare. These functions have been combined with others inherited from the provincial government units, and new ones have been added growing out of the new division of function between the Bonn government and the several states.

There are still numerous conflicts and considerable uncertainty concerning the jurisdiction of state and federal governments, since the Bonn Constitution does not reveal with absolute clarity the areas in which federal legislation[23] and standard-setting should be accepted. While there is no question that earlier federal legislation will continue to be valid so long as it is not in conflict with the constitution (Art. 123), all subject matter in health and social welfare is within the competence of both the state and federal governments (Art. 74). States are now interested in developing a pattern of voluntary co-operation which will yield a higher degree of unity and thus facilitate the handling of numerous problems affecting a highly mobile population but still preserve at least a modicum of decentralized control.[24]

National Level—Several federal departments give special attention to health and welfare. The Ministry of the Interior has a Bureau of Public and Child Welfare and a Bureau of Public Health. The former federal Health Institution (*Reichsgesundheitsamt*), which also functioned under the Ministry of the Interior, has been re-established. The functions of the Bureaus for Social Welfare and Health Affairs are complex and are expanding.[25] They do not include operational responsibilities, but serve in the main as co-ordinating, standard-setting, and planning units. The bureaus also give expert consultation to other federal bureaus and ministries in relation to legislation and other projects involving health and welfare matters. They are also visualized as the key agencies involved in planned co-operation with international agencies, such as those of the United Nations, or with international voluntary agencies engaged in specific service programs in German territory.

[23] The German Association for Public and Private Welfare has been much concerned with the possible danger of losing the progressive concepts embodied in the federal social welfare legislation of the Weimar period, if the priority of the federal government should not be recognized in social legislation. See among others the association's memorandum entitled "Entschliessung des Vorstands des Deutschen Vereins zur Vorranggesetzgebung des Bundes," published in *Nachrichtendienst*, April, 1949.

[24] See Chapter IV above for discussion of the wider aspects of the same problem.

[25] The ministry's functions and plans in the area of social welfare were presented by the chief of the Bureau of Public and Child Welfare and supplemented by a representative of the Bureau of Public Health at the National Social Welfare Conference, October, 1950. See *Nachrichtendienst*, November, 1950.

In co-operation with the state departments of social welfare, the federal bureaus attempt to work out a partnership which will facilitate voluntary agreements and the location and definition of such continuing problems as may call for new regulations. Such co-operation is particularly important and needed since uniform procedures have been discarded under the impact of differing occupation practices and the introduction of more decentralized concepts of federal administration. The recently established Federal Institution for Employment and Unemployment Compensation (with headquarters in Nuremberg) and corresponding organizations on the state level deal with many issues of equal concern to public welfare agencies.

The Labor Ministry also has responsibilities in some parts of this field. Its activities are concentrated in bureaus dealing with employment, unemployment insurance, and general social insurance affairs. Because of the great importance of social insurance benefits in cash, kind, and service which underpin practically all other health and welfare services in Germany and represent the most important community resource, a brief additional statement may also be in order.

In the western zone the structure and organization of the several social insurance schemes still reflect their different historical origins and the traditional German emphasis on utilizing industrial and other vocational units as agents of health and accident insurance, thus operating through many different outlets on the local and regional levels.

In contrast, old age, disability, and survivors insurance and employees insurance are each structured as national schemes, with very limited operating units on the local levels. Though federally supervised, most of their operations are centered in their important regional units (*Landesversicherungsanstalten*), which administer all types of claims and also a wide range of preventive and rehabilitative services. The latter group includes institutional treatment and vocational rehabilitation for tuberculosis, crippling conditions, and numerous other severe disabilities which may be dealt with constructively and thus may lead to increased capacity for work and self-support. These comprehensive treatment programs (*Heilverfahren*) are available for both children and adults, for the insured worker as well as for the dependent members of his household, and represent one of the most important services available to the population. In many instances they are matched by practically identical rehabilitation programs for those who are not insured directly or indirectly, the cost in such cases being borne by the public welfare units operating on the regional level (*Landesfürsorgeverband*). In all cases, applications for these rehabilitation programs are registered with the local units of the public health service which work out the treatment plan, assisted by its own diagnostic facilities, and initiate the filing of the claim to the insurance or public welfare agency concerned. These rehabilitation programs are considered of such importance that they have received substantial federal subsidies when the insurance funds were not able to cope adequately with the number of requests. They illustrate effectively the principle of dealing with the roots of the incapacity in order to prevent temporary damage from deteriorating into permanent incapacity.

Two other organizations on the national level should be mentioned which also have certain responsibilities in the social welfare area. The development of a Bonn Ministry for the Affairs of Expellees and Refugees—whose chief has cabinet rank—recognizes the political, economic, and social importance of the refugee problem, involving at least one-sixth of the resident population of the western zones. Corresponding to the federal position, state commissioners for refugees and expellees have also been appointed. On all levels of government the operating programs of these units are in the main, however, carried on through the channels of traditional agencies. Most of the material aid both for their current support and for rehabilitation and resettlement was first derived from a temporary program of emergency aid, based on a law for the Mitigation of Urgent Social Needs (August, 1949). While this temporary program of limited aid, providing maintenance benefits and grants, was administered through the channels of the local social welfare departments which had set up special bureaus for this purpose, a Main Office for Emergency Aid was established on the federal level, with corresponding state offices in each of the states. In 1952 the emergency program was replaced by the Equalization Law which operates on the federal level through the Federal Equalization Office. These units, on the national and state level, are affiliated with the Ministry of Finance. The emergency aid program represents a preliminary payment on account, in recognition of the most urgent claims for the equalization of war and war-related burdens and in advance of more comprehensive regulations to affect both tax collection and compensation of the victims. It is not planned to structure the compensation scheme as if it were a plan of individualizing assistance to be based on current need. All claimants will have a legal right to compensation for specific loss or damage suffered, limited only by the funds which the economy of the country will be able to yield toward the important objective of fair and just equalization (*Lastenausgleich*).

CONCLUSION

In appraising Germany's long tradition in the fields of health and welfare, one cannot but be impressed both by its outstanding contributions and by some of its more recent failures to follow its own good examples. Thus, while older legislation contains a clear statement of sound principles, current practice frequently pays them little heed. Furthermore, whereas fundamental and comprehensive social legislation of earlier days provides an emphatic statement of principles and objectives of service which are centered upon the capacity for growth and the differential needs of each individual, today's practice gives insufficient recognition to individual capacities for adjustment, for reorientation to drastic change, and for self-help.

Germany had early developed an excellent principle of client participation in administration. This included utilizing many self-governing units in social insurance and the inclusion of representatives of beneficiary groups in claims procedures. Yet for all this the splendid tradition today seems nearly lost. Here, as elsewhere, the current tendency is to leave matters to the bureaucrats and the experts for attention.

Much of this may be interpreted as the natural consequence of present living conditions and of the drastic recent experiences which the entire population has undergone. Most people are still involved in rebuilding their own homes, their health, their own opportunities for a meaningful life. Personal and family problems may absorb so much of their remaining power that there is nothing left for community concern and service. Difficult economic conditions, combined with the pressure on all social agencies of many needy and desperate people, are usually given as an explanation of the failure to provide a much more individualizing and truly rehabilitative service, which would develop the client's potential capacity. The same conditions also interfere with the more positive and valid use of client participation, individually and in the form of organized self-help groups. There can hardly be any question that all these factors are important and that agencies as well as the community's social leadership are doing most difficult work against tremendous odds and in a setting which hardly makes it possible to think calmly about priorities. They are constantly confronted with urgent problems resulting from the utter inadequacy of financial resources at their disposal; from the maldistribution of the masses of expellees and refugees, increased daily by new arrivals from areas behind the iron curtain; and from jurisdictional conflicts in the wake of the reorganization of the national territory into new state units, with new legislators and new administrators. They are also deeply involved in striving for a new and much more valid balance between pension, insurance, and assistance programs, each corresponding to a rather different concept of the relationship between the individual and the state. Only when these ideological conflicts—in a most sensitive area affecting the major part of the population—have been worked out and the new solutions have gained the sanction of the legislators will it be possible to overhaul, to streamline, and to integrate the structure of the total health and welfare programs.

Foreign observers and students of the German scene should not fail to take these realities into account when they attempt an evaluation. They will, however, also wonder whether some of the difficulties and deficiencies would not be overcome more promptly if German social welfare policy could become more convincingly focused on a goal. This, however, must be widely shared by sensitive and responsible citizens and by government as a whole, in co-operation with the experts and social welfare specialists. The spiritual and physical rebuilding of people—individual by individual and family by family—and their social reintegration with the community as active, respected, and personally responsible members would seem a rather obvious goal.

If such a goal is actually considered of supreme importance, it can be realized only if the best possible personnel and methods are utilized. It must also be backed by deep convictions, by some hope, and by faith in a future which can be more constructive than the past only if built on a new quality of interaction and on new human relations.

16

Police Administration

ROBERT M. W. KEMPNER

THE defeat of Germany in May, 1945, brought to an end a police system that over a period of twelve years had taken total control of all phases of individual and civic life. The two-million-man police machinery, headed by Heinrich Himmler, "*Reichsfürer* of the SS (Elite Guards) and the Police," was a State upon the State, a structure superimposed upon all other governmental agencies, for the establishment, development, and enforcement of the National Socialist new order. It was a perfect example of a totalitarian police system. Changing it to operate in the interests of a democratic citizenry required the incorporation of the best principles that could be drawn from other parts of the democratic world. But it also meant finding roots in German tradition which would assure sound organic growth.

GERMAN POLICE SYSTEMS BEFORE 1933

Such a police tradition, although differing from Anglo-Saxon concepts, could be found in pre-Nazi police systems and practices of Germany, especially as developed during the period of the Weimar Republic from 1918 to 1933, under the Social Democratic police ministers Carl Severing and Albert Grzesinski. During this period the functions of the police were limited to the maintenance of public safety and order and were subject to judicial review. All activities of the police in the various German *Länder* were statutorily defined by section 14 of the Prussian Law for Police Administration of June 1, 1931, on the drafting of which the author was privileged to work. Section 14, paragraph 1, reads as follows: "The police authorities shall

[403]

take the necessary measures in order to protect the general public and the individual citizen from dangers which threaten the public safety or order. They shall take these measures in accordance with the laws in effect and they shall be in duty bound to use proper discretion."[1] The same statute, in its sections 24-69, gave the police the authority to issue police decrees, orders, and subpoenas and to impose minor penalties for the enforcement of the "necessary measures" defined above. A number of provisions to ensure freedom of person and property are also included in this law. Similar statutes were in effect in the other German states. All these police laws, defining and limiting the power and duties of the police, were actually restatements of royal ordinances limiting the jurisdiction of the police.[2] They had long been observed in practice and had been tested in many rulings of administrative courts.

Before the Nazis came to power in January, 1933, Germany had never had a federal police system, either in the Empire or in the Weimar Republic. Only in very limited emergency cases did the constitution of the *Kaiserreich* and the Weimar Constitution allow for the exercising of certain limited police functions, and then only for a carefully defined period of emergency. Otherwise, federal police jurisdiction existed only in such special fields as customs and railway police. Traditionally, the maintenance of public safety and order had been for centuries under the jurisdiction of the *Länder*. Even when, after 1808, the larger cities in Prussia and the other German states became autonomous, the field of public safety remained in the hands of the states, with a few exceptions south of the Rhine-Main line. Section 1 of the Prussian police law of June 1, 1931, stated categorically: "The police shall be a function of the State."[3] The same principle obtained in the other German states and proved a magic formula again after World War II among state administrators as well as among the police officers unions.

Thus, although cities were allowed to set up their own public safety forces, the operatives down to the last traffic policeman remained officials of the states. All police forces were controlled by the ministries of the interior of the individual *Länder*. As a consequence, the ministers of the interior, called police ministers, were the most powerful members of their respective state governments. From the *Länder*

---

[1] *Polizeiverwaltungsgesetz, Preussisches,* of June 1, 1931, in *Preussische Gesetz-sammlung* (1931), p. 77.

[2] Klausener, Kerstiens, Kempner, *Das Polizeiverwaltungsgesetz mit Quellen-material,* 3rd ed. (Berlin, 1931), pp. 98 ff.

[3] *Preussische Gesetzsammlung* (1931), p. 77.

capitals of Berlin, Munich, Stuttgart, and so on, the ministers of the interior exercised their control through district police authorities, having their seats at the district governments (*Regierungsbezirke*). From the district government level, the line of control went down on the local level to the state police commissioners (*Polizeipräsidenten*) in the big cities having a state police administration, to the mayors (*Bürgermeister*) in the smaller cities having their own police forces, and to the county managers (*Landräte*) in the rural counties. During the period of the Weimar Republic, almost twenty separate state police forces served the needs of their respective states and of the Free Cities Hamburg, Bremen, and Lübeck.

In this period the number of police officers in Germany totaled about 200,000, more than two-thirds of them in Prussia, the largest German state. The major part of these police officers were uniformed police troopers, known as security police (*Schutzpolizei*). Large units of them were quartered in barracks and were called out only in emergencies. Battalions of the *Schutzpolizei* were stationed mainly in the large cities and in the big industrial areas of the Ruhr Valley, Thuringia, and Upper Silesia. The public safety needs of the rural areas were served by the so-called *gendarmerie* forces, uniformed state troopers organized during the nineteenth-century Napoleonic occupation of wide parts of Prussia and other German territories.

In addition, each German state had its detective force (*Kriminalpolizei*), charged with the prevention and investigation of crimes. In personnel and disciplinary matters and as far as crime prevention was concerned, the *Kriminalpolizei* was also controlled by the minister of the interior of each state. As far as investigative work was concerned, the ministries of justice of the various German *Länder* were their supervisory authorities. In this phase of their work, the *Kriminalpolizei* served as an auxiliary agency to the state attorneys (*Hilfsbeamte der Staatsanwaltschaft*). As in many European and South American countries, the police of the German *Länder* exercised a considerable number of administrative functions not regarded as police functions in Anglo-Saxon thinking. A so-called administrative police (*Verwaltungspolizei*) handled these matters, which included supervision of business and industry (with the authority to issue trade and business licenses), supervision of fairs, markets, public health, and passport and alien matters, and the maintenance of a residence registration system.

THE POLICE OF THE NAZI REGIME

With the advent of Hitler, this police system was centralized into a Reich police force, and the German *Länder* police systems, which had been traditional for more than two hundred years, were abolished. Under the National Socialist regime, the police had aggrandized to itself powers unprecedented in the police history of Germany or any modern western state. Beyond traditional police duties, it exercised unlimited and ever-expanding legislative, judicial, and executive functions.

The new gargantuan police machinery comprised two main branches: the order police (*Ordnungspolizei*) and the security police (*Sicherheitspolizei*). The order police carried out functionally most of the duties normally associated with a modern police system, but was organized as a centralized, uniformed, para-military force, closely affiliated with the black-shirted SS-guards of the *Schutzstaffeln* of the National Socialist German Workers party (NSDAP).[4] The security police embraced the secret state police (*Gestapo*), the criminal police (*Kriminalpolizei*), and a number of less important sections. It was the security police that had the power to arrest persons without warrant and without judicial control, to search houses, and to confiscate property, for a wide variety of reasons falling under the elastic heading "political." It was this branch that engineered and managed the nation-wide system of concentration camps and political prisons. This police agency organized, co-ordinated, and enforced programs for the annihilation of political enemies of the Nazi regime and of minority groups, such as members of the intelligentsia, Catholic priests in Nazi-occupied countries, sick people designated as "useless eaters," Jews, and gypsies.

The uprooting and demolition of this Nazi police system, which had been in power from 1933 to 1945, a declared war aim of the Allied powers, was one of the primary tasks facing the occupation governments. The unconditional termination of this police machinery was marked by the judgment of the International Military Tribunal of Nuremberg, handed down on October 1, 1946.[5] The Nuremberg judgment stigmatized as criminal organizations the *Gestapo,* the SS and the affiliated SD (*Sicherheitsdienst*), and the special intelligence service of the *Gestapo,* and the SS. Membership in these organizations, under certain provisos of knowledge, was declared to constitute a crime —a decision which was to have far-reaching consequences in the building up of new democratic police forces for postwar Germany.

OCCUPATION IMPACT UPON THE POLICE SYSTEM

Faced with the German police tradition and with the remnants of

[4] See Werner Best, *Die Deutsche Polizei* (Darmstadt, 1940).
[5] International Military Tribunal, *Trial of the Major War Criminals* (Nurem-

the Nazi police system, the western occupational administrations and the reawakening democratic forces in Western Germany found the building up of a new police according to modern and democratic concepts an almost insurmountable task. However, in the eight years 1945 through 1952, this task was accomplished to a highly satisfactory degree. Today, throughout Western Germany democratic police systems have been established that combine the best of Anglo-Saxon and of continental police tradition and practice. While in the American and British zones of occupation Anglo-Saxon traits have come more to the fore in post–World War II German police development, continental police characteristics predominate in the French Zone. The development of a new police came about gradually and hesitantly, but from the outset was directed towards certain cardinal objectives commonly embraced and energetically pursued by the three western occupying powers. These were the big D's: Demilitarization, Denazification, Decentralization, Democratization, and, last but not least, a functional Delimitation of the Nazi-style police by a removal from the public safety forces of all those judicial, legislative, and administrative functions not rightly in the province of an executive police.

The policy governing the formation of the new police was laid down by the western occupational powers in a number of basic orders.[6] With the founding of the Federal German Republic in September, 1949, the three Allied High Commissioners restated their policy in a letter, dated September 21, 1949, to the Allied *Land* commissioners concerning the organization, control, and administration of police within the *Länder*.[7] In order to implement the policy of demilitarization, all military ranks in the police systems of the three western zones were abolished; strict limitations were set upon the numbers and types of weapons that could be carried by the police; all practices and cus-

---

berg, 1947), 262 ff.

[6] For the American Zone, the statement of policy can be found in Title 9, Military Government Regulations on Public Safety, dated February 1, 1946, and in the amendments thereof, dated May 22, 1947, and January 19, 1948. For the British Zone, the statement of policy is contained in the Instructions of the Military Government on the Reorganization of the German Police System, dated September 25, 1945, BAOR/38708/30/G (SDO 1b), and in Order No. 135 of the British Military Government, dated March 1, 1948 (*Official Military Government Gazette for the British Zone*, 1948, p. 713). The basic instruction for the French Zone is given in Circular OPA 1, issued by the French Administrator General, dated January 15, 1946. The special problem of developing a new police for the City of Berlin under the auspices of all four occupational powers was dealt with in an order of the Allied *Kommandantura* Berlin, dated October 4, 1946, BK/0(46)391.

[7] HICOM/P(49)10(Final)–TRIB/P(49)100(Final).

toms were banned that "might in any way serve as cover for secret military organizations or military practices."

The denazification of the German police was carried out in accordance with the denazification laws severally applying in the U.S., British, and French zones. Although it cannot be said that the post–World War II German police forces do not contain many members who, in varying degrees, have had Nazi records, still an earnest attempt was made in all three western zones to weed out the grosser cases from the new German police and to place police personnel held over from the Nazi system under sanctions of good behavior. The thoroughness of the police denazification program has varied from zone to zone and within each zone, from area to area. The larger cities, such as Berlin, Hamburg, Frankfurt, and Nuremberg, have had, in general, better success in removing Nazi influences from their police than have the state governments.

The decentralization of the German police has been accomplished in the American Zone by restoring governmental controls of the police at communal or, in special instances, at *Land* levels and in the British Zone by decentralizing the police into forty separate and independently controlled forces, one for each city with a population of 100,000 or more and one for each district government area (*Regierungsbezirk*). Only in the French Zone have the police been centralized at *Land* level.

As late as September 21, 1949, the desirability of decentralizing police forces below the *Land* level was restated in a letter from the Allied High Commission to the *Land* commissioners. This letter instructed specifically that formation or maintaining of forces on the *Land* level must be authorized by the High Commission. At the same time, the development of independent communal police forces was encouraged in the following words: "Independently administered communities have the right to establish their own independent police units. Two or more neighboring communities may join together, by mutual agreement, to form a common police force. However, such police forces may in no case total more than two thousand members."

However, as a result of political developments, the decentralization policy was subsequently modified in a decision of the High Commission, made public on June 21, 1950. The modified policy authorized the ministers of the interior of the *Länder* to instruct the local police forces of their respective *Länder* to give mutual assistance, within the *Land,* in the event of a disturbance or threat of disturbance that could not be dealt with effectively by the police force at hand. The authority exercised by the minister of the interior must be based on *Land* legislation providing that police transferred to a troubled area come under the command of the chief police official of the area concerned.

But this deviation from the principle of police decentralization below *Land* level did not satisfy a movement of certain German police experts and *Land*-level government officials, among them Dr. Walter Menzel, North Rhine–Westphalia minister of the interior. These men have argued with increasing emphasis[8] that in times of political tension, of possible riots, sabotage, and infiltration, the public safety forces cannot perform the duties required of them with adequate flexibility and power unless further concessions by the Allied authorities are made in the direction of centralizing police organizations at *Land* level.

The weight of these arguments and the stresses of the times led the High Commission to form a new policy on *Land* police organization, set forth in a letter of instruction to the *Land* commissioners, dated November 14, 1950. The new policy provided that after the passing of appropriate *Land* legislation, the organization of police forces in the *Länder* may be centralized at *Land* level, subject to the proviso that such legislation guarantee independent municipalities the right to maintain their own forces. *Land* governments may also introduce legislation permitting themselves to direct the police to enforce particular provisions of law and to advise the police on the interpretation of law.

As a result of this new policy, the ministers of the interior are again regaining a position equivalent to that of the police ministers of the state governments under the Weimar Republic, with the one exception that independently governed municipalities continue to have the right to maintain independent municipal police forces. But even this one remaining prerogative of the municipalities is limited by the fact that the *Land* may issue regulations on recruiting, training, and promoting in the ranks of local police forces, and the *Land* may assume operational control of all police forces in case of emergency.[9]

One of the most essential tasks in building up the new German police was to establish that body as a genuine public safety force devoting itself solely and completely to the maintenance of public safety and order and to the prevention and investigation of crimes. To bring this about it was necessary to strip away the vast agglomeration of judicial, legislative, and nonpolice executive functions that had marked the Third Reich police and even found some tradition in pre-Hitler times. Therefore, all judicial functions exercised before 1945 by the

[8] Record of Session 97 of the *Bundestag*, November 7, 1950, pp. 3538 ff.
[9] *New York Times*, February 10, 1951.

German police, such as the authority to impose fines and penalties, were transferred from the police to the criminal courts. The legislative powers of the police, for example the authority to issue police decrees and orders, were handed over to city, county, or state governments. Thus, the police power was limited to purely executive functions. Even with regard to these functions the police were no longer allowed to handle matters which did not have a direct bearing on the protection of persons and property, the maintenance of peace and order, and the prevention and investigation of crimes. Such matters as the supervision of public works and buildings, public health and veterinary services, fire protection, and licensing of trade were transferred to other branches of the local or state administration. In a number of cities the functions of the former administrative police were transferred to especially created city government sections, organized as *Ordnungämter*. These new offices were distinct from the police organization, and it was expressly ordered that they refrain from using the term "police" in carrying on their work. Removing from the functions of the police those activities not directly related to public safety and order contributed to putting an end to the paternalistic control exercised formerly by the German police over the normal everyday activities of every average law-abiding citizen.

Beyond defining legally the limited police functions of the new German public safety forces, however, much work had to be done to bring police practice into line with the legal basis of police authority. For, in Germany, police practice had traditionally overreached the limitations placed upon the police by the provisions of the federal and state constitutions, the German code of criminal procedure, and the German laws of police administration. Indeed, arbitrary police actions in the field of arrests and searches had been taken so much for granted by both police and public in Germany that it was an uphill struggle to persuade the police to abide by the statutory and constitutional limitations on their authority. In 1948, for example, the U.S. Military Government made a survey of 10,631 searches of private dwellings occurring over a six-month period in Württemberg-Baden.[10] This survey indicated that a judicial search warrant had been obtained in only 8 cases: searches without warrants appeared to have been justified in 228 cases at the most. Similar military government surveys showed that in a six-month period only one-third of 11,266 searches in Hesse had been authorized by the issue of judicial search warrants, while in Ba-

[10] *4th Quarterly Report on Germany,* Office of the U.S. High Commissioner for Germany (Frankfurt, 1950), p. 54.

varia 50,033 searches had taken place in the course of 1948, of which 42,228 were conducted without warrants.[11]

The goal of democratizing the German police progressed with the goals of denazifying, demilitarizing, decentralizing, and delimiting the functions of the police. But in addition new doctrines and professional ideas were brought into the training of the police. An effort was made to teach both new and old police personnel democratic practices of law enforcement and police activity and to develop in them a recognition of the position of the police as the servants and protectors of the community rather than as sub-*Führers* and dictators of the population. The lecture material used in the newly established police schools in the German *Länder* gives these principles their proper emphasis.

In addition, new devices were applied for the reorientation of the German police. The *4th Quarterly Report on Germany* issued by the Office of the U.S. High Commissioner for Germany on September 30, 1950, outlines these methods in the following words:

With Allied encouragement a number of police associations dedicated to professional improvement and fellowship have been formed [an example: the Association of Police Chiefs]. They circulate new ideas to police officials. Through such associations contact is established with other civic groups and with the public, in order that public knowledge and understanding of police functions and problems may improve. Such contacts, in turn, make the police more conscious of their obligations to the community.

Through the Exchange of Persons Program, German police officials have been taken to the United States to study police methods. . . . Because of impressions they gathered there many of them have become convinced supporters of the reform measures that are an American reorientation goal. From the United States and Great Britain, on the other hand, leading experts in the field have been brought to Germany to work with German police authorities and citizen groups. The visitors have served as an inspiration to German police officials.

Not only do these exchanges improve the operating efficiency of the German police force, they also bring German police officials, many of them of policy-making rank, into contact with Anglo-Saxon law enforcement agencies permeated by a sense of responsibility to all the people. German police officials who have returned from the United States have been instrumental in bringing police practice in the search of private dwellings into line with German law.[12]

POLICE FUNCTIONS AND ORGANIZATION TODAY

With the work of the three military governments of the western

[11] *Ibid.*, p. 55.   [12] *Ibid.*

powers and the trizonal efforts of the High Commission now at an end, how does the organization of the German police look today? In all three zones the police systems are now full-fledged organizations, all built in part upon German tradition, all reflecting the Allied objectives for them, but each differing from the others in certain respects.

American Zone—Characteristic of the police in Bavaria, Württemberg-Baden, Hesse, and Bremen is the large number of independent municipal police systems. A strongly developed police system at the municipal level is no innovation in the southern parts of Germany, and the American concept of police has found relatively ready reception here. Throughout the American Zone, police systems are organized in all cities and in other communities with more than 5,000 inhabitants. These police forces are under direct policy and administrative control of the local government. The chief of police, called *Polizeidirektor* or, in the larger cities, *Polizeipräsident*, is responsible to the mayor, who in turn is responsible to the city or town council. Only the city detectives, when working on crime investigation, are under some operational control by the state attorneys.

Jurisdiction over its own police system is an integral part of the autonomy of the individual community. In Bavaria, this basic principle is expressly provided for in section 83 of the *Land* constitution as adopted on December 2, 1946. Nevertheless, despite the successful organization of independent community-level police systems and despite the German legal underwriting of their existence, increasing tendencies can be observed towards state control over these municipal police systems in the *Länder* of Bavaria, Württemberg-Baden, and Hesse. In part, these inroads into local domain were made possible by the financial weakness of local governments, which must depend on state funds for grants averaging about DM3,000 for every municipal police officer. The needs of the rural areas in the American Zone are served by state police forces, called *Landpolizei* or *Landesgendarmerie*. Each of the *Länder* has its own police force, administered by the ministers of the interior of the *Länder* who, as cabinet members, are responsible to their respective *Landtage*.

In each police force in the U.S. Zone all police branches, the uniformed protection forces and the investigative forces, are consolidated under one executive head. There are no separate criminal police forces. However, there is in each *Land* a central Bureau of Criminal Identification and Statistics, partly with police power and operational responsibility. These offices provide technical services, laboratory and other scientific crime detection devices, a central identification service, and consolidated crime statistics for the service of all police forces of the *Land.* There are also a number of special state police organizations in some of the *Länder,* such as the frontier police forces in Bavaria and Hesse, forces for policing the inland waterways, forest police forces, and police training schools. All these police organizations have limited jurisdiction and responsibility and are administered on *Land* level. The combined police strength of the four *Länder* in the American Zone is about 40,000, representing 2.3 police officers for every thousand inhabitants.

British Zone—North Rhine–Westphalia, Lower Saxony, Schleswig-Holstein, and Hamburg, the *Länder* of the British Zone, until 1953 had decentralized police systems that had broken more with the past than have those of any other section of Germany. Most of the area constituted by these *Länder* (Hamburg is an exception) formerly belonged to the State of Prussia, whose police system was highly centralized. Thus the police forces throughout the British Zone were, in accordance with Order No. 135 of the British Military Government, organized in specially demarcated police districts. These police districts are formed either by cities of more than 100,000 inhabitants—neighboring cities may join together to constitute such a police district —or by the district government (*Regierungsbezirk*). As a result, forty separate and independently controlled police forces have been established, called *Stadtkreispolizei* (S/K police) in the cities and *Regierungsbezirkspolizei* (R/B police). Each police force is made up of uniformed police officers and its own internal criminal investigation, traffic, and administrative branches. The combined police strength of the three *Länder* and the *Hansestadt* Hamburg is approximately 45,000.

Each force is under the command of a chief of police, who had sole responsibility for executive control of the force, its internal administration, maintenance of discipline, and appointments to and promotion within the force up to the rank of *Obermeister.* The chief of police was in turn responsible to the Police Committee (*Polizeiausschuss*) of his district. The institution known as the Police Committee as established in the British Zone was something completely new in Germany. It was a body constituted from the freely elected representatives of the communities making up the *Regierungsbezirk* or *Stadtkreis.* In the cities, these committees, while not identical with the city council, may have some members who also serve on the city council. The Police Committee had no executive powers with regard to the operational control of its police force. Its responsibilities were maintenance of an effective police force, provision of buildings, equipment, and budgetary requirements—other than a 50 per cent grant-in-aid provided from

Länder funds—the making of promotions above the rank of *Ober-meister,* and the appointment and dismissal of the chief of police.

This system of setting up police districts whose boundaries are not identical with the established political demarcations for municipal governments had, however, not taken any strong roots. While it had its basis in British Order No. 135 and in German *Länder* legislation, popular demand was growing throughout the zone for making the police districts again contiguous with the political municipalities. This popular demand has now resulted in marking off police districts in the traditional way, a changeover which has also resulted in increased central police control at *Land* level.

At present, the British Zone *Länder* governments have the general responsibility to maintain law and order. The ministers of the interior are responsible for the general supervision of all police forces within their respective *Länder,* exercising this general supervision through nonexecutive *Land* inspectors of police. The ministers of the interior can issue instructions providing for uniform conditions of service, a uniform discipline, and a uniform system of promotions. Other prerogatives of the state administrations are the sanctioning of all police budgets and the confirmation of appointments and dismissals of chiefs and deputy chiefs of police. Aside from exercising these controls, the *Länder* maintain forces for the protection of inland waterways, police training schools, and a central office giving technical assistance in criminal investigations.

French Zone—Rhineland - Palatinate, Württemberg - Hohenzollern, and Baden, the three *Länder* making up the French Zone, have state police systems. From the outset, French occupational authorities did not undertake to decentralize police systems below *Land* level and adopted no program to develop independent communal police systems. Indeed, quite the contrary—in line with their own tradition and practice, the French supported German police systems centralized at *Land* level though they were at the same time insisting upon the decentralization of other functions of government which are equally centralized in France. A few exceptions to this practice exist, for instance in those communities of Rhineland-Palatinate having a population between 5,000 and 10,000, whose needs are served by municipal police forces. Even here, however, direct control is exercised by the Rhineland-Palatinate *Land* government.

The three centralized state police systems, with about 7,500 officers, are composed of (1) the *Schutzpolizei,* a uniformed police for the maintenance of order in towns and large and medium-sized population centers, totaling about 4,000; (2) the *gendarmerie,* a uniformed police for the maintenance of order in rural areas, totaling about 2,200; and (3) the *Kriminalpolizei,* a judicial police without uniform, stationed in towns and other centers of population, totaling about 600. In addition, the *Länder* maintain special small police forces for the protection of waterways and frontiers. As in the American and British zones, those extra-police functions belonging more properly to other executive agencies, such as the licensing of trade and business enterprises, public health inspection, and so on, have been transferred to other governmental agencies.

At *Land* level, the head of personnel of the police is a *Landespolizeidirektor,* taking his orders from the Ministry of the Interior. He performs administrative duties, such as preparing the police budget for the *Land,* directing the *Land* police schools, and standardizing the rules for management and discipline. Operationally, the uniformed forces, *Schutzpolizei* and *gendarmerie,* are organized at *Kreis* level; the *Kriminalpolizei* is organized at *Land* level and directed in each *Land* by a *Landeskriminalpolizeidirektor.*

*Berlin—*Berlin, with its four occupational sectors within the one metropolis, has had a police development peculiar to itself in the period since the end of World War II. After the end of the war, the Berlin police was reorganized on October 4, 1946, by an order of the Allied *Kommandantura.*[13] The order directed that the Berlin police be organized in such a way as to "guarantee the four-powered control of police, bring about the betterment of police practices in the interest of the city population, and safeguard the prerogatives of the chief of police, as delegated to him by the Allied *Kommandantura.* The order also provided that the chief of police for the City of Berlin should have four subchiefs, one for each of the four sectors. The same order authorized the new police force in this city of 3,200,000 to reach a strength of 15,000 police officers and 1,600 auxiliary police employees. Until 1948, this unique four-sector Berlin police met the stipulations of the order governing its formation and carried on its work, under very trying circumstances, with relative adequacy. More than any other branch of the new city government, the police was subject to the frictions and disagreements besetting the Four Power city.

When, in 1948, the split came between East and West in Berlin,[14] the division of the police meant an overnight reorganization to create an independent service for the 2,200,000 citizens of the western sectors of the city. In a matter of days, Dr. Johannes Stumm, the newly appointed police chief for the three western sectors, organized a new police with those parts of the Berlin police personnel who elected to

[13] BK/0(46)391. [14] See Chapter 4 above for further discussion.

join with the West. The old police headquarters, located in the Soviet Sector, had to be abandoned and new central offices established in the American Sector.

This western-sector Berlin police consists of about 9,500 uniformed police officers, among them 200 women and about 1,000 city detectives. Various administrative services, separated elsewhere in the western parts of Germany, have in Berlin remained under the control of the police and are performed by 1,000 police administrative personnel. In addition, about 2,000 auxiliary police employees do guard duty at certain city installations (*Wachpolizei*). In addition there also exists special mobile emergency forces.

The formal Three Power provision for the administration of the new police of West Berlin has recognized the special security needs of Berlin. It also provides a greater independence of the police system from general city government controls than other western police forces enjoy.[15]

Today, the police system of the western sectors of the City of Berlin is one of the best-organized and most effectively functioning metropolitan police systems in all Europe. In addition, this police force has a number of unique functions in the field of international co- or counteroperation.

The Federal Republic—The Basic Law for the Federal Republic of Germany has no provision for the organization of a federal public safety system. The federal government is entitled to exercise, without limitation, only a few specified police functions. In addition, it may exercise a limited police authority in certain specified emergency situations. According to Article 87 of the Bonn Constitution, the federal finance administration, the federal railways, and the federal waterways shall be conducted by a direct federal administration, with its own lower-level administrative offices. As a consequence of these provisions, the federal government has jurisdiction over the railway police, the water protection police, and the border police. The railway police, controlled by the Ministry of Traffic, consists of uniformed and plainclothes railway police officers, organized on the level of the administrative districts of the Federal Railway (*Reichsbahn*). The railway police forces, reorganized after the end of World War II by Allied authorities, are responsible for the protection of the railway service, for the preservation of law and order within the confines of the *Reichsbahn*, and for the investigation of crimes committed on railway premises.

The water protection police is responsible for the policing of inland

[15] See BK/0(49)123, *Official Gazette for Greater Berlin*, 1949, p. 194.

waterways and certain coastal waters and the enforcement of laws affecting the safety of vessels. At the present time, however, these functions are delegated to the existing water police forces of the *Länder* for the most part.

A border protection police, provided for under Article 87, has been established by law,[16] and this police will supersede and gradually take over the function of the various border police forces of the *Länder*. The strength of this force has been set at 10,000 men. The force is charged with the protection of the 2,800 miles of border of the Federal Republic. Their main task is the prevention of illegal border crossings and foreign infiltration.

Article 73 (10) of the Bonn Constitution provides for the "establishment of a Federal Office of a Criminal Police." In addition, Article 87 provides that federal legislation may establish "central offices for police information and communication, for the compilation of data for purposes concerning the protection of the Constitution, and for the Criminal Police." A Federal Office of Criminal Police (*Bundeskriminalamt*), under the control of the federal minister of the interior, has been established by statute. This agency has no executive or investigative power. It is authorized to give directives to the central criminal police offices of the states, but upon issuing such directives must inform the respective *Land* governments. The main tasks with which the agency is charged are the maintaining of liaison with the criminal police forces of other countries, the establishment of card indices on persons with criminal records, and the disseminating of lists of persons wanted by the police. In addition, the agency maintains a criminological institute (*Kriminaltechnisches Institut*) with various laboratories.

A Federal Office for the Protection of the Constitution (*Bundesamt für Verfassungsschutz*) has been established by statute.[17] This agency, which is also under the control of the minister of the interior, is an agency for collecting and disseminating information on any activities endangering the German federal constitution. The agency has no executive power and is therefore not authorized to apprehend or detain persons or to question any individual against his will. It aids and cooperates with similar agencies established at *Länder* level, but is not entitled to issue directives to them.

The emergency police powers of the federal government are limited by the provisions of Article 91 (2) of the constitution which provides

[16] Law for the Organization of a Border Protection Force for the *Bund*, February 15, 1951.
[17] Law for the Establishment of a Federal Office for the Protection of the Constitution, September 27, 1950.

as follows: "If the *Land* in which the danger is imminent is not itself prepared, or in a position to combat the danger, the Federal Government may place the police in that *Land* and the police forces of other *Länder* under its instructions. The order (*Anordnung*) shall be rescinded after the elimination of the danger, otherwise at any time on demand from the *Bundesrat.*" However, the emergency police powers contained in Article 91 (2) were suspended by the military governors "until specifically approved by the occupation authorities."[18] This suspension was lifted on February 9, 1951, by specific authorization of the Allied High Commission in response to Chancellor Adenauer's request and in accordance with decisions made at the New York meeting of the three Foreign Ministers in September, 1950.

The result of this decision, made in view of the East-West tension, was the organization of a veritable police division in the Federal Ministry of the Interior (*Bundesinnenministerium*) in Bonn. Minister of the interior, Dr. Robert Lehr, his undersecretary Ritter von Lex, and the director of the police division, Dr. Hans Egidi, are, as far as their emergency powers go, in control of the entire federal, state, and municipal police forces of Western Germany, in all about 130,000 police officers. But even in normal times the federal police administration now will exercise great influence—without interfering with the *Länder* police powers—in the advising, training, and co-ordinating of the police systems of the *Länder* and municipalities and serve as a clearing center for all basic police problems.

Yet despite the trend toward centralization here undeniably in evidence, there remains a fair balance between federal, state, and municipal systems. Even more important for the maintaining of democratic practices within the German police systems is the right of the individual citizen to have police measures and actions reviewed by the administrative, constitutional, civil, or criminal courts. This right, it is encouraging to observe, is being increasingly made use of by the citizenry of the *Bundesrepublik*.

[18] See letter to the Parliamentary Council of May 12, 1949, Appendix J.

17

Currency, Banking, Domestic and Foreign Debt

HOWARD PALFREY JONES

G ERMANY emerged from the war a broken country. Not only was her army destroyed, a large part of her plant capacity wiped out or earmarked for reparations, her transportation system crippled, her bridges smashed, her housing seriously curtailed; equally serious, she was a country without a government, a country adrift save for the military government imposed upon her by the occupying powers. Paralleling the physical chaos was economic chaos; paralleling the economic chaos was financial chaos; and with all this were bewilderment and hopelessness and shock.

A few comparatives will serve to picture the financial situation in terms of its over-all magnitudes. In 1945, in contrast with 1935, Germany's real wealth decreased by one-third, from approximately RM370 billion to RM250 billion, and her capacity to produce was cut to about one-half. Yet during the same period, her public debt (Reich only) increased from RM15 billion to RM400 billion, not counting potential war-damage claims of about an equal amount, and her currency and bank deposits jumped from about RM35 billion to more than RM200 billion. At the same time, her population increased perhaps 25 per cent, due largely to the artificial introduction of huge numbers of refugees into a country without adequate facilities for taking care of the people already there. Germany, in a postwar situation of critical scarcity in almost everything that people needed to live and work, had more money than she could use. The country was suffering from a tremendous monetary overhang that threw the relationship between money with which to buy and goods available for purchase so badly out of line that money had no meaning.

CURRENCY REFORM

The runaway inflation of 1923 had taught the Germans to beware of deteriorating currency. They had reached a stage where they were afraid of money but were uncertain as to what should be substituted for it as a medium of exchange. They wanted something which was in universal demand, which could always be exchanged for goods needed. They found it in cigarettes. And so the famous "cigarette currency" of Germany developed. Illegal product of black-market operations though it was, it nevertheless proved to be the most stable medium of exchange in this "Alice in Wonderland" country over a period of nearly three years during which the German people in fact if not in law repudiated the official reichsmark.

In this period the tragedy of Germany from a financial and economic standpoint lay in the unjustifiable delay in adopting measures to correct a situation which obviously was subject to ready repair. When the Allied armies marched into Belgium, a currency conversion program was ready to hand, having been prepared in London; indeed, the author in September, 1944, ran the gantlet of the German blockade to transport across the English Channel, from a London printing plant to the *Banque Nationale de Belgique* in Brussels, forty-three tons of notes necessary for the conversion. On October 8, 1944, hardly one month subsequent to the liberation of Belgium, currency reform was launched in that country by then Finance Minister Gutt. The postwar economic condition of Belgium, in contrast to most European countries, was at least partial testimony to this prompt and effective action.

Efforts at Quadripartite Reform—There was no such fortune for Germany or its equivalent relief for the American taxpayer who was forced to rush to the aid of a defeated and helpless foe. Germany's finances became in a very real sense America's sacrifice to a three-year frustrating effort to assist Four Power control of Germany. Not that a financial solution was all that was needed—it was, however, the foundation that had to be laid. The United States Military Government representatives fought long and hard at Four Power council tables to reach agreement on an all-German currency reform and related measures. The prevention of inflation and the establishment of a sound financial basis for economic recovery in Germany were the object of a comprehensive program, outlined in the Colm-Dodge-Goldsmith report, which was put forward early in 1946 as the U.S. answer to the question raised by the financial aftermath of the war. The plan[1] included three major proposals:

a. The elimination of the monetary overhang by the creation of a new currency, to be called the *Deutsche* mark (DM), and the reduction of existing monetary claims and obligations to the ratio of ten old reichsmarks to one new mark. Cancellation of the existing national debt would accompany this action, with the assumption by Germany as a whole of a new debt allocated to banks and other financial institutions in amounts which would enable them to balance their books after the devaluation of the mark.

b. The equalization of the burdens imposed by the war and by currency reform, in connection therewith the imposition of mortgages on real estate, plant equipment, and inventories at 50 per cent of the value. Title to the mortgages would be placed in a War Loss Equalization Fund which would issue certificates to persons who had suffered losses from war damage and monetary devaluation.

c. The imposition of a progressive capital levy, with rates ranging from 10 to 90 per cent on the remaining net worth of individuals after the first two proposals had been put into effect, to assist in financing the equalization program; the levy to be paid into the War Loss Equalization Fund over a ten-year period. An exemption limit would have relieved the majority of the population from the levy.

The plan also proposed a number of important corollary measures to be taken, including the following:

a. Adjustments in banking organization and credit structure.
1. Creation of a new bank of issue and credit control.
2. Liquidation of part of the excessive banking structure.
3. Provision of working capital and medium and long-term credits to industry.
4. Introduction of deposit and mortgage insurance.
5. Creation of small-amount life and burial insurance.
b. Adjustments in price and wage structure.
c. Adjustment in government budgets and the tax structure.
1. Limitation of war-damage payments, pensions, benefit payments, and occupation costs and economies by reason of reductions in expenditures and consolidation of governmental agencies.

[1] OMGUS, *Special Report: A Plan for the Liquidation of War Finance and the Financial Rehabilitation of Germany,* May 20, 1946.

    2. Moderate reductions in income and property taxes and possible increase in excise and luxury taxes.

    d. Determination of the rate of exchange of the new *Deutsche* mark.

The program was destined never to be adopted in full, although its principles served as the basis of the currency conversion which eventually took place in the three western zones. Meanwhile, Four Power negotiations, seemingly often on the verge of successful conclusion, finally broke down over what might seem a minor matter, the question as to where the currency should be printed. The western Allies urged the use of the former Reich printing plant in Berlin—a modern, well-equipped plant—under strict quadripartite supervision. Berlin, being the only quadripartite city in Germany, seemed the logical place since facilities were available. The Soviet delegation, however, insisted that the printing take place in Leipzig in their zone at a plant dubiously equipped therefor. The unreasonableness of this position, for which they were unable to muster any arguments that seemed logical to western minds, made it appear as though their real purpose lay in planned secret manipulation of the currency in their own interest. This view was supported by western experience with the Soviets in the matter of printing Allied Military Marks for use in Germany.[2] It should be added that just before the Soviet delegation walked out of the currency negotiations, it had presented a compromise plan under which a German department of finance would be created to issue and manage the new currency that would then be printed in Berlin. Whether or not this might have been the basis for a solution, whether or not, indeed, it was a genuine offer in view of the fact that agreement had not been reached on basic questions of governmental structure and policy to which the establishment of a German department of finance was subsidiary, will never be known, since the Soviet delegation chose this moment to terminate the discussions.[3] When the break finally came, after protracted effort had made it clear that the men in the Kremlin were delaying in the belief that an economic breakdown in the western zone would provide a fertile field for communism, it meant that Germany would have two currencies. One was to be created in the Germany comprising the three western zones, and another for the eastern zone under Soviet control, with Berlin the meeting ground and the battleground.

Reform in Western Germany—It is with the currency reform programs in the western zones that we are primarily concerned here, with

[2] Jack Bennett, "The German Currency Reform", *Annals of the American Academy of Political and Social Science*, CCLXVII (Jan., 1950), p. 44.
    [3] *Ibid.*

its objectives, terms, and conditions, with its effects, in so far as effects can be isolated from other contemporary factors, and with the corollary conditions which were essential to make it a firm success. The currency reform program as finally put into effect in the three zones of Western Germany during the week of June 20 to 26 of 1948 was the most drastic operation of its kind ever performed on a nation where runaway inflation had not already taken its toll. True, Germany had been suffering from black markets and gray markets and had reached a stage of economic paralysis in which barter and compensation trading had become the order of the day. Nevertheless, runaway inflation had been successfully avoided by the price-wage freeze which was fastened on the economy in the early days of the occupation. In terms of money in circulation, what this financial operation actually accomplished in Germany was to reduce, subsequent to "C" day, June 20, 1948, the RM130 billion in currency and bank deposits in Western Germany to somewhere between DM12 and 13 billion (*Deutsche* marks). In terms of psychology, what happened was that the Allies breathed the breath of life into a new money, in which the German people suddenly acquired confidence—so significant is scarcity in a commodity even when that commodity is money.

A series of laws, promulgated simultaneously by the military governors of the three zones, constituted the legal basis for the conversion.[4] Their contents represented the utmost in monetary sophistication, since the architects of the program had been enabled to take advantage of the experience of the half-dozen European nations which had adopted conversion programs since the war. The plan provided for a provisional supply of money in the hands of the population to see them through the week of conversion. Each person received 40 new marks, which at the precurrency reform military rate would have been $4 and at the postconversion 30-cent rate was $13.30. The old money was no longer valid after June 21, 1948. It was required that by the end of the week which began on that date all old currency must be deposited for subsequent conversion at a rate to be announced later. Thus, the population was required to deposit all old currency before the basic conversion rate or the other features of the plan were known. This prevented much of the manipulation which ordinarily

[4] First Law for Monetary Reform (currency law), Military Government Law No. 61, June 18, 1948; Second Law (issue law), Military Government Law No. 62, June 20, 1948; Third Law (conversion law), Military Government Law No. 63, June 27, 1948; Fourth Law (supplementary), Military Government Law No. 65, October 4, 1948; Provisional Revision of Taxation, Military Government Law No. 64, June 20, 1948.

accompanies a monetary conversion. The program as finally announced would in any other country have been a terrific shock, but the Germans had so long awaited a currency reform that the whole country was relieved, not over its terms, but over the fact that it had finally come.

Although the basic tenet of the program was the reduction in value of individual holdings of currency and bank deposits from 10 to 1, in the implementation of the plan a person actually received considerably less. Before the blocked half of the accounts had been released, it became evident by the rise in prices that sufficient money was already in circulation. The 5 per cent that had been blocked was then distributed as follows: 3.5 billion marks were canceled, an additional billion was put into circulation and available for consumption purposes immediately, and 500 million marks were set aside for capital investment. It meant that the individuals affected received only .65 to 10 rather than 1 to 10.

It would manifestly have been inequitable to write down an individual's cash holdings and at the same time neglect the other side of his ledger—what he owed. Debt was treated as follows. A moratorium of one week was declared on all debt, wages, and other contractual payments, and at the same time all debt and contractual obligations were written down by the same 90 per cent liquidation rate that was applied to money, with certain unavoidable exceptions. Wages themselves were continued at the same rates, and there was no alteration in prices except those resulting from a decontrol program which was put into effect simultaneously. The entire internal debt of the Reich and its agencies, estimated at approximately RM400 billion, was invalidated. Since the banks, insurance companies, and other financial institutions had heavy holdings of this paper, provision was made for liquid assets and new public securities to keep these institutions solvent.

One of the interesting features of the program was the apparent inconsistency between the provision for tax reduction and the provision that all governmental budgets must be balanced while imposing severe restrictions on borrowing. One of the precurrency reform accomplishments in the field of public finance which had astounded observers of the German scene was the fact that an economy so badly damaged had since the occupation been able to balance governmental budgets. One of the reasons for this was the high tax rates imposed by the Allied Control Council. The best estimates available indicate that prior to currency reform approximately 40 per cent of the national income was taken in taxes. This was obviously too high: many a businessman found himself in the position of paying more in taxes than he earned. Had it not been for the tremendous monetary overhang that existed and the lack of confidence in the currency generally—so that there was in fact no financial foundation on which to base economic recovery in Germany—the tax burden alone would have impeded recovery. A 33⅓ per cent reduction in taxes lightened this burden and gave the entrepreneur additional encouragement to go to work. The requirement that governmental budgets must continue to be balanced was an anti-inflationary measure to force down governmental expenditures as required, although governmental officials optimistically predicted that a reduction in tax rates would actually bring in more revenue. Additional inducement to the entrepreneur was provided in the form of decontrol of prices in all but essential food items, coal, steel, oil, and rents. Every effort was made, in other words, to provide a normal climate in which normal economic relationships would operate up to the point of extreme short supply such as existed in the case of foodstuffs.

The immediate results of currency reform were so dramatic as to be almost unbelievable. One day there was nothing to buy in the shops; the next day the shops were full of merchandise. One day nobody would sell anything for marks; the next day no one would sell except for marks. Goods which had not been seen since the war appeared in the shops; new shops were opened; people were again willing to work and sell both goods and services for this new money. There was, of course, some bitter with the sweet. Previously, everyone had money but there was little to buy. Now, no one had very much money and there was almost everything to buy. Though there was also a sharp rise in unemployment during the period of initial readjustment, the best measure of the success of the reform is the extent to which Germany eventually went back to work. In June of 1948, the index of industrial production (1936=100) stood at 45; in June of 1949, it had doubled to nearly 90; by mid-1951 it was over 130 and still rising. Because of extensive black-market operations before the currency reform, the precurrency reform index does not completely reflect output. The comparison of indices somewhat magnifies the improvement in west German industry, since extensive black-market operations before currency reform had drained off production from legitimate and measured channels. Additional evidence of the success of the reform is to be found in the fact that the *Deutsche* mark officially has the value of 23.8 cents, and by mid-1951 it was selling at slightly over 19 cents on the Swiss free exchange. Caution should be taken at this point not to credit currency reform alone with this tremendous achievement. The Marshall Plan, stimulating German initiative, energy, and capacity by contributing the tools with which to work, must be credited with primary responsibility for the result. Without a sound money in which people had confidence, however, even the Marshall Plan could not have been so effective.

Aside from the fact that it should have come much earlier to speed the postwar economic recovery of Germany, the currency reform was nicely timed in the light of the situation then existing. It came exactly three months to the day (March 20, 1948) after the Russians walked out of the Allied Control Council meeting. (Fortunately the new money had already been printed in the United States in 1947 in preparation for a quadripartite currency reform, and no delays were necessary because of printing problems.) It was timed to take effect after seedtime but before harvesttime so that the farmer would receive new money for his crops. It would manifestly have been disastrous on future food production if the farmer had had the product of his year's labor and his working capital liquidated at a 90 per cent rate. The harvesting of the small grains (wheat, rye, and barley), hay, potatoes, and hops begins in Germany in July so that the program could not have waited much longer. Meanwhile, too, a central bank for the three western zones, the *Bank Deutscher Länder,* had been set up and had begun operations, so that a central banking system was now available to handle the mechanics of a great currency conversion operation. Finally, the first quarter of the European Recovery Program was under way but substantial shipments had not yet begun to arrive.

Governmentally, the situation was not quite so ripe. A provisional German organization, the Bizonal Economic Council,[5] which bridged the gap between zonal administration by the Allies and the establishment of the Federal Republic of Germany in the three western zones, had not yet been converted into a full-fledged government. This meant that both the currency reform and tax reform measures had to be military government regulations, although there was considerable German participation in the planning and implementation. Last-minute currency reform negotiations were proceeding with the French when there was still no positive indication that the National Assembly would approve the Six Power Agreement, providing for economic integration of the French Zone with the other two western zones.[6] The situation in Berlin was one of tension; the full-scale blockade was not

[5] See Chapter 2 above.
[6] London Conference recommendation on economic organization of Germany in the combined U.S.-U.K. zones and the French Zone: communiqué of June 2, 1948. *Germany, 1947-1949: The Story in Documents* (Washington, D.C., 1950).

yet in effect, but Four Power negotiations had broken down and the Soviets were interfering with traffic to and from Berlin. In addition to nonpropitious political and governmental situations, the banking and credit picture was not complete. A new Office of Debt Administration had been authorized but was not yet ready to take over its duties. A Reconstruction Loan Corporation had been authorized by military government on June 2, but no action had been taken to create such a public loan corporation, and legislation setting up agricultural credit banks was still in the discussion stages. The Bizonal Economic Administration had not established its 1948/49 budget or authorized any public borrowing. Under these circumstances, considerable credit is due the men who engineered the currency reform, both Allied and German. Many men worked night and day and some under highly disadvantageous circumstances. For secrecy purposes, the group of German technical experts working on currency reform and tax reform were segregated at a "Shangri-La" behind barbed wire and under armed guard, a voluntary submission to a temporary concentration camp.

Reform in the Western Sectors of Berlin—The three western sectors of Berlin were not included in the currency reform program for the western zones, but three days after the announcement of the western currency reform, the Russians announced a new currency reform for the Eastern Zone applicable also to Greater Berlin. This was an attempt to incorporate all of Berlin economically into the Eastern Zone. The three western Allies two days later proclaimed a new currency for the three western sectors of Berlin. The basic conception was the same, but the *Deutsche* mark for the three western sectors of Berlin was specially marked with a "B" although freely convertible into the western zone *Deutsche* mark. Many complications have resulted from the competition of two currencies, existing side by side in the same city but each circulating only in part of the city. Suffice to say here that over a long period of time the East mark which was launched at par has had a relation to the west mark of about 5 to 1, a rough measurement of the purchasing power of each.

REORGANIZATION OF THE GERMAN BANKING SYSTEM

On the theory that the centralization of the German banking system played into the hands of Adolph Hitler and enabled him to utilize machinery already created to gain complete control over Germany's financial resources, Allied policy in Germany was directed toward the establishment of a new decentralized banking system, modeled somewhat on American experience. Emphasis on political decentralization in the Potsdam Agreement was matched by the article[7] which required that "at the earliest possible date, the German economy shall be decentralized for the purpose of eliminating the present excessive concentration of economic power." This was spelled out more specifically by United States policy directives, the 1947 directive stating unequivocally that the U.S. Commander "will take such action as may be necessary to prevent the establishment of a centralized German banking system and an undue concentration of financial power."[8] Background for the Allied conclusion that the entire banking system had served as Hitler's funnel for the control of the nation's financial resources is found in the long history of German financial institutions culminating in the empire built by Dr. Schacht.

Historical Development of the German Banking System—Except for the famous fifteenth-century merchant banking house of Fugger at Augsburg, financiers to the Hapsburg kings, there were no banks in Germany until the seventeenth century when the Hamburger Bank was founded, modeled after a similar bank in Amsterdam. The principal problem then as now—three hundred years later—was monetary stability and convertibility. Each city had its own currency, which was subject to violent fluctuations. The Hamburger Bank, which existed until the *Reichsbank* was founded, became a clearinghouse for all kinds of money and for this purpose created a fictitious but stable unit of value based upon a quantity of silver, known as the *Mark Banko*. About a hundred and fifty years later, a century after the Bank of England was founded, the first banks of issue were finally established in Germany. In 1785 Frederick the Great established the Royal *Giro* and Loan Bank in Berlin. It became the leading bank of issue, survived upheavals, and in 1846 became the Prussian State Bank, predecessor to the *Reichsbank*. Numerous small German kingdoms and duchies followed suit, and royal families founded some thirty additional banks which issued over a hundred different types of money. Consolidation proceeded only gradually, and it was not until 1935 that the *Reichsbank* became the sole bank of issue.

From 1875 until 1922 the *Reichsbank* was under the supervision and management of the German Reich. It struck gold and silver coins and issued paper money which was covered by gold, commercial papers, and government bonds. Paper money was convertible into gold upon demand until the outbreak of World War I. In 1923, at the time

[7] Protocol of the Proceedings of the Berlin (Potsdam) Conference, July 17-August 2, 1945, par. 12.

[8] 1947 Directive to the Commander in Chief of the U.S. Forces of Occupation (JCS 1779), July 15, 1947, par. 19b (3).

of the postwar inflation in Germany, the Dawes Commission was established with financial objectives in part similar to those of the present occupation, namely, balanced budgets and a sound currency in a stabilized economy. One of the first acts under the Banking Law of 1924, which resulted from the work of the Dawes Commission, was to make the *Reichsbank* completely independent from the German government. In 1933 one of the first acts of the Nazi regime was to do exactly the opposite, and the *Reichsbank* was placed under the direct control of Adolf Hitler. This enabled the Nazi dictator, through Dr. Schacht, then head of the *Reichsbank,* to carry on secret operations and finance German rearmament without public knowledge. The *Reichsbank* was continued after the occupation until Military Government Laws 60 and 66 went into effect establishing the *Land Central Bank* and the *Bank Deutscher Länder* in its place, thus creating a federal reserve type of central banking system.

Commercial banking in the eighteenth and nineteenth century in Germany was principally in the hands of famous Jewish private banks, who reputation was such as to command respect throughout the financial world. The same cannot be said of the incorporated banks in Germany whose history is not an enviable one. Unhampered by restrictive legislation, many banks were established, prospered for a time, and then frequently failed or were taken over by other banks. This was principally due to their assumption of large risks in almost any type of business that appeared to offer quick profits. By a process of consolidation and elimination, these private institutions were reduced in number so that in 1918 only eight highly centralized, extremely powerful banking institutions remained. These controlled 87 per cent of the capital of all banks, and with over one thousand branches throughout Germany, probably an equally high percentage of all the business. In 1931, Germany experienced a bank crisis almost simultaneously with that in the United States, which was set off by failure of one of the Darmstatt banks. A few large banks survived this crisis and became more powerful than ever. They were principally the banks known as the *Deutsche Bank,* the *Dresdner Bank,* and the *Commerzbank,* all three of which survived World War II and were decentralized into regional independent banks under Military Government Law No. 57.

In addition to the large commercial banks Germany has numerous savings banks which as a rule are municipally owned by the *Gemeinde* or *Kreis* in which they operate. These banks are usually the depository for *Gemeinde* and *Kreis* public funds, and the local government is responsible for their liabilities. Credit co-operatives also play an important role in Germany. They were founded in 1860 by Raiffeisen and became extremely popular in Württemberg-Baden and Bavaria. In North Württemberg alone, there were some 800 rural credit co-operatives. These tiny mutual banks work closely together through large central co-operative banking associations. Finally, the postal savings and the postal check system have become widely used in Germany. These systems were copied after the Austrian model and following the German-Austrian *Anschluss* were actually operated from Vienna.

Postwar Banking Reform—When the Allied armies entered Germany in the fall of 1944, they found no banks: the buildings themselves were for the most part buried under heaps of rubble, the personnel had fled with the records and what assets they could lay their hands on. Occupation currency had to be used in the early stages to meet payrolls of local governments, industries, and coal mines which it was deemed essential to keep operating. The speed of the Allied advance across Germany was such that conditions were less acute as deeper penetration was effected. Nevertheless, by the end of the war, such banking operations as were in existence, were directly supervised by Allied Military Government. The stage thus was set for the sweeping reform that was in contemplation. The United States proposed quadripartite legislation to close the *Reichskreditgesellschaft* and the *Bank der Deutschen Arbeit*—both Nazi-created institutions—and break up the other big three private banking systems by (a) abolishing their national head offices and (b) limiting branch banking to the confines of a single state. The U. S. proposals originally contemplated going even further, decentralizing to a city or country basis under local ownership and control.

Progress was slow. By December, 1945, agreement had been reached on one item, a plan for clearings between the four zones of Germany. Shortly thereafter, two other relatively noncontroversial items were agreed: "the Elimination of Bank Power to Invest in Stocks and Engage in Stock Exchange Transactions" and a paper on "Uniform Banking Statistics in Germany."[9] Meanwhile, the German economy was crippled by the lack of central banking machinery of any kind, and representatives of the Four Powers were struggling over the question as to which should take precedence—the establishment of a central bank or the decentralization of all banking, the U.S. view being that, of these two vital questions, the first must, as a matter of practical operation, take precedence. It was not as apparent then as it later became that the Soviets were playing a blocking game. United States authorities, impatient at seemingly unwarranted delay

[9] CORC/MC 46/15, March 18, 1946.

in reaching agreement on basic questions, adopted Military Government Law No. 57 in the U.S. Zone in 1947 which provided for breakup and curtailment of the activities of the large banks, the appointment of custodians for the separate posts, and a change of names for the new institutions created by this dismemberment. This law, considerably modified, later served as the basis for legislation in all three western zones in 1949. It provided that no bank might have branches in any state other than that in which its head office is located, except that banks with operations confined to medium- and long-term credit extension might obtain approval of the *Bank Deutscher Länder* for such purpose. Banks were also made subject to the technical supervision of the Ministry of Finance through the Bank Supervisory Authority in each *Land* and regulated also by the *Bank Deutscher Länder*. The changes in the names of the banks were confirmed and the custodianships continued.[10]

Though still in the process of transition, the banking system which has thus far emerged for Western Germany may be described as a system generally patterned after that of the United States. The central bank of this federal reserve type system is the *Bank Deutscher Länder* with its seat in Frankfurt am Main. It is the bank of issue and has wide discretion in directing and controlling banking and credit policies in Western Germany. The bank has also the function of administering the foreign exchange transactions of Western Germany, one of its most important responsibilities. Finally, the handling of money transfer and clearing operations between the various states and the power to fix uniform discount and minimum reserve policy give the institution powers in this respect equivalent to those of the Federal Reserve Board in the United States. It further holds the cash reserves required of the *Land* central member banks and rediscounts eligible papers for these banks.[11]

The bank is restricted to dealing with the state central banks which have been established in each state and lacks the power of the old *Reichsbank* to compete with other banks for private business. The capital of the bank was originally established at RM100 million to be paid by the member *Land Central Banks* in proportion to their own deposits. The president of each *Land Central Bank* is a member of the governing board of the *Bank Deutscher Länder*. These plus a president and chairman of the board, elected by the eleven *Land* bank

[10] Decentralization of Banks, Military Government Law No. 57 (Revised), April 15, 1949.

[11] Establishment of a *Bank Deutscher Länder*, Military Government Law No. 60, February 15, 1948.

presidents, make up the thirteen members of the governing board.

The *Land Central Banks* in turn have power to:

a. Exercise qualitative and quantitative control over the supply of money and credit within their territory.

b. Promote the solvency and liquidity of financial institutions and ensure the required minimum reserves against deposits.

c. Act as the sole fiscal agent of the *Land* in respect of funds supplied as new currency or obtained from taxation. This involves also executing financial transactions for, or granting short-term credits to, the *Land* or other public corporations.

d. Aid in clearing operations within the *Land* and assist in financial transactions with other German *Länder* and with foreign countries under the direction of the *Bank Deutscher Länder*.

e. Handle the safekeeping and management of securities and their transfer.[12]

The president and vice-president of the *Land Central Bank* are appointed by the minister-president of the *Land* upon recommendation of the minister of finance. The board of nine directors is chosen in a manner to assure broad representation: a chairman appointed by the minister-president upon recommendation of the minister of finance; a vice-chairman who shall be the president of the bank; the head of the Bank Supervisory Authority; one representative each from agriculture, trade and industry, workers and employees, appointed by the minister having competence in these respective fields; one representative each from co-operative, private, and public law credit institutions elected by the respective shareholders. The board of directors determines policy and appoints the remaining members of the board of managers (of which the president and vice-president are two) which is the agency that really runs the bank. The board of managers is composed of the officers of the bank as required under its bylaws.

Discussion of the program for decentralization of the German banking system would be incomplete without frank recognition that it has constituted one of the most controversial of all programs adopted by the occupying powers. It was subjected to sharp criticism from within as well as without the Allied circle, and many leading German monetary and banking experts continue to criticize it as a program based on false promises and one which creates a banking system ill adapted to a nation of the size and complexity of Germany and ill designed to meet the special problems of strain inherent in the German economy. One school of thought has held that in a diversified economy such as Germany's with its high concentration of industry in the Ruhr it

[12] *Land Central Banks,* Military Government Law No. 66, April 15, 1949.

was unsound to decentralize both public and private finance, on the ground that in a depression period neither the public fiscal authorities nor the private banking system could come to the rescue of a depressed area. This, it is argued, would have the inevitable result of human suffering forcing a return to a higher degree of centralization than would have been the case had more moderate measures been adopted.

Some German bankers also take issue with the premise on which the three big banks were broken up—that is, their importance in financing the Nazi war effort. They insist that these banks had no more decisive a role in the financing of the war than did the savings banks, credit co-operatives, and regional banks which were not centrally organized; they point out that on September 30, 1944, when the total indebtedness of the Reich amounted to approximately RM300 billion the savings banks held approximately 53 billion in treasury certificates and Reich loans and in addition had approximately 35 billion on deposit with the *Girozentralen* which in turn invested the major part of these funds in Reich obligations. Furthermore, they insist the Reich issued strict regulations which prevented banks and insurance companies from free choice in investment decisions and forced the acquisition of Reich securities upon them. This would have happened regardless of the degree of centralization, these critics say.

Regardless of these criticisms, however, and regardless, too, of a host of legal problems created by the breakup of the big banks, there seems a disposition on the part of most German bankers to accept the present decentralized banking structure as a foundation upon which to build a new type of system that ultimately will have to adjust itself to the requirements of the German economy serviced by it. To say this, however, is not to imply that there is general satisfaction with the present system. Leading German bankers have been discussing for some time proposals to reorganize the banking system in an effort to strike a compromise between the present and prewar systems. They recognize frankly that a re-establishment of the prewar banking system would be blocked by the Allies but maintain, on the other hand, that permanent decentralization to a *Land* level is excessive in a relatively small country like Germany. "Midget banks," they insist wryly, can neither enjoy sufficient credit abroad nor fulfill the domestic credit requirements. The latest German thinking proposes the creation of three regional banks for each of the big prewar banks, each regional bank to maintain branches in neighboring *Länder*. There would be three groups of *Länder*, a north group, a south group, and a west group. There would be nine regional banks, each operating in one group of *Länder*. To the charge that this would cut into the effectiveness of the *Land Central Banks*, those advocating this plan insist that the *Land Central Banks* would retain the same authority over these regional banks as they now have over banks operating in their territory—that is, control over rediscount facilities and minimum reserves as well as the monopoly on making remittances between *Länder*. The proposal contemplates distribution of the shares of the regional banks to stockholders of the prewar banks. There are other problems to be solved, among them the question of applicability of the Currency Conversion Law to the prewar banks; and also the diffi-culties arising from debts of the prewar banks. These problems, how-ever, would be outside of the scope of any such proposal.

DOMESTIC AND FOREIGN INDEBTEDNESS

The huge military effort by Germany prior to and during six years of war could only in small part be financed from normal government revenues. By far the greater portion of war expenditures was financed by means of currency expansion and loans which, however, did not stem from savings. As pointed out above, insurance companies and other financial institutions were required to invest their funds in treasury bills and treasury bonds which they could resell to the *Reichsbank* at any time. Without running any risk as to their liquidity, the banks could thus freely expand their credit volume, and the state had the benefit of the increased credits. At the end of the war the internal debts of the former *Deutsche Reich* were estimated at upwards of RM400 billion. This huge debt—representing five times the amount of the national income of 1938—was eliminated with one stroke of the pen through currency reform.

To offset the liabilities of the banks and other financial institutions, so-called equalization claims were created, which for all practical purposes can be considered both as a cover for the new currency and as a bankruptcy quota of the old Reich debts. This sum totals more than DM16 billion, of which DM6 billion represent liability of the Federal Republic and the balance an obligation of the *Länder*. It is interesting to note that this amount of 16 billion in equalization claims is a perpetual debt because no provision has been made for its repay-ment. At an average rate of 3 per cent, the interest required to be paid on this debt totals approximately DM500 million per annum, some DM350 million of which have to be raised by the *Länder*, the remaining DM150 million being paid by the Federal Republic.

There is also a floating debt resulting from the loans that have been made since currency reform, in an amount of approximately DM2 billion. In theory, this debt can be acquired only in anticipation of revenues, since the currency laws explicitly prohibit any budgetary deficits and provide that public borrowing is limited to provisional cash advances. Actually, however, this proved to be too inflexible and German legislation approved by the Allied High Commission eased this situation somewhat, albeit at the expense of acquisition of a permanent short-term debt which appears to be increasing slowly but steadily. The resulting indebtedness is, however, relatively inconsiderable, amounting to less than one-quarter of the present national income, and only some 3 per cent of the budgetary funds of the *Bund* and the *Länder* are required to meet the interest on this debt.

The currency reform laid to rest the problem of the domestic debts of the Reich, but did nothing to solve the delicate and complex problem of Germany's foreign indebtedness. Foreign creditors, quite understandably, began to show interest in their old claims only after the almost valueless reichsmark had been replaced by the new *Deutsche mark*, that is, they remembered the debtor only after he was on his way out of bankruptcy toward solvency. The question is a vital one for Germany too. Foreign investment capital, much needed, will hardly venture into Germany again until the old debts are settled. Up to the present writing, settlement of these obligations has been impossible, since military government law prohibited such transactions, primarily to prevent the exploitation of Germany and an illicit transfer of property to foreign countries.

In terms of the present rate of exchange, Germany's entire prewar liabilities vis-à-vis foreign countries amount to some DM15 billion, including about DM3 to 4 billion of public debts and DM5 to 7 billion of private debts plus unpaid interest. The problem of settlement is complicated by the unpleasant fact that in some cases the debtor no longer exists. This is true, for example, of the former Reich which, from the point of view of international law, must be considered as having perished and which, in view of the division of Germany in two parts, has not found an official successor in the German Federal Republic. As far as private debtors and the public corporations are concerned, claims can also be advanced only if they are located in Western Germany, and it is not possible at least for the time being, to enforce any claims vis-à-vis debtors residing in East Germany or the cut-off areas in the East.

In spite of these and many other difficulties, the German Federal Republic, in an official letter of March 6, 1951, addressed to the Allied High Commission, declared its readiness to assume the liability for the prewar debts of the *Deutsche Reich*. However, the Federal Republic pointed out that due consideration must be given to territorial changes and the solvency of Germany. At the same time, the letter acknowledged the liabilities resulting from the economic aid received after the war. This assistance amounts also to some DM15 billion, so that all foreign debts, both prewar and postwar, can be estimated to amount to some DM30 billion. It is obvious that such a burden—corresponding to something like three times the amount of all German imports for 1950—would be too heavy for the debtor if its full weight were brought to bear. This is recognized by her creditors, and it will be necessary to work out a formula providing for the resumption of interest payments in the first instance and a gradual amortization as soon as her balance of payments position makes this feasible.

EQUALIZATION OF BURDENS

It was generally recognized in Germany that justice demanded some equalization of the burdens resulting from war losses and losses sustained through currency reform. It has already been noted that this was also included as a fundamental part of the original financial planning of the Allies. The caprice of fortune emphasized this situation in dramatic ways. One man's house would stand unharmed, while his neighbors on both sides were completely destroyed. One man's factory would be severely damaged, while a neighboring plant stood intact. Everyone in Germany, it is true, had lost something. But some—indeed many—had lost everything. Essentially, however, the straightening out of the situation, the effort to render approximate justice, was a German task, calling for German decisions; consequently this part of the program was left to the Germans themselves to work out.

Since June, 1948, the date of currency reform, the Germans have been endeavoring to draft legislation which would untangle the skein of this problem. It should be appreciated that a genuine equalization of war burdens in Germany amounts to a redistribution of property on a broad scale. It is literally taking away from those who have and giving to those who have not. Its effects, consequently, approach those of a social revolution, and its political as well as economic consequences are tremendous. The major political parties, therefore, have been approaching the problem somewhat warily, recognizing that their constituencies are composed of both those who have suffered losses and those who still own property. Finally, the implementation of such a program involves many complex questions as to how in fact to bring about a redistribution of properties over a period of time without upsetting the economic machinery of the nation. If the burden is to be imposed gradually, then a capital levy at the rate of a given per cent a year is probably the most practical answer. If wealth remaining after the war were to be levied upon at a 50 per cent rate, it would take approximately twenty-five years to settle the matter. If installment payments are made from this levy each year, then the equalization of burdens becomes a form of social relief and not a genuine redistribution of wealth as originally contemplated. Owners of properties, furthermore, could be counted upon to consider the 2 per cent as an additional tax levy and to pay it from income rather than capital.

The Germans are invariably meticulous and thorough, and they have in this case made strenuous efforts to work out a practical program with all possible refinements; but a capital levy at best can only approximate justice, and the endeavor to refine it may only result in additional complexities which make the program even more difficult of implementation. It was obvious by the fall of 1949 that legislation to attack the problem head on would not be ready for some time. Meanwhile, the pressure for some relief was steadily increasing from those who had suffered losses. A stopgap aid program was, therefore, initiated which took the form of an emergency relief tax to provide the needy with basic essentials (that is, furniture, clothing, and shelter), to enable juveniles to obtain an education, and to ensure a subsistence standard of living for the aged and the handicapped. This program is costing approximately DM1.5 billion annually.

It is now some years since the end of the war. Germany has recovered economically to the point where its industrial production index has reached 130 (1936=100). It remains to be seen whether the German parliament will attempt to turn the clock back and spread the burden as it existed at the end of the war. Many changes have taken place in the status of individuals and groups since 1945. The country is prospering again. There is considerable sentiment in favor of leaving the economic machinery much as it is by those who take the point of view that even those who suffered serious losses as a result of the war would gain less by being partly repaid than by sharing in the economic recovery now under way. For, this group argues, the readjustments and uncertainties created by the equalization program would constitute a serious brake on economic progress. Then, too, there are millions of refugees. These, certainly, have lost everything, and are beginning to be a political force to be reckoned with. But no program of equalization of burdens will touch them. Thus, in all, the outlook for legislative action on this problem is not too bright, although there will continue to be strong pressure from the individuals and groups which suffered most.

BERLIN

The exposed position of Berlin means that any economic or financial calculations are subject to assumptions as to the extent of Soviet harassment in any given period. However, the dependence of the Soviet Zone of Germany on trade with the West is so great that it may reasonably be assumed that Soviet interference with Berlin trade will not reach the point at which the western Allies will be aggravated into taking strong countermeasures. With this as a basic assumption, the program of external financial aid to Berlin has been designed to bring about gradual economic recovery in the city. It is difficult to see how any fundamental change in the relationship between the Allies and the Berlin city government can take place in the near future for both political and economic reasons. So long as Berlin is not a part of the German Federal Republic, so long as substantial aid is required to meet Berlin's deficit, just so long will it be necessary for the Allies to retain greater power of action in Berlin.

18

Education

ALONZO G. GRACE

EDUCATION under the National Socialist party was not limited to formal educational facilities such as schools, universities, or research institutions. It comprised every means by which the party and state could dominate the minds and souls of an entire nation. Hitler proclaimed that education does not begin or end with a certain age. The National Socialist revolution imposed upon education clearly defined tasks and made these independent of any age group. Every field or medium of education was considered within the scope of the state's obligation. Schools, books, newspapers, theaters, films, were recognized and used as educational media. Hitler youth, labor service, party, armed forces, were regarded as educational institutions and as such helped to mold the minds of the German people. All media were controlled, and any external influence, whether exerted by family, private societies, or churches was eliminated. Hence, the final aim of education under the Nazis was political, that is, the creation of a political National Socialist human being.

If the democratic reorientation of German education involved nothing more than the restoration of the pre-Hitler educational system and practices, the task would be less difficult. While the great mass of German educators would be content to re-establish the situation as it had been, the fact is that the democratic reorientation of German education involves much more than the elimination of Nazism;[1] it involves the creation of a democratic philosophy of education, a democratic plan of school organization, and democratic practices, for Ger-

[1] Alonzo G. Grace, "If I Had Ten Lives," *Educational Forum*, January, 1951.

man education never has been democratic. There was before Hitler, and is now, a sincere minority of German liberal educational leaders who have the democratic point of view. It is in this relatively small group that hope lies.

Economic recovery and material reconstruction of a conquered people in an occupied country may be easily observed and evaluated. But what happens to the minds and the hearts of a people under these circumstances is more difficult to measure. An "eye for an eye" policy or concept of directing Germany to the democratic road never could succeed. While it is wrong to condemn the entire German people for the domination of the Nazi party and the reverence for Hitler, perhaps the Norwegians' phrase, "We can forgive but we shall never forget," represents the feeling in most of the citizens of the free western nations of Europe. It may be a generation before we shall know whether or not the education and cultural mission of the three democratic powers of the west has made any substantial impact on the German educational system. It may be a considerably shorter period if the East dominates.

Before considering education prior to and during the Hitler era or describing the progress of education in postwar Germany, a review of the attitude of American educators toward German education a hundred years ago has a significant bearing on understanding the problem.

AMERICANS TO GERMANY—A CENTURY AGO

Over a hundred years ago several of America's educational pioneers, including Horace Mann, Henry Barnard and Calvin Stowe, traveled to Europe and especially to Germany to study the most liberal practices in education. Subsequently, in a lecture to a convention of teachers at Columbus entitled "The Prussian System of Public Instruction and Its Applicability to the United States," Stowe said, "The Kingdom of Prussia, at the present time, affords the rare spectacle of an absolute sovereign exerting all his power for the intelligence and moral improvement of his people. The government of Prussia, in which the voice of the King is everything and the voice of the people nothing, does more for education of the whole people than has ever been done by any other government on earth." He then enumerated several characteristics of the Prussian system which he recommended for adoption in this country: (1) the recognition of the duty and obligation of every parent to educate his children; (2) the proper training of teachers; (3) extensive and thorough instruction; (4) proper supervision.[2]

[2] Henry Barnard, *Normal Schools and Other Institutions, Agencies, and Means*

In the summer of 1843, Horace Mann, in his seventh annual report as secretary of the Board of Education in Massachusetts, said:

Among the nations of Europe, Prussia has long enjoyed the most distinguished reputation for the excellence of its schools. In reviews, in speeches, in tracts, and even in graver works devoted to the cause of education, its schools have been exhibited as models for the imitation of the rest of Christendom. For many years, scarce a suspicion was breathed that the general plan of education in that kingdom was not sound in theory and most beneficial in practice. Recently, however, grave charges have been preferred against it by high authority. The popular traveler, Laing, has devoted several chapters of his large work on Prussia to the disparagement of its school system .... and during the pendency of the famous "Factories Bill" before the British House of Commons in 1843, numerous tracts were issued from the British Press, not merely calling in question, but strongly denouncing the whole plan of education in Prussia as being not only designed to produce, but as actually producing a spirit of blind acquiescence to arbitrary power in things spiritual as well as temporal—as being, in fine, a system of education adapted to enslave and not to enfranchise the human mind, and even in some parts of the United States the very nature and essence of whose institutions consist in the idea that the people are wise enough to distinguish between what is right and what is wrong—even here some have been illiberal enough to condemn in advance everything that savors of the Prussian system because their system is sustained by arbitrary power.[3]

After considering certain other matters in this report, Mann continues:

But allowing all these charges against the Prussian system to be true, there are still two reasons why I was not deterred from examining it. In the first place, the evils imputed to it were easily and naturally separable from the good which it was not denied to possess. If the Prussian schoolmaster has better methods of teaching writing, drama, arithmetic, geography, and so on, so that in half the time he produces greater and better results, surely we may copy his mode of teaching these elements without adopting his notions of passive obedience to government, of blind adherence to articles of a church. ... In the second place, if Prussia can pervert the benign influences of education to the support of arbitrary power, we surely can employ them for the support and perpetuation of republican institutions. A national spirit of liberty can be cultivated more easily than a national spirit of bondage, and if it may be made one of the great prerogatives of education to perform the unnatural and unholy work of making slaves, then surely it must be one of the noblest instrumentalities for rear-

Designed for the Professional Education of Teachers (Greeley, Colo., 1929), Part II, p. 35.
[3] *Ibid.,* p. 39.

ing a nation of free men. If moral power over the understandings and affectation of people may be turned to evil, may it not also be employed for the highest good?[4]

It is more important, then, to realize that Hitler was a symbol for a condition which has existed for generations and which was not removed by the defeat of Nazism. On the other hand, some of the most liberal contributions to education in the United States have come from Germany. To Germany belongs the credit for the first thoroughly organized system of public education under the administration of the civil authority.[5] Here, too, education first assumed the form and name of a science. The concept of a state education authority, kindergartens, compulsory school attendance, contributions to psychology, university seminars, research, and the doctor of philosophy degree are among many German contributions to our own practice.

Charles Brooks, who was instrumental in establishing the first state normal school in Massachusetts, wrote three long lectures in which the Prussian state system was described. The program of studies, books, classification, mode of teaching, rewards, punishment, were presented. He showed how the system could be adjusted to Massachusetts and in the third lecture "showed that all these great practical Christian results could be realized by establishing State Normal Schools and could not be realized without them, and therefore, the proposed school reform must begin with introducing such normal schools." He continued, "From what I have learned it is now my opinion that the Prussian system is to make a new era in the public education of the United States." Says Brooks after the establishment of the first state normal school, "I say it was the Prussian system which brought out the educational regeneration of New England."[6]

GERMAN EDUCATION PRIOR TO HITLER

Aims and Spirit—While it is not possible in this chapter to record the history of education in Germany, a review of the general organization and objectives before the Nazis came to power will throw some light on the problems involved in a policy of educational redirection. All German children attended the *Volksschule* or the elementary school for at least four years. At the close of the fourth year, when the child was about ten, the decision as to whether he was to

[4] *Ibid.*, pp. 39-40.
[5] Henry Barnard, *National Education in Europe* (Hartford, 1854). Also see *Papers on Froebel's Kindergarten.*
[6] John Walz, *German Influence in American Education and Culture* (Philadelphia, 1936), pp. 25-27.

prepare himself for a profession or a trade was made. By selective procedures influenced in part by the social-economic status of the parents, those who were to prepare for the professions entered one of the higher schools of which the *gymnasium* is most commonly known. These were tuition institutions. The others continued in the *Volksschule* for another four years; they then selected their future vocation with the assistance of the labor office, which is not connected with the schools. Although 10 to 25 per cent, the number varying in the different states, entered the higher school-university preparatory program, by the close of the program their number had been reduced to less than 5 per cent. Fewer than 10 per cent of all vocational school children attended full-time vocational schools; the others were in part-time school programs an average of five hours per week and spent the remainder of their time in on-the-job apprenticeship training. Because of emphasis on specialized vocational preparation in all these schools, there was little time for general education, health education, education for citizenship, or other phases of functional education.

Basic to this emphasis on specialized vocational preparation was the assumption that there are two groups of people, the intellectually gifted who were to become the leaders and the less gifted, incapable of scientific thinking, who were to carry on the work of commerce and industry. Emphasis for the first group was on academic education; for the second group the emphasis was on specific job preparation.

German educational psychology, which was comparable to the faculty psychology of 1900 in the United States, contended that the ability to think developed at about the age of ten and that this necessitated the segregation of the intellectually gifted into separate programs and in separate buildings. As a result, a multiple-track overlapping system of schools developed. After a child had moved ahead on one track, it became increasingly difficult for him to transfer to another. Thus there developed two kinds of education of different quality for two kinds of people—leaders and followers.

Consistent with this concept of leadership was a concept of authority that was focused not in the masses but in the specialist. The teacher and the administrator were appointed and assigned by the central authority. Authority in education was centered in the state ministry of education. As experts within their realms, the administrator and the teacher, too, were authorities. The public, the parents, and the pupils had little or no responsibility for the educational program or opportunity to make their wishes known. As might be expected, there was little or no democracy in the classroom.

Administrative Responsibility—Before 1937, education in Germany was a state responsibility. There was a federal department identified only as Department III in the Reich Ministry of the Interior which served as a clearinghouse. There was no federal control or authority over the schools. The ministry of education of each *Land* was responsible with two exceptions for school within the *Land*. Public kindergartens were under the ministry of the interior, and the agricultural vocational schools and schools for the preparation of teachers of agriculture were under the ministry of agriculture.

Responsibility for the administration of the schools in each German *Land* was centered in the ministry of education, cultural, and religious affairs. The ministry was headed by a *Kultusminister*, who was an executive member of a political party. He was appointed by the executive board of the party which, according to the election returns, was authorized to nominate the *Kultusminister*. He remained in office unless a vote of distrust was brought against him by at least a two-third vote of the *Landtag* or until there was a change in the political status of his party.

The ministry determined the basic features of the curriculum, including the subjects to be taught, their grade placement, the number of lessons per week, and methods of instruction. Educational standards subject to constitutional limitations were imposed at the ministry level.

Below the *Land* level came the *Regierungsbezirk* with its *Regierungsschulrat*, the equivalent of a regional superintendent of schools, who was responsible for the vocational schools. All higher schools, except in the largest cities, which had a *Stadtschulrat* or city superintendent of schools, were under the direct administrative authority of the state ministry. In some *Länder* the ministry appointed a deputy for each *Regierungsbezirk* who was in charge of the higher schools. The lowest level of school administration was the *Kreis*, or county. The largest cities and some smaller cities which historically were independent had their separate administrations comparable to the *Kreis*. The *Kreisschulrat* and the *Stadtschulrat* were appointed by the ministers of education and were responsible to him. There were no school administration officials at the Gemeinde level. The administrative functions at this level were taken care of by a school principal who was also a member of the teaching staff.

With all authority concerning educational policies and the organization and administration of education centered in the ministry, there was practically no opportunity for the citizens in the local community to participate in matters affecting the local schools, except in connection with student welfare, school feeding, vacation trips, and other matters not interfering with the educational program.

Again, the policy of central school administration permitted no recognition of co-operative planning and decision making by groups on the community level. The responsibility of the local school administrator was to carry out the policy established by the ministry of education and given to him. The teacher received his orders from the school principal and was not supposed to question anything decreed from above. Just as the teacher and the local citizen had little or nothing to say about the administration of the school, the boys and girls had no responsibility or privileges in that connection. As a rule, students recognized their incompetence and looked to the teachers for decisions; they, in turn, looked to the principal, who received his instruction from the ministry.

Parent-School Co-operation—The earlier disregard for the participation of parents in school matters gave way during the short period of the Weimar Republic to encouragement to parents to co-operate with the schools. After 1920, most of the German states established by ministerial decree local community-parent councils for the higher schools. All parents of children enrolled in higher schools were invited to elect those who were to represent them on the parents' councils.

These parent councils served in an advisory capacity; they were privileged to discuss and make recommendations on all matters relating to the higher schools. Neither the school principal nor the ministry, however, was bound to follow or even to consider their recommendations. On the contrary, their resolutions were for the most part completely disregarded by those in authority. As a result, the initial interest of parents soon disappeared. They were most successful in their work on student welfare, such as providing help for needy students and arranging vacation trips for students who were not well. They were also especially successful in advising teachers on problems involving individual children and in promoting a better understanding of children by the teacher.

Teachers' Organizations—Voluntary associations of teachers had their beginning in Germany over a hundred years ago. The development of such associations originated with the teachers themselves. As a result, they were organized on the basis of the different kinds of schools, subjects taught, church affiliation, political party membership, age, and sex. These organizations held regular meetings, published professional magazines, and carried on programs to improve the economic status of their professional group. Some of them were active in the promotion of school reform movements and in the recommendation of improvements in the school program. Their relationship with the ministries of education was not close, and their actual influence in bringing about changes in organization, administration, and curriculum practices was limited.

School Finance—The financial support of the *Volksschule* was a joint responsibility of the state and the community. *Volksschule* teachers' salaries were paid by the state. Provision for buildings, equipment, and maintenance was the responsibility of the local community. Only in rare cases, when it had a particular interest in the establishment of a school, did the state assist in the building of a *Volksschule* building. Most higher schools for boys were established and supported completely by the state. Most higher schools for girls were established and supported by the communities in which they were located. The school budget was determined by the supporting unit, the state or the community.

There was no tuition charge for enrollment in the *Volksschule,* the elementary school, or in the *Berufsschule,* the part-time vocational school, throughout the period of compulsory school attendance. All higher schools and the *Berufsfachschule,* the full-time vocational school, however, charged tuition which ranged from five to forty marks per month in different schools and communities. A reduction or complete cancellation of the tuition charge was granted upon request to able and needy students. Only about three-fourths of the possible tuition income, if all students had paid full tuition, was actually collected.

Students in all schools purchased their own textbooks. Most schools had textbook libraries which would lend books to needy students. Efforts were made to reduce the cost of textbooks by collective ordering, and students were encouraged to sell their books at the completion of a grade to those who were entering that grade. It was the responsibility of the student, however, to supply himself with the needed textbooks. Such materials as visual aids for demonstration or display purposes and laboratory and shop equipment and supplies were provided without charge. All other learning materials were paid for by the student. A small fee per month was collected from each student to support the educational film and slide program.

Many children, though they might have been given tuition scholarships, were unable to enter the full-time higher school program at the close of the fourth grade because their parents felt that they could not afford to pay such costs as transportation and textbooks over a six to nine year period or that they needed their help or that the parents needed the additional income the boys would earn as apprentices beginning at age fifteen. Assistance from public funds was available to a limited number of such students. Upon the special recommendation of the teacher and approval by the school administration, especially talented students were given maintenance grants by the state or the community to make possible their attendance at a full-time academic or vocational school. The amount of the grant was usually small. In most cases the normal income of an apprentice during his first year of apprenticeship was approximately twenty marks per month.

Financial assistance to parents in the education of their children, which had the effect of maintenance grants, was given in two different ways. First, the taxes collected from individuals on any kind of income took into consideration the number of children in the family. For each child a tax reduction was automatically granted. For the ordinary worker with a low income, this reduction would amount to as much as ten marks per month for the first child and a little less for each additional child. Second, civil servants, who made up 10 per cent of the population in normal times, and a large proportion of private employees permanently employed by the larger corporations received a salary increase for each child, amounting to as much as thirty marks per month at the lower salary and wage levels. This reduction in income tax and increase in salary or wages was continued up to age twenty-five as long as the child was enrolled in school.

The Universities—In 1932, when the total German population was 65,000,000, there were 23 universities and 56 other institutions of higher learning such as technical universities, theological institutions, academies of music, and colleges of commerce. The total enrollment in all these institutions was 138,000, of which 131,000 were enrolled in the universities. The annual entering group was less than 20,000, which was about one in two of those completing the programs of the higher schools.

The search for truth generally is considered the chief concern and ultimate purpose of the university. In the field of pure research the German universities have been outstanding. The German concept of academic freedom and its strict application to the universities over a long period of time have made it possible for German university scholars to make discoveries, to develop philosophical systems, to gain and to commmunicate insights without which the total sum of human knowledge would today be much less than it is.

Along with the search for truth, *Forschung*, there is often mentioned a second activity of the university, namely, *Lehre*. English-speaking persons must be on their guard against misunderstanding this term. In Germany there are two words which may be used to translate the English word *teaching,* namely, *Lehre* and *Unterricht. Lehre* includes only that teaching which consists of the communication of the results of research. The concept of *Forschung und Lehre,* therefore, means the search for truth and the communication of its results. *Lehre* does not include instruction intended to develop skills. That kind of instruction is called *Unterricht,* which is said to be the business of the schools; only *Lehre* is held to be worthy of the universities.

While the confinement of university teaching to *Lehre* seems to be the ideal of many German university teachers, actually the universities are not exclusively concerned with this aspect of teaching. Those who feel that only *Lehre* can be the concern of the universities and who would relegate *Unterricht* exclusively to the schools disregard the fact that a large amount—probably more than half—of the time and energy of university teachers is invested in the kind of teaching which is properly called *Unterricht.*

The greatest shortcoming of the German universities in the training of professional personnel is their tendency toward overspecialization. The force which motivates most students during their university study is the examinations which they must pass at the end of their course. Since economic circumstances now demand of most students that they finish their university course and establish themselves in their profession in the shortest possible time, there is a strong tendency to eliminate from the course of study all subject matter which is not specifically included in the usual examinations. Prospective physicians pursue almost exclusively the study of strictly medical courses; prospective preachers neglect all courses which are not theological. The result is that the young practitioners of these professions are trained to perform the technical functions of their profession but are not prepared to assume the position of leadership in contemporary society which one should expect them to take.

The desire to confine university teaching to *Lehre* results in an overemphasis on courses of theoretical and historical content. The curricula in law, for instance, stress Roman and Egyptian law sometimes apparently at the expense of the social aspects of legal practice in our day; theological faculties stress church history, dogmatics, and systematic theology more than they do pastoral theology and the study of religious institutions as social forces; the philosophical faculties offer a large number of courses in ancient languages and dialects of purely historical importance.

The first step in admission to the university and other higher institutions was taken by the student at the close of the fourth grade when he entered one of the higher schools. About one student in five did this. The second step came at the close of the thirteenth grade when it was required that the student satisfactorily pass the *Abitur,* a final examination. The mortality rate in the higher academic schools was very high. Of the students who entered these schools at the close of the fourth grade, only one in four completed the nine-year program. At the end of the program, they took written examinations in about six academic subjects. A whole day would then be spent in an oral examination of about twenty students. A ministerial delegate was present on the examination board. The subject teachers asked specialized questions first; the school principal and the ministerial delegate would then ask questions of a more general nature. If a student failed in the *Abitur,* he was permitted to repeat it in the next year; in individual instances he was even admitted a third time.

The institutions followed a policy which limited the number of students admitted each year to specialized professional fields on the basis of the replacement needs of the professions involved. Only during periods of high prosperity, as in 1926 to 1928, and during the Nazi period was this restriction lifted. This policy was established following World War I as a result of the critical overcrowding of the professions. The problem created by the overcrowding of the professions was a much more serious problem in Germany than it would have been in the United States because of the traditional attitude of the professionally trained person. Only an exceptional German with legal training and a university degree, for example, would consider employment at any type of work other than in one of the professions. A large number of such unemployed professional people, referred to as "the academic proletariat," were regarded as dangerous to the stability of the country. Consequently, it was the accepted point of view that admission to the higher institutions had to be restricted.

Adequate personnel information was not collected by German institutions of higher learning which would make possible a very exact analysis of the social composition of the student body. Upon entrance into a higher institution, the student indicated the occupation of his parents by categories of vocations. Some of these categories, however, were so general that great variation existed in the income of different groups within the category. For example, a storekeeper with an annual income of perhaps five thousand marks and an industrialist with an annual income of a million marks would both be classified as businessmen.

About 50 per cent of the German population in the early 1930's consisted of laborers, farmers, and low-ranking civil servants such as post-men, streetcar conductors, and clerks in government offices. Approximately 10 per cent of the university students came from families on this level. About one-third of the university students were sons and daughters of lawyers, doctors, and other professional workers who made up less than one-twentieth of the gainfully employed population. The remaining students, between 50 and 60 per cent, came from the middle classes. Of the total gainfully employed population, 10 per cent were civil servants, and from this group came 50 per cent of the university students. This disproportion in the student composition is evidence of a greater desire for financial security on the part of civil servants than in any other vocational group.

German universities were made up of four departments, called "faculties"—theology, law, medicine, philosophy. After the student was admitted to the university and had selected the faculty in which he wished to study, he was, except for clearing any minimums such as a required language which he might not have studied in his higher school program, relatively free to do as he pleased.

There were, except in the medicine and chemistry departments, no periodic examinations and no accumulations of class credits. The students spent most of their time in research work in seminars or in laboratories. These seminars or laboratory courses were obligatory, and students had to give evidence of successful attendance before they were admitted to the final examination. In the upper semesters, however, students could select their special field of interest from among the many seminars offered. In the courses or seminars, the student was treated as a mature person who had come to the institution for a serious purpose. At the end he was responsible for demonstrating by dissertation and a very extensive examination that he was qualified for the degree in the particular field which he had selected for specialization. The examination would, however, also include the more general aspect of the field in which he specialized. A graduate of organic chemistry, for instance, had to take examinations in all other fields of chemistry and physics.

German universities had no special department or school of education; consequently, in spite of the great emphasis which was put on scientific research in all other fields, there was no department responsible for the promotion of educational research on the university level. Some of the larger universities had a full professor of pedagogy. These professors sometimes promoted research in the field of educational psychology, but the opportunities for educational and sociological research were extremely limited and very little encouraged.

NAZI SCHOOL REFORM

The National Socialist school reform embraced four principles: (1) uniformity in the meaning and objectives of all instruction in accordance with National Socialist ideology; (2) reformation of the organization, curriculum, and teaching methods in accordance with this policy; (3) breaking down the "aloofness" of the schools by establishing a close contact between the schools and the realities and exigencies of national life; (4) consolidation of the separate courses of study in a single over-all curriculum consistent with reality and ideology.

These principles were discussed in considerable detail by Professor Krieck, who referred to Hitler as the Messiah of National Socialist education. Krieck maintained that, as far as he could see from the history and the life of the various nations, there had never before been a political philosophy and a government so closely and thoroughly connected with the idea of education, as under Adolf Hitler. He also claimed that it was the aim of the National Socialist movement to bring about a revival of the German people on its natural foundations of race, blood, and soil and to lead it toward its goal of perfection and its historical mission in the world through a reorganization of the national and governmental structures and by means of a culture and a scale of values corresponding to the fundamental German character. He added that it was for this reason that the National Socialist revolution was a milestone in the history of the Occident and of all mankind. The work, he continued, of bringing about a revival of the German people through blood and soil, of elevating them to the realization of new national and political concepts, had been started by the leader of the movement from the political angle in such a way that the political philosophy was unsolubly intertwined with that of education. He said that the third Reich found its fulfillment within the heart and soul of the German man with a new attitude and an ideology which bound the whole nation into a real community, a unified and living whole, and thus paved the road for the German's Day in history.[7]

Although the Nazis endeavored to bring about changes in all spheres of public life, they did not change the organizational structure of most schools until about 1937. Some curriculum reforms were effected prior to this date which placed strong emphasis on gymnastics and history instruction. The trends towards unification, however, occurred after 1937 only and produced a number of new school types. Perhaps the most illustrative statement concerning the objectives of the German schools during the Nazi time is set forth by Paul Kretius and

[7] Ernst Krieck, *Nationalpolitische Erziehung* (Leipzig, 1936), p. 25.

Martin Spielhagen. According to these authors, "it is the task of the German schools, together with the other National Socialist powers, to educate—in line with its characteristic methods—the youth of our nation to become physically, spiritually and mentally healthy and strong German men and women who, deep-rooted in their home and race, are willing to serve, each in his place, the *Führer* and the people."[8]

The Volksschule—The organizational structure of the *Volksschule* remained unchanged during the Nazi period. The four lower grades continued to be the *Grundschule* (common basic school), which was compulsory for all children, while the upper four grades represented the final schooling of more than 80 per cent of all children. Religious instruction was cut down by 50 per cent, and a slight increase is evident in history, drawing, and gymnastics. The over-all picture, however, is not very revealing because elements of National Socialist and militaristic education were included in every subject—not even the arts were excluded. Thus, curriculum for the first and second grades includes the drawing of swastikas; in the upper grades, soldiers represented a substantial part of the formative arts instruction; and almost 50 per cent of the music curriculum was devoted to the singing of Nazi and soldiers' songs. Only one reader was provided for the *Volksschulen* throughout Germany, and of course this book contained an enormous number of lessons emphasizing Nazism and the Nazi ideology. An appendix devoted to home studies was attached to this book. This was the only part that made provision for some differences according to the regional districts in which the book was used.

The Höhere Schulen—in 1937, a drastic change aimed at unification of high schools occurred. The only school type that remained intact after this radical conversion was the *Gymnasium*, although but a very few of them remained. All other school types were dissolved and replaced by one common high school type, the *Deutsche Oberschule*. Though a school with the same name had been in existence since 1924, the Nazi school was of an entirely different nature. The *Deutsche Oberschule* of the Nazi period included a "common basic track" which extended over the first four classes (grades five to eight) and three specialized upper tracks—the linguistic tracks for both boys and girls, the science track for boys, and the home economics track for girls.

Gymnastics ranked as one of the predominant subjects. The offerings in German history and geography were the same in all tracks and represented 25 per cent of the total schedule. Only in this respect does

[8] Paul Kretius and Martin Spielhagen, *Zicke und Wege des Neuen Volksschulunterrichts.*

the *Oberschule* of the Nazi time correspond to the *Deutsche Ober-schule* of the Weimar period, where 29 per cent of the total offerings were devoted to these subjects. However, the subjects, while retaining their old names, had undergone drastic reforms. There was hardly any subject in any of the eight grades of the *Höhere Schulen* which did not provide substantial offerings in Nazi ideology, militarism, or the like.

Universities—The changes in universities during the Nazi time were primarily concerned with the introduction of the "leadership principle" in the administration. Many of the responsibilities of the Senate of the universities were transferred to the *Rektor*, who in turn was directly subordinate to the Reich minister of education. Thus, the universities' self-administration was changed into a "command-line" system, and the *Länder* were practically eliminated in the administrative pattern.

With respect to admission of new lecturers of students, leaders of the Nazi Lecturers' League and the Nazi Students' League had a decisive voice in the selection policy. The "Reich Law on Habilitation" of February 17, 1949, illustrates what the "requirements" for admission of new lecturers were. It stated that "the habilitated Doctor can only obtain authorization to teach if he fulfills certain conditions. He must meet the requirements of a German civil servant with respect to descent, public position, qualification, and political attitude." Although the character of the universities thus was changed completely, little influence was exercised on its scientific and research activities, except that many institutions carried out research tasks which were in direct connection with the war effort. Student fraternities were dissolved, and the Nazi Students' League took their place. Membership during the first term of study was compulsory at most of the German universities. In addition, no student was admitted to the fourth semester unless he gave evidence of successful participation in gymnastics and sports courses during the first three terms.

Nazi Party Schools—There were several types of full-time party schools which actually deserve the name of a school.[9]

(1) *The National Political Education Institutions*—On April 20, 1933, three existing state educational institutions (Köslin, Plön, and Potsdam) which formerly had been officer candidates' schools were converted into "National Political Education Institutions." A number of institutions of this type had been organized. These schools, which were boarding schools, closely followed the pattern of the old Prussian officer candidates' schools. The main educational objective was the "formation of militant men and conscious promoters of Germandom,

[9] The authority for this description was taken from the official Nazi publication *Erziehungsmächte und Erziehungshoheit im Grossedutschen Reich.*

and the development of those qualities which enable the young men to become leaders in Party, State and Industry. Strict principles of selection were applied. Attendance was voluntary; tuition fees were for the most part borne by the state. German boys who had successfully completed three or four years of the *Grundschule* were admitted if they had the necessary racial, physical, mental, and spiritual qualifications and passed an admission examination which extended over at least one week.

The instruction in the schools was not confined to mental and spiritual education only. Physical education in every form was emphasized: there were courses in swimming, fencing, boxing, rowing, sailing, riding, motoring, gliding. A number of institutions joined in summer camps where they carried on all kinds of sports activities and contests. In every year, the boys for a certain period were assigned to work in agriculture, industry, and mining. During this time they had to live with the farmers' or laborers' families in order to study the living conditions of the working classes. In addition to these activities, extensive study trips were made through Germany, particularly to the border districts. Finally, these boys were sent to foreign countries for one year or more by way of student exchange.

The teaching staff was composed of carefully selected, politically reliable teachers, former army officers, engineers, artists. The supervision of the schools was under the Inspection of the National Political Education Institutions, attached to the Office of the Reich Education Minister.

(2) *The Adolf Hitler Schulen and the Ordensburgen*—These "political universities" were supervised by the offices of the main education office of the Nazi party, subordinate to the Reich organization leader (Robert Ley), and were thus exclusively party-supervised institutions. The Reich education minister had no jurisdiction over these schools. The "Office of the *Ordensburgen*," in view of their over-all importance, was headed by the chief of the Main Education Office himself (until 1937 Rosenberg; later a Dr. Friedrich Schmidt). Their objective was the training of future Nazi party leaders (Adolf Hitler School as the preschool, *Ordensburgen* as the advanced school). Great emphasis was placed on the study of rhetoric. Instruction was offered in the way of speeches, lectures, work-study groups, sports, drills, contests, and festive performances. The faculties were composed of old party members and political leaders who worked either full time or part time at these schools. The strictest possible standard of selection from the political and racial standpoint was applied.

THE PERIOD OF OCCUPATION

The authority of the United States government to initiate, sponsor, and conduct a so-called reorientation program in Germany was contained in a series of policy statements issued over a period of four years. These statements reflect not merely the basic intentions of the United States and the other occupying powers with respect to the treatment of Germany, but also the major modifications which Allied policies have undergone since VE-Day.

The objectives of the first stage were characterized by punitive action and gradual reconstruction of physical facilities. The authority for these measures for all four powers was contained in the Potsdam Agreement and for the United States in the Directive to the Commander in Chief regarding the occupation of Germany (JCS 1067). The Potsdam Agreement called upon the Control Council "to so control German education that Nazi and militarist doctrine will be eliminated and the successful development of democratic ideas will be made possible." The basic tenets of the Potsdam Agreement were incorporated in the Directive on U.S. Objectives and Basic Policies in Germany (JCS 1067) which instructed the Commander in Chief that: "The principal Allied objective is to prevent Germany from ever again becoming a threat to the peace of the world. Essential steps in the accomplishment of this objective are the elimination of Nazism and militarism in all their forms . . . and the preparation for an eventual reconstruction of German political life on a democratic basis."

In order to guide German educators in their efforts to accomplish the needed reforms, American authorities proposed the "Basic Principles for Democratization of Education in Germany" to the Allied Control Council. In June, 1947, this body adopted the proposed principles. They served in all zones as a standard by which to judge and evaluate the effectiveness of a school reform program to develop democratic ideas and processes.[10] This basic policy statement includes the following:

1. There should be equal educational opportunity for all.

2. Tuition, textbooks and other necessary scholastic material should be provided free of charge in all educational institutions fully supported by public funds which cater mainly for pupils of compulsory school age; in addition, maintenance grants should be made to those who need aid. In all other educational institutions, including universities, tuition, textbooks, and necessary material should be provided free of charge together with maintenance grants for those in need of assistance.

[10] Military Government Regulations, Ch. 24 to Title 23-161, July, 1947.

3. Compulsory full-time school attendance should be required for all between the ages of six and at least fifteen—and thereafter, for those pupils not enrolled in full-time educational institutions, at least part-time compulsory attendance up to the completed age of eighteen years.

4. Schools for the compulsory periods should form a comprehensive educational system. The terms "elementary education" and "secondary education" should mean two consecutive levels of instruction, not two types or qualities of instruction which overlap.

5. All schools should lay emphasis upon education for civic responsibility and a democratic way of life, by means of the content of the curriculum, textbooks and materials of instruction, and by the organization of the school itself.

6. School curricula should aim to promote understanding of and respect for other nations and to this end attraction should be given to the study of modern languages without prejudice to any.

7. Educational and vocational guidance should be provided for all pupils and students.

8. Health supervision and health education should be provided for all pupils and students. Instruction will also be given in Hygiene.

9. All teacher education should take place in a university or in a pedagogical institution of university rank.

10. Full provision should be made for effective participation of the people in the reform and organization as well as in the administration of the educational system.

Principles and Policy, 1948—It is obvious that with the formation of a western German government, the acceleration of the so-called "cold war," the early withdrawal of our armed services in alarming numbers, and the evident desire of reducing the dollar cost of occupation a more effective policy and program were essential. The probable adoption of an occupation statute which would omit the educational and cultural relations effort called for a drastic redirection of policy. It was at Berchtesgaden that the basic principles on which policy and program would be based in this new era in Western Germany were set forth.[11] Basic among them were:

1. The true reform of the German people will come from within. It will be spiritual and moral. The types of school organization or structure, for example, are of less importance to the future of Germany and the world than what is taught, how it is taught, and by whom it is taught.

2. The solution to the so-called "German problem" will be more readily attained when we recognize that it is a part of the entire

[11] Alonzo G. Grace, *Basic Principles of Educational Reconstruction in Germany,* Berchtesgaden Conference Report, October, 1948; Office of Military Government for Germany, Education and Cultural Relations Division.

European problem. We will not enlist the support of the German people in the struggle of ideologies or prevent them from arising again by superimposing an educational structure, or program, which ignores the history of this and other European countries.

3. It will not be the purpose of Military Government to superimpose an American system of education on the German people. It is our purpose to indicate to the German people that the education of children and youth should be so organized and developed:

    a. That each individual, irrespective of race, class, creed, or economic status, shall have equal access to education.

    b. That each individual be allowed to pursue that form or type of educational opportunity for which he is endowed.

    c. That each individual shall, as a result of his schooling, be able to make the maximum contribution toward the maintenance of world peace and international understanding, the maintenance of law and order, and the development of social justice.

4. The most effective method of establishing a society based on the democratic ideal is to abandon the use of the term as such and, by practice and precept, lead the German people to accept this ideal.

5. The provision for a corps of educated teachers and leaders in Germany is a primary necessity. We must observe that schooling does not necessarily guarantee education; that the acquisition of knowledge does not indicate the possession of wisdom; that instruction does not necessarily mean learning; that schooling, instruction, and knowledge without moral responsibility, spiritual enlightenment, and intellectual integrity will fail to produce the character necessary to resist the effort of those who would destroy the dignity of the individual.

6. We must not be guilty of attempting to develop in Germany the ideal, which may not have been accomplished elsewhere, in the midst of an environment frought with confusion and uncertainty.

7. The redirection of the goals, programs, or policies of social institutions must grow from the people. Wide citizen participation in community planning, in the discussion of community problems, and in aiding in the formulation of public policy is one guarantee that no one individual can dominate the thinking and living habits of the people. Power *through* people must supplant power *over* people.

8. No army of occupation has or possibly ever will successfully superimpose an educational and cultural pattern on a conquered people. Military Government will be regarded as military government, irrespective of the high motives of those who would "re-educate or re-orient" a defeated, conquered, occupied Germany. It will be the purpose of Military Government, therefore:

a. To bring into co-operation with the German people the voluntary nongovernmental organizations that are able to contribute toward the attainment of the common goals.
b. To encourage an effective German program by UNESCO.
c. To identify and encourage known democratic elements in the German population.
d. To support the development or re-establishment of institutions and organizations in Germany which will contribute toward the accomplishment of the purposes of this mission.

9. The more rapid the material reconstruction and economic recovery, the more difficult becomes the problem of intellectual, moral, and spiritual redemption. The United States will have failed in Germany if materialism is allowed to supersede moral values. A concurrent program of educational and cultural reconstruction on a long-time basis is required.

These principles became the basis of policy, and a systematic program of education and cultural relations was inaugurated. The emphasis was removed from structural change in education and placed on the aim and spirit of education, the equalization of opportunity, the importance of the human element in educational systems, the importance of co-operation.

Seven years, the first three of which were more or less devoid of an educational and cultural relations effort, is a short time in which to expect any profound democratic impact on Germany. It is difficult to believe that after fifteen years of Nazi indoctrination, youth could be so readily recruited to the democratic ideal. There are, however, islands of democratic ferment. German educators in increasing numbers have entered the open doors of the free and democratic countries of the West. They have found that in most nations substantial educational progress has occurred during the period of the Nazi blackout. Norway, for example, has adopted a seven-year elementary school program based on the premise that this basic general education is the minimum required for national security and the development of happy, independent, thinking human beings. The philosophy of separating children into groups at the end of the fourth year in school on the basis that it is the period at which the child begins to think has been rejected by most of the world. It is evident, under any circumstances, that educational systems and cultural patterns cannot be imposed on an entire people. It also is evident that the democratic ideal cannot be established overnight or by some magic formula. It takes a long period of time as we in the United States are aware. Perhaps in a generation we may know what happened in Germany during this occupation period.

School Reform—In the early years of any program as comprehensive and as difficult as the democratic reorientation of German education, real progress is more dependent upon the building of a sound base for future development and the formulating of an intelligent long-range program than upon results which might be achieved immediately. Progress in basic matters, although observable, does not readily lend itself to statistical presentation. The number of new history textbooks published is an objective fact of significance, but the really significant achievement is in the improvement of the content and method of teaching history.

Historically, the first job was the reopening of schools and provision for teaching personnel and instruction material. Schools were reopened with limited staffs, excessive pupil-teacher ratio, and almost no instructional materials. Since then the supply of teachers has increased greatly, but the problem of an adequate supply of well-qualified teachers will continue for some years. By 1948, the pupil-teacher ratio had been reduced but it was still in excess of 50 to 1. The limitation of the number of classrooms, which will continue to be a serious problem for years, imposes a limitation on the number of teachers regardless of the number that might be available. In the supplying of instructional materials, greater progress was made in the year 1948-49 than in the entire period of occupation up to that time.

Provision for equal educational opportunities involves many different aspects, such as the elimination of tuition charges for all programs during the compulsory school period, the provision of instructional materials without charge, and the elimination of discrimination with reference to certain groups of students as represented by differences in the preparation of teachers and the quality of facilities. Legislation providing for free tuition and free textbooks and learning aids has been enacted in the west sectors of Berlin and in the *Länder* of the U.S. Zone. Provision for free tuition has been extended to include students at the university level in one *Land*.

Compulsory full-time school attendance to the age of fifteen, a common provision of the school regulations in all *Länder*, has been extended by one year in Bremen and West Berlin. The upward extension of traditional four-year *Grundschule* to a six-year common school program has met with serious objection in all states except Bremen and the west sectors of Berlin. The objection has its basis in the conviction of German educators that the intellectually gifted child must be identified as early as the close of the fourth class and that he must then enter into an academic program in which the course of study must emphasize the languages. This position taken by German leaders is wholly consistent with their classical philosophy of education, their social philosophy of a special education for the intellectually gifted, and their concepts of the psychology of learning. In one *Land* the proposal has been made that this issue be submitted to extensive scientific investigation. The elimination of the overlapping multiple-track pattern of school organization and provision for a common educational program through six years is, however, an objective which will not be fully realized in the immediate future.

The emphasis given to specialized education of an academic nature in the preparatory schools and of a job-training nature in the vocational schools leaves little time for an adequate program of general education. The social studies as developed in America are unknown in Germany. American occupation efforts have placed great emphasis upon the development of the social studies, and some progress has been made. Improvement in this area is dependent not only upon the preparation of new materials of instruction but also upon the development of a new philospohy of education.

The centralization of educational authority in the ministries of education thus far has been little affected. Progress in this area is necessarily dependent upon creation of new patterns of administration and increased interest of the lay public in the schools. In this respect it is also possible to report that there has been progress in recent years. Community meetings, open to the public, have been held throughout the former U.S. Zone. The interest of parents and citizens in the schools has been greatly increased. Parent-teacher associations are being organized, and teachers are becoming more and more interested in teacher organizations.

Perhaps the greatest progress in the development of school reform programs has been the democratic organization of educators. This achievement is probably best illustrated in Bavaria, which until the spring of 1948 had done little or nothing in school reform. With the advice and assistance of American personnel, the Bavarians set up an organization for school reform which operates with facilities and under conditions which surpass such provisions in many of our own states. A full-time school-planning committee, with its members released from their positions with full pay by the ministry, was set up. More than fifteen major school committees with membership including as many as twenty teachers and administrators from all parts of the *Land* were organized. Members of these committees, too, were relieved of their regular duties with full pay to engage in school reform planning for whatever length of time might be necessary. The Bavarians, while opposing the extension of a common elementary school program to include six years, have requested that a thorough scientific investigation be conducted to determine the validity of their philosophy and psychology. Further, they have established a Demonstration *Kreis* which puts into operation on a *Kreis*-wide basis the reforms proposed by the school reform committee, including a new general education track, which will do much to increase the in-school experience of a great proportion of the vocational school students who now spend five hours or less per week in school.

Hochschule für Internationale Pädagogische Forschung—The announcement on December 14, 1951, by the Hessian minister of education that the *Hochschule für Internationale Pädagogische Forschung* (Institute for International Educational Research) of Frankfurt had been established as a corporate foundation under public law constitutes one of the most promising achievements of the postwar education program. This action had been pending since early 1951 when the German sponsor of the institute, the Society for Educational Research and Advanced studies in Education, submitted the proposed statutes for approval. The first discussions on research in education began in 1948.

The new institution is the first of its kind in Germany in the field of higher education. For the attainment of its purpose of promoting international educational research, the *Hochschule* assumes the following tasks:

1. To engage in educational research, publish its results, and use them for the improvement of education.
2. To promote advanced preparation of specialists in educational research and to prepare persons for special tasks in education, school administration, and supervision.
3. To advise and assist educators and educational organizations in the conduct of educational research studies as well as in the utilization of the results of such studies and to co-operate with other German, foreign, and international agencies and organizations in the conduct of comparative studies in education.
4. To promote the theoretical and practical introduction of teachers in all types of schools to the methods of educational research.

Cultural Co-operation—It frequently happens that cultural relations are closely tied to the foreign policy of a nation, and the process becomes one of cultural penetration rather than cultural co-operation. The United States sought a program of cultural co-operation through which an understanding and appreciation of the culture of each nation could be developed. It was not the intention of the United States to transplant our own American cultural pattern. To attain the goal, the program included a series of international conferences, the exchange of persons, exchange of materials, the artists' program, the scholars' consulting program, and so on. The International Conference on education held at Chiemsee in 1949 was the first time in over fifteen years that German educators had had an opportunity to discuss the educational progress and the forces affecting education in adjacent European countries.

No scientific evaluation of the results of an exchange program as yet is available. While several thousand Germans have come to the United States, the result of this one-way exchange will not be known for many years to come. These visitors to the United States have included labor, religious, and youth leaders, public officials, industrialists, educators, and university students, and they have come from every phase of German life. A wide two-way exchange of persons is one of the methods by which peoples can speak to one another and thereby become more conscious of the goals of a free people. In spite of frequent recommendations, it was not until late in the occupation that the United States was able to send Germans to other free democratic countries of Europe. Equally important in the area of exchange was the invitation to nongovernmental voluntary American organizations to participate in the cultural program. This involved bringing artists and scholars to meet with Germans in communities, in recitals, at lectures, in various centers in Germany.

Youth Organization—At the conclusion of the war, German youth was, for the most part, without goals of any kind; the collapse of the huge 10,000,000 Hitler Youth Organization, together with the invalidation of the Nazi teaching of the organization, left vast numbers of young people without goals or a means of generating more positive ideals and programs. Such problems of the postwar period as unemployment, housing, educational opportunity, and general disorder fall with special weight on the youth of Germany. Can we now paraphrase the Schirach statement of 1936 and say, "What was formerly the teaching and spirit of the Hitler Youth Movement is dead"? The role of the occupation powers has been threefold: first, to assist those forces inside Germany to provide leadership and direction to the citizens of tomorrow; second, to foster an atmosphere in which the positive elements can find expression in society; and third, to prevent the recurrence of any totalitarian or militaristic tendencies among youth organizations. Since 1945, for example, the total membership of voluntary youth organizations has increased 700 per cent. Of the young people between the ages of ten and twenty-five, 1,500,000 or approximately 25 per cent belong to one or more organizations. Voluntary citizen participation on behalf of youth has been encouraged, and at the present time, youth committees consisting of representative citizens from the community have been formed in 266 *Kreise* in the American Zone. Five leadership training schools have been established in which over 4,000 youth leaders have received training in the fundamentals of democratic youth work.

The self-help program for German youth is one of the most encouraging and one of the most important developments in recent months. Over a hundred projects have been developed by German leadership without the aid of publicity and without the knowledge of the general population. These programs in Germany consist in the rebuilding of damaged buildings, in new dormitories and new homes. This becomes most important, because it is estimated that perhaps as many as 100,000 youth are homeless and wandering from one place to the other throughout the zone. The *Studentenhaus* at Aachen, with the financial aid of the state ministry of education, has been completely restored by student help. This self-help program includes the re-establishment of self-governing youth homes and an extensive student-worker exchange program, self-help, and a scholarship program. A western German association for youth reconstruction work has been formed to co-ordinate and advance the program.

The *Wohnheimsiedlung Maszmannplatz* in Munich is a housing colony for young men of all social classes, especially for young workers and students. Responsible for the origin of the project was a group of students and workers, who began the building of the colony themselves in the summer of 1948 and by means of self-help attained a new and contemporary form of community living. Youth from foreign countries, both students and workers, also live in the *Wohnheimseidlung Maszmanplatz* for shorter or longer periods of time and share the life of young Germans of their own age. This gives the colony the opportunity to promote contact with other countries and to arrange jobs outside Germany for its members. Serving the same purpose of broader international contacts are the many international work camps in operation in Western Germany. At these camps are representatives from many European nations and the United States. Youth from many nations live and work together.

The last several years have also seen the development of work-study programs involving an international exchange of selected students based upon a program developed between 1919 and 1932 in Germany. It provides for sending German students to the United States and other countries for a two-year period, during which time these youth work on farms and in factories, studying, working, and observing the way of life in the United States or in whatever country is participating in the program. Of the 500 work students who participated in this work plan between 1925 and 1932, only one ever became a Nazi, and dozens died in concentration camps or in the war. Many hold positions of importance in Germany today. While there are many problems connected with the development of such a program on any extensive scale, widespread interest has been expressed in the plan.

It is certain that only those things will remain which a considerable number of German leaders have come to believe in and which are closely related to German needs and desires.

Universities—Four important programs have been established in cooperation with the universities. Briefly, these are:

(1) *Frankfurt–University of Chicago Experiment*—The relationship between the University of Chicago and the University of Frankfurt is one of the notable developments in the field of German university education. Some American experts in earlier days, in spite of their knowledge of the German university, hoped to create in Germany a mass education institution. The Germans fail to recognize that "equality of opportunity" should mean that the youth from all classes including the working class should have an opportunity to enter not only the humanistic *Gymnasium* but also the university. Only 4 per cent of the university enrollment today comes from this particular young group.

One of the most important contributions of the Chicago group has been the opportunity for Germans to learn from scholars about the scholarly attainments in America. The frequent informal social gatherings, the opportunity to meet with groups outside of the University of Frankfurt, the relationship between students and professors—all are important contributions to German university life. It is hoped that this program will be organized on a permanent basis.

(2) *The American Institute*—Again by virtue of Foundation assistance together with a grant of some 250,000 marks from the Bavarian government to repair a building at the University of Munich, the American Institute has been established. It is an institute in which American civilization will be studied by German students. It will be the first institute in any German university devoted to the study of American civilization.

(3) *The Nauheim Resolutions*—At a conference of the rectors of all German universities held in Bad Nauheim during the latter part of 1949 a series of resolutions was adopted. These in brief state that:

1. If corporations of fraternities are to be eliminated, a positive

program is needed; therefore, the erection of dormitories and student unions is urged. This is under progress in a small way.

2. An institute on international education should be established.

3. Wide student-professor exchange on a two-way basis with other countries should be developed.

4. The self-help program should be expanded.

Some positive advances have been accomplished by German students, and they must be given the credit due them even if the moving forces usually have been small and not always representative of general student opinion. The courage, tenacity, ingenuity, and above all real understanding of democracy exhibited by the student governments in most of the universities leave much room for improvement, but they are remarkable if one remembers that until a few years ago the concept of parliamentary procedure was totally unknown to these students.

A positive concept of democracy has so far not caught hold of many German students, nor have they had much opportunity to learn its meaning. This means that the bulk of student opinion is committed to no side and that it is not possible to predict the future development. The over-all attitude of German students is thus one of general disillusion, cynicism, and apathy. If they have a positive attitude, it is one of sitting back and waiting to be shown. That this indifference is a dangerous attitude cannot be denied. The implementation of the Nauheim Resolutions is of the utmost importance.

(4) *The Free University of Berlin*—Soviet interference with the intellectual life of faculty and students in the Humboldt University, the old University of Berlin, caused the Germans to organize the so-called "Free" University. This is a thrilling story of the fight for freedom to teach and to learn. The Manifesto issued by the German Forming Committee in 1948 set forth the position of several thousand moral supporters of the plan. It asserts the importance of the independence of schools from limitations in their search for truth and the right of every student to grow in the spirit of democratic inquiry. Unquestionably the Free University of Berlin, therefore, represents one of the most important developments in postwar Germany. Early in 1948 three students were expelled from the University of Berlin by the Soviet-controlled rector. The story of how these three students surrounded themselves with courageous Berlin leadership and appealed to the free citizens of the West to provide for them an educational opportunity which is free of political indoctrination and in which the spirit of freedom to seek the truth would prevail is a remarkable story. It is a remarkable example of courage, faith, and devotion to true scholarship. This entire development was accomplished by the Germans with

some financial assistance by military government and subsequently by the Office of the High Commissioner. From a faculty of three and a student body of perhaps a hundred, the Free University has grown to a faculty of 300 and student body of over 5,000.

Other Evidences of Democratic Ferment—It is not only impossible, but perhaps imprudent, to indicate either that any of these surface demonstrations of important educational patterns in Germany will be permanent or that they will be extended to all of Germany in the West. These are merely examples of new programs that seem to be accepted by German educators. Further evidence of change is to be found in many directions. Almost at random one thinks of the Esslingen workshop for teachers, which brought together outstanding specialists in education and psychology not only from the United States but also from Europe, and of the educational service centers that provide not only for co-operative curriculum planning and for many other services which can be rendered to communities, but also a bridge between the parent and the school. The International Youth Library at Munich will become one of the most important libraries for youth in Europe. One thinks also of the opportunities for co-operative program planning provided by the Weilburg teacher training and of the manner in which Bremen, through a democratically organized local citizens' council, has been able to set a new pattern for school buildings and school sites for Germany. It is encouraging, too, to observe that there is no centralized minister of education in the federal government at Bonn. The attitude of the state ministers is opposed to any effort to secure such centralization. The state constitutions provide amply for freedom in education, equalization of opportunity, and parental responsibility. Finally, even this brief outline of hopeful developments must note the work of the community council in Fellbach. This effort in a city of about 20,000 affords an excellent example of the beginning of community initiative and co-operation. After explanatory discussions with community officials and leaders, a council was organized in 1949. After some discussion of problems it was decided to appoint committees to study the following projects and to report progress toward their realization: (a) to establish a small community sales store where women and handicapped persons could sell the products of their home industry; (b) to establish a small community laundry room where housewives could do their laundry work; (c) to organize a program of practical instruction and practice in traffic control for school children; and (d) to investigate the possibilities of organizing an effective reorientation program in Fellbach for young adults, many of whom are disillusioned war veterans or former members of the Hitler Youth organization.

Fellbach citizens for some time had been discussing these problems informally, but no action was taken toward their solution until the founding of the community council. The council's accomplishments were apparent in a short time. Within several months a community salesroom had been selected, equipped, stocked, and started in business; more than half the funds needed to purchase equipment for a community laundry had been pledged; and plans had been completed for the traffic and adult education programs.

A program of mass public interpretation is required in order to convey the spirit and idea of "community" as well as the necessity of broadening the relationship between separate groups and agencies. There are few or no courses on these subjects in German teacher-training institutions. The resistance of German official agencies and governments toward using citizens' groups in the planning of their policies and toward extending their own staffs by the use of volunteers is a block to progress in civic improvement and initiative. Efforts such as this one in Fellbach will help mitigate that resistance.

CONCLUSION

This chapter, as previously indicated, has been limited almost wholly to the consideration of the aims, spirit, and organization of formal education and the identification of certain islands of democratic ferment that appear to be the result of seven years of occupation. No consideration has been given to the many other facets of the occupation organization that contributed or attempted to contribute to the development of the democratic ideal as part of the German way of life. Specialists in religion, civil administration, and agriculture, the local American *Kreis* officer working at the grass roots, and many others contributed in their respective areas to the better understanding of the democratic ideal on the part of the German population.

There had been islands of democratic ferment in the past, notably during the Weimar period of German history. However, the liberal elements of a population who sincerely and devotedly understood the concept of the dignity of the individual, of the incompatibility of authoritarianism with the democratic idea, of the importance of a state serving men rather than men serving a state, always were subordinated. In considerable measure the same elements which struggled for freedom in Germany over a generation ago or who left Germany in the middle of the nineteenth century to seek freedom are the same elements that seek the same goal today. What happened in Germany could happen elsewhere and inevitably does happen when the state becomes the master of the individual and when a party subordinates both. The same elements prevail in the totalitarian formula, wherever it may exist.

It is exceedingly difficult to understand why a people who a century ago contributed so substantially to the advancement of education in so many countries including the United States would succumb to the forces of Nazism. The future of Germany with respect to the application of the democratic ideal will depend largely on what happens if and when unification comes, on the objectives of the political parties that may succeed in the West, on the opportunity that the government and people will afford youth, on the willingness to recognize talent irrespective of the class in which talent is located, and on many other unpredictable factors. Whether or not these organized programs have been as effective as the face to face personal relationships of Americans and Germans is a matter that cannot be answered today. It will be many years before the real impact of this occupation is known. One of the most important scientific studies which presently should be undertaken is an evaluation of the cultural relations program of the government and of the nongovernmental voluntary associations. In the meantime, there may have been some intellectual, spiritual, and cultural impact made on the German people by the three occupying powers in the West. It is clearly evident, however, that the democratic ideal never will be implanted by use of totalitarian methods. It is not something that emerges overnight; it is not something that is accomplished in a short period of time as we in the United States have occasion to know. Seven years, indeed, is a very short time.

Part V

POLITICS

19

Political Parties

RICHARD M. SCAMMON

U NLIKE its Weimar predecessor, the Bonn Basic Law contains definite reference to political parties and to their position in the political life of democratic, federal Germany. Most democratic constitutional documents have ignored the role of the political party as the bridge between governmental formalism and political reality, and the between-the-wars constitution of Weimar Germany was no exception. Though nearly all political leadership is exercised through party leadership and though nearly all governmental policies stem from party policies, the tradition of the democracies has been to pass over this aspect of the art of governance and to limit constitutions and basic laws to the more formalistic aspects of political organization.

Article 21 of the Bonn document, however, recognizes the right to form freely political parties, requiring that their internal organization conform to democratic principles and specifying that a public accounting of funds be made. Additionally the present Basic Law grants the Federal Constitutional Court the right to decide if parties "according to their aims and the behaviour of their members, seek to impair or abolish the free and democratic basic order or to jeopardize the existence of the Federal Republic of Germany." The court has used this power but once, to outlaw an extremist party of the right. As yet no legislation has been enacted to regulate the organization or finances of political parties.

Even were such implementing legislation to be undertaken, however, it is doubtful if it would have any far-reaching effect on the pattern of west German political party organization and program.

Communists and minor splinter groups of the extreme right might be concerned over legislation against "antidemocratic" parties, but even the complete elimination of these organizations would not basically alter the present party system of non-Soviet Germany. This party system has grown and developed in the years since the end of the war from roots lying deep in the history of Weimar and Imperial Germany and is the product of a historical evolution going back well into the nineteenth century.[1]

DEVELOPMENT OF POLITICAL PARTIES

Major Imperial Parties—In the Bismarckian era may be found the clear indication of the party system that was to mature in the latter days of the Empire. On the right came the Conservatives and Free Conservatives, in general representing large landowners and most frequently elected from the rural areas of eastern Germany in which great estates were important and often the dominant social and political element. Further towards the center came the National Liberals, broadly representative of *status quo* upper and middle class, financial, trade, and industrial interests, and the Center party itself. This last group was a purely Catholic party, first organized to join with the Church in fighting Bismarck's *Kulturkampf* in the seventies and eighties. After this conflict ended, the Center party continued its existence as a defender of the Church and an exponent of its doctrines in political life. Naturally, the party drew its strength from the Catholic population, and most of its *Reichstag* members came from the Catholic areas of south Germany, Rhineland-Westphalia, and Silesia.

Slightly left of center was the middle-class group of Progressives (*Fortschrittliche Volkspartei*), with a program of moderate social and political reform calculated to appeal especially to professional men and those seeking a modest "social conscience" liberal doctrine. On the left itself sat the Social Democrats, especially strong in the latter years of the Empire, with socialism in economic life and full democracy in politics the principal parts of their domestic policy. As elsewhere on the continent, the Social Democrats drew their greatest strength from the working class in the large cities and such industrial complexes as Saxony and the Ruhr.

Aside from these five major groups the *Reichstag* always contained a small representation of local parties (usually agrarian and conservative) and a somewhat larger delegation from national minority groups

[1] As with most continental countries, Germany has functioned during her democratic period with a multi-party system; the two-party plan known in the United States is unknown on the continent.

—the Poles, the members from Alsace-Lorraine, the lone Danish member from the northern border constituency in Schleswig-Holstein, and a half-dozen Guelph members urging the restoration of the Hanoverian sovereignty taken over by Prussia in the sixties.[2]

Weimar Parties—With the collapse of the Imperial structure in 1918, most of the parties associated with the Empire disappeared, but disappeared in name only, for the interests and doctrines which they represented under the Kaiser continued to exist and the party pattern of the Weimar Republic period closely paralleled that of the Empire. On the right the most conservative elements—landowners, army, industrialists, conservative *Beamten*—were grouped into the German National People's party, the less extreme conservatives forming the German People's party as an inheritor of the mantle of the old National Liberals. In the middle of the political spectrum the Centrists continued to defend Church interests, minus their Bavarian colleagues, who split off to form a more conservative Bavarian People's Party, but continued to co-operate with the larger Center party on most occasions. To the left of center the German Democratic party (known in its last years as the German State party) represented a segment of socially liberal traders, industrialists, and professional people (the prewar Progressives), and on the left proper the Social Democrats continued as the mass representative of working-class democratic socialism. However, the world-wide split of left and right in the international socialist movement was faithfully reproduced in Germany; from a series of wartime and early postwar splits, the Communists made their electoral appearance in the early twenties and represented the only addition to the five Imperial political parties until the rise of the Nazis in the early thirties. Smaller political groups continued to be active and *Reichstag* elections were contested by as many as thirty or more parties,[3] but these six (seven with the NSDAP from 1930

[2] The Imperial *Reichstag* was made up of members elected from 397 single-member districts under a majority system with a runoff if no candidate achieved a majority on the first vote. The last elections (January, 1912) before World War I chose 110 Social Democrats, 91 Centrists, 57 Conservatives and Free Conservatives, 45 National Liberals, 42 Progressives, 33 representatives of national minorities (including five Hanoverian Guelphs), and 19 from smaller, local parties, mainly conservative and agrarian in character.

[3] With the detachment of the territories they represented, the Danish, Alsace-Lorraine, and Polish minority *Reichstag* members disappeared, though the persistent Guelphs continued to represent Hanoverian autonomous sentiment. Most of these multitudinous splinter parties of the Weimar period, however, were based on economic, not racial or national, concepts. Many—for example the Economic party—represented efforts to defend the lower middle class from inflation and proletarianization. Others continued the Imperial tradition of local farmer parties

onwards) retained the support of the vast majority of the electors, as the accompanying table demonstrates.[4]

Table 8. Membership in the German *Reichstag*, 1919-1933

Party*	January 1919	June 1920	May 1924	December 1924	May 1928	September 1930	July 1932	November 1932	March 1933
SPD	185	186	100	131	153	143	133	121	120
Z-BVP	91	85	81	88	78	87	97	90	92
KPD	–	4	62	45	54	77	89	100	81
DNVP	44	71	95	103	73	41	37	52	52
DVP	19	65	45	51	45	30	7	11	2
DDP	75	39	28	32	25	20	4	2	5
NSDAP	–	–	32	14	12	107	230	196	288
Others	7	9	29	29	51	72	11	12	7
Total	421	459	472	493	491	577	608	584	647

* Party abbreviations used here are: SPD—*Sozialdemokratische Partei Deutschlands;* Z-BVP—*Zentrumspartei-Bayerische Volkspartei;* KPD—*Kommunistische Partei Deutschlands;* DNVP—*Deutschnationale Volkspartei;* DVP—*Deutsche Volkspartei;* DDP—*Deutsche Demokratische Partei;* NSDAP—*Nationalsozialistische Deutsche Arbeiterpartei.*

As may be seen, the early majorities of the so-called "Weimar Coalition" of Democrats, Centrists, and Social Democrats diminished with time, especially in so far as the Democrats were concerned, but the struggle of left versus right was the basic conflict in the political life of Germany in the twenties. As Hitlerism gained, the Centrists, Social Democrats, and Communists managed to hold the larger part of their support, but the Democrats, the People's party, and the small local parties were almost wiped out, finally producing an NSDAP-DNVP majority in the March, 1933, Hitler-organized "election."

With the advent to power of the Nazis, the non-Hitlerian parties either dissolved or were forcibly liquidated; remnants of leadership remained, but no active work could be undertaken with the *Gestapo* in power. Some underground organization was maintained, especially on the left, and much information and propaganda material was smuggled out of Hitler's Germany, but widespread activity was out

such as the Württemberg *Bauern und Weingärtnerbund.*

[4] The first of these elections (that of January, 1919) was to the National Assembly which drafted the constitution; the others were to the *Reichstag.* Under the proportional 60,000 votes per seat system of election used during the Weimar period the seat totals for the various parties represent their actual vote strength, as contrasted to the Imperial single-member district system which constantly discriminated against the Social Democrats. This voting system also accounts for the shifting total number of seats, since the total number of *Reichstag* members depended on how many electors voted for the various party lists.

of the question. During the war period the situation for the old democratic parties and their leaders was no better, and the July, 1944, insurrectionary movement was a conspiracy in which the old political parties did not figure. Individual Weimar political leaders were among those seeking to eliminate the Hitler regime, but the police state had suppressed political organisms of the normal type so effectively that these leaders participated in the movement as individuals, not as party personalities.

POLITICAL PARTIES UNDER
MILITARY GOVERNMENT CONTROL

Beginning of Postwar Politics—A rebirth of democratic political party life had to await a physical ending of Hitler control and came only when Nazi Germany had been defeated militarily and the exercise of power had passed to the Allies. While the western Allies—France, Great Britain, and the United States—had envisaged a temporary suspension of politics in Germany until life had returned to some measure of normalcy, the Soviet authorities quickly announced their approval of the resumption of political activity. In June, 1945, the Soviet Commander in Chief authorized the organization of "antifascist" parties in the Soviet Zone of Occupation (then including Berlin), and four such parties were immediately licensed "from above" by the Soviet Military Government. In view of this circumstance the Potsdam conference agreed to proceed with the normalization of political life immediately, and the Potsdam Agreement of August, 1945, provided that "all democratic political parties with rights of assembly and of political discussion shall be allowed and encouraged in Germany."[5]

Zonal Organization—In the American Zone, local *Gemeinde* and *Kreis* political organizations were authorized in the summer, *Land* organizations in the fall, and zonal organizations in February, 1946. In the British Zone the local level organization was permitted in October, zonal organization two months later; for the French area of control all levels of organization were authorized in December, 1945. While the Potsdam Agreement and subsequent Allied conferences envisaged some sort of all-German policy with respect to political activity and political parties, such a policy never developed. In the early days of

[5] The authorization of political activity was linked with elections in the following phrases: "local self-government shall be restored throughout Germany on democratic principles and in particular through elective councils" and "representative and elective principles shall be introduced into regional, provincial, and state (*Land*) administration as rapidly as may be justified by the successful application of these principles in local self-government."

the Allied *Kommandatura* in Berlin, a multipartite policy was concerted which recognized—for Berlin—both the Soviet-sponsored Socialist Unity party (SED) and the Social Democratic party suppressed by the Soviet authorities in their zone, but this agreement collapsed with the splitting of the city into its present democratic West and totalitarian East. At the 1947 Moscow session of the Council of Foreign Ministers there was some discussion of political parties, but the course of Soviet policy in Germany obviously made impossible any sort of democratic policy towards the organization of political life. At the following session of the Council—in London—the matter was not discussed.

As a consequence of these failures to reach any agreed quadripartite policy towards political parties, each zone developed its own implementation of the Potsdam Agreement. In East Germany the U.S.S.R. representatives set about to establish the political base for a fascio-communist regime, and the development of political activities there followed this intent. In the West, however, policy was not so clear-cut. The military authorities generally sought to develop a political life cleansed of Nazis, neo-Nazis, and Nazi influences, and to this end they adopted a licensing system by which persons seeking to organize political parties were required to apply to military government for an authorization. This general attitude was supplemented by a desire to see political parties emerge "from the grass roots" rather than from the top down, as had been done in the Soviet Zone, and this "grass roots" viewpoint was especially prevalent among American Zone Military Government authorities. On the French side there was a definite feeling that any prospective federalists ought to get substantial encouragement; and amongst all the western military government political personnel, there persisted a hope that not too many political parties would be licensed lest the political life of postwar Germany be fragmentized as was that of Weimar.[6]

As far as the "grass roots" question was concerned, the realities of politics soon indicated that German politicians would meet together and organize on *Land,* zonal, and national bases long before the formalities of military government recognition permitted them to do so. The Social Democrats and Communists, first to apply for local licenses

---

[6] The American Military Government regulations with respect to political party activity spelled out in some detail the necessity that political parties licensed to operate in the American Zone must have certain democratic characteristics. Among these were requirements that the party officers and candidates for office be chosen by the party members or by delegates elected by the party members, a clause which has been translated over into many of the German election laws.

everywhere in the West, were also the first to so foregather, and within six months the "grass roots" concept had gone by the board in fact, though the official fiction that no national political organizations existed continued. Actually, the "grass roots" theory was aided more by the shortage of transportation and the economic difficulties of the early postwar period than by any official dogma that political parties should grow out of local groupings of like-minded citizens. It was soon realized that historic lines of political cleavage dating back to the Weimar Republic and the Empire would continue whether the ruler of the moment was an Allied occupation, an elected President, or a Kaiser.

Effect of Licensing—In several ways, however, the system of licensing and authorizing political parties had substantial effects on German political life. First and foremost it cut down the number of political competitors in the early days of the occupation. By screening out the Nazis, militarists, and those of similar political belief the extreme right existed only *in suspenso;* the paper work involved in getting a military government authorization was substantial and kept potential fragmentary parties from organizing. In the French Zone it was clearly indicated that minor parties would not be welcome, and indeed none were authorized in that area until well after the *Landtag* elections of 1947. In the British Zone the military government authorities adopted a more lenient attitude, but limited the number of licenses granted. In the American Zone a policy comparable to that of the British Zone was adopted save that *Land*-wide licenses were granted only to a party which demonstrated a measure of local strength and organization in a number of local areas, a part of the "grass-roots" theory.

Refugee Parties Banned—Although the party competition was thus somewhat circumscribed, no substantial non-Nazi group of political activists was denied the right to form a party save in one instance. From the beginning of political activity in the western zones there was agitation for the licensing of refugee-expellee political parties. Applications for such licenses were denied by the respective military governors in the hope that the refugees and expellees would find a place in German political life aside from special party representation of their interests. There is no doubt that this decision prevented the development of purely refugee-expellee parties prior to the organization of the present German Federal Republic. With the elimination of licensing consequent upon the organization of the west German government, however, such parties immediately emerged and are playing an important role in contemporary German political life.

During the period in which licensing was in force, the western powers followed varied zonal policies with respect to control of political activity once licensed, as well as to the original authorization of political organizations. In the British and American zones the parties were relatively free to do what they wished, and authorizations were suspended or revoked only in a few exceptional cases.[7] Though permits for political meetings were required for a time, these were largely matters of formality and had little meaning. In the French Zone the military government authorities applied stricter controls in fear of an "anti-French" movement. Restrictions were placed on the activities of several of the political leaders of such nationalist parties as the Social Democratic. Until the union of the three zones the French policy refused to sanction affiliation of parties in the French control area with those in other zones, and party leaders sometimes had difficulty getting the necessary papers for interzonal travel. It was only after much consideration that the French Zone state delegations were permitted to proceed to the SPD national *Parteitag* in 1947.

Occupation Policies—During this whole period of licensing there were often accusations that one occupation power or another was favoring this group or that in the matter of licensing.[8] Specifically, the French and the Americans were accused of favoring the Christian Democrats and the British of favoring the Social Democrats. The evidence indicates little support for these accusations. Many of the French authorities undoubtedly had personal preferences for the CDU as a party, for it was much more federalistic than the SPD, and the French were concerned over what they regarded as the highly inflammatory and nationalistic speeches of Dr. Kurt Schumacher, then national SPD leader. Nonetheless, there is no evidence that the French authorities exceeded their publicly announced political activity control policies.

As for the Americans, most United States occupation authorities were uninterested in "politics" and whatever reaction they had towards political activity was largely one of apathy. In the interim period between the beginning of licensed political activity and the coming into force of the Occupation Statute, it is probably correct to say that most American officials who considered the matter at all would have

[7] The license of the *Koenigs- und Heimatpartei* was revoked in Bavaria; that of a right-wing group was suspended in a part of the British Zone. Such instances were rare, however.

[8] In addition to the criticisms of favoritism, there was a strong attack on the American Zone policy of not licensing political party newspapers. In the other zones—including the Soviet—either the parties had their own newspapers (as in pre-Hitler days) or certain ones were generally regarded as on their side. The American Zone policy was to develop nonparty journals and restrict parties to the issuance of newsletter-type sheets within the limits of their paper allowance.

preferred the CDU as a "free enterprise" party over the SPD, but the actual attitude towards licensing was one of neutrality. This may be said as well for the British, accused at one time of favoring the SPD because of their own Labor government at home. There is little question that leading British political figures favored Schumacher and the SPD and, indeed, consulted with that party in preference to—even in exclusion of—its opponents. Comments of these Labor party leaders and their associates gave every evidence of their being personally well disposed toward their fellow Socialist. Alternatively, the SPD leadership certainly had many grievances against British Military Government in the latter's policies and day-to-day operations, and there is no evidence that any feeling of comradeship between the SPD and British political leaders led to unfair paper allocations, license favoritism, or other similar marks of political brotherhood. Like the Americans, the British were neutral.

There were certainly instances, especially in the early months of military government, of political favoritism by military government officers of all the western occupation powers. Interference by occupation authorities was not infrequent in the earliest days of German political activity, and many of these interferences seem on later examination to have been improper and arbitrary. Most of these activities, however, were the product of a lack of thorough political training and lack of understanding rather than deliberate policy, and they had virtually vanished by the ending of the political party licensing system.

Naturally, the development of the "cold war" has had its repercussions in Western Germany, but the freedom of the Communist party has remained despite the attacks of its Soviet parent on the western powers. In several instances, issues of Communist party journals have been confiscated for unsubstantiated attacks on the occupation authorities, but the party's licenses to engage in political activity remained valid until licensing itself ceased. Communist efforts to change the party name were, however, denied. An effort to gain a license for the Socialist Unity party in Western Germany was refused because the party claimed to be an amalgamation of the SPD and the Communists, which, in the West at least, it was not. In denying this application the authorities indicated they would approve the new name if any such amalgamation actually took place.[9]

[9] A later effort to change the party name from Communist to Socialist People's party was also refused as an attempt to confuse the electorate and as a ruse to get around the previous decision, since it was understood that the Socialist Unity party in the Soviet Zone would quickly change its name to Socialist People's party once the adjustment had been made in the western zones.

*Development of Responsible Parties—*As the political parties developed under the military government licensing system in Western Germany, frequent comment was made that these newly licensed political parties were unreal and that they worked in a dreamworld, without authority, without power, and without responsibility. In the earliest days of the occupation these observations had some truth; the parties had little opportunity to convene national representative bodies to establish doctrine and set up organizations. Most of them were largely pre-1933 in their personnel, and their authority was certainly limited. However, with the establishment of *Land* governments in the three western zones, with the election of the various *Landtage,* and especially with the transfer of larger and larger areas of authority to German control, this became less and less true. The governments of the various states became responsible to their own parliaments rather than to the military governments which had originally put them into office, and the vitality of the political parties increased from month to month via this transfusion of power to German agencies.

POSTWAR PARTY PROGRAMS

*Social Democratic Party—*These political parties as they emerged during the occupation in the various zones and states followed a fairly uniform pattern and one that has become national for the new west German republic. Oldest of the parties is the Social Democratic, dating its parliamentary history back to the leadership of Ferdinand Lassalle and the North German Federation and its actual organization to the 1869 Workers' Congress at Eisenach. In its early years, repressed by the antisocialist laws of Bismarck, the new party nevertheless managed to gain strength in the rapidly expanding industrial areas of Germany. Though proclaiming a vigorous Marxist socialist program, the party as it grew veered more and more towards social reformism, and the struggle for control of the party between the maximalists of Bebel and the "revisionists" of Bernstein never ceased. With the outbreak of World War I the contest developed into more open splitting and finally led to the secession of the leftist "Independent Socialists" and the eventual establishment of the German Communist party.

During the Weimar period the SPD was a bulwark of the republic, though never able to offer a really challenging and dynamic leadership to the forces that might have kept the new democracy alive and fought off the advent of Hitlerism. Following World War II the party immediately reorganized and today continues the old party name and tradition of democratic socialism as the second largest of the present-day west German political parties. The basic strength of the SPD lies in its representation of the interests of the industrial working class. Though much of its leadership comes from intellectuals, as with other European socialist parties, and though it draws some strength from the middle class, the white-collar workers, and the farmers, its base lies in the industrial worker. An examination of the directly elected membership of the *Bundestag* will show that the large majority of the SPD members so chosen come from cities and from industrial areas like the Ruhr. Since the Eastern Zone of Germany has been cut off from the democratic western zones, many of these centers of SPD strength are denied the party, but the areas in which it has most strength today are those in which the worker predominates. Despite this connection with the worker and his organized trade unions, the SPD maintains no formal contact with the trade unions as does the British Labor party. SPD membership—which varies from around 750,000 to 850,000—is entirely personal and direct. This means that the weight of the trade unions in party decisions is made personally, not institutionally as in the British party.[10]

Programmatically, the party has always maintained the traditional socialist doctrine of public ownership of the basic means of production, a doctrine to be achieved via the winning of political power in a democratic struggle with the forces of capitalism. Governmentally, the SPD has always favored a strong central authority and socially stands for a wide range of programs of social improvement. In foreign policy the party has taken a strong line since the end of the war in urging abandonment of occupation controls, German unification, and the re-establishment of full German sovereignty.

Communist Party—The German Communist party during the Weimar period began as an advanced working-class revolutionary party seeking to extend the political revolution of 1918 into the economy and social system of the republic. While the party, like its counterparts throughout the world, was advocating a proletarian revolution and the establishment of the workers' state, its real policies by the end of the twenties were being determined by the Communist International, in complete authority over Communist parties everywhere. Though movements of revolt started from time to time within the

---

[10] In the British Labor party, trade unions are directly affiliated to the party on a national basis and have as many votes as they possess members. In voting at party conventions such unions may thus cast several hundred thousand votes each, and the total of such affiliated trade-union members (and votes) considerably exceeds the 700,000 to 900,000 individual, direct members of local, district organizations.

KPD, they never succeeded. In the period of the early thirties the KPD gained some strength as a more militant foe of Hitlerism than the SPD, even despite occasional Nazi-Communist co-operative efforts. As soon as the Nazis came to power, however, the KPD was suppressed.

The party has been active in Western Germany since the first authorization of political activity, but without success. Its strength in elections has declined steadily and continuously in each election until today it represents some 5 per cent of the electors. It is strongest in the Ruhr and in large industrial centers elsewhere in West Germany, especially amongst workers in heavy industry; it is weakest among Catholics and farmers. Despite its electoral weakness, the party membership—something between 100,000 and 125,000—is active, perhaps more active than that of any other group in Western Germany. Naturally the aim of the Soviet-type totalitarian state is played down in party propaganda, and most of the contemporary Communist program emphasizes German unity and peace. These two points represent real drives for general support, but the fate of KPD appeals in the past indicates that the handicaps to Communist campaigning are formidable. These handicaps include the obvious and clear association of the KPD with the Soviet Union and the real hatred and fear of the average German for Russia. Another difficulty for the KPD has been the insistence of Moscow on "signing away" the eastern territories to Poland; a third is the factual information about conditions in the Soviet Zone of Germany available to those living in the west. So long as these factors work in force against the Communists they will remain a minor political party, though their over-all political influence as an outpost of Soviet colonialism may be large.

This special character of the KPD as an agent of Soviet policy makes out of date the old (and simple) classification of left-right in German politics, a classification in any event much in doubt in postwar Germany. The political spectrum has no firm locus on which the KPD can now be placed though tradition still gives it the seats at the extreme left. In the sense that the KPD represents the line of alleged proletarian dictatorship, it is the extreme left. Actually, however, it remains outside the scope of democratic political life as its counterpart, the NSDAP, did before it. Thus, while it would have been correct some years ago to speak of the SPD and KPD as the parties of the left and the CDU and FDP as the right, it is better now to speak of the CDU and the FDP as the "parties of the government" and the SPD as the opposition, with the various minor parties filling in on both sides as their aims and interests dictate.

Christian Democratic Union—The "parties of the government," that is, those contributing the basic support of the Adenauer government installed in September, 1949, are the Christian Democratic Union, the Free Democratic party, and the *Deutsche Partei*. The first of these, the CDU, appeared early on the occupation political scene under the sponsorship of the old Center party Catholic leaders. In its early days, before time had developed any competition on the center or right of the political stage, the CDU polled the majority of the non-Communist, non-Social Democratic votes in Western Germany.[11] It developed primarily as a *Land* and zonal group of parties held together by a more or less common desire to maintain a *status quo* and, within Catholic circles, to defend Church interests. Today a good deal of its non-Catholic support has dwindled away—to its FDP partner or to other conservative groups—and the great majority of its directly elected members of the *Bundestag* come from the Catholic districts of Rhineland-Westphalia and southern Germany, though it still has numerous Protestant adherents.

Like the Imperial and Weimar Center party in which its present leader—Dr. Konrad Adenauer—was active, the present CDU has internal problems on economic questions. Especially in the Ruhr area, the direction of CDU policy is challenged from the left, but not to the point of leaving the organization. This type of internal economic struggle comes naturally enough in a party which includes conservative Catholic farmers and trade-union-minded Catholic Ruhr workers. So far the common interest of both in the Church has kept them together though their economic instincts might have otherwise kept them apart. In its general program the CDU (and with it must be included the CSU of Bavaria, where the traditions of the Weimar Bavarian People's party and local provincial interests have prevented full amalgamation) tends to defend the economic *status quo*. In such matters as schools and in social questions generally it naturally supports the Catholic Church position, but sometimes the exigencies of political life modify its economic line. On such contemporary matters as the problem of codetermination of plant policy by workers, the CDU has sought to find a line of compromise between its own left and right. Its position in this and similar questions has sorely tried the undoubted political talents of its present leadership.

[11] The drop in this monopoly of the non-Socialist, non-Communist vote may be best illustrated in Bavaria. In the Constitutional Assembly elections of June, 1946, the CSU polled 58.3 per cent of the votes; in the *Landtag* voting of December, 1946, this had dropped to 52.3. By the *Bundestag* election of August, 1949, it was down to 29.2 and finally fell to 27.4 in the November, 1950, *Landtag* elections.

Free Democratic Party—The Free Democratic party, the other major party in the present Adenauer government, contains within it as many divergent elements as the CDU-CSU, perhaps more. It was the last of the major parties to organize, and its voting strength has been more recently developed as a result of this late arrival on the political scene. Like the CDU-CSU, it is organized primarily on a *Land* and zonal basis, and its national organization is not comparable to that of the SPD or KPD. Though the FDP has often been regarded as the lineal descendent of German liberalism and nonsocialist democratic thought, it now contains more conservativism than liberalism in its program. It represents a modern-day amalgam of the Weimar German People's and Democratic parties, appealing especially to the middle class, professional people, and small business man in the tradition of the latter and to financial and large business interests in the line of the former. This complexity of program in the FDP leads to considerable variation in program from state to state. In the southwest the party follows a liberal social doctrine and can make common cause on occasion with the SPD. In the north and in central Germany its conservative economic interests prevail and shape its line of thought. From a religious viewpoint the party is overwhelmingly Protestant and opposes the denominational schools favored by the CDU-CSU, though not to the point of breaking relations with its partner in federal politics.

These four—SPD, KPD, CDU-CSU, and FDP—are the major parties of contemporary German political life. The Social Democrats and Christian Democrats are by far the larger of the four and represent a sort of "Big Two" in terms of current politics, though the FDP is now so closely associated with the CDU-CSU in most states and in the federal political arena that the political fight is really between these two as "parties of the government" and the Social Democrats as the opposition.

Minor Political Parties—Other political parties, however, are active in West Germany. The activity of the four major organizations has eclipsed but not eliminated their smaller competitors. Among the more important of these minor groupings are to be listed the Bavarian party, a conservative, nativistic group with special concern for Bavaria's rights. It naturally opposes any federal interference in Bavaria, but otherwise generally supports the CDU-FDP right coalition with its seventeen *Bundestag* members. It is strongly Catholic, as the locus of its strength would indicate, and tends to act in terms of rural rather than urban interests, though it does have a following in cities as well as in the smaller communities.[12]

[12] The Bavarian party has been well compared with such political movements as

Somewhat akin to the Bavarian party is the *Deutsche Partei*, the German party. This organization emerged after the war as the Lower Saxon State party—descendent of the Guelphs—dedicated to carrying on the struggle for freeing old Hanover from the Prussians. This aim was accomplished in the setting up of Lower Saxony as one of the states of the west German republic, but the party did not cease its activities. It had found a niche as representative of conservative, Protestant farmers and business elements in Lower Saxony and now is expanding into other parts of northern Germany with a view to increasing its national position. While the Bavarian party seeks to maintain "Bavaria for the Bavarians," the German party has a definitive doctrine to preach outside its former limits of Lower Saxony. Aside from its conservatism and defense of rural interests, the party stresses federalism and, as a specifically Protestant party, joins with the Catholics in seeking a church school system. So far it has had little success outside Lower Saxony, but it has at least gained a foothold elsewhere in north Germany, is in the Adenauer cabinet, and now holds seventeen seats in the *Bundestag*.

Another political party with its beginnings in a north German *Land* is the new Center party, not to be confused with the older Imperial and Weimar party of the same name. The new center party is definitely left-of-center and through the years has consistently rejected efforts to merge it with the CDU on the grounds that the latter was a "reactionary" organization. The Centrists are active in North Rhine–Westphalia and Lower Saxony, but represent a political force only in the latter, from which they have elected ten *Bundestag* members. The party was originally organized by left-wing members of the old Center party and is almost entirely Catholic in make-up. Despite this fact, its economic doctrine usually brings it to the support of the SPD in such matters as socialization, codetermination, land reform, and the like. Essentially the new Center is an organization representing Catholic workers and lower-middle-class groups, and since it is Catholic in membership and orientation, it follows a strong antistate line on school questions and upholds Church doctrine on social questions generally.

Still other minor parties are active besides the Bavarian, German, and Center parties, but they play only a small role. The Economic Reconstruction party in Bavaria is a personal creation of Alfred Loritz;

the *Union Nationale* of Maurice Duplessis in Quebec, and the relation of the Bavarian party to the larger CDU-CSU is quite comparable with that of Duplessis' organization to the larger Liberal party for the whole of Canada. The problems of nativism in a native organization which is a part of a larger federal group as opposed to those of a nativist party *qua* nativist party are almost exactly similar.

its fortunes have declined in recent years, though it still holds twelve seats in the *Bundestag*. Loritz was a member of the prewar Economic party, and his postwar organization is best known for his scathing attacks on all political personalities and his adventures in escaping arrest on black-market charges. The party has no especial program and has recently lost heavily to other political organizations with something more definite to offer the voters, especially refugee voters to whom Loritz made a special appeal in 1949.

Besides these parties there are a number of miscellaneous groups, associations, *Kreise,* and parties of all shades of opinion from Titoist and Trotskyite to neo-Nazi. Fear has been expressed that a new fascist organization might be able to unite various small quasi-Nazi groups into a new NSDAP, but so far the "radical right" has been unable to find any over-all leadership. The only extremist party of the right which developed any real mass support was the *Sozialistische Reichspartei* (SRP). This party polled well in the *Landtag* elections in Lower Saxony in May, 1951, and might have become the nucleus of a united radical right movement. In October, 1952, however, acting under Article 21 of the Basic Law, the Federal Constitutional Court declared the SRP *verfassungswidrig*—"inimical to the constitution"—and ordered it dissolved, its activities ended, and its various *Bundestag* and *Landtag* seats vacated.

The only important political party to emerge as a result of this change in policy was one whose growth had been anticipated—the refugee-expellee party. The *Block der Heimatvertriebenen und Ent-rechteten* (BHE) activities in *Land* elections in Schleswig-Holstein, Baden-Württemberg, and Bavaria[13] have been significant, and in other areas their alignments with older parties have done much to influence the course of elections. This group represents a single interest, improved conditions for the refugee, the expellee and, incidentally, the native dispossessed. The BHE seeks to help these groups in such matters as civil service appointments, housing, employment opportunities, pensions and the like, matters which have little to do with broad political doctrine but a great deal to do with the everyday life of Western Germany's "new citizens."[14] How the BHE may affect older

[13] The BHE polled 23.4 per cent of the vote in Schleswig-Holstein in *Land* elections in 1950, 14.9 per cent in Lower Saxony (1951), 9.5 per cent in Baden-Württemberg (1952), and 12.3 per cent in Bavaria (1950).

[14] The BHE, while aiming primarily at the refugees and expellees, does not ignore its appeal to the native dispossessed. Its very name, literally the "League of the Expelled and Those Deprived of Their Rights," emphasizes the BHE's effort to get nonexpellee support. Especially important in this regard is the BHE campaign for a liberal *Lastenausgleich* or equalization of burdens measure which

and more traditional political alignments remains to be seen. Naturally this party seeks power by way of a coalition with one or the other of the major groups with which it competes—the CDU-FDP on the one hand, the Social Democrats on the other. So far it has refused to be drawn into so tight an embrace by either that it cannot escape if its interests so dictate. Nationally the BHE is very weak in the *Bundestag*, but its national influence is substantial and may be expected to increase as the elections begin to reflect more accurately its strength among the voters. What this influence may eventually mean in terms of foreign policy is obscure, though there is no uncertainty about the desire of a large majority of refugees and expellees to return to their various homelands.

The success of the BHE has indicated that new parties can develop in postwar Germany if they have substantial support, but the short history of most of the newer political parties indicate this support is essential. The high mortality rate of new groups or parties is due to the general indifference of the public to individual personalist parties and a popular antipathy to the fragmentization of political life. From an electoral viewpoint the prevalence of minimal clauses in election legislation is a handicap to representation in elective bodies, but no bar to candidacy itself. The number of signatures which must be secured to put a candidate's name on the ballot varies from state to state and between the various levels of election—federal, state, *Kreis*, and communal—but the requirements are not so rigid that a party or group with any sort of following encounters insuperable obstacles. Most of the newest crop of small political parties and groups die early because they have no program which appeals to a group of citizens who cannot find representation of their interests elsewhere.

POSTWAR PARTY ORGANIZATION

Organizationally the Social Democrats are the prototype of efficient organization of a mass political party. Under the Empire, in the Weimar Republic, and today the SPD remains the largest in membership and the best organized of the German political parties. From the *Parteihaus* in Bonn an experienced group of party organizers and functionaries co-ordinates the work of a party machine extending into nearly every community of Western Germany. At the base of this organization are the local dues-paying, card-holding party members, organized regionally into some twenty-three districts or *Parteibezirke* following roughly *Land* and *Regierungsbezirk* boundaries. These mem-

---

would tax those who lost little or nothing during the war to pay for the losses of those who suffered severely, especially in property loss.

bers are represented upwards through a series of district and *Land* organizations to the topmost party authority, the annual *Parteitag* or national convention. At this convention delegates from the districts meet to hear reports and discuss the year's work of the party and its agencies, to consider policy questions, and to elect the permanent officials of the party. In the SPD these last consist of the party leader, his deputy, and the members of the party executive and control commission.

Party Hierarchy—These officials and comparable personalities in smaller offices at the district and/or *Land* level conduct the day-to-day work of the party organization. Unlike the large political parties of the United States, German party work is organized on a year-round basis. Not only is the party active on a permanent basis, it is active in a whole series of fields of youth work, women's activities, sport, welfare, and similar areas which would be foreign to the American party organizer save perhaps on a highly personal basis in a city party machine.[15] This party work is conducted on a national and local basis and, like the purely political effort of the organization, is co-ordinated by the national and regional party headquarters. Between these headquarters and the actual party member stand a host of lesser party officials, not salaried as are the full-time regional and national party workers, but active in multitudinous party affairs at the local and county level. The party members may have enthusiasm and faith, and the top officialdom may have the organizational skill, the staff, the professional party workers, and the apparatus; but it is these noncommissioned officers of the party who bring the two together, get nominations made for local elections, organize local campaign work, maintain local educational work in times of slack interest, collect dues, distribute literature, interest young people in joining and working with the party—in short, keep the organization running smoothly and efficiently. The ability of the SPD to function through the past eighty years has been based on the ability of these men and women to do the job of maintaining the organization and carrying its appeal to the citizenry.

Communist Organization—When the German Communists split off

[15] The participation of women and young people in political activities in postwar Germany is generally comparable to that of the average in the western democracies. Within the political parties men are much more numerous than women though the present *Bundestag* of 402 members includes 28 women, as compared with 21 of 625 in the British House of Commons and 8 of 435 in the American House of Representatives. The age factor in political leadership is about that of the pre-Hitler period. Of Western Germany's *Bundestag* members 14.4 per cent are under forty, as compared with 17.8 in Great Britain, and 13.8 in the United States.

from the parent SPD to set up the new KPD, they carried with them this concept of a highly organized doctrinal party apparatus, though the Communists went much further. For the essentially democratic character of the SPD party organization they substituted a new idea: "democratic centralism," a mixture of one-third internal party democracy, one-third bureaucratic rule from the top, and one-third Soviet infallibility. As time progressed and the U.S.S.R. came into full control of the Communist parties everywhere in the world, the KPD, like those elsewhere, emphasized the last two elements of its formula. The Communist party in Western Germany today numbers some 100,000 to 125,000 members, with an organization active in all states, but especially so in industrial areas. The internal organization and operation of the party has always been obscure, conditioned as it has been by its semiconspiratorial role, but the party apparatus—the hierarchy and the functionaries—is placed and displaced from the top down. Expulsions and "reductions in rank" have been common in the postwar KPD, especially since the Titiost break away from orthodox Communism in Yugoslavia, and scarcely a week passes without the press's noting some new purging of KPD ranks. While it might seem that this process would eventually defeat its own end, it must be remembered that the KPD is not a political party in the normally accepted sense of the word; its primary purpose is to train a cadre of disciplined, completely malleable adherents in the struggle to establish a Soviet state. Under these conditions, the purge marks almost the normal type of party life inside the KPD. Party members are not important as such but active and fanatically loyal party-line militants are, and the membership effort of the KPD is primarily to develop inside the party these activist elements.

Middle-Class Party Organization—In contrast to the traditional left parties (the SPD and the KPD), the so-called *bürgerliche* parties are weak in formal organization and in formal membership. Though both the CDU-CSU and the FDP maintain formal membership lists, dues-paying is not enforced as it is in the parties making their basic appeal to the worker. Moreover, the parties themselves tend much more to local autonomy than to national central direction of party work. Though the heart of the SPD and the KPD may be said to be their respective national offices, these are secondary institutions with the CDU and the FDP. In both parties the postwar trend has been to regard the national organization as a sort of co-ordinating committee of state parties rather than a centralized national party authority.

In the CDU this attitude was modified several years ago; at the

Goslar Conference in October, 1950, a formal "all-German" CDU was established with a national party constitution and organization. At this meeting all the state organizations of the CDU were merged into a single party, excepting only the Bavarian CSU, with which close relations are maintained though it remains formally outside the national organization. Thus the CDU is now established nationally as a single party rather than as a confederation of state units, and the party central organization may be expected to develop in importance and authority, though not so far as in the tightly organized SPD. As with the Social Democrats, the national *Parteitag* is a sort of combined highest party authority and national rallying point, the year-round leadership of the party being exercised through a chairman, two deputies, and a national party executive elected by this national convention.

In one rather small but significant point the processes of the CDU and SPD conventions differ. In the latter representation is based upon the number of dues-paying party members in each party district; in the former the size of delegations depends on the vote cast for the CDU in the last federal election in each *Land*.[16] In this variation lies one of the keys to the organizational differences of the two parties— the SPD a dues-paying centralized, highly organized, programmatic party, the CDU a less tightly knit, less programmatic, more localized group with a national organization and central office maintained more as a necessary nuisance than as an integral part of the organizational concept of the party itself.

The Free Democratic partners of the CDU and CSU in the present Adenauer government are even less organized than their more numerous colleagues. Membership as membership is less important to the FDP than to any of the other major parties. Although a national convention is held by the FDP, the party maintains only a nominal national organization, and the supra-*Land* apparatus of this party functions as a *"Dachorganization,"* a "roof" organization, rather than as a true national central office. Essential policies are determined in the various state organizations and among the *Bundestag* delegates rather than by means of discussion within a recognized mass party rank-and-file. While occasional efforts are made to strengthen the membership and organizational position of the FDP, these have come to naught and are unlikely to progress far in the future. In a sense this is a concomi-

---

[16] The Goslar constitution of the CDU also provides for special representation from the "CDU in Exile," that is, the organization as it existed in the Soviet Zone of Occupation until forced into a puppet status with respect to the dominant Socialist Unity party.

tant of the individualist character of the party's general political view-point; in part it is due to the apparent reluctance of middle-class voters in all countries to join in mass-type political parties of the Social Democratic pattern, a reluctance which affects the CDU and FDP alike.

Parties since the end of the war have developed organizationally along much the same lines as under the Weimar period, though not to the point of maximum intensity of the republican era. Under the Empire the SPD was the only effectively organized national mass party, but with the revolution of 1918 came tighter forms of organization, emphasis on large membership and on continuous year-round party work, and large national central offices comparable to the British party headquarters. Since 1945 this type of organization has been reintroduced by the SPD and KPD, but the *"bürgerliche"* parties (large and small, confessional and otherwise) have tended to go slower than they did during the Weimar years.

POLITICAL PARTY CAMPAIGNING

As far as campaigning itself is concerned, the postwar parties have not essentially varied the techniques of Weimar. The primary emphasis of each campaign is the party, not the individual. The change-over from closed list proportional systems of election to combined majority proportional methods has changed this emphasis very little.[17] Some attention is now paid to the individual candidate in *Bundestag* voting and in those states electing a part of their local representation directly, but the candidate personally is much less important than the appeal to vote for the party, an appeal often coupled with the number of the party on the ballot.[18]

The party campaign is waged primarily by literature, meetings, and the loud-speaker truck. As in most democratic nations, the facilities of the state radio are made available to the parties, or at least to the larger ones, on an agreed basis for a limited number of talks by the party leaders. The prolific literature varies between the colored poster pasted on kiosks, walls, and empty buildings and the throw-away leaflet. Meetings are generally small affairs and, like similar gatherings in elections elsewhere, are more rallies of the convinced than efforts to persuade the uncertain voter. As such, they serve a

[17] See Chapter 20 below for full discussion.
[18] This emphasis on party rather than on individuals is not a German innovation; in all European democracies the voter ballots for the party rather than for a specific personality. No matter what election system is used, this party-over-candidate emphasis is dominant nearly everywhere.

purpose in bringing the faithful together for a mutual pledge of re-doubled efforts and as a reindoctrination into the party campaign. Most larger cities will also be the scene of several larger, public-square meetings, with one of the "name" national or state leaders addressing a larger audience on his party's program.

Party Finances—To finance these campaigns and to carry on their regular party work between elections the parties have varied systems of fund-raising. For the SPD, reliance is placed on dues paid by the membership and on election-time contributions, usually small. On the Communist side there is much less clarity as to money and where it comes from, but lack of funds has certainly been no great barrier to postwar KPD activity. Part of this Communist treasury comes from party dues and the contributions of supporters, but a substantial part comes from the east German SED and possibly even from Russia. The nonsocialist parties, lacking the dues support of mass membership, have necessarily to rely on private contributions, and these come in the largest part from businessmen or organizations of means. The SPD has consistently charged that big business and industry finances the CDU, the FDP, and other nonsocialist parties. In the absence of any legal requirement that parties or candidates submit public statements of revenue and expenses, the SPD claims have remained but allega-tions, though it is generally agreed that the expenses of the nonsocialists, especially campaign expenses, have been usually met by those with a stake in keeping the Socialists out of office. This matter of expenses often crops up in connection with party nominations of candidates; although the SPD and KPD will normally finance their candidates from the party treasury, it is not uncommon for more conservative groups to have the candidate share in the party's election costs.[19]

Party Nominations—Nominations of candidates by the parties have been perhaps less affected by postwar conditions than any other as-pect of German political life. Though the final control of nominations is democratic, especially in the SPD, there is no question that party leadership exerts considerable influence in the selection of candidates. Under the Weimar list systems of election, the vital point in nominat-ing candidates lay in deciding the order in which individual candi-dates' names would appear on the list, since the persons to sit in

[19] Total German campaign expenses are impossible to establish, but they certainly run lower than during the Weimar Republic. Twenty years ago party expenditures in a national campaign were the highest on the continent, though still well behind the level in the United States. Today, with currency reform stabilizing the mark and making money hard to come by, budgets are much restricted over the postinflation campaigns of the late twenties.

elective bodies were picked in that order, once the number of seats to which their party was entitled was determined. Lists were therefore made up with extreme care to see that the most important party interests were represented—trade unions, women's and youth groups, business interests, the farmers, a representative of the bureaucracy— whatever the composition of the party required.[20] With the changes made since the war in the system of election, this nomination problem has altered somewhat, but not basically. *Land* reserve lists still provide for the indirect, proportional election of a number of party candidates in *Bundestag* and state elections, and local candidates running for direct election are not necessarily nominated where they live. Normally these local candidates will seek election in their home districts, but there are many exceptions. The influence of the party leadership is probably less today in nomination matters than it was twenty years ago, but it is still substantial.[21]

PARTY DEVELOPMENT IN SOVIET GERMANY

In direct contrast to the movement towards freedom from control which has characterized political party development in Western Germany, the Soviet Zone of Occupation has been steadily pushed into a totalitarian frame of organization. In June, 1945, the Soviet military authorities first permitted political party organization, and four groups were licensed from the top down—CDU, SPD, KPD, and LDP. These four came into being with a central leadership appointed by the Soviet authorities to function for the whole zone, including the City of Berlin, at that time still occupied in its entirety by the Red Army.

Forced SPD-KPD Merger—In the early days of the occupation Communist policy emphasized the independence of the KPD and the carrying on of broad Communist aims through committees of the four parties. It soon became obvious, however, that this technique would not provide an adequate mechanism of control, and a policy of "amal-

---

[20] This process of drawing up a list for a German party nomination is almost exactly comparable to the "slate-making" problem of the American party leadership. Racial groups must be provided for and religious representation not slighted. Urban and rural candidates must be provided and no substantial part of the state left out in the making up of a "ticket."

[21] This influence is not necessarily bad; often it serves to balance the party appeal and give representation to groups who would otherwise have no voice. In Great Britain the views and suggestions of the party central office are often sought as to a suitable candidate for Parliament, and frequently a candidate will carry the party's banner in a district which never heard of him until a few days after the party central office has "suggested" his nomination to the local party organization.

gamation" of the two working-class parties was put into effect. The merger of the SPD and KPD in the Soviet Zone was accomplished by a wholesale campaign of the Soviet occupation authorities involving bribery, cajolery, threats, and physical force. In the sectors of Berlin taken over by the three western powers, a free vote referendum of the SPD membership was held on the amalgamation question, and merger was voted down overwhelmingly.[22] In the Soviet Zone itself no such referendum was held. Vote on the issue was by open show of hands, and it was plain what the fate of those opposing the will of the Soviet would be.

In April, 1946, the Soviet campaign to merge the Social Democratic and Communist parties into a new mass state party was brought to its anticipated conclusion and the SED—the Socialist Unity party of Germany—was formally proclaimed. As for the old SPD, some of its leaders and members fled to the West or relapsed into the political coma of the Hitler days. A few opportunists took governmental or party office under the auspices of the new organization, and others went along with it in the hope that the Soviets really did not mean to make of East Germany a standard satellite state. For most, however, political activity simply ceased.

1946 Elections—With the formal organization of the SED, the official state party of the Soviet military authorities was ready to expand its work. Elections were established for the fall of 1946 for local and state authorities, and these votes were marked by the appearance in the political arena of the so-called "mass organizations"—the unified trade union, the youth league, the women's union, a farmers' group, the cultural association, and the like. Set up under SED sponsorship and controlled by SED leaders, these groups are comparable to similar cogs in the highly developed Hitler system. For the Hitlerite single trade union there was now a Stalinist single trade union; for the old *Hitler Jugend* there was now the *Freie Deutsche Jugend*. But the introduction of these groups into the 1946 local and state elections produced little political effect. The voters still preferred the parties as parties.

In the campaign that fall the advantages of the SED were incalculable. Besides the fully appreciated knowledge that behind its banners stood the Soviet secret police, the Red Army, and indeed the Soviet

[22] The referendum of SPD members in West Berlin was held at the end of March, 1946, with 19,526 votes cast against merger with the KPD and 2,937 favor. Of the SPD membership in the whole City of Berlin, about half lived in the three western sectors. The other half, living in the Eastern, or Soviet, Sector, were forbidden to vote by Soviet order.

state, the SED had specific advantages everywhere. It could nominate candidates virtually at will, while the CDU and LDP, only remaining "free" political parties, could nominate only where they had local groups registered. Not only did it take a good measure of courage to organize officially and register such a group, but also the registrations often were denied, or were delayed, by the Soviet authorities. CDU and LDP party meetings were often forbidden or their approval delayed. Party newspapers of the old SPD and the KPD had been allocated to the new SED, and paper allocations to these papers were increased while those of non-SED papers were decreased.[23] The discrimination was so complete in the matter of paper for leaflets and posters that the ratio of the material posted on the walls of the Soviet Zone was easily 20 to 1 in favor of the SED.

Terror against the CDU and LDP—Despite all these handicaps, the non-SED parties did very well in these elections. From 1946 onwards the Soviet authorities pursued a policy of coercion and terror toward the CDU and LDP which reduced those parties beyond the status of subservience to that of trained collaborators. Leaders of any independence or character were terrorized into silence, "disappeared," or fled to the West. Scarcely a week has passed in the last few years in which the flight of one or another of the CDU or LDP's leading personalities has not been noted. Most of these were men who had sought to work with the regime in the hope of gaining some compromise from the Soviet, some mitigation of the condition of their people, some amelioration of the full effect of Soviet imperialism. They found this was impossible, and East Germany soon had a complete satellite state apparatus.

The elimination of the CDU and LDP as political elements of any independence was accompanied by an expansion of the role of the SED-controlled "mass organizations" and the founding of two new parties in 1948. Of these the National Democratic was designed to weave ex-Nazis into the state system and to give them a kind of junior political party of their own, and the Democratic Farmer's party was set up as a political addendum to the Farmer's Mutual-Aid Association. Both parties were organized by the Soviet authorities from the top down, and trained Communist functionaries were assigned as their official leaders.[24]

[23] Thus in Saxony the SED daily newspaper printed some million copies while the LDP was limited to a journal appearing three times a week in an edition of 50,000 copies. The CDU newspaper for this state came out only twice a week and was limited to 20,000 copies.

[24] When the National Democratic party was founded and licensed by the Soviet

National Front System—These measures were consolidated in 1949 and 1950 by the appearance of the Soviet-*cum*-satellite "National Front," co-ordinating all political activities under a single leadership and presenting single lists of candidates for election. The front concept developed from the old local anti-fascist committees and the unity committees of all four parties set up in 1945, but the only unity it now possesses is the unity of the police state. In its organization for electoral "campaigns" the front is almost the complete replica of the Soviet Union's electoral "Block of Communists and Non-Party People," and it functions in a society designed to reproduce as much as possible the conditions of life of the U.S.S.R.

With the organization of the national front-type political system the SED completed its course of movement from an old-line revolutionary communist party to the new version satellite managerial complex. When the SPD was merged with the KPD in the spring of 1946, the resultant SED began its life with some 1,500,000 members; since that time the membership figure has somewhat increased, though present emphasis in the SED is not so much on massive membership figures as on an increasing number of "activists" on the party rolls. But if the figures of membership have changed only slightly in the past five years, the character of the party has altered considerably.

In its earliest form the SED represented a direct descendant of the pre-Hitler Communist party; as such it was made up largely of workers seeking a militant and revolutionary socialism. Today it is essentially a state party, based on a core of old KPD revolutionaries, especially those who refugeed eastward when Hitler came to power, young people, and state employees, with a considerably reduced representation of industrial workers.[25] Naturally many of the present members hold cards because it is expedient to do so rather than through any fervent belief in communism or the SED, though such elements tend to be reduced by the frequent party purges, extending from the well-pub-

---

authorities in June, 1948, the party leadership announced that they were not going to compete with other parties and that they would find their function in co-operation with "all progressive democratic organizations." The organization of both the National Democratic and National Farmer's parties was preceded by "meetings in factories and on the farms in which thousands upon thousands demanded the formation of new parties."

[25] At the July, 1950, SED congress the delegate list was made up of 39 per cent industrial workers, 12 per cent farmers and agricultural workers, 5 per cent professionals, and 40 per cent employees of the state, the party, party front organizations, and state enterprises, with the balance being miscellaneous. Two out of every five delegates were under thirty, and only one-third of the delegates were KPD or SPD members before 1933.

licized liquidation of leading officials right down to purges in the smallest party cell.

SED Organization—The SED is today organized in thousands of relatively small units at the factory, town, farm, block, and similar level, co-ordinated upward through a complex hierarchy of organizations to the top Politburo of the party's Central Committee. Though the Party Congress and the large Central Committee are the official governing organs of the SED, real power lies in the Politburo, even as it does in East Germany's prototype, the U.S.S.R. More specifically, real power rests in the hands of the Politburo member who is also Secretary-General of the SED's Central Committee.

The party apparatus directs its own members from the top down, and every party member is obligated to accept higher decisions. It also controls the satellite National Democratic and National Farmer's parties and the various front organizations in addition to the older CDU and LDP. The program and policy of the apparatus are announced as moving on the road to socialism in the footsteps of Lenin and Stalin. In fact, what this means is the development of a Communist economic, social, and political system inside East Germany and slavish obedience to the needs of Soviet foreign policy inside and outside the new "German Democratic Republic," the whole welded together by a police state.

POLITICAL PARTIES IN BERLIN

While the SED has been able via Soviet control to maintain and develop its position in the Soviet Zone proper and in the eastern sector of Berlin, it has failed miserably in West Berlin. On a compromise arrangement amongst the occupying powers the SPD and the SED were *both* authorized to carry on political activity in West Berlin after the merger of SPD and KPD in the Soviet Zone in April, 1946. In its first—and only—direct election contest with the Social Democrats, the new Soviet state party was badly beaten. In the Berlin city elections in the fall of 1946 the SED polled just under 20 per cent of the vote, less than the KPD alone had obtained in the Weimar period. The lesson to the Soviet authorities was obvious: the weaknesses of the SED must not again be exposed to public gaze. Eventually this determination not to engage in free political competition with the West led the Soviets to split the city administration. East Berlin was given a separate, special regime; though not fully integrated into the Soviet Zone, it was brought into the police system of East Germany and the free SPD was proscribed and persecuted there as it had been in the Soviet Zone itself.

In the West the three remaining political parties, SPD, CDU, and

LDP, continued their work and affiliated with sister parties in the west German republic, the LDP eventually changing its name to FDP lest it be considered as having any connection with the Soviet party in the East. These parties were the only ones licensed in West Berlin until 1950, when several minor party organizations made their appearance in the city elections of that year, but none of these is as yet of any great significance. Organizationally and program-wise the present SPD, CDU, and FDP in West Berlin are comparable to their sister parties in Western Germany with the exceptions and alterations which might be expected, given Berlin's peculiar international position.

CONCLUSION

In Berlin specifically and in Germany generally the contrast between Sovietism and democracy is clearly drawn. In the West—in federal Western Germany and in democratic Berlin—the political parties have emerged from the years of occupation as free instruments for the wielding of democratic political authority. They compete freely with one another, and often within themselves, to determine the policies and personnel of government. The parties of Western Germany are not significantly different from those of other western European democracies and, like their contemporaries, are not ideal institutions, but human ones.

Most of the leaders of democratic Germany's postwar parties come from the ranks of the pre-Hitler political leadership; some new faces have appeared, some young people are active, some women have become politically active, but basically today's pattern of German politics is the pattern of the twenties, altered, of course, by the fact of occupation. The general public votes and takes a measure of interest in politics, but it does not feel vitally concerned with political affairs any more than it feels so in other western democracies. It has, in short, the freedom to take politics or to leave them alone.

In their internal organization and activities the parties of the West remain democratic, but with a strong leadership factor. The possibility of rank-and-file revolt exists in the typical German party organization, but it almost never happens, one of the functions of politics—in Germany as elsewhere—being to maintain and develop an internal unity system against just such breakdowns. But these can happen, and do happen, in free party activity.

Certainly the experiences of the Hitler regime have left one mark on the German public: a caution with respect to party membership and party activity. Though membership figures are higher than in many other democratic states, memory of the penalties of being a known anti-Nazi once Hitler came to power are very much alive. This factor tends to strengthen the natural inclination of many citizens to "leave politics to the professionals."

In the Soviet Zone of Germany the citizen has no such choice. There communism has created the complete police state and a typical fascio-communist apparatus to run it; the state party (the SED) dominates all political life and operates, through its subsidiary "mass" organizations, many facets of the citizen's daily life. Behind the party stand the "dedicated" government and the terror system of a well-trained secret police. In Soviet Germany, communism repeats Hitlerism, and political life under the SED daily grows more like that under the NSDAP.

20

Postwar Elections and

Electoral Processes

RICHARD M. SCAMMON

IN THE summer of 1949, fifty months after the end of World War II, Western Germany—federal, democratic Germany—was in the midst of its first free national election campaign in seventeen years. In the middle thirties Germany had known the *Ja* or *Nein* type of totalitarian vote, and her eastern states under Soviet control were to know this kind of forced plebiscite again, but in the newly organized western republic, free elections, free campaigns, and a free vote had returned. They returned to a Germany which had no small measure of experience with popular government and with popular elections. Though the Reich of the Kaisers made no pretense to full responsible government, the German adult male population of the late nineteenth and early twentieth century did possess the right to vote and the right to elect the popular chamber of the national legislature, the *Reichstag*. In the revolution which swept away the Empire in 1918 the matter of elections was not ignored. The franchise was broadened to include women as well as men; the age of voting was reduced to twenty; and a party vote, closed list, proportional representation system of election was substituted for the prewar single-member district method. State legislatures (*Landtage*) and local councils, many of which had been chosen on the basis of highly undemocratic suffrage and election systems under the Empire,[1] were brought into line with the national proportional plan.

[1] The best known of this type of election system was the "three-class" method used to elect the Prussian House of Representatives. Electors were separated into

Germans of the post-1945 period could call upon a wide experience with democratic practice in the electoral field when in 1949 it became necessary to draft a code for the election of the first national legislative body of postwar Germany. Not only had the German lawmakers this experience from pre-Hitler and even pre-Weimar days; they had also passed through a period of some three and one-half years of miscellaneous local and *Land*-wide elections under the occupation, and these had produced a number of new electoral arrangements for their consideration. But the matter of federal elections in the to-be-organized west German republic did not wait, of course, on the framing of an electoral law. Directly the Bonn Parliamentary Council began its work on the Basic Law, questions arose as to the manner in which that constitution would deal with the problem of representation and popular control and the most democratic and most effective method that might be devised to secure this representation and control.

FEDERAL ELECTIONS

Constitutional Basis—As finally agreed, the Bonn Constitution treated the electoral questions in much less detail than its predecessor drafted at Weimar thirty years before. The nation-wide popular election of the President used under the first republic was a dead issue, and the new constitution now provides that the choice of the head of state rests with a specially convened Federal Convention. This Convention, called into being solely for the purpose of choosing a President, includes all members of the *Bundestag* and an equal number of delegates elected by the *Landtage* of the various states by proportional representation. To choose a President the constitution provides that a clear majority of all members of the Convention be secured for election on the first or second ballot. If no candidate is so elected, then a mere plurality suffices on the third ballot.

Just as the experiences of the Weimar period with national popular elections to the presidency led to the quick abandonment of this practice at Bonn, so also the maintenance of the national initiative and referendum provisions of the Weimar period found little support at Bonn and were therefore left entirely outside federal attention in the new

---

three classes on the basis of their tax returns. The electors who paid the highest taxes up to one-third of the total elected one-third of the members, those who paid a middle third chose another third, and the small taxpayers whose total payments made up the last third of the total collected chose the final third of the membership. Naturally the electorate for the first third of taxes paid was tiny, the middle third larger, and the last third huge. By this method a permanent antisocialist majority was guaranteed.

constitution.[2] Several of the states still maintain these special institutions, but they have ceased to exist on a national basis.

But the presidency and the national initiative and referendum were secondary in the minds of those who drafted the Bonn Constitution. On these questions the elimination of popular voting was a matter of general agreement. There was little regret at the passing of what was regarded as an unhealthy superabundance of voting due to execessive zeal on the part of the Weimar Constitution makers. The major area of interest and concern at Bonn was in the manner of election to the *Bundestag.* For some years before the rise of Hitler and especially in the years following the end of the war, many Germans sought to abolish the Weimar-instituted system of party vote, closed list proportional representation and revert to some sort of majority election plan of the kind used in Germany before World War I. Although the final election law adopted for the first *Bundestag* voting was a compromise of viewpoints, at least the advocates of majority voting did keep the Bonn Constitution from committing the new federation to a proportional system. The Weimar document had specifically required that not only the *Reichstag,* but also the popularly elected chamber of all state legislatures must be elected "in accordance with the principles of proportional representation." In its references to elections the present constitution requires only that the *Bundestag* be elected by the people "in universal, free, equal, direct, and secret elections"; it requires no specific type of election system in the states.

Federal Electoral Law—As the Weimar drafters reduced the voting age from twenty-five to twenty, those at Bonn raised it to twenty-one and made twenty-five the minimum age for election to the *Bundestag;* but otherwise they left the details of election regulation to an Electoral Law. This law the Parliamentary Council adopted in May, 1949. Though some changes were later made as a result of correspondence between the military governors and the ministers-president of the various states, it was not fundamentally altered by these amendments and was proclaimed in June, 1949, by the ministers-president, acting on authority of the military governors. The law was the basis for the first national elections in Germany, though its brevity and limitation of scope were such that the states themselves were required to adopt detailed implementing ordinances. For the voting in August, 1949, all Germans of twenty-one who had a minimum residence of three months

[2] One exception should be noted—Article 29 of the Bonn Constitution provides that territorial changes of area as between the states are subject to referendum. The states of Württemberg-Baden, Württemberg-Hohenzollern, and Baden voted in December, 1951, to consolidate into a single *Land.*

in Western Germany and who were registered could vote. Candidates were voters of twenty-five who were eligible for election to their respective *Landtage*, without any requirement of residence within the *Land* or the district from which election was sought.

The "60-40" System—The number of *Bundestag* members was set at 400, with 60 per cent directly elected from single-member districts by a plurality vote and the remaining 40 per cent taken from *Land* "reserve" lists of party candidates, the *Land* list members acting as a pool to make the party representation of each *Land* proportional to the party vote cast in it. This uniformity of election procedure was something of a concession on the part of the military governors, for the more federal-minded of the occupation authorities would have preferred an electoral code which left determination of election system to each *Land* individually; but uniformity was finally secured on the basis of the Electoral Law with its 60-40 division of members. Thus, the system under which members of Germany's first postwar legislature were selected was a compromise between the views of those who sought complete proportionality and those who wanted a return to the single-member district "first-past-the-post" system. The plan thus introduced was one which had been used in elections of *Landtage* in the British Zone and had the virtue of being a method on which the supporters of personal election and the proportionalists could agree, for it provided a majority of the *Bundestag* members elected from single-member districts while still keeping, within each *Land*, a relatively proportional distribution of actual seats by way of the *Land* reserve list.

The Electoral Law made no effort actually to draw up the single-member districts from which the directly elected members would be chosen. This task it left to the individual states, merely allocating the total number of representatives to which each state was entitled and requiring that this number be divided in the proportion of 60-40 as to direct and *Land* reserve list election. In order to guard against later multiplication of parties, the law also provided that no party might be allocated seats on its *Land* reserve list unless it had polled a minimum of 5 per cent of the valid vote within the *Land* or had won at least one of the directly elected members. Minimal clauses of this sort had become common in postwar German electoral legislation, and there was no difficulty in inserting this provision in the federal code.

Since the participation of political parties in this first election was limited to those authorized by the various military governments,[3] the

---

[3] Licensing of political parties by the occupation authorities was not abandoned until after the establishment of the federal government and the coming into force of the Occupation Statute. While the federal law specified that only political

arrangements for independent candidates were especially important. For the authorized parties, nominations had to be attested only by the appropriate *Land* or district authority of the party concerned, though it was required that party nominations be made "by secret vote at a meeting of the political party concerned to which a number of delegates corresponding either to the number of members or to the statutory provisions of the party concerned shall be duly invited." Since independent candidates were presumably not concerned with a party organization, such candidates were to be accepted if they filed, in the district for which they sought election, a petition with the signatures of at least 500 electors of the district. Since this figure represented well under 1 per cent of the electorate of the average district, no special hardship was imposed on those nonparty candidates who had any real measure of support. Since such independent candidates were nonparty, they could not, of course, file *Land* reserve lists.

Operation of the 1949 Election—In its actual operation in the election in August, 1949, the Electoral Law worked about as anticipated.[4] The districts set up by the various states for the members to be directly elected were fairly uniform.[5] The registration of over 31,000,000 electors proceeded without undue difficulty, and the campaign itself was hard-fought. The percentage of the electorate voting was high,[6]

---

parties licensed at the *Land* level could submit *Land* reserve list nominations, the effect would have been the same without such a provision, for the filing of a *Land* list would have constituted the act of a political party and the lack of a license would have rendered the participants liable to penalties under military government law. For a full discussion of the problem of licensing of political parties, see Chapter 19, pp. 475-480 above.

[4] Statistics for this and the elections mentioned later in the chapter will be found in Appendix O.

[5] Most districts fell in the 175,000 to 225,000 population group, but population variations were not vital in a system of this sort, in which at least the major parties ended up with an approximation of their proportionate share of the seats in any given *Land* by reason of the *Land* reserve clause. In the pre-Weimar *Reichstag*, elected on a single-member district system in its entirety, there had been no redistricting of constituencies from the time of the Empire's founding to the end of World War I; as a consequence of the growth of industrialism and urbanism in Germany during this period, there were vast inequities in representation. In 1912 there were eleven districts with an electorate of over 100,000 and ten with under 15,000. The largest—one of the Potsdam districts embracing part of suburban Berlin—had 339,256; the smallest, Schaumburg-Lippe, had 10,709. Since the eleven largest districts returned eight Social Democrats and the ten smallest all returned nonsocialists, the party interest in this matter is obvious and explains some of the vigor with which Social Democrats at Weimar demanded proportional representation.

[6] The participation percentage, 78.5, approximated that of the twenties—the

and there was widespread interest in the contest and in the result (see table 9). The invalid vote was high, but lower than in many of the *Land* and local elections in the 1946-1948 period.[7] The combination of proportional representation and direct election helped the large parties generally and the smaller groups with heavy regional concentrations. Thus the CDU-CSU won 139 seats, as compared with 125 which it would have obtained under straight proportionalism; the Social Democrats, who won 131, would have had 117. The FDP and the minor parties with a regional *Bayernpartei*—DP, WAV, and *Zentrum*— won about the same number of seats that they would have had under pure proportional representation. The DRP-DKP won five instead of seven, but the real losers were the Communists and the nonparty and independent candidates. The KPD, which failed to win a single seat directly, was eliminated from several *Land* reserve list distributions by failure to poll the 5 per cent minimum and had to accept fifteen reserve seats, nine of them from North Rhine–Westphalia. But the greatest losers were, naturally, the independents.[8]

---

stablest period of the Weimar Republic (77.4 and 78.8 in the two *Reichstag* votes of 1924; 75.6 in 1928). Participation had been somewhat higher in Imperial elections, but it has been almost universally true that the general enfranchisement of women has reduced participation percentages. The German *Bundestag* participation figure is somewhat higher than the American, similar to that in France (78.0 for the National Assembly election in 1951), higher than in Canada (74.9 for Dominion elections in 1949), and under that of Great Britain (84.0 for the 1950 general election). Within the federal territory, the highest participation in 1949 was in urban areas (Hamburg, Bremen, North Rhine–Westphalia) and in those areas with the largest number of refugees. Lowest figures for participation were in the southern French Zone states of Baden and Württemberg-Hohenzollern.

[7] Three-quarters of a million votes were invalid, a percentage of 3.1 of the total votes cast. This figure was highest in Rheinland-Pfalz (5.5), Hesse (5.3), Baden (4.8), and Württemberg-Baden (4.2) and lowest in the north. Weimar and Imperial German statistics show that the invalid vote of past elections rarely exceeded one per hundred and very often fell below that figure. While American statistics are not comparable owing to the large number of offices filled at elections, invalid ballots in any British Parliamentary election running over 1 per cent would be most unusual. In Canada, in the June, 1949, Federal House of Commons election, 54,601 of 5,903,572 ballots were invalid—just under 1 per cent. Where large invalid vote percentages are found, these represent a form of political protest. This has been the case in certain constituencies in elections to the House of Commons of Northern Ireland and is best illustrated in postwar Germany in a special election held in September, 1947, to select a member of the Rheinland-Pfalz *Landtag* to represent *Gemeinden* transferred from the Saar back to German jurisdiction. In this vote 15,360 electors participated, with 4,500 votes being invalid, nearly 30 per cent. Those who invalidated their ballots did so in protest against the transfer, preferring to remain with the Saar.

[8] The rounded average vote cast for each member elected to the *Bundestag*

Nonparty Candidates—While the federal election law gave every opportunity to independent and nonparty candidates to present themselves to the voters, the evidence of this polling indicated there is little chance, in the near future, of wide-scale acceptance of independents in the *Bundestag*. While a large vote—over a million—was polled

Table 9. Bundestag Election, August, 1949

Eligible Electors			31,207,620		
Voters Participating			24,495,614		78.5%
Valid Votes Cast			23,732,398		
Invalid Votes Cast			763,216		3.1%

	Votes	Per Cent	Total Seats	Direct Seats	Land Seats
CDU-CSU°	7,359,084	31.0	139	115	24
SPD	6,934,975	29.2	131	96	35
FDP	2,829,920	11.9	52	12	40
KPD	1,361,706	5.7	15	0	15
Bayernpartei	986,478	4.2	17	11	6
DP	939,934	4.0	17	5	12
Zentrum	727,505	3.1	10	0	10
WAV	681,888	2.9	12	0	12
DRP-DKP	429,031	1.8	5	0	5
RSF	216,749	.9	0	0	0
SSW	75,388	.3	1	0	1
Independent and Miscellaneous	1,189,740	5.0	3	3	0

° A key to party abbreviations will be found in Appendix O, p. 637.

by so-called independent candidates, many of these were refugee and expellee candidates seeking separate representation at Bonn. Though the established political parties made an effort to nominate refugees on their *Land* reserve lists and occasionally in individual constituencies, many of the refugees felt the fullest representation of their interests impossible, save through candidates not connected with these older parties. In certain of the states, refugees organized and presented their candidates as a group. Though such groups were not licensed as political parties and, therefore, could not present a *Land* list and benefit from the application of proportional representation, they polled well. In still other states the refugee-expellee representatives ran simply as independent, nonparty candidates.

Among the 242 directly elected members of the *Bundestag* only

---

was as follows (abbreviations are identified in Appendix O, p. 637): CDU-CSU, 53,000; SPD, 53,000; FDP, 54,000; *Bayernpartei*, 58,000; *Deutsche Partei*, 55,-000; WAV, 57,000; *Zentrum*, 72,500; SSW, 75,000; DRP-DKP, 85,000; KPD, 90,000; Independents, 380,000.

three were chosen from other than licensed-party nominees and none of these three could actually claim to be a true independent.[9]

Though the workings of direct election imposed very real handicaps on the Communists and the independents, there was general satisfaction with the over-all result. While the technique of seat distribution was naturally more complex than that in a legislative body elected solely from single-member districts, final results were available on the afternoon following the voting and the distribution had but to be made official later. To indicate just how the division of seats worked out in practice, a typical *Land,* Lower Saxony, may be used as an example.

Method of Seat Distribution—In this *Land* there were 4,425,610 eligible voters (third in size after North Rhine–Westphalia and Bavaria), and 77.7 per cent of those voted, just under the national average. Of these some 75,000 were invalid, and the remainder were cast for candidates in the *Land's* 34 single-member districts. In each of these districts the voter cast a single vote for the individual he wanted as his district member, with the knowledge, of course, that this would additionally help that candidate's party list at the *Land* level, except in the case of the independents. (See Figure 4.) While each party did not contest every seat, the eight *Land*-wide parties nearly did so and independents entered in 10 of the 34 districts. Each voter thus had eight or nine names from which to choose. For the whole *Land* the valid votes were divided amongst the candidates as shown in Table 10.

Within the various districts the Social Democrats elected 24 of their candidates, the *Deutsche Partei* 5, the CDU 4, and the FDP 1. Only two of these candidates were elected with an absolute majority, that is, with more than half the valid votes cast. The typical winner polled between 30 and 40 per cent of the vote but was "first past the post" and won the seat. For the distribution of the 24 *Land* reserve seats, calculations were made as to what the result would have been had all

[9] This small figure for independents is normal for countries employing the single-member district system of election. In the November, 1952, elections to the United States House of Representatives but one member of this classification was chosen—Frazier Reams, who defeated both Republican and Democratic candidates in the ninth Ohio district. In the October, 1951, elections to the British House of Commons no independents were chosen. Two Irish Nationalist members were returned for constituencies in Northern Ireland, but as party representatives, not as nonparty, uncommitted independents. The Speaker of the House, Col. D. Clifton Brown, was returned from the Hexham division of Northumberland simply as "Mr. Speaker," in deference to a rarely challenged custom of offering no party opposition to the incumbent Speaker of the House. Independent members are more numerous in the Canadian House of Commons, but they are almost all representatives of deviations from the overwhelming Liberal majority in the Province of Quebec.

Figure 4. Ballot used in *Bundestag* election, August, 1949.

58 seats been distributed proportionately, but with the parties eliminated that failed to win a single seat directly and polled less than the

Table 10. Votes Cast for Parties in Lower Saxony
Bundestag Election, 1949

	Votes	*Per Cent of Total*
SPD	1,125,295	33.4
Deutsche Partei	597,542	17.8
CDU	593,691	17.6
DRP	273,129	8.1
FDP	252,141	7.5
Zentrum	113,464	3.4
KPD	104,132	3.1
RSF	33,275	1.0
Independents	273,296	8.1

minimal 5 per cent (*Zentrum*, KPD, and RSF). With these limitations the proportional distribution of 58 seats would have given the Social Democrats 24, the CDU and *Deutsche Partei* 12 each, and the FDP and DRP 5 each.[10] Since the SPD had already won its quota of 24 by direct election, the 24 *Land* reserve seats were therefore divided up among the last four parties to bring their totals up to what they would have been under pure proportionalism with the stated minimal clauses, 8 going to the CDU, 7 to the *Deutsche Partei*, 5 to the DRP, and 4 to the FDP. The final distribution is shown in Table 11.

Once the number of reserve seats to go to each party *Land* reserve

Table 11. Distribution of Seats in Lower Saxony
Bundestag Election, 1949

	Direct	Reserve	Total
SPD	24	0	24
Deutsche Partei	5	7	12
CDU	4	8	12
FDP	1	4	5
DRP	0	5	5
	—	—	—
	34	24	58

[10] The federal election code provides for proportionalism to be determined by the D'Hondt method, and this is the system generally used in the German states (except in the southwest, where a quota method is employed) and on the continent. Briefly, it provides for the assignment of seats on the basis of each list's getting the number of seats which would give it the highest average of votes per seat. The totals of each party are successively divided by whole numbers to produce this average, as in the following example:

Divisor	Party A	Party B	Party C	Party D
1	102,000	216,000	90,000	69,000
2	51,000	108,000	45,000	34,500
3	34,000	72,000	30,000	23,000
4	23,000	54,000	22,500	17,250
5	20,400	43,200	18,000	13,800

With nine seats to be distributed, Party B would get the first with its average of 216,000 and the second with 108,000. The third would go to Party A with 102,000, the fourth to Party C with 90,000, and the fifth back to Party B since, if it got this seat, its average per seat would be 72,000 greater than the average for any other party list if it should have obtained the seat. Similarly, the sixth seat goes to Party D, the seventh to Party B, the eighth to Party A, and the ninth to Party C, its average of 45,000 for two seats beating out Party B's average of 43,200 for five seats. The party distribution would thus be four seats to Party B, two each to Party A and Party C, and one to Party D. This system tends to give the larger parties an advantage in areas with a relatively small number of seats to be filled, but differs little from an ordinary quota system if the number of seats is large.

list was determined, these seats were assigned to individuals in the order in which their names appeared on the party nomination papers. Thus, for the *Deutsche Partei,* candidates listed in order numbering one through seven were elected. Had any of these already been elected in one of the districts (candidacy both in the district and on the *Land* reserve list was permitted), the district election took priority and the next candidate on the *Land* list moved up to the place thus vacated.

This sample is typical of election performance in the whole west German territory. In several of the states, especially in the French and American zones, the number of candidates was not as great as in Lower Saxony, but the number everywhere was substantial. The four principal parties (SPD, CDU, FDP, and KPD) contested nearly every seat—if not in the hope of winning it directly, at least to add to the total vote of their respective *Land* lists. The regional parties naturally contested in their own areas of strength, and a sufficient number of minor party and independent candidates appeared to make clear majority election in the constituencies the exception rather than the rule. Though a number of seats found in heavily Catholic areas, and especially rural Catholic areas, were won on a majority and there were other exceptions, the typical seat was won on a plurality of the vote cast, the *Land* reserve list serving to restore a proportionality that would otherwise have been lost.

Result of Plurality System—Much speculation may be undertaken as to what the result would have been had all the seats been filled directly, without any reserve seats to maintain proportionalism, but it is difficult to assess what electoral coalitions would have been formed in the absence of proportional representation. As it was, the CDU and CSU won 115 of the 242 direct seats, the SPD took 96, the FDP 12, the *Bayernpartei* 11, the *Deutsche Partei* 5, and 3 went to independents. Since it may be presumed that the more conservative parties would have formed electoral blocks in support of single nonsocialist candidates if the full membership of the *Bundestag* were elected directly, their share of the seats in such a body would undoubtedly have risen. Such minor groups as the WAV in Bavaria, the *Zentrum,* and the DRP-DKP might well have vanished from the *Bundestag,* as would the KPD, with perhaps the first three amalgamating into the nonsocialist block. Since KPD-SPD alliances would have been almost impossible given the strong anti-Communist feeling of the Social Democrats, the SPD would have been faced in most districts with a united conservative opposition and would, on the evidence, have been badly beaten in the actual distribution of seats. Of course, it is not certain that all who supported the various conservative candidates as individual nominees of their parties would have voted for a single block candidate, but the evidence at hand would indicate that direct election of all members of the *Bundestag* would have produced a heavy conservative majority. Indeed, lopsided majorities are the normal result of a single-member district system of election and are a major reason why it is supported by those who claim that it results in the formation of strong governments with strong majorities.

"Extra" Seats Problem—Given the type of system used, there was one special problem which the drafters of the Electoral Law had to face: that of the situation arising should a party win more seats directly than it deserved on a proportional distribution of direct and reserve seats taken together. This situation arose in two states in the August voting, in Baden and in Bremen, both of them states with small *Bundestag* delegations in which all the directly elected members were won by a single party—by the CDU in Baden and by the SPD in Bremen. In Baden there were a total of 11 seats, 7 direct and 4 reserve. In this Catholic and rural *Land* the CDU candidates won each of the 7 direct seats, but the over-all *Land* vote, divided proportionately, should have given the CDU 6, the SPD 3, and the FDP 2. But the CDU already had 7, so Baden was simply assigned an extra seat, raising her *Bundestag* delegation from 11 to 12. Similarly, in the case of Bremen the delegation was raised from 4 to 5, so that the *Bundestag* elected in August, 1949, finally totaled 402, not 400, members.[11] Naturally this situation is most likely to arise in small states in which one party dominates the direct election, but it is not impossible to imagine circumstances in which the number of *Bundestag* members so added might considerably exceed two. Contemporary German thinking, however, regards the raising of the *Land* delegation as a better solution than keeping the *Land* delegation to a fixed figure and letting the largest party get whatever advantage it can from this possible overrepresentation.

But such circumstances will presumably not basically affect the over-all character of the *Bundestag* election plan as it now exists. However, the field of *Land* and local electoral legislation is one in which changes are constantly being made, and it may well be that new experiments in smaller jurisdictions will bring national adjustments comparable to the adoption of the original law itself, stemming as it did from the experiences of British Zone *Landtag* elections.

[11] Eight additional members were selected in Berlin by the city assembly of the three western sectors, but these 8 have an associate, rather than full, status. Five of the 8 were SPD, 2 CDU, and 1 FDP. In 1952 Berlin representation was increased to 19.

STATE ELECTIONS

As for the individual states, the Bonn Constitution made no effort to fasten on them the voting system it adopted. Indeed the *Landtage* had been elected long before the *Bundestag* existed, the first being the Hamburg and Bremen local assemblies dating from October, 1946, and each of the states had a definitive body of postwar electoral law before the constitutional debates began at Bonn. The experience of the various German states with elective legislative bodies goes back well into the nineteenth century.[12] In the Imperial period a vast and complex set of election laws governed franchise and representation in the various components of the Empire. With the revolution of 1918, however, these became much alike, tending to follow the *Reichstag* pattern of closed list proportional systems in which the elector cast his ballot for a party ticket, with that ticket receiving a share of the total seats equal to its share of the total vote.

In 1946 the first of the postwar *Landtage* were elected in the American Zone states, in Bremen and Hamburg. These were soon followed in the spring of 1947 by the French Zone states, and Schleswig-Holstein, Lower Saxony, and North Rhine–Westphalia, so that all eleven states had popularly elected legislative bodies by the summer of 1947. Though there are variations in the laws of the various states, many aspects of election procedure have received identical treatment in the various jurisdictions, some indeed in identical language, for the interchange of ideas has been considerable. At the present time all states have a voting age of twenty-one, plus a requirement for residence within the state ranging from three months to one year. All require electors to be registered before being permitted to vote, though in some instances an exception is made for those who can present some reasonable excuse for not being able to get their names on the voters' list; all use an "election certificate" system of absentee voting. All have the usual disqualifications of the mentally incompetent, those serving prison sentences, and the like; all provide for polls to be open on a Sunday between approximately the same hours (eight or nine in the morning to five or six in the evening). The administration of elections varies little from *Land* to *Land;* the greatest differences exist in election methods and systems of seat distribution.

PR Standard in State Elections—All the *Landtage* are elected by some sort of proportional representation, with a minimal clause in all save Lower Saxony and Hamburg. The minimal clause, the device to limit participation in the distribution of "reserve" or "surplus" seats.

[12] See Chapter 4 above for further discussion.

came into prominence as a result of the *Bundestag* voting. But by that time it had already developed in postwar German election legislation as a nearly universal practice—a practice itself stemming from the great fear of many Germans of a splintering of the political parties and the growth of a huge number of contesting political groups comparable to the twenty-five or thirty regularly appearing on Weimar *Reichstag* ballots. Since minimal clauses also tend to protect the existing political parties, these organizations have an additional stake in limiting competition; but most of the sentiment for a minimal clause in state and national electoral legislation is genuinely a product of the era of the tiny fragment political parties rather than an effort to advance party interests. In most states the clause requires that a party poll 5 per cent of the total *Land* vote before it may obtain any reserve seats and is sometimes supplemented by the proviso that any party electing a direct member is exempt. In Bavaria it is varied to provide that a party must poll at least 10 per cent in one of the seven regions into which that *Land* is divided.[13]

State Systems Similar to Federal—The proportional systems of six of the states are now comparable to that used for *Bundestag* elections. A majority of the members are directly elected by plurality from single-member districts; a minority are selected from *Land* "reserve" lists. Of these, Lower Saxony, North Rhine–Westphalia, and Baden-Württemberg use the federal system of distributing *Land* list seats. A true proportion is determined in terms of the over-all party vote for the whole *Land;* from these, proportionate seat totals are subtracted whatever seats have been won in direct election. The *Land* reserve list is then utilized to bring the district seat totals up to what the over-all

[13] In several states recent legislation has introduced a new device—no party is permitted to participate in the distribution of *Land* reserve list seats unless it has nominated candidates in *all* districts. This was originally put into the Schleswig-Holstein law to forestall a conservative coalition and was designed to force the conservative parties to fight one another as well as the Social Democrats, then in sole control of the *Land* government. Its special purpose was underlined by a provision exempting "national minority" parties, that is, the SSW, from its application. To defeat the workings of this law the conservative parties (CDU-FDP-DP) took their chances on getting no seats from the *Land* list by not fighting one another, that is, by agreeing on which party should contest each seat. In this way the coalition won 31 direct seats. Since its various parties had not each put up a candidate in each district, they were legally banned from getting any seats from the *Land* list, but undoubtedly the decision was wise. Had each of the parties of the coalition put up candidates in each district, the splitting of the antisocialist vote would have greatly reduced the number of direct seats the conservatives would have won, reduced it beyond the number that could have been gained by participating in the *Land* list distribution.

Land figures would have been under true proportionalism. In the other three a special system of reserve list distribution is used in which a pool of votes is formed by adding all the votes cast for defeated candidates to the margin of victory represented by the plurality of all elected candidates. This device, a hang-over from the British Zone system of municipal elections, is taken from the Hare system of single transferable vote proportional representation, but has been twisted out of any resemblance to its original purpse. Under this system both the party winning a large number of direct seats and those losers who have met the requirements of the minimal clause[14] are given a share of the *Land* list seats. This "losers and surplus" method is used in Hamburg, Schleswig-Holstein, Hesse.

Other Systems in Use in the States—In other states like Bremen and Rheinland-Pfalz, older systems of proportional election are used. In these states each party puts up its list and the elector marks his choice, not for a single candidate, but for the list as presented. In Bremen the whole of Bremen city is one district, the city of Bremerhaven another, and each elects to the *Bürgerschaft*, without any *Land*-wide "reserve" list arrangements. Much the same system exists in Rheinland-Pfalz, which is divided into seven regions, each of which returns from 8 to 19 members.

Bavaria has experimented with several methods of electing its *Landtag*, the largest in Western Germany, and now uses a system in which each elector has two votes. One he casts for a directly elected member in one of 100 districts, the other he uses to vote for an "at-large" member in one of the *Land*'s seven regions. The district members win their seats on a "first-past-the-post" basis; then a proportion

[14] The operation of this system is illustrated by the Hesse *Landtag* election of November, 1950. The *Land* was divided into 48 districts returning a single member each. The vote cast in these 48 districts was: SPD, 820,444, electing 36 direct members; FDP, 588,191, electing 8 direct members; CDU, 347,803, electing 4 direct members; KPD, 87,446, electing 0 members; all others, 5,046, electing 0 members. With the minimal clause operating, only the SPD, FDP, and CDU were qualified to obtain seats from the *Land* reserve list. Under a completely proportional system, most of the 32 *Land* reserve seats (in a total *Landtag* of 80) would have been divided between CDU and FDP to bring their seat total up to its true proportion of the membership. With the "losers and surplus" system working, however, the reserve pool was made up of the votes of all defeated SPD, FDP, and CDU candidates plus the surplus of winners above what they needed to be elected. The result was that the *Land* reserve seats were split fairly evenly among the three parties (13 to the FDP, 11 to the SPD, and 8 to the CDU), so that the final result gave the SPD 47 members (in a *Landtag* of 80), the FDP 21, and the CDU 12. Thus, with 44.4 per cent of the votes cast, the Social Democrats obtained 58.75 per cent of the seats.

is calculated for what the total distribution of seats ought to be in each region. From this "correct" proportion of seats among the parties is subtracted the number of seats already won in the 100 districts, and the regional seats are used to make up the difference. The significant change which the Bavarians have introduced is that the regional seats are separately balloted for. The individuals elected on regional lists are determined by the number of votes they receive, not by their order on the party list. Despite these differences, however, the system has the same basic purpose as the federal and generally prevailing pattern, that of providing a compensatory mechanism by which to offset the distortions of the "first-past-the-post" method. While emphasizing the importance of party nominees in the matter of proportional representation, all states have fairly liberal provisions as to independent nomination. The most restrictive, Baden, requires a thousand signatures in a district for nonparty candidates, but most are lower. In almost all cases the nominees of a recognized party (usually defined as one represented in the last *Landtag*) has his name placed on the ballot by certification of the appropriate party authorities, without the necessity of filing a signature petition. The whole tendency of current state practice in Germany is to make candidature a matter of responsibility, with restrictions designed to keep fragmentary parties from cluttering up the ballot. No substantial group has difficulty in presenting its case, however, and the rapid rise of refugee and expellee parties since the abandonment of military government restrictions upon them is an evidence of this situation.

State Referenda—Aside from the *Landtag* itself, most of the west German states also have made provision for a certain measure of popular initiative and referendum. Though the referendum concept is missing from the Bonn Constitution, it still exists in most of the states, and the majority of these (including all in the French and American Zones) have passed their own *Land* constitutions by popular referendum. In several of these referenda, special parts of the constitution were put to a special vote. This procedure was followed in Rheinland-Pfalz for those sections of the constitution dealing with schools and in Bremen and Hesse for parts involving codetermination by works councils (Bremen) and socialization (Hesse).[15] Apart from these constitutional referenda, however, the use of the referendum has been limited; in July, 1950, a proposed amendment to the Hesse constitution was put to a popular vote but excited little interest. Bavaria has voted on the general advisability of joining a federation of Europe, and subsequently, in December, 1951, there occurred a three-*Land*

[15] See Chapter 4 above for further discussion.

joint referendum held in Württemberg-Baden, Württemberg-Hohen-zollern, and Baden on the territorial reorganization issue discussed elsewhere in this volume. It seems clear that there will be little re-course to the referendum in future German political life, even less than in the Weimar period. Save for Switzerland, this tendency fol-lows a general European pattern of doubt about the widespread con-sultation of the people on specific issues and a desire to leave these matters to elected representatives.[16]

LOCAL ELECTIONS

But if this picture of *Land* and federal election systems appears to be moving towards a uniformity of system, the local elective methods of Western Germany do not. Below the federal and *Land* level the basic units of representation are the *Kreistag* (in the county) and the *Stadtrat* or *Gemeinderat* for the city or village.[17] Here variety is com-plete, ranging all the way from closed lists to the complex Swiss-type local election codes of the southern states, including popular election of local *Bürgermeisters*. However, a certain trend is to be seen in that the closed list system, with the elector voting for a party list, is much less in favor now than before the war and is giving way to newer methods calculated to maximize the individual voter's control over local political personalities.

Postwar Voting at Local Level—Chronologically, local level elec-tions were the first to be held in postwar Germany, beginning in Jan-uary, 1946, less than a year after the close of hostilities. The first series of these local contests was held in the American Zone, but the French and British areas soon followed, and local authorities were completely elective by the end of 1946. Though the American and French author-ities made some small changes in pre-Hitler local election methods, only in the British Zone were substantial alterations undertaken. The British Military Government, working with a specially nominated German committee, established a whole new system of local voting, drawing heavily on British local government experience. The British Zone sys-tem used in the fall of 1946 set up a technique of direct election, with a limited number of reserve seats allocated on what was to become known as the "losers and surplus" system, later (as already noted) to be adopted in many states for *Landtag* elections. The British plan also envisaged annual elections of one-third of the membership of local

[16] See Chapter 4.

[17] See Chapter 3 above for detailed description of the varied forms of local government.

councils, so that the first election required voting for candidates in multiples of three. This device caused much confusion amongst German electors and was one of the factors underlying the eventual abandonment of the plan; the annual elections which would have taken place in the fall of 1947 were postponed, and entirely new systems were devised by the various states of the British Zone for new local elections in 1948. The present systems of local election in the states of the British Zone include single-member districts with reserve lists (North Rhine–Westphalia), and single or multiple voting in single or multi-member districts with reserve lists (Schleswig-Holstein). There is also a special Lower Saxony system involving three votes per elector (not necessarily in an area with three members) with lists receiving seats in proportion to their total vote but with the choice among individuals within each list being determined by the number of votes received. This Lower Saxony system is supplemented for *Kreistag* voting by a *Kreis* reserve list.

Southern State Systems—In the French and American zones older systems of local election are preserved in Hesse, Baden, and Rheinland-Pfalz based on Weimar proportional methods, but in Württemberg-Hohenzollern, Württemberg-Baden, and Bavaria the Swiss-type system introduced in Württemberg before World War I is used. Under this system each elector has as many votes as members to be elected, and he is not bound to any one list. He may vote for any candidate and may accumulate as many as three votes to those he especially prefers.[18] Thus, for a village council of twelve, he might cast single votes for four Social Democrats and a Christian Democrat, accumulate three votes for a candidate on an independent list, and put down two votes for each of two Free Democrats. Seats are distributed among the various lists proportionately in accordance with votes cast, the individuals getting the seats assigned to their list being those with the highest number of votes. This system has been long used in Württemberg and was recently introduced in local elections in Bavaria. Naturally it produces huge vote totals (in Stuttgart in 1946 some 180,-000 voters cast over 8,000,000 votes), but the communities that have

[18] In nominating its list the party or sponsoring group may also "officially' accumulate votes so that in a *Gemeinde* with twelve council members to be elected it may plump three votes for each of two candidates and follow these with six additional single-vote nominees. Since the ballot will show the favored candidate with his name printed three times or with some other indication that three votes go to him, the elector who votes the ticket "as is" accepts this as a sort of party recommendation and automatically casts the votes as "officially" accumulated. The voter can, of course, change this if he wishes.

used it a long time seem pleased with the results it gives in balancing party and personal considerations.[19]

In states using this system and in several of the closed list states as well, straight majority voting is used if only one list is filed or if none are presented. This is often the case, especially in small rural *Gemeinden*. Under these circumstances the elector can vote for anyone he chooses, official candidate or not, and those with the highest vote are elected. (See Figure 5.) He cannot, however, accumulate votes as he would in a proportional election, since there are no lists in the distribution of seats for which he is invited to indicate his favorites. In addition to electing local councils, voters in the southern states also elect

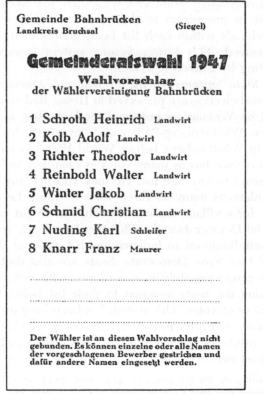

Figure 5. Ballot used in *Gemeinderat* elections, 1947.

[19] The amount of alteration in ballots varies considerably from area to area. In a large city, the tendency for the majority of electors is to vote the ticket as nominated, without change. In smaller communities, and especially in those accustomed to the workings of this method, altered ballots may run as high as nine out of every ten. The percentage can normally be equated with city size, with voter familiarity, and with the personalities seeking office.

their *Bürgermeisters* by direct popular vote. In areas which do elect *Bürgermeisters* directly, a majority system is used with a runoff if no candidate secures a clear majority on the first ballot.

GERMAN ELECTION ADMINISTRATION

Registration of Voters—These elections, federal, state, and local, are the basis of postwar German representative democracy, and their administration has been maintained at a uniformly efficient and corruption-free level, beginning with the first step in the electoral process, registration of voters. Unlike the American practice, but according to what has long been the custom in Europe, the register of voters is made up by the municipal authorities. There are official lists of residents at hand for various purposes. The old voters' list is usually kept up to date from time to time by striking out the names of those who have moved from the area or died and by adding new arrivals and those coming of age. This is a simple enough task in a small rural village and is not too burdensome even in a large city, for in the latter the small town hand-written list of electors is usually replaced by a card-catalog system which can be easily altered as each new election approaches.

Officially the voters' list must be made up anew for each election and posted for public inspection, with time allowed for objections and changes. Actually it is almost always up to date, comparable to an American city system of permanent registration. The registers used in any election will be "live" ones and the voter will have no difficulty with an out-of-date register. Although there was some suggestion that early elections of 1946 were handicapped by the inexperience of registration compilers and the necessity of making lists anew for a rapidly shifting population, this has ceased to be a criticism for contemporary practice and there are few, if any, objections entered to the list of voters once it is officially posted for one and all to examine.

Denazification—One special problem of the earliest of the occupation elections was the enforcement of franchise denazification provisions in the various *Land* electoral codes. These provisions were strictest in the American Zone. To cite one example: in Württemberg-Baden in the June, 1946, Constitutional Assembly elections, 105,032 otherwise eligible electors were disfranchised on political grounds, 5.5 per cent of the potential eligibles. With the passage of time, the operation of the various denazification tribunals, and the liberalization of state laws, this figure has now been reduced to insignificant proportions, and only those persons most heavily incriminated in the Nazi regime are now prevented from voting. The law for the *Bundestag* election in August, 1949, made no special provisions for denazification but left this matter up to the contemporary state law.

As election day approaches, each elector on the list is usually notified by a postcard of the fact of the election, the date and hours of polling, and the place at which he is to cast his ballot. If he expects not to be able to come to his voting place, he may apply for a special election certificate (*Wahlschein* or *Stimmschein*) to vote elsewhere. This certificate is issued by the municipal authorities where he is registered, and his name is stricken from the local voters' list for that particular election. On election day he may take this certificate into any polling place in a similar jurisdiction and cast his vote there, even though the candidates are not the same as those for whom he would vote at home. This easy device for absentee voting undoubtedly has helped increase voter participation and avoids the technicalities of the American system of postal absentee balloting.[20]

Voter Facilities—Whether by certificate or on the regular register, the voter always goes to the polls on a Sunday. It is generally felt that Sunday polling is an inducement to high participation, though a Sunday in the spring or summer often produces conflicts with holiday-makers. If the city elector wants to take a Sunday trip, however, he will often find that the railway station has a special polling station for certificate voters, and this will frequently be opened as early as 4 A.M. to accommodate transients. Facilities are also made available to take votes from patients in hospitals and sanatoria. These are special arrangements, however, and most voters will simply walk to their assigned polling place to cast their ballots. They can do this at any time during the day, for the polls are normally open from eight or nine in the morning until five or six in the evening. In some local

[20] In *Reichstag* elections of the Weimar period there was little problem about the *Wahlschein*. Since votes were cast in every instance for lists rather than for individuals, it was not important that a Berlin lawyer cast his vote at home or at a holiday resort in the Bavarian Alps. All votes were pooled in the final analysis, and the fact that his ballot went first to some local Bavarian list was unimportant. With the introduction of district voting and individual candidates this situation was altered. Now the absentee *Wahlschein* voter was not only voting for his party; he was also electing an individual member of a *Landtag* or of the *Bundestag*. In the German view, however, the voting was still primarily party, and the *Wahlschein* has been retained in its old form. For the *Bundestag* election one change was made at the insistence of the military governors—election certificates were valid only within the *Land* in which issued. Thus a Munich truck driver could vote in New Ulm, in Bavaria, but not in Ulm, Baden-Württemberg. This ruling caused confusion amongst German voters, and many who sought to vote in such a transient center as Frankfurt were turned away when it became evident that their election certificates were from states other than Hesse.

elections, especially in rural areas, this time may be shortened, for the majority in the villages vote in the morning after church services. In these villages and small towns the polling places will normally be located in the town hall or *Rathaus,* even if this be but a room or two in a building combined with a school. In the larger cities, where a number of polling places are used, the majority of these will be found in public buildings. Where public facilities are not available, the poll will be located in private premises, and a number will be found in local restaurants, coffeehouses, and taverns.

*State and Local Administration—*Once in his assigned polling place, the voter will come under the jurisdiction of the local election board, headed by an election chairman (*Wahlvorsteher*). This chairman has been appointed by the district election officer, and he in turn by the chief state election official (*Landeswahlleiter*). The *Landeswahlleiter* is always a senior state civil servant, an expert in election questions and trained to handle the myriad details involved in organizing an election. His work is immediately supervised by a state election committee (*Landeswahlauschuss*) of half-a-dozen members. The committee is not necessarily made up of party representatives, but this is almost always the practice followed, though the administrative work of the voting process is left in the hands of the *Landeswahlleiter.* The district election officers are appointed, like the *Landeswahlleiter,* by the *Land* interior ministry and will also be experienced permanent civil servants working under a district election committee (*Kreis-wahlauschuss*). At the lowest point of the administrative pyramid is the local *Wahlvorsteher* and his committee charged with carrying out the election in a single polling place. The *Wahlvorsteher* will not normally be a civil servant, but competent people of all walks of life are secured for these posts, and little complaint is ever heard against their work.

*Ballots—*When he arrives in the polling place the voter will secure his ballot from a table and take it away to mark. The typical German ballot is officially printed (as opposed to privately printed "tickets"), but is not as carefully controlled as are ballots in American, British, and Canadian elections. Security against fraud is not obtained by controlling the ballots themselves, but by giving each voter a small, non-transparent envelope along with his ballot. After it is marked, he places this ballot in the envelope and hands it to the *Wahlvorsteher* or his assistant. These officials can readily determine that only one envelope is handed them without being able to see for whom the elector has voted. This one envelope is then put into the ballot box. The use of the envelope is not required in certain local elections, especially in Bavaria, and has been replaced by or combined with the American-British-Canadian system in certain of the British Zone states. But whether the voter is issued a ballot or simply picks one up on his way to a voting booth, secrecy is not violated in German elections. This secrecy remains secure despite the rather flimsy character of the average "booth" provided, often no more than a screen.

Since the voter is working with a "short" ballot involving only one office, the time he requires to mark his ballot is not long and he soon has done his civic duty, been marked off the electoral register, and is on his way home. Even where several elections are held at once—and this is not the normal procedure and in any event never exceeds two or three—the time required is not great. The elector is not required to fight his way through a long American "jungle" ballot to vote for dozens of state, county, and local offices and referenda. Though each city polling station is expected to serve a fairly large number of electors, often up to 2,000, and they are nearly always crowded, there is no confusion and voting proceeds without disorder.[21]

Administrative Efficiency—This efficiency of the German election apparatus is largely a product of good administrative work and the high capacity of every level of election official. It is a very real tribute to the German civil service that it has been able to conduct in the past few years a whole series of electoral consultations from the lowest to the highest level without any serious complaint from the voting public. Nor can this matter of efficiency alone be considered. Fraud is virtually absent from German elections. No extensive and complex legislation exists on election frauds in any of the German states because such evils are unknown. Nor are the elections themselves costly. The ballots are simple and easy to print. Candidates are not rotated as in some American states but are listed either alphabetically or in respect to their party strength, based on representation in the *Landtag*

[21] Although not a part of the voter's work on election day, the proceedings of the *Wahlvorsteher* and his board after the polls close should be noted. Counting of ballots in German elections is generally done locally. However, an effort was made in the British Zone elections of 1946 to introduce the central count used in elections in Great Britain. The count itself is normally fairly rapid, involving as it usually does only a single "short" ballot. In certain districts the authorities may have directed that votes by men and women be cast and counted separately, and such an arrangement will take somewhat longer, but not much. Decisions on invalid ballots are made on the spot by the election board, and rules in this regard are interpreted liberally, the main effort being to find the will of the voter rather than enforce complex invalidity regulations. With these matters out of the way, the board members enter their proceedings on the official papers provided them and close up shop, telephoning or telegraphing the results to the appropriate local authority and taking their election materials to the district election office.

or votes cast in the last state election. As an aid to identification each party is usually assigned a number, and this appears on the ballot along with its name to help the voter find his party choice. As ballot cost is low, so are the other expenses. Service of election officials is *ehrenamtlich*—comparable to jury duty—and unpaid. Since schools and other public buildings are used most frequently as polling places, rent for such quarters is low. These facets of German elections, low cost, freedom from fraud, and efficiency, are not new with the occupation. They existed under the Weimar regime and under the Empire. The really new contribution that Germany has made to election practice since the end of World War II has not been in these fields but in the larger one of systems of representation.

ELECTION METHODS

Prior to the rise of Hitler, but especially during the Hitler period, there was very strong criticism of the election method and system of representation used from 1919 to 1933. Many critics asserted that the type of closed list proportionalism prevalent in republican Germany was one of the significant causes of Hitler's coming to power. It was claimed that the closed list, with the elector voting for party instead of individual, removed the voter from any contact with his representatives and put the *Reichstag* or *Landtag* member under the direct control of the executives of his party—the *Parteibonzen*—without any feeling of responsibility to the electorate as such. The proportional system, which for *Reichstag* elections assigned each list a seat for every 60,000 votes cast, was alleged to have produced a host of minor parties, fragmented the larger ones, made working legislative majorities of the British type impossible, and frustrated the functioning of both legislature and executive. So it was that the first proposals to hold democratic elections in occupied Germany were immediately greeted with widespread argument over method, an argument carried on both inside and outside Germany, in German and in military government circles. The antiproportionalists argued that future German elections should be held on a majority system. Some favored a straight "first-past-the-post" plurality method on American, British, and Canadian lines. Others sought a runoff plan in which failure to get a clear majority on the first ballot would lead to a runoff vote between the top two candidates. The last system had been used to elect the Imperial *Reichstag* and was used in French Chamber of Deputies elections before World War I and in the late twenties and thirties.

Supporters of PR—Against this view the proportionalists maintained that a majority method was no guarantee of a two-party system, even if such a system were admitted to be the most desirable, for German and French experience had shown that the runoff plan did nothing to cut down the number of political parties. As for the election of representatives by mere plurality, the proportionalists argued that this produced so distorted an electoral picture as to negate the whole idea of representative democracy. The opponents of majority voting also argued that much of the argument against proportional representation based on the special relationship established between elector and representative by majority systems was in fact taken from non-European experiences in the United States. It was urged that the European voter sought to vote for party, not for individuals, and that he ought not to be forced into a system based on North American personalist traditions. It was suggested that the British voter is far more conscious of "voting Labor" or "voting Conservative" than of any particular individual candidate. In the view of one advocate, the "single-member district system is a list system with but one name on the list."

These arguments on majority versus proportional election were not new in Germany, any more than they might be new today in some other country. The new factor introduced in the German decision on these matters was the position of the occupation powers. Though later years were to reduce their powers, in 1946 their directives were authoritative, and it was in their hands that the final decision rested on this question.

French and American Zonal Solutions—In the French and American zones the matter was solved by leaving the matter to German jurisdiction. Basically the line of thought developed was that the question of electoral systems was a matter of free choice in a democracy. Were the Germans to adopt electoral practices obviously undemocratic by the standards of contemporary practice in democratic states—for example, were they to seek the disfranchisement of all persons of a single religious belief or of all those with incomes under 2,000 marks per year —then such German measures would be vetoed. If, however, the Germans made a choice as between electoral practices generally used in democratic states, then such actions of the German authorities would be approved. Thus the Germans might permit or not permit absentee voting; they might use official ballots or privately printed "tickets"; they might adopt the American "primary" system if they desired or the British practice of requiring candidates in Parliamentary elections to poll one-eighth of the vote or pay a £150 forfeit. This line of thought held that it would be undemocratic either to compel or to forbid the Germans to adopt proportional voting systems of the sort used in Switzerland, Ireland, Holland, Belgium, Italy, France, Denmark, Sweden, Norway, and other democratic states. Against this doctrine it was argued by the antiproportionalists that this matter was so important that it must be legislated into the Germans despite what they themselves might want.

German Opinion—Within the German community itself opinion was divided; in those early days there were no elective bodies to make their views known, and even had these existed, it would be presumed that their views would be prejudiced in favor of the system under which they had obtained office. Under these circumstances this decision was put in the hands of the nominated state authorities in the French and American zones. In the latter this was done as a firm matter of policy; in the former it was regarded as less important and as secondary to such questions as federalism and the building of strong local feeling as a bulwark against new German centralism. Thus, the early elections in these zones were held under the older Weimar systems, somewhat altered by circumstances and with some adjustments by the military governments concerned, for these older codes had almost all been the choice of the German authorities.

British Zone Approach—In the British Zone, however, an entirely different approach was used. The British authorities felt that their plurality system was so vital that they were prepared to legislate it into German practice themselves. Working with a committee of nominated Germans they developed the plan for local elections previously outlined, drawing heavily upon British electoral practice and instituting such innovations as the central count, annual renewal by thirds of local councils, election of individuals in districts, and the like. At one time the British concept involved no concession to proportionalism whatsoever and in the matter of the parties went so far as to ban even the appearance of the party name on the ballot. These matters were changed by the time the first local elections were held in the fall of 1946, however, and a system of reserve seats in each area was established, these to be assigned on the previously described "losers and surplus" system. By the time of the *Landtag* elections in the British Zone, in the spring of 1947, a strong German reaction had developed against these British innovations and new plans of election were devised; but some of the old features were retained, especially the overall idea of a combination of district and reserve seats.

German Decision—By 1948, with the *Landtage* all elected and discussion beginning on the character of the election method to be used for a national legislature, the debate on election systems was virtually over. Though the British occupation authorities openly sought a plurality election system and though most individual Americans concerned with the question were personally opposed to PR and favored plurality election, the Germans determined to follow PR methods in choosing their representative bodies. The method upon which they appear to have come to a measure of agreement—a combination of direct and "reserve list" election—has some aspects of majoritarianism about it, but these should not conceal the essential character of pro- portionalism. The fact that one-half, or two-thirds, of the members of a representative body are elected directly and personally by the voters in single-member districts cannot obviate the proportional character of the decision postwar Germany has made.

The development of this system was hastened, of course, by the fact that it maintained proportionalism while taking from the majoritar- ians one of their strongest arguments, that of the alleged personal relationship between representative and elector. Although it may be argued that this is important or unimportant, the fact remains that those opposing proportional representation had developed it as a major doctrine and the district-plus-reserve plan took this argument from them. Then, too, the widespread adoption of minimal clauses in the states demonstrated that it was possible to check the growth of a vast number of fragmentary political parties without adopting a plu- rality vote system.

Perhaps the most significant fact in the development of this new district-and-reserve method in postwar German election doctrine is that both major parties now appear committed to its use. While for some time it was felt that the Christian Democrats were favorably dis- posed towards majority rule, and indeed there was much evidence to support this view, the adoption by CDU majorities of the district-and- reserve system for *Landtag* elections in Baden and Württemberg- Hohenzollern would appear to indicate acceptance of the new method in place of straight majority voting. These two states could have adopted majority systems had the CDU so wished, for their margins of control in the *Landtage* were more than adequate. Naturally the minor parties constantly urge full PR—and join this with appeals to abolish all minimal clauses—in the interest of self-preservation. But even the major SPD and CDU refuse to endorse full plurality voting of the English or American variety. Though the parties will naturally seek whatever advantage there may be in this variation or that, neither is ready to run the risks of doing away with proportionalism.

ELECTIONS IN SOVIET GERMANY

While the democratic election process was being debated in the west German republic, the electoral function was not overlooked in its totalitarian neighbor to the east. The Soviet Zone had been the first to license political party activity and organized its first elections in the fall of 1946 at the time of those held in the French and British zones.[22] Unlike the latter, however, the Soviet Zone vote included *Landtage* as well as local government bodies. These first elections in the Soviet Zone were held under a single set of electoral laws and ordinances, all proclaimed by the Soviet Military Government. These laws required closed list proportional voting for communal, county, and state representatives, with nomination limited to the licensed political parties and to so-called "mass organizations"—the Farmers' Mutual Aid Association, Women's Committees, Cultural League, and the like. (See Figure 6.) No provision for independent or nonparty candidacy was

Provinz Sachsen			Kreis: Bitterfeld
Stimmzettel			
für die Wahlen zum Kreistag am 20. Oktober 1946			
Wahl vorschlags-nummer	Kennwort	Namen der Kandidaten	Wille des Wählers
1	Sozialistische Einheitspartei Deutschlands (SED)	Paul Taube Bernh. Moder Helene Elteste Alfred Baudl	◯
4	Vereinigung der gegenseitigen Bauernhilfe (VdgB)	Otto Mieth Werner Kochniss Ernst Kläring Hilda Frömmichen	◯

7267/46. MDV. 43

Figure 6. Ballot used in *Kreistag* elections, 1946, Soviet Zone (an old-style closed list PR ballot).

[22] These fall elections were preceded by a referendum in the Soviet Zone *Land* Saxony on the "nationalization of properties of war criminals and Nazis." This referendum was held in June, 1946, with a 94.1 per cent participation. The proposal was approved by a vote of 2,683,401 to 571,600 and is noteworthy primarily for the fact that half-a-million people in a Soviet Zone state were willing to say that they opposed such a measure.

made, and the voter was required to put his cross on the ballot after the list of one of these parties or authorized "mass organizations."[23]

Since the Soviet military authorities had suppressed the Social Democratic party early in 1946 by forcing it to merge with the Communists into the SED, or Socialist Unity party, these local and state elections were contested by only the SED, the CDU, and the LDP as major participants, with a few lists put up by authorized front organizations. The election regulations for both the September *Gemeinde* elections and those in October for *Kreistage* and *Landtage* were taken from the Weimar pattern and differed little in content from those used in similar closed list elections in the West. Registration of voters, polling arrangements, balloting, *Wahlscheine,* organizational administration of the vote—all these were similar.

The SED as a Soviet State Party—The great differences lay in the character of the SED as a "state party" and the official and unofficial favoritism shown it during the campaign in the matter of paper, position on the ballot, and preferential local treatment of various sorts. Actual voting in the 1946 elections was relatively free. If the voter was assailed on all sides by SED propaganda, if non-SED party meetings had a way of not being approved by the Soviet authorities, if CDU and LDP local organizations were unrecognized so that they might not put up competing candidates, nonetheless the voter could vote in secret; and in those constituencies where non-SED parties were permitted to nominate he could vote against the state party of the Soviet administration. The full corrupting influence of totalitarianism was just beginning in these elections, and it had not yet come to the full flavor which East Germany had known under Hitler and was to know later under the SED and its Soviet masters.

Election participation was high in the September communal elections, and with this high participation came a large number of invalid protest ballots, especially in those *Gemeinden* and cities in which the Soviet authorities had refused to license local units of non-SED parties and so had prevented the opposition from expressing itself. In the

[23] In quadripartite discussion the U.S.S.R. consistently favored proportional representation as a desirable system of election for Germany. The Soviets especially attacked the British Zone system of 1946 local elections in which, by the operation of the "surplus and losers" system of combined direct-and-reserve election, the Communists were much underrepresented on local councils. With the full development of totalitarianism in the Soviet Zone, little has been heard of PR. In the Soviet Union itself a so-called majority system of election operates, with members of the two houses of the Supreme Soviet elected from individual single-member districts. Of course only a single candidate appears at election time in each of these districts.

following month's elections, however, the CDU and LDP had better opportunities, for in *Land*-wide voting the possibility existed for every elector to vote for non-SED parties, though restrictions against the CDU and LDP were still applied in a number of instances to the *Kreistag* voting which took place simultaneously. Participation was high, and the number of invalid votes much lower than in September.

Development of Nonrepresentative Institutions—These elections had, however, indicated to the Soviet authorities and their German associates that the time had come to do away with the "bourgeois" idea of party competition for public support. So it was that the elections which would have been held in 1948 were postponed by the Soviet military authorities in August of that year,[24] and in the spring of 1949 it was announced that elections would be held to a People's Congress (*Volkskongress*) for Eastern Germany and the eastern sector of Berlin. This Congress had been first organized in December, 1947, on the basis of "delegates" sent from the parties and SED-front "mass organizations" to provide an extraparliamentary body for the whole of Eastern Germany, a body not subject to the whims of a not-yet-completely cowed electorate. The second session of the Congress was held in the spring of 1948, and arrangements were now undertaken to "elect" the membership of the third session in May, 1949.

Though the technical arrangements for this first zone-wide election in the Soviet area were not unusual, two special items were introduced. The polling was to last for two days, Sunday and Monday, fifteenth and sixteenth of May, so that every voter could be pushed to the polls, and the voting age was brought down to eighteen. More important, the voter was not to be concerned with the "outmoded" and "undemocratic" idea of competing political parties, groups, and independents. He was presented with but a single list of candidates, allegedly representing the various political parties, "mass organizations," and even independents, and to this list he could reply with the old-time Hitler *Ja* or *Nein*. Naturally all candidates had the approval of the SED and its various subsidiary and front organizations.

[24] In announcing his decision to postpone these elections (due with the expiration of the terms of office of those elected in 1946), Marshal V. D. Sokolovsky stated that this postponement was being ordered "lest the attentions of democratic organizations and the people in general be diverted from a practical solution of their economic problems and the task of improving the general living standard." What Marshal Sokolovsky meant, of course, was that the Soviet-SED leadership feared that they would suffer prestige-wounding losses in elections held under competitive circumstances, no matter how limited, and that they were not yet ready to install a completely fascio-communist totalitarian election system. See Chapter 6 above for further discussion.

1949 Volkskongress "Election"—This *Ja* or *Nein* election was the last even remotely free vote to be held in Eastern Germany; though the whole weight of the state and party apparatus was thrown into the effort to get a unanimous *Ja* vote, the east Germans showed an unmistakable lack of enthusiasm for the benefits of the emerging fascio-communist state. Election results would normally be available the same night as the election—at latest the following morning—but in this case there was an unexplained delay of twenty hours in the announcement of results, and finally it was declared that the list had been approved, but only by a two-to-one vote and with over 800,000 invalid ballots cast. This was, of course, a shocking blow to the SED and to its Soviet controllers. Under the Communist methodology any vote less than 99 per cent affirmative was a failure, and it was a mistake which the east German regime was not to repeat again. The basic error of the SED in its election arrangements lay, of course, in the need for the voter to go into a booth to mark a cross opposite either *Ja* or *Nein*. No matter how much intimidation might exist outside the booth, the elector still had his precious second of freedom actually to mark a choice.

1950 "Elections"—By the summer of 1950, however, these errors in tactics had been remedied. The elections due in 1946 had been postponed in 1948 by Marshal Sokolovsky and again were postponed in 1949, but in 1950 the ground was ready. On October 15 of that year "elections" were held at all governmental levels—to a *Volkskammer* for the new east German satellite state, to *Landtage,* to *Kreistage,* and to communal councils. Again the voter was presented with a single block list of candidates for each level or representation, but no opportunity was given him to vote even *Ja* or *Nein*. There was no need to mark his ballot at all. He had but to drop it in the box. The only way in which the voter could indicate his disapproval was to stay away from the polls entirely or deface his ballot. The Soviet-SED regime was ready for both possibilities. In the days before the "voting" took place the electorate were warned and threatened by press and radio that those who failed to vote would be regarded as having "fallen for the propaganda of American warmongers" and "obviously" to be voting for remilitarization, war, the atomic bomb, and the "destruction of our people." The voters took the warnings to heart, for they knew well that far less serious "crimes" against the new fascio-communist state resulted in concentration camps.

For the voter who actually appeared at the polls—and this included nearly everyone, since the Interior state secretary had added to the press and radio campaign by announcing that those who failed to vote were "enemies of peace, unity, and prosperity"—the task at hand was simple. He had but to stand in line, identify himself, get his ballot, hand it back to the election chairman to be put in the ballot box, and go about his business. While most polling places actually provided voting booths, the use of these would naturally attract attention, and each voter using one would have his name entered for future attention of the sort so well known in the modern totalitarian state. Though this whole proceeding was clothed in a most attractive, holiday-like garb, it had a hollow ring throughout.[25] The method was too familiar, and the view of the Soviet army newspaper in Berlin, "German elections have never been so well prepared before," was echoed by the comment of the west German Chancellor, Dr. Konrad Adenauer, "They can do it better than the Nazis."

BERLIN ELECTIONS

While the eastern (Soviet) sector of the City of Berlin had been included in the May, 1949, *Ja* or *Nein* voting for the *Volkskongress*, it was spared having to participate in the melancholy work of the October, 1950, "elections." The whole of the City of Berlin, including all four occupation sectors, had been put under at least semieffective Four Power control in the summer of 1945 and under this control voted for its city assembly and for local district assemblies in October, 1946.[26] In these elections a compromise was worked out in which both the SED and the SPD participated in all four sectors, as well as the two nonsocialist parties, but nominations were limited to these four authorized political parties—there were no independents, no front organization nominees.

Early Berlin Four-Power Elections—These first Berlin elections were carried through under a closed list proportional system, with the elector marking his choice of party, seats distributed proportionally to votes polled, and individual members elected from lists in the order in which their names appeared on those lists. Administratively the election had little to distinguish it from any other in Germany, and the laws and regulations applied in the city were comparable to those employed in other jurisdictions. The participation in this first postwar Berlin election was very high (92.3 per cent), and the number of in-

[25] The finally announced figures for this "election" were 12,097,105 votes for the lists of 12,144,597 voters participating. This compares with similar results for Fascist Italy (March, 1934; 10,045,477 favorable of 10,061,978 voting), Hitler Germany (March, 1936; 44,411,911 favorable of 44,954,937), and the Soviet Union (March, 1950; 110,788,377 favorable of 111,090,010).

[26] For full discussion of circumstances of Four Power control within which these elections were conducted, see Chapter 4 above.

valid ballots low (2.0 per cent), this last largely owing to a vigorous campaign and to the strong views held by the electorate towards one or another of the parties presenting candidates. SED adherents did rather worse than they had expected, and it became obvious that they could not hope to control Berlin via democracy and the ballot. Therefore it was necessary to apply other measures in the eastern sector of the city where the Soviet Military Government maintained police control.

Eventually relationships between the three democratic western sectors on the one hand and the totalitarian eastern sector on the other became so bad that the east split off and organized a minority rump government of its own. The majority, the western democratic sectors, have maintained the organization first set up after the 1946 elections.

Western Sector Elections—Elections have been held under the same closed list system as that operating in 1946, save that in 1950 restrictions against minor parties were removed and several such organizations put up candidates. Though the SED sought to effect a general boycott of the 1948 and 1950 elections in West Berlin, participation continued to be very high, and the number of invalid ballots increased only insignificantly. As for the Soviet Sector, save for its participation in the May, 1949, *Volkskongress* "election" no voting has been held in East Berlin since the original city assembly vote of October, 1946.

CONCLUSION

The experience of Germany with elections since the end of World War II has been marked by the emergence of new forms of proportional election in the West, forms designed to stress the tie between voter and party and to reduce somewhat the overwhelming power of the Weimar "*Parteibonzen*," but forms also designed to retain the bases of PR in popular elections. Nowhere in postwar Germany has there been an adoption of the Anglo-American majority election idea for policy-making bodies. Though many individual Germans have urged an abandonment of PR, the major party organizations—the SPD and the CDU—continue to support it though they might gain party advantage by shifting over to a majority single-member district system.

In Western Germany the election experience of the postwar years has been a democratic experience; candidates have been freely nominated and have freely campaigned for public office. The elections in which they have sought support have been free elections, efficiently and honestly administered.

In Soviet Germany the pattern of elections has followed that so well known in other satellite countries—the first elections held honestly, but under considerable pressure on behalf of the Soviet state party, in this case the SED. Later elections, as in other satellites, have degenerated into typical totalitarian "roll-call" votes, with opposition parties silenced and the voter marched to the polls.

The possibility of a bringing together of the two Germanies for united elections is always held up as something for the future, but the issue here is not one of election systems or of election law and election administration. The problem is a basic political one, and so long as Eastern Germany exists as a satellite of the Soviets it is impossible to imagine free, democratic, competitive elections taking place in a united Germany.

APPENDICES AND INDEX

Appendices

A

Letter of Approval of United States Zone

Land *Constitution*

24 October 1946

Dr. Michael Horlacher, President
Bavarian Constitutional Assembly
Munich, Bavaria

Dear Mr. President:

On behalf of United States Military Government, I have examined the provisions of the proposed Constitution of the State of Bavaria which was passed by the Constitutional Assembly on 20 September 1946. I am informed that the Drafting Committee of the Assembly at its meetings of 11 and 22 October 1946 has recommended amendment in certain Articles. The amendments have been submitted to this office and are listed in an appendix attached hereto.

United States Military Government recognizes the Constitution of the State of Bavaria to represent the will of the State of Bavaria as expressed through the elected representatives of the citizens of the State. Moreover, it is convinced of the evident purpose of the drafters that the Constitution should embody the fundamentals of democracy and safeguard the rights of individuals.

Therefore, if the full Assembly shall adopt the changes referred to above and listed in the appendix, and subject to the reservations set out below, the Constitution is approved for presentation to the people so that they may express their views at the polls. Naturally it is understood that no further changes will be made other than those purely formal and textual in character.

The approval which Military Government gives to this Constitution must, of course, be subject to the international agreements to which the United States Government is a party, to quadripartite legislation, and to the powers which Military Government must reserve in order to effectuate the basic policies of the occupation. Moreover, it must be pointed out that in approving the Constitution, Military Government does not thereby express any approval of separatism for Bavaria or any other German State. The use of the term "Bavarian National" is, therefore, accepted only as it imports a citizen of Bavaria who is also a citizen of Germany as it is administered by the Allied Control Council, and as later it may be administered by some form of German government. Likewise, the expressed will to join in a federal German State must be interpreted as an instruction to the representatives of Bavaria who may later participate in a determination of the form of future German government, and not as a right to refuse to participate in whatever form of German government may be established as an interim measure by Allied authorities or as a lasting form of government by the German people as a whole.

I wish to take this occasion to compliment the members of the Assembly on the manifest care and thoroughness with which they have done their work, and on their devotion to the democratic ideals toward the achievement of which we are all striving.

Sincerely,

(Signed) LUCIUS D. CLAY
Lieutenant General, U.S. Army
Deputy Military Governor

B

Directive concerning "Relationship between

Military and Civil Government (U.S. Zone)

Subsequent to Adoption of Land *Constitutions"*

30 September 1946

TO   : Directors,
Office of Military Government for Bavaria
Office of Military Government for Wuerttemberg-Baden
Office of Military Government for Greater Hesse
Office of Military Government for Bremen Enclave
Office of Military Government for Berlin District
Regional Government Coordinating Office

1. U. S. policy requires that the German people be permitted increasingly to govern themselves. The elections held in the U. S. Zone in 1946, and the constitutions which have been adopted are implementations of this policy. The subsequent operation of both Civil and Military Governments will be based upon this objective.

2. *Adoption of Land Constitutions Will Change Civil-Military Government Relations.* The adoption of constitutions in the Laender of the U. S. Zone marks the beginning of a new period in the relationships between Military and Civil Government. All military and civil authorities must clearly understand those relationships.

3. *Specific Restrictions Which Will Continue to be Imposed Upon Civil Governments.* While self-government is the object of U. S. Military Government policy, it must nevertheless be understood that there are certain restrictions which will continue to apply to the actions of all levels of civil government in the U. S. Zone. The basic occupation policies announced from time to time, as in the case of the Berlin Protocol and Secretary of State Byrnes' Stuttgart speech, will, of course, continue to be enforced by Military Government. Furthermore, the specific restrictions set forth below must be considered as superior to the authority of any German governmental agency, and to both statutory and constitutional law. Those restrictions are:

a. All international agreements regarding Germany which have been or may be concluded;

b. All present and future quadripartite policy decisions, laws and regulations;

c. All basic policy decisions of the U. S.-British Bipartite Board affecting the fields of central agencies;

d. The rights of an occupying power under international law to maintain an occupying force within the zone, to preserve peace and order, to reassume at any time full occupation powers in the event the purposes of the occupation are jeopardized;

e. The specific occupation purposes of the U. S. Government which, in addition to those set forth above, shall consist of the following basic tenets:

    (1) *Democracy*—All levels of German government in the U. S. Zone must be democratic to the extent that:

    (a) All political power is recognized as originating with the people and subject to their control;

    (b) Those who exercise political power are obliged to renew their mandates regularly by frequent references of their programs and leadership to popular elections;

    (c) Popular elections are conducted under competitive conditions in which not less than two effectively competing political parties submit their programs and candidates for public review;

    (d) Political parties must be democratic in character and must be recognized as voluntary associations of citizens clearly distinguished from, rather than identified with, the instrumentalities of government;

(e) The basic rights of the individual including free speech, freedom of religious preference, the rights of assembly, freedom of political association, and other equally basic rights of free men are recognized and guaranteed;

(f) Control over the instrumentalities of public opinion, such as the radio and press, must be diffused and kept free from governmental domination;

(g) The rule of law is recognized as the individual's greatest single protection against a capricious and willful expression of governmental power.

(2) German governmental systems must provide for a judiciary independent of the legislative and executive arms in general and of the police activity in particular. U. S. policy does not demand the rigid separation of legislative and executive powers. It has no objection to the cabinet or parliamentary type of government in which the executive and legislative branches are interdependent. Where a governmental system does provide for a separation of the executive and legislative, there must be no provision which would enable the executive to rule without the approval and consent of the legislative branch.

(3) *Intergovernmental Distribution of Powers*—German governmental structure shall be federal in character (Bundesstaat), and the constituent units thereof shall be States (Staaten not Laender). The functions of government shall be decentralized within that structure to the maximum degree consistent with the modern economic life. U. S. policy concerning the relationships between levels of government requires that:

(a) All political power is recognized as originating with the people and subject to their control;

(b) Power shall be granted by the people primarily to the States (Staaten), and subsequently only in specifically enumerated and limited instances to a federal government;

(c) All other grants of governmental power by the people shall be made to the States;

(d) All powers not granted by the people shall be reserved to the people;

(e) A substantial number of functions shall be delegated by the States to the local governments. These should include all functions which may be effectively determined and administered by local governments;

(f) Governmental powers may not be delegated to private or quasi-public economic bodies;

(g) Pending the establishment of a federal government, the popularly responsible governments and Landtage of the States shall act as the people's agents for the conferring of powers requiring central execution upon such transitional federal or central body or bodies as may be agreed upon by civil government and military government, or as may be directed by the latter.

(4) *Economic Unity*—Economic unity through the establishment of German central administrative agencies, particularly in trade, industry, food and agriculture, finance, transportation, and communications, is a controlling objective of our occupation. Pending quadripartite agreement for the establishment of such agencies, the U. S. Government offered to join with any one or two of the other occupying powers in the establishment of such administrative agencies to cover such zones as would accept. The administrative agencies now established for the British and U. S. Zones are an important step toward the economic unity agreed to by the occupying powers at Potsdam. Accordingly, the furtherance of their successful operations is a major policy of the U. S. occupation. When agreement is reached with either or both of the other powers for the establishment of German administrative agencies covering the wider areas involved, the implementation of such agreements will constitute a part of the fundamental policy of the U. S. occupation.

f. All limitations upon governmental action which may be set out as specific qualifications to the approval of the State constitutions;

g. Such proclamations, laws, enactments, orders, and instructions of U. S. occupation authorities as continue in force or shall hereafter be promulgated.

4. *Subsequent Functions of Military Government Will Be Limited to:* Subsequent to the adoption of these constitutions, Military Government will obtain its objective by means of:

a. Observation, inspection, reporting and advising;

b. Disapproval of only such economic, social and political and governmental activity as it may find to clearly violate those objectives;

c. Removal of public officials whose public activities are in violation of those objectives;

d. The establishment of full Military Government controls in any area in the U. S. Zone where the objectives of the occupation as herein defined or provided for may be endangered;

e. Military Government courts;

f. Direct administration of such activities as demilitarization and reparations which cannot be assumed entirely by German civil governmental agencies but which are necessitated by international agreements, quadripartite action, or U. S. occupation policy.

5. Subsequent directives will implement the foregoing statements insofar as modifications or revisions in Military Government practices may be required.

6. The Land Directors of Military Government will advise the appropriate German officials of the content of this directive. It is desirable that the widest possible distribution to both civil and military authorities be given it. However, the directive will be considered a restricted document to be used for information of Military Government only until you are subsequently authorized to release it.

BY DIRECTION OF THE MILITARY GOVERNOR:

(Signed) G. H. GARDE
Lieutenant Colonel, AGD
Adjutant General

C

Documents I, II, III, Including the Principal Provisions of the London Tripartite Agreements regarding Germany

MEETINGS OF THE
MILITARY GOVERNORS AND MINISTERS-PRESIDENT OF
THE WESTERN ZONES ON FUTURE GERMAN POLITICAL
ORGANIZATION

DOCUMENT I

MGMP/P(48)1

1 July 1948

SUBJECT: Constituent Assembly

The Military Governors of the US, UK and French Zones of Occupation in Germany, in accordance with the decisions of their respective Governments, authorize the Ministers-President of the states of their respective zones to convene a constituent assembly to be held not later than 1 September 1948. The delegates to this assembly will be chosen in each of the existing states under such procedure and regulations as shall be adopted by the legislative body of each of these states. The total number of delegates to the constituent assembly will be determined by dividing the total populations at the last census by 750,000 or some similar figure as may be recommended by the Ministers-President and approved by the Military Governors. The number of delegates from each state will be in the same proportion to the total membership of the constituent assembly that its population is to the total population of the participating states.

The constituent assembly will draft a democratic constitution which will establish for the participating states a governmental structure of federal type which is best adapted to the eventual re-establishment of German unity at present disrupted, and which protect the rights of the participating states, provide adequate authority, and contain guarantees of individual rights and freedoms.

If the constitution as prepared by the constituent assembly does not conflict with these general principles, the Military Governors will authorize the submission for ratification. The constituent assembly will thereupon be dissolved. The ratification will take place by each participating state by means of a referendum requiring a simple majority of the voters in each state under such rules and procedure as it may adopt. When the constitution has been ratified by two-thirds of the states, it will come into force and be binding upon all states. Thereafter, any amendment to the constitution must be ratified by a like majority of the states. Within thirty days following the coming into force of the constitution, the institutions for which it provides shall be established.

MEETINGS OF THE
MILITARY GOVERNORS AND MINISTERS-PRESIDENT OF THE WESTERN ZONES ON FUTURE GERMAN POLITICAL ORGANIZATION
DOCUMENT II

MGMP/P(48)2

1 July 1948

SUBJECT: Land Boundaries

The Ministers-President are asked to examine the boundaries of the several states in order to determine what modifications they may want to propose. Such modification should take account of traditional patterns, and avoid, to the extent feasible, the creation of states which are either too large or too small in comparison with the other states.

If these recommendations are not disapproved by the Military Governors, they should be submitted for the approval of the people of the affected areas not later than the time when the members of the constituent assembly are chosen.

Prior to the completion of the work of the constituent assembly, the Ministers-President will take the necessary steps for the election of the assemblies of those states, the boundaries of which have been modified, so that these assemblies and those of the states, the boundaries of which have not been modified, will be in a position to determine the electoral procedure and regulations for the ratification of the constitution.

MEETINGS OF THE
MILITARY GOVERNORS AND MINISTERS-PRESIDENT OF
THE WESTERN ZONES ON FUTURE GERMAN POLITICAL
ORGANIZATION

DOCUMENT III

MGMP/P(48)3

1 July 1948

SUBJECT: Occupation Statute

The establishment of a constitutional German government will necessitate careful definition of the relationship between this government and the Allied Authorities.

It is the view of the Military Governors that this relationship should be based on the following general principles:

A. The Military Governors will grant legislative, executive and judicial power to German governments and reserve to themselves such powers as are necessary to ensure the fulfilment of the basic purpose of the occupation. Such powers are those necessary to enable the Military Governors to:

(a) Conduct or direct for the time being Germany's foreign relations;

(b) Exercise the minimum control over German foreign trade, and over internal policies and measures which could adversely affect foreign trade, necessary to ensure a respect for obligations entered into by the Occupying Powers in regard to Germany and the proper use of funds made available to Germany;

(c) Exercise such controls as have been or may be agreed upon, as for example, regarding the international authority for the Ruhr, reparations, the level of industry, decartelization, disarmament and demilitarization, and certain aspects of scientific research.

(d) Protect the prestige and ensure the security of the Occupation Forces and the satisfaction of their requirements within defined limits agreed upon between the Military Governors;

(e) Ensure the observance of the constitutions which they have approved.

B. The Military Governors will resume their exercise of their full powers in an emergency threatening security, and if necessary to secure compliance with the constitutions or the occupation statute.

C. The Military Governors will exercise the above-mentioned controls, according to the following procedure:

(a) Any amendments to the constitutions will be submitted to the approval of the Military Governors;

(b) In the fields mentioned in (a) to (e) of paragraph A. above, the German authorities will comply with the decisions or directions of the Military Governors;

(c) Unless otherwise provided, in particular for implementation of paragraph (b) above, all laws and regulations emanating from the federal government shall come into force automatically within 21 days unless disapproved by the Military Governors.

The Military Governors will have a special responsibility to observe, advise and assist the federal and state governments in regard to the democratization of political life, social relations and education. This shall not imply any restriction of the legislative, executive and judicial competence accorded to such governments in these matters.

The Military Governors request the Ministers-President to submit their observations on the above principles. The Military Governors will then communicate these broad principles, modified as they may then agree, to the constituent assembly, as a guide to that body in its work of preparing the constitution, and will receive from it the observations which it may wish to put forward. When the Military Governors announce their approval for the submission of the constitution to the states, they will publish simultaneously an occupation statute incorporating these principles as finally modified in order that the people of the states may understand that they accept the constitution within the framework of this occupation statute.

D

Coblenz Resolutions of the Ministers-President

July 10, 1948

The ministers-president of the *Länder* of the three western zones of occupation were assembled in Koblenz from 8th to 10th July this year in order to deliberate the answers requested of them to the documents handed to them on 1st July of this year. They subjected the mandate of the military governors contained in them to a thorough discussion and unanimously arrived at the opinions expressed in the appendices to this letter which they asked to be examined.

The proposals are an expression of the intent to collaborate creatively in the solution of the problems which pose themselves and to reach the goal set in the documents as quickly and as effectively as possible.

The ministers-president are convinced that the exceptional difficulties under which Germany suffers today can be overcome only if the German people is enabled to administer its affairs on the broadest possible territorial basis. Therefore they welcome the fact that the occupying powers are determined to combine the areas of Germany which are subject to their jurisdiction into a unified territory to which the population itself shall give a vigorous organization which makes it possible to preserve the interest of the whole without endangering the rights of the *Länder*.

However, the ministers-president believe that nothing should be done to give the character of a state to the organization which is to be formed, not withstanding the granting of the fullest possible autonomy to the population of this territory. Therefore, they are of the opinion that the procedure followed for this purpose should make it clear that what is in question is a provisional establishment only, and also an institution which owes its origin exclusively to the temporary state of the conditions related to the present occupation of Germany.

Because thus far unanimity of the four occupying powers regarding Germany was impossible the ministers-president have to be particularly anxious to avoid anything which during the pending reorganization could increase to the rift between west and east. They are convinced that the procedure they suggest will under the given circumstances provide within the shortest period of time an instrument best suited to overcome the existing difficulties and to serve the administrations of that part of Germany which is under the three western powers of occupation.

The same considerations were decisive for the proposal of the ministers-president to refrain from a referendum. A referendum would give to the basic law the kind of weight which should be reserved to a final constitution. The ministers-president want to repeat on this occasion that in their opinion a German constitution cannot be created until the whole German people finds it possible to constitute itself through free self-determination; until this time comes only provisional organization measures can be taken.

With regard to the change of *Land* boundaries the ministers-president unanimously reached the conclusion that a basic and final solution is required but needs thorough investigation.

The boundaries of the individual *Länder* should be reviewed with the purpose in mind to create for the united Germany the kind of internal structure which takes into account what is needed for a well-functioning federal system. Attention should be paid to the needs of the present and in particular to the development of viable and well-balanced *Länder* as well as to traditional patterns. Such review and reorganization of the *Länder* in the combined area of administration is a German task. It presupposes the existence of common organs of democratic parliamentary character. Therefore it cannot be solved within a short period of time.

This should not prevent the elimination by the *Länder* of those particularly regrettable territorial conditions which exist in the South West of Germany.

The ministers-president gave their especially serious consideration to the problems related to the regulation of the exercise of the occupation authority. They noted with satisfaction the intention to put the relations to the occupying powers on a clear legal basis. However, the ministers-president think that it is urgently necessary that the military governors proclaim an occupation statute before the body which is entrusted to draft the basic law for the area of the three western zones starts its activities; only then will this body have a firm foundation for its work. Furthermore they think that the Occupation Statute should express clearly that the organizational changes which are now intended are ultimately based on the will of the occupying powers. This must lead to consequences different from those which would follow if the changes were an act of free self-determination of the German people.

In making these detailed proposals the ministers-president want to express their conviction that the German organs should have all those competences which are not kept from them by the Occupation Statute itself; save for definite exceptions the actions of the occupying powers should be limited in principle to the supervision of the activities of the German organs with a view to ensuring the fulfilment of the occupation purposes.

In this connection it seems particularly important that the German foreign trade be freed from the restrictions under which at present its productivity is suffering—notwithstanding an effective supervision by the occupation authorities. The ministers-president believe that beyond the provisions of the Occupation Statute it should soon be made possible to enter into trade negotiations which should be conducted by German agencies the results of which, however, should be subject to ratification by the occupying powers.

Furthermore they think that it might be appropriate to leave the international Ruhr authority out of the Occupation Statute because of its peculiar functions. Concerning the resumption of the full occupation powers by the military governors in case of emergencies the ministers-president believe that the military governors share their opinion that in case of mere police emergencies it should be for the German governments to do what is necessary to overcome them.

Finally, the ministers-president address to the military governors the request to examine at regular intervals whether developments permit a further extension of German powers and a further decrease of control.

At the end the ministers-president express their wish and their expectation that by decision of the governments of France, Great Britain and the United States the state of war be ended.

In view of the wealth of problems which are posed by the intended reorganisation the ministers-president could comment only on the most important points in the attached appendices. Therefore they express the wish that they may have an opportunity to explain orally to the military governors the opinions and requests laid down in the appendices and in this letter.

The ministers-president do not want to end this letter without thanking the military governors that through their initiative they widened the possibilities for a progressive democratic development which can proceed only when a freely deciding people can accept responsibility and determine its own affairs. They affirm that they as much as the military governors will do everything which can serve the peace of the world and the unity of a free and democratic Germany.

MINISTERS-PRESIDENT CONFERENCE
COMMENTS ON DOCUMENT I

1. The ministers-president will assume the powers delegated to them on 1 July 1948 by the Military Governors of the American, British and French Zones.
2. The convening of a German National Assembly and the preparation of a German constitution shall be postponed until a solution for all of Germany is possible and until German sovereignty has been sufficiently restored.
3. The ministers-president will recommend to the *Landtage* of the three zones to elect a representation (Parliamentary Council) which has the task
   a) to draft a basic law for the uniform administration of the occupation zones of the western powers;
   b) to enact an election law for a popular representation based upon general and direct elections.

   The participation of the *Land* Governments in the deliberations of the Parliamentary Council must be assured.

   The representation shall be formed in accordance with the figures proposed in Document No. I and shall convene not later than 1 September 1948. Each *Land* puts up at least one delegate; for a fraction of at least 200,000 votes another delegate shall be appointed.
4. The elections for the popular representation shall be carried through during the year 1948.
5. The basic law must provide in addition to a popular representation elected directly by the people, for *Länder* representation which participates in the legislation.
6. As soon as the delegates elected by the *Landtage* have accomplished their task (para. 3), the ministers-president, after consultation of the *Landtage*, will submit the basic law with their comments to the military governors and ask them to authorize the ministers-president to promulgate the law.
7. The popular representation shall have all functions exercised by a democratically elected parliament.
8. The common executive organ provided for the occupation area of the western powers shall be established in accordance with the basic law.

MINISTERS-PRESIDENT CONFERENCE
COMMENTS ON DOCUMENT II

The ministers-president agree with the military governors that a re-examination of the German *Länder* boundaries is advisable.

They are, however, of the opinion that this question requires careful investigation, which cannot be accomplished within a short time.

Under these circumstances the ministers-president cannot at present propose a general solution. They are, however, of the opinion that a revision of the boundaries of the southwestern *Länder* is urgently required. [The solution of this problem is to be left to the Parliamentary Council which is to submit to the ministers-president proposals on the need for such a revision and on the manner of its execution.]

The right of the *Länder* concerned themselves to arrive at a solution remains unaffected.

MINISTERS-PRESIDENT CONFERENCE
COMMENTS ON DOCUMENT III

Basic Principles for an Occupation Statute

I.

1. In order to realise the economic and administrative unity of all German territory occupied by Great Britain, France and the United States this territory should be formed into a unified area, the organisation of which should be entrusted by the occupying powers to its population.

2. German legislative, administrative and judicial powers should be limited only by the powers of the occupying authorities as defined in the text of the Occupation Statute. In any event presumption is that the German organs are competent (*Die Vermutung spricht für die Zustandigkeit der deutschen Organe*).

3. The occupying authorities reserve the right to take action only insofar as is necessary to realise the purposes of the occupation.

4. These measures may consist of
   (a) direct administration by organs of the occupation,
   (b) control,
   (c) supervision,
   (d) observation, advice and assistance.

5. The purposes of the occupation are
   (a) ensuring the security of occupying troops,
   (b) ensuring the existence of a democratic order in Germany,
   (c) the demilitarisation of Germany,
   (d) ensuring the fulfillment of Germany's treaty (*vertraglichen*) obligations.

6. Direct administration will be exercised by the occupying authorities for the temporary conduct of foreign affairs; nevertheless German

representation abroad for the protection of economic and trade interests will be permitted. The heads of such German offices abroad have a legal status corresponding to that of a consul.

7. Measures to be taken by the occupying authorities are limited in principle to general supervision of the activity of German organs. In respect of German foreign trade the right of control may be exercised, but only in so far as there is reason to fear that the obligations which the occupying powers have undertaken in relation to Germany are not being observed, or that the means placed at Germany's disposal are not being used in an appropriate manner. Such control shall not extend to deciding whether German measures are technically correct and appropriate.

Furthermore such control may be concerned with the safeguarding of German reparations obligations still in force, for maintaining the regulations limiting the level of German industry, for carrying out decartelisation, for disarmament and demilitarisation and for scrutinizing such activities of scientific research as served the German war economy.

This statute is not concerned with the powers of an international Ruhr authority.

8. Instructions within the framework of the above principles will be issued only by the highest organs of the occupying authorities and only to the highest German Regional authorities.

9. The right of veto shall only be employed against duly enacted German law if it is likely to endanger the realisation of the purpose of the occupation. Unless within twenty-one days of the enactment of the law the military governors acting together do not object to it, the law enters into force.

10. In the sphere of democratisation of political and social life, and of education, the occupying authorities will restrict themselves to observation, advice and assistance.

11. The independence and the territorial and material universality (*territoriale und sachliche Universalitat*) of the German preservation of justice should be acknowledged.

12. The jurisdiction of Occupation Courts is limited to
    (a) non-German members of the occupying forces and the occupation administration and members of their families,
    (b) crimes and offences against the security or property of the occupying powers or against the persons of those belonging to them.

13. For litigation between Germans and nationals of the occupying powers mixed courts shall be established.

II.

The universal human rights as well as civil rights and freedoms shall be guaranteed to the German population, also in its relations with the organs of the occupying powers.

III.

1. Material and personal services shall be demanded only on such

a scale as is necessary to satisfy the requirements of the forces and administration of the occupying powers. They must be in proportion to the resources of the country.

2. The nature and scope of material and personal services to be rendered and the way in which they are to be paid for will be determined by the military governors acting together. A special procedure for the making and meeting of such demands will be established, in the execution of which German authorities are to take part.

3. Occupation costs shall be established for one year in advance. All German services described in the previous two sub-paragraphs are to be included. Occupation costs shall be a fixed sum and cannot exceed a fixed percentage of the regular expenditure under the normal budget. They shall be determined in consultation with the competent German authorities.

IV.   A special procedure shall be provided for to guarantee the payment of reparations and the advance performance of such German reparation obligations as have not yet been fixed. The same applies to restitutions. Such a procedure shall provide for the effective participation of German organs.

V.   Arbitration and conciliation authorities shall be established for settling differences of opinion on the interpretation and application of the Occupation Statute.

VI.   Should the military governors regard it necessary to resume the exercise of their full powers they will do so only as an emergency measure and as a result of a decision taken in common, and only if an emergency situation threatens security or it appears necessary to enforce respect for the constitution and the Occupation Statute.

E

Minutes of the Third Meeting of the Military Governors and Ministers-President of the Western Zones on the Future Political Organization of Germany

held on 26th July 1948, at 15:00 hours
in the Headquarters Building at Frankfurt

26 July 1948   *MGMP/M(48)3**

PRESENT

General KOENIG   Chairman
General CLAY
General ROBERTSON

ALSO PRESENT

FRANCE	UNITED STATES	GREAT BRITAIN
Ambassador TARBE	Ambassador MURPHY	Mr. STEEL
de ST-HARDOUIN	Major General HAYS	Mr. CHAPUT
General NOIRET	Dr. LITCHFIELD	de SAINTONGE
M. SEYDOUX	Dr. SIMONS	
M. de LABOULAYE		

MINISTERS-PRESIDENT PRESENT

French Zone	*U. S. Zone*	*British Zone*
Herr ALTMEIER	Dr. EHARD	Herr ARNOLD
Herr WOHLEB	Herr STOCK	Herr KOPF
Dr. BOCK	Dr. MAIER	Herr LUEDEMANN
	Herr KAISEN	Herr BRAUER

SECRETARIAT

M. JOOS (Deputy Secretary) (FR)
Mr. FOREST (US)
Mrs. HAMILTON-STOKES (UK)

Note: The second meeting of the Military Governors and Ministers-President took place in closed session. Minutes were prepared unilaterally by each delegation.

REPLY OF THE MINISTERS-PRESIDENT TO THE PROPOSALS MADE BY THE MILITARY GOVERNORS FOLLOWING THE LONDON DECISIONS

26 July 1948 MGMP/M(48)3

General KOENIG, as Chairman, opened the Meeting. He stated that the meeting had been called to allow the Ministers-President to give their final reply concerning Documents I, II and III (MGMP/P(48) 1, 2, 3 and 4) and he therefore asked Minister-President STOCK (Hesse) to speak.

Herr STOCK stated that the Ministers-President had examined very closely the observations made at the last meeting. They were glad to be able once again to discuss the problems as a whole with the Military Governors. The Ministers-President were prepared to create, within the framework of the London Agreements, a political and economic organization for Western Germany and they were very anxious to reach agreement with the Military Governors. They had chosen two from amongst their number to discuss the specific questions. Minister-President ARNOLD, would present the point of view of his colleagues on Document I (MGMP/P(48)1) and Minister-President LUEDEMANN would discuss Document II (MGMP/P(48)2). As far as Document III (MGMP/P (48)3) was concerned the Ministers-President had not found it necessary to discuss this for the present.

Herr STOCK further stated that he and his colleagues would be glad to hear the comments of the Military Governors after the statements of Herr ARNOLD and Herr LUEDEMANN and to be able to withdraw for a final consultation after having heard them. The Military Governors stated that they were in agreement with this procedure and the Chairman asked Minister-President ARNOLD to speak.

Herr ARNOLD (North Rhine-Westphalia) wished, first, to make a few general remarks on the question of the referendum and the "Basic Law". He indicated that there was general agreement that a solution must be reached as quickly as possible. According to the original proposals, the "Basic Law" or "Provisional Constitution" should be accepted by the population by means of a referendum. Obviously the problem of the referendum was of the greatest importance. The Ministers-President were also of the opinion that the Basic Law should be ratified on as broad a democratic basis as possible.

They had, however, certain serious objections to the referendum as provided in Document I. The Ministers-President feared, in fact, that the submission of the "Basic Law" to a referendum might provoke a very violent electoral campaign throughout Western Germany. The communists and all other destructive elements would certainly take advantage of this electoral campaign to aggravate the schism which already existed between the West and the East. In particular, in view of the position of the communists, it was very probable that they would do their utmost to present the "Basic Law" not as a German Law, but as a law imposed by the Allied Powers. There was therefore a risk that an electoral campaign, in these conditions, would result in a vote against the Occupying Powers. The destructive forces of the left as well as of the right would combine to destroy the proposals made. Recalling that in conformity with the original proposals, the veto of one-third of the Laender would be sufficient to overthrow the proposals, Minister-President ARNOLD stressed that if, as a result of an electoral campaign, the "Basic Law" was rejected, this would mean not only the rejection of the Koblenz proposals but also the rejection of the London decisions. Such a development would be a catastrophe not only for Germany but for the whole of Europe. But whatever the results of such an electoral campaign, it was certain that it entailed the risk of introducing an element of uncertainty into any future development.

Minister-President ARNOLD repeated that he and his colleagues were entirely in agreement with General CLAY on the point that this "Basic Law" should be ratified on as broad a popular basis as possible but after having closely examined the psychological conditions and the political situation the Ministers-President wondered whether it would not be preferable to have the "Basic Law" ratified by the Landtage of the different Laender instead of having it ratified by means of a referendum. The members of the Landtage had been elected by general and secret ballot and could therefore be considered as the legitimate and democratic representatives of 45,000,000 inhabitants. If, therefore, as was probable, the Landtage accepted this "Basic Law" by a large majority, it could be said that it had been adopted on a broad democratic basis. The Ministers-President were of the opinion that this proposal took more into account the interests both of the Military Governments and of the German people than did the initial proposal.

As far as the "Basic Law" itself was concerned Herr ARNOLD recognized that this was not a question of the statutes of a private organization. This, moreover, would become clear, without any doubt, in the text of the articles which it would contain.

Regarding the title, there was no objection to adding in brackets after the words "Basic Law" the words "Provisional Constitution" and especially since there was general agreement on the fact that the whole organization to be created would be of a temporary nature only.

In conclusion, Minister-President ARNOLD wished to stress that the amendments proposed by himself and his colleagues could be made to concur with the London decisions.

General KOENIG thanked Herr ARNOLD for his statement and asked Minister-President LUEDEMANN to speak.

Minister-President LUEDEMANN (Schleswig-Holstein) stated that during the previous meeting new statements had been made about the modification of the Land boundaries. From these statements it was clear that the Military Governors attached particular importance to this question. The Ministers-President had been asked for a specific reply on this subject and they had done their best to give this reply. Two questions had been asked:

1. Did the Ministers-President recognize the necessity for modifying the Land boundaries?
2. Were the Ministers-President themselves prepared to submit proposals on this subject?

The reply of the Ministers-President to these two questions was in the affirmative.

The Ministers-President were asked, moreover, to state on what date they would be able to make these proposals. It was difficult to reply to this last question for the following reasons: In the document transmitted on 1st July it was stipulated that such proposals should be made before the convening of a constituent Assembly. Since the Assembly was to meet before 1st September, there remained only four weeks or less to consider the question of modifications of the Land boundaries. This period was too short to reach a satisfactory solution of the problem and to make concrete proposals in view of the numerous difficulties which were implicated in this question.

In the Koblenz decisions the Minister-President had suggested that this Assembly which they had called "Parliamentary Council" should be composed of delegations of the Landtage of the different Laender and that, in conformity with the London decisions, there should be one delegate to every 750,000 inhabitants. The situation could have changed if the Koblenz proposals had been accepted by the Military Governors. The Ministers-President supposed that there was agreement on this point although this had not been specifically stated. For that reason they had been unable to commit themselves on the question of the date. The Ministers-President had, however, decided at their last meeting to form a committee to deal with this problem and this committee had set to work immediately. The task of the Ministers-President would be made considerably lighter if the two problems which were at present connected could be treated separately.

Buergermeister BRAUER (Hamburg) wished to complete the statement of his two colleagues. To begin with he stressed that the attitude of the Ministers-President as a whole to the London decisions was fundamentally positive. In their opinion it was in the interests of Germany to reach as quickly as possible a solution to all the problems within the framework of these decisions.

Herr BRAUER wished to go even further. He considered indeed that if a quick solution was not found there was a risk that the application of the Marshall Plan, and the economic recovery made by Germany since the currency reform, would be jeopardized. For these reasons it was of the greatest interest to Germany to reach a solution in the shortest possible time. The remaining divergencies concerned only the methods to be adopted and not the objects in view. The Ministers-President were prepared not to insist on these points of method and procedure if there was a risk of jeopardizing the whole. Therefore, the Ministers-President wished to reach agreement today within the framework of the instructions of the Military Governors.

Regarding the Constituent Assembly or rather the Parliamentary Council, it could be said that ever since Koblenz the Ministers-President had accepted the London proposals. They had recommended that the delegates who were to draw up the "Basic Law" should be designated by the different Landtage before 1st September.

The Ministers-President, when translating the word "Grundgesetz" into English had chosen the term "Basic Law". They felt, however, that a more adequate translation would be "Basic Constitutional Law". The term "Grundgesetz" had only been chosen in order to avoid aggravating the condition of the Eastern struggle and of the struggle which the Ministers-President were obliged to carry on against the propaganda of the SED and the parties of the Eastern Zone. This struggle would be made easier if the terms chosen by the Ministers-President could be accepted by the Military Governors.

Concerning the crucial point of the referendum, the point of view of the Ministers-President was as follows:

If it was a question of principle, the direct vote based on universal suffrage should have been applied already for the election of the members of the Constituent Assembly.

Herr BRAUER recalled, in this connection, the campaign for the "Volksbegehren" in Germany. The states of the West had defended themselves against the introduction in their territory of this "Volksbegehren" which was of SED inspiration. By accepting the referendum as a means of ratification they would be giving to the Communists just that popular vote which up to the present they had not obtained. This was for the Ministers-President of the West a question of political and psychological tactics. In support of his statement Herr BRAUER quoted a press commentary from the San Francisco Chronicle.

"There lies a deep and devilish irony in the fact that the Germans are defending their undemocratic actions by using such democratic methods as the referendum in order to make their attitude palatable to the United States. This is a powerful weapon which is being utilized with great skill."

On the question of boundary modifications Herr BRAUER re-affirmed that the Ministers-President were equally desirous of settling it quickly so that there would be no delay in the application of Document II.

Finally, as concerned the Occupation Statute, the Ministers-President noted with satisfaction the decision of the Military Governors to take into consideration the German proposals.

In conclusion Herr BRAUER stressed once more that the Ministers-President, like the Military Governors, wished the present discussion to reach a satisfactory conclusion as soon as possible in order to end the state of uncertainty.

General KOENIG thanked the Ministers-President for their statements and on his proposal the meeting was adjourned for 45 minutes in order that the Military Governors might have time to consult.

The meeting adjourned at 15:45 hours.

* * *

The meeting continued at 16:30 hours.

General KOENIG, on behalf of his colleagues and of himself, again thanked the Ministers-President for the opinions expressed by them. He indicated that, since these proposals differed on certain points from the London decisions, the Military Governors were obliged to refer to their respective Governments so that the Governments might examine whether they could consider them.

In reply to Minister-President STOCK as to the date of the next meeting, General KOENIG stated that another meeting would be called as soon as the three Allied Governments had made known their points of view.

Minister-President STOCK wished then to know what were the points on which the Ministers-President differed from the London decisions to such an extent that an adjournment for Governmental consultation became necessary.

General KOENIG indicated that the points on which he and his colleagues were obliged to consult their respective Governments were the following:

1. The question of the referendum.
2. The question of the name to be given to the "Basic Law" — "Basic Constitutional Law."
3. The question of co-ordination in the time of the modifications to be made to the Land boundaries and for the meeting of the Constituent Assembly.

Minister-President EHARD (Bavaria) then asked to be heard.

He stated that it was not the intention of the Ministers-President to end the present discussion in this manner. The Ministers-President had felt obliged to set forth the reason for their attitude; they would have liked to know whether these reasons were acceptable in principle or not, and whether the appreciation by the Military Governors of these reasons would not permit them, within the framework of the London agreements, and their own instructions, to take into account the proposals of the Ministers-President. If the Military Governors could affirm that on certain points they had no freedom of action, the Ministers-President would find themselves in a new situation. In this case the Ministers-President should be given a fresh opportunity for consultation in order that the discussion might be continued, but first he wished to be allowed to discuss quickly the points of divergence.

As regards the name to be given to the Basic Law, the Ministers-President saw no real difficulty in this question of terminology. In their opinion it was simply a bad translation and an addition or explanation should be sufficient to clear up this point. They suggested that the Military Governors should make a proposal on this point compatible with their instructions.

The second point was that of co-ordination in the time of modification of Land boundaries and of the convening of the Constituent Assembly. There again, Dr. EHARD saw no real divergence and considered that this difficulty could easily be resolved.

Therefore, the only question on which there was serious difficulty was that of the referendum. The Ministers-President would have acted in contradiction to their duty if they had not explained to the Military Governors their objections to the principle of the referendum. If the Military Governors could not accept these reasons the Ministers-President would like them to say so clearly. They would also like to know why the Military Governors were unable to accept these reasons. Perhaps they were bound, on this point, by the very specific provisions of the London Agreement. This point was very important for the Ministers-President. If, finally, the questions of the referendum was the only divergence which made it necessary for the case to be referred to the three Governments this created a new situation and in such a case the Ministers-President wished to consult, amongst themselves, once more in order to modify, if necessary, their attitude.

Dr. EHARD stressed once again that the Ministers-President would be very glad if the discussion could continue today on this basis.

Finally, Dr. EHARD asked the Military Governors to state precisely the points of divergence and their demands on those points.

On the proposal of General KOENIG the meeting adjourned for ten minutes, it being understood that the Military Governors would reply to Dr. EHARD's questions when meeting resumed.

* * *

The meeting resumed at 17:15 hours.

General KOENIG stated on behalf of his colleagues and of himself that:

1. The question of the term "basic law" or "Basic Constitutional Law" or "Basic Law (Provisional Constitution)" was not very important and the Military Governors considered that, in fact, an arrangement was possible on this point.

2. Concerning the question of the referendum, the Military Governors

had heard of the explanations given, in particular those of Herr AR-NOLD, on this point and if the Ministers-President insisted on ratification by the Landtage the Military Governors would be obliged to refer to their Governments. This did not, however, signify a refusal.

3. Concerning the question of the modification of boundaries, the Military Governors understood the reasons given by the Ministers-President; in particular they understood that it was a question of time. The Military Governors were, however, bound by the London agreements. They were therefore obliged to inform their Governments of this question and ask them for instructions but, here again, this did not constitute a refusal.

General KOENIG added that, in referring to their Governments, the Military Governors promised to request that a reply be given as early as possible.

Senator President KAISEN (Bremen) then asked to be heard. He stated that the reply of General KOENIG was very clear. It signified, as far as the Germans were concerned, that an unnecessary loss of time would ensue before it was possible to proceed. The opinion of the world, and particularly of the masses, would not understand that the application of the London decisions had been held up for minor divergencies of this nature. The Chairman had himself said that the question of terminology did not constitute a difficulty which could not be easily smoothed out.

On the question of the referendum, the London agreements of course provided the framework which, in a general manner, was binding upon the Germans insofar as their requests for modification might be unsuccessful. The Germans would consider, therefore, that for the question of the referendum they were bound by the London agreements and they would prefer to accept the referendum rather than waste time. If the referendum was to be the stumbling block which risked upsetting the whole, the Ministers-President would be ready to accept it. They wished only that the Allied Governments should be informed of the reasons brought forward by the Ministers-President against this referendum.

The Ministers-President asked only that they be allowed to begin applying the London decisions for they had already taken certain preparatory measures, in particular with regard to the Constituent Assembly, and they wished to know whether the time limits fixed for them were to be observed.

General KOENIG asked if this reply given by Herr KAISEN represented the reply of the Ministers-President as a whole.

The Ministers-President replied in the affirmative.

General KOENIG, having summed up the situation created by the last statement of Minister-President KAISEN and after having asked the opinion of his two colleagues, stated that the Military Governors wished to consult quickly on this new situation.

After consultation, General KOENIG stated on behalf of his two colleagues and of himself that:

[Appendix E]

THE MEETING:

2. (a) agreed:

(1) That there was no longer any serious difficulty about the name to be given the proposed "Grundgesetz".

(2) That, as far as the question of the referendum was concerned, the Ministers-President accepted the London decisions. It was understood, however, that their wishes in regard to this question would be submitted by the Military Governors to the three Allied Governments and that the Ministers-President would be informed in due time of the position taken by the (respective) Governments.

(3) That, as far as the question of co-ordination in the time of carrying out the boundary modifications and convening the Constituent Assembly was concerned, the Military Governors would also submit to the three Allied Governments the wishes of the Ministers-President. The Commanders-in-chief promised to support this request. The reply of the Governments would be communicated to the Ministers-President as soon as possible. In the case these Governments should refuse to grant an additional extension of time to the Ministers-President, the latter would be obliged to observe the dates provided for in London.

General KOENIG added that the three Military Governors had thus given a clear reply to the three questions. If they accepted points 1, 2 and 3 above, and if they undertook entire responsibility for them, they could begin to apply the London decisions . . . In particular, they could allow their Landtage to choose the method of election of the Delegates to the Constituent Assembly.

Minister-President STOCK asked to speak once again in order to state in the name of all the Ministers-President that they felt that considerable progress had been made that day. The Ministers-President would take the first measures for the nomination of delegates to the Constituent Assembly. They believed that agreement was complete as far as the question of the "Grundgesetz" was concerned, and of the date of convening the Constituent Assembly. As to the referendum, they had presented their arguments with a view of permitting co-operation between the Germans and the Occupying Powers. They were glad to know that these arguments would be submitted by the Military Governors to their Governments, and they agreed to abide forthwith by the decision which would be taken. Regarding the modifications of the Land boundaries, they noted the intention of the Military Governors to inform their Governments of their wish to extend the time limits fixed, and they were glad to know that the Military Governors were disposed to recommend that the German proposals on this matter be taken into consideration. In the meantime, the work on this question would be begun without delay and a Sub-Commission would start work on this problem the next day. The Ministers-

President were of the opinion that a very satisfactory solution had thus been found and they wished that a Press communique be drawn up at the end of the present discussion.

On the proposal of the Chairman it was agreed that a Press communique should be drawn up by the three Political Advisers and Dr. Litchfield in collaboration with Herr ARNOLD, Herr BRAUER, and Herr STOCK, representing the Ministers-President' Group.

Minister-President STOCK wished to thank the Military Governors in the name of all the Ministers-President for the patience which they had shown in following up the discussion, although at the beginning of the meeting they might have feared that a solution would not be reached.

He expressed especial gratitude to General CLAY for his endurance and for the active part which he had taken in the discussions despite his sickness. He wished him a speedy recovery, hoping that the result of the present meeting would constitute for General CLAY the best remedy.

General KOENIG thanked Minister-President STOCK for his kind words and, on behalf of his colleagues and himself, expressed to the Ministers-President their thanks for the comprehensive work which they had done during the past weeks.

The meeting closed at 17:55 hours.

F

Ministers-President Protocol of August 8, 1948

I

On 1 July 1948 the Military Governors of the American, British and French Zones of Occupation have authorized the Ministers-President of the Laender in their Zones to convene an assembly which is to create the legal basis for a community of the Laender. On 26 July 1948 the Ministers-President informed the Military Governors that they would make use of this authority in order to restore provisionally at least for a part German unity at present disrupted.

II

The Ministers-President have agreed to convene forthwith a Parliamentary Council which has the exclusive task to create a Basic Law for the area designated above. After the conclusion of the work of the Parliamentary Council, the Ministers-President will lay before the Military Governors the agreed Basic Law in order to get the authorization for the ratification in each individual Land. In doing so they will examine whether the decision of the Parliamentary Council creates for the participating Laender a form of Government of the Federal type provides for appropriate central power, safeguards the rights of the Laender, and guarantees the individual rights and freedoms.

III

Every Minister-President will lay before the Landtag of his Land a draft law for the election of representatives to the Parliamentary Council. The number of the representatives to be elected will be established according to the following principles: Each Land has at least one representative. For each 750,000 inhabitants one representative will be elected. For a fraction of at least 200,000 inhabitants one representative is added. The up-to-date population figures as of 1 July 1948 are the basis for calculating the number of inhabitants.

IV

Not later than 16 August 1948 the Ministers-President will communicate the names of the elected representatives to the common office which they set up on 15 July 1948. The Ministers-President intend to convene the Parliamentary Council on 23 August for a meeting on 1 September 1948 in a place still to be agreed.

V

Compensation for the personal expenses incurred by the representatives will be regulated by Land law. The other costs of the Parliamentary Council and of the office of the Ministers-President will be allocated to the individual Laender by agreement of the Ministers-President according to a plan still to be determined.

G

Text of Aide Memoire Left with the President

of the Parliamentary Council at Bonn

Frankfurt   *22 November 1948*

1. "As you are well aware, the Parliamentary Council was convened in order to draft a democratic constitution which will establish for the participating states a governmental structure of federal type, will protect the rights of the participating states, provide adequate central authority and contain guarantees of individual rights and freedoms. During the last eleven weeks the Parliamentary Council in plenary session as well as in its several committees has freely discussed those principles and drafted a basic law (provisional constitution) which is now before the main committee.

2. In view of the advanced stage now reached in the work of the Parliamentary Council, the Military Governors consider it advisable at this time to give the Council some indication of the interpretation which they will apply to the general principles set out in Document No. 1. Since there are several ways in which democratic federal government can be obtained, they intend to consider the provisions of the basic law in their whole context. Nevertheless, they believe that the basic law should, to the maximum extent possible, provide:

   (a) for a Bicameral legislative system in which one of the houses must represent the individual states and must have sufficient power to safeguard the interests of the states;
   (b) that the executive must only have those powers which are definitely prescribed by the constitution, and that emergency powers, if any, of the executive must be so limited as to require prompt legislative or judicial review;
   (c) that the powers of the federal government shall be limited to those expressly enumerated in the constitution and in any case, shall not include education, cultural and religious affairs, local government and public health (except in this last case, to secure such coordination as essential to safeguard the health of the people in the several states) that its powers in the field of public welfare be limited to those necessary for the co-ordination of social security measures,

that its powers in the police field be limited to those especially approved by the Military Governors, during the occupation period;

(d) that the powers of the federal government in the field of public finance shall be limited to the disposal of monies, including the raising of revenue for purposes for which it is responsible; that the federal government may set rates and legislate on the general principles of assessment with regard to other taxes for which the uniformity is essential, the collection and utilization of such taxes being left to the individual states, and that it may appropriate funds only for the purpose for which it is responsible under the constitution;

(e) that the constitution should provide for an independent judiciary to review federal legislation, to review the exercise of federal executive power, and to adjudicate conflicts between federal and Land authorities as well as between Land authorities, and to protect the civil rights and freedom of the individual;

(f) that the powers of the federal government to establish federal agencies for the execution and administration of its responsibilities should be clearly defined and should be limited to those fields in which it is clear that state implementation is impracticable;

(g) that each citizen has access to public office, with appointment and promotion being based solely on his fitness to discharge the responsibilities of the position, and that the Civil Service should be non-political in character;

(h) that a public servant, if elected to the federal legislature, shall resign his office with the agency where he is employed before he accepts election.

The Military Governors will be guided by these principles in their final examination of the basic law (provisional constitution) and any subsequent amendments thereto, and they will consider the basic law (provisional constitution) as a whole in order to determine whether or not the broad requirements of Document 1 have been met."

H

Memorandum on the Basic Law

handed by the Military Governors to a Parliamentary Council Delegation
(As read by the Chairman of the Meeting, General Robertson)

Frankfurt   *2 March 1949*

1. My colleagues and I have asked you to come here today in order
that we might comment to you upon several provisions of your proposed
Basic Law as it was passed by the Main Committee of the Parliamentary
Council. We have studied this document in the light of the Aide Memoire
which our Liaison Officers delivered to you on 22 November 1948.

2. There are a number of provisions in the Basic Law which deviate
from detailed principles set forth in that Aide Memoire. However, in
viewing the document as a whole we are prepared to disregard some of
these deviations but at the same time feel it necessary again to call your
urgent attention to other provisions which, in our opinion, depart too far
from these principles.

3. In the first place, we would like to point out that the powers of the
federal government as now set forth in Article 36 are not defined with
sufficient clarity adequately to safeguard the position of the states in a
federal system. To correct this we suggest that you delete present Articles
36 and 36a and substitute therefor a new Article 36 based very largely
upon your own language and which might read substantially as follows:

Article 36

(1) The Laender shall retain the right to legislate in the fields hereinafter enumerated except where it is clearly impossible for a single Land
to enact effective legislation or where the legislation if enacted would be
detrimental to the rights or interests of other Laender; in such cases, and
provided that the interests of several Laender are clearly, directly and
integrally affected, the Federation shall have the right to enact such
legislation as may be necessary or appropriate:

1. Civil law, criminal law and execution of sentences, constitution of
   courts, court procedure insofar as the Laender are not competent
   according to Article 112/2, the bar, notaries and legal advice
   (Rechtsberatung);
2. Census and registry matters;

3. Associations and assemblies;
4. The right of sojourn and settlement of aliens;
5. The protection of German works of art against removal abroad;
6. Matters relating to refugees and expellees;
7. Public welfare;
8. War damages and compensation (Wiedergutmachung);
9. Provisions for war-disabled persons and surviving dependents, the welfare of former prisoners of war and the care of war graves;
10. Law relating to the economy (mining, industry, power supply, crafts, trades, commerce, banking and stock exchanges, private insurances);
11. Labor law, including the legal organisation of enterprises, protection of workers and provision of employment as well as social insurance including unemployment insurance;
12. The furtherance of scientific research;
13. Expropriation in matters on which the Federation has legislative power;
14. Transfer of land and landed property, natural resources and means of production to public ownership or to other forms of publicly controlled economy;
15. Prevention of the abuse of economic power;
16. Promotion of agricultural and forestry production, safeguarding of food supply, import and export of agricultural and forestry products, deep-sea and coastal fisheries and coastal preservation;
17. Transactions in landed property, law concerning land and agricultural lease, housing, settlements and homesteads;
18. Measures against epidemic and infectious diseases affecting humans and animals, the licensing for medical and other healing professions and the healing trade and traffic in drugs, medicines, narcotics and poisons;
19. Protection relating to traffic in food and stimulants as well as in necessities of life, in fodder, in agricultural and forestry, seeds and seedlings, and protection of trees and plants against diseases and pests;
20. Ocean and coastal shipping and aids to navigation, inland shipping, meteorological services, ocean channels and inland waterways used for general traffic;
21. Road traffic, motor transport and the construction and maintenance of highways used for long-distance transport;
22. Railways other than federal railways, except mountain railways;
23. Citizenship of the Federation and the Laender;
24. Hunting, protection of nature and care of the countryside;
25. Land distribution, regional planning and water conservation;
26. Matters relating to registration and identity cards.

4. In the second place, my colleagues and I would like you to under-

stand that we are ultimately responsible for security and that the powers contained in Article 118c may not be exercised until specifically approved by the Occupation Authorities. This reservation upon the exercise of these police powers will be repeated at the time when you are formally advised of our action with regard to the constitution as a whole.

5. In the third place, we have noted with concern the extent to which the provisions regarding finance powers depart from the criteria agreed upon in London and transmitted to you in paragraph (d) of the Aide Memoire. We have already had occasion to advise you that in our opinion substantially the same provisions would result in "the Laender being left without adequate independent sources of revenue for the conduct of their affairs". We would suggest, therefore, several changes in Articles 122a, 122b and 123 which would enable these articles more nearly to satisfy the principles of financial organization which we believe to be of primary importance in a federal system. We suggest that these be re-worded to read substantially as follows:

Article 122a

The Federation shall have powers of exclusive legislation in customs and financial monopolies (Federal taxes) and of priority legislation on the following taxes (concurrent taxes):

1. Excise taxes and taxes on transactions, with the exception of taxes (Land taxes) with localised application, in particular the taxes on real estate acquisition, incremental value and on fire protection.
2. The taxes on income, property, inheritance and gifts (or donations),
3. "Realsteuern" (taxes on real estate and on businesses), with the exception of the fixing of tax rates.

Article 122b

The Federation shall exercise priority legislation in the field of concurrent taxes only to the extent that it may require the whole or any portion of the proceeds of any concurrent tax or taxes to cover its responsibilities. If the Federation takes over a portion of a concurrent tax the remaining portion shall be retained by the Laender as and where collected.

Article 123

1. The federal taxes shall be administered by federal finance authorities. The Federal Government may, if it so desires, administer, through federal financial authorities, those taxes which it imposes for authorized Federal purposes in their entirety, and the tax on income to the extent that such a tax is for federal purposes. The structure of the Federal finance authorities and the finance courts and the procedure to be applied by them shall be regulated by Federal law. The heads of the finance and customs authorities in the Laender shall be appointed by agreement with the governments of the Laender involved.

2. The Land taxes and concurrent taxes other than those referred to in Article 123 (1), shall be administered by Land finance authorities.

3. The raising of the "Realsteuer" shall be regulated by Land legislation.

To be consistent with what has been said above we wish to call your attention to the need for deleting Article 138c (4) and substituting a detailed specification of Land taxes.

6. In the fourth place, we wish to draw your attention to the fact that Article 129—1 (2) is not entirely clear as to the extent to which the independence of the judiciary is insured. We urge you to give it your thoughtful attention particularly as to the safeguards provided in connection with the dismissal of judges.

7. In the fifth place, we consider that the possibilities for the Federation to establish its own administrative agencies (Articles 112/2 and 116) are wide. We would therefore like to point out that the Military Governors will have to give careful consideration at the time when such agencies are established to ensure that they do not represent too great a centralisation of power.

8. In the sixth place, we should like to clarify our position with regard to the question of the federal civil service. If principles with regard to the civil service as set out in Articles 27 (b) and 62 are to be embodied in the Constitution, they must be modified to conform to the principles enumerated in paragraphs (g) and (h) in our Aide Memoire of 22 November 1948.

9. A seventh matter which has concerned us is the question of the reorganization of the territories of the Laender as set out in Articles 25 and 26. In this connection we wish to draw your attention to the statements which we made to the Ministers President on the 20th of July, the pertinent portions of which were as follows:

"We wish you to appreciate that the question of Land boundaries is one of great importance to us. We feel that the present is an appropriate time to deal with it, and we are ready to do so. However, it would be much more difficult for us to deal with it later on. It has, for example, reactions with regard to our own zonal boundaries. We do not feel that we should be willing to deal with the subject again at a later date prior to the conclusion of a peace treaty.

"Moreover, the fixing of Land boundaries is important in relation to the constitution itself. We believe that we should recommend to our Governments that the boundaries which were recognized during the drafting of this constitution should remain unchanged, at least until a peace treaty is signed."

Our position today is the same as it was at that time and we feel we must now advise you that unless we unanimously agree to change this position it must remain so until the peace treaty. In this case also we will remind you of this decision at the time formal action is taken with regard to the Constitution as a whole.

10. Finally, my colleagues and I would like you to know that we understand the solicitude which the Parliamentary Council has shown for Berlin. However, in view of the existing situation, that portion of Article 22 which refers to Berlin must be suspended. Nevertheless, there would be no objection to the responsible authorities in Berlin designating a small number of representatives to attend the meetings of the parliament.

I

Text of Proposals Made by the Parliamentary Council Committee of Seven on the Basis of the Memorandum of 2 March 1949

Bonn   *10 March 1949*

Article 95a

1. The Laender shall have the right of legislation insofar as this Basic Law does not give legislative powers to the Federation.

2. The delimitation of the competence between Bund and Laender shall conform to the provisions of this basic Law on the exclusive and concurrent legislation.

Article 95b

Within the exclusive legislation of the Federation, the Laender shall have the power to legislate only if and insofar as they are expressly authorized by a Federal law.

Article 95c

(1) Within the limits of the concurrent legislation of the Federation, Laender shall have the power to legislate, as long and insofar as the Federation does not make use of its right to legislate.

(2) Within this sphere the Federation has the right to legislate

1. If a matter cannot be effectively regulated by the legislation of one or several Laender or

2. If the regulation of a matter by a Land law would be harmful to the interests of other Laender or

3. If the purpose of the law can only be achieved by a Federal law or
4. If the preservation of the legal or economic unity requires the regulation by a Federal law.

Article 96 (former Art. 35)

The Federation shall have exclusive legislation on:
1. Foreign affairs;
2. Freedom of movement, passports, immigration and emigration and extradition;
3. Currency, money and coinage, weights and measures and regulation of time and calendar;
4. The unity of customs and commercial territory, commercial and navigation agreements, the freedom of traffic in goods and the traffic in goods and payments with foreign countries;
5. Federal railways and air traffics;
6. Post and telecommunications;
7. The legal status of persons in the employment of the Federation and of public law corporations under direct supervision of the Federal government;
8. Trade marks, copyright, and publishing rights;
9. Co-operation of the Laender in the criminal police and the establishment of a Federal Office for Criminal Affairs;
10. Statistics for federal purposes.

Article 97 (former Art. 36)

(1) The Federation shall have concurrent legislation on:
1. Civil law, criminal law and execution of sentences, constitution of courts, court procedure insofar as the Laender are not competent according to Article 112/2, the bar, notaries and legal advice (Rechtsberatung);
2. Census and registry matters;
3. Associations and assemblies, press and motion pictures;
4. The right of sojourn and settlement of aliens;
5. The protection of German works of art against removal abroad;
6. Matters relating to refugees and expellees;
7. Public welfare;
7a. Citizenship of the Federation and the Laender;
8. War damages and compensation (Wiedergutmachung);
9. Provisions for war-disabled persons and surviving dependants, the welfare of former prisoners of war and the care of war graves;
10. Law relating to the economy (Mining, industry, power supply, crafts, trades, commerce, banking and stock exchanges, private insurances);
11. Labor law, including the legal organization of enterprises, pro-

tection of workers and provision of employment as well as social insurance including unemployment insurance;

12. The furtherance of scientific research;
13. Expropriation in matters on which the Federation has legislative power;
14. Transfer of land and landed property, natural resources and means of production to public ownership or to other forms of publicly controlled economy;
15. Prevention of the abuse of economic power;
16. Promotion of agricultural and forestry production, safe-guarding of food supply, import and export of agricultural and forestry products, deep-sea and coastal fisheries and coastal preservation;
17. Transactions in landed property, law concerning land and agricultural lease, housing, settlements and homesteads;
18. Measures against epidemic and infectious diseases affecting humans and animals, the licensing for medical and other healing professions and the healing trade and traffic in drugs, medicines, narcotics and poisons;
19. Protection relating to traffic in food and stimulants as well as in necessities of life, in fodder, in agricultural and forestry seeds and seedlings, and protection of trees and plants against diseases and pests;
20. Ocean and coastal shipping and aids to navigation, inland shipping, meteorological services, ocean channels and inland waterways used for general traffic;
21. Street traffic, motor transport and the construction and maintenance of highways used for long-distance transport;
22. Railways other than federal railways, except mountain railways.

Article 98 (former Article 36a)

The Federation shall have the right to issue general provisions (Rahmenvorschriften) concerning:

1. The legal status of persons employed in the public service of the Laender, Gemeinden and other public law corporations;
2. Hunting;
3. Land distribution, regional planning and water conservation;
4. Matters relating to registration and identity cards.

PROPOSALS OF THE COMMITTEE OF SEVEN

Bonn   *17 March 1949*

Article 95a

(1) The Laender shall have the right to legislate, insofar as this Basic Law does not give legislative powers to the Federation.

(2) The delimitation of the competence between the Federation and

the Laender shall conform to the provisions of this Basic Law on the exclusive and concurrent legislation.

Article 95b

Within the sphere of the exclusive legislation of the Federation the Laender shall have the power to legislate only if and insofar as they are expressly empowered by a federal law.

Article 95c

(1) Within the sphere of the concurrent legislation of the Federation the Laender shall have the power to legislate as long and insofar as the Federation does not make use of its legislative power.

(2) Within this sphere the Federation shall have legislative power,

1. If a matter cannot be effectively regulated by the legislation of individual Laender or
2. if the regulation of a matter by a Land law would impair the interests of other Laender or of the entirety or
3. if the preservation of the legal or economic unity requires the regulation by a federal law.

Article 96 (former Article 35)

The Federation shall have exclusive legislation on

(1) Foreign affairs;
(2) *Citizenship of the Federation;* (rest of the item omitted)
(3) Freedom of movement, passport, immigration and emigration, and extradition;
(4) Currency, money and coinage, weights and measures and regulation of time and calendar;
(5) The unity of customs and commercial territory, commercial and navigation agreements, freedom of traffic in goods and the traffic in goods and payments with foreign countries;
(6) Federal railways and air traffic;
(7) Post and telecommunications;
(8) The legal status of persons in the employment of the Federation and of public law corporations under direct supervision of the Federal Government;
(9) Trade marks, copyright and publishing rights;
(10) Cooperation of the Laender in the criminal police and the establishment of a Federal Office for Criminal Affairs;
(11) Statistics for federal purposes.

Article 97 (former Article 36)

The concurrent legislation shall apply to the following fields:

(1) Civil law, criminal law and execution of sentences, constitution of courts, court procedure, insofar as the Laender are not competent according to Article 111, the bar, notaries and legal advice (Rechtsberatung);

(2) Census and registry matters;
(3) *Associations and assemblies;* (rest of the item omitted)
(4) The right of sojourn and settlement of aliens;
(5) The protection of German works of art against removal abroad;
(6) Matters relating to refugees and expellees;
(7) *Public welfare;* (the word "the entire" omitted)
(7a) *Citizenship of the Laender;*
(8) War damages and compensation (Wiedergutmachung);
(9) Provisions for war-disabled persons and surviving dependants, the welfare of former prisoners of war and the care of war graves;
(10) Law relating to the economy (mining, industry, power supply, crafts, trades, commerce, banking and stock exchanges, private insurances);
(11) Labor law, including the legal organization of enterprises, protection of workers and provision of employment as well as social insurance including unemployment insurance;
(12) The furtherance of scientific research;
(13) *Law relating to expropriation;* (rest of the item omitted)
(14) Transfer of land and landed property, natural resources and means of production to public ownership or to other forms of publicly controlled economy;
(15) Prevention of the abuse of economic power;
(16) Promotion of agricultural and forestry production, safeguarding of food supply, import and export of agricultural and forestry products, deep-sea and coastal fisheries and coastal preservation;
(17) Transactions in landed property, law concerning land and agricultural lease, housing, settlements and homesteads;
(18) Measures against epidemic and infectious diseases affecting humans and animals, the licensing for medical and other healing professions and the healing trade and traffic in drugs, medicines, narcotics and poisons;
(19) Protection relating to traffic in food and stimulants as well as in necessities of life, in fodder, in agricultural and forestry seeds and seedlings, and protection of trees and plants against diseases and pests;
(20) Ocean and coastal shipping and aids to navigation, inland shipping, meteorological services, ocean channels and inland waterways used for general traffic;
(21) Street traffic, motor transport and the construction and maintenance of highways used for long-distance transport;
(22) Railways other than federal railways, except mountain railways. (paragraph 2 omitted)

Article 98 (former Article 36a)

Under the conditions of Article 95c, paragraph 2, the Federation shall have the right to issue general provisions (Rahmenvorschriften) concerning:

(1) The legal status of persons employed in the public service of the Laender, Gemeinden and other public law corporations;

(1a) *The general legal status of press and motion pictures;*

(2) *Hunting;* (rest of the item omitted)

(3) Land distribution, regional planning and water conservation;

(4) Matters relating to registration and identity cards.

Article 138 (former Articles 132 and 129-1)

(1) Judges shall be independent and subject only to the law.

(2) If a federal judge, in his official or unofficial capacity infringes the principles of the Basic Law or the constitutional order of a Land the Federal Constitutional Court may, on the application of the Volkstag, with a two-thirds majority order that the judge be transferred to another office or placed on the retired list. In the case of a wilful infringement, dismissal may be decided upon.

Article 139 (former Articles 129-1 and 129a)

(1) The legal status of the federal judges must be regulated by a special federal law.

(2) The legal status of the judges in the Laender shall be regulated by special Land legislation. The Federation may issue general provisions (Rahmenvorschriften).

(3) The Laender may determine that the Land Minister of Justice shall, together with a committee for the election of judges, decide on the appointment of judges in the Laender.

(4) The Laender may make an appropriate regulation for Land judges in accordance with Article 138, paragraph 2. Existing Land constitutional law shall remain unaffected.

Article 65 (former Article 62)

An official exercising public powers (Hoheitsbefugnisse) must, before accepting his election to the Volkstag, request his transfer to the inactive status. The transfer shall be valid for the duration of his membership in the Volkstag, without a claim to inactive status pay; the claim to re-employment, however, shall be maintained. These provisions shall apply appropriately to employees in public service. The provisions of sentence 1 shall not apply to officials elected for a limited period of time. Details shall be regulated by a federal law.

Article 120 (former Article 122)

To cover the expenditures of the Federation, in particular:

(1) The costs of federal administration,

(2) Federal outlay on occupation costs and other external and internal war-induced burdens,

(3) Federal grants towards the burdens of social insurance, including unemployment insurance and public assistance for the unemployed, the following revenues shall serve:

[574]

1. The statutory contributions of the federal railways and the federal postal services, the profits of federally owned enterprises, the yields from participations of the Federation, its share in the profits of the federal currency bank and bank of issue and the yields from other federal property,
2. the revenues of the federal administration,
3. *customs, the yields from financial monopolies and the taxes accruing to the Federation.*

Article 121 (former Article 122a)

The Federation shall have exclusive legislation on customs and financial monopolies.

Insofar as the Federation uses the taxes entirely or partly to cover federal expenditures or considers necessary a uniform regulation with regard to the legal and economic unity, the Federation shall have concurrent legislation on:

(1) excise taxes and taxes on transactions, with the exception of taxes with localized application, in particular the taxes on real estate acquisition, incremental value and on fire protection,
(2) the taxes on income, property, inheritance and donations,
(3) "Realsteuern" (taxes on real estate and on businesses), with the exception of the fixing of tax rates.

Article 122 (former Article 122b)

(1) Of the taxes subject to concurrent legislation of the Federation the following taxes shall, until otherwise regulated by law, accrue to the Laender and, in accordance with Land legislation, to the Gemeinden (Gemeindeverbaende) to cover their expenditures:
   1. The beer tax, race-betting tax, motor vehicle tax, property tax (with the exception of the non-recurrent property tax serving the equalization of burdens), the inheritance tax and the "Realsteuern".
   2. Shares in the turnover tax and the income and corporation taxes,

and (the following taxes) shall accrue to the Federation to cover its expenditures:
   1. The other excise taxes and taxes on transactions,
   2. Shares in the turnover tax and the income and corporation taxes.

(2) The shares in the turnover tax and in the income and corporation taxes accruing to the Federation or the Laender shall be fixed by a federal law which shall require the approval of the Bundesrat.

(3) To secure the capacity even of the Laender with little tax revenue, the Federation may, by a federal law which shall require the approval of the Bundesrat, determine that, with regard to individual taxes and tax shares accruing to the Laender, the yields or a part of the yields shall be compensated between the Laender on another basis than that of local yields.

(4) The taxes and tax shares which, according to these provisions, accrue to the Laender shall not be federal revenues but shall be directly and currently delivered to the Laender.

(5) The final distribution of the taxes subject to the concurrent legislation of the Federation shall be effected by 31 December 1952. The federal law concerning this matter shall require the approval of the Bundesrat.

Article 123 (former Article 123)

(1) Customs and financial monopolies as well as the taxes subject to the concurrent legislation of the Federation shall be administered by federal finance authorities. The structure of the federal finance authorities and the finance courts and the procedure to be applied by them shall be regulated by federal law. The heads of the finance and customs authorities in the Laender shall be appointed by agreement with the Governments of the Laender involved.

(2) The implementing regulations shall be issued by the Federal Government, insofar as the taxes entirely or partly accrue to the Laender, with the approval of the Bundesrat.

(2) The impending regulations shall be issued by the Federal Government, insofar as the taxes entirely or partly accrue to the Laender, with the approval of the Bundesrat.

(3) The taxes subject to Land legislation shall be administered by Land finance authorities.

(4) The raising of the "Realsteuern" shall be regulated by Land legislation.

J

Letter of Approval of the Basic Law

Frankfurt   *12 May 1949*

Dr. Konrad Adenauer
President of the Parliamentary Council
Bonn

Dear Dr. Adenauer:

1. The Basic Law passed on 8 May by the Parliamentary Council has

received our careful and interested attention. In our opinion it happily combines German democratic tradition with the concepts of representative government and a rule of law which the world has come to recognize as requisite to the life of a free people.

2. In approving this constitution for submission to the German people for ratification in accordance with the provisions of Article 144(1) we believe that you will understand that there are several reservations which we must make. In the first place, the powers vested in the Federation by the Basic Law, as well as the powers exercised by Laender and local Governments, are subject to the provisions of the Occupation Statute which we have already transmitted to you and wish is promulgated as of this date.

3. In the second place, it should be understood that the police powers contained in Article 91(2) may not be exercised until specifically approved by the Occupation Authorities. Likewise the remaining police functions of the Federation shall be governed by our letter to you of 14 April 1949 on this subject.

4. A third reservation concerns the participation of Greater Berlin in the Federation. We interpret the effect of Articles 23 and 144(2) of the Basic Law as constituting acceptance of our previous request that while Berlin may not be accorded voting membership in the Bundestag or Bundesrat nor be governed by the Federation she may, nevertheless, designate a small number of representatives to attend the meetings of those legislative bodies.

5. A fourth reservation relates to Articles 29 and 118 and the general question of the reorganization of Laender boundaries. Excepting in the case of Wuerttemberg-Baden and Hohenzollern our position on this question has not changed since we discussed the matter with you on 2 March. Unless the High Commissioners should unanimously agree to change this position the powers set forth in these articles shall not be exercised and the boundaries of all of the Laender excepting Wuerttemberg-Baden and Hohenzollern shall remain as now fixed until the time of the peace treaty.

6. Fifthly, we consider that Article 84, paragraph 5 and Article 87, paragraph 3, give to the Federation very wide powers in the administrative field. The High Commissioners will have to give careful consideration to the exercise of such powers in order to insure that they do not lead to excessive concentration of authority.

7. At our meeting with you on 25 April, we proposed to you a formula to interpret in English the intention of Article 72(2), 3. This formula which you accepted as conveying your meaning reads as follows:

". . . because the maintenance of legal or economic unity demands it in order to promote the economic interests of the Federation or to insure reasonable quality of economic opportunity to all persons."

We wish you to know that the High Commissioner will interpret this article in accordance with this text.

8. In order to eliminate the possibility of future legal controversy, we would like to make it clear that when we approved constitutions for the Laender we provided that nothing contained in those constitutions could be interpreted as restricting the provisions of the Federal constitution. Conflict between Laender constitutions and the provisional Federal constitution must, therefore, be resolved in favor of the latter.

9. We should also like it to be clearly understood that upon the convening of the legislative bodies provided for in the Basic Law, and upon the election of the President and the election and appointment of the Chancellor and the Federal Ministers, respectively, in the manner provided for in the Basic Law, the Government of the Federal Republic of Germany will then be established and the Occupation Statute shall thereupon enter into force.

10. On the completion of their final task as laid down in Article 145, 1, the Parliamentary Council will be dissolved. We wish to take this occasion to compliment the members of the Parliamentary Council on their successful completion of a difficult task performed under trying circumstances, on the manifest care and thoroughness with which they have done their work and on their devotion to the democratic ideals toward the achievement of which we are all striving.

B. H. ROBERTSON   PIERRE KOENIG
General   General d'Armee
Military Governor   Military Governor
British Zone   French Zone

LUCIUS D. CLAY
General, US Army
Military Governor
US Zone

K

Basic Law for the Federal Republic of Germany

PREAMBLE

Conscious of its responsibility before God and before man, inspired by the resolve to preserve its national and political unity and to serve world peace as an equal partner in a united Europe, the German people in the Laender Baden, Bavaria, Bremen, Hamburg, Hesse, Lower Saxony, North-Rhine-Westphalia, Rhineland-Palatinate, Schleswig-Holstein, Wuerttemberg-Baden and Wuerttemberg-Hohenzollern has, by virtue of its constituent power, enacted this Basic Law of the Federal Republic of Germany to give a new order to political life for a transitional period.

It has also acted on behalf of those Germans to whom participation was denied.

The entire German people is called upon to achieve, by free self-determination, the unity and freedom of Germany.

I BASIC RIGHTS

Article 1

(1) The dignity of man is inviolable. To respect and protect it is the duty of all state authority.

(2) The German people therefore acknowledges inviolable and inalienable human rights as the basis of every human community, of peace and of justice in the world.

(3) The following basic rights are binding on the legislature, on the executive and on the judiciary as directly valid law.

Article 2

(1) Everyone has the right to the free development of his personality, insofar as he does not infringe upon the rights of others or offend against the constitutional order or the moral code.

(2) Everyone has the right to life and to physical inviolability. The freedom of the individual is inviolable. These rights may be interfered with only on the basis of a law.

Article 3

(1) All men are equal before the law.

(2) Men and women have equal rights.

(3) No one may be prejudiced or privileged because of his sex, his descent, his race, his language, his homeland and origin, his faith or his religious and political opinions.

Article 4

(1) Freedom of faith and conscience and freedom of creed in religion and in philosophy of life (weltanschauliche) are inviolable.

(2) The practice of religion without interference is guaranteed.

(3) No one may be compelled against his conscience to perform military service as an armed combatant. Details are regulated by a federal law.

Article 5

(1) Everyone has the right freely to express and to disseminate his

opinion through speech, writing and pictures and, without hindrance, to instruct himself from generally accessible sources. Freedom of the press and freedom of radio and motion-pictures reporting are guaranteed. There is no censorship.

(2) These rights are limited by the provisions of the general laws, the legal regulations for the protection of juveniles and by the right to personal honor.

(3) Art and science, research and teaching are free. Freedom of teaching does not absolve from loyalty to the Constitution.

Article 6

(1) Marriage and family are under the special protection of the state.

(2) The care and upbringing of children are the natural right of parents and their duty, incumbent upon them primarily. The state watches over their performance (of this duty).

(3) Children may be separated from the family against the will of those entitled to bring them up only on the basis of a law, if those so entitled fail to perform their duty, or if, on other grounds, the children are in danger of falling into neglect.

(4) Every mother has a claim to the protection and assistance of the community.

(5) For their physical and mental development and for their position in society, illegitimate children shall, by legislation, be given the same opportunities as legitimate children.

Article 7

(1) The entire educational system is under the supervision of the state.

(2) Those entitled to bring up a child have the right to decide whether it shall receive religious instruction.

(3) Religious instruction shall form part of the curriculum in state and municipal schools, with the exception of non-denominational schools. Religious instruction shall, without prejudice to the state's right of supervision, be given according to the principles of the religious denominations. No teacher may against his will be placed under an obligation to give religious instruction.

(4) The right to establish private schools is guaranteed. Private schools as a substitute for state or municipal schools require the approval of the state and are subject to Land legislation. The approval must be given if the private schools, in their educational aims and facilities, as well as in the professional training of their teaching personnel, are not inferior to the state or municipal schools and if a segregation of the pupils in accordance with the (financial) means of the parents is not fostered. The approval must be withheld if the economic and legal status of the teaching personnel is not adequately ensured.

(5) A private elementary school is to be permitted only if the educational authority recognizes a specific pedagogic interest or if, at the

request of those entitled to bring up children, it is to be established as an inter-denominational school (Gemeinschaftsschule), as a denominational or an ideological school, and if a state or municipal elementary school of this type does not exist in the Gemeinde.

(6) Preparatory schools (Vorschulen) remain abolished.

Article 8

(1) All Germans have the right, without prior notification or permission, to assemble peacefully and unarmed.

(2) In the case of open-air meetings this right may be restricted by legislation or on the basis of a law.

Article 9

(1) All Germans have the right to form associations and societies.

(2) Associations, the objects or activities of which conflict with the criminal laws or which are directed against the constitutional order or the concept of international understanding, are prohibited.

(3) The right to form associations to safeguard and improve working and economic conditions is guaranteed to everyone and to all trades and professions. Agreements which restrict or seek to hinder this right are null and void; measures directed to this end are illegal.

Article 10

Secrecy of the mail as well as secrecy of the postal services and of telecommunications is inviolable. Restrictions may be ordered only on the basis of a law.

Article 11

(1) All Germans enjoy freedom of movement throughout the federal territory.

(2) This right may be restricted only by legislation and only for the cases in which an adequate basis of existence is absent, and, as a result, particular burdens would arise for the general public or in which it is necessary for the protection of juveniles from neglect, for combatting danger of epidemics or in order to prevent criminal acts.

Article 12

(1) All Germans have the right freely to choose their trade or profession, place of work and place of vocational training. The exercise of an occupation or profession may be regulated by legislation.

(2) No one may be compelled to perform a particular kind of work except within the scope of a customary general compulsory public service equally applicable to all.

(3) Forced labor is admissible only in the event of deprivation of freedom ordered by a court.

Article 13

(1) The home is inviolable.

(2) Searches may be ordered only by a judge or, in the event of danger in delay, by other authorities provided by law, and may be carried out only in the form prescribed therein.

(3) In other cases interferences with, and restrictions of, this inviolability may be undertaken only to avert a common or mortal danger to individuals and, on the basis of a law, also to prevent imminent danger to public safety and order, especially for the relief of the housing and space shortage (Raumnot), for combatting the danger of epidemics or for the protection of endangered juveniles.

Article 14

(1) Property and the right of inheritance are safeguarded. (Their) scope and limitations are determined by legislation.

(2) Property commits to duties. Its use should at the same time serve the general welfare.

(3) Expropriation is admissible only for the welfare of the community at large. It may be effected only by legislation or on the basis of a law regulating the nature and extent of compensation. The compensation shall be determined after just consideration of the interests of the general public and the parties concerned. In case of dispute regarding the amount of compensation, there is recourse to the ordinary courts.

Article 15

Land, natural resources and means of production may, for the purpose of socialization, be transferred to public ownership or other forms of publicly controlled economy by means of a law regulating the nature and extent of compensation. For the compensation, Article 14, paragraph (3), sentence 3 and 4, applies correspondingly.

Article 16

(1) No one may be deprived of his German citizenship. A person may be deprived of citizenship only on the basis of a law and, against his will, only if he is not thereby rendered stateless.

(2) No German may be extradited to a foreign country. The politically persecuted enjoy the right of asylum.

Article 17

Everyone has the right, individually or jointly with others, to address written requests or complaints to the competent authorities and to the popular representative bodies.

Article 18

Whoever abuses freedom of expression of opinion, in particular freedom of the press (Article 5, paragraph (1)), freedom of teaching (Article 5, paragraph (3)), freedom of assembly (Article 8), freedom of association

(Article 9), the secrecy of the mail, of the postal services and of telecommunications (Article 10), the (right of) property (Article 14), or the rights of asylum (Article 16, paragraph (2)), in order to attack the free democratic basic order, forfeits these basic rights. The forfeiture and its extent shall be pronounced by the Federal Constitutional Court.

Article 19

(1) Insofar as, under this Basic Law, a basic right may be restricted by legislation or on the basis of a law, this law must be of general application and not applicable solely to an individual case. Furthermore, the law must specify the basic right and indicate the Article (concerned).

(2) In no case may a basic right be infringed upon in its essential content.

(3) The basic rights also apply to domestic juridical petitions insofar as the former, according to their nature, are applicable to the latter.

(4) Should any person's rights be infringed by public authority, he shall have recourse to the courts. Insofar as there is no other jurisdiction, the recourse shall be to the ordinary courts.

II. THE FEDERATION AND THE LAENDER

Article 20

(1) The Federal Republic of Germany is a democratic and social federal state.

(2) All state authority emanates from the people. It is exercised by the people by means of elections and plebiscites and through specific legislative, executive and judicial agencies.

(3) Legislation is subject to the Constitution; the executive power and the administration of justice are subject to the Law.

Article 21

(1) The parties participate in the forming of the political will of the people. They can be freely formed. Their internal organization must conform to democratic principles. They must publicly account for the sources of their funds.

(2) Parties which, according to their aims and the conduct of their members, seek to impair or abolish the free democratic basic order or to jeopardize the existence of the Federal Republic of Germany are unconstitutional. The Federal Constitutional Court shall decide on the question of unconstitutionality.

(3) Details are regulated by federal legislation.

Article 22

The federal flag is black-red-gold.

[Appendix K]

Article 23

For the time being, this Basic Law applies in the territory of the Laender Baden, Bavaria, Bremen, Greater Berlin, Hamburg, Hesse, Lower-Saxony, North-Rhine-Westphalia, Rhineland-Palatinate, Schleswig-Holstein, Wuerttemberg-Baden and Wuerttemberg-Hohenzollern. It is to be put into force in other parts of Germany on their accession.

Article 24

(1) The Federation may, by legislation, transfer sovereign powers to international institutions.

(2) For the maintenance of peace, the Federation may join a system of mutual collective security; in doing so it will consent to those limitations of its sovereign powers which will bring about and secure a peaceful and lasting order in Europe and among the nations of the world.

(3) For the settlement of disputes between nations, the Federation will accede to conventions concerning a general, comprehensive obligatory system of international arbitration.

Article 25

The general rules of international law form part of federal law. They take precedence over the laws and directly create rights and duties for the inhabitants of the federal territory.

Article 26

(1) Activities tending to disturb, and undertaken with the intention of disturbing, the peaceful relations between nations, especially of preparing the conduct of an aggressive war, are unconstitutional. They are to be subject to punishment.

(2) Weapons designed for warfare may be manufactured, transported or marketed only with the permission of the Federal Government. Details are regulated by a federal law.

Article 27

All German commercial vessels constitute a (federally) unified merchant fleet.

Article 28

(1) The constitutional order in the Laender must conform to the principles of the republican, democratic and social state based on the rule of law (Rechtsstaat) within the meaning of this Basic Law. In the Laender, Kreise and Gemeinden, the people must be represented by a body created by universal, direct, free, equal, and secret elections. In Gemeinden, the assembly of the Gemeinde may take the place of an elected body.

(2) The Gemeinden must be safeguarded in their right to regulate, under their own responsibility, all the affairs of the local community within the limits of the laws. The Gemeindeverbaende also shall have

[584]

the right of self-government within the legally established scope of their functions and in accordance with the laws.

(3) The Federation guarantees that the constitutional order of the Laender conforms to the basic rights and the provisions of paragraphs (1) and (2).

Article 29

(1) The federal territory is to be reorganized by a federal law with due regard to regional ties, historical and cultural connections, economic expediency and social structure. The reorganization should create Laender which, by their size and potentiality, are able to fulfill efficiently the functions incumbent upon them.

(2) In areas which, at the time of the reorganization of the Laender after 8 May 1945, became part, without popular initiative, of another Land, a specific change of the decision reached concerning this jurisdiction can be demanded by popular initiative within one year of the coming into force of this Basic Law. The popular initiative requires the consent of one-tenth of the population qualified to vote in Landtag elections. Should the popular initiative materialize, the Federal Government must, in the draft law regarding the reorganization, include a provision determining to which Land the area concerned shall belong.

(3) After adoption of the law, that part of the law which concerns an area which it is proposed to join to another Land must in each such area be submitted to a referendum. If, pursuant to paragraph (2), a popular initiative has materialized, a referendum must be held in any case in the area concerned.

(4) Insofar as the law is rejected in at least one area, it must then be reintroduced in the Bundestag. Insofar as it is then re-enacted, it shall to that extent require acceptance by referendum in the entire Federal territory.

(5) In a referendum, the majority of the votes cast is decisive.

(6) The procedure is regulated by a federal law. The reorganization should be concluded before the expiration of three years after promulgation of the Basic Law and, should it be necessary in consequence of the accession of another part of Germany, within two years after such accession.

(7) The procedure regarding any other change in the existing territory of the Laender is regulated by a federal law which shall require the approval of the Bundesrat and of the majority of the members of the Bundestag.

Article 30

The exercise of the powers of the state and the discharge of state functions is the concern of the Laender, insofar as this Basic Law does not otherwise prescribe or permit.

Article 31

Federal law overrides Land Law.

Article 32

(1) The maintenance of relations with foreign states shall be the concern of the Federation.

(2) Before the conclusion of a treaty affecting the special interests of a Land, this Land must be consulted in good time.

(3) Insofar as legislation falls within the competence of the Laender, these may, with the approval of the Federal Government, conclude treaties with foreign states.

Article 33

(1) Every German has in every Land the same civic (staatsbuergerliche) rights and duties.

(2) Every German has equal access to any public office in accordance with his suitability, ability and professional achievements.

(3) Enjoyment of civil and civic rights (buergerliche und staatsbuergerliche Rechte) and access to public offices as well as the rights acquired in the public service, are independent of religious denomination. No one may suffer prejudice on account of his adherence or non-adherence to a denomination or philosophy of life (Weltanschauung).

(4) The exercise of state authority (hoheitsrechtliche Befugnisse) as a permanent function, shall, as a rule be entrusted to members of the public service who are pledged to service and loyalty by public law.

(5) Law regarding the public service shall be regulated with due regard to the traditional principles concerning the status of professional civil servants (Berufsbeamtentum).

Article 34

If any person, in exercising a public office entrusted to him, violates his official duty to a third party, responsibility (liability) rests in principle with the state or the public body which employs that person. In a case of willful intent or gross negligence, the (employing body's) right of recourse (against the civil servant or employee) is reserved. With respect to the claim for compensation of damage and to the right of recourse, the jurisdiction of the ordinary courts must not be excluded.

Article 35

All Federal and Land authorities render each other mutual legal and administrative assistance.

Article 36

Civil servants (Beamte) from all Laender shall be employed by the highest Federal authorities in appropriate ratio. Persons employed with the other Federal authorities should, as a rule, be taken from the Land in which they are employed.

Article 37

(1) If a Land fails to fulfill its obligations towards the Federation under the Basic Law or any other Federal law, the Federal Government

may, with Bundesrat approval, take the necessary measures to force the Land by way of Federal compulsion (Bundeszwang) to fulfill its duties.

(2) For the implementation of federal compulsion, the Federal Government or its commissioner has the right to give instructions to all Laender and their administrative agencies.

III. THE BUNDESTAG

Article 38

(1) Representatives to the German Bundestag are elected by the people in universal, direct, free, equal, and secret elections. They are representatives of the whole people, not bound by orders and instructions, and subject only to their conscience.

(2) Any person who has reached the age of 21 years is entitled to vote, and any person who has reached the age of 25 years may stand for election.

(3) Details are determined by a federal law.

Article 39

(1) The Bundestag is elected for a four-year term. Its legislative term ends four years after its first convention, or with its dissolution. The new election takes place in the last three months of the legislative term or, in case of a dissolution, after sixty days at the latest.

(2) The Bundestag convenes not later than thirty days after the election, but in no case before the end of the legislative term of the previous Bundestag.

(3) The Bundestag determines the closure and resumption of its meetings. The President of the Bundestag may convoke it at an earlier date. He is bound to do so if one-third of the members, the Federal President or the Federal Chancellor so demand.

Article 40

(1) The Bundestag elects its President, his deputies and the secretaries. It draws up its Rules of Procedure.

(2) The President has charge of, and exercises police power in the Bundestag building. No search or seizure may take place in the premises of the Bundestag without his permission.

Article 41

(1) The scrutiny of elections is the responsibility of the Bundestag. It also decides whether a representative has lost his seat in the Bundestag.

(2) An appeal to the Federal Constitutional Court against the decision of the Bundestag is admissible.

(3) Details are regulated by a federal law.

Article 42

(1) The deliberations of the Bundestag are public. Upon a motion of

one-tenth of its members, or upon a motion of the Federal Government, the public may, by a two-thirds majority, be excluded. The motion is decided in a closed meeting.

(2) Decisions of the Bundestag require the majority of votes cast insofar as this Basic Law does not otherwise provide. For the elections to be held by the Bundestag, exceptions in the Rules of Procedure are admissible.

(3) True records of the public meetings of the Bundestag and of its committees do not entail any responsibility.

Article 43

(1) The Bundestag and its committees may demand the presence of any member of the Federal Government.

(2) The members of the Bundesrat and of the Federal Government as well as persons commissioned by them have access to all meetings of the Bundestag and its committees. They must be heard at any time.

Article 44

(1) The Bundestag has the right and, upon the motion of one-fourth of its members, the obligation to set up an investigating committee which shall take the necessary evidence in public proceedings. The public may be excluded.

(2) In principle, the provisions relating to criminal procedure shall essentially apply to the taking of the evidence. Secrecy of the mail, postal services and telecommunications remains unaffected.

(3) The courts and administrative authorities are bound to provide legal and administrative assistance.

(4) The decisions of the investigating committee are not subject to judicial review. The courts are free to appraise and judge the facts on which the investigation is based.

Article 45

(1) The Bundestag appoints a Standing Committee which shall safeguard the rights of the Bundestag in relation to the Federal Government in the interval between two legislative terms. The Standing Committee has also the powers of an investigating committee.

(2) Any wider powers, in particular the right to legislate, to elect the Federal Chancellor, and to impeach the Federal President, are not vested in the Standing Committee.

Article 46

(1) A representative may at no time be proceeded against in the courts or be subjected to disciplinary action or otherwise called to account outside the Bundestag on account of a vote given or an utterance made by him in the Bundestag or one of its committees. This shall not apply in the case of defamatory insults.

(2) A representative may be called to account or arrested for a punish-

able act only with the permission of the Bundestag, unless he be apprehended while committing the act or in the course of the following day.

(3) Furthermore, the permission of the Bundestag is required in respect of any other restriction of the personal freedom of a representative or for the initiation of proceedings pursuant to Article 18 against a representative.

(4) Any criminal proceedings and any proceedings pursuant to Article 18 against a representative, any detention and any other restriction of his personal freedom, shall be suspended upon the demand of the Bundestag.

Article 47

Representatives are entitled to refuse to give evidence concerning persons who have confided facts to them in their capacity as representatives or to whom they have entrusted facts in this capacity, as well as concerning those facts themselves. Within the scope of this right to refuse to give evidence, the seizure of documents is inadmissible.

Article 48

(1) Any person standing for election to the Bundestag is entitled to the leave necessary for the preparation of his election.

(2) No one may be prevented from accepting and exercising the office of representative. Notice of dismissal or dismissal (from employment) for this reason shall be inadmissible.

(3) Representatives are entitled to a remuneration adequate to ensure their independence. They are entitled to free travel in all state-owned transport. Details are regulated by a federal law.

Article 49

Articles 46, 47, and paragraphs (2) and (3) of Article 48 apply to the members of the Presidium and the Standing Committee, as well as to their chief deputies, also in the interval between two legislative terms.

IV. THE BUNDESRAT

Article 50

By means of the Bundesrat, the Laender participate in the federal legislation and administration.

Article 51

(1) The Bundesrat consists of members of the Laender Governments which appoint and recall them. Other members of their Governments may represent them.

(2) Each Land has at least three votes; Laender with more than two million inhabitants have four, Laender with more than six million inhabitants, five votes.

(3) Each Land may delegate as many members as it has votes. The

votes of each Land may be given only as a block vote and only by members present or their substitutes.

Article 52

(1) The Bundesrat elects its President for one year.

(2) The President convokes the Bundesrat. He must convoke it if the members for at least two Laender or the Federal Government so demand.

(3) The decisions of the Bundesrat are taken by at least the majority of its votes. It draws up its Rules of Procedure. It deliberates in public. The public may be excluded.

(4) Other members of the Laender Governments or persons commissioned by Laender Governments may belong to the committees of the Bundesrat.

Article 53

The members of the Federal Government have the right and, on demand, the duty to participate in the deliberations of the Bundesrat and its committees. They must be heard at any time. The Bundesrat must be kept currently informed, by the Federal Government, of the conduct of federal affairs.

V. THE FEDERAL PRESIDENT

Article 54

(1) The Federal President is elected, without debate, by the Federal Convention (Bundesversammlung). Every German is eligible who is entitled to vote for the Bundestag and has reached the age of 40 years.

(2) The term of office of the Federal President is five years. Re-election for a consecutive term is admissible only once.

(3) The Federal Convention consists of the members of the Bundestag and an equal number of members elected by the popular representative bodies of the Laender according to the principle of proportional representation.

(4) The Federal Convention meets not later than thirty days before the expiration of the term of office of the Federal President and, in the case of premature termination, not later than thirty days after this date. It is convoked by the President of the Bundestag.

(5) Upon expiration of the legislative term, the time period provided for in paragraph (4), sentence 1, begins with the first meeting of the Bundestag.

(6) The person receiving the votes of the majority of the members of the Federal Convention is elected. If such majority is not obtained by any candidate in two ballots, the candidate receiving most votes in a further ballot is elected.

(7) Details are regulated by a federal law.

Article 55

(1) The Federal President must not be a member of either the Government or a legislative body of the Federation or a Land.

(2) The Federal President must not hold any other salaried office, nor engage in a trade, nor practice a profession, nor belong to the management or the supervisory board (Aufsichtsrat) of a profit-making enterprise.

Article 56

On assuming office, the Federal President takes the following oath in the presence of the assembled members of the Bundestag and the Bundesrat:

"I swear that I shall dedicate my efforts to the well-being of the German people, enhance its prosperity, protect it from harm, uphold and defend the Basic Law and the laws of the Federation, fulfill my duties conscientiously and do justice to all. So help me God".

The oath may also be taken without the religious asseveration.

Article 57

In the event of the Federal President's being prevented from exercising the authority of his office, or in the event of a premature vacancy in the office, this authority shall be exercised by the President of the Bundesrat.

Article 58

Orders and decrees of the Federal President become valid only when countersigned by the Federal Chancellor or the competent Federal Minister. This does not apply in the case of the appointment and dismissal of the Federal Chancellor, of the dissolution of the Bundestag pursuant to Article 63, and of the request pursuant to Article 69, paragraph (3).

Article 59

(1) The Federal President represents the Federation in matters concerning international law. He concludes treaties with foreign states on behalf of the Federation. He accredits and receives envoys.

(2) Treaties which regulate the political relations of the Federation or refer to matters of federal legislation require, in the form of a federal law, the approval or the participation of the respective bodies competent for federal legislation. For administrative agreements the provisions concerning the federal administration apply correspondingly.

Article 60

(1) Unless otherwise provided by law, the Federal President appoints and dismisses the federal judges and the federal civil servants.

(2) In individual cases, he exercises the right of pardon on behalf of the Federation.

(3) He may delegate these powers to other authorities.

(4) Paragraphs (2) to (4) of Article 46 apply to the Federal President correspondingly.

Article 61

(1) The Bundestag or the Bundesrat may impeach the Federal President before the Federal Constitutional Court for willful violation of the Basic Law or any other federal law. The motion for impeachment must be introduced by at least one-fourth of the members of the Bundestag or one-fourth of the votes of the Bundesrat. The decision to impeach requires a majority of two-thirds of the members of the Bundestag or of two-thirds of the votes of the Bundesrat. The prosecution is conducted by a person commissioned by the impeaching body.

(2) If the Federal Constitutional Court finds the Federal President guilty of a willful violation of the Basic Law or of any other federal law, it may declare him to have forfeited his office. Upon institution of impeachment proceedings, the Federal Constitutional Court may, by interim order, rule that the Federal President shall be debarred from exercising the authority of his office.

VI. THE FEDERAL GOVERNMENT

Article 62

The Federal Government consists of the Federal Chancellor and the Federal Ministers.

Article 63

(1) The Federal Chancellor is elected, without debate, by the Bundestag on the proposal of the Federal President.

(2) The person obtaining the majority of votes of the Bundestag members is elected. He is to be appointed by the Federal President.

(3) If the person proposed (for appointment) is not elected, the Bundestag may, within fourteen days after the ballot, elect a Federal Chancellor by more than one half of its members.

(4) If the Federal Chancellor is not elected within this time period, a new ballot shall take place without delay, in which the person receiving the greatest number of votes shall be elected. If the person elected obtains the votes of the majority of the Bundestag members, the Federal President must, within seven days of the election, appoint him. If the person elected does not obtain this majority, the Federal President must, within seven days, either appoint him or dissolve the Bundestag.

Article 64

(1) The Federal Ministers are appointed and dismissed by the Federal President upon the proposal of the Federal Chancellor.

(2) The Federal Chancellor and the Federal Ministers, on assuming office, take before the Bundestag the oath provided in Article 56.

Article 65

The Federal Chancellor determines, and assumes responsibility for, general policy. Within the limits of this general policy, each Federal Minister conducts the business of his department independently and on his own responsibility. The Federal Government decides on differences of opinion between the Federal Ministers. The Federal Chancellor conducts the business of the Federal Government in accordance with Rules of Procedure adopted by it and approved by the Federal President.

Article 66

The Federal Chancellor and the Federal Ministers may not hold any other salaried office, nor engage in a trade nor practise a profession nor belong to the management or, without Bundestag approval, to the supervisory board (Aufsichtsrat) of a profitmaking enterprise.

Article 67

(1) The Bundestag may express its lack of confidence in the Federal Chancellor only by electing, by the majority of its members, a successor and by submitting a request to the Federal President for the dismissal of the Federal Chancellor. The Federal President must comply with the request and appoint the person elected.

(2) There must be an interval of forty-eight hours between the motion and the election.

Article 68

(1) If a motion of Federal Chancellor for a vote of confidence does not obtain the support of the majority of the members of the Bundestag, the Federal President may, upon the proposal of the Federal Chancellor, dissolve the Bundestag within twenty-one days. The right to dissolve lapses as soon as the Bundestag, with the majority of its members, elects another Federal Chancellor.

(2) There must be an interval of forty-eight hours between the introduction of the motion and the vote thereon.

Article 69

(1) The Federal Chancellor appoints a Federal Minister as his deputy.

(2) The Federal Chancellor's or a Federal Minister's tenure of office ends in any case with the convening of a new Bundestag; a Federal Minister's tenure of office ends also with any other termination of the tenure of office of the Federal Chancellor.

(3) At the request of the Federal President, the Federal Chancellor or, at the request of the Federal Chancellor or of the Federal President, a Federal Minister, is bound to continue to transact the business of his office until the appointment of his successor.

VII. THE LEGISLATION OF THE FEDERATION

Article 70

(1) The Laender have the power to legislate insofar as this Basic Law does vest legislative powers in the Federation.

(2) The delimitation of competence between the Federation and the Laender is determined in accordance with the provisions of this Basic Law concerning exclusive and concurrent legislation.

Article 71

In the field of exclusive legislation of the Federation, the Laender have the power to legislate only if, and insofar as, they are expressly so empowered by a federal law.

Article 72

(1) In the field of concurrent legislation, the Laender have the power to legislate as long as, and insofar as, the Federation makes no use of its legislative power.

(2) The Federation has legislative power in this field insofar as a need for regulation by federal law exists because:

1. a matter cannot be effectively regulated by the legislation of individual Laender, or
2. the regulation of a matter by a Land law might prejudice the interest of other Laender or of the community at large, or
3. the preservation of legal or economic unity demands it, in particular the preservation of uniformity of living conditions beyond the territory of an individual Land.

Article 73

The Federation has exclusive legislation on:

1. foreign affairs;
2. citizenship in the Federation;
3. freedom of movement, passports, immigration and emigration and extradition;
4. currency, money and coinage, weights and measures and regulation of time and calendar;
5. the unity of the territory as regards customs and commercial purposes, commercial and navigation agreements, the freedom of traffic in goods, and the exchanges of goods and payments with foreign countries, including customs and border control;
6. federal railways and air traffic;
7. postal services and telecommunications;
8. the legal status of persons in the service of the Federation and of public law corporations directly controlled by the Federal Government;
9. industrial property rights (including patents and trade marks), author's copyrights and publisher's copyrights;

10. co-operation of the Federation and the Laender in the field of criminal police and in matters concerning the protection of the Constitution, the establishment of a Federal Office of Criminal Police, as well as international prevention and repression of crime;
11. statistics for federal purposes.

Article 74

Concurrent legislation extends over the following fields:

1. Civil law, criminal law and execution of sentences, the constitution of courts and their procedure, the Bar, notaries and legal advice (Rechtsberatung);
2. census and registry matters;
3. law pertaining to associations and assemblies;
4. the right of sojourn and of settlement of aliens;
5. the protection of German works of art and of cultural (historic) significance against removal abroad;
6. matters relating to refugees and expellees;
7. public welfare;
8. citizenship in the Laender;
9. war damage and compensation (Wiedergutmachung);
10. assistance to war-disabled persons and to surviving dependents, the care of former prisoners of war and the care of war graves;
11. law relating to the economy (mining, industry, power supply, crafts, trades, commerce, banking and stock exchange, insurance to which civil and not public law applies);
12. labor law, including the legal organization of enterprises, the protection of workers and provision of employment, as well as social insurance, including unemployment insurance;
13. the furtherance of scientific research;
14. law regarding expropriation insofar as it is concerned with the matters enumerated in Articles 73 and 74;
15. transfer of land and real estate, natural resources and means of production to public ownership or to other forms of publicly controlled economy;
16. prevention of the abuse of economic power;
17. furtherance of agricultural and forestry production, safeguarding of food supply, import and export of agricultural and forestry products, deep-sea and coastal fishing and the guarding and preservation of the coasts;
18. transactions in real estate, law concerning land and matters concerning agricultural leases, housing, settlements and homesteads;
19. measures against, epidemic and infectious diseases affecting human beings and animals, the admission to medical and other healing professions and healing practices and the traffic in drugs, medicines, narcotics and poisons;
20. protection concerning traffic in food and stimulants as well as in

necessities of life, in fodder, in agricultural and forestry seeds and seedlings, and protection of trees and plants against diseases and pests;

21. ocean and coastal shipping and aids to navigation, inland shipping, meteorological services, sea waterways, and inland waterways used for general traffic;
22. road traffic, motorized transport and the construction and maintenance of highways used for long-distance traffic;
23. railroads other than federal railroads, except mountain railroads.

Article 75

Within the conditions set forth in Article 72, the Federation has the right to issue general provisions concerning:
1. The legal status of persons employed in the public service of the Laender, Gemeinden and other public law corporations;
2. the general law to govern the press and motion pictures;
3. hunting, the preservation of nature and the care of the countryside;
4. land distribution, regional planning and water conservation;
5. matters relating to registration and identity cards.

Article 76

(1) Bills are introduced in the Bundestag by the Federal Government, by members of the Bundestag or by the Bundesrat.

(2) Bills of the Federal Government are to be submitted first to the Bundesrat. The Bundesrat is entitled to give its opinion on these bills within three weeks.

(3) Bills of the Bundesrat are to be submitted to the Bundestag by the Federal Government, which must add a statement of its own views.

Article 77

(1) Federal laws are passed by the Bundestag. After their adoption, they shall, without delay, be submitted to the Bundesrat by the President of the Bundestag.

(2) The Bundesrat may, within two weeks of the receipt of the adopted bill, demand that a committee composed of members of the Bundestag and Bundesrat be convoked to consider the bill jointly. The composition and the procedure of this committee is regulated by Rules of Procedure which shall be agreed by the Bundestag and shall require the approval of the Bundesrat. The members of the Bundesrat delegated to this committee are not bound by instructions. If the approval of the Bundesrat is required for a law, both the Bundestag and the Federal Government may demand the convocation of the committee. Should the committee propose amendments to the adopted bill, a new vote must be taken by the Bundestag.

(3) Insofar as the approval of the Bundesrat is not required for a law, the Bundesrat may, if proceedings pursuant to paragraph (2) are completed, veto within one week a law passed by the Bundestag. The time period for a veto begins in the case of paragraph (2), last sentence, with the receipt of the bill as readopted by the Bundestag; in all other cases, with the conclusion of the proceedings before the committee provided for in paragraph (2).

(4) Should the veto be adopted by a majority of the Bundesrat votes, it may be rejected by the decision of a majority of the Bundestag members. If the Bundesrat has adopted the veto by at least a two-thirds majority of its votes, the rejection by the Bundestag shall require a majority of two-thirds, and at least the majority of the members of the Bundestag.

Article 78

A law adopted by the Bundestag is deemed to have been passed if the Bundesrat approves it, does not introduce a motion pursuant to Article 77, paragraph (2), does not impose a veto within the time period provided by Article 77, paragraph (3), or withdraws its veto; or, if the veto is overridden by the Bundestag.

Article 79

(1) The Basic Law may be amended only by a law expressly amending or amplifying the text of the Basic Law.

(2) Such a law requires the approval of two-thirds of the Bundestag members and two-thirds of the Bundesrat votes.

(3) An amendment to this Basic Law affecting the organization of the Federation into Laender, the basic participation of the Laender in legislation, or the basic principles laid down in Articles 1 and 20, is inadmissible.

Article 80

(1) The Federal Government, a Federal Minister or the Land Governments may be empowered by a law to issue decrees having the force of law (Rechtsverordnungen). In such cases, the contents, purpose and scope of such powers must be specified in the law. The legal basis must be cited in the decree. If a law provides that such power may be further delegated, such delegation shall require a decree having the force of law (Rechtsverordnung).

(2) Bundesrat approval is required, unless otherwise provided by federal legislation, for decrees having the force of law (Rechtsverordnungen) issued by the Federal Government or a Federal Minister, concerning basic principles and charges for the use of facilities of the federal railroads, of the postal services and of telecommunications, concerning the construction and operation of railroads, as well as for decrees having the force of law (Rechtsverordnungen) issued on the basis of federal laws which require Bundesrat approval or which are executed by the Laender on behalf of the Federation or as matters of their own concern.

Article 81

(1) Should the Bundestag not be dissolved as provided for in Article 68, the Federal President may, at the request of the Federal Government and with Bundesrat approval, declare a state of legislative emergency with respect to a bill, if the Bundestag rejects the bill although the Federal Government has declared it to be urgent. The same applies if a bill has been rejected although the Federal Chancellor had combined with it the motion provided for in Article 68.

(2) If the Bundestag, after a state of legislative emergency has been declared, again rejects the bill or passes it in a version declared to be unacceptable to the Federal Government, the law shall be deemed passed provided that the Bundesrat approves it. The same applies if the bill has not been passed by the Bundestag within four weeks after its reintroduction.

(3) During the term of office of a Federal Chancellor, any other bill rejected by the Bundestag may be passed within a period of six months after the first declaration of a state of legislative emergency in accordance with paragraphs (1) and (2). After expiration of this period, a further declaration of a state of legislative emergency is inadmissible during the term of office of the same Federal Chancellor.

(4) The Basic Law must neither be amended nor wholly or partially repealed or suspended by a law enacted pursuant to paragraph (2).

Article 82

(1) Laws enacted in accordance with the provisions of this Basic Law shall, after countersignature, be engrossed by the Federal President and published in the Federal Gazette. Decrees having the force of law (Rechtsverordnungen) shall be signed by the issuing authority and, unless otherwise provided by law, published in the Federal Gazette.

(2) Every law and every decree having the force of law (Rechtsverordnungen) should specify the date of its becoming effective. In the absence of such a provision, it shall become effective on the fourteenth day after the end of the day on which the Federal Gazette was issued.

VIII.   THE EXECUTION OF FEDERAL LAWS AND THE FEDERAL ADMINISTRATION

Article 83

The Laender execute the federal laws as matters of their own concern insofar as this Basic Law does not otherwise provide or permit.

Article 84

(1) If the Laender execute the federal laws as matters of their own concern, they determine the establishment of authorities and adminis-

trative procedures insofar as federal laws approved by the Bundesrat do not otherwise provide.

(2) The Federal Government may, with Bundesrat approval, issue general administrative provisions.

(3) The Federal Government exercises supervision to ensure that the Laender execute the federal laws in accordance with the legislation in force. For this purpose the Federal Government may send commissioners to the highest Land authorities and, with their approval or, if this approval is refused, with Bundesrat approval, also to subordinate authorities.

(4) Should shortcomings in the execution of Federal Laws which the Federal Government has found to exist in the Laender not be corrected, the Bundesrat shall decide, upon request of the Federal Government or of the Land, whether the Land has infringed the law. A decision of the Bundesrat may be challenged in the Federal Constitutional Court.

(5) For the execution of federal laws the Federal Government may, by federal legislation requiring Bundesrat approval, be granted the power to give individual instructions in special cases. They are, except if the Federal Government considers a case to be urgent, to be addressed to the highest Land authorities.

Article 85

(1) Where the Laender execute the federal laws on behalf of the Federation, the establishment of the administrative agencies remains a concern of the Laender insofar as federal legislation approved by the Bundesrat does not otherwise provide.

(2) The Federal Government may issue, with Bundesrat approval, general administrative provisions. It may regulate the uniform training of civil servants (Beamte) and government employees (Angestellte). The heads of the administrative agencies at intermediate level shall be appointed with its agreement.

(3) The Land authorities are subject to the instructions of the competent highest federal authorities. Except if the Federal Government considers the matter urgent, the instructions are to be addressed to the highest Land authorities. Execution of the instructions is to be ensured by the highest Land authorities.

(4) Federal supervision extends to the legality and suitability of the manner of execution. The Federal Government may, for this purpose, require the submission of reports and documents and send commissioners to all authorities.

Article 86

Where the Federation executes the laws by direct federal administration or through public law corporations or institutions directly under the Federation, the Federal Goverment issues, insofar as the Law does not make any special provisions, general administrative provisions. It determines, insofar as it is not otherwise provided by the law, the establishment of the administrative agencies.

Article 87

(1) The foreign service, the federal finance administration, the federal railroads, the federal postal services and, in accordance with the provisions of Article 89, the administration of the federal waterways and shipping are conducted as integral parts of the federal administration with their own subordinate administrative offices. Federal border control authorities and central offices for police information and communications, for the compilation of data for the purpose of protecting the Constitution, and for the criminal police may be established by federal legislation.

(2) Social insurance institutions, the sphere of competence of which extends beyond the territory of a Land, are conducted as public law corporations directly under the Federation.

(3) In addition, independent central federal administrative agencies and new public law corporations and institutions directly under the Federation may be established by federal legislation for matters on which the Federation has the power to legislate. Should new functions arise for the Federation in matters in respect to which it has legislative competence, federal administrative agencies at intermediate and lower levels may, in case of urgent need, be established with the approval of the Bundesrat and of the majority of the Bundestag.

Article 88

The Federation establishes a bank of issues as a federal bank.

Article 89

(1) The Federation is the owner of the former Reich waterways.

(2) The Federation administers the Federal waterways through its own agencies. It exercises those state functions relating to inland shipping which extend beyond the territory of a Land and the functions relating to sea-going shipping which are conferred on it by legislation. Upon request, the Federation may delegate the administration of federal waterways, insofar as they lie within the territory of a Land, to this Land, in administration by commission (Auftragsverwaltung). Should a waterway touch the territories of several Laender, the Federation may delegate the administration of it to the Land which is proposed in a request submitted by the Laender concerned.

(3) In the administration, development and construction of waterways, the requirements of soil cultivation and of water conservation shall be safeguarded in agreement with the Laender.

Article 90

(1) The Federation is the owner of the former Reich Autobahn (auto-highways) and Reich highways.

(2) The Laender, or such self-governing corporations as are competent under Land public law, administer on behalf of the Federation the

federal Autobahnen (auto-highways) and other federal highways used for long-distance traffic.

(3) At the request of a Land, the Federation may take under direct federal administration federal Autobahnen (auto-highways) and other federal highways used for long-distance traffic, insofar as they lie within the territory of the Land.

Article 91

(1) In order to avert any imminent danger to the existence or the free democratic basic order of the federation or of a Land, a Land may appeal for the services of the police forces of other Laender.

(2) If the Land in which this danger is imminent is not itself prepared or in a position to combat the danger, the Federal Government may place the police in that Land and the police forces of other Laender under its instructions. This order (Anordnung) has to be rescinded after the elimination of the danger otherwise at any time on the demand of the Bundesrat.

IX. THE ADMINISTRATION OF JUSTICE

Article 92

Judicial authority is vested in the judges; it is exercised by the Federal Constitutional Court, by the Supreme Federal Court, by the federal courts provided for in this Basic Law and by the courts of the Laender.

Article 93

(1) The Federal Constitutional Court decides:
1. on the interpretation of this Basic Law in the event of disputes concerning the extent of the rights and duties of any of the highest federal agencies or of other parties granted independent rights by this Basic Law or by Rules of Procedure of the highest federal agencies;
2. in case of differences of opinion or doubts as to the formal and material compatibility of federal law or Land law with this Basic Law or on the compatibility of Land law with other federal law, at the request of the Federal Government, of a Land Government or of one-third of the Bundestag members;
3. in case of differences of opinion on the rights and duties of the Federation and the Laender, particularly in the execution of federal law by the Laender, and in the exercise of federal supervision;
4. on other public law disputes between the Federation and the Laender, between different Laender or within a Land, insofar as recourse to another court is not provided for;
5. in all other cases provided for in this Basic Law.

(2) Furthermore, the Federal Constitutional Court shall act in such cases as are otherwise assigned to it by federal legislation.

Article 94

(1) The Federal Constitutional Court consists of federal judges and other members. Half of the members of the Federal Constitutional Court are elected by the Bundestag and half by the Bundesrat. They may not belong to the Bundestag, the Bundesrat, the Federal Government or corresponding agencies of a Land.

(2) A federal law determines the constitution and procedure of the Federal Constitutional Court and specifies in what cases its decisions shall have the force of law.

Article 95

(1) A Supreme Federal Court is established for the maintenance of the unity of federal law.

(2) The Supreme Federal Court decides cases in which the decision is of fundamental importance for the uniformity of the administration of justice by the high federal courts.

(3) The appointment of the judges of the Supreme Federal Court is decided jointly by the Federal Minister of Justice and a committee for the selection of judges consisting of the Land ministers of Justice and an equal number of members elected by the Bundestag.

(4) In other respects, the constitution of the Supreme Federal Court and its procedures are regulated by federal legislation.

Article 96

(1) High federal courts shall be established in the spheres of ordinary, administrative, finance, labor and social jurisdiction.

(2) Article 95, paragraph (3), applies to the judges of the high federal courts with the proviso that the Federal Minister of Justice and the Land Ministers of Justice shall be substituted by the Ministers competent in the particular matter. Their service status must be regulated by a special federal law.

(3) The Federation may establish federal disciplinary courts for disciplinary proceedings against federal civil servants and federal judges.

Article 97

(1) Judges are independent and subject only to the law.

(2) Judges definitively appointed on a full-time basis to established court offices may, against their will, be dismissed before the expiration of their term of office, or permanently or temporarily suspended from office or transferred to another position or placed on the retired list, only by the decision of a court and only on grounds and according to the procedures provided for by law. Legislation may set age limits for the retirement of judges who have been appointed for life. In the case of changes

in the structure of the courts or their area of jurisdiction, judges may be transferred to another court or suspended from office with the retention, however, of their full salary.

Article 98

(1) The legal status of the federal judges is to be regulated by a special federal law.

(2) If a federal judge, in his official capacity or unofficially, infringes on the principles of the Basic Law or the constitutional order of a Land, the Federal Constitutional Court may, upon request of the Bundestag, rule, with a two-thirds majority, that the judge be transferred to another office or placed on the retired list. In a case of willful infringement, dismissal may also be ordered.

(3) The legal status of the judges in the Laender is to be regulated by special Land legislation. The Federation may issue general provisions.

(4) The Laender may determine that the Land Minister of Justice shall, together with a committee for the selection of judges, decide on the appointment of judges in the Laender.

(5) The Laender may, in conformity with paragraph (2) provide a regulation for Land judges. Land constitutional law in force remains unaffected. The decision concerning a case of impeachment of a judge rests with the Federal Constitutional Court.

Article 99

The decision on constitutional disputes within a Land may be assigned by Land legislation to the Federal Constitutional Court, and the decision of last instance, on such matters as involve the application of Land law, to the high federal courts.

Article 100

(1) If a court considers unconstitutional a law the validity of which is pertinent to its decision, proceedings must be stayed and, if a violation of a Land Constitution is at issue, the decision of the Land court competent for constitutional disputes shall be obtained and, if a violation of this Basic Law is at issue, the decision of the Federal Constitutional Court shall be obtained. This also applies if the violation of this Basic Law by Land law or the incompatibility of a Land law with a federal law is at issue.

(2) If, in litigation, it is doubtful whether a rule of international law forms part of federal law and whether it directly creates rights and duties for the individual (Article 25), the court has to obtain the decision of the Federal Constitutional Court.

(3) If the constitutional court of a Land, in interpreting the Basic Law, intends to deviate from a decision of the Federal Constitutional Court or of the constitutional court of another Land, the (said) constitutional court must obtain the decision of the Federal Constitutional Court. If, in in-

terpreting other federal law, it intends to deviate from the decision of the Supreme Federal Court or a high federal court, it must obtain the decision of the Supreme Federal Court.

Article 101

(1) Extraordinary courts are inadmissible. No one may be removed from the jurisdiction of his lawful judge.

(2) Courts dealing with matters in special fields may be established only by law.

Article 102

The death sentence is abolished.

Article 103

(1) Everyone is entitled to a proper hearing before the courts.

(2) An act may be punished only if the Law defined it as punishable before it was committed.

(3) On the basis of the general criminal laws, no one may be punished for the same act more than once.

Article 104

(1) The freedom of the individual may be restricted only on the basis of a formal law and only with due regard to the forms prescribed therein. Detained persons may be subjected neither to mental nor physical ill-treatment.

(2) Only a judge is (entitled) to decide on the admissibility and extension of a deprivation of liberty. In the case of every such deprivation which is not based on the order of a judge, a judicial decision must be obtained without delay. The police may, on its own authority, hold no one in its own custody beyond the end of the day following the arrest. Further details are to be regulated by law.

(3) Any person temporarily detained on suspicion of having committed a punishable act must, at the latest on the day following the detention, be brought before a judge who shall inform him of the reasons for the detention, interrogate him and give him an opportunity to raise objections. The judge must, without delay, either issue a warrant of arrest, setting out the reasons thereof, or order the release.

(4) A relative of the person detained or a person enjoying his confidence must be notified without delay of any judicial decision ordering or extending a deprivation of liberty.

X. FINANCE

Article 105

(1) The Federation has exclusive legislation on customs and fiscal monopolies.

(2) The Federation has concurrent legislation on:

1. excise taxes and taxes on transactions, with the exception of taxes with localized application, in particular the taxes on real estate acquisition, incremental value and fire protection;
2. the taxes on income, property inheritance and donations;
3. taxes on real estate and on businesses (Realsteuern), with the exception of the fixing of tax rates;

if it claims the taxes in their entirety or in part to cover federal expenditures, or if the conditions set forth in Article 72, paragraph (2), exist.

(3) Federal legislation on taxes the yield of which accrues in their entirety or in part to the Laender or the Gemeinden (Gemeindeverbaende) require Bundesrat approval.

Article 106

(1) Customs, the yield of monopolies, the excise taxes with the exception of the beer tax, the transportation tax, the turnover tax and levies on property serving non-recurrent purposes accrue to the Federation.

(2) The beer tax, the taxes on transactions with the exception of the transportation tax and turnover tax, the income and corporation taxes, the property tax, the inheritance tax, the taxes on real estate and on businesses (Realsteuern) and the taxes with localized application accrue to the Laender and, in accordance with provisions of Land legislation, to the Gemeinden (Gemeindeverbaende).

(3) The Federation may, by means of a federal law requiring Bundesrat approval, claim a part of the income and corporation taxes to cover its expenditures not covered by other revenues, in particular to cover grants which are to be made to Laender to meet expenditures in the fields of education, public health and welfare.

(4) In order to ensure the working efficiency also of the Laender with low tax revenues and to equalize the differing burdens of expenditure of the Laender, the Federation may make grants and take the funds necessary for this purpose from specific taxes accruing to the Laender. A federal law, requiring Bundesrat approval, shall determine which taxes shall be utilized for this purpose and in what amounts and on what basis the grants shall be distributed among the Laender entitled to equalization; the grants must be transferred directly to the Laender.

Article 107

The final distribution, as between the Federation and the Laender, of the taxes subject to concurrent legislation shall be effected not later than 31 December 1952 and by means of a federal law requiring Bundesrat approval. This does not apply to the taxes on real estate and on businesses (Realsteuern), and the taxes with localized application. Thereby, each party should be assigned a legal claim to certain taxes or shares in taxes commensurate to their tasks.

Article 108

(1) Customs, fiscal monopolies, the excise taxes subject to concurrent legislation, the transportation tax, the turnover tax and the non-recurrent levies on property are administered by federal finance authorities. The organization of these authorities and the procedure to be applied by them are regulated by federal legislation. The heads of the authorities at intermediate level shall be appointed in agreement with the Land Governments. The Federation may delegate the administration of the non-recurrent levies on property to the Land finance authorities as administration by commission (Auftragsverwaltung).

(2) Where the Federation claims part of the income and corporation taxes it shall thus far administer them; it may, however, delegate the administration to the Land finance authorities as administration by commission (Auftragsverwaltung).

(3) The remaining taxes are administered by Land finance authorities. The Federation may, by federal legislation requiring Bundesrat approval, regulate the organization of these authorities, the procedure to be applied by them and the uniform training of the civil servants. The heads of the authorities at intermediate level must be appointed in agreement with the Federal Government. The administration of the taxes accruing to the Gemeinden (Gemeindeverbaende) may be delegated by the Laender in entirety or in part to the Gemeinden (Gemeindeverbaende).

(4) Insofar as taxes accrue to the Federation, the Land finance authorities shall act on behalf of the Federation. The Laender are liable with their revenues for an orderly administration of these taxes; the Federal Minister of Finance may supervise the orderly administration through authorized federal agents who have the right to give instructions to the authorities at intermediate and lower levels.

(5) The jurisdiction of Finance Courts shall be uniformly regulated by federal legislation.

(6) The general administrative provisions shall be issued by the Federal Government and, insofar as the administration is incumbent upon the Land finance authorities, will require Bundesrat approval.

Article 109

The Federation and the Laender are self supporting and mutually independent with regard to their respective budgets.

Article 110

(1) All revenues and expenditures of the Federation must be estimated for each fiscal year and included in the budget.

(2) The budget shall be established by law before the beginning of the fiscal year. Revenue and expenditure must be balanced. Expenditures shall, as a rule, be approved for one year; in special cases, they may be approved for a longer period. Otherwise, the federal budget law may contain no provisions which extend beyond the fiscal year or which do not

concern the revenues and expenditures of the Federation or its administration.

(3) The assets and liabilities shall be set forth in an appendix to the budget.

(4) In the case of federal enterprises commercially operated, only the final result, and not the detailed revenues and expenditures, need be included in the budget.

Article 111

(1) If, by the end of a fiscal year, the budget for the following year has not been established by law, the Federal Government shall, until such a law comes into force, be empowered to effect such payments as are necessary:

(a) to maintain existing institutions established by law and to carry out measures adopted by law;

(b) to meet legal obligations of the Federation;

(c) to continue building projects, procurements and other services, or to grant further subsidies for these purposes, provided that funds have already been approved in the budget of a previous year.

(2) Insofar as revenues, provided by special legislation and derived from taxes, dues and other sources, or working capital reserves do not cover the expenditures mentioned under paragraph (1), the Federal Government may, by way of credits, procure the funds, up to one-fourth of the total amount of the previous budget, which are necessary to conduct current operations.

Article 112

Expenditures exceeding the budget and any extraordinary expenditures require the approval of the Federal Minister of Finance. It may only be given in case of unforeseen and compelling necessity.

Article 113

Decisions of the Bundestag and Bundesrat which increase the budget expenditure proposed by the Federal Government, or include or imply new expenditures for the future, require the approval of the Federal Government.

Article 114

(1) The Federal Minister of Finance must submit to the Bundestag and the Bundesrat an annual account of all revenues and expenditures as well as of assets and liabilities.

(2) This account shall be audited by an Audit Office (Rechnungshof) the members of which shall enjoy judicial independence. The general account and a survey of the assets and liabilities have to be submitted to the Bundestag and the Bundesrat in the course of the following fiscal year, together with the comments of the Audit Office, in order to secure a

discharge (Entlastung) for the Federal Government. The auditing of accounts shall be regulated by a federal law.

Article 115

Funds may be obtained by way of credits only in the case of extraordinary requirements and as a rule only for expenditure for productive purposes and only on the basis of a federal law. The granting of credits and providing of securities as a charge on the Federation, the effect of which extends beyond the fiscal year, may be undertaken only on the basis of a federal law. The amount of the credits or the extent of the obligation for which the Federation assumes liability must be determined in the law.

XI. TRANSITIONAL AND CONCLUDING PROVISIONS

Article 116

(1) Unless otherwise provided by law, a German within the meaning of this Basic Law is a person who possesses German citizenship or who has been accepted in the territory of the German Reich, as it existed on 31 December 1937, as a refugee or expellee of German ethnic stock (Volkszugehoerigkeit) or as the spouse or descendent of such person.

(2) Former German citizens, who, between 30 January 1933 and 8 May 1945, were deprived of their citizenship for political, racial or religious reasons, and their descendents, shall be regranted German citizenship on application. They are considered as not having been deprived of their German citizenship if they have taken up residence in Germany after 8 May 1945 and have not expressed a desire to the contrary.

Article 117

(1) Legislation which conflicts with Article 3, paragraph (2), remains in force pending harmonization with this provision of the Basic Law, but not beyond 31 March 1953.

(2) Laws restricting the right of freedom of movement, by reason of the present housing and space shortage (Raumnot), remain in force until repealed by federal legislation.

Article 118

The reorganization of the territory comprising the Laender Baden, Wuerttemberg-Baden and Wuerttemberg-Hohenzollern may be effected, by agreement between the Laender concerned, in a manner deviating from the provisions of Article 29. Failing agreement, the reorganization shall be regulated by federal legislation which must provide for a referendum.

Article 119

In matters relating to refugees and expellees, in particular as regards their distribution among the Laender, the Federal Government may, with Bundesrat approval, issue decrees having the force of law (Verordnungen mit Gesetzeskraft), pending a settlement of the matter by federal legislation. In special cases, the Federal Government may be empowered to issue individual instructions. Except in case of danger in delay the instructions are to be addressed to the highest Land authorities.

Article 120

(1) In accordance with more detailed provisions of a federal law, the Federation bears the expenses for occupation costs and the other internal and external burdens caused by war, and for the subsidies to (alleviate) the burdens of social insurance, including unemployment insurance, and public assistance for the unemployed.

(2) The revenues are transferred to the Federation at the same time as the Federation assumes responsibility for the expenditures.

Article 121

Within the meaning of this Basic Law, a majority of the members of the Bundestag and of the Federal Convention (Bundesversammlung) is the majority of the statutory number of their members.

Article 122

(1) As from the convening of the Bundestag, laws shall be passed exclusively by the legislative authorities recognized in this Basic Law.

(2) Where the competence of legislative bodies and of bodies participating in legislation in an advisory capacity ends in accordance with paragraph (1), such bodies shall be dissolved as of the same date.

Article 123

(1) Law in existence prior to the (first) convening of the Bundestag remains in effect, insofar as it does not conflict with the Basic Law.

(2) The state treaties concluded by the German Reich concerning matters for which, under this Basic Law, Land legislation is competent, remain in force if they are valid and continue to be valid in accordance with general principles of law, subject to all rights and objections of the interested parties, pending the conclusion of new state treaties by the authorities competent under this Basic Law or until they are otherwise terminated pursuant to the provisions that they contain.

Article 124

Legislation concerning matters within the exclusive legislative competence of the Federation shall become federal law within the area of its application.

Article 125

Legislation concerning matters of concurrent federal legislation shall become federal law within the area of its application

1. insofar as it uniformly applies within one or more zones of occupation,
2. insofar as it concerns legislation by which former Reich law has been amended since 8 May 1945.

Article 126

Differences of opinion concerning the continuing validity of legislation as federal law are settled by the Federal Constitutional Court.

Article 127

Within one year of the promulgation of this Basic Law, the Federal Government may, with the approval of the Government of the Laender concerned, extend, to the Laender Baden, Greater Berlin, Rhineland-Palatinate and Wuerttemberg-Hohenzollern, legislation of the Bizonal Economic Administration insofar as it continues to be in force as federal legislation under Articles 124 or 125.

Article 128

Insofar as legislation continuing in force provides for powers to give instructions within the meaning of Article 84, paragraph (5), these powers remain in effect until otherwise provided by law.

Article 129

(1) Insofar as legal provisions continuing in force as federal law contain an authorization to issue decrees having the force of law (Rechtsverordnung) or general administrative provisions, and to perform administrative acts, this authorization passes to the (administrative) agencies henceforth competent in such matters. In cases of doubt, the Federal Government decides in agreement with the Bundesrat; the decision must be published.

(2) Insofar as legal provisions continuing in force as Land law contain such an authorization, it shall be exercised by the (administrative) agencies competent according to Land law.

(3) Insofar as legal provisions within the meaning of paragraphs (1) and (2) authorize their amendment or amplification or the issue of legal provisions in lieu of laws, these authorizations have expired.

(4) The provisions of paragraphs (1) and (2) apply correspondingly whenever legal provisions refer to regulations no longer valid or to institutions no longer in existence.

Article 130

(1) Administrative agencies and other institutions which serve the public administration or the administration of justice and are not based on Land law or state treaties between Laender, as well as the amalgamated management of the South West German railroads and the Administrative Council for the postal services and telecommunications of the French Zone of Occupation, are placed under the Federal Government. The latter, with Bundesrat approval, regulates their transfer, dissolution or liquidation.

(2) The highest disciplinary authority over the personnel of these administrations and establishments is the competent Federal Minister.

(3) Public Law corporations and institutions not directly under a Land, and not based on state treaties between Laender, are under the supervision of the competent highest federal authority.

Article 131

The legal status of persons, including refugees and expellees, who on 8 May 1945, were employed in the public service and who have left service for reasons other than those based on legal provisions concerning civil service or agreed employment regulations (Tariff), and who till now have not been employed or are not employed in a position corresponding to their former position, is to be regulated by federal legislation. The same applies to persons, including refugees and expellees, who, on 8 May 1945, were entitled to a pension or other assistance and who no longer receive any assistance or any adequate assistance for reasons other than those based on legal provisions concerning civil service or agreed employment regulations (Tariff). Pending the coming into force of the federal law, no legal claims may be made, unless otherwise provided by Land legislation.

Article 132

(1) Civil servants (Beamte) and judges who, at the coming into force of this Basic Law, hold appointments for life may, within six months after the first convening of the Bundestag, be placed on the retired list or waiting list or be transferred to another office with lower remuneration, if they are personally or professionally unsuitable for their office. This provision applies correspondingly also to government employees (Angestellte) whose service cannot be terminated by notice of dismissal. In the case of government employees (Angestellte) whose service conditions provide for termination by notice of dismissal, the period of notice exceeding that required by agreed rules of employment (Regelung) may be cancelled within the same period (of six months).

(2) These provisions do not apply to members of the public service who are not affected by the provision regarding the "liberation from national socialism and militarism" or who are recognized victims of national socialism, insofar as no serious grounds are to be found in their character.

(3) Persons affected (by the above) have recourse to the courts in accordance with Article 19, paragraph (4).

(4) Details are determined by a decree (Verordnung) of the Federal Government, requiring Bundesrat approval.

Article 133

The Federation succeeds to the rights and obligations of the Bizonal Economic Administration.

Article 134

(1) Reich property becomes in principle federal property.

(2) Insofar as such property was originally intended mainly for ad-

ministrative functions which, under this Basic Law, are not administrative functions of the Federation, it is, without compensation, to be transferred to the authorities hereafter competent to carry out such functions, and to the Laender insofar as, according to its present, not merely provisional, use, it serves for administrative functions which, under this Basic Law, are hereafter to be fulfilled by the Laender. The Federation may also transfer other property to the Laender.

(3) Property which was placed at the disposal of the Reich by the Laender and Gemeinden (Gemeindeverbaende) without compensation shall again become the property of the Laender and Gemeinden (Gemeindeverbaende), insofar as it is not required by the Federation for its own administrative functions.

(4) Details are regulated by a federal law requiring Bundesrat approval.

Article 135

(1) If, between 8 May 1945 and the coming into force of this Basic Law, a territory has passed from one Land to another, the property in this territory of the Land to which this territory had belonged devolves on the Land to which this territory now belongs.

(2) Property of no longer existing Laender or other public law corporations and institutions, insofar as it was originally intended mainly for administration functions, or in accordance with its present not merely provisional use serves mainly for administrative functions, devolves on the Land or public law corporation or institution henceforth performing these functions.

(3) Insofar as it is not already included among property within the meaning of paragraph (1), real estate of no longer existing Laender, including appurtenances, devolves on the Land in the territory of which it is located.

(4) Where an overriding interest of the Federation or the particular interest of a territory so requires, an arrangement deviating from paragraph (1) to (3) may be adopted by federal legislation.

(5) Moreover, the legal succession and the settlement (of property), insofar as it has not been effected by 1 January 1952 by agreement between the Laender or public law corporations or institutions concerned, shall be regulated by federal legislation requiring Bundesrat approval.

(6) Participation of the former Land Prussia in civil law enterprises devolves on the Federation. Details shall be regulated by a federal law which may make deviating provisions.

(7) Insofar as, at the time of the coming into force of the Basic Law, property devolving on a Land or a public law corporation or institution under paragraphs (1) and (3) has been disposed of by the party thereby authorized through a Land law, on the basis of a Land law or in another way, the transfer of property is deemed to have taken place before the act of disposal.

Article 136

(1) The Bundesrat convenes for the first time on the day of the first convening of the Bundestag.

(2) Pending the election of the first Federal President, his functions shall be exercised by the Bundesrat President. He does not have the right to dissolve the Bundestag.

Article 137

(1) The right of civil servants (Beamte), of employees (Angestellte) of the public services and of judges of the Federation, of the Laender and of the Gemeinden to stand for election may be restricted by legislation.

(2) The Electoral Law to be adopted by the Parliamentary Council applies for the election of the first Bundestag, of the first Federal Convention and of the first Federal President of the Federal Republic.

(3) Pending its establishment, the functions of the Federal Constitutional Court, pursuant to Article 41, paragraph (2), shall be exercised by the German High Court for the Combined Area, which shall decide in accordance with its Rules of Procedure.

Article 138

Changes in the regulations of notaries, as they now exist in the Laender Baden, Bavaria, Wuerttemberg-Baden and Wuerttemberg-Hohenzollern, require the approval of the Government of these Laender.

Article 139

The legal provisions enacted for the "liberation of the German people from national socialism, and militarism" shall not be affected by the provisions of this Basic Law.

Article 140

The provisions of Articles 136, 137, 138, 139, and 141 of the German Constitution of 11 August 1919 are an integral part of this Basic Law.

Article 141

Article 7, paragraph (3), first sentence, finds no application in a Land where another regulation by Land law existed on 1 January 1949.

Article 142

Notwithstanding the provision of Article 31, provision of Land Constitutions remain in force also insofar as they guarantee basic rights in conformity with Articles 1 to 18 of this Basic Law.

Article 143

(1) Whoever, by force or by threat of force, changes the constitutional order of the Federation or of a Land, deprives the Federal President of the powers accorded to him by this Basic Law, or, by force or by danger-

ous threats, compels him to exercise his powers or prevents him from exercising them altogether or in a specific manner, or separates from the Federation or from a Land a territory belonging to them, shall be sentenced to penal servitude for life or for not less than ten years.

(2) Whoever publicly incites to an action, within the meaning of paragraph (1), or plots it in connivance with another person, or otherwise prepares it, shall be sentenced to penal servitude up to ten years.

(3) In less serious cases, a sentence of not less than two years' penal servitude in the cases specified in paragraph (1), and of not less than one year's imprisonment in the cases specified in paragraph (2), may be imposed.

(4) Whoever of his own free will abandons an activity (of this sort) or, in case of participation of several persons, prevents the execution of a plot (of this sort), may not be punished in accordance with the provisions of paragraphs (1) to (3).

(5) Where such an action is directed exclusively against the constitutional order of a Land, the highest Land court competent for criminal cases shall, in the absence of any other provision in Land law, be competent to decide. In other cases, the Land superior court (Oberlandesgericht), in the district of which the first Federal Government has its seat, is competent.

(6) The aforementioned provisions apply pending other regulations by federal law.

Article 144

(1) This Basic Law requires acceptance by the popular representative bodies in two-thirds of the German Laender in which it shall for the time being apply.

(2) Insofar as restrictions are imposed on the application of the Basic Law in any of the Laender enumerated in Article 23, paragraph (1), or in a part of any of these Laender, that Land or that part of a Land has the right, in accordance with Article 38, to send representatives to the Bundestag and, in accordance with Article 50, to the Bundesrat.

Article 145

(1) The Parliamentary Council, with the participation of the representatives of Greater Berlin, confirms in a public meeting the adoption of this Basic Law, engrosses and promulgates it.

(2) This Basic Law becomes effective at the end of the day of its promulgation.

(3) It is to be published in the Federal Gazette.

APPENDIX TO BASIC LAW

Articles 136-137-138-139 and 141
of the Section on "RELIGION AND RELIGIOUS ASSOCIATIONS"
of the Weimar Constitution incorporated into the Basic Law for the
Federal Republic of Germany pursuant to Article 140 thereof

Article 136

Civil and political rights and duties are neither qualified nor limited by the exercise of religious belief.

The enjoyment of civil and political rights, and eligibility to public offices, are independent of religious belief.

No one is obliged to reveal his religious convictions. The authorities have the right to inquire into membership in a religious association only so far as rights and duties depend thereon, or a legally ordered statistical investigation makes it necessary.

No one may be compelled to perform any religious act or ceremony, or to participate in religious exercises, or to use a religious form of oath.

Article 137

There is no state church.

Freedom of membership in religious associations is guaranteed. The combination of religious associations within the domain of the Reich is subject to no limitations.

Every religious association regulates and administers its affairs independently within the limits of the law valid for all. It chooses its officers without the intervention of the state or the civil commune.

Religious associations effect incorporation according to the general provisions of the civil law.

Religious associations remain public-law corporations in so far as they were such heretofore. Other religious associations are to be granted the like rights upon their application, if through their organization and the number of their members they offer a guarantee of permanency. If several such public-law religious associations join in a union, this union is also a corporation of public law.

The religious associations which are public-law corporations are entitled to levy taxes on the basis of the civil tax list, according to the standards of the provisions of the state law.

Associations whose function is the common cultivation of a philosophy of life have the same status as religious associations.

In so far as the execution of these provisions requires further regulation, this is a function of state legislation.

Article 138

Public contributions to religious associations, which rest upon law, contract, or special legal title, are abrogated by state legislation. The fundamental provisions for this are established by the Reich.

Property and other rights of the religious associations and religious unions, in respect to their institutions, foundations, and other property devoted to purposes of worship, education, and benevolence, are guaranteed.

Article 139

Sunday and the recognized public holidays remain under legal protection as days of freedom from labor and of spiritual edification.

Article 141

In so far as there exists a need for religious service and spiritual care in the army, in hospitals, penal institutions, or other public institutions, the religious associations are to be given an opportunity for religious exercises, in connection with which there is to be no compulsion.

L

Occupation Statute

Washington
8 April 1949

Berlin
11 April 1949

DEFINING THE POWERS TO BE RETAINED BY THE OCCUPATION AUTHORITIES

In the exercise of the supreme authority which is retained by the Governments of France, the United States and the United Kingdom,

We, General Pierre KOENIG, Military Governor and Commander-in-Chief of the French Zone of Germany,

General Lucius D. CLAY, Military Governor and Commander-in-Chief of the United States Zone of Germany, and

General Sir Bryan Hubert ROBERTSON, Military Governor and Commander-in-Chief of the British Zone of Germany,

DO HEREBY JOINTLY PROCLAIM THE FOLLOWING OCCUPATION STATUTE:

1. During the period in which it is necessary that the occupation continue, the Governments of France, the United States and the United Kingdom desire and intend that the German people shall enjoy self-government to the maximum possible degree consistent with such occupation. The Federal state and the participating Laender shall have, subject only to the limitations in this instrument, full legislative, executive and judicial powers in accordance with the Basic Law and with their respective constitutions.

2. In order to insure the accomplishment of the basic purposes of the occupation, powers in the following fields are specifically reserved, including the right to request and verify information and statistics needed by the Occupation Authorities:

(a) Disarmament and demilitarization, including related fields of scientific research, prohibitions and restrictions on industry, and civil aviation;

(b) Controls in regard to the Ruhr, restitution, reparations, decartelization, deconcentration, nondiscrimination in trade matters, foreign interests in Germany and claims against Germany;

(c) Foreign affairs, including international agreements made by or on behalf of Germany;

(d) Displaced persons and the admission of refugees;

(e) Protection, prestige, and security of Allied Forces, dependents, employees and representatives, their immunities and satisfaction of occupation costs and of their other requirements;

(f) Respect for the Basic Law and the Land Constitutions;

(g) Control over foreign trade and exchange;

(h) Control over internal action, only to the minimum extent necessary to ensure use of funds, food and other supplies in such manner as to reduce to a minimum the need for external assistance to Germany;

(i) Control of the care and treatment in German prisons of persons charged before or sentenced by the courts or tribunals of the Occupying Powers or Occupation Authorities; over the carrying out of sentences imposed on them; and over questions of amnesty, pardon or release in relation to them.

3. It is the hope and expectation of the Governments of France, the United States, and the United Kingdom that the Occupation Authorities will not have occasion to take action in fields other than those specifically reserved above. The Occupation Authorities, however, reserve the right, acting under instructions of their Governments, to resume, in whole or in part, the exercise of full authority if they consider that to do so is essential to security or to preserve democratic government in Germany or in pursuance of the international obligations of their Governments. Before so doing they will formally advise the appropriate German authorities of their decision and the reasons therefor.

4. The German Federal government and the governments of the Laender shall have the power, after due notification to the Occupation Authorities, to legislate and act in the fields reserved to these authorities, except as the Occupation Authorities otherwise specifically direct, or as such legislation or action would be inconsistent with decisions or actions taken by the Occupation Authorities themselves.

5. Any amendment of the Basic Law will require the express approval of the Occupation Authorities before becoming effective. Land constitutions, amendments thereof, all other legislation, and any agreements made

between the Federal state and foreign governments, will become effective twenty-one days after official receipt by the Occupation Authorities unless previously disapproved by them, provisionally or finally. The Occupation Authorities will not disapprove legislation unless in their opinion it is inconsistent with the Basic Law, a Land constitution, legislation or other directives of the Occupation Authorities themselves or the provisions of this instrument or unless it constitutes a grave threat to the basic purposes of the occupation.

6. Subject only to the requirements of their security, the Occupation Authorities guarantee that all agencies of the occupation will respect the civil rights of every person to be protected against arbitrary arrest, search or seizure; to be represented by counsel; to be admitted to bail as circumstances warrant; to communicate with relatives; and to have a fair and prompt trial.

7. Legislation of the Occupation Authorities enacted before the effective date of the Basic Law shall remain in force until repealed or amended by the Occupation Authorities in accordance with the following provisions:

(a) Legislation inconsistent with the foregoing will be repealed or amended to make it consistent herewith;

(b) Legislation based upon the reserved powers, referred to in para 2 above, will be codified;

(c) Legislation not referred to in (a) and (b) will be repealed by the Occupation Authorities on request from appropriate German authorities.

8. Any action shall be deemed to be the act of the Occupation Authorities under the powers herein reserved, and effective as such under this instrument, when taken or evidenced in any matter provided by any agreement between them. The Occupation Authorities may in their discretion effectuate their decisions either directly or through instructions to the appropriate German authorities.

9. After 12 months and in any event within 18 months of the effective date of this instrument the Occupying Powers will undertake a review of its provisions in the light of experience with its operation and with a view to extending the jurisdiction of the German authorities in the legislative, executive and judicial fields.

M

Petersberg Protocol

(Protocol of Agreements Reached
Between the Allied High Commissioners
and the Chancellor of the German Federal Republic
on the Petersberg on November 22, 1949)

Following upon the meeting of the three Foreign Ministers in Paris on November 9th and 10th the U.K., French and U.S. High Commissioners were authorised to discuss with the Federal Chancellor the letters which he had addressed to them on the subject of dismantling with a view to a final settlement of this problem. The instructions to the High Commissioners also covered a wider field and required them to examine with the Chancellor other points to be included in a general settlement. Discussions took place accordingly on November 15th, 17th and 22nd on the Petersberg.

The discussions were animated throughout by the desire and the determination of both parties that their relations should develop progressively upon a basis of mutual confidence. Meanwhile, their primary objective is the incorporation of the Federal Republic as a peaceful member of the European community and to this end German association with the countries of Western Europe in all fields should be diligently pursued by means of her entry into the appropriate international bodies and the exchange of commercial and consular representation with other countries. Both the High Commissioners and the Chancellor appreciate that progress toward this objective must depend upon the re-establishment of a true sense of security in Western Europe and they have addressed themselves particularly to this end. In all these matters they have been encouraged to find a wide community of ideas and intention and they have in particular agreed upon the following:—

I. The High Commission and the Federal Government are agreed to promote the participation of Germany in all those international organisations through which German experience and support can contribute to the general welfare.

They record their satisfaction at the various steps already achieved in this direction including German participation in OEEC, the desire expressed on both sides that the Federal Republic should be promptly admitted to the Council of Europe as an associate member and the proposed signature of a bilateral agreement with the Government of the United States of America covering ECA assistance.

II. The Federal Government, appreciating the desirability of the closest possible cooperation by Germany in the rehabilitation of Western European economy, declares its intention of applying for membership of the International Authority for the Ruhr in which, at present, the Federal Government is only represented by an Observer, it being understood between both parties that German accession will not be subject to any special conditions under Article 31 of the Agreement for the establishment of the Authority.

III. The Federal Government further declares its earnest determination to maintain the demilitarization of the Federal territory and to endeavour by all means in its power to prevent the re-creation of armed forces of any kind. To this end the Federal Government will cooperate fully with the High Commission in the work of the Military Security Board.

IV. It is further agreed between them that the Federal Government shall now initiate the gradual re-establishment of Consular and Commercial relations with those countries where such relations appear advantageous.

V. The Federal Government affirms its resolve as a freely elected democratic body to pursue unreservedly the principles of freedom, tolerance and humanity which unite the nations of Western Europe and to conduct its affairs according to those principles. The Federal Government is firmly determined to eradicate all traces of Nazism from German life and institutions and to prevent the revival of totalitarianism in this or any form. It will seek to liberalize the structure of government and to exclude authoritarianism.

VI. In the field of decartelization and monopolistic practices the Federal Government will take legislative action corresponding to decisions taken by the High Commission in accordance with Article 2(b) of the Occupation Statute.

VII. The High Commission has communicated to the Chancellor the terms of an agreement reached by the three Powers for the relaxation of the present restrictions on German shipbuilding:

The main provisions now agreed are as follows:-

The construction of ocean-going ships, excluding those primarily designed for passengers, and tankers up to 7,200 tons, fishing vessels up to 650 tons and coastal vessels up to 2,700 tons not exceeding 12 knots service speed may begin forthwith. The number of such ships to be constructed shall not be limited.

The Federal Government may, with the approval of the High Commission, acquire or construct before December 31st, 1950 six special ships exceeding these limitations of size and speed. Further particulars on this point were communicated to the Chancellor.

The Federal Chancellor raised the question of the construction and repair of ships in German shipyards for export. The High Commissioners informed him that this matter was not discussed by the Committee of Experts and that they were not in a position to give him a final decision on it. However, they will meanwhile authorise German shipyards to construct for export ships of the types and within such limits of numbers as are applicable to construction for the German economy; they will authorise repair of foreign ships without restriction.

VIII. On the question of dismantling, the High Commission has reviewed the present position in the light of the assurances given by the Federal Government and has agreed to the following modification of the programme. The following plants will be removed from the reparations list and dismantling of their equipment will cease forthwith.

a. *Synthetic oil and rubber plants.*

Farbenfabriken Bayer, Leverkusen ⎫
Chemische Werke, Huls ⎬ except for certain research equipment at these plants involving an important security element ⎭

Gelsenberg Benzin, A.G., Gelsenkirchen.
Hydrierwerke Scholven, A.G., Gelsenkirchen-Buer
Ruhroel G.m.b.H., Bottrop
Ruhrchemie, A.G., Oberhausen-Holten
Gewerkschaft Viktor, Castrop-Rauxel
Krupp Treibstoff-Werke, Wanne-Eickel
Steinkohlenbergwerk, Rhein Preussen, Moers
Dortmunder Paraffin Werke, Dortmund
Chemische Werke Essener Steinkohle, Bergkamen.

b. *Steel Plants*
August Thyssen Huette, Duisburg, Hamborn
Huettenwerke Siegerland, A.G., Charlottenhuette, Niederschelden
Deutsche Edelstahlwerke, Krefeld
Huettenwerk Niederrhein, A.G., Duisburg
Kloeckner Werke, A.G., Düsseldorf
Ruhrstahl, A.G., Henrichshuette, Hattingen
Bochumer Verein, A.G., Gusstahlwerke, Bochum.

except that electric furnaces not essential to the functioning of the works will continue to be dismantled or destroyed.

c. Further dismantling at the I.G. Farben plant at Ludwigshafen-Oppau will not take place except for the removal of the equipment for the production of synthetic ammonia and methanol to the extent provided for in the reparations programme.

d. All dismantling in Berlin will cease and work in the affected plants will be again rendered possible.

It is understood that equipment already dismantled will be made available to IARA except in the case of Berlin. The present modification of the reparations list will not affect the existing prohibitions and restrictions upon the production of certain materials. Dismantled plants may be re-constructed or re-equipped only as permitted by the Military Security Board and those plants at which dismantling has been stopped will be subject to suitable control to ensure that the limitation on the production of steel (11.1 million tons per annum) is not exceeded.

IX. The question of the termination of the state of war was discussed. Although such termination may be regarded as consistent with the spirit of this Protocol, it presents considerable legal and practical difficulties which need to be examined.

X. The High Commissioners and the Federal Chancellor have signed this Protocol with the joint determination to carry into effect the purposes stated in the preamble hereof and with the hope that their understandings will constitute a notable contribution to the incorporation of Germany into a peaceful and stable European community of nations.

B. H. ROBERTSON
A. FRANÇOIS-PONCET   K. ADENAUER
J. J. McCLOY

N

Convention on Relations between the Three

Powers and the Federal Republic of Germany

THE United States of America,
the United Kingdom of Great Britain and Northern Ireland
and the French Republic,
    of the one part, and
the Federal Republic of Germany,
    of the other part;

WHEREAS a peaceful and prosperous European community of nations firmly bound to the other free nations of the world through dedication to the principles of the Charter of the United Nations can be attained only through united support and defence of the common freedom and the common heritage;

WHEREAS it is the common aim of the Signatory States to integrate the Federal Republic on a basis of equality within the European Community itself included in a developing Atlantic Community;

WHEREAS the achievement of a fully free and unified Germany through peaceful means and of a freely negotiated peace settlement, though prevented for the present by measures beyond their control, remains a fundamental and common goal of the Signatory States;

WHEREAS the retention of the Occupation Statute with its powers of intervention in the domestic affairs of the Federal Republic is inconsistent with the purpose of integrating the Federal Republic within the European Community;

WHEREAS the United States of America, the United Kingdom of Great Britain and Northern Ireland and the French Republic (hereinafter referred to as "the Three Powers") are therefore determined to retain only those special rights of which the retention is necessary, in the common interest of the Signatory States, having regard to the special international situation in Germany;

WHEREAS the Federal Republic has developed free and responsible political institutions and is determined to maintain the liberal-democratic federal constitution which guarantees human rights and is enshrined in its Basic Law;

WHEREAS the Three Powers and the Federal Republic recognize that both the new relationship to be established between them by the present Convention and its related Conventions and the Treaties for the creation of an integrated European community, in particular the Treaty on the Establishment of the European Community for Coal and Steel and the Treaty on the Establishment of the European Defence Community, are essential steps to the achievement of their common aim for a unified Germany integrated within the European Community;

HAVE entered into the following Convention setting forth the basis for their new relationship:

Article 1

1. The Federal Republic shall have full authority over its internal and external affairs, except as provided in the present Convention.

2. The Three Powers will revoke the Occupation Statute and abolish the Allied High Commission and the Offices of the Land Commissioners upon the entry into force of the present Convention and the Conventions listed in Article 8 (hereinafter referred to as "the related Conventions").

3. The Three Powers will thenceforth conduct their relations with the Federal Republic through Ambassadors who will act jointly in matters the Three Powers consider of common concern under the present Convention and the related Conventions.

Article 2

1. The Three Powers retain, in view of the international situation, the rights, heretofore exercised or held by them, relating to (a) the stationing

of armed forces in Germany and the protection of their security, (b) Berlin, and (c) Germany as a whole, including the unification of Germany and a peace settlement.

2. The Federal Republic, on its part, will refrain from any action prejudicial to these rights and will cooperate with the Three Powers to facilitate their exercise.

Article 3

1. The Federal Republic agrees to conduct its policy in accordance with the principles set forth in the Charter of the United Nations and with the aims defined in the Statute of the Council of Europe.

2. The Federal Republic affirms its intention to associate itself fully with the community of free nations through membership in international organizations contributing to the common aims of the free world. The Three Powers will support applications for such membership by the Federal Republic at appropriate times.

3. In their negotiations with States with which the Federal Republic maintains no relations, the Three Powers will consult with the Federal Republic in respect of matters directly involving its political interests.

4. At the request of the Federal Government, the Three Powers will arrange to represent the interests of the Federal Republic in relations with other States and in certain international organizations or conferences, whenever the Federal Republic is not in a position to do so itself.

Article 4

1. The mission of the armed forces stationed by the Three Powers in the Federal territory will be the defence of the free world, of which the Federal Republic and Berlin form part.

2. The Three Powers will consult with the Federal Republic, insofar as the military situation permits, regarding the stationing of such armed forces in the Federal territory. The Federal Republic will cooperate fully, in accordance with the present Convention and the related Conventions, in facilitating the tasks of such armed forces.

3. The Three Powers will obtain the consent of the Federal Republic before bringing into the Federal territory, as part of their forces, contingents of the armed forces of any nation not now providing such contingents. Such contingents may nevertheless be brought into the Federal territory without the consent of the Federal Republic in the event of external attack or imminent threat of such attack but, after the elimination of the danger, may only remain there with its consent.

4. The Federal Republic will participate in the European Defence Community in order to contribute to the common defence of the free world.

Article 5

1. In the exercise of their right to protect the security of the armed

forces stationed in the Federal territory, the Three Powers will conform to the provisions of the following paragraphs of this Article.

2. In case the Federal Republic and the European Defence Community are unable to deal with a situation which is created by

an attack on the Federal Republic or Berlin,

subversion of the liberal democratic basic order,

a serious disturbance of public order or

a grave threat of any of these events,

and which in the opinion of the Three Powers endangers the security of their forces, the Three Powers may, after consultation to the fullest extent possible with the Federal Government, proclaim a state of emergency in the whole or any part of the Federal Republic.

3. Upon the proclamation of a state of emergency, the Three Powers may take such measures as are necessary to maintain or restore order and to ensure the security of the Forces.

4. The proclamation will specify the area to which it applies. The state of emergency will not be maintained any longer than necessary to deal with the emergency.

5. The Three Powers shall consult the Federal Government to the fullest extent possible while the state of emergency continues. They will utilize to the greatest possible extent the assistance of the Federal Government and the competent German authorities.

6. If the Three Powers do not terminate a state of emergency within thirty days after a request by the Federal Government to do so, the Federal Government may submit a request to the Council of the North Atlantic Treaty Organization to examine the situation and consider whether the state of emergency should be terminated. If the Council concludes that continuance of the state of emergency is no longer justified, the Three Powers will restore the normal situation as promptly as possible.

7. Independently of a state of emergency, any military commander may, if his forces are imminently menaced, take such immediate action appropriate for their protection (including the use of armed force) as is requisite to remove the danger.

8. In all other respects, the protection of the security of these forces is governed by the provisions of the Convention on the Rights and Obligations of Foreign Forces and their Members in the Federal Republic of Germany referred to in Article 8 of the present Convention.

Article 6

1. The Three Powers will consult with the Federal Republic in regard to the exercise of their rights relating to Berlin.

2. The Federal Republic, on its part, will cooperate with the Three Powers in order to facilitate the discharge of their responsibilities with regard to Berlin. The Federal Republic will continue its aid to the political, cultural, economic and financial reconstruction of Berlin and, in

particular, will grant it such aid as is set out in the annexed Declaration of the Federal Republic (Annex A to the present Convention).

Article 7

1. The Three Powers and the Federal Republic are agreed that an essential aim of their common policy is a peace settlement for the whole of Germany, freely negotiated between Germany and her former enemies, which should lay the foundation for a lasting peace. They further agree that the final determination of the boundaries of Germany must await such a settlement.

2. Pending the peace settlement, the Three Powers and the Federal Republic will cooperate to achieve, by peaceful means, their common aim of a unified Germany enjoying a liberal-democratic constitution, like that of the Federal Republic, and integrated within the European Community.

3. In the event of the unification of Germany the Three Powers will, subject to such adjustments as may be agreed, extend to a unified Germany the rights which the Federal Republic has under the present Convention and the related Conventions and will for their part agree that the rights under the Treaties for the formation of an integrated European Community should be similarly extended, upon the assumption by such a unified Germany of the obligations of the Federal Republic toward the Three Powers or to any of them under those Conventions and Treaties. Except by common consent of all the signatory states the Federal Republic will not conclude any agreement or enter into any arrangement which would impair the rights of the Three Powers under those Conventions and Treaties or lessen the obligations of the Federal Republic thereunder.

4. The Three Powers will consult with the Federal Republic on all other matters involving the exercise of their rights relating to Germany as a whole.

Article 8

1. The Three Powers and the Federal Republic have concluded the following related Conventions which will enter into force simultaneously with the present Convention:

> Convention on the Rights and Obligations of Foreign Forces and their
> Members in the Federal Republic of Germany;
> Finance Convention;
> Convention on the Settlement of Matters Arising out of the War and the Occupation.

2. During the transitional period provided for in paragraph 4 of Article 6 of Chapter One of the Convention on the Settlement of Matters Arising out of the War and the Occupation, the rights of the Three Powers referred to in that paragraph shall be deemed to be included within the exception set forth in paragraph 1 of Article 1 of the present Convention.

Article 9

1. There is hereby established an Arbitration Tribunal which shall function in accordance with the provisions of the annexed Charter (Annex B to the present Convention).

2. The Arbitration Tribunal shall have exclusive jurisdiction over all disputes arising between the Three Powers and the Federal Republic under the provisions of the present Convention or the annexed Charter or any of the related Conventions which the parties are not able to settle by negotiation, except as otherwise provided by paragraph 3 of this Article or in the annexed Charter or in the related Conventions.

3. Any dispute involving the rights of the Three Powers referred to in Article 2, or action taken thereunder, or involving the provisions of paragraphs 1 to 7 inclusive of Article 5, shall not be subject to the jurisdiction of the Arbitration Tribunal or of any other tribunal or court.

Article 10

The Three Powers and the Federal Republic will review the terms of the present Convention and the related Conventions

(a) upon the request of any one of them, in the event of the unification of Germany or the creation of a European federation; or

(b) upon the occurrence of any other event which all of the Signatory States recognize to be of a similarly fundamental character.

Thereupon, they will, by mutual agreement, modify the present Convention and the related Conventions to the extent made necessary or advisable by the fundamental change in the situation.

Article 11

1. The present Convention and the related Conventions shall be ratified or approved by the Signatory States in accordance with their respective constitutional procedures. The instruments of ratification shall be deposited by the Signatory States with the Government of the Federal Republic of Germany.

2. The present Convention shall enter into force immediately upon

(a) the deposit by all the Signatory States of instruments of ratification of the present Convention and of all the Conventions listed in Article 8; and

(b) the entry into force of the Treaty on the Establishment of the European Defence Community.

3. The present Convention and the related Conventions shall be deposited in the Archives of the Government of the Federal Republic of Germany, which will furnish each Signatory State with certified copies thereof and notify each such State of the date of the entry into force of present Convention and the related Conventions.

IN FAITH WHEREOF the undersigned representatives duly authorized thereto by their respective Governments have signed the present Convention.

Done at Bonn this twenty-sixth day of May, 1952 in three texts, in the English, French and German languages, all being equally authentic.

DEAN ACHESON   ANTHONY EDEN

For the United States of America: For the United Kingdom of

                                 Great Britain and Northern Ireland:

ROBERT SCHUMAN   ADENAUER

For the French Republic: For the Federal Republic of Germany:

ANNEX A

TO THE CONVENTION ON RELATIONS BETWEEN THE THREE POWERS AND THE FEDERAL REPUBLIC OF GERMANY

DECLARATION OF THE FEDERAL REPUBLIC ON AID TO BERLIN

In view of the special role which Berlin has played and is destined to play in the future for the self-preservation of the free world, aware of the ties connecting the Federal Republic with Berlin, and motivated by the desire to strengthen and to reinforce the position of Berlin in all fields, and in particular to bring about insofar as possible an improvement in the economy and the financial situation in Berlin including its productive capacity and level of employment, the Federal Republic undertakes

(a) to take all necessary measures on its part in order to ensure the maintenance of a balanced budget in Berlin through appropriate assistance;

(b) to take adequate measures for the equitable treatment of Berlin in the control and allocation of materials in short supply;

(c) to take adequate measures for the inclusion of Berlin in assistance received by the Federal Republic from outside sources in reasonable proportion to the unutilized industrial resources existing in Berlin;

(d) to promote the development of Berlin's external trade, to accord Berlin such favoured treatment in all matters of trade policy as circumstances warrant and to provide Berlin within the limit of possibility and in consideration of the participation of Berlin in the foreign currency control by the Federal Republic, with the necessary foreign currency;

(e) to take all necessary measures on its part to ensure that the city remains in the currency area of the Deutsche Mark West, and that an adequate money supply is maintained in the city;

(f) to assist in the maintaining in Berlin of adequate stockpiles of supplies for emergencies;

(g) to use its best efforts for the maintenance and improvement of trade and of communications and transportation facilities between

Berlin and the Federal territory, and to cooperate in accordance with the means at its disposal in their protection or their re-establishment;

(h) to facilitate the inclusion of Berlin in the international agreements concluded by the Federal Republic, provided that this is not precluded by the nature of the agreements concerned.

ANNEX B

TO THE CONVENTION ON RELATIONS BETWEEN THE THREE POWERS AND THE FEDERAL REPUBLIC OF GERMANY

CHARTER OF THE ARBITRATION TRIBUNAL

PART I

Composition, Organisation and Seat of the Tribunal

Article 1

1. The Tribunal shall be composed of nine members who shall have the qualifications required in their respective countries for appointment to the highest judicial offices or shall be lawyers of recognized competence in international law.

2. The nine members of the Tribunal shall be appointed as follows:

(a) Three members, appointed by the Governments of the Three Powers, one by each Government;

(b) Three members appointed by the Federal Government;

(c) Three members (hereinafter referred to as "the neutral members") appointed by agreement between the Governments of the Three Powers and the Federal Government, none of whom shall be a national of any one of the Three Powers or a German national.

3. The Governments of the Three Powers and the Federal Government shall make known their first appointments not later than sixty days after the entry into force of the present Charter. Within the same period the Governments of the Three Powers and the Federal Government shall agree upon the three neutral members. If, after the expiry of such period, one or more of the neutral members shall not have been appointed, either the Governments of the Three Powers or the Federal Government may request the President of the International Court of Justice to appoint such neutral member or members.

4. Appointments to fill vacancies shall be made in the same manner as the appointment of the member to be replaced. However, if a vacancy to be filled by the Government of one of the Three Powers or the Federal Government is not so filled within one month of its occurring, either the

Governments of the Three Powers or the Federal Government may request the President of the International Court of Justice to make an interim appointment to the vacancy of a person who shall not be a national of any one of the Three Powers or a German national and who shall serve for a period of six months or until the vacancy is filled in the normal manner, whichever is longer. If the member to be replaced is a neutral member, the Governments of the Three Powers or the Federal Government may request the President of the International Court of Justice to make such appointment, if the agreement envisaged by sub-paragraph (c) of paragraph 2 of this Article has not been reached within one month of the vacancy occurring.

5. The Tribunal may, by majority vote, declare a vacancy if, in its opinion, a member has, without reasonable excuse, failed or refused to participate in the hearing or decision of a case to which he has been assigned.

Article 2

1. The members of the Tribunal shall be appointed for four years. They may be reappointed after the expiration of their terms of office.

2. A member whose term of office has expired shall nevertheless continue to discharge his duties until his successor is appointed. After such appointment he shall, unless the President of the Tribunal directs otherwise, continue to discharge his duties respecting pending cases in which he has participated until such cases have been finally decided.

3. Members of the Tribunal shall not engage in any activity incompatible with the proper exercise of their duties, nor shall they participate in the adjudication of any case with which they have previously been concerned in another capacity or in which they have a direct interest. Differences of opinion regarding the applicability of this paragraph shall be resolved by the Tribunal.

4. (a) During and after their terms of office, the members of the Tribunal shall enjoy immunity from suit in respect of acts performed in the exercise of their official duties.

   (b) The members of the Tribunal who are not of German nationality, shall, moreover, enjoy in the Federal territory the same privileges and immunities as are accorded chiefs of diplomatic missions. If sittings or official acts take place in the territory of one of the Three Powers, the members of the Tribunal who are not of the nationality of the country in which the sitting or act takes place shall enjoy diplomatic privileges and immunities in such country.

5. Every member of the Tribunal shall, before taking office, make a declaration at a public session that he will exercise his duties impartially and conscientiously.

6. Subject to the provisions of paragraph 5 of Article 1 of the present Charter, no member may be dismissed before the expiry of his term of

office, or before the termination of his duties in accordance with paragraph 2 of this Article, except by agreement between the Governments of the Three Powers and the Federal Government; or, in the case of a member appointed by the President of the International Court of Justice, by agreement between the Governments of the Three Powers and the Federal Government, with the consent of the President of the International Court of Justice.

Article 3

The Tribunal shall elect from the neutral members a President and two Vice-Presidents to serve as such for two years.

Article 4

1. The Tribunal, presided over by the President or one of the Vice-Presidents, shall sit either in plenary session or in Chambers of three members.

2. A plenary session shall, in principle, include all the members of the Tribunal. A quorum of five members shall suffice to constitute a plenary session; it shall be composed of an uneven number of members and in any case shall consist of an equal number of the members appointed by the Governments of the Three Powers and of those appointed by the Federal Government, and at least one neutral member.

3. Chambers shall be composed of one of the members appointed by the Governments of the Three Powers, one of the members appointed by the Federal Government and one neutral member.

4. The Tribunal in plenary session shall nominate the members of such Chambers, define the categories of cases with which a Chamber will be concerned or assign a particular case to a Chamber.

5. Any decision of a Chamber, on a case assigned to it, shall be deemed to be a decision of the Tribunal.

6. The final decision on a case assigned to a Chamber must be taken by the Tribunal in plenary session, if one of the parties so requests before the Chamber itself has pronounced a final decision.

Article 5

The Tribunal shall sit in public unless it decides otherwise. The deliberations of the Tribunal shall be and shall remain secret as shall all facts brought to its attention in closed session.

Article 6

1. A Registrar shall be responsible for the administration of the Tribunal; he shall have the necessary staff at his disposal. The Registrar shall handle the transmission of documents, keep a record of petitions submitted to the Tribunal and be responsible for the archives and accounts of the Tribunal.

2. The first Registrar shall be appointed by agreement between the Three Powers and the Federal Republic. The Registrar shall be a perma-

nent official subject to dismissal and replacement only by the Tribunal.

Article 7

The seat of the Tribunal shall be located within the Federal territory at such place as shall be determined by a subsidiary administrative agreement between the Governments of the Three Powers and the Federal Government. The Tribunal may, however, sit and exercise its functions elsewhere, when it deems it desirable to do so.

Article 8

Questions pertaining to the operating costs of the Tribunal, including the official emoluments of members, as well as arrangements for securing the inviolability of the premises of the Tribunal, shall be regulated by the subsidiary administrative agreement referred to in Article 7 of the present Charter.

PART II

Competence and Powers of the Tribunal.

Article 9

1. The Tribunal shall have jurisdiction over all disputes arising between the Three Powers and the Federal Republic under the provisions of the Convention on Relations between the Three Powers and the Federal Republic of Germany (hereinafter referred to as "the Convention") or the present Charter or any of the related Conventions, listed in Article 8 of the Convention, which the parties are not able to settle by negotiation, except disputes expressly excluded from its jurisdiction by the provisions of the Convention or the present Charter or any of the related Conventions.

2. (a) The Tribunal shall, moreover, have jurisdiction in respect of any question as to the extent of the competence of the following authorities:

   The Board of Review referred to in Chapter Two of the Convention on the Settlement of Matters Arising out of the War and the Occupation;

   The Supreme Restitution Court referred to in Chapter Three of that Convention;

   The Arbitral Commission on Property, Rights and Interests in Germany referred to in Chapters Five and Ten of that Convention.

   (b) A question as to the extent of the competence of these authorities may be raised at any time after the institution of proceedings before them and also after a final decision.

   (c) The decisions of the Tribunal on these questions shall be binding on the authorities whose competence has been questioned.

3. The decisions of the authorities specified in sub-paragraph (a) of

paragraph 2 of this Article shall be subject to the jurisdiction of the Tribunal and to the provisions of sub-paragraph (a) of paragraph 5 of Article 11 of the present Charter only to the extent contemplated in sub-paragraph (a) of paragraph 2 of this Article, unless the contrary is expressly provided in one of the related Conventions.

4. Decisions of the authorities provided for or referred to in the related Conventions, other than those specified in sub-paragraph (a) of paragraph 2 of this Article, shall be subject to review by the Tribunal, whether on questions as to the extent of competence or on the merits, only to the extent contemplated by paragraph 1 of this Article, unless the contrary is expressly provided in one of the related Conventions.

5. Only the Governments of one or more of the Three Powers, on the one hand, and the Federal Government, on the other, may be parties before the Tribunal. If the Federal Government brings a complaint against one or two of the Governments of the Three Powers, or if one or two of the Governments of the Three Powers brings a complaint against the Federal Government, the other Government or Governments of the Three Powers may apply to the Tribunal to be joined as parties.

Article 10

The Tribunal shall render its decisions in the form of judgments or directives which shall be binding on the parties.

Article 11

1. The Signatory States undertake to comply with the decisions of the Tribunal and to take the action required of them by such decisions.

2. The Tribunal may set a period of time for the execution of its decisions.

3. If a judgment of the Tribunal establishes that the provisions of a law or ordinance, applicable in the Federal territory, are in conflict with the provisions of the Convention or the present Charter or the related Conventions, it may order the party which has enacted such provisions to deprive them of effect, in whole or in part, in the Federal territory. Should this party fail to comply with the judgment of the Tribunal, the Tribunal may, at the request of the successful party, declare the provisions null, in whole or in part, in the Federal territory with binding effect.

4. If a judgment of the Tribunal establishes that an administrative measure applicable in the Federal territory, is in conflict with the provisions of the Convention or the present Charter or the related Conventions, it may order the party which has taken such measure to annul it, in whole or in part, in the Federal territory. Should this party fail to comply with the judgment of the Tribunal, the Tribunal may, at the request of the successful party, declare the measure null, in whole or in part, in the Federal territory, with binding effect.

5. (a) If a judgment of the Tribunal establishes that a judicial decision, enforceable in the Federal territory, is in conflict with

the basic principles of the Convention or the present Charter or the related Conventions, it may annul such decision, in whole or in part, in the Federal territory. In such case the judicial proceedings shall be restored to the position in which they were before the judicial decision was given; in further proceedings the Tribunal's findings of fact and law shall be binding in the Federal territory.

(b) The provisions of sub-paragraph (a) of this paragraph shall not apply to decisions of Service Tribunals.

6. If a judgment of the Tribunal establishes that a party has failed to take action which it is obliged to take by the Convention or the present Charter or the related Conventions, the Tribunal may, in its judgment or, on the application of a party, in a second judgment, specify special measures which must be taken by the unsuccessful party in order to remedy the situation in compliance with the judgment. Should this party fail to take such special measures within the time specified by the Tribunal, the Tribunal may, on the application of the other party, authorize the latter to take appropriate measures to remedy the situation in compliance with the judgment. If, however, the measures which the unsuccessful party fails to take consist in the issue of legal provisions, the Tribunal may embody in its judgment provisions, not inconsistent with the Basic Law of the Federal Republic, creating rights and obligations for all persons and authorities in the Federal territory.

Article 12

1. The Tribunal or, in a case of urgency, the President shall have the power, by the issue of directives, to take such measures as may be necessary to conserve the respective rights of the parties pending the judgment of the Tribunal. Any directive issued by the President under this Article may be confirmed, amended or annulled by the Tribunal within seventy-two hours after the notification thereof to the parties.

2. The parties shall be afforded an opportunity to be heard prior to the issue of any directive by the Tribunal or by the President under this Article.

3. In the absence of the President, his powers under this Article shall be exercised by one of the Vice-Presidents to be designated by the President for this purpose.

PART III

Proceedings

Article 13

The official languages of the Tribunal shall be French, English and German.

Article 14

Proceedings before the Tribunal shall be instituted by a written petition filed with the Tribunal which shall contain a statement of the facts giving rise to the dispute, reference to the provisions of the Convention or the present Charter or the related Conventions which are invoked, legal argument, and conclusion.

Article 15

1. The parties shall be represented by agents. They may be assisted by counsel.

2. Such agents and counsel shall enjoy immunity from suit in respect of acts performed in the exercise of their duties.

Article 16

1. The presiding member may summon the agents in order to be informed of their wishes concerning the time limits and conduct of the proceedings.

2. The presiding member shall set the time limits for the submission of pleadings and shall prescribe all the measures necessary for the conduct of the proceedings.

3. Certified copies of all documents submitted by either party shall be immediately forwarded to the other party through the Registrar.

Article 17

The proceedings shall consist of two parts; written and oral. Oral proceedings may be dispensed with if both parties so request.

Article 18

1. Written proceedings shall consist of a statement of the complainant's case, the defendant's answer and, unless the Tribunal directs otherwise, a reply and a rejoinder.

2. Counterclaims shall be permissible.

Article 19

1. Oral proceedings shall consist of the complainant's argument, the defendant's argument and, unless the Tribunal directs otherwise, a reply and a rejoinder, as well as hearings of witnesses and experts.

2. The Tribunal shall have power to demand the production of evidence, documentary or other, to require the attendance of witnesses to testify, to request expert opinion, and to direct inquiries to be made.

3. In the event that a party does not produce evidence which in the opinion of the Tribunal is relevant to the issues before it and which such party possesses or is in a position to procure, the Tribunal shall proceed to give its decision notwithstanding the absence of such evidence.

4. The presiding member or any other member of the Tribunal may put questions to the parties, witnesses and experts.

5. A written record of the oral proceedings shall be kept and shall be signed by the presiding member and the Registrar.

Article 20

All decisions of the Tribunal shall be based on the Convention, the present Charter and the related Conventions. The Tribunal shall, in the interpretation of such Conventions, apply the generally accepted rules of international law governing the interpretation of treaties.

Article 21

1. The Tribunal shall decide by majority vote.
2. Judgments shall state the reasons on which they are based.
3. Judgments shall be signed by the presiding member and by the Registrar.
4. Judgments shall be final and not subject to appeal.
5. In the case of a difference of opinion as to the meaning or scope of a judgment, the Tribunal may construe it by an interpretative judgment, on the application of either party and after having heard both parties.

Article 22

The revision of a judgment may not be requested of the Tribunal except upon the grounds of the discovery of a fact which is of such a nature as to exercise a decisive influence, and of which the Tribunal and the party requesting revision had been unaware before the pronouncement of the judgment always provided that such ignorance was not due to negligence on the part of the party requesting the revision.

Article 23

1. Unless the Tribunal directs otherwise, each party to proceedings before the Tribunal shall pay its own costs.
2. The Tribunal shall bear the costs in respect of witnesses whose attendance it has required and expert opinions and inquiries which it has ordered.

Article 24

The Tribunal shall determine its own rules of procedure consistent with the present Charter.

PART IV

Advisory Opinions

Article 25

1. The Tribunal may, at the joint request of the Governments of the Three Powers and of the Federal Government give an advisory opinion on any matter arising out of the Convention or the present Charter or the related Conventions, with the exception of those questions with which

it would not have been competent to deal if they had been referred to it in the form of a dispute.

2. The Tribunal may, at the request of an authority referred to in paragraph 2 of Article 9 of the present Charter or at the request of the presiding member of such an authority, give an advisory opinion on the competence of such authority.

3. Advisory opinions shall not be binding.

O

Election Statistics in Postwar Germany

ABBREVIATIONS

SPD — Sozialdemokratische Partei Deutschlands
CDU — Christlich-Demokratische Union (in early elections in some areas also CSVP — Christlich-Soziale Volkspartei)
CSU — Christlich-Soziale Union
WAV — Wirtschaftliche Aufbauvereinigung
FDP — Freie Demokratische Partei (known as LDP in some areas in early elections and still as DVP — Demokratische Volkspartei — in others)
LDP — Liberal-Demokratische Partei
SED — Sozialistische Einheitspartei Deutschlands
KPD — Kommunistische Partei Deutschlands
VdgB — Vereinigung der gegenseitigen Bauernhilfe
DG — Deutsche Gemeinschaft
BHE — Block der Heimatvertriebenen und Entrechteten
DP — Deutsche Partei (formerly NLP — Niedersächsische Landespartei)
SSW — Südschleswigscher Wählervereinigung (also SSV — Südschleswigscher Verein)
DRP — Deutsche Reichspartei
DKP — Deutsche Konservative Partei
SRP — Sozialistische Reichspartei
RSF — Radikal-Soziale Freiheitspartei
VBH — Vaterstädtischer Bund Hamburg

SOVIET ZONE OF OCCUPATION
LANDTAG ELECTIONS, OCTOBER, 1946

Länder

	Brandenburg	Mecklenburg	Sachsen-Anhalt	Thuringen	Sachsen
Eligible Electors	1,652,985	1,301,703	2,700,633	1,911,682	3,803,416
Voters Participating	1,515,987	1,172,831	2,473,184	1,735,197	3,518,108
Per Cent Participating	91.7	90.1	91.6	90.7	92.5
Valid Votes Cast	1,446,819	1,107,303	2,330,511	1,657,196	3,290,995
Invalid Votes Cast	69,168	65,528	142,673	78,001	227,113
Per Cent Votes Invalid	4.6	5.6	5.8	4.7	6.5

Party or Group	Brandenburg		Mecklenburg		Sachsen-Anhalt		Thuringen		Sachsen	
	Votes	Per Cent	Votes	Per Cent	Votes	Per Cent	Votes	Per Cent	Votes	Per Cent
SED	634,787	43.9	547,663	49.5	1,068,703	45.8	816,864	49.3	1,616,068	49.1
CDU	442,634	30.6	377,808	34.1	507,765	21.8	313,824	18.9	766,859	23.3
LDP	298,607	20.6	138,572	12.5	696,669	29.9	471,415	28.5	813,224	24.7
VdgB	70,791	4.9	43,260	3.9	57,374	2.5	55,093	3.3	57,356	1.7
Kulturbund									19,148	.6
Landesfrauenausschuss									18,340	.6

LANDTAG MEMBERSHIP

Party or Group	Brandenburg	Mecklenburg	Sachsen-Anhalt	Thuringen	Sachsen
SED	44	45	51	50	59
CDU	31	31	24	19	28
LDP	20	11	33	28	30
VdgB	5	3	2	3	2
Kulturbund					1

ZONAL ELECTIONS
Elections to the Third Volkskongress, May, 1949

Eligible Electors	13,533,071	
Voters Participating	12,887,234	95.2%
Valid Votes Cast	12,024,221	
Invalid Votes Cast	863,013	6.7%
Votes Cast "Yes"	7,943,949	66.1%
"No"	4,080,272	33.9%

In this election voters were presented with a single list of officially sponsored candidates and could vote only "Yes" or "No." This election was the first legalization of the *Volkskongress*, the first and second Congress meetings having been gatherings of delegates from the approved political parties and so-called "mass organizations."

The Soviet (eastern) sector of Berlin was included in the polling as well as the Soviet Zone of Occupation proper.

GENERAL ELECTION, OCTOBER, 1950

Eligible Electors	12,325,168	
Voters Participating	12,144,597	98.5%
Valid Votes Cast	12,131,165	
Invalid Votes Cast	13,432	.1%
For the National Front List	12,097,105	99.7%
Against the List	34,060	.3%

The electorate in this vote was required to vote on a single list of National Front candidate groups for zonal representation (the *Volkskammer* of the newly organized German Democratic Republic), for each *Landtag*, and for local *Kreis* and *Gemeinde* representatives. The Soviet sector of Berlin was excluded from this polling.

BERLIN

CITY ASSEMBLY ELECTION, OCTOBER, 1946

Eligible Electors 2,307,122
Voters Participating 2,128,677   92.3%
Valid Votes Cast 2,085,338
Invalid Votes Cast   43,339   2.0%

	Votes	Per Cent	Seats
SPD	1,015,609	48.7	63
CDU	462,425	22.2	29
SED	412,582	19.8	26
LDP	194,244	9.3	12

This was the only election held for the whole area of Berlin. In the next scheduled voting, in December, 1948, the Soviet sector was prevented from participating and a separate rump city government was established for the Soviet (eastern) sector of the city. No further elections have been held in this Soviet sector save for its participation in the Soviet zonal election of the third *Volkskongress* in May, 1949.

WEST BERLIN

	City Assembly December, 1950			City Assembly December, 1948		
Eligible Electors	1,663,995			1,586,461		
Voters Participating .	1,504,539	90.4%		1,369,492	86.3%	
Valid Votes Cast . . .	1,463,861			1,331,270		
Invalid Votes Cast . .	40,678	2.7%		38,222	2.8%	
	Votes	Per Cent	Seats	Votes	Per Cent	Seats
SPD	654,025	44.6	61	858,461	64.5	60
CDU	360,864	24.6	34	258,664	19.4	21
LDP(FDP in 1950) . .	337,493	23.1	32	214,145	16.1	17
DP	53,749	3.7	0	. . . . . .	. . .	. .
BHE	31,885	2.2	0	. . . . . .	. . .	. .
Miscellaneous	25,845	1.8	0	. . . . . .	. . .	. .

These elections included only the French, British, and American occupation sectors of the city.

BADEN

	Bundestag August, 1949			Landtag May, 1947		
Eligible Electors	815,221			694,953		
Voters Participating .	570,238	70.0%		471,389	67.7%	
Valid Votes	542,218			427,824		
Invalid Votes Cast . .	27,520	4.8%		43,565	9.2%	
	Votes	Per Cent	Seats	Votes	Per Cent	Seats
CDU	277,274	49.6	7	239,312	55.9	34
SPD	128,608	24.0	3	95,829	22.4	13
FDP	94,601	19.3	2	60,980	14.3	9
KPD	22,754	3.8	0	31,703	7.4	4
Sammlung zur Tat . .	19,481	3.3	0	. . . . . .	. . .	. .

BAYERN

	Landtag November, 1950			Bundestag August, 1949			Landtag December, 1946			Constitutional Assembly June, 1946		
	Votes	Per Cent	Seats	Votes	Per Cent	Seats	Votes	Per Cent	Seats	Votes	Per Cent	Seats
Eligible Electors........	6,025,798			5,980,683			4,170,054			3,884,158		
Voters Participating.....	4,819,904	80.0%		4,351,324	81.0%		3,197,578	76.7%		2,785,661	71.7%	
Valid Votes Cast........	9,237,840			4,727,623			3,048,337			2,721,114		
Invalid Votes Cast.......	401,968	4.2%		123,701	2.5%		149,241	4.7%		64,547	2.3%	
SPD..................	2,588,549	28.0	63	1,075,416	22.8	18	871,760	28.6	54	785,620	28.9	51
SCU..................	2,527,370	27.4	64	1,380,448	29.2	24	1,593,908	52.3	104	1,585,772	58.3	109
Bayernpartei...........	1,657,713	17.9	39	985,478	20.9	17	....	....	..	....	....	..
FDP..................	653,741	7.1	12	404,145	8.5	7	172,242	5.6	9	69,037	2.5	4
WAV.................	259,687	2.8	0	681,888	14.4	12	225,404	7.4	13	136,627	5.0	8
KPD..................	177,768	1.9	0	195,852	4.1	0	185,023	6.1	0	144,058	5.3	8
BHE-DG..............	1,136,148	12.3	26	....	....	..	....	....	..	....	....	..
Independent and Miscellaneous..........	236,864	2.6	0	3,396	.1	0	....	....	..	....	....	..

In the *Landtag* elections of 1950 each elector had two votes, one cast for a local district member, one for an "at-large" member.

[*Appendix O*]

BREMEN

	Bundestag August, 1949				Bürgerschaft October, 1947		
Eligible Electors........................	379,639				338,011		
Voters Participating....................	311,481	82.0%			229,245	67.8%	
Valid Votes Cast.......................	304,368				218,858		
Invalid Votes Cast.....................	7,113	2.3%			10,387	4.5%	
	Votes	Per Cent	Seats		Votes	Per Cent	Seats
SPD............	104,509	34.3	3		91,235	41.7	46
DP.............	54,569	17.9	1		8,442	3.9	3
CDU............	51,192	16.8	1		48,118	22.0	24
FDP............	39,229	12.9	0		42,539	19.4	17
KPD............	20,530	6.7	0		19,290	8.8	10
RSF............	7,046	2.3	0		2,410	1.1	0
Independent......	27,293	9.1	0		6,824	3.1	0

The vote listed for the FDP is the total of the FDP proper and of the Bremen Democratic People's party. The elections to the *Bürgerschaft* held in October, 1946, are not included in this compilation since the electoral area at that time was limited to Bremen City and excluded parts of what were to become *Land* Bremen in January, 1947.

HAMBURG

	Bürgerschaft October, 1949			Bundestag August, 1949			Bürgerschaft October, 1946		
Eligible Electors	1,151,566			1,141,214			968,454		
Voters Participating	811,778	70.5%		926,435	81.2%		765,008	79.0%	
Valid Votes Cast	789,240			905,444			735,593		
Invalid Votes Cast	22,538	2.8%		20,991	2.3%		29,415	3.8%	

	Votes	Per Cent	Seats	Votes	Per Cent	Seats	Votes	Per Cent	Seats
SPD	337,697	42.8	65	358,873	39.6	6	1,210,010	43.1	83
VBH	272,649	34.5	40	.....	.....	..	.....	.....	..
CDU	.....	.....	..	178,786	19.8	3	749,153	26.7	16
FDP	.....	.....	..	143,371	15.8	2	509,632	18.2	7
DP	104,728	13.2	9	118,583	13.1	1	.....	.....	..
KPD	58,314	7.4	5	76,747	8.5	1	291,701	10.4	4
RSF	15,505	2.0	1	13,830	1.5	0	20,034	.7	0
DRP-DKP	.....	.....	..	10,838	1.2	0	9,625	.3	0
Independent and Miscellaneous	527	.1	0	4,416	.5	0	17,650	.6	0

The vote for *Bürgerschaft* members in October, 1946, was held under the British Zone local government multi-member district system, with each elector having four votes. The 735,593 valid ballots at this election included 2,807,805 valid votes, thus the discrepancy between party vote totals for this election and for subsequent ballotings in which each elector had but a single vote.

HESSE

	Landtag November, 1950			Bundestag August, 1949			Landtag December, 1946			Constitutional Assembly June, 1946		
Eligible Electors........	2,982,232			2,906,239			2,380,109			2,174,759		
Voters Participating.....	1,935,591	64.9%		2,247,390	77.3%		1,741,416	73.2%		1,559,027	71.7%	
Valid Votes Cast........	1,848,930			2,128,278			1,609,388			1,478,373		
Invalid Votes Cast......	86,661	4.5%		119,112	5.3%		132,028	7.6%		80,654	5.2%	
	Votes	Per Cent	Seats	Votes	Per Cent	Seats	Votes	Per Cent	Seats	Votes	Per Cent	Seats
SPD.........	820,444	44.4	47	684,042	32.1	13	687,431	42.7	38	655,090	44.3	43
FDP.........	588,191	31.8	21	597,081	28.1	12	252,207	15.7	14	120,346	8.1	6
CDU.........	347,803	18.8	12	454,437	21.3	9	498,158	30.9	28	550,342	37.2	34
KPD.........	87,446	4.7	0	142,539	6.7	2	171,592	10.7	10	144,272	9.8	7
Independent and Miscellaneous.........	5,046	.3	0	250,179	11.8	0	....	....	..	8,323	.6	0

By far the largest number of the Independent and Miscellaneous group of votes listed for the *Bundestag* election were cast for refugee and expellee candidates.

NIEDERSACHSEN

	Bundestag August, 1949			Landtag April, 1947		
Eligible Electors..................	4,425,610			3,956,845		
Voters Participating.............	3,439,964	77.7%		2,576,368	65.1%	
Valid Votes Cast.................	3,365,965			2,459,479		
Invalid Votes Cast...............	73,999	2.2%		116,889	4.5%	
	Votes	Per Cent	Seats	Votes	Per Cent	Seats
SPD............................	1,125,295	33.4	24	1,066,380	43.4	65
DP.............................	597,542	17.8	12	440,467	17.9	27
CDU............................	593,691	17.6	12	489,322	19.9	30
DRP-DKP.......................	273,129	8.1	5	7,245	.3	0
FDP............................	252,141	7.5	5	215,805	8.8	13
Zentrum........................	113,464	3.4	0	101,283	4.1	6
KPD............................	104,132	3.1	0	138,977	5.6	8
RSF............................	33,275	1.0	0	....	....	..
Independent.....................	273,310	8.1	0	....	....	..

NORDRHEIN-WESTFALEN

	Landtag June, 1950			Bundestag August, 1949			Landtag April, 1947		
Eligible Electors............	8,892,305			8,678,335			7,860,608		
Voters Participating.......	6,433,003	72.3%		6,906,019	79.1%		5,291,111	67.3%	
Valid Votes Cast...........	6,201,117			6,722,800			5,028,892		
Invalid Votes Cast.........	231,886	3.6%		183,219	2.7%		262,219	5.0%	

	Votes	Per Cent	Seats	Votes	Per Cent	Seats	Votes	Per Cent	Seats
CDU...................	2,286,644	36.9	93	2,481,354	36.9	43	1,889,581	37.5	92
SPD...................	2,005,312	32.3	68	2,107,898	31.4	37	1,607,487	32.0	64
FDP...................	748,926	12.1	26	580,275	8.6	10	298,995	5.9	12
Zentrum...............	466,497	7.5	16	601,278	9.0	10	491,138	9.8	20
KPD..................	338,862	5.5	12	512,489	7.6	9	702,410	14.0	28
RSF...................	122,878	2.0	0	142,507	2.1	0	.....	....	..
DRP-DKP.............	107,104	1.7	0	118,005	1.7	0	24,879	.5	0
DP...................	106,351	1.7	0	.....	....	.	.....	....	..
Independent and Miscellaneous...	18,543	.3	0	21,910	.3	0	14,402	.3	0

RHEINLAND-PFALZ

	Bundestag August, 1949				Landtag May, 1947		
Eligible Electors...........	1,902,150				1,644,128		
Voters Participating.......	1,513,842	79.6%			1,284,070	78.7%	
Valid Votes Cast..........	1,431,080				1,151,438		
Invalid Votes Cast........	82,762	5.5%			132,632	10.3%	
	Votes	Per Cent	Seats		Votes	Per Cent	Seats
CDU..................	701,943	49.1	13		539,791	46.9	47
SPD..................	408,752	28.6	7		398,225	34.6	34
FDP..................	226,562	15.8	4		112,980	9.8	11
KPD..................	88,948	6.2	1		100,442	8.7	8
Independent...........	4,875	.3	0		.....	.....	.....

The vote for the FPD in the May, 1947, *Landtag* election represents 70,946 Liberal ballots in the Rhineland and 42,034 for the Social Peoples' League in the Pfalz. These two parties had an electoral arrangement not to oppose one another and merged after the *Landtag* voting.

SCHLESWIG-HOLSTEIN

	Landtag July, 1950			Bundestag August, 1949			Landtag April, 1947		
Eligible Electors	1,715,496			1,731,022			1,594,794		
Voters Participating	1,341,835	78.2%		1,431,020	82.7%		1,113,005	69.8%	
Valid Votes Cast	1,310,758			1,397,671			1,073,204		
Invalid Votes Cast	31,077	2.3%		33,349	2.3%		39,801	3.6%	
	Votes	Per Cent	Seats	Votes	Per Cent	Seats	Votes	Per Cent	Seats
SPD	360,188	27.4	19	413,257	29.6	8	469,994	43.8	43
BHE	306,570	23.4	15	....	..	..	....	..	..
CDU	258,907	19.7	16	428,956	30.7	8	365,534	34.0	21
DP	125,663	9.6	7	169,240	12.1	3	....	..	..
FDP	92,454	7.1	8	103,492	7.4	2	53,359	5.0	0
SSW	71,811	5.5	4	75,388	5.4	1	99,500	9.3	6
DRP-DKP	37,106	2.8	0	27,070	1.9	0	32,848	3.0	0
KPD	28,344	2.2	0	43,744	3.1	0	50,398	4.7	0
SRP	21,041	1.6	0	....	..	..	....	..	..
RSF	....	....	..	18,144	1.3	0	....	....	..
Zentrum	....	....	..	12,580	.9	0	1,082	.1	0
Independent	8,674	.7	0	105,800	7.6	1	489	.1	0

WÜRTTEMBERG-BADEN

	Landtag November, 1950			Bundestag August, 1949			Landtag November, 1946			Constitutional Assembly June, 1946		
	Votes	Per Cent	Seats	Votes	Per Cent	Seats	Votes	Per Cent	Seats	Votes	Per Cent	Seats
Eligible Electors	2,563,402			2,519,244			1,875,074			1,771,337		
Voters Participating .	1,476,865	57.2%		1,825,344	71.3%		1,344,602	71.7%		1,208,481	68.2%	
Valid Votes Cast....	1,442,058			1,747,995			1,269,764			1,161,578		
Invalid Votes Cast . .	34,807	2.4%		77,349	4.2%		74,838	5.6%		46,903	3.9%	
SPD............	476,262	33.0	34	441,094	25.2	10	404,716	31.9	32	374,739	32.3	32
CDU............	379,487	26.3	28	542,208	31.0	12	487,085	38.4	39	474,878	40.9	41
FDP............	303,510	21.1	22	318,424	18.2	7	247,710	19.5	19	195,440	16.8	17
BHE-DG..........	212,431	14.7	16	......	......	2	......	......	..	......	......	..
KPD............	70,368	4.9	0	129,239	7.4	2	130,253	10.2	10	116,521	10.0	10
Independent and Miscellaneous......	......	......	..	317,030	18.1	2	......	......	....	......	......	....

By far the largest number of the Independent and Miscellaneous group of votes listed for the *Bundestag* election were cast for refugee and expellee candidates.

WÜRTTEMBERG-HOHENZOLLERN

	Bundestag August, 1949	Landtag May, 1947
Eligible Electors...........	727,948	616,593
Voters Participating.......	469,518 64.6%	408,956 66.3%
Valid Votes Cast...........	453,774	378,333
Invalid Votes Cast.........	15,744 3.4%	30,623 7.5%

	Bundestag August, 1949			Landtag May, 1947		
	Votes	Per Cent	Seats	Votes	Per Cent	Seats
CDU.................	268,044	59.1	7	205,037	54.2	32
SPD.................	85,780	18.9	2	78,707	20.8	12
FDP.................	69,385	15.3	1	67,018	17.7	11
KPD.................	23,891	5.3	0	27,571	7.3	5
Sammlung zur Tat....	6,674	1.4	0	....	.....	..

Index

[Index]

[Index]

German Trade Union Federation, 172, 365-366, 367, 369, 374-375, 376, 379
German Zonal Advisory Council, 88
Gestapo, 269, 270, 406
GGO, *see* Common Code of Administrative Procedure
Ghandi, 118
Gleitze, Vice-President, 162
Gniffke, Erich, 155
Goebbels, Dr. Paul Josef, 110
Grotewohl, Otto, 155, 169, 177
Grundschule, 452, 454, 459
Gutt, Finance Minister, 420
Gymnasium, 443, 452

Hague Convention on the Laws and Customs of War on Land, 11, 12, 15, 51
Hague Conventions of 1899 and 1907, 12
Hamburg, 87-88, 105, 107, 108, 374, 413
Hanover, 79, 87-88
Health and welfare services: administration of, 388-391; empire, 382-387; on local level, 392-397; on national level, 398-400; National Socialist regime, 391; on regional level, 397; on state level, 397-398; Weimar, 387-391; after World War II, 391-403
Heinemann, Dr., 138, 145
Hesse, 91, 97, 102-103, 106-108, 129, 140, 232, 288; approval of *Land* constitutions, 35; local government 70-71; police system, 412-413; territorial changes, 47, 89; works council and codetermination law, 373-374
Hesse-Nassau, 91
Hesse-Palatinate, 91
Heuss, Theodor, 137-138
Himmler, Heinrich, 403
Hindenburg, Field Marshal Paul von, 61, 118
Hitler, Adolf, 61, 64, 97, 110, 264, 266, 362
Hochschule für Internationale Pädagogische Forschung, 461
Hohenzollern, 47, 91, 93; *see also* Württemberg-Hohenzollern
Holy See, 188
Hopker-Aschoff, Dr., 144
Hottenheimer Conference, 371
Human Rights, Charter on, 199

IAR, *see* International Authority for the Ruhr
Immunities of members of *Bundestag*, 213-215
Impeachment of judges, 259
Imperial Ministry of Finance, 328-329, 334
Independent personnel agency, 275, 277
"Independent Socialists," 480
Independent Trade-Union Organization, 172, 366
Individual rights, 22, 199, 239-241, 259, 404, 406, 410-411
Initiative and referendum, 129, 501-502, 515
Institute for International Educational Research, *see* Hochschule für Internationale Pädagogische Forschung
Institute of Public Affairs, 82, 278
Instrukteure, 176
International Authority for the Ruhr, *see* Ruhr, International Authority for
International Bank for Reconstruction, 201
International Confederation of Free Trade Unions, 366
International Labor Organization, 201
International Military Tribunal of Nuremberg, 406
International Monetary Fund, 122, 201
International Telecommunications Union, 202
International Wheat Council, 202
International Youth Library, 466
Internship training, 281-282
Interpellation: in *Bundestag*, 218

Jefferson, Thomas, 57
JEIA, *see* Joint Export-Import Agency
JFEA, *see* Joint Foreign Exchange Agency
Joint Chiefs of Staff 1067, 7, 236
Joint Export-Import Agency, 33
Joint Foreign Exchange Agency, 33
Joint Municipal Office for Administrative Simplification, 303
Judicature Act of 1877, 238
Judiciary: independence of, 41, 250-255; independence of in Soviet Zone, 172; under the Basic Law, 255-261
Jury system, 261

[Index]